This Book Comes With Lots of FREE Online Resources

Nolo's award-winning website has a page dedicated just to this book. Here you can:

KEEP UP TO DATE. When there are important changes to the information in this book, we'll post updates.

GET DISCOUNTS ON NOLO PRODUCTS. Get discounts on hundreds of books, forms, and software.

READ BLOGS. Get the latest info from Nolo authors' blogs.

LISTEN TO PODCASTS. Listen to authors discuss timely issues on topics that interest you.

WATCH VIDEOS. Get a quick introduction to a legal topic with our short videos.

And that's not all.
Nolo.com contains thousands of articles on everyday legal and business issues, plus a plain-English law dictionary, all written by Nolo experts and available for free. You'll also find more useful **books, software, online apps, downloadable forms,** plus a **lawyer directory.**

With **Downloadable FORMS**

Get forms and more at
www.nolo.com/back-of-book/EVTEN.html

NOLO **The Trusted Name**
(but don't take our word for it)

"In Nolo you can trust."
THE NEW YORK TIMES

"Nolo is always there in a jam as the nation's premier publisher of do-it-yourself legal books."
NEWSWEEK

"Nolo publications…guide people simply through the how, when, where and why of the law."
THE WASHINGTON POST

"[Nolo's]…material is developed by experienced attorneys who have a knack for making complicated material accessible."
LIBRARY JOURNAL

"When it comes to self-help legal stuff, nobody does a better job than Nolo…"
USA TODAY

"The most prominent U.S. publisher of self-help legal aids."
TIME MAGAZINE

"Nolo is a pioneer in both consumer and business self-help books and software."
LOS ANGELES TIMES

9th Edition

Every Tenant's Legal Guide

Attorney Janet Portman and Marcia Stewart

NINTH EDITION	APRIL 2018
Cover Design	SUSAN PUTNEY
Book Design	SUSAN PUTNEY
Proofreading	IRENE BARNARD
Index	VICTORIA BAKER
Printing	BANG PRINTING

Names: Portman, Janet, author. | Stewart, Marcia, editor.
Title: Every tenant's legal guide / Attorney Janet Portman and Marcia Stewart.
Description: 9th edition. | Berkeley, CA : Nolo, 2018. | Includes index.
Identifiers: LCCN 2017047706 (print) | LCCN 2017050198 (ebook) | ISBN
    9781413325065 (ebook) | ISBN 9781413325058 (paperbook)
Subjects: LCSH: Landlord and tenant--United States--Popular works.
Classification: LCC KF590.Z9 (ebook) | LCC KF590.Z9 P67 2018 (print) | DDC
    346.7304/34--dc23
LC record available at https://lccn.loc.gov/2017047706

This book covers only United States law, unless it specifically states otherwise.

Quantity Sales: For information on bulk purchases or corporate premium sales, please contact the Special Sales Department. For academic sales or textbook adoptions, ask for Academic Sales. Call 800-955-4775 or write to Nolo at 950 Parker Street, Berkeley, CA 94710.

Please note

We believe accurate, plain-English legal information should help you solve many of your own legal problems. But this text is not a substitute for personalized advice from a knowledgeable lawyer. If you want the help of a trained professional—and we'll always point out situations in which we think that's a good idea—consult an attorney licensed to practice in your state.

About the Authors

Janet Portman, an attorney and Nolo's Executive Editor, received undergraduate and graduate degrees from Stanford and a law degree from Santa Clara University. She is an expert on landlord-tenant law and the coauthor of *Every Landlord's Legal Guide, The California Landlord's Law Book: Rights & Responsibilities, California Tenants' Rights, Renters' Rights: The Basics, Leases & Rental Agreements,* and *Negotiate the Best Lease for Your Business.* As a practicing attorney, she specialized in criminal defense before joining Nolo.

Marcia Stewart is the coauthor of *Every Landlord's Legal Guide, Renters' Rights: The Basics, Leases & Rental Agreements, First-Time Landlord,* and *Nolo's Essential Guide to Buying Your First Home.* Marcia received a Master's degree in Public Policy from the University of California at Berkeley.

Table of Contents

Your Tenant Companion 1

1 Finding a Place to Rent 3

Setting Your Rental Priorities 4

How to Find an Apartment or House for Rent 5

Visiting Prospective Rentals 13

Checking Out the Landlord and Manager 14

Checking Out Other Tenants and the Neighbors 15

Rental Applications and Credit Reports 16

How Landlords Reject Tenants 26

Finder's Fees and Holding Deposits 27

Choosing Roommates 30

2 Leases and Rental Agreements 31

How Leases and Rental Agreements Differ 33

Oral Leases and Rental Agreements 36

Typical Provisions in Leases and Rental Agreements 36

Negotiating With the Landlord 53

Changing a Lease or Rental Agreement 56

Signing a Lease or Rental Agreement 56

Cosigners 57

3 Basic Rent Rules 59

How Much Can Your Landlord Charge? 60

Rent Control 61

When Is Your Rent Due? 64

Grace Periods for Late Rent 65

Where and How Rent Is Due 66

Late Charges and Discounts for Early Payments 68

Returned Check Charges 70

Negotiating Partial or Delayed Rent Payments 70

Rent Increases 71

Talking the Landlord Out of a Rent Increase 75

4 Security Deposits 77

Dollar Limits on Deposits 78

How Landlords May Increase Deposits 80

Last Month's Rent 80

Nonrefundable Deposits and Fees 81

Interest on Deposits and Separate Accounts 82

How the Deposit May Be Used 83

If Your Landlord Sells the Property 83

5 Discrimination 85

Kinds of Discrimination Prohibited by Federal Laws 87

Kinds of Discrimination Prohibited by State and Local Law 97

How to Fight Back 99

6 Inspecting the Rental Unit and Moving In 107

How to Inspect the Rental Unit 108

Photographing the Rental Unit 114

How to Handle Problems 114

Clarifying Important Terms of the Tenancy 115

Organizing Your Rental Records 116

Using Email or Text Messages for Notice or a Letter of Understanding 116

7 Roommates, Guests, and Airbnb 119

Renting a Place With Others 120

Adding a New Roommate 129

Guests 131

Tenant Rights to Use Airbnb and Similar Vacation Rental Services 131

Taking In a Roomer 132

8 Major Repairs and Maintenance 133

Your Basic Right to Livable Premises 134

State Laws and Local Housing Codes 135

Court-Imposed Rules 136

Your Repair and Maintenance Responsibilities 137

Making Tenants Responsible for Repairs 137

How to Get Action From Your Landlord 138

What to Do If the Landlord Won't Make Repairs 141

9 Minor Repairs and Maintenance 151

Minor Repairs: What Are They? 152

The Landlord's Responsibilities 152

Tenant Responsibilities 155

Getting the Landlord to Make Minor Repairs 157

Making Minor Repairs Yourself 161

10 Making Improvements and Alterations 163

Improvements That Become Part of the Property 164

Improving Your Rental Unit Without Enriching Your Landlord 165

Cable TV Access 167

Satellite Dishes and Other Antennas 168

11 Your Right to Privacy 173

Entry by the Landlord 174

Entry by Others 179

Other Invasions of Privacy 181

What to Do About Invasions of Privacy 182

12 Injuries on the Premises 187

What to Do If You're Injured 188

Is the Landlord Liable? 191

If You're at Fault, Too 197

How Much Money You're Entitled To 198

13 Environmental Hazards 201

Asbestos 203

Lead 208

Radon 217

Carbon Monoxide 219

Mold 221

Bedbugs 225

14 Crime on the Premises 231

The Landlord's Basic Duty to Keep You Safe 232

Problems With Other Tenants 235

Illegal Activity on the Property and Nearby 237

Getting Results From the Landlord 240

Protecting Yourself 245

15   How Tenancies End or Change 247

Changing Terms During Your Tenancy 248

How Month-to-Month Tenancies End 250

How Fixed-Term Leases End 254

Retaliation and Other Illegal Tenancy Terminations 257

How to Stay When Your Landlord Wants You Out 258

Getting Out of a Lease 259

Condominium Conversions 270

If the Landlord Sells or Goes Out of Business 271

If the Landlord Declares Bankruptcy 271

If the Rental Property Is Foreclosed 272

16   Moving Out and Getting Your Security Deposit Back 275

Basic Rules for Returning Deposits 276

Deductions for Cleaning and Damage 279

Deductions for Unpaid Rent 281

Avoiding Fights Over Deposits 283

Security Deposits From Cotenants 290

How to Handle Deposit Disputes 291

Suing Your Landlord in Small Claims Court 293

If Your Deposit Doesn't Cover What You Owe 296

Your Abandoned Property 297

17   Termination Notices Based on Nonpayment of Rent and Other Illegal Acts 303

Termination Notices 304

Other Violations of the Lease or Rental Agreement 306

Violations of Your Legal Responsibilities as a Tenant 307

Illegal Activity on the Premises 308

Negotiating With the Landlord 308

Getting Help From a Mediator 310

Refusing to Move Out 310

Cutting Your Losses and Moving 312

18   Evictions 315

When to Fight—And When to Move 316

Illegal "Self-Help" Evictions 316

How Eviction Lawsuits Work 317

Stopping Eviction by Filing for Bankruptcy 323

19 Resolving Problems Without a Lawyer 325

How to Negotiate a Settlement 326

Using a Mediator 327

Suing in Small Claims Court 328

Tenants Working Together 329

20 Lawyers and Legal Research 335

How a Lawyer Can Help You 336

Finding a Good Lawyer 336

Fee Arrangements With Lawyers 339

Resolving Problems With Your Lawyer 340

Doing Your Own Legal Research 341

Appendixes

A State Landlord-Tenant Law Charts 347

State Landlord-Tenant Statutes 348

State Rent Rules 349

State Rules on Notice Required to Change or Terminate a Month-to-Month Tenancy 351

State Security Deposit Rules 354

Required Landlord Disclosures 364

State Laws in Domestic Violence Situations 378

State Laws on Rent Withholding and Repair and Deduct Remedies 383

State Laws on Landlord's Access to Rental Property 385

State Laws on Handling Abandoned Property 387

State Laws Prohibiting Landlord Retaliation 388

State Laws on Termination for Nonpayment of Rent 390

State Laws on Termination for Violation of Lease 393

State Laws on Unconditional Quit Terminations 395

State Small Claims Court Limits 402

Landlord's Duty to Rerent 408

Consequences of Self-Help Evictions 410

B How to Use the Downloadable Forms on the Nolo Website 413

Editing RTFs 414

List of Forms Available on the Nolo Website 414

Index 415

Your Tenant Companion

Dealing with your landlord or property manager can be challenging, to say the least. Doing it successfully requires not only knowing the basics of landlord-tenant law, but also coping with your landlord's business policies and idiosyncrasies and keeping your cool at the same time you protect your rights.

This book is based on the view that your life will be much easier if you are both a responsible tenant and legally knowledgeable—that is, if you pay the rent on time and comply with your lease rules. It includes important state-specific information, with dozens of detailed charts on everything from state security deposit rules to state laws prohibiting landlord retaliation.

If you are also savvy enough to send written requests—for example, when repairs are needed or you want to add a roommate—your landlord is far more likely to respond positively to your request. And if you keep records of all communications with your landlord, you'll be in good shape if a dispute occurs later and you need backup documentation. (Just be careful you don't rely only on email or text messages for sending important notices and letters; we explain why in "Using Email or Text Messages for Notice or a Letter of Understanding" in Chapter 6.)

This book includes dozens of forms, sample letters, notices, and checklists to help you through the entire rental process—from a rental priorities worksheet to help organize your search for housing, to a notice informing your landlord of your intent to move out. Each form is easy to customize for your particular situation. There are filled-in samples in the text, and you'll find the key forms on the companion page for this book on the Nolo website (see below for details).

But let's face it—even a conscientious and knowledgeable tenant can't always get good results. Some landlords are stingy, petty, and obnoxious, bent on extracting the last dollar from their tenants at the least possible cost to themselves. Trying to deal with them reasonably just doesn't work. If that sounds like your landlord, this book may become a combat manual, something you study closely to discover legal weapons to protect your rights. You'll probably find there is much you can do to fight back.

But even if the law is 110% on your side, there may be times when avoiding conflict (finding a new place to live) is wiser than engaging in a drawn-out, costly, and risky legal dispute with your landlord.

We hope that by reading this book you'll find the information you need to make an intelligent decision about whether to stay or go—and even better, that you'll learn strategies that will help you avoid these conflicts in the first place.

CAUTION

Who shouldn't use this book? Don't use this book if you are renting commercial property or space in a mobile home park, hotel, or marina. If you are a tenant in government-subsidized or -owned housing (including the "Section 8" program), your lease may contain terms required by the government, which neither you nor your landlord can change. Tenants who lease a home in a condominium complex are generally on the same legal footing as those who rent single-family houses, which means that this book will apply to them. However, condo tenants are also subject to the condominium's operating rules and regulations (known as "CC&Rs"), which may impose obligations or restrictions on tenants and landlords in addition to those found in federal, state, and local law.

Get Legal Updates, Forms, and More at This Book's Companion Page on Nolo.com

This book includes several useful forms, such as a rental application and a demand for the return of a security deposit. You can download any of the forms and worksheets in this book at

www.nolo.com/back-of-book/EVTEN.html

When there are important changes to the information in this book, we'll post updates on this same dedicated page. See Appendix B, "How to Use the Downloadable Forms on the Nolo Website" for a list of forms available on Nolo.com.

Finding a Place to Rent

Setting Your Rental Priorities...4

How to Find an Apartment or House for Rent..5

    Personal Contacts..9

    Craigslist...10

    Pound the Pavement..10

    Classified Ads...10

    Online Apartment and Rental Listings...10

    Advertising Yourself to Landlords..11

    Real Estate Brokers...12

    Management Companies..12

    University, Alumni, and Corporate Housing Offices...12

Visiting Prospective Rentals...13

Checking Out the Landlord and Manager..14

    Ask Current Tenants...14

    Ask Neighbors in Nearby Buildings...15

    Check Out www.apartmentratings.com..15

    Google the Landlord or Manager..15

    Check for Any Notices of Default..15

Checking Out Other Tenants and the Neighbors...15

Rental Applications and Credit Reports..16

    Rental Applications...17

    The Importance of Your Credit History...24

How Landlords Reject Tenants..26

    Permissible Reasons for Rejecting Tenants...26

    What Landlords Must Tell You..27

    Illegal Discrimination...27

Finder's Fees and Holding Deposits..27

    Finder's Fees..27

    Holding Deposits..29

Choosing Roommates...30

It goes almost without saying that choosing a place to live is an extremely important decision. A good apartment or house should provide more than shelter, warmth, and a place to lay your head; it should be a true home. Yet many people make bad choices—spending too much money; picking the wrong location, landlord, or neighbors; or settling on a place that's too small, dreary, noisy, unsafe, or in bad shape. Sure, if you're in a tight rental market, such as those in New York City, San Francisco, or Chicago, you can have an extremely difficult time finding a good place to live at a reasonable price, but it's still possible to find decent housing.

Finding a good place to live is rarely a lucky accident. Whether rental housing is plentiful or scarce, there are specific steps you can take to find an apartment or house that meets your needs and budget. Most important, you need to take your time. One of the worst—and most costly—mistakes you can make is to sign a lease or put down a hefty deposit at the end of a long, frustrating day of apartment-hunting, only to realize later that the place is completely unsuitable. Even if it means staying with friends for a few weeks, finding a short-term rental or house-sitting arrangement, or (horrors) moving back in with your parents temporarily, it may be well worth it.

Whether you're looking for your first or tenth rental, living by yourself or with others, this chapter shows you how to find a good place to live within your price range, by:

- setting clear priorities before you start looking for a place to rent
- using a variety of resources to tap into available rentals, and
- beating the competition by pulling together the information landlords want to see—good references and credit information—before you visit prospective rentals.

This chapter also explains your legal rights and responsibilities regarding the rental application process, credit reports, credit-check fees, and holding deposits. (For details on antidiscrimination laws that limit what landlords can say and do in the tenant selection process, see Chapter 5.)

RELATED TOPIC

Preparing for a move. If you're moving from one rental to another, be sure you understand all the legal and practical rules for ending a tenancy, getting your deposit returned, and moving out. See Chapters 15 and 16 for details.

Check Your Credit Rating Before You Start Your Housing Search

Your credit report contains a wealth of information that landlords use to choose (or reject) tenants—for example, the report lists any bankruptcy filings, uncollected child support, and unpaid debts that have been reported to the credit reporting agency. It will also reflect favorable information, such as your ability to pay your card balances and other debts on time. To make sure your credit report is accurate—or to give yourself time to clean it up if there are problems or errors—get a copy of your report before you start looking. "Rental Applications and Credit Reports," below, provides complete details.

Setting Your Rental Priorities

While most people start their housing search with some general idea of how much they can afford to pay, where they want to live, and how big a place they need, that doesn't guarantee good results. The best way to find an excellent rental home is to set specific guidelines in advance, being realistic, of course, both as to your budget and what's available for rent.

Here's our approach to finding a rental house or apartment you can afford and will enjoy living in:

Step 1: Firmly establish your priorities—such as maximum rent, desired location, and number of bedrooms—before you start looking. The list below, Rental Priorities, will help you do this.

TIP

If you're renting with one or more other people, review the Rental Priorities list together and make sure you agree on the basics. Always consider each person's strong likes and dislikes when you're choosing a rental. For example, you might care most about a modern kitchen and a sunny deck or patio. If so, you'll surely be miserable if you allow your spouse or partner to talk you into renting an older apartment with its original 1960s kitchen because it has a great view (but no deck).

Step 2: Once you've set your priorities, you'll want to see how prospective rental units measure up. To make this simple, we've prepared a Rental Priorities Worksheet, shown below. There's space for you to write down your mandatory ("must have") priorities, as well as secondary ("it would be nice, but aren't crucial") priorities and your absolute "no ways." Try to limit your mandatory priorities to those features your rental unit must have, such as "less than $1,000 a month rent," "two or more bedrooms," and "near the bus line to work." Take time developing your list of "no ways." Avoiding things you hate—for example, a high-crime area or noisy neighborhood—may be just as important as finding a place that meets all your mandatory priorities.

FORM

The Nolo website includes a downloadable copy of the Rental Priorities Worksheet. See Appendix B for the link to the forms in this book.

Step 3: Once you complete the priorities section of the Worksheet, make several copies for use when looking at apartments or rental houses.

Step 4: Complete a Worksheet for each rental unit you're seriously considering, as follows:
- Enter the address, contact person, phone number, email, rent, deposit, term (month-to-month or year lease), and other key information on the top of the form.

- As you walk around the rental unit and talk with the landlord or manager, indicate the pluses and minuses and the mandatory and secondary priorities (as well as "no ways") that apply.
- Make notes next to a particular feature that can be changed to meet your needs—for example, "Rent is high, but space is fine for an extra roommate."
- Jot down additional features in the section for Other Comments, such as "Neighbors seem very friendly" or "Tiny yard for kids to play, but great park is just a block away."

Step 5: If at all possible (but it may not be, especially in tight rental markets), insist that any apartment or house meets at least your most important priorities.

Check Out All Important Conditions of the Tenancy

Leases and rental agreements cover many issues, such as the amount of rent and deposits, length of the tenancy, number of tenants, and pets. In addition, some rental agreements may include provisions that you find unacceptable—for example, restrictions on guests, design alterations, or the use of an apartment for your home business. Ask for a copy of the lease or rental agreement early on, so you are not reading it for the first time with a pen in your hand. Be sure to read Chapter 2 for details on leases and rental agreements and how to negotiate terms before you sign on the dotted line.

How to Find an Apartment or House for Rent

You've just done an important part of the job of finding a place to live by creating your list of Rental Priorities. Now you need a plan to find a place that matches it as closely as possible. Focus on your time and financial constraints and consider how

Rental Priorities

When you're making your list of priorities, consider these issues:

Rent

Figure out the maximum you can afford to pay. Be sure to include utilities, Internet, and any additional charges, such as for parking. As a broad generalization, you probably don't want to spend more than 25% to 35% of your monthly take-home pay on rent, but this will obviously depend on your expenses. Be careful about overspending—you don't want to live in a penthouse if it means you need to eat popcorn for dinner every night.

Deposits

Depending on state law and landlord practices, you may need to pay as much as two months' rent as a security deposit. (Chapter 4 covers security deposits.) If you have limited cash to pay deposits and other up-front fees, include the maximum you can pay in the Priorities list on your worksheet.

Location and Neighborhood

Where you live is often more important than the size and amenities of the unit you rent. If you know the exact area you want, list it. If you don't, think of the features that are important. If living in a low-crime area or being able to walk to grocery stores, restaurants, athletic facilities, or a kid-friendly park are important, don't end up renting a nicer apartment in a neighborhood with none of these features.

Schools

If you have school-age children, the proximity and quality of local schools are very important considerations. If you're new to the area, start by contacting your state department of education. It should be able to provide data for individual schools and districts, including academic test scores, enrollment figures, racial and ethnic information, and even dropout rates. Your next step is to call and visit local schools and school districts to learn about class size, class offerings, instructional practices, and services. Finally, check out resources such as newspaper articles on the local school board or PTA at public libraries and online sites.

Work or School Commute

If you're looking at a potentially long commute, note the maximum times or distance you're willing to travel to and from work or school.

Ability to Work From Home

If you're planning to run a business from home, make sure local law or landlord policies don't prohibit your home-based business. See Chapter 2 for more information on this topic.

Public Transit

Do you need to be close to a bus line, subway, train, or airport? Write it down.

Pets

If you have a dog, cat, or other pet, you'll need to make sure the landlord allows pets. (See Chapter 2 for suggestions on how to negotiate with landlords who don't normally allow pets.)

Number of Tenants

If you want to live with an unusually large number of people, given the size of the rental you can afford, you must make sure the landlord will allow it. (Chapter 5 discusses occupancy standards many landlords set, limiting the number of tenants in a particular rental unit.)

Rental Term

Do you want the flexibility of a short-term rental agreement, or the security of a long-term lease? (Chapter 2 discusses the pros and cons of leases and rental agreements. Also, Chapter 15 discusses sublets, which may be a short-term rental option.)

Move-In Date

If you need a place immediately, write "Must be available now" in your priority list. But don't be too quick to pass up a great place that's not available for several weeks. It might be worth your while. (Remember the importance of patience.) Also, if a fantastic apartment is available now, but you have to give 30 days' notice on your current place, it might be worth paying double rent for a while rather than give up a terrific apartment.

Rental Priorities (continued)

Number and Type of Rooms

How many bedrooms, baths, or other rooms do you need? Do you need suitable space for your home office? Is a finished basement important—for your pottery studio or band practice or kids' playroom? Is a modern kitchen with lots of counter space and good light ideal? How about a large living room for entertaining? List what you can't live without.

Furnishings

If you want something completely furnished, make this a priority. Remember, however, you can always rent furniture yourself if you can't find a furnished apartment—in fact, it might be cheaper. A few calls to local furniture rental places will quickly give you the information you need.

Other Interior Needs

Other priorities may include good space separation for roommates, a fireplace, lots of closets, air conditioning, or laundry facilities in the building. For some people, satellite TV is important. (Chapter 10 explains your right to install a satellite dish.) If you need multiple phone lines, make sure your building (and budget) can accommodate them. If you are disabled and have special needs, and want a rental that is already compatible with your needs, mark these as priorities. (For more on rights of the disabled, see Chapter 5.)

Type and Style of Building and Rental Unit

Do you have a clear idea of the type of place you want to live in? One-family house, duplex, six-to-ten-unit apartment building, high-rise, or gated community? If you have your heart set on a flat in a Victorian house, a loft, a small cottage, or a modern apartment with lots of windows and a great view, note that, too.

Security

For many people, a top-notch security system for the building and rental unit is important—for example, bars on all windows, a doorman or a front gate security system with intercom that allows you to screen visitors before they actually get to the front door of your apartment.

Quiet

If you can't stand the idea of living on a busy street with lots of traffic or in an apartment with paper-thin walls, make this a priority.

Yard and Outdoor Space

If you have a large dog or want room for a garden or for kids to play, a fenced-in yard will be important. Or maybe a deck, patio, or balcony ranks high on your wish list.

Parking

Parking can be a critical consideration, especially if you live in an urban area. Write down how many vehicles you have and whether you need garage parking or easy street parking with no restrictions.

Other Tenants

While we'd all like quiet, considerate neighbors, you may prefer a building with certain types of tenants—for example, mainly seniors, college students, or families with children. While your landlord cannot deliberately choose tenants because they belong to these groups (and exclude others) without courting a lawsuit, sometimes renters tend to choose, on their own, certain properties. For example, affordable housing near a college will be filled with students, and pricey buildings in spruced-up business or financial areas are likely to be peopled with older, professional types.

Landlord and Manager

Maybe you don't want to share a duplex house with the landlord. Or you want a place with an on-site manager who's always available to make repairs.

Purchase Potential

If you want to move into a rental you can eventually buy, such as a condo, co-op, or lease-option-to-buy house, investigate this from the start. This book does not cover these options, so you'll need to do additional research for advice on these subjects.

Rental Priorities Worksheet

Address: 178 Park St., #4F, Springsteen, New Jersey 00000

Contact: Emily Greenwood (Owner)   Email: emily@greenwood.com   Phone: (609) 555-1212

Rent: $3,200/month   Deposit: $3,200   Other fees:

Term: one year lease   Date seen: February 15, 20xx   Date available: March 1, 20xx

Brief description of rental unit and building: Sunny three-bedroom apt. in four-story brownstone. Recently remodeled kitchen. One and one-half baths. Lots of charm. Great location!

Mandatory Priorities:

☑ Close to university (a 10-minute walk!)

☐ Maximum $3,000 rent (over our limit, but it's worth the price)

☑ Modern kitchen

☑ Lots of light

☑ Three bedrooms

☑ Two bathrooms

☐

Secondary Priorities:

☑ Hardwood floors

☑ Small building

☐ Allows pets

☐ Fireplace

☐

☐

Absolute No Ways:

☐ High-crime area

☐ Run-down area

☐

☐

☐

☐

Other Comments: Neighbors seem very friendly. Noisy dog next door. Train station a few blocks away. Last vacancy was two years ago.

they will influence your search. For example, the housing search of a well-paid couple with money in the bank who wants to move to a bigger apartment sometime in the next six months should differ tremendously from that of a graduate student on a limited budget with a small child who has only a few weeks to find a place before school starts.

What type of search will work best for you will also depend on a number of factors, most importantly where you want to live and whether you want a lease for a year or more or prefer a month-to-month rental agreement. In many cities, Craigslist is your best resource. In others, you may want to work with a real estate broker. In all areas, it always makes sense to assertively and creatively use your own personal contacts and networks. Of course, the tighter the rental market you face, the more important it will be to pursue as many search options as possible. Here's a rundown of your choices.

Personal Contacts

If you know people who live or work near where you want to live, ask them for leads. Using personal contacts as housing scouts can be quite effective, because when people plan to move, friends, neighbors, and business associates almost always know about it before a for-rent sign goes up.

Prepare a brief description of exactly what you want (your rental priorities). Send this to friends, coworkers, and your social media networks. Don't forget local businesspeople with whom you have a friendly relationship—doctors, shopkeepers, lawyers, and insurance brokers may all have good leads for available rentals. If your company has an employee grapevine (possibly part of your internal email system), get the word out this way. Let as many people know of your housing search as possible. You never know who may come through with the perfect apartment—it might be the woman with the flower stand down the block or your dental hygienist.

See the sample Apartment-Hunting Note, below, for a good way to describe your housing needs and priorities. This Sample Apartment-Hunting Note is for a couple with professional jobs and excellent credit and references, who are looking in a moderately-priced rental market in northern New Jersey. If you are in your 20s and just out of college, have a limited budget, and are looking in an expensive and tight rental market, a detailed note like this to a handful of friends probably won't do the trick. Getting the word out on social media ("Help! I need a one-bedroom apartment that allows cats, in North Oakland by May 1, maximum $1,500 per month.") might be your best bet.

If you decide to offer a reward, such as a $50 restaurant gift certificate to the person who finds you the apartment you end up renting, mention this in your apartment-hunting note.

Sample Apartment-Hunting Note

Dear Friends:

We're in the market for a new apartment and hope you can help. We're looking for a three-bedroom, two-bath place near the university. We can afford up to $3,000 per month. We'd like to move within the next few months, but definitely by April 1 when Hannah starts her new job in New Brunswick.

It is important that the apartment be light and airy, in good condition and in a secure building (doorman preferred). We love to cook, so a decent kitchen is a must. Hardwood floors and a fireplace would be great. We don't have any pets but are thinking of getting a cat in the future, so we'd like a place that allows pets.

We have always been good tenants and can provide excellent references and credit.

If you hear about a rental unit that seems likely, please phone us at 609-555-3789 (home). Here are our work numbers:

Dennis: phone 609-555-2345; email Dennis@work.com

Hannah: phone 609-555-4567; email Hannah@work.com

Thanks so much for your help!
Regards,

Dennis Olson and Hannah Silver

Craigslist

Craigslist is enormously popular in the hundreds of cities it serves, and is the best place to begin your housing search, whether on your computer (www.craigslist.org) or via an app on your smart phone. Craigslist is free to both landlords and tenants.

If you respond to a Craigslist ad, be on the lookout for scams. If there are no images or information on the rental location, or the place sounds too good to be true, be wary. In all cases, be cautious about giving out personal identifying information, such as your Social Security number and even your phone number, before you're reasonably sure that there's no shady business going on. While the majority of advertisers are legit, a few have used the service for scams and worse. Arrange to talk with the owner or property manager before you view the rental; once you're comfortable, you can proceed with an application.

Pound the Pavement

In addition to enlisting the help of friends, you can do much looking on your own. In some neighborhoods, landlords simply post "Apartment For Rent" signs in front of the building or in one of the windows. Others put notices on neighborhood bulletin boards, such as the local laundromat or coffee shop.

Many tenants find great apartments or houses to rent by posting their own "Apartment Wanted" signs (sometimes offering a finder's fee) in local stores or businesses, such as a dance studio, a health club, or even an auto repair shop. You might also consider buying a classified ad in the local weekly paper or putting a notice in the newsletter of a community organization. Some enterprising tenants go so far as to track down the owners of houses that have been for sale for a long time, hoping to work out a rental arrangement.

If you want to live in a particular apartment building or complex, but there's no sign listed, stop by anyway and talk to the manager or doorman. (A generous tip might just do the job!) Also, try to talk with some of the other tenants. You might just get a good lead on someone who's planning to move soon. Spend a lot of time walking around the neighborhood you want to live in—this will give you a chance to meet local people who may know about available rentals before they're advertised.

Classified Ads

Many landlords in smaller cities advertise their rental units in the newspaper real estate classified ads. The largest section usually runs in the Sunday paper. The classifieds are usually organized by city or neighborhood and include basic information such as rent, location, number of bedrooms and baths, and any special features such as a fireplace or view.

Get early editions of papers (for example, Sunday papers are available late Friday night in some areas) and start calling as soon as possible to get a jump on the competition. Better yet, go online. Many papers post their classifieds before the information hits the streets.

 RELATED TOPIC

Illegal ads. Classified ads run by landlords should never mention sex, race, religion, disability, or age (unless the rental is really legally sanctioned senior citizens housing). Chapter 5 discusses the topic of discriminatory advertising.

Online Apartment and Rental Listings

For many tenants, Craigslist will be the best place to find an apartment or rental housing. Local online services may also be available, particularly in large urban areas, such as Apartable.com in New York City and San Francisco or Westside Rentals in Southern California.

There are also many websites that offer national listings, including:
- www.hotpads.com (a Zillow company)
- www.zumper.com
- www.apartments.com
- www.apartmentguide.com
- www.rentals.com

- www.forrent.com
- www.apartmentsearch.com, and
- www.rent.com.

Many of these sites provide more than apartment listings, offering information and links covering renters' insurance, moving tips, and more. Useful iPhone and Android apps are free for some of these sites, such as apartmentguide.com.

> ⓘ **CAUTION**
>
> **Before you use any online apartment rental service, make sure it's reputable.** Check how long the company has been in business, who owns it, and how they handle problems with apartment listings. Check for any consumer complaints, and avoid paying any hefty fees without thoroughly checking out a company and its services.

Advertising Yourself to Landlords

While the Internet is full of websites that landlords use to post rentals, only a few offer the opposite service: Letting people who are searching for a rental describe themselves, their needs, and their price range, hoping that a landlord in the area will see their post and contact them. The idea is similar to the practice in adoptions, where would-be adopting parents produce glossy and glowing descriptions of themselves and the family they want to raise, aimed at women who will choose the family that will get their child.

Craigslist offers this service, and their pages are chock-full of posts that run the gamut from sophisticated to self-defeating. If you decide to place an ad for yourself in this manner, follow the tips below. They're geared to these twin goals:

- giving a potential landlord relevant information about your needs and nature, so that the landlord doesn't waste time calling someone who isn't suited for the rental—and you don't waste time taking these calls, and
- painting an accurate picture of yourself that fits every landlord's search for tenants who are stable, clean, and honest.

With these goals in mind, design your ad as follows:

- Describe what you're looking for. Make it clear whether you need a quiet, secluded home, or a utilitarian studio downtown. But resist listing all of your "must-haves." You're likely to appear as a demanding tenant (a landlord's worst nightmare).
- Describe your job, your interests, and how you spend your free time carefully. Any activities that spell "property damage" or "party animal" may backfire. You'd be surprised at how many tenant-advertisers describe their love of alcohol and music (without mentioning that they use earbuds).
- Include a photo, and use some common sense. Far too many look like they were taken at a wild party or look downright scary.
- Don't play the sympathy card. You may be down on your luck, but don't expect landlords to choose you because they feel sorry for you. Instead, emphasize the positive—your respect for your neighbors, longevity at your current rental, and so on.

Use a new and dedicated email account for your posting. That way, you will avoid getting scammed by people who will use the email to find you on Facebook, intending to do all sorts of damage.

What the Words Really Mean

With online ads, as with print ads, you need to watch for misleading statements or just plain puffery. We took a look at ads for rentals in the Bay Area and came up with this gem for a Marin County apartment:

Closest train: BART

Distance to train: More than 5-minute drive.

Nearest highway: 101 Freeway

Distance to nearest highway: Less than 5-minute drive.

The real story: The closest BART station is in the next county, over a bridge that has poor public transit—more like an hour's trip on the bus. The freeway is, indeed, less than five minutes away—it's directly across the street!

TIP

Looking for a pet-friendly rental? Go to a local park or veterinarian's office and talk to people with animals. They may have some good leads. Also, check out www.humanesociety.org (search "renting with pets"). They provide helpful advice on how to put your best paw forward, with links to sites listing animal-friendly apartments.

Real Estate Brokers

Some local real estate offices, especially in large cities, also handle rental properties, often exclusively for a property owner. If you're moving into a new area, especially someplace like New York City, or have limited time to apartment-hunt, real estate brokers can be very useful. A good broker should do lots of legwork for you. The more prepared you are (by setting priorities as we discuss above), the more helpful a broker can be.

As with apartment-finding services, choose your broker carefully:

- **Get full information about all fees, which can be quite hefty.** In New York City, for example, real estate brokers often charge either a fee that is tied to the rent (for example, 15% of the first year's rent) or a flat fee of $1,000 or more for a rental. Sometimes the property owner covers the real estate broker's fee, but typically the tenant pays.

CAUTION

Avoid brokers who try to pressure you into paying their fee before you sign a lease or rental agreement. Don't pay until the deal is final.

- **Ask about the type and exclusivity of the broker's listings.** Why pay a hefty fee if you can find the same place through Craigslist, or for a lower price through an apartment-finding service? And don't waste your time with a broker whose properties don't meet your needs as to neighborhood, type of unit, or budget.

- **Choose a broker with lots of experience and a good reputation.** The best way to do this is through recommendations from people who have used the particular broker in the last few years and whose judgment you trust. Interview a few brokers and ask a lot of questions about their services, how long they've been in business, and their knowledge of the area. Be sure to check Yelp reviews and see if any complaints are on file with the Better Business Bureau.

Management Companies

Property management companies often contract with landlords to rent units and manage all aspects of the rental property. In many areas, a handful of management companies control a significant number of rental properties. You can find the names of the bigger companies just by driving around and looking at signs posted outside apartment buildings. Or, check online (or in your local phone book) under "Real Estate Management."

You can usually approach management companies directly. When choosing a property management company, follow our advice on real estate brokers (discussed above).

TIP

Beat the competition by getting on a waiting list. If you want to rent in a particular big complex and you have a little time, you may be able to prequalify and get on a waiting list for the next available rental unit. To convince the landlord to screen you now (and to allay his fears that he would be wasting his time because you'll probably end up living elsewhere before he has a vacancy), assure him that you are in no hurry and are not considering other properties.

University, Alumni, and Corporate Housing Offices

College housing offices can be an excellent source of rentals, especially services geared to faculty members. If you want a short-term rental, you can often find places that never appear on

Craigslist—for example, the home of a professor who's going on sabbatical for six months. If you're not affiliated with a university, try to find someone who is. The same holds true for housing offices available to employees of local corporations. And don't forget to check out your college alumni association. It may also provide information on rentals in the area (or you can contact fellow alumni for leads).

Renting a Place When You're New in Town

If you're completely unfamiliar with the area you're moving to, you're at an obvious and serious disadvantage —you simply don't have the basic information normally considered essential to locating a good place in a congenial location at a fair price. Your HR office at work or college housing office are good places to start. Also, check online community resources and websites such as www.streetadvisor.com and City-Data.com for street, neighborhood, and city reviews.

But there's no substitute for your own legwork. Ask your friends and colleagues, walk and drive around neighborhoods, talk to local residents and shop owners, read local newspapers, check the library's community resources file, visit the local planning department and chamber of commerce, and do whatever else will help you get a better sense of a neighborhood or city. Also, a good real estate broker can be invaluable.

If you're in a hurry to move, one sensible alternative is to leave your furniture in storage and stay in a hotel or take a short-term furnished rental. Check out Airbnb, VRBO, and similar services for good leads. While finding a temporary rental means moving twice, it's far better than settling on an apartment or area that's not to your taste.

Visiting Prospective Rentals

Everyone needs a home-hunting strategy—whether you make an appointment to see an apartment by yourself or attend an open house with dozens of others. Here are some basic tips:

Visit promising rentals as soon as they come on the market. Especially in college towns and popular neighborhoods, apartments and rental houses move fast. If a place sounds good, schedule a visit as soon as it's listed.

Be prepared. Come equipped with your own handy-dandy apartment-hunter's kit. Include a street map, notebook, pen or pencil, pocket calculator, tape measure (to make sure the living room is big enough for your carpet), graph paper, and camera. (You may want to take pictures if it's okay with the landlord.) Your smartphone may have everything you need. Most important, bring your Rental Priorities Worksheet as discussed above. Don't forget your checkbook. (You may fall in love with a place and need to leave a holding deposit while the landlord checks out your credit history and references. Holding deposits are covered below.)

Impress the landlord by showing up with everything you need to fill out a rental application, including references and credit information. (See "Rental Applications and Credit Reports," below, for more on these issues.)

Be on your best "good tenant" behavior. Clearly understand that while you're looking at a rental unit, the landlord or manager will be looking at and evaluating you. This means showing up on time, dressing neatly, and presenting yourself as being both conscientious and agreeable. (This also means keeping your love of drums to yourself.) Realize that landlords live in fear of overly demanding and fussy tenants who will give them constant headaches by ceaselessly complaining about trivial things. So while we recommend checking out the rental unit's condition (see below) and making sure significant defects are being remedied, it's usually a mistake to ask for a long list of upgrades and repairs before you're even offered the place. Better to save your requests until the landlord makes you an offer. But make sure you do your essential negotiating before you sign a lease or rental agreement.

Look around carefully for tell-tale signs of problems in the rental unit and building. While you don't want to come across as a nit-picking housing inspector with white gloves, do keep your eyes open. Don't broadcast your concerns (subtlety is a strong point here), but try to check as many of the following things as possible:

- Look for obvious damage, such as loose steps, torn carpet, or shaky handrails.
- Check for dirt, mildew, and signs of insects or rodents. (But try to overlook the sloppiness of a current tenant. Piles of dishes in the sink and mounds of clothes on the floor are only temporary.)
- Flush the toilet and run water in the shower and sinks. Check the water temperature and pressure.
- Make sure the windows and doors are in good shape, open and close easily, and have secure locks.
- Walk around the building, checking out any elevators and common areas such as stairs, laundry rooms, and lobbies, as well as the parking area, garage, and yard. Again, check for general cleanliness and repair. Good lighting is especially important in common areas.
- Ask about building and neighborhood security, especially if you have concerns about the area. Get neighborhood crime stats from the local police department. If there have been criminal incidents on the property, find out what kind and when, and what steps have been taken to provide reasonable safety to tenants and guests. If you learn later that the answers were not accurate, you may have grounds for getting out of your lease or rental agreement. Chapter 14 gives more information on your rights to a safe place to live.

At this point, you're just trying to get a general sense of the place. Ask yourself: Does this feel safe and comfortable? Clean and in good repair? If you decide you want the rental unit, and before you actually sign a lease or rental agreement, you will want to do a more detailed inventory of the condition of the rental unit, completing the Landlord-Tenant Checklist we recommend in Chapter 6. (You want your landlord to acknowledge any existing defects so he or she can't blame you later for causing them.)

If there are some minor problems, or improvements you want—for example, a new coat of paint in the living room—you may be able to negotiate with the landlord on this before you move in. (Chapter 2 shows how.) Major problems, such as lack of heat, may be the landlord's legal responsibility to fix. (For details on housing standards and landlords' responsibility to provide habitable housing, see Chapter 8.) Also, see Chapter 2 for information on disclosures landlords must tell prospective tenants, such as the presence of lead-based paint in the rental unit.

Think of creative ways to use space. You may need to compromise on the number and type of rooms in exchange for a great location or lower rent. Use your imagination or check out home design books, magazines, and websites such as www.apartmenttherapy.com for ideas on how to make the most of your living space. For example, you might be able to carve out a study at the end of an extra-large living room, using bookcases or screens to divide the space. Rolling carts with butcher block tops can add instant space to a kitchen with limited counters.

Walk, drive, and/or bike around the neighborhood. If you're not familiar with the area, check out restaurants, shops, local businesses and schools, and bus, subway, and train stops. Do this at night (ideally, by car and with a friend) as well as the daytime. You might find that the neighborhood doesn't seem quite as safe and friendly at night as it does during the day.

Checking Out the Landlord and Manager

Your prospective landlord will probably check you out pretty thoroughly (asking for references and getting a credit report); turnaround is not only fair play, but is also a good way to find out what it's like to live in your landlord's building.

Ask Current Tenants

Visit the building after work and ask residents, especially the person whose unit you're considering, about pluses and minuses of living in the building. Inquire about security and noise in the building or neighborhood and if there are any problems regarding repairs and basic services such as heat and hot water. See if you can get a sense of the landlord's personality and style of operating. An excellent indicator of whether you can expect smooth sailing is to find out how often there are vacancies in the building and, in particular, how often your prospective landlord has had to evict tenants. A low rate of turnovers and evictions suggests that tenants like living there and that the landlord has chosen considerate, law-abiding renters who will be good neighbors.

Ask Neighbors in Nearby Buildings

Other people and businesses in the neighborhood may know something about the reputation of the building, landlord, or manager. Ask if tenants seem to stay more than a year—if so, that's the mark of a well-run building. By speaking with neighbors, you can confirm the truthfulness of the landlord's or property manager's representations, such as a claim that there have been no recent incidents requiring a police response.

Check Out www.apartmentratings.com

This comprehensive website has hundreds of thousands of renter reviews of individual apartments and property managers nationwide. It includes other information useful to new tenants, such as noise and safety ratings of each rental.

Google the Landlord or Manager

Don't let your interest in a particular rental go too far without running a Google search on the owner and/or property manager, and even the address. If the property has been in the news lately, you'll read all about it, and chances are, the story won't be comforting. Likewise with the owner or manager—you don't want to rent a place whose management has been the subject of a feature article on the woes of renting, or a property with terrible Yelp reviews.

Check for Any Notices of Default

If you're concerned about the landlord's financial stability, find out whether the property you're considering is the subject of a notice of default (the first public step toward foreclosure). Banks and other lenders must file these notices, in the courthouse of the county in which the property is located, when the owner has failed to make payments on a loan or mortgage for a specified number of months (two is common). Obviously, renting a property that's liable to be foreclosed upon during your tenancy is not a good idea—even if you get to stay, you may end up with an owner (especially if it's the bank itself) who will not be a conscientious landlord.

Checking Out Other Tenants and the Neighbors

Not surprisingly, many tenants are as concerned about who their potential neighbors will be (and what kind of background they have) as they are about the physical aspects of the prospective rental. Anyone who has lived in close proximity to others, be they down the hall, on the other side of the wall, or over the fence, knows that a law-abiding, considerate neighbor is every bit as important as a view, a second bathroom, or a parking spot.

If you visited the rental and had a chance to talk with other residents, you may already have a rough impression of your prospective neighbors. But depending on your situation, you may want to learn more. In particular, if you're a single female or have young children, you may want reassurance that the tenant next door doesn't have a dangerous criminal background. How much information can you expect to learn from your landlord and from law enforcement? In general, here's what you can expect.

First, there is no law requiring your landlord to investigate the criminal history of his tenants. Of course, many landlords do inquire or run background checks, and most will decline to rent to those with violent criminal backgrounds. But if you ask and are told, "I have no idea," you have no legal basis to press your landlord for more. And even if the landlord does know about a tenant's unsavory past, there is no law requiring him to disclose it to you (though the landlord may be held liable if you are later injured by this tenant, as the example below illustrates).

> **EXAMPLE:** Nancy and her daughter rented an apartment from Lester. When Nancy applied for the apartment, she told Lester that she was not home in the afternoon and that her daughter would be on her own until Nancy came home from work. Nancy was concerned for her daughter's safety and asked Lester if any of the other tenants had criminal histories or had done anything to suggest that they would act inappropriately with children.
>
> Lester told Nancy she had nothing to worry about from the neighbors. In fact, however, Lester knew that a downstairs tenant had a conviction, albeit an old one, for child molestation. Tragically, this neighbor molested Nancy's daughter. Nancy sued the offender and Lester, on the grounds that he knew about and failed to disclose a dangerous condition—namely, the presence of a known molester. Lester's insurance company settled the case in Nancy's favor for a large sum.

Although you cannot count on your landlord for a full answer to your questions, you may be able look online for help. Every state has a version of "Megan's Law," a federal law passed in 1996 and named after a young girl who was killed by a convicted child molester who lived in her neighborhood. The original law charged the FBI with keeping a nationwide database of persons convicted of sexual offenses against minors and violent sexual offenses against anyone (42 U.S.C. §§ 14701 and following). The state versions typically require certain convicted sexual offenders to register with local law enforcement officials, who keep a database on their whereabouts.

If you are concerned about whether prospective neighbors are registered sex offenders, you can search for their names on your state's database.

To find out how to access your state's sex offender registry, contact your local law enforcement agency, or call the Parents for Megan's Law Hotline at 888-ASK-PFML, or check www.parentsformeganslaw.org. Of course, it's unlikely that you'll know the full names of all the residents of a large apartment complex. Even when you do have that information, keep in mind that a database search may not give you accurate information. In many states, the databases are not current, or have mistaken information, which may result in both false positives (typical when dealing with common names) and false negatives.

 TIP

Concerned about too many Airbnb guests in the rental property? Many tenants rent out their apartments on a short-term basis through websites such as Airbnb. While that might be fine with you (maybe you even hope to do the same), you may not want to live someplace where lots of different people are coming and going. At any rate, be sure you know your landlord's policies on Airbnb and common tenant practices. See Chapter 7, "Tenant Rights to Use Airbnb and Similar Vacation Rental Services," for more on the subject.

Report Deceptive Advertising

If a rental unit is unavailable, inferior, or higher priced than advertised, contact the consumer fraud division of the local district attorney's office. Such deceptive advertising is illegal, and many property owners have been prosecuted for such practices.

Rental Applications and Credit Reports

Once you find a place you like, you're part, but not all, of the way home. First, you will probably be asked to fill out a rental application. Landlords use rental applications to screen potential tenants and select those who are likely to pay the rent on time, keep the rental in good condition, and not cause problems. Conscientious landlords will insist on checking your references and credit history before signing a lease or rental agreement. You should be happy they do so. You'll probably have fewer problems with other tenants in the building if the landlord is strict about screening. Who wants to move into a great building where one tenant is dealing drugs, holding midnight rehearsals for her rock band, or otherwise causing trouble that the landlord could have averted by proper screening?

Rental Applications

On a written rental application, you must provide information on your employment, income, credit history (including any bankruptcies), and rental housing history (including evictions), as well as any criminal convictions. If you are self-employed, the landlord may require the last few years' tax returns and other documentation of income. It's legal to ask for your Social Security number, driver's license number, or other identifying information (such as an Individual Taxpayer Identification Number, or ITIN). Except in California and New York City, landlords may also ask for proof of an applicant's right to be in the United States under U.S. immigration laws. Under federal fair housing laws, landlords who ask for such immigration information must ask all tenants, not just those whom they suspect may be in the country illegally. It is, however, illegal to discriminate on the basis of national origin. (See Chapter 5.)

A sample Rental Application is shown below, so that you can get an idea of the information you will need. It may be a good idea to complete this rental application and take it with you when you see a potential rental unit. This type of information is sure to impress a landlord.

Most careful landlords will make a few calls to confirm that the information you've supplied on the Rental Application is correct. Current and past landlords, credit sources, and employers will normally request permission from you before

they'll talk to a prospective landlord. Along with the Application, you'll want to give your landlord a Consent to Background and Reference Check, which supplies this permission. This consent form carefully limits the information that sources are authorized to give to that pertaining only to your qualifications as a tenant. In other words, you aren't giving the landlord carte blanche to inquire about extraneous matters, such as "Where is this fellow from?" or "Do you think there is a boyfriend in the picture?" While such irrelevant questions are often illegal (because they're discriminatory), they're annoying even if they're not. Hopefully, the wording on the form will remind (or instruct) both the reference and the inquiring landlord that only tenant-related questions should be asked.

The landlord can make copies and mail, email, or fax them to the sources he wishes to speak with. A sample Consent to Background and Reference Check is shown below; note how the applicant has filled in her own information but left blank the lines for the prospective landlord's name, the date, and her signature.

Keep in mind that even with your consent to a reference check, you cannot force a prior landlord or an employer to provide information.

 FORM
The Nolo website includes a downloadable copy of the Rental Application and the Consent to Background and Reference Check forms. See Appendix B for a link to the forms in this book.

TIP
Fill out applications only when you're truly interested. Don't waste your time (or money, if the landlord charges a credit-check fee) filling out a rental application unless you really want a place. If you are interested, but still want to keep your options open, go ahead and fill out an application. Don't worry that this will lock you into taking a place—only signing a lease or rental agreement does so.

Rental Application

Separate application required from each applicant age 18 or older.

Date and time received by landlord _____

Credit check fee ___$40___ Received _____

THIS SECTION TO BE COMPLETED BY LANDLORD

Address of Property to Be Rented: ___178 Park St., Apt. 4F, Springsteen, NJ 00000___

Rental Term: ☐ month-to-month ☑ lease from ___March 1, 20xx___ to ___February 28, 20xx___

Amounts Due Prior to Occupancy

First month's rent	$ ___3,200___
Security deposit	$ ___3,200___
Credit-check fee	$ ___40___
Other (specify): _____	$ _____
TOTAL..	$ ___6,440___

Applicant

Full Name—include all names you use(d): ___Hannah Silver___

Home Phone: ___609-555-3789___ Work Phone: ___609-555-4567___ Cell Phone: ___609-555-6543___

Email: ___hannah@coldmail.com___ Fax*: _____

Social Security Number: ___123-00-4567___ Driver's License Number/State: ___D123456/New Jersey___

Other Identifying Information: _____

Vehicle Make: ___Toyota___ Model: ___Corolla___ Color: ___White___ Year: ___2015___

License Plate Number/State: ___NJ1234567/New Jersey___

Additional Occupants

List everyone, including minor children, who will live with you:

Full Name	Relationship to Applicant
Dennis Olson	Husband

Rental History

FIRST-TIME RENTERS: ATTACH A DESCRIPTION OF YOUR HOUSING SITUATION FOR THE PAST FIVE YEARS.

Current Address: ___39 Maple St., Princeton, NJ 00000___

Dates Lived at Address: ___May 2011–date___ Rent: $ ___2,000___ Security Deposit: $ ___4,000___

Landlord/Manager: ___Jane Tucker___ Landlord/Manager's Phone: ___609-555-7523___

Reason for Leaving: ___New job in northern New Jersey___

* By providing this fax number I agree to receive facsimile advertisements from the landlord or management company.

Previous Address: _____1215 Middlebrook Lane, Princeton, NJ 00000_____

Dates Lived at Address: _____June 2008–May 2011_____ Rent: $ _____1,800_____ Security Deposit: $ _____1,000_____

Landlord/Manager: _____Ed Palermo_____ Landlord/Manager's Phone: _____609-555-3711_____

Reason for Leaving: _____Better apartment_____

Previous Address: _____1527 Highland Dr., New Brunswick, NJ 00000_____

Dates Lived at Address: _____Jan. 2007–June 2008_____ Rent: $ _____800_____ Security Deposit: $ _800_

Landlord/Manager: _____Millie & Joe Lewis_____ Landlord/Manager's Phone: _____609-555-9999_____

Reason for Leaving: _____Wanted to live closer to work_____

Employment History

SELF-EMPLOYED APPLICANTS: ATTACH TAX RETURNS FOR THE PAST TWO YEARS.

Name and Address of Current Employer: _____Argonworks, 54 Nassau St., Princeton, NJ 00000_____

_____ Phone: _____609-555-2333_____

Name of Supervisor: _____Tom Schmidt_____ Supervisor's Phone: _____609-555-2333_____

Dates Employed at This Job: _____2008–date_____ Position or Title: _Marketing Associate_

Name and Address of Previous Employer: _____Princeton Times_____

_____13 Junction Rd., Princeton, NJ 00000_____ Phone: _____609-555-1111_____

Name of Supervisor: _____Dory Krossber_____ Supervisor's Phone: _____609-555-2366_____

Dates Employed at This Job: _____June 2007–Feb. 2008_____ Position or Title: _Marketing Associate_

ATTACH PAY STUBS FOR THE PAST TWO YEARS, FROM THIS EMPLOYER OR PRIOR EMPLOYERS.

Income

1. Your gross monthly employment income (before deductions): $ _____8,000_____

2. Average monthly amounts of other income (specify sources): $ _____

 Note: This does not include my husband's income. See his application. $ _____

 _____ $ _____

 TOTAL: $ _____8,000_____

Bank/Financial Accounts

	Account Number	Bank/Institution	Branch
Savings Account:	1222345	N.J. Federal	Trenton, NJ
Checking Account:	789101	Princeton S&L	Princeton, NJ
Money Market or Similar Account:	234789	City Bank	Princeton, NJ

Credit Card Accounts

Major Credit Card: ☑ VISA ☐ MC ☐ Discover Card ☐ Am Ex ☐ Other: _____

Issuer: __City Bank_____   Account No.: __1234 5555 6666 7777_____

Balance: $ __1,000_____   Average Monthly Payment: $ ___1,000_____

Major Credit Card: ☐ VISA ☐ MC ☐ Discover Card ☐ Am Ex ☑ Other: ____Dept. Store_____

Issuer: __City Bank_____   Account No.: __2345 0000 9999 8888_____

Balance: $ __500_____   Average Monthly Payment: $ __500_____

Loans

Type of Loan (mortgage, car, student loan, etc.)	Name of Creditor	Account Number	Amount Owed	Monthly Payment

Other Major Obligations

Type	Payee		Amount Owed	Monthly Payment

Miscellaneous

Describe the number and type of pets you want to have in the rental property: __None now, but we might want to get a cat some time__

Describe water-filled furniture you want to have in the rental property: __None_____

Do you smoke?   ☐ yes ☑ no

Have you ever:

Filed for bankruptcy?	☐ yes	☑ no	How many times	_____
Been sued?	☐ yes	☑ no	How many times	_____
Sued someone else?	☐ yes	☑ no	How many times	_____
Been evicted?	☐ yes	☑ no	How many times	_____
Been convicted of a crime?	☐ yes	☑ no	How many times	_____

Explain any "yes" listed above: _____

_____

_____

_____

References and Emergency Contact

Personal Reference: Joan Stanley   Relationship: Friend, coworker

Address: 785 Spruce St., Princeton, NJ 00000

                                          Phone: 609-555-4578

Personal Reference: Marnie Swatt   Relationship: Friend

Address: 82 East 59th St., #12B, NYC, NY 00000

                                          Phone: 212-555-8765

Contact in Emergency: Connie & Martin Silver   Relationship: Parents

Address: 7852 Pierce St., Somerset, NJ 00000

                                          Phone: 609-555-7878

Source

Where did you learn of this vacancy? Craigslist

I certify that all the information given above is true and correct and understand that my lease or rental agreement may be terminated if I have made any material false or incomplete statements in this application. I authorize verification of the information provided in this application from my credit sources, credit bureaus, current and previous landlords and employers, and personal references. This permission will survive the expiration of my tenancy. I give permission for the landlord or its agent to obtain a consumer report about me for the purpose of this application, to ensure that I can continue to meet the terms of the tenancy, for the collection and recovery of any financial obligations relating to my tenancy, or for any other permissible purpose.

Hannah Silver   *February 15, 20xx*
Applicant   Date

Notes (Landlord/Manager):

Consent to Background and Reference Check

I authorize _____ to obtain information about me from my credit sources, current and previous landlords, employers, and personal references, to enable _____ to evaluate my rental application. I authorize my credit sources, credit bureaus, current and previous landlords, and employers and personal references to disclose to _____ information about me that is relevant to _____'s evaluation of me as a prospective tenant.

_____
Applicant's Signature

Hannah Silver
_____
Printed name

39 Maple Street. Princeton, NJ 00000
_____
Address

609-555-3789
_____
Phone Number

_____
Date

How to Impress Prospective Landlords

Bringing the following information when you first meet prospective landlords will give you a competitive edge over other applicants:

- a completed rental application
- written references from landlords, employers, friends, and colleagues, and
- current copy of your credit report.

If you have a pet, you might even bring a completed pet application form (find one at www.humanesociety.org).

Landlord References

Landlords usually want references from your current and previous landlords, and details on your rental history. In talking with your past landlord or manager, prospective landlords will ask the following types of questions:

- Did you pay rent on time?
- Were you considerate of neighbors (no loud parties; you cleaned up after your dog)?
- Did you make any unreasonable demands or complaints?
- Did you take good care of the rental property?
- In general, were you a good (ideally, great) tenant?

Do You Need References for Your Dog (or Cat)?

If you have a dog or cat, don't be surprised if the landlord wants to meet your pet, to make sure it's well-groomed and well-behaved, before making a final decision. If pet-friendly apartments are especially tight in your area, be prepared to make the best case you can for Max or Bella. Here are some ideas for doing so:

- Get written references from current and previous landlords and neighbors saying how sweet and well-mannered your dog (or cat) is.
- Bring a cat or dog résumé, describing your pet, favorite activities, and health. See the San Francisco SPCA website (www.sfspca.org) for samples.
- Pull together any materials that support your pet's good behavior, such as paperwork that shows your dog passed obedience training classes.

See the "Pets" section in Chapter 2 for more advice on negotiating with landlords on pets. Also, see the discussion of tenant rights when it comes to service and support animals in Chapter 5.

If you are leaving a current rental because the neighbors, the landlord, or the manager was awful, prepare your defense in advance—by mounting a preemptive offense. Explain the difficulty and offer evidence to bolster your version, such as a letter from other dissatisfied tenants, police reports chronicling disturbances at the property, a list of the times the former landlord was hauled before the local rent board for violations, or, if problems rose to the point of litigation, a copy of a court judgment in your favor. No matter how righteous your position, however, be advised that it won't count for much unless you can show that, aside from your use of legal tenant remedies such as rent withholding, you always paid the rent on time, left voluntarily, and left a clean and undamaged apartment or house.

Extra-picky landlords may actually want to visit your current rental to see how it looks. If your place usually looks like a cyclone just hit it, either clean up or forget it.

Employer References

Conscientious landlords will usually want to speak with your current employer to verify your income and length of employment and to get a better sense of your character—for example, to see if you're a responsible person.

Before talking with a prospective landlord, your employer may require your written permission. Use the Consent to Background and Reference Check, explained above.

Character References

Some landlords also want character references from people (nonrelatives) who know you well. Below is an example of the type of letter that will help you beat the competition.

TIP

Alert references. Make sure that all of your references know to expect a call or email from a potential landlord. Even better, get written references first. And obviously, only give out the names of people who know you well and who have positive things to say about you— anticipate the crafty landlord who asks for four references and calls only the fourth one on the list.

CAUTION

Complete all rental applications truthfully. Prospective landlords will be able to verify much of the information you give by ordering a credit report. Nothing will hurt your chances of getting a place more than lying, whether it be by failing to reveal a previous eviction,

providing the name of a friend as a landlord reference, or overstating your income.

Sample Character Reference

February, 20xx

To Whom It May Concern:

I am writing to recommend Hannah Silver for the rental unit you have available. I have known Hannah for ten years and I cannot recommend her too highly. You won't find a better tenant.

I know Hannah as both a close personal friend and a colleague. We first met in 2009 when I started work as a technical writer at Argonworks in Princeton. Hannah has been the marketing director at Argonworks since 2008.

Hannah is extremely reliable and responsible. She's not the type of person who will pay her rent late (or come up with excuses why she needs a few extra days), bother you about small things, annoy other tenants with loud music, or generally cause you problems. I have been to her apartment many times, and she is a meticulous housekeeper and very organized. She will take excellent care of your rental property.

Hannah is trustworthy, and she keeps her commitments. She has always worked 100% plus on marketing Argonworks products, consistently meets her deadlines, and gives her best. She is a wonderful person to work with, a talented businesswoman, and a cooperative team player. I am confident that Hannah will be one of your best tenants.

All in all, Hannah is a fantastic person who will be greatly missed when she moves out of the area.

I will be happy to provide further information about Hannah. If you have any questions, please feel free to call me at work (609-555-1232) or home (609-555-4578), or email me at Joan @Joan.com.

Sincerely,

Joan Stanley

Joan Stanley
785 Spruce St.
Princeton, NJ 00000

The Importance of Your Credit History

Many landlords find it essential to check a prospective tenant's credit history with at least one credit reporting agency to see how responsible you are at managing money and whether you will be a reliable tenant who pays rent on time. This credit check can be the most important part of the rental application process.

How Far Can Credit Reporting Agencies Go?

Some landlords—especially those who rent luxury units or insist on long-term leases—may go beyond a routine credit report and ask a screening agency to pull together detailed information about your character, general reputation, personal characteristics, or mode of living.

Almost all such checks are considered "investigative consumer reports" under federal law (15 U.S.C. §§ 1681 and following, as amended by the Fair and Accurate Credit Transactions Act of 2003). Legally, a landlord does not need your permission before asking for one; however, a landlord who requests a background check on a prospective tenant must tell you within three days of requesting the report that the report may be made and that it will concern your character, personal characteristics, and criminal history. This gives you an opportunity to withdraw your rental application if you don't want the credit reporting agency to proceed with the report. The landlord must also tell you that more information about the nature and scope of the report will be provided upon your written request. The landlord must provide this added information within five days of your request.

If you are turned down wholly or in part based on information contained in the investigative report, the landlord must tell you this and give you the name and address of the agency that prepared the report.

A landlord can find out your credit history over the past seven years, including whether you have ever been:

- late or delinquent in paying rent or bills, including student or car loans
- convicted of a crime or, in many states, even arrested
- evicted, or
- involved in another type of lawsuit, such as a personal injury claim.

A credit report will also state whether you have filed for bankruptcy in the past ten years.

If a landlord does not rent to you because of negative information in your credit report, or charges you a higher rent because of such information, he is legally required (under the federal Fair Credit Reporting Act, 15 U.S.C. §§ 1681 and following) to give you the name and address of the agency that reported the negative information. Landlords must tell you that you have a right to obtain a free copy of your file from the agency that reported the negative information. You must request it within 60 days of being rejected by the landlord. Landlords must also tell you that the credit reporting agency did not make the rejection decision and cannot explain it, and that if you dispute the information in the report, you can provide a consumer statement setting forth your position.

What Happens to Your Application

Tenants and applicants are justifiably concerned that the information landlords gather during screening be kept safe and secure from would-be identity thieves. A federal law, known as the "Disposal Rule," addresses this concern. (Fair and Accurate Credit Transactions Act of 2003, 69 Fed. Reg. 68690.) Landlords and managers must share sensitive information only on a "need to know" basis, keep all documents in a locked, secure location, and destroy any unneeded documents. Applications and credit reports from rejected applicants should be destroyed routinely; whether landlords have a legitimate reason to hang on to tenants' applications and credit reports is not so clear.

Credit-Check Fees

It is legal for a prospective landlord to charge you a fee for the cost of the credit report itself and the landlord's time and trouble. Some states regulate the exact amount of the fee by statute; others require landlords to charge reasonably. Any credit-check fee should be reasonably related to the cost of the credit check—$30 or $50 is common. California sets a maximum screening fee and requires landlords to provide an itemized receipt when accepting a credit check fee. If you think you're being charged too high a fee, call your city or district attorney's office for advice.

Be sure you understand the purpose of any fee you are charged and whether or not it is any kind of guarantee that you will get the rental unit. Don't confuse the fee with a holding deposit, which is normally a separate charge.

CAUTION

Watch out for fraudulent credit-check fees. Some landlords have been known to take credit-check fees from several prospective tenants and never run the credit checks, pocketing the money instead. You can easily find out if this has happened to you by contacting a credit reporting agency as soon as you've been rejected by a landlord. As discussed above, you're entitled to a free copy of your credit report if a landlord rejects you because of information in it, which should indicate who's requested your report recently. It is illegal for a landlord to charge a credit-check fee and not use it for the stated purpose. Problems can also develop if the landlord takes a long time to check a tenant's credit and the tenant, not knowing whether the rental will be approved, rents another place. To avoid these and other possible areas of dispute, it is wise to sign a brief agreement with a landlord, clarifying the purpose of any up-front fee and whether or not it will be refunded if you don't get the place. (See the discussion of holding deposits below.) If you have any problems, contact your city or district attorney's office or a tenants' rights group for advice.

Check Your Credit Rating and Clean Up Your File

Because your credit report is so important, you should always check it before you start your housing search. This will give you the opportunity to correct or clear up any mistakes, such as out-of-date or just plain wrong information. It's all too common for credit bureaus to confuse names, addresses, Social Security numbers, or employers. Especially if you have a common name (say John Brown), chances are good you'll find information in your credit file on other John Browns, or even John Brownes or Jon Browns. Obviously, you don't want this incorrect information given to prospective landlords, especially if the person you're being confused with is in worse financial shape than you are.

The three largest credit bureaus, with offices throughout the United States, are Experian, Equifax, and TransUnion. As mentioned above, you are entitled to a free copy of your report when you are denied credit (including a place to live) because of information in your credit report. You can also get a free copy once every 12 months. Go to www.annualcreditreport.com to place your request.

Once you get your report, if you find errors, check your files at the other two agencies. You have the right to insist that the credit bureau verify anything that's wrong, inaccurate, or out of date. Information that can't be verified must be removed.

If the credit reporting agency fails to remove inaccurate or outdated information, lists a debt you refused to pay because of a legitimate dispute with the creditor, or reports a bogus lawsuit against you that was abandoned, you have the right to place a 100-word statement in your file, giving your version of the situation. Do so immediately.

If the credit bureau fails to cooperate, and the information is really wrong, contact the creditor that reported the information for help in getting it out. If that doesn't work, you have several options:

- Contact the Federal Trade Commission (FTC) for advice. Check their website (www.ftc.gov) or the government section of your phone book, or call the national office at 877-FTC-HELP.
- Threaten to sue the credit reporting agency in small claims court. (Chapter 19 discusses small claims suits.)
- Complain to your Congressional representative, who might be able to put pressure on the FTC to fix your problem.

TIP

Bring copies of your recent credit report with you when you apply for a rental. If you're submitting multiple applications, the credit check fees will mount up. Most landlords insist on running the check themselves, because they're afraid that applicants will doctor their reports, but you may be able to persuade some to accept yours. (In Wisconsin, a landlord cannot charge you for a report if, before the landlord asks you for the fee, you offer a report that's less than 30 days old from a consumer reporting agency. (Wis. Admin. Code ATCP 134.05(4)(b).) And in Washington, landlords must advise tenants whether they will accept a screening report done by a consumer reporting agency (in which case the landlord may not charge the tenant a fee for a screening report). Landlords who maintain a website that advertises residential rentals must include this information on the home page. (Wash. Rev. Code Ann. § 59.18.257)

How to Deal With Problems in Your Credit Report

If your credit file shows negative but accurate information, or you have no credit history because you're a first-time renter and have never borrowed money or used a credit card, there are steps you can take to look better to prospective landlords:

- Get a creditworthy person to cosign the lease or rental agreement. (See Chapter 2 for details on cosigners.)
- Pay a large deposit, or offer to prepay rent for several months. (Chapter 4 discusses security deposits and state limits.)
- Show proof of steps you've taken to improve bad credit—for example, your enrollment in a

debt counseling group, your recent history of making and paying for purchases on credit and maintaining a checking or savings account.
- Get more positive references from friends, colleagues, employers, and previous landlords.

RESOURCE

For more information on obtaining your credit file, getting out of debt, and rebuilding your credit, see *Solve Your Money Troubles: Strategies to Get Out of Debt and Stay That Way* and *Credit Repair*, both by Amy Loftsgordon and Cara O'Neill (Nolo). For useful articles or consumer credit and credit reports, see the Debt Management and Personal Finance sections of www.nolo.com.

How Landlords Reject Tenants

Federal and state antidiscrimination laws limit what landlords can say and do in the tenant selection process. (See Chapter 5.) Basically, a landlord is legally free to choose among prospective tenants as long as all tenants are evaluated more or less equally. For example, a landlord can probably refuse to rent to a smoker, as long as this no-smoking policy applies to all tenants.

Permissible Reasons for Rejecting Tenants

A landlord is entitled to reject you for any of the following reasons:

- poor credit history, which leads the landlord to believe that you will be unable to pay rent
- income that the landlord reasonably regards as insufficient to pay the rent
- negative references from previous landlords indicating problems—such as property damage or consistent late rent payments
- previous eviction lawsuits
- convictions for criminal offenses, unless the conviction was for past drug use (see Chapter 5 for a discussion of illegal discrimination on the basis of disability)
- current illegal behavior, such as dealing drugs

- your inability to meet terms of the lease or rental agreement—for example, if you want to keep a pet and the landlord's policy is no pets (assuming you do not have a disability, as discussed in Chapter 5)
- more people than the landlord wants to live in the unit—assuming that the limit on the number of tenants is clearly tied to health and safety or legitimate business needs (Chapter 5 discusses occupancy limits), or
- untruthful responses on the rental application.

What Landlords Must Tell You

You are entitled to certain information from a landlord who turns you down based on information in your credit report, even if other factors also played a role in the rejection. Known as an "adverse action report," the landlord must tell you the name and address of the agency that supplied the report, as well as that:

- you may request a copy of your report from the agency that reported the negative information, by asking within the next 60 days (or one year after receiving your last free annual credit report)
- the agency didn't make the decision not to rent to you and cannot explain the reason for the rejection, and
- you can dispute the accuracy of the information in the report and attach your own consumer statement (Fair Credit Reporting Act, as amended by the Fair and Accurate Credit Transactions Act of 2003, 15 U.S.C. §§ 1681 and following).

Landlords must also supply an adverse action report when they rent to applicants but do so with negative or onerous qualifications, such as demanding a higher rent, larger security deposit, or a cosigner. If the landlord rejects you or demands tougher terms based on information the landlord developed or learned independent of the credit report or a background screening report, the landlord need not give you the adverse action report.

Illegal Discrimination

Antidiscrimination laws specify clearly illegal reasons to refuse to rent to a tenant. The federal Fair Housing Acts (42 U.S.C. §§ 3601–3619) prohibit discrimination on the basis of race, color, religion, national origin, gender, familial status (children), or physical or mental disability (including alcoholism and past drug addiction). Many states and cities also prohibit discrimination based on marital status, gender identity, or sexual orientation. (Chapter 5 discusses illegal discrimination and how to file a complaint with a fair housing agency.)

Also, landlords risk violating the law if they screen certain categories of applicants more stringently than others—for example, requiring credit reports or a higher income level only from racial minorities.

Finder's Fees and Holding Deposits

Almost every landlord requires tenants to give a substantial security deposit. The laws concerning how much can be charged and when deposits must be returned are discussed in Chapters 4 and 16. Here we discuss some other fees and deposits that are occasionally required.

Finder's Fees

Real estate brokers may legitimately charge a fee for their services. And there's nothing wrong with a landlord charging you for the actual cost of performing a credit check.

Less legitimate, however, is the practice of some landlords, especially in cities with a tight rental market, of collecting "finder's fees" just for renting the place to a tenant. Unlike brokers, which actually do some work for their money, a finder's fee charged by a landlord just for the privilege of being offered a rental is nothing short of a rip-off. You should suspect this ploy if you're told to pay a finder's fee directly to the landlord or management company to get a particular unit. You should also be suspicious if you're directed to pay a finder's fee to an apartment locator "service" set up by the

Receipt and Holding Deposit Agreement

This will acknowledge receipt of the sum of $ 500 _____ by Jim Chow _____

_____ ["Landlord"] from Hannah Silver _____

_____ ["Applicant"] as a holding deposit to hold vacant

the rental property at 178 Park St., #4F, Springsteen, NJ 00000 _____

_____ ,

until ____ February 20, 20xx _____ at ____ 5 P.M. _____ . The property will be rented to Applicant

on a _____ one-year _____ basis at a rent of $ 3,200 _____ per month, if Applicant signs

Landlord's written _____ lease _____ and pays Landlord the first month's rent and a

$ _____ 3,200 _____ security deposit on or before that date, in which event the holding deposit will be

applied to the first month's rent.

This Agreement depends upon Landlord receiving a satisfactory report of Applicant's references and credit

history. Landlord and Applicant agree that if Applicant fails to sign the lease or rental agreement and pay the

remaining rent and security deposit, Landlord may retain of this holding deposit a sum equal to the prorated

daily rent of $ _____ 103 _____ per day plus a $ _____ 75 _____ charge to compensate Landlord for his or her

time and labor.

Hannah Silver _____   _February 16, 20xx_ _____
Applicant   Date

Jim Chow _____   _February 16, 20xx_ _____
Landlord/Manager   Date

landlord as a front to collect the fee (as opposed to really being in the business of locating apartments).

What can you do about this blatant nonsense? If the rental is a good one and the fee something you can afford without too much pain, perhaps it's in your best interests to shut up and pay up. However, if you want to challenge this "pay me for nothing" fee, consider the following avenues.

Read your state's security deposit statutes and the cases that have interpreted them. (The citations are found in "State Security Deposit Rules" in Appendix A; Chapter 20 explains how to find cases that explain statutes.) If your state prohibits nonrefundable security deposits (security deposits are explained at length in Chapter 4), look for a case where the judge ruled that the term "security deposit" includes a finder's fee. Because the fee is kept by the landlord, a landlord who collects a finder's fee violates the statute. This theory was used successfully by a group of tenants in California. (*People v. Sangiacomo,* 129 Cal.App.3d 364 (1982).)

Sue in small claims court. You might argue that you're being forced to pay for a nonexistent service —in legalese, it's a case of fraud. You could also point out that it's a matter of bait-and-switch: Charging a finder's fee is the same as charging a higher rent for the first month, which your landlord probably has not made clear in ads for the unit. (Chapter 19 gives advice on using small claims court.)

Contact your city attorney or district attorney's office (consumer fraud unit) for advice, or your local rent control board. Especially in areas with rent control, finder's fees may be illegal by statute or court decision.

Holding Deposits

Sometimes, if you make a deal with a landlord but don't actually sign a lease or rental agreement, she will want some type of cash deposit, then and there, to hold the rental unit. This might happen when the landlord wants time to do a credit check or call your references. Or it can happen if you need to borrow money (or wait for a paycheck) to come up with enough to cover the rent and security deposit. For example, a landlord might ask for $500 cash to hold the place for you until you bring your first month's rent and any deposits you agreed on, pending the results of a credit check.

If you give a landlord a holding deposit and later decide not to take the place, there is a good chance you won't get most or all of your deposit back. So be sure you really want the place before making this kind of deposit. The laws of most states are unclear as to what portion of a holding deposit a landlord can keep if a would-be tenant changes his mind about renting the property or doesn't come up with the remaining rent and deposit money, or if your credit doesn't check out to the landlord's satisfaction. And even if the law does limit the landlord to keeping a "reasonable" amount (often based on how long the unit was kept off the market), you may have to go to small claims court to force the landlord to actually return your money.

In California, for example, the basic rule is that a landlord can keep an amount that bears a "reasonable" relation to the landlord's costs—for example, for more advertising and for prorated rent during the time the property was held vacant. A California landlord who keeps a larger amount may be sued for breach of contract. A few states require landlords to provide a receipt for any holding deposit and a written statement of the conditions under which the fee or deposit is refundable.

Most states, however, do not have specific laws on holding deposits. So, whatever you and a landlord agree on, such as your right to get half of the holding deposit back if you decide not to take the place within a certain number of days, be sure to write your agreement down. Include:

- the amount of the deposit
- the dates the landlord will hold the rental property vacant, and
- the conditions for returning the deposit or applying it to the security deposit.

Also, be sure you and the landlord understand what is to happen to the deposit when you take the place. Usually, it will be applied to the first month's rent. To make this clear, have the landlord give you a receipt for the deposit and have her write on the receipt what is to happen to the deposit when you come back with the rent.

A sample Receipt and Holding Deposit Agreement that you might want to adapt to your own situation is shown above.

FORM

The Nolo website includes a downloadable copy of the Receipt and Holding Deposit Agreement. See Appendix B for the link to the forms in this book.

Choosing Roommates

The greatest place in the world won't make up for an obnoxious, inconsiderate, or financially irresponsible roommate. Whoever you live with, make sure you're compatible, particularly with respect to issues such as neatness and privacy needs.

How to Find a Roommate

You may want to find a rental where current tenants need a roommate, or you may be looking for a roommate to share a rental you've found. Either way, there are lots of sources for finding roommates, including Craigslist and university housing offices. You may also want to check out roommate sites such as www.roomster.com or www.roommates.com. Check online under under Roommate Assistance or Referral Services for others. Many services will screen and match compatible roommates, based on detailed questionnaires you fill out. Some groups—senior or religious organizations, for example—may keep lists or help you to find a compatible person.

Whether you're filling out an application with an agency that matches roommates, or responding to a "Roommate Wanted" notice at university housing, be honest and try to make sure you're getting clear answers from prospective roommates. It might sound excessive, but checking references is always a good idea. Talk to former landlords and other roommates, following our advice above on how landlords screen tenants.

Before you move in with roommates, or even friends, it's always a good idea to make a written agreement of important issues, including:

- neatness and cleaning standards
- financial responsibility
- privacy
- noise
- amount of entertaining, including overnight guests
- pets
- food tastes and sharing
- political preferences or strong personal beliefs
- children, and
- smoking.

No, this isn't overkill—after all, you routinely sign an agreement with the landlord, whom you won't see a fraction as often as a roommate. Roommate referral services often have form agreements, or you can use the sample roommate agreement in Chapter 7.

CAUTION

Always know your legal status when you move into an existing rental with roommates. Are you a full-fledged cotenant (having signed the lease or rental agreement) or a subtenant (responsible to the other tenant, not the landlord)? You have very different legal rights and responsibilities depending on your status. (See the detailed discussion of roommates in Chapter 7.)

Leases and Rental Agreements

How Leases and Rental Agreements Differ 33

    Month-to-Month Rental Agreement 33

    Fixed-Term Lease 34

    Lease or Rental Agreement: What's Better for You? 34

Oral Leases and Rental Agreements 36

    Should You Use an Oral Rental Agreement? 36

    How to Make Oral Understandings Binding 36

Typical Provisions in Leases and Rental Agreements 36

    Identification of Landlord and Tenant 37

    Identification of the Premises 37

    Restrictions on Home Businesses 37

    Limits on Occupants 38

    Guest Policies 39

    Term of the Tenancy 39

    Rent, Late Fees, and Grace Periods 40

    Deposits and Fees 40

    Utilities 41

    Assignment and Subletting 41

    Condition of the Rental Unit and Landlord's Responsibilities 42

    Tenant's Repair and Maintenance Responsibilities 42

    Renters' Insurance 43

    Violating Laws and Causing Disturbances 46

    Pets 47

    Landlord's Right of Access 47

    Extended Absences by Tenant 48

    Possession of the Premises 48

    Tenant Rules and Regulations 49

    Attorneys' Fees in a Lawsuit 50

    Disclosures 51

    Authority to Receive Legal Papers 51

    Grounds for Termination of Tenancy 52

    Mediation 52

    Additional Provisions 52

    Validity of Each Part 52

    Entire Agreement 52

    Miscellaneous Clauses 53

Negotiating With the Landlord 53

   Four Types of Lease Clauses 54

   Concluding Your Negotiations 55

Changing a Lease or Rental Agreement 56

   Deleting Language 56

   Adding Language 56

Signing a Lease or Rental Agreement 56

Cosigners 57

The lease or rental agreement you and your landlord sign defines your legal relationship. It is a contract in which:

- you agree to pay rent and abide by other terms (such as no pets and no additional roommates), and
- your landlord agrees to provide you with a place to live, often with listed amenities.

If you don't pay rent, or you violate another contract provision, the landlord will have grounds to end your tenancy. If your landlord violates a lease or rental agreement term, you also have certain rights. Depending on the situation, you may have the right to break the lease or sue the landlord for damages.

Because it is so important, you should never sign a lease or rental agreement until you understand what's in it. Also remember that, unlike a tax return, there is no one officially blessed form, so you can negotiate terms with your landlord.

This chapter discusses the key provisions typically included in leases and rental agreements, and explains the differences between these two documents. We highlight terms that are unfair to tenants and show how to bargain for better provisions when you start a tenancy, and know when to turn down an agreement altogether.

 RELATED TOPIC
Other chapters in this book go into greater detail on topics covered in leases and rental agreements, including:

- Rules involving rent, including late fees, grace periods, and rent control: Chapter 3.
- Use and return of security deposits: Chapters 4 and 16.
- Occupancy limits and policies: Chapter 5.
- Tenants, cotenants, sublets, and assignments: Chapters 7 and 15.
- Landlord's repair and maintenance responsibilities, and how to enforce your rights: Chapters 8, 9, and 10.
- Landlord's right to enter rental property and tenant privacy rights: Chapter 11.
- Notice and procedures for changing a lease or rental agreement after you have begun your tenancy: Chapter 15.
- Impact of a rental property sale or foreclosure on a tenant's lease: Chapter 15.
- How to break a lease as painlessly as possible: Chapter 15.
- Grounds and procedures for terminating tenancies: Chapters 17 and 18.

Appendix A includes details on state laws regarding many of the topics covered in this chapter, such as security deposit limits and access rules.

How Leases and Rental Agreements Differ

Leases and rental agreements usually look so much alike they can be hard to tell apart. Both cover nitty-gritty issues, such as the amount of rent and deposits you must pay and the number of people who can live in the rental unit. The primary difference between the two is the length of the tenancy. A rental agreement lasts only from one month to the next, while a lease almost always covers a longer, fixed term. It's crucial that you understand this difference because it affects not only how long you can stay but, even more important, the strength of your bargaining position if you and your landlord get into a dispute.

Month-to-Month Rental Agreement

A written rental agreement provides for a tenancy for a short period of time, usually one month. The law refers to these agreements as periodic or month-to-month tenancies, although it is usually legal for landlords to base rental agreements on other time periods—for example, if the rent were due every two weeks.

A month-to-month rental agreement is auto-matically renewed each month unless you or your landlord gives the other the proper amount of written notice (typically 30 days) to terminate the agreement. A landlord can also raise the rent or change other terms of the month-to-month rental agreement with proper written notice. (Chapter 15 discusses these changes.)

If you live in an urban area with a tight rental market, where new tenants are easy to find, you may be offered a rental agreement. Landlords sometimes prefer to use a rental agreement because it:

- gives them the right to raise the rent as often as they wish (unless there is a local rent control ordinance), and
- usually allows them to easily get rid of problem tenants without the need to give a reason, because in most states, rental agreements can be terminated for no reason.

But of course, not all landlords think this way. Some wisely prefer to find and keep good long-term tenants and avoid the hassles of new tenants coming and going—even if it means less flexibility in terms of increasing rent or terminating the tenancy.

Smart landlords have figured out how to have the security of a long-term rental *and* rent increases—they use a lease clause that specifies a rent increase after a certain amount of time, such as $100 after six months.

Fixed-Term Lease

A lease is a contract that obligates both you and the landlord for a set period of time, usually a year. With a lease, your landlord can't raise the rent or change other terms of the tenancy until the lease runs out, unless the lease itself provides for an increase.

Many landlords prefer the stability of renting to long-term tenants. As a result, landlords who use leases will probably take an extra measure of care when choosing tenants who will be around for a while. Sometimes external factors influence the landlord's choice. If you live in an area with a high vacancy rate or where it is difficult to find tenants for a particular season of the year—for example, a college town, where most students are gone during the summer, or a resort town, where residents leave for part of the year—many landlords insist on a fixed-term lease, usually for one year. Single-family houses are likely to come with leases, since the landlord will want to minimize the number of times the house must be prepared for new tenants. Preparing an apartment, by contrast, is not as big a job.

A lease has a definite beginning and ending date. Your landlord can't force you to move out before the lease term expires unless you fail to pay the rent or violate another significant term of the lease or state law, such as repeatedly making too much noise, damaging the rental unit, or selling drugs on (or even near) the property. (Chapter 18 discusses evictions for lease violations.)

What happens when a lease expires? At the end of the lease term, your landlord may decline to renew the lease, or may opt to negotiate with you to sign a new lease with the same or different terms. If you stay and keep paying monthly rent, most states will consider you a month-to-month tenant renting under an oral lease. (Chapter 15 discusses what happens at the end of a lease period.)

Tenants Who Enlist or Enter Active Duty May Break a Lease

The War and National Defense Servicemembers' Civil Relief Act helps active duty military personnel handle legal affairs. (50 App. U.S.C. Ann. §§ 530 and following.) Among its provisions, it allows tenants who enter active military service after signing a lease or rental agreement to break the lease or agreement. Chapter 15, How Tenancies End or Change, gives details.

Lease or Rental Agreement: What's Better for You?

You may not have the bargaining power to insist on one arrangement (lease or rental agreement) over the other. But you'll want to recognize situations in which a rental agreement or lease is a clear necessity or a definite problem.

For example, if you may want to move soon, you'll prefer the flexibility of a rental agreement. But if you plan to stay put for the foreseeable future, it's often better to have a lease, because of the security it provides. There is the enormous practical advantage to having the right to occupy your rental unit for an extended time. If you ask for needed repairs or protest unreasonable landlord conduct (for example, entering your home without notice when there isn't an emergency), the landlord can't respond by giving you a 30-day notice to move—something that's generally allowed if you have a month-to-month tenancy. (If your state protects you against landlord retaliation, you can fight a spiteful landlord, but it will cost you time and money.) Even if your landlord decides to sell the property halfway into the lease, the new owner usually must honor existing leases.

Should you feel nervous about seeing your future (or at least one year of it) set in concrete by virtue of a lease, you can relax. Most leases don't lock you in nearly as much as you might think. If you need to break your lease before the term ends, you can often avoid or substantially limit your financial obligation. In most states, the landlord must try to find another suitable tenant as soon as is reasonably possible in order to "mitigate" (minimize) the loss suffered as a result of a broken lease. If the landlord rerents the unit fairly quickly, your financial exposure may not be that great.

Nolo's Tenant-Friendly Leases and Rental Agreements

Nolo has developed standard lease and rental agreement forms that are clearly written, fair to both landlords and tenants, and good in all 50 states. If your landlord does not give you a written lease or rental agreement, or hands you one that is clearly unfair, you might suggest using Nolo's forms.

Our forms are available online and with *Every Landlord's Legal Guide*, by Marcia Stewart, Ralph Warner, and Janet Portman, and *Leases & Rental Agreements*, by the same authors. Nolo also publishes interactive state-specific leases and rental agreement forms. For more information on these products, go to www.nolo.com.

 RENT CONTROL

Rent control gives you many of the protections of a lease. If your unit is covered by a local rent control ordinance that limits the landlord's ability to raise rent or terminate the tenancy without a good reason, your need for the protection a lease provides is lessened. On the other hand, many rent control ordinances do allow some rent increases—for example, if the landlord's operating costs, such as taxes and major capital improvements, have risen. Also, rent control ordinances usually allow a landlord to evict a tenant in order to move himself or a relative in or to make certain repairs. A lease normally protects you against these dangers. (Chapter 3 discusses rent control.)

Lease With Option to Purchase

If you want to buy a single-family rental, especially in a rising market, and you expect to stay in the area and have more money soon, consider a lease-option. It's a possibility if your landlord wants to sell you the rental house, and you're in general agreement about the price and terms but can't come up with the necessary financing now. Here are the basics.

Under a lease-option contract, you lease a house for a set period of time—usually from one to five years—and get the right (option) to buy the house for a price established in advance.

The rent you pay may increase during the contract term. In addition to rent, you pay some money for the option: a lump-sum payment at the start of the contract, or in the form of higher-than-market rent.

You may pay only a few hundred dollars—or thousands—for tying up the property with the option. You are not entitled to a refund of your option fee or any refund in rent if you do not exercise the option.

Depending on the terms of the contract, you can exercise the option to buy the property:

- at any time during the lease period
- at a date specified in the contract, or
- when another prospective buyer makes an offer on the house. The owner must give you a chance to match the offered price.

In some states, leasing a home with an option to purchase triggers the owner's duty to disclose important information about the property, just as he or she must do when selling the home. For this reason, and because it's so important to get the terms and conditions right, it's a good idea to work with an experienced real estate lawyer if you plan on signing a lease-option.

Oral Leases and Rental Agreements

Oral leases or rental agreements are perfectly legal for month-to-month tenancies and, in most states, for leases of a year or less. If you have an oral lease for a term exceeding one year, it becomes an oral month-to-month agreement after the first year is up.

Under an oral understanding, the period between rent payments typically determines how much notice your landlord must give you before increasing the rent or terminating your tenancy. For example, if you pay monthly, you are entitled to 30 days' notice.

Should You Use an Oral Rental Agreement?

While an oral agreement is legal and enforceable as explained above, it's usually unwise to rely on one. You don't necessarily need a full-blown complicated legal document, especially if you know and trust your landlord, but you should at least get the basic terms in writing. If you want long-term security from rent increases and termination of tenancy, you'll most certainly prefer a fixed-term lease of one year or more. And even with month-to-month rental agreements, you'll want the clarity of having everything written down.

Oral agreements often lead to disputes. As time passes, people's memories (even yours) have a funny habit of becoming unreliable. And you can almost count on your landlord forgetting key agreements—for example, an oral promise that there would be no rent increase the first six months or that your unit would be completely repainted within 60 days. And with oral agreements, other important issues—for example, your landlord's policies on returning security deposits—probably won't be discussed at all. If you and your landlord disagree about a particular policy or procedure, you will not be able to settle it by referring to your written agreement. Instead, you are likely to end up in court arguing over who said what to whom, when, and in what context.

How to Make Oral Understandings Binding

An effective way to lock in your landlord's oral promises is to write a letter of understanding, in which you relate your understanding of what was discussed and agreed to, and invite the landlord to respond if he feels that you have misrepresented the conversation and conclusion. Whether you hand-deliver the letter to the landlord, mail it return-receipt requested, or mail it first class, the laws in most states will presume that your landlord received the letter and agrees with your version unless you promptly hear otherwise. If you hear nothing back, and the landlord fails to make good on his promise and you end up in court, your letter should help you prove your version of the facts. It's almost as good as getting the promise into a lease or rental agreement. (See the sample Letter of Understanding, below.)

Typical Provisions in Leases and Rental Agreements

Here are the most important provisions found in most leases and rental agreements. Unfortunately, these are often dressed up with legal frills and frou-frous (like calling the landlord the "party of the first part") or buried in paragraph-long sentences. Hang in there and follow along with the lease your prospective new landlord has given you. We'll strip pretentious phrases and verbose clauses down to their usually simple legal meanings.

If you run across terms or whole clauses not discussed here, get more information before you sign. Tenants' rights groups, which exist in many areas, will be able to answer your questions. Or, if you're signing a long-term lease for a valuable property, you may even want to see a lawyer. (See Chapter 20 for how to find and work with an attorney and do your own legal research, including online resources for doing so.)

RENT CONTROL

If you are protected by rent control, there will be additional information in your lease or rental agreement, such as the name and address of the rent control board, a citation to the ordinance itself, and sometimes basic information on how to enforce your rights under the ordinance. (Chapter 3 provides details on rent control.)

Identification of Landlord and Tenant

Every lease or rental agreement must identify the tenant and the landlord or the property owner—often called the "parties" to the agreement. The tenant may be referred to as the "lessee" and the landlord as the "lessor."

Any competent adult—at least 18 years of age—may be a party to a lease or rental agreement. A teenager who is under 18 may also be a party to a lease in most states if she has achieved legal adult status through a court order (called emancipation), military service, or marriage.

Landlords typically want all adults who will live in the premises, including both members of a couple, to sign the lease or rental agreement. Doing this makes everyone who signs responsible for all terms, including the full amount of the rent.

To remind tenants of this rule, many leases and rental agreements state that all tenants are "jointly and severally" liable for paying rent and abiding by terms of the agreement. This bit of legalese means that each tenant is legally responsible for the whole rent, and that the misdeeds of one tenant—for example, keeping a pet in violation of a no-pets clause—will allow the landlord to evict all of you.

Identification of the Premises

Your lease or rental agreement will state the address of the property being rented (often called "the premises") and should provide details on any furnishings, parking space, storage areas, or other extras. In addition, your landlord may require you to sign a separate inventory of the rental furnishings, as discussed in Chapter 6.

Some lease or rental agreements also specify that you will use the premises as your "primary residence." This condition would exclude, for example, the tenant who lives primarily with his girlfriend but still wants to keep his own place, or the businessperson who travels to the same city a few times a month and needs a regular home away from home. From a landlord's point of view, the primary residence requirement makes sense because landlords worry that:

- You won't pay the rent on time if you are responsible for rent or house payments elsewhere.
- A home that is infrequently occupied will not be kept up with the same care as you would give a steady residence.
- A vacant unit will be an easy mark for a burglary.
- You'll advertise your rental unit on Airbnb or a similar online service (see "Tenant Rights to Use Airbnb and Similar Vacation Rental Services" in Chapter 7, for more on this).

If in fact your rented home will *not* be your primary residence, you'll need to think about how to deal with this issue. If the landlord lives at a distance and you are sure that you can always pay the rent on time, you might decide to take a chance and remain mum. But if your landlord or manager lives nearby or is often on-site, your absence will be noticed. As long as you always pay rent on time, every time, your tenancy probably won't be terminated—especially if you let the landlord know when you will be out of town for extended periods of time. In fact, this type of notification might even be a lease requirement or a state law. (See "Extended Absences by Tenant," below.)

Suppose now that your landlord lets you stay, knowing full well that you're in violation of the "primary residence" provision. If the landlord decides to terminate your tenancy on this ground many months down the line, it may be too late. If you fight an eviction action you may be able to convince a judge that since your landlord knowingly let you stay, she waived her right to enforce that provision.

Restrictions on Home Businesses

If you are one of the millions of Americans who run a business from your house or apartment, make sure your lease or rental agreement doesn't specify that the premises are "for residential purposes only." If you're working alone or your job primarily consists of making phone calls or using your computer, you've probably got nothing to worry about. But if clients or deliveries will be coming on a regular basis, you'll want to discuss the issue with your landlord. Obviously, you don't want to print stationery or business cards listing your new address only to be given notice to move based on your violation of your agreement.

Your landlord's concerns will rise especially if neighboring tenants may be inconvenienced. Where will your visitors park, for example? Will your piano students disturb the neighbors?

A landlord who does allow you to run a business from your rental unit may require that you maintain certain types of liability insurance. That way, the landlord won't wind up paying if someone gets hurt on the rental property—for example, a business customer who trips and falls on the front steps. Also, be aware that if you use your residence as a commercial site, the property may need to meet the accessibility requirements of the federal Americans with Disabilities Act (ADA). For more information on the ADA, contact the U.S. Department of Justice, 950 Pennsylvania Avenue, NW, Civil Rights Division, Disability Rights Section, Washington, DC 20530; or call 800-514-0301 (800-514-0383 TTY). The ADA website is quite helpful: www.ada.gov.

Child Care Operations

If you want to do child care or day care in your rental, you may be entitled to do so despite the landlord's general prohibition against businesses. In California and New York, legislators and the courts have declared a strong public policy in favor of home-based child care, and have limited a landlord's ability to say no. (California Health & Safety Code § 1597.40; *Haberman v. Gotbaum*, 698 N.Y.S.2d 406 (N.Y. City Civ. Ct., 1999).) Local laws may address this situation as well. If you intend to do regular child care, check with your state's office of consumer protection to find out if there are laws that cover in-home child care in residential rentals.

Zoning Laws

Finally, even if it's okay with your landlord, your home-based business may violate local zoning laws restricting the type of businesses allowed (if any) in your residential neighborhood. The ordinances are often vague as to the type of business you can operate—for example, many allow "traditional home-based businesses," whatever they are. They are usually tighter when it comes to:

- restricting the amount of car and truck traffic the business can generate
- barring outside signs
- prohibiting employees or at least limiting their number, and
- setting a limit on the percentage of the floor space that can be devoted to the business.

In some cities, for example, dentists, physicians (except for psychiatrists), and unlicensed massage therapists may not operate home offices. In others, photo labs and recording studios are banned.

Homeowner Association Rules

If your rental unit is in a planned unit or condominium development, be sure to check if the covenants, conditions, and restrictions (CC&Rs) of the homeowners' association restrict home businesses.

Limits on Occupants

You probably encountered your landlord's occupancy policy (the limit on the number of occupants for your unit) when you visited the rental. Many landlords limit occupants in the lease or rental agreement to remind tenants that they may not bring in additional roommates without permission.

Occupancy limits are legal as long as they are tied to health and safety needs, such as the size and number of bedrooms, or the landlord's legitimate business needs, such as limitations of the plumbing or electrical systems. They are not legal if based on the age or sex of the occupant or the whim of the landlord. For example, restricting a spacious two-bedroom flat to one occupant would be illegal under federal law if it were imposed because the landlord simply preferred to have fewer people living on the property.

⚠ **CAUTION**

Landlords cannot use overcrowding as an excuse for refusing to rent to tenants with children. Discrimination against families with children is illegal, except in housing reserved for senior citizens only. (Chapter 5 discusses antidiscrimination laws.)

Guest Policies

Most landlords do not want people living in their building unless they are full-fledged tenants who have been screened and approved, and who have signed the lease or rental agreement. There are several reasons for this:

- More people cause more wear and tear; if there are more permanent residents living in the unit, landlords want to increase the rent.
- It's harder for landlords to get unauthorized occupants to pay for rent or repairs.
- Unapproved guests, especially if they are frequent and short-term, may annoy other tenants in the building who don't like the idea of strangers coming and going.
- Unapproved residents can create legal hassles in the event of an eviction.

To deal with these potential problems, some landlords go so far as to set a time limit for guest stays, such as no more than ten days in any six-month period, with written approval required for longer stays. This type of provision can be annoying because it allows your landlord to nose into your private affairs.

If you plan on having regular guests—for example, your college roommate stays with you two weekends a month when she's in town on business, or your boyfriend sleeps over a few nights a week—you'll need to think about how to handle this issue. If your landlord lives far away and doesn't have a resident manager, you may decide to take a chance that you'll never be found out. You might get away with it if you're always current with the rent and have no hassles with other tenants. (Be assured that the first words out of a disgruntled neighbor's mouth will be a description of your boyfriend's overnight stays, even if they have nothing to do with your problem with the neighbor.) But if the landlord lives downstairs, ask her to revise this clause. If she resists, consider looking for another rental.

Term of the Tenancy

Your agreement will state whether it's a month-to-month tenancy or a fixed-term lease. "How Leases and Rental Agreements Differ," above, discusses the differences between these two approaches to renting.

Lease Provision

A lease obligates both you and the landlord for a specific term, typically one year. It sets a definite date for the beginning and expiration of the lease. It may also cover

- what happens at the end of the lease—for example, there may be a built-in option to extend the lease at the same or a higher rent.
- monetary consequences if you "hold over," or fail to leave, after the lease ends—for example, the monthly rent may increase if you stay without permission. These clauses are not always legal. (See the discussion on penalties for holding over in Chapter 15.)
- periodic rent increases, perhaps tied to a consumer price index or the landlord's operating expenses. Without this type of built-in rent increase, your landlord can't increase the rent until the lease ends. Landlords in rent control cities may build-in the rent board's annual allowable increase.
- financial penalties if you break the lease. Most of these penalties (called liquidated damages) are illegal. See "Watch Out for Termination Fees," below.

Rental Agreement Provision

Rental agreements usually provide for a month-to-month tenancy. They also specify how much written notice your landlord must give to change or end the tenancy—most commonly, 30 days. See Chapter 15 for details.

Rent, Late Fees, and Grace Periods

Your lease or rental agreement will specify the amount of rent, when it's due (typically the first of the month), and where it's to be paid (via mail to the landlord's office or home is common). Your agreement may also include details on how rent is to be paid, such as by personal check or money order. Many landlords spell out their policies on late fees (if rent is not paid on time) or if your rent check bounces. In most states, there are legal limits on the amount that can be charged for late fees. (See Chapter 3.) The agreement may list any extra items that are included in the rent, such as parking, cable TV hookup, or water.

A grace period is a promise by the landlord that he won't terminate the tenancy until you are a certain number of days late with the rent. Except for a few states that impose mandatory grace periods, you'll almost never encounter a grace period spelled out in a rental agreement. You may see something like a "late fee after five days" clause, but this is not the same thing as a grace period—that is, your landlord can take steps to terminate your tenancy if you don't pay rent on the due date.

Deposits and Fees

All states allow landlords to collect a deposit when a tenant moves in and hold it until the tenant leaves. This may be called a security deposit, cleaning deposit, or last month's rent. The general purpose of a deposit is insurance: It's a financial cushion for the landlord should you fail to pay the rent when it is due or leave the rental unit filthy or in poor repair.

State laws typically control the amount landlords can charge, how deposits may be used, when they must be returned, and what type of itemization a landlord must provide to a tenant when deductions are made. In addition, some states allow landlords to charge a nonrefundable fee such as for cleaning or pets, while others specifically prohibit nonrefundable fees. Several cities and states require landlords to put deposits in a separate bank account and pay tenants interest on them.

If your lease or rental agreement is a good one, it may provide lots of helpful details on deposits—for example, where they will be held, interest payments, and the conditions under which the security deposit will be returned or withheld. A few states require specific information like this to be included in leases and rental agreements, but most don't, so most agreements simply state the dollar amount of the deposit.

The use and return of security deposits is a frequent source of disputes between landlords and tenants. To avoid confusion and legal hassles, be sure you get all the information you need on security deposits before you sign a lease or rental agreement, especially as to what deductions are allowed, how the landlord expects you to clean the rental unit when you leave, when the deposit must be returned, and whether the deposit can be used for last month's rent. If this information isn't spelled out in the lease or rental agreement, ask your landlord to add it.

CAUTION
Watch out for automatic lien provisions. Your lease may have a clause that gives the landlord an "automatic lien" on your possessions if you fail to pay the rent or damage the unit. The purpose of this clause is to give your landlord the right to seize and sell your property without first going to court to prove the debt and give you a chance to hang on to certain property that is protected by state law. If you are presented with a lease that has an automatic lien provision (sometimes called a "distraint" or "distress" power), you should be concerned. Reputable landlords don't attempt to use them. While you may ultimately prevail in a lawsuit to compensate you for your seized possessions, that will be cold comfort when you return home to find your stereo, computer, or other personal items missing.

Utilities

Your lease or rental agreement may specify who pays for the utilities. Normally, landlords pay for garbage, and sometimes for water, if there is a yard. Tenants usually pay for other services, such as phone, gas, and electricity.

CAUTION
Make sure you're not paying anyone else's utility bills. Some older buildings and some duplexes and triplexes do not have separate gas and electric meters for each unit. In other situations, your meter may also measure gas or electricity used in areas outside of your unit—such as a water heater that serves several apartments or lighting in a common area. Whenever you'll be required to pay for utilities that are not 100% under your control, your landlord should disclose this in your lease or rental agreement. (This type of disclosure is required by law in some states.) To avoid hassles later on with neighbors who are wasteful of energy, your best approach is to ask the landlord to install a separate meter for all areas served outside your unit—but be forewarned, it's expensive, and the landlord is likely to say no. Alternatively, your landlord should place the particular utility in his name and pay the bill.

Assignment and Subletting

Most leases and rental agreements include a clause forbidding sublets—for example, having someone stay in your place and pay rent while you're gone for an extended period of time—without the prior written consent of your landlord. Also common is a prohibition against "assignments," a legal term that describes what happens when you transfer your entire tenancy to someone else. Landlords include these clauses to prevent you from bringing in tenants whom they haven't approved, and to preserve their occupancy policies.

Even if your lease or rental agreement prohibits sublets and assignments without consent, however, state law usually prohibits your landlord from arbitrarily withholding consent to your request to sublet or assign your lease to someone else.

If your lease or rental agreement doesn't specifically prohibit sublets or assignments, you can do so without your landlord's consent (except in Texas). Nevertheless, it's always wise to get the landlord's permission first, since most landlords will want to know whom they're renting to.

CAUTION
What about using Airbnb? Before you list your apartment on Airbnb or a similar service, be sure to check your lease or rental agreement (see "Tenant Rights to Use Airbnb and Similar Vacation Rental Services" in Chapter 7, for more on this).

Condition of the Rental Unit and Landlord's Responsibilities

Many leases and rental agreements include a clause in which you agree that the premises are in habitable (livable) condition. Before you sign off on a clause like this, we strongly recommend that you inspect the rental unit and note any problems, using the Landlord-Tenant Checklist in Chapter 6. Doing so will help you identify problems that need fixing before you move in, and help you avoid losing your security deposit over a problem that was present when you moved in. It's best to insist that this Checklist be made a part of your lease or rental agreement. You can add a clause like this:

> Tenant has examined the premises, including appliances, fixtures, carpets, drapes, and paint, and has found them to be in good, safe, and clean condition and repair, except as noted in the attached Landlord-Tenant Checklist.

If the landlord won't do this, at least include the landlord's specific promises in the lease or rental agreement. If the landlord promises to fix the oven or install security bars on the ground floor windows, for example, write this into the lease or rental agreement, and set a deadline for work to be completed (ideally, before you move in). (Chapter 6 includes sample agreements regarding repairs.) You could also use a letter of understanding, as explained below.

Some states require landlords to notify tenants in writing, usually in the lease or rental agreement, of procedures for making complaints and repair requests and to alert landlords to defective or dangerous conditions. Even where it is not required, good leases and rental agreements include this information.

CAUTION

Know your rights to live in a habitable rental unit—and don't give them up. As a general rule, landlords are legally required to offer livable premises when a tenant originally rents a rental unit and to maintain the premises throughout the rental term. Your lease or rental agreement will probably provide very few details on the landlord's exact repair and maintenance responsibilities. And you'll probably never see a clause that describes your options, such as withholding rent, if the landlord fails to provide habitable premises. To protect your rights, it is crucial you know the laws on these issues. (See Chapter 8 for details.)

Also, in most states, language a landlord sticks in a lease or rental agreement saying a tenant gives up his right to habitable housing won't be effective. By law, the landlord has to come through with habitable housing, no matter what the agreement says. And even if your state law allows such clauses, as is true in Maine and Texas, in limited situations, you'll want to avoid any landlord who operates this way.

Landlord's Responsibility for Repairs Caused by Natural Disasters

Many leases and rental agreements outline the landlord's responsibilities if the rental property is damaged or destroyed by a natural disaster, such as an earthquake or flood. For example, the landlord might have the right to declare the lease terminated if the premises are totally destroyed, or the option to simply suspend the lease and begin repairs reasonably quickly. If your lease has no provision regarding destruction, it's likely that state law has something to say on the subject. See Chapter 8.

Tenant's Repair and Maintenance Responsibilities

Most leases and rental agreements state that you are responsible for keeping the rental premises clean, sanitary, and in good condition, and that you must reimburse the landlord for the cost of repairing damage caused by your abuse or neglect. Some clauses go beyond a general statement and actually detail tenants' responsibility for problems like broken windows, clogged drains, or snow removal. And a few landlords go so far as to delegate some of their own repair and maintenance responsibilities to tenants. This is most common, and most practical, for single-family houses or duplexes, because owners of these properties seldom have on-site managers or maintenance people. See "Making Tenants Responsible for Repairs" in Chapter 8 for more on this issue.

Your lease or rental agreement will probably also tell what you what you *can't* do in the way of repairs. Typically, it will prohibit you from making alterations or repairs, such as painting or nailing holes in the walls or fixing the broken heater, without your landlord's consent. In addition, your lease or rental agreement may specify that if you add any "fixtures"—a legal term that means any addition that is attached to the structure, such as a bolted-on bookcase or built-in dishwasher—they will become the landlord's property and may not be removed without permission. And because your landlord has the legal right to enter your unit in an emergency, there may be a clause specifically forbidding you from adding or rekeying locks or installing a burglar alarm system without your landlord's consent.

Who's Responsible for Appliance Repair?

Most state laws do not require landlords to provide major appliances such as refrigerators or stoves, although many landlords do. So, if you see a refrigerator or stove in a rental unit, you would naturally expect it comes with the deal, and that if an appliance breaks through no fault of your own, it's the landlord's job to repair it. Think again. Some landlords, trying to save a buck, include a clause in the lease or rental agreement stating that the appliances are there for the tenant's use but are not part of the rent. The clause goes on to say that if you use the appliances, you are responsible for their repair and maintenance.

This kind of clause is a clear sign that you're dealing with a cheap landlord who's almost certain to do a poor job in the repairs and maintenance department. If the apartment is otherwise terrific and the appliances in pretty good shape, you might decide to put up with this nonsense, but it probably makes more sense not to rent from someone who pinches pennies this hard. (Chapter 9 gives advice on how to pry appliance repairs out of a reluctant landlord.)

Regardless of what the lease or rental agreement says, tenants have certain limited rights to alter or repair the premises. For example:

- In most states, tenants have the right to repair defects or damage that makes the premises uninhabitable.
- Texas law specifically allows tenants to install security devices without the landlord's prior consent. (Texas Security Devices Act, Tex. Prop. Code §§ 92.151–170.)
- In California, a tenant may install statutorily required door and window locks if the landlord has refused to do so. (Cal. Civ. Code § 1941.3(c).)
- Disabled tenants have certain rights to modify rental living space under the Federal Fair Housing Act. (42 U.S.C. §§ 3601–3619.)
- Federal law gives tenants limited rights to install wireless antennas and small satellite dishes. See "Satellite Dishes and Other Antennas," in Chapter 10, for details.

Renters' Insurance

Your lease or rental agreement may include a clause alerting you to the fact that your landlord's property insurance will not cover any losses to your personal property that might result from an accident on the premises. For example, if a fire that's the fault of the landlord destroys part of your unit and damages your possessions, the landlord's policy will not cover you—it will compensate only the landlord for the cost of repairing the structure. You could demand compensation from the landlord and sue if necessary, but the source of any recovery will be the landlord, personally, not his insurance company.

Similarly, the landlord's liability policy won't cover you if property is damaged or someone is injured on the property as the result of your carelessness. This means that you may be personally responsible if your actions cause:

- damage to the rental unit or other tenants' property
- loss of or damage to your belongings, or
- injuries to yourself or others.

Because of these realities, you may see a clause requiring you to obtain renters' insurance, which will cover losses to your belongings as a result of fire or theft and also provides coverage if your

How to Choose Renters' Insurance

When considering renters' insurance, follow these steps:

Take a property inventory. In order to choose a policy limit, you'll need to know the value of the items that you'll insure. (The smallest amount of coverage is usually $20,000 to $30,000.) You will be surprised at how fast the totals will mount up, given our ever-expanding inventory of modern necessities—computers, phones, bicycles, cameras, clothing, stereos, even pets. Also, taking an inventory will make it easier to make a claim, should you need to do so. The nonprofit organization United Policyholders has useful home inventory worksheets on its website (www.uphelp.org), as well as information on apps for taking a home inventory. Make a copy of your inventory and keep it in a safe place *away* from home.

Shop around. Find an agent or company representative you trust—possibly your automobile insurance agent, or one recommended by friends or relatives. Keep your inventory handy so that you can compare premiums.

Check what's covered. Ask about things not covered by the policy or where dollar limits are low. Cash is usually not covered and jewelry, computer, and table silver coverage typically is limited, but you may be able to buy additional coverage (called a "floater" policy). Bicycles are usually covered (but not cars, vans, boats, or trucks). If you run a home business, you may need to purchase additional coverage for office equipment.

Determine whether the policy is for replacement value. If you suffer a loss, your renters' policy can cover your belongings in one of two ways. It can reimburse you for the actual cash value (what your three-year-old computer would sell for today on the open market) or pay replacement value (what you would have to spend today to get a comparable computer). Obviously, a replacement value policy is preferable but is likely to cost more.

TIP

If you aren't worried about your property, get a high deductible. If your landlord requires renters' insurance to cover any damage you cause to his property, but you really aren't worried about the theft or loss of your own goods (maybe they aren't worth much, or you live in an extremely safe area), you can save a bundle by getting the highest deductible the insurance company offers.

Add your lease guarantor. If the landlord has required a cosigner or guarantor, be sure to add this person as an additional insured to your policy. Although a cosigner's primary role is to provide a source of money if you can't pay the rent, the cosigner could also be sued, along with you, by someone who claims that your negligence caused an injury. Do not expose your generous cosigner to this risk—adding a cosigner to your policy will cost only a few dollars.

Read your policy. Don't assume that the fine print exactly mirrors what you and the insurance agent discussed. Unless you check the important points (and complain, if there are any discrepancies), you'll be stuck.

RESOURCE

More information on renters' insurance. United Policyholders, a highly regarded consumer advocacy group, has helpful articles on renters' insurance on its website at www.uphelp.org. Also, check out www.rentersinsurance.net, and the Insurance Information Institute website (www.iii.org). Many of the apartment-listing websites referred to in Chapter 1 have links to companies that sell renters' insurance.

negligence causes property damage or injury to other people. Landlords with exclusive properties are especially likely to require renters' insurance. Typically, they'll ask for a copy of your policy's face sheet or a certificate of insurance from your company, which lists the type of policy, its coverage limits, and its expiration date. Whether it's legal to require tenants to purchase liability insurance is a topic of hot debate among lawyers; one state, Virginia, has explicitly legislated that it is. (Va. Code Ann. § 55-248.7:2.)

Is It Legal for Landlords to Require Renters' Insurance?

Whether it's legal to require tenants to purchase renters' insurance is a topic of hot debate among lawyers. Judges in some states, including Oklahoma, have held that, by implication, tenants are coinsured under their landlords' own property policy, because their rent helps pay the landlords' premiums. Unfortunately, only Virginia has clear statutory law on the subject: Virginia allows a landlord to require a tenant to pay for renters' insurance that's obtained by the landlord. However, if the landlord also requires a security deposit in Virginia, the combined cost of the insurance premiums and the security deposit cannot exceed two months' rent. (Va. Code Ann. §§ 55-248.2 to 248.9.) Oregon also regulates landlords' requirements for renters' insurance. (Or. Rev. Stat. § 90.367.)

The real reason landlords insist on renters' insurance has little to do with concern for your personal property. Rather, they want it in place so that if you damage the rental property, or if someone is hurt due to your carelessness, your insurance company, not the landlord's, will foot the bill. If you let your renters' policy lapse and refuse to reinstate it, landlords have little recourse other than to terminate your tenancy (assuming their lease or rental agreement provides for that consequence). If you're an otherwise good tenant, landlords will not want to take this ultimate step.

However, the insurance industry handed landlords a way to keep your insurance alive and pressure you to pay the premiums. Landlords can buy a type of insurance called "Apartment Owners Limited Building Policy" that will, if needed, provide you with liability insurance—but not property insurance—if your renters' insurance policy has lapsed. The landlord sets the rent to include both the rent and a "rent credit" equal to the monthly cost of such a policy, plus a little to cover the landlord's administrative costs. If your insurance policy remains in effect, you get a rent credit every month and pay just the regular rent. But if you can't prove that you have a current policy, the landlord will buy the coverage for you and you'll pay rent plus the "credit." A scheme like this will have a hard time surviving a legal challenge in cities with rent control, unless the rent plus the rent credit is within the rent allowed by law.

What Does Renters' Insurance Cover?

Even if your landlord does not require renters' insurance, buying it can be a good idea if you can afford it. The cost depends on the location and size of the rental unit and the value of your possessions. Renters' insurance typically costs a few hundred dollars a year for a $50,000 policy. Some insurance companies offer discounts if you already have another type of insurance with the company or if you have risk-reduction measures in place such as a security system.

Renters' insurance covers the following:
- loss due to theft, including some losses that occur away from home
- negligent destruction of your or the landlord's property (for example, you start a fire that destroys your kitchen)
- liability for injuries or losses to others (a guest slips and breaks her leg on your freshly washed kitchen floor, or you leave the water on, ruining the downstairs tenant's computer), and
- natural disasters or damage to your property caused by other people (the creek rises, flooding the building, or your neighbor starts a fire that damages your unit).

CAUTION

Renters' insurance will not cover intentional damage. It also will not pay back rent, nor will it cover any sums you might owe the landlord in excess of your security deposit. It probably won't cover if an Airbnb "guest" causes damage.

Buying Renters' Insurance With Cotenants

If you rent a place with other people (your cotenants), you may want to explore purchasing one policy that will cover all of you. You shouldn't have a problem getting a joint renters' insurance policy. Under a joint policy, if someone's personal property is stolen or damaged, the insurance company will write just one check for the value of the property. It will be up to you and your cotenants to give the money to the cotenant who suffered the loss. Or, if a fire damages a jointly owned sofa, you'll get one check and you and your roommates will have to apportion the money fairly. The advantage of having one joint policy is that you'll have to satisfy only one deductible. For example, if a burglar steals your bike, one roommate's climbing rack, and another roommate's computer, you'd make one claim for all three items and face only one deductible.

You and your cotenants can also purchase individual policies that cover your individual property, as well as your share of jointly owned property. For instance, if you and your roommate buy a sofa together and each pay half, your individual policy would cover you for up to half the sofa's value. If a fire were to damage the sofa, you could submit a claim for half its value, but you'd probably have to document the fact that you paid for half of it. (You can document your ownership share by signing an agreement with your roommate at the time of sale, or by showing that you wrote a check or incurred a credit card charge for half the price.)

In sum, having just one policy that all cotenants share is cheaper because there's only one premium and one deductible, but having two may be less hassle when it comes to dividing up the proceeds. Whether you get a joint policy, or each buy an individual policy, it's important to keep clear records of who owns what.

Watch Out for Hold-Harmless and Exculpatory Clauses

Many form leases include illegal provisions that attempt to absolve the landlord in advance from responsibility for all damages, injuries, or losses, including those caused by the landlord's misdeeds. These clauses come in two varieties:

- Exculpatory: "If there's a problem, you won't hold me responsible."
- Hold-harmless: "If there's a problem traceable to me, you're responsible."

For example, the lease generated by one popular legal software package contains an exculpatory provision so broad that it states that your landlord is not responsible, period, for injuries to tenants and guests. If enforced, this would mean that if you fall down broken stairs and break your leg, the landlord isn't responsible (even, apparently, if the landlord personally littered the stairs with banana peels).

Such pro-landlord language is blatantly illegal. If your landlord assaults you, or you're injured because of a dangerous or defective condition the landlord failed to fix for several months, no boilerplate lease provision will protect your landlord from civil and possibly even criminal charges. To this end, most states have laws that declare that exculpatory clauses in residential leases and rental agreements are void. This means that a judge will not enforce them.

Violating Laws and Causing Disturbances

Most form leases and rental agreements contain a clause forbidding you from using the premises or adjacent areas, such as the sidewalk in front of the building, in such a way as to:

- violate any law or ordinance, including laws prohibiting the use, possession, or sale of illegal drugs
- seriously damage the property (sometimes called "committing waste" in legalese), or
- create a nuisance by annoying or disturbing other tenants or nearby residents—for example, by continuous loud noise.

You may also see reference to tenants' right to "quiet enjoyment" of the premises. This bit of legal jargon amounts to a promise that your landlord will not act (or fail to act) in a way that seriously interferes with your ability to use the rented premises—for example, by allowing garbage to pile up, tolerating a major rodent infestation, or failing to control (or evict) a neighboring tenant whose constant loud music makes it impossible for tenants to sleep (or even think). Fortunately, you have the right to quiet enjoyment even if your lease or rental agreement doesn't mention it.

Many landlords also include specific rules—for example, no loud music played after midnight—in a separate set of rules and regulations. As discussed below, as long as these rules are fairly reasonable— and sometimes even if they are not—your landlord can enforce them.

Pets

In most situations, your landlord has the right to prohibit all pets, or restrict the types allowed— for example, no dogs or cats, but birds are okay, or dogs are okay, but none of a particular breed. However, a landlord may not prohibit trained service animals used by physically or mentally disabled people, or emotional support animals, as provided by the federal Fair Housing Amendments Act, discussed in Chapter 5.

Many landlords spell out pet rules—for example, that the tenants will keep the yard free of all animal waste, or that dogs will always be on leash—in a separate set of rules and regulations.

Some landlords allow pets but require tenants to pay a separate deposit to cover any damage that may be caused by the pet. The laws of a few states specifically allow separate, nonrefundable pet deposits. In others, charging a designated pet deposit is legal only if the total amount your landlord charges for all deposits does not exceed the state maximum for all deposits. Also, it is illegal to charge an extra pet deposit for people with trained guide dogs, signal dogs, or service dogs.

Opening Landlords' Doors to Pets

Several humane societies across the country offer pet-owning tenants helpful materials on how to negotiate with a landlord who doesn't normally allow pets. Here are a few examples:

- The San Francisco Society for the Prevention of Cruelty to Animals' website (www.sfspca.org) includes a sample pet agreement and cat and dog résumés.
- The Hawaiian Humane Society (www.hawaiian humane.org) includes a special section ("Pets Are Family") that offers lots of useful resources for tenants, including a pet addendum to a rental agreement; the site also includes information on state laws in Hawaii, such as regards pet deposits.
- The Humane Society of the U.S. (www.humane society.org) includes useful tips for tenants, and a sample pet application form.

Landlord's Right of Access

Some leases and rental agreements spell out rules covering the landlord's right to enter your rental unit, including circumstances allowing access and the minimum amount of notice the landlord must provide. Others are silent on the subject. Even if the lease tries to restrict your right to privacy, however, most states with laws guaranteeing a tenant's privacy prohibit a landlord from enforcing unreasonably strict rules.

Nearly every state clearly recognizes the right of a landlord to enter rented premises while a tenant is still in residence, under certain narrow circumstances, such as to deal with a genuine emergency (for example, a fire or broken pipe) and when the tenant gives permission. Many states have access laws specifying the other circumstances under which landlords may legally enter rented premises—for example, to make repairs and inspect the property and to show property to prospective tenants or buyers. State access laws often require the landlord to give the tenant at least 24 hours' notice for nonemergency entries. A few states simply require the landlord to provide "reasonable" notice, often presumed to be 24 hours. Many states have no statutes covering landlord's access.

To protect your privacy, particularly if your state does not set specific rules on landlords' entry, be sure your lease or rental agreement covers the subject. Here's an example of the kind of lease clause you should get your landlord to write into your lease or rental agreement:

"Landlord or Landlord's agent will not enter tenant's home except to deal with an emergency; to make necessary or agreed repairs; to supply necessary or agreed services; or to show the unit to potential purchasers, tenants, or repairpersons. Unless there is an emergency, or it is impractical to do so, Landlord will give tenant at least 24 hours' written notice of the date, time, and purpose of the intended entry."

Extended Absences by Tenant

Some leases and rental agreements require you to notify the landlord in advance if you will be away from the premises for a certain number of consecutive days (often seven or more). Such clauses may give the landlord the right to enter the rental unit during your absence to maintain the property as necessary and to inspect for damage and needed repairs. You'll most often see this type of clause if you live in a cold-weather place where, in case of extreme cold weather, landlords want to check the pipes in rental units to make sure they haven't burst. By state law in Alaska, a rental agreement or lease must say that you need to inform the landlord of any planned absences over seven days (Alaska Stat. § 34.03.150).

Possession of the Premises

Many leases and rental agreements include a clause explaining what happens if you choose not to move in after signing the lease or rental agreement. Generally, you will still be required to pay rent and satisfy other conditions of the agreement. This does not mean, however, that your landlord can sit back and expect to collect rent for the entire lease or rental agreement

term. Instead, as we explain in Chapter 15, landlords in most states must take reasonably prompt steps to rerent the premises, and must credit the rent they collect against your rent obligation under the lease.

Most leases and rental agreements also cover situations when the landlord is unable to turn over possession of the unit to the tenant on time after having signed the agreement or lease. This clause is included in case fire destroys the building, contracted repairs aren't done on time, or a prior tenant illegally fails to leave as expected. In the absence of a clause like this, the law would usually consider the landlord's failure to allow you to move in on time to mean that the lease was breached, justifying your walking away and looking for another place. But landlords hate to lose a new tenant just because the old one failed to leave or the contractor didn't get the refurbishing done on time. So they typically insert a clause that states that the lease will be considered breached only if *the landlord* says it is. Usually, they give themselves ten to 30 days to make up their minds. In the meantime, you are obligated to honor the lease—even though you can't move in! You may be able to sue the landlord for reasonable costs of temporary housing, although some particularly nasty leases attempt to eliminate that remedy, too.

Another common approach to the "not ready" apartment is to allow the new tenant to walk away—in other words, to acknowledge that the lease has been breached—but to try to limit the landlord's liability for failing to have the unit ready on move-in day. This is done with a clause that limits the landlord's financial liability to new tenants to the return of any prepaid rent and security deposits (the "sums previously paid" is the language common in this type of clause). If you have a limiting clause like this in your lease, you won't be able to sue the landlord for temporary housing while you wait for repairs or for the prior tenant to move out. You could, however, file a small claims court case and sue the hold-over tenant himself or the person who caused the delay for your inconvenience and expenses, although your chances of winning are slight.

Tenant Rules and Regulations

Many landlords don't worry about detailed rules and regulations, especially when they rent single-family homes or duplexes. However, in large multitenant buildings, landlords usually set out rules to control the use of common areas and equipment and to protect the rental property from damage. Rules and regulations also help avoid confusion and misunderstandings about day-to-day issues such as garbage disposal and use of recreation areas.

What's Covered in Tenant Rules and Regulations

Tenant rules and regulations typically cover issues such as:

- elevator safety and use
- pool rules
- garbage disposal and recycling
- vehicles and parking regulations—for example, restrictions on repairs on the premises or types of vehicles (such as no RVs), or where guests can park
- lock-out and lost-key charges
- pet rules
- security system use
- no smoking—either in common areas in multi-unit buildings (including the hallways, lobby, garage, or walkways), or even in individual units (see "Marijuana Smoking," below)
- specific details on what's considered excessive noise (for example, playing loud music after 10 p.m.)
- dangerous materials—nothing flammable or explosive should be on the premises
- storage of bikes, baby strollers, and other equipment in halls, stairways, and other common areas
- specific landlord and tenant maintenance responsibilities (such as stopped-up toilets or garbage disposals, broken windows, rodent and pest control, lawn and yard maintenance)
- use of the grounds
- maintenance of balconies and decks—for instance, no drying clothes on balconies
- display of signs in windows
- laundry room rules
- waterbeds, and
- no business (or very limited types).

Marijuana Smoking

Many states have decriminalized the recreational use of marijuana, often defined as personal possession of a specified, small amount. You surely know if your state is among them. And you may be wondering if your landlord can legally prevent your lighting up in your rental. The answer is yes.

Although possession and use of a small amount may be legal, smoking that amount will still create smoke. Because landlords can legally designate their properties as smoke-free (common areas and individual units), they can consider marijuana smoke a violation of that policy.

Now, what about medical marijuana? The states that provide for legal use do not require landlords to allow such users to smoke on otherwise smoke-free properties. These laws simply protect the users from prosecution by the state; they do not interfere with a landlord's ability to maintain a smoke-free property. The wise practice of a medical marijuana user is to consume the substance in food or liquid, which will not impinge on other tenants' rights to a smokeless property.

Many landlords spell out their rules and regulations right in their lease or rental agreement. However, if the rules and regulations are lengthy, a clause in the agreement usually refers to them as a separate document (lawyers call this "incorporating by reference").

Unlike the terms and conditions contained in the rental agreement or lease, rules and regulations can be changed by the landlord without waiting until the end of the rental term (for leases) or without giving proper notice (for rental agreements). The landlord has this freedom, however, only if the change is minor and not apt to significantly affect the tenant's use or enjoyment of his tenancy. For example, shortening the pool hours by a few hours in the winter is rather inconsequential; on the other hand, announcing that the pool will be permanently closed is major—and a tenant would have a good argument that this change constitutes a breach of the rental agreement or lease, even if the landlord characterizes the change as a mere rule change.

Chapter 15 covers your options when important amenities or services are withdrawn.

Tenant rules and regulations can have a significant impact on your daily life and enjoyment of the rental premises. Be sure to read them carefully.

Attorneys' Fees in a Lawsuit

People who sign contracts, including leases and rental agreements, sometimes end up in a legal dispute involving lawyers and courts. Usually, each side pays for his or her own attorney and court costs, unless a judge orders the losing side to pay the winner's expenses. This happens only rarely, and only when the law that the winner relied upon authorizes attorneys' fees, or when the conduct of the loser was particularly outrageous—for example, filing a totally frivolous lawsuit. If your lease or rental agreement has no "attorneys' fees" clause in it, then you'll be playing by the general rules if you end up in a court spat with your landlord.

But parties to a contract can decide in advance that they would like the rules to be otherwise. Many leases and rental agreements specify who will pay the costs of a lawsuit, by including one of two types of attorneys' fee clauses:

- **The "Loser Pays" Attorneys' Fees Clause.** A common and evenhanded attorneys' fees clause requires the losing side in a landlord-tenant dispute to pay attorneys' fees and court costs (filing fees, service of process charges, deposition costs, and so on) to the winning ("prevailing") party in a lawsuit. With an attorneys' fees clause of this type, if you hire a lawyer to sue your landlord (for example, over the security deposit) and win, the judge will order your landlord to pay your costs and attorneys' fees. A "loser pays" clause is attractive if you're confident that you will be a law-abiding and conscientious tenant—in other words, if you expect to be in the right.

  On the other hand, if you qualify for legal aid or just feel confident about representing yourself in most situations, you may prefer

not to have an attorneys' fees clause, reasoning that your landlord may be more willing to compromise any dispute if he can't sue you and recover his attorneys' fees.

- **"Losing Tenant" Pays.** Some landlords aren't content to make the loser (possibly themselves, after all) pay for lawyers' fees. Instead, they write a clause that obligates the tenant to pay the landlord's fees and costs if the landlord wins. But if the landlord loses, the clause says the landlord isn't obligated to pay the tenant's expenses.

This is a pretty shifty arrangement, and it hasn't gone down well. By law in California, New York, Oregon, Washington, and a number of other states, any attorneys' fees clause in a lease or a rental agreement must work both ways, even if it's not written that way. That is, even if the lease states that only your landlord is entitled to attorneys' fees for winning a lawsuit, you will be entitled to collect your attorneys' fees from your landlord if you prevail. Your landlord would be ordered to pay whatever amount the judge decides is reasonable.

Assuming you have any choice in the matter (you often won't), is it a good idea to include an attorneys' fees clause in your lease? It depends. The presence of an attorneys' fees clause will make it far easier for you to find a willing lawyer to take a case that does not have the potential for a hefty money judgment. For example, if you successfully defend against an eviction, you're likely to get the right to stay, but you probably won't be entitled to any money from the landlord. If your lease has a clause providing that the winner pays the loser, your attorney will get paid by the landlord. Knowing this, a lawyer will be more likely to take your case. Similarly, if your case has the potential for only a small monetary award but will involve a lot of work, a lawyer will be more willing to take it knowing that the fees will come from the landlord and not from your modest winnings.

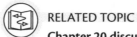 **RELATED TOPIC**
Chapter 20 discusses how to find and work with a lawyer.

CAUTION

Attorneys' fee clauses don't cover all legal disputes. They cover fees only for lawsuits that concern the meaning or implementation of a rental agreement or lease—for example, a dispute about rent, security deposits, or the landlord's right to access (assuming that the rental document includes these subjects). The clause would not apply in a personal injury or discrimination lawsuit.

Disclosures

Federal, state, or local laws may require your landlord to make certain disclosures before you sign a lease or rental agreement or move in. Some disclosures that may be required include:

- the name of the owner and the person authorized to receive legal papers, such as a property manager

- any known lead-based paint hazards in the rental premises (discussed in Chapter 13)
- hidden (not obvious) defects of the rental property that could cause injury or substantially interfere with your safe enjoyment and use of the dwelling—for example, a warning that the building walls contain asbestos insulation, which could become dangerous if disturbed
- the name and address of the bank where security deposits are held, and the rate of interest and its payment to the tenant (see Chapter 4)
- planned condominium conversions (discussed in Chapter 15), and
- the presence of a methamphetamine lab at the rental in a prior tenant's occupancy.

 **RELATED TOPIC**

State disclosures. See "Required Landlord Disclosures" in Appendix A for a list of the disclosures required in your state. Your city may impose additional disclosures—call your city attorney or city manager's office for details.

 **RENT CONTROL**

Rent control ordinances typically include additional disclosures, such as the name and address of the government agency or elected board that administers the ordinance and special rules governing sublets and assignments.

Authority to Receive Legal Papers

It's the law in many states, and a good idea in all, to know whom you should send legal papers to. For example, you may need to send a notice that you are ending the tenancy, or you may even need to sue the landlord one day. Leases and rental agreements typically include the name and address of the landlord or whoever is authorized to receive notices and legal papers on the landlord's behalf, such as a property manager.

Grounds for Termination of Tenancy

There is usually a clause stating that any violation of the lease or rental agreement by you, or by your guests, is grounds for terminating the tenancy, according to the procedures established by state or local laws.

RELATED TOPIC
Chapters 17 and 18 discuss grounds and procedures for terminating tenancies.

Mediation

Some landlords have wisely learned that disputes that can't be worked out between the landlord and tenant are often best resolved without lawyers, but with the help of a skilled, professional mediator. You may see a clause obligating you to go through mediation "in good faith" if a dispute arises over the meaning or implementation of your lease or rental agreement. All this means is that you agree that you won't rush off and sue until you have met with the landlord and a mediator and have genuinely tried to work out a solution to your dispute. This is an excellent requirement from your point of view, since it also gives you a way to get help with your grievance. Mediation is not binding—if you don't come to an agreement, you can assert your rights in court.

A mediation clause covers only lease and rental agreement disputes. A provision requiring good-faith mediation requires you to mediate disputes that arise from the lease or rental agreement itself. For example, if you intend to sue your landlord for discriminating against you in violation of federal or state fair housing laws, you need not mediate first, because that behavior is not connected with the meaning or implementation of the lease or rental agreement.

RELATED TOPIC
Mediation is explained in more detail in Chapter 19.

Additional Provisions

Some form lease and rental agreements include a blank space for any other agreement you and your landlord wish to make. For example, your landlord may want to add a provision that prohibits smoking in your apartment or in the common areas, or spells out lost key charges.

Write down any agreement that's important to you, such as a landlord's promise to paint the unit before you move in or replace the deck within two months. If you don't, and the promised improvement is put off or not done as promised, you'll be left with little more than your word against the landlord's.

If there is no place on the form to add your own clause, you can modify the lease as shown below in "Changing a Lease or Rental Agreement."

CAUTION
If you don't get everything added to the agreement you sign, be sure to send your landlord a letter of understanding. See the discussion in "Oral Leases and Rental Agreements," above, and the sample Letter of Understanding, below.

In Chapter 6, "Using Email or Text Messages for Notice or a Letter of Understanding" explains why it's best to send this kind of letter by mail or delivery service, rather than email or text messages.

Validity of Each Part

Leases and rental agreements commonly include what lawyers call a "savings" clause, which means that, in the event that one of the other clauses in the lease or rental agreement is found to be invalid by a court, the remainder of the agreement will remain in force. Given the number of blatantly illegal clauses that lots of landlords stick in their agreements, it's not hard to see why they need this one.

Entire Agreement

Somewhere in the fine print, usually at the end, most leases have a provision that says that the agreement, and any attachments such as rules and regulations, is the entire agreement of the parties. That means that if the landlord (or you) made any promises that weren't in or attached to the lease or rental agreement, then they don't count and can't be enforced.

Does this clause mean that your landlord's oral promises ("Of *course* I'll fix the ice maker before you move in!") will never be enforced? Probably not, but if the landlord claims he never promised you anything, it will make it harder for you to convince a judge that he did. For this reason, we counsel you again to get all promises from the landlord in writing and part of or attached to the lease.

Sample Letter of Understanding

777 Walnut Street
San Gimo, Arizona 00000

January 20, 20xx

Manny Money
125 Capitol Mall
San Gimo, Arizona 00000

Dear Mr. Money,

Thank you for showing me Apartment #3 today at your apartment complex, Willow Run. As you doubtless remember, we discussed the poor condition of the living room carpet, which you said you were planning to replace within two months. Since I was very pleased with every other aspect of the apartment and the building, I signed a lease, based on your promise that the carpet would in fact be replaced within two months of my starting date of February 1, 20xx.

Please let me know immediately if your understanding of your promise regarding the living room rug differs from mine. As I mentioned today, I would not want to live with that stained carpet for more than two months, and would consider the lease to be breached if the carpet were not replaced by April 1, 20xx. I have every hope that you will attend to the matter as promised and that I will fully enjoy my tenancy at Willow Run.

Yours truly,

Sally Smart

Sally Smart

Miscellaneous Clauses

If the landlord's lease has been prepared by a lawyer or trade organization, there's a good chance that you'll see these additional clauses at the end.

- **Successors.** Many leases state that the lease will be binding on the "successors, heirs, assigns, administrators, and executors" of the parties. This simply means that if the owner dies and the property passes to someone else, or if the owner voluntarily sells the building or assigns the right to receive rent to someone else, all of these persons will be bound by the agreement. The same goes for you—if you assign the lease (turn it over to a new tenant), you understand that the new tenant will be bound by the lease. (Assignment is explained in Chapter 15.)

- **Applicable law.** Your lease may state that it will be construed according to the laws of a particular state. Most of the time, this will be the state where the property is located. If another state is listed, beware. That state may be where the landlord's business is located, and the landlord may simply want to play by the laws that he (and his lawyer) are more familiar with (and, no surprise, that state probably has less tenant-friendly laws than your state). In a business-to-business context, this type of choice is often allowed, but it's doubtful that a court would permit a residential landlord to choose another state's law to govern the rental relationship. Any attempt to do so is not a good sign; you'll want to consider whether to negotiate this one away.

Negotiating With the Landlord

Your lease or rental agreement is probably loaded with clauses written to maximize the landlord's rights and minimize yours. That's because these rental documents are typically written by lawyers hired by landlords or their trade associations.

Don't assume, however, that every clause is written in stone. Armed with a little legal knowledge, you'll be able to figure out whether the terms and conditions of your lease or rental agreement—its clauses—are legal or illegal, subject to negotiation or not. Here's how to do it.

> **TIP**
> **Knowing *when* to negotiate is as important as knowing *how*.** Don't start bargaining the minute you see a promising rental. Take some time to establish a rapport with the landlord and give him reason to want to choose you over other applicants. Even seemingly implacable rules, especially no-pets restrictions, may melt away if the landlord likes and wants you as a tenant.

Four Types of Lease Clauses

Every rental clause falls into one of four categories, depending on the issue's connection to any federal, state, or local laws on that subject. Determining how (or whether) to negotiate with your landlord over a rental clause will depend on which category the issue fits into.

Category 1: A Restatement of Your Guaranteed Legal Rights

Many states have passed tenant-friendly laws covering key areas such as landlords' access to rental property, the amount and use of security deposits, and your right to a livable home. In addition, you may have important legal rights under federal law (particularly in the area of discrimination) and local law (especially if your community has rent control). *Your landlord cannot legally diminish these rights and cannot ask you to waive them.* This book explains which important tenant rights belong in this category; below, we provide further clarification.

Your landlord is obliged to comply with these tenant rights, but is not usually required to inform you of them in your lease or rental agreement. You don't have to bargain for legal rights that are guaranteed under local, state, or federal law. If your landlord spells out guaranteed tenant rights in your rental document, fine, but you've got them regardless.

Category 2: A Variation of a Negotiable State or Local Law

Not all tenant-protection laws are off-limits to landlord tinkering, as are the ones in Category 1, above. For example, in some states a landlord and tenant may agree that the statutory notice periods for changing or ending a tenancy may be shortened if *both* agree. If the rental document doesn't mention the issue, however, state law prevails.

If you see a clause that restricts rights that are given you by a state or local statute, you'll obviously need to know whether this restriction is allowed in your state—in other words, whether the subject instead fits within Category 1, above.

If your state or local law allows the landlord some wiggle room on a tenant-friendly procedure, he's allowed to take advantage of that liberty. You can't force him back to the original law. If he's stubborn, you must be prepared to offer reasons why the variation is either not necessary or not fair. You may be able to work out a compromise or offer a concession of your own in exchange for your full rights under the law. Ultimately, however, if a landlord won't budge and you feel very strongly about the issue, you'll have to look elsewhere.

Category 3: Illegal Clauses

Landlords cannot diminish certain tenant-protection laws, such as your rights to a habitable rental unit and to be free from illegal discrimination. These are the rights that fit within Category 1, above. Nonetheless, many landlords attempt to circumvent the law by rewriting it. The best example of this is when landlords try to limit their responsibility to provide habitable housing, despite the laws that exist in the vast majority of states to the contrary. Incredible though it may seem, you'll see rental clauses in which the landlord states that the premises are not warranted as fit, safe, secure, or in good repair. Most states will not uphold these clauses. This means that even if you sign a lease or rental agreement that contains a clause absolving the landlord of the duty to offer and maintain fit housing, you can still complain (or use a tenant remedy such as repair and deduct, explained in Chapter 8) and a court will not hold you to your "waiver."

A misstatement of a guaranteed tenant right isn't the only kind of illegal clause you may encounter. Some clauses are illegal because they violate an important public policy. For example, many landlords use a lease clause that states that the tenant will not hold the landlord responsible for injuries the tenant may suffer as a result of the landlord's negligence or carelessness. Most courts will not enforce these clauses because our society expects that, for the most part, people should be held accountable for their screw-ups.

Remember that we are dealing here with tenant rights that can't be waived or diminished—in other words, they are *nonnegotiable*. If your landlord nevertheless attempts to avoid his responsibilities, it means that he is either unaware of your rights or deliberately violating the law. Your response will depend on your reading of the landlord.

- **The landlord doesn't know the law.** If you think the landlord has made an honest mistake, and especially if your options as to other rentals are narrow, you may decide that it's worth pointing out to the landlord that his clause is invalid. Doing so lets him know that he's not dealing with a dummy or a pushover, and hopefully he'll be more careful in the future. There is a risk, however: You may discover that he'll do everything possible to get rid of you, preferring to rent to people who don't know their rights.

- **The landlord is deliberately violating the law.** If every sign suggests that the landlord has deliberately circumvented the law, the wise course is clear: Move on. If you don't, you can count on problems ahead.

Category 4: A Policy or Rule Not Covered by State or Local Law

Finally, you'll see lots of lease clauses that are not regulated in the slightest by your local or state laws

or court decisions. Examples include provisions for parking spaces, amount of rent (rent control excepted), rent due date, move-in date, rules regarding common area use, and procedures for registering complaints and repair requests. Some of these issues are written as clauses in the lease or rental agreement itself, but many are covered in "house rules," which landlords attach to leases.

But minor, day-to-day issues aren't the only ones that may be untethered to a federal, state, or local law. In some states, extremely important issues, such as security deposit limits or rules governing landlords' access to rental property, are not governed by law. For example, New York (for nonregulated units) and Texas do not limit the amount of money a landlord may demand as a security deposit. Clearly, before sounding off with a haughty demand to reform an "illegal" clause, you'll need to know whether your state law does, in fact, regulate the issue.

Issues that aren't governed by law are the truly negotiable ones. Here you are both free to bargain, restrained only by the strength of your position. If it's a renters' market and the landlord's property is littered with "Vacancy" signs, you can expect more cooperation than if there are 17 professional couples lined up waiting to take the unit with no demands. Rather than push now for a better deal, it sometimes makes sense to get the rental and then, after you have established yourself as a stable, desirable tenant, ask the landlord to revisit the issue and possibly change that lease clause (changing rental agreements and leases is covered in Chapter 15).

Concluding Your Negotiations

Negotiation with your landlord should always end with a written version of what the two of you agreed to. Never, ever walk away from a negotiation session without reducing your deal to writing, either by changing the rental document or adding to it. Follow our instructions for changing a lease or rental agreement, below.

Changing a Lease or Rental Agreement

If you and your landlord agree to make changes to your lease or rental agreement, the process is simple.

Deleting Language

You may be able to convince your landlord that a particular clause need not be in your lease—for example, perhaps you have successfully shown that your four-legged pal is friendlier and better behaved than most of the existing tenants, so that your landlord is willing to delete the no-pets clause. Never rely on the landlord's sincere promise that he won't enforce that part of the lease (he may change his mind or sell the building). To protect yourself, all you do is cross out the unwanted portion, write in desired changes (if any) and have everyone who is going to sign the document initial and date the changes. If your landlord has the lease in a computer, he will probably want to print out a clean copy to sign.

Adding Language

You or your landlord may write or type in minor changes to your lease or rental agreement, as explained above. If the proposed changes are fairly lengthy, however, either your landlord will need to prepare a new agreement, or prepare an amendment page (lawyers use the word "addendum") to the original document.

 FORM

The Nolo website includes a downloadable Amendment to Lease or Rental Agreement form that you can tear out, copy, and use to make changes or insert additions before you sign a lease or rental agreement. A sample is shown in Chapter 15. See Appendix B for the link to the forms in this book.

To use the amendment form, follow these steps:

Step 1: On the original document, at the end of the rental provisions and before your signature, add the sentence "See Amendment A for additional provisions." That way, if the attachment gets lost (or the landlord removes it), the fact that it ought to be there will be recorded on the lease, and the landlord cannot claim that it never existed.

Step 2: Fill out the Amendment form included on the Nolo website. If it is the only addition, label it "A" in the space provided in the title and set out the additional lease provision in the space below. (If you later add more provisions, label them "B," "C," and so on, and refer to them on your copy at least of the original lease or rental agreement.) See the sample in Chapter 15. Include a date by which the landlord is to accomplish the promise, if appropriate.

Step 3: Consider what you want to happen if the landlord fails to follow through. If the amendment is absolutely essential to you—for example, you simply must have a parking space within three months—and you want to be able to legally move out if the landlord doesn't follow through, add this sentence: "Failure of the Landlord to comply with the terms and conditions of this Amendment constitutes a material breach of the Lease/Rental Agreement." This means that the landlord's breach excuses your obligations to stay and pay rent. On the other hand, if noncompliance would not be so devastating to your ability to stay and enjoy your home, specify another consequence, such as that your rent will be reduced a certain amount per day or week until the provision is complied with.

Step 4: Sign and date the amendment. Since it's part of your lease or rental agreement, store it carefully with the other important documents relating to your tenancy, as suggested in Chapter 6.

Signing a Lease or Rental Agreement

At the end of the lease or rental agreement, there will be space to include your landlord's signature, street address, and phone number, or that of the person she authorizes to receive legal papers, such as a property manager. There's also space for your and other tenants' signatures and phone numbers, as well as any cosigner. (Cosigners are discussed below.)

If your landlord has altered a preprinted form by writing or typing in changes, be sure that you and the landlord initial and date the changes when you sign the document.

Make sure you sign the lease or rental agreement at the same time as the landlord and that you get a copy then and there. This assures both sides that no changes can be made after only one party has signed.

Cosigners

A cosigner is someone who agrees to make good on your financial responsibilities under a lease or rental agreement should you fail to do so. If you fail to pay the rent, or to replenish your security deposit after the landlord has used it to fix something you've damaged, the landlord can demand that sum from your cosigner. If the cosigner doesn't pay up, the landlord can terminate your tenancy.

Tenants who are students and supported in whole or in part by their parents often ask landlords to accept their parents (or others) as cosigners, hoping that the parents' or friend's financial solidity will make up for the student's meager income. Landlords who accept cosigners typically have the cosigners fill out a separate rental application and agree to a credit check.

With one exception (explained below), landlords do not have to accept cosigners. Many feel that it just isn't worth the hassle of trying to reach someone who may live out of state to pay a tenant's late rent. But the reality of the marketplace usually dictates the practice—in a college town full of rentals, many landlords will accept cosigners because students are overwhelmingly the ones who rent their units.

There is an important exception to the landlord's ability to say no to all cosigners. If an applicant with a disability does not meet the landlord's income threshold but is otherwise qualified, a landlord must at least consider the applicant's proffered cosigner. If that cosigner is financially solvent and stable, the landlord would have to accommodate the applicant by accepting the cosigner. (*Griebeler v. M & B Associates*, 343 F.3d 1143 (9th Cir. 2003).)

Basic Rent Rules

How Much Can Your Landlord Charge?..60

Rent Control...61

    Property Subject to Rent Control...62

    Limits on Rent...62

    Evictions in Rent Control Areas..63

    Interest Payments on Security Deposits 64

    Special Notice Requirements...64

When Is Your Rent Due? 64

    When Rent Is Due Under an Oral Lease..65

    When the Due Date Falls on a Weekend or Holiday 65

Grace Periods for Late Rent 65

Where and How Rent Is Due 66

    Where Rent Must Be Paid 66

    Form of Rent Payment 66

    The Landlord's Right to Change Where and How Rent Is Due........................67

Late Charges and Discounts for Early Payments 68

    Are Late Fees Legal?..68

    Limits on Late Fees..68

    Late Fees Disguised as Early Payment Discounts...69

    Avoiding Late Fees...69

Returned Check Charges 70

Negotiating Partial or Delayed Rent Payments..70

Rent Increases..71

    When Your Landlord Can Raise the Rent..72

    How High Can the Rent Go?...73

    Rent Increases as Retaliation or Discrimination...73

Talking the Landlord Out of a Rent Increase 75

This chapter shows how to get accurate answers to important questions about rent, including the following:

- How much rent can my landlord charge?
- Am I allowed a grace period to pay rent?
- What happens if I can't pay on time?
- Are there any limits to late fees a landlord charges?
- How much notice must my landlord give before increasing my rent?
- What are my options if I think the rent increase is unfair?

Normally, you'll need to look at your lease or rental agreement, refer to your state's law (you'll find handy charts in Appendix A), and consider your landlord's unwritten business practices.

Paying rent on time is the most important thing you can do to establish a good relationship with your landlord. By paying your rent in full on time every month, you meet the legal requirements of your lease or rental agreement. But you do something else that can be almost as important: You establish yourself in your landlord's mind as a conscientious, reliable person. Put another way, you identify yourself as one of your landlord's best customers. Although this reputation is only occasionally of legal importance, it is likely to be of great practical help when you make a repair request or ask for a favor such as a little extra time to pay the rent one month.

 RELATED TOPIC
Also covered in this book:

- Lease and rental agreement provision or rent, late fees, and grace periods: Chapter 2.
- Paying first and last month's rent: Chapter 4.
- Negotiating a late rent payment and eviction for nonpayment of rent: Chapter 17.

How Much Can Your Landlord Charge?

Except for the cities and counties with rent control ordinances, landlords are free to charge as much rent as they like. (In Connecticut, however, tenants may challenge a rent that they believe is excessive. Conn. Gen. Stat. Ann. §§ 7-148b and following. And most states prohibit rent gouging following a natural disaster.) Most landlords monitor the rental market and price their rental units accordingly. To make sure you're not overpaying, you should do the same thing: Check rentals on Craigslist and other sites and visit a few similar-sounding places to make sure your rent isn't out of line. Real estate offices are also good sources of information on area rents. (See Chapter 1 for a discussion of how to find an apartment or house.) In addition, local tenants' associations can be a terrific resource. See the "Tenants Working Together" section in Chapter 19 for advice on finding a local tenants' group.

"Section 8"

Many tenants with low incomes qualify for federally subsidized housing assistance. The most common is the Section 8 program of the federal Department of Housing and Urban Development (HUD). ("Section 8" refers to Section 8 of the United States Housing Act of 1937, 42 U.S.C. § 1437f.) That program determines a "market rent" for each rental property and then pays a percentage of the rent directly to the landlord, with the tenant paying the rest. The local housing authority, the landlord, and the tenant enter into a one-year agreement, using a written lease supplied by the county housing authority.

Section 8 housing can often be a good deal, since "market rent" for a unit is often set at a fairly low rate and, of course, part of this amount is subsidized. In addition, Section 8 tenants cannot be evicted except for nonpayment of rent or other serious breaches of the lease. Under federal law, landlords are not required to participate in Section 8, but at least four states—New Jersey, Maryland, Massachusetts, and Connecticut—require landlords to do so.

If you think you may be eligible for Section 8 assistance, contact your local HUD office. (Find yours at www.hud.gov.)

TIP

If the rent seems low, find out why. When you're apartment-hunting, keep in mind that a lower rent does not always reflect less value. Many wise landlords charge a little less than the going rate as part of a policy designed to find and keep excellent tenants. On the other hand, if you find an attractive unit at an unbelievably low rent, be sure to ask the landlord when the rent last went up. If it's been more than 18 months since rent was raised, you can bet an increase will happen soon. For reassurance, you might want to ask the landlord for a lease of a year or more at the existing rent.

Rent Control

SKIP AHEAD

Unless you live in California, the District of Columbia, Maryland, New Jersey, or New York, you aren't affected by rent control. You can skip this section.

Some cities and counties in California, Maryland, New Jersey, New York, and Washington, DC, have laws that limit the amount of rent landlords may charge. Local rent control ordinances (also called "rent stabilization" or "maximum rent regulation") are now in effect in some of the country's largest cities, including New York City, Washington, DC, Los Angeles, San Francisco, Newark, San Jose, and Oakland.

Rent control ordinances vary widely. Some, like the ones in New York, have real teeth, while others (in San Jose and Oakland, for example) are practically useless. And rent control is increasingly unpopular politically—so any changes to existing ordinances are likely to be prolandlord. State law often restricts local rent control rules or bans them altogether; over 30 states have laws prohibiting local rent control ordinances.

RESOURCE

New York and California rent control. Rent control laws for New York are extremely complicated. If

you are a New York tenant, consult your local tenants' organization (start by going to www.tenant.net). If you live in a community with rent control in California, be sure to check out the Nolo book *California Tenants' Rights*, by Janet Portman and J. Scott Weaver, which includes details on local rules.

Where to Get Information About Rent Control

If you are protected by a rent control ordinance, use these resources to get straight information:

- **Your city rent control board.** It can supply you with a copy of the current local ordinance, and possibly also with a brochure explaining the main features of the ordinance.
- **Your local tenants' organization.** Virtually every city with a rent control ordinance has an active and vocal tenants' group. (In many cases, the pressure from these groups is why the city has rent control in the first place.) These organizations typically are vigorous watchdogs of the rent board and monitor court decisions and any political goings-on (such as proposed ballot amendments) that affect the ordinance. Most important, tenant organizations can usually provide a written explanation of the ordinance and how it works, and many have volunteer staff available to explain ambiguous or complex facets of the ordinance.
- **Local attorneys who specialize in landlord-tenant law.** Chapter 20 discusses how to find and work with a lawyer.

Rent control laws commonly regulate much more than rent—for example, they may limit the circumstances under which landlords may evict tenants. Because local ordinances are complicated, vary widely, and change often, this book cannot provide fine details on each city's program. Instead, we give a good general description of what rent control ordinances cover and an outline of seven big-city ordinances.

Property Subject to Rent Control

Not all rental housing within a rent-controlled city is subject to rent control. Commonly, ordinances exempt:

- new buildings
- owner-occupied buildings with no more than three or four units, and
- single-family houses and luxury units that rent for more than a certain amount.

Limits on Rent

Rent control comes in two basic styles: one that protects only the present tenant, and one that regulates rent over the long term, regardless of turnover. In rent control jargon, these varieties are known as "vacancy decontrol" and "vacancy control" statutes. Here's how they work.

Vacancy Decontrol Statutes: Protecting Current Tenants

In most rent control areas, landlords may raise rent —either as much as they want or by a specified percentage—when one tenant moves out and a new one moves in. This feature, called "vacancy decontrol" or "vacancy rent ceiling adjustment," means that rent control applies to a particular rental unit only as long as a particular tenant (or tenants) stays there. If a tenant voluntarily leaves or, in some cities, is evicted for a legal or "just" cause (discussed below), the rental unit is not subject to rent control again until the new (and presumably higher) rent is established.

Some ordinances automatically allow a specific percentage rent increase each year for existing tenants. This may be set by the rent control board as a fixed percentage of the rent or a percentage tied to a local or national consumer price index.

In addition to built-in annual increases, some rent control boards allow landlords to petition for a rent hike based on an increase in costs, such as taxes or capital improvements.

> **EXAMPLE:** Marla has lived in Edward's apartment building for seven years. During that time, Edward has been allowed to raise the rent only by the modest amount authorized by the local rent board each year. Meanwhile, the market value of the apartment has gone up significantly.
>
> When Marla finally moves out, Edward is free to charge the next tenant the market rate. But once set, that tenant's rent will also be subject to the rent control rules, and Edward will again be limited to small annual increases as approved by the rent control board.

Vacancy Control Statutes: Protecting Future Tenants

These rent control ordinances set a base rent for each rental unit. (The brute forces of the market have no place here.) The base rent usually takes into account several factors, including the rent that was charged before rent control took effect, the landlord's operating and maintenance expenses, inflation, and housing supply and demand. The base rent may be raised during the tenancy under certain circumstances, such as an increase in inflation. When the tenant moves out, a landlord cannot raise the rent to market level. Rent stays controlled, subject to the formula of the rent control ordinance.

EXAMPLE: Sergei has been a tenant in Rudolph's apartment complex for two years. Every year on January 1, Rudolph raises the rent according to the rate set by the rent control board. When Sergei moves out on June 1 and Sasha moves in, Rudolph must charge her the same rent as Sergei paid during that year. He cannot raise her rent until the following January 1.

TIP

Slumlords can't raise the rent. Even if your landlord is entitled to raise the rent under the terms of your rent control ordinance, the rent board may deny permission if the landlord hasn't adequately repaired and maintained the rental property. Read your ordinance carefully to see if you have the right to protest a rent increase based on a pattern of substandard conditions in your building or unit. If your landlord doesn't keep the premises habitable, you probably have other remedies—for example, you may be able to withhold rent—independent of the rent control ordinance. (Chapter 8 discusses your options.)

Evictions in Rent Control Areas

For rent control to work—especially if the ordinance allows rents to rise when a tenant leaves—it must place some restrictions on eviction. Otherwise, landlords have an incentive to create a vacancy by throwing out existing tenants. Recognizing this, many local ordinances require landlords to have a "just cause"—that is, a good reason—to evict.

Rent control ordinances specify a limited number of reasons that justify eviction, including:

- You violate a significant term of the lease or rental agreement—for example, by failing to pay rent, causing substantial damage to the premises, or allowing unauthorized people to live in the rental unit. However, in many situations, state law requires that a landlord must first give you a chance to correct the problem. (See Chapter 17.)

- The landlord wants to move into the rental unit or give it to an immediate family member.

TIP

"Relative move-ins" are often bogus. Unscrupulous landlords often cite the need for a relative (or personal) move-in as the reason for evicting a tenant. Then, after a ridiculously short tenancy (or none at all), the relative or landlord moves out. In areas with vacancy control, this enables the landlord to raise the rent to market rate for the next tenant.

If you suspect an illegitimate relative move-in, investigate further. See if you can find out whether the landlord or a real relative actually moved in and, if so, for how long. If the tenancy is patently short or the "relation" isn't one at all, consider seeing a lawyer or suing in small claims court to recoup your moving costs and higher new rent. Some rent control ordinances presume that the move-in is fraudulent if the landlord or relative stays less than a prescribed amount of time.

Additional "just cause" reasons include:
- The landlord wants to substantially remodel the property, which requires you to move out. Under some ordinances, a landlord who rents a number of units (for example, in a good-sized apartment building) must make available to you another similar unit or give you first chance to move back in after the remodeling. In some cases, the landlord may raise the rent based on the improvements.
- You create a serious nuisance—for example, by repeatedly disturbing other tenants or engaging in illegal activity, such as drug-dealing or prostitution, on the premises.

CAUTION

Rent control ordinances affect renewals as well as evictions. Rent control ordinances typically protect you not only from an eviction in the middle of a tenancy, but from a landlord's decision not to renew your lease. Unless the landlord can point to a "just cause" for tossing you out, you are entitled to renew under the same terms and conditions, including the length of the rental term. Landlords often refer to this aspect of a rent control ordinance as "the endless lease."

Your Landlord's Right to Go Out of Business

It's not uncommon for landlords in rent-controlled cities to decide to get out of the residential rental business entirely. To do so, however, they must evict tenants, who will protest that the eviction violates the rent control ordinance.

A rent control ordinance cannot force an unwilling landlord to stay in business, though an ordinance may attempt to restrict the number of condominium conversions (the number-one reason most landlords withdraw from the rental market). However, a landlord who withdraws rental units from the market must usually have plenty of evidence that his motive is not to evade the rent control ordinance: Rent control boards do not want landlords to use going out of business as a ruse for evicting long-term tenants, only to start up again with a fresh batch of tenants whose rents will be substantially higher.

If your landlord files an eviction lawsuit because he is going out of business, check your ordinance carefully. It may require the landlord to offer you relocation assistance, and may impose a minimum time period during which the landlord may not resume business. A landlord who owns multiple units may be prohibited from withdrawing only a portion of the units; and if the premises are torn down and new units constructed, the ordinance may insist that the landlord offer former tenants a right of first refusal. State law may also address these issues. Contact your local tenants' group or rent control board for details.

Interest Payments on Security Deposits

Local rent control ordinances sometimes impose rules regarding security deposits that supplement those set out by state law. For example, San Francisco landlords are required to put security deposits in interest-bearing bank accounts, something not required under California law. Check your ordinance to see whether similar protections apply to you. (Chapter 4 discusses interest payments on security deposits.)

Special Notice Requirements

State laws typically require landlords to give a specified amount of notice when it comes to raising the rent or terminating the tenancy. (Notice requirements are explained in Chapter 15.) In rent control situations, however, the notice requirements are often tighter in two respects:

- **Raising the rent.** State law typically requires a 30-day notice for a rent increase. A local rent control law might also require the notice to tell the tenant that the rent control board can verify that the new rental amount is legal under the ordinance.
- **Terminating the tenancy.** Most rent control ordinances forbid the landlord from terminating (or refusing to renew) a tenancy without a "just cause," as explained above. And even where the landlord does have a just cause, the termination or nonrenewal period is longer than that required under general state law.

When Is Your Rent Due?

Most leases and rental agreements call for rent to be paid monthly, in advance, on the first day of the month. However, landlords are normally legally free to establish a different monthly payment date—or even to require that rent be paid weekly or biweekly. Some landlords make the rent payable each month on the date the tenant first moved in. Most find it easier, however, to prorate rent for a short first month and thereafter collect rent on the first of the month.

A twice-a-month schedule is the most common variation on the standard monthly payment arrangement. This is often imposed by landlords on tenants who have relatively low-paying jobs and get paid twice a month. Some landlords assume that a tenant can't be trusted to save the needed portion of the midmonth check until the first of the month. Can your landlord require bimonthly checks from you, yet let a wealthier tenant pay once a month? Under certain circumstances, yes; in others, this would be an act of illegal discrimination. (Chapter 5 discusses discrimination in detail.)

> **TIP**
> **Special provisions for public assistance recipients.** If you receive public assistance in Hawaii, for example, you may choose to establish a due date for your rent that is on or before the third day after the day you usually receive your public assistance check. (For more information, check your state's rent rules. Citations are listed in "State Rent Rules" in Appendix A.)

When Rent Is Due Under an Oral Lease

Oral leases, though never a good idea, are legal for tenancies of up to one year. If you have an oral lease and you and your landlord have not discussed when the rent is due, how do you know when to pay?

The safest route is to raise the issue immediately with the landlord. (And, in the process, get a written lease!) Failing that, consider the due date to be the same as it would be if you did, in fact, have a written lease that was silent on the issue (see "When Is Your Rent Due?" above). For example, a tenant with an oral lease in Oregon (and the majority of states) would have to pay at the beginning of the term, but a tenant in California would consider rent to be due at the end. But if you live in a state where rent is due at the end of the rental period, unless otherwise arranged, heed this word of advice: Your landlord probably doesn't know the law, and probably expects rent at the start of the term.

If you live in a state that has no law on the subject, we suggest paying at the start of the term.

When the Due Date Falls on a Weekend or Holiday

Most lease and rental agreements state that when the rent due date falls on a weekend day or legal holiday, the tenant must pay rent by the next business day. This sensible practice is legally required in some states and is the general practice in most. If your landlord insists on receiving the rent check by the first of the month (or other due date), even if mail is not delivered on that day, you may want to check your written agreement. If you get no help there, take a look at the law in your state; you may find that your landlord is violating it. If not, you may have to bite the bullet and get your rent in early.

Grace Periods for Late Rent

Lots of tenants are absolutely convinced that if rent is due on the first, they actually have until the fifth (or sometimes the seventh or even the tenth) of the month to pay, because they are within a legal grace period. Sorry, but this is not true. Rent is legally due on the date specified in your agreement or on the next business day, if your state's law contains that rule.

Landlords May Wink at Late Rent—For a While

Many landlords do not get upset about late rent or impose a late fee (discussed below), until the rent is a few days past due. And most states actually require the landlord to give you a written notice granting you a few days (typically three to five) in which to pay the rent or move out before beginning eviction procedures. But even if you believe nothing will happen if you pay rent a few days late, this does not mean that it's a good idea. You're far better off consistently paying the rent on time. If, on rare occasions, you can't do so, follow our suggestions for promptly and courteously informing your landlord of your money troubles. (See "Negotiating Partial or Delayed Rent Payments," below.) This will keep you straight with the law and help avoid spats with your landlord about late fees.

A landlord who must repeatedly deliver pay-the-rent-or-leave notices may simply decide to end your tenancy—even if you always come up with the rent within the notice period.

See Chapter 17 for details on tenancy terminations for nonpayment of rent.

Where and How Rent Is Due

Your lease or rental agreement probably states where you should pay the rent and how it should be paid—for example, by check or money order only.

> ⊘ CAUTION
> **In most states, landlords must inform tenants of where and how rent is paid.** Laws typically require landlords to notify tenants (either in a separate writing or in a written rental agreement or lease) of the name and street address of the owner or manager responsible for collection of rent, how rent is to be paid, and who is available for services of notices.

Where Rent Must Be Paid

Many, if not most, leases and rental agreements specify where you are to pay the rent, such as:

By mail to the landlord's business address. This is the most common method of rent payment. If you mail your rent check, make sure that it arrives on or before the date the rent is due—it is not sufficient to post your check on that date. Given the sluggishness of the U.S. mail, you should obviously allow at least three days for a local delivery. If your rent check will be in the mail on a Sunday or holiday, give yourself an extra day. If the due date is a Sunday or holiday, usually the following business day will suffice— but check your lease or rental agreement and your landlord's policy on this.

At your home. Your landlord may send someone to each unit every month to pick up the rent. This old-fashioned way of collecting the rent isn't well-suited to modern life, since in most households it's hard to find someone at home during the day. On the other hand, it's a tried-and-true method to pressure a tenant who is chronically late with the rent.

At your landlord's—or manager's—office. This option is practical only for those owners with on-site offices. Often, there is a drop box or mail slot—but if the office is open when you come by with the rent, spend a few minutes talking with your landlord or manager. It's a perfect time to raise any concerns, suggest improvements, or thank the landlord for attention to previous requests. A conscientious landlord will appreciate the feedback and the opportunity to discuss little problems before they become big ones. Of course, don't make every visit a gripe session, or your landlord will come to dread your visits.

Easy Ways to Pay the Rent

More and more owners, especially those with large numbers of rental units, are looking for ways to ensure that rent payments are quick and reliable. There are two common methods:

Credit card. Some landlords offer tenants the option of using credit cards. Some may even insist on an automatic billing to your credit account at the same time every month, which means you do not have to show up at the rental office with your card. This is an extremely convenient arrangement, assuming your credit card can support it. It is obviously not a good idea if you are regularly over your credit limit or if you consistently pay interest on your balance.

Automatic debit. At the time you move in, your landlord may ask your permission—or even require you—to have rent payments debited automatically each month from your bank account and transferred into the landlord's account. This is also convenient but, like the automatic use of your credit card, should not be used by tenants whose checking accounts are thin or often overdrawn. (If your account cannot honor the automatic debit, it's just like having written a bad check.)

Form of Rent Payment

Most leases and rental agreements also specify how rent must be paid. Cash, check, and money order are most common, but many landlords now allow payment by credit card, automatic debit, or other electronic funds transfer.) Tenants often feel that the form of payment should be up to them, but, just like restaurants and shops, landlords are usually legally free to insist on a particular form of payment (exceptions involve government-subsidized rent payments). California landlords may not require cash rent unless a tenant has bounced a check, and then only for three months. (Cal. Civ. Code § 1947.3.)

For most landlords, personal checks are the norm—but, folk wisdom to the contrary, your landlord does *not* have to accept your personal checks. If you don't have a checking account (or if you have bounced a few checks), your landlord may legally require a certified check or money order. (Below, we explain landlords' rights to change the method of rent payment.)

There is no legal requirement that a landlord accept postdated checks, and most won't, because there's absolutely no assurance that necessary funds will ever be deposited in the account. If you are short on funds, far better to handle it in a straightforward manner. See "Negotiating Partial or Delayed Rent Payments," below, for advice on paying late rent.

CAUTION
Don't pay rent in cash unless you have no choice. These days, few landlords will accept rent in cash—they are justifiably wary of the risks of keeping large amounts of cash on hand. Your safety, too, will be imperiled if the word gets out that you regularly make a trip to the manager's office carrying several hundred dollars in cash. If you must pay in cash, be sure to get a written, dated receipt stating your name and the amount paid. It's your only proof that you did, indeed, pay the rent.

The Landlord's Right to Change Where and How Rent Is Due

If you've bounced a check or two, chronically pay rent late, or have lost your job, can your landlord suddenly refuse personal checks and accept only certified checks or money orders? Or, if you've been paying by mail as specified in your lease or rental agreement, can your landlord now require you to bring your rent to the manager's office?

Legally the answer is usually no. Your landlord may not unilaterally change terms in the lease or rental agreement. This means that if you have a year's lease, the payment arrangement is in force for a year; and if you rent month to month, most states require your landlord to give at least 30 days' written notice before changing a rental agreement clause.

How Landlords May Change Lease or Rental Agreement Terms

To change the terms and conditions of your lease or rental agreement—such as how and where you pay the rent, pet policies, or late rent policies—your landlord must give you proper notice. Here are the basics, which are explained in detail in Chapter 15.

Type of tenancy	Amount of notice
Rental Agreement	Typically 30 days, although some states require as much as 45 or 60 days
Lease	Lease provisions cannot be changed until the lease runs out and a new tenancy begins

If your lease or rental agreement doesn't say where and how rent is to be paid, your landlord's past practice is more likely to legally control how rent is paid. For example, a landlord who has always asked for your rent check on the first of the month has established a due date that you must honor until the landlord formally changes the system with proper notice (in most states, 30 days).

Don't be too quick to assert your rights. It may be a mistake to point out to your landlord that the rent payment clause cannot be changed without proper notice, or at all if you have a lease. Especially if you have been habitually late paying rent or have broken some other significant provision for which you could be evicted (for example, your boyfriend has moved in, violating your lease's restrictions on occupants), you may end up winning the battle but losing the war. In short, if the landlord has a legal ground for eviction (or may be considering giving you a 30-day notice to end a month-to-month tenancy), it is probably far better to go along with the rent payment change than to stand on your rights and invite the end of your tenancy. Similarly, if, after several bounced checks, a landlord demands a certified check or money order, it can make sense to go along for a few months. When you have paid on time for several months and hopefully things have calmed down, your landlord may once again be willing to accept your personal check.

If, however, the proposed change is both inconvenient to you and not motivated by your violation of a lease clause (but perhaps by the landlord's fear that because you lost your job you are or may become insolvent), you are within your rights to just say no. As long as you have a lease, the landlord can't evict you, because you've done nothing wrong. But if you have a month-to-month agreement, you may as well go along with the new system; the landlord can change it easily, anyway, by giving you proper notice.

A landlord who has been allowing you to pay rent in a different way than is required by the lease or rental agreement can probably start enforcing the written policy at any time. For example, suppose your lease or rental agreement specifies that rent be paid by certified check, but your landlord regularly and happily accepts your personal checks. Can the landlord suddenly decide to enforce the clause, even if your checks have not bounced? There is no clear answer. If such a dispute ended up in court, it would depend on whether the judge concluded that regular acceptance of your personal checks constituted a valid oral amendment of the written lease or rental agreement. Since your ability to prevail in court is unpredictable, unless you are very seriously inconvenienced by the change it's probably best to accept your landlord's insistence that the written agreement be followed.

Late Charges and Discounts for Early Payments

Rare is the tenant who's never had a problem paying rent on time. If you are a conscientious and honest tenant who is temporarily short on funds, most landlords won't evict you for paying rent a little late one month. However, landlords are wary of sending a message that late payments are okay, and often impose a late fee when rent is even a few days late. But the size of the late fee is subject to legal limits, and in some situations it's not legal to impose one at all.

Are Late Fees Legal?

If your lease or rental agreement says nothing about late fees, your landlord may not impose one, no matter how reasonable it is. For example, if you hand your rent check to the landlord two days late and he tells you he will accept it only if you pay an additional $10, you may refuse unless your lease or rental agreement includes a late fee clause. But don't be too hasty to assert your rights if you live in a state that allows landlords to refuse late rent and begin eviction proceedings as soon as the rent is even one day late. (Chapter 17 explains your landlord's legal options when you are late with the rent.)

Limits on Late Fees

Some states put dollar limits on late fees. (See "State Rent Rules" in Appendix A.) But even if your state doesn't, general legal principles still prohibit unreasonably high fees. Courts in a number of states have ruled that contracts that provide for unreasonably high late charges are not enforceable. In other words, if you refuse to pay an outlandish late fee and your landlord attempts to evict you because of it, you should survive the eviction.

 RENT CONTROL

Rent control protections. Some rent control ordinances also regulate late fees. If you are covered by rent control, check the ordinance.

Of course, the crucial question in any court fight is: How big a fee is "unreasonable"? To make that determination, many courts use these guidelines:

- **The fee shouldn't begin immediately.** Normally, a late fee should not apply until at least three days after the rent due date.

- **The fee should not exceed a certain percentage of your rent.** Your landlord is always on shaky ground if the late charge exceeds 5% of the rent. That's $50 on a $1,000-per-month rental. And a few states set lower limits. Even in the majority of states with no statutory limits, a higher late charge, such as 10%, might not be upheld in court, unless the rent was extremely late—at least ten days.

- **The fee should not increase without limit.** Late fees that increase a little bit each day the rent is late are likely to be upheld only if the increase is moderate and there is an upper limit to the total charge. For example, $5 per day for the first four days the rent is late, and $10 for each subsequent day up to a $50 limit on a rent of $1,000 would amount to a maximum fee of 5% and would probably be accepted by a court. However, a late charge that increases fast and has no limit is likely to be considered too high.

If you evaluate your late fee in light of these guidelines and conclude that it is clearly too high, communicate your reasons in writing to your landlord. If you decide not to pay it, be prepared to be asked to move at the first legal opportunity—with proper notice if you rent with a rental agreement, or by the landlord refusing to renew your lease when it expires. A sufficiently annoyed landlord might even initiate eviction proceedings against a tenant with substantial time remaining on the lease. To avoid the risk of eviction, it may make more sense to pay the fee and challenge it in small claims court, where the worst-case scenario is losing your time, the court filing fee, and the offer of a renewal when the lease is up.

Late Fees Disguised as Early Payment Discounts

Some landlords try to disguise excessive late charges by giving a so-called "discount" for on-time rent payment. Here's how this dodge is often structured: A landlord who knows that he can't get away with charging a $100 late charge on an $850 monthly rent payment will set the rent at $900 and offer a $50 discount if the rent is no more than three days late. Fortunately, this bit of landlord subterfuge is unlikely to stand up in court unless the discount for on-time payment is modest. Giving a discount of more than 4% to 5% is in effect the same as charging an excessive late fee, and a judge is likely to see it as such.

Of course, if you are always prompt with the rent, a "discount" for prompt payment may not be a problem—after all, if you argue the point with the landlord when you sign the lease or rental agreement, you might end up with a reasonable late fee but a higher rent. And you can still complain about paying an overly high fee if, unfortunately, you *are* late with the rent a time or two. Most courts will still invalidate an unreasonable late fee although you may have in a sense benefited from its prompt payment "discount" by paying rent on time, or even if you have paid the late fee once or twice before complaining.

Avoiding Late Fees

Obviously, the surest way to avoid a late fee is to pay your rent on time. But if you cannot do this, don't automatically assume that there's nothing you can do about the penalty. Negotiation is often the tenant's best friend.

You should handle the late fee in the same manner that you handle the late rent payment itself: If you know that you will not be able to make the rent due date, notify your landlord in advance, explain the situation, suggest a payment schedule, and get it in writing. (We explain this process in detail below.) As part of your negotiations, ask for a waiver or reduction of any late penalty—many landlords, appreciating your advance notice, will be willing to forgo that extra nickel. (The sample letter below shows how.)

Returned Check Charges

Like any other business, your landlord has the legal right to charge an extra fee if your rent check bounces, but only if you knew in advance (in the lease or rental agreement, orally, or by means of an obvious sign in the rental office where you bring your monthly check) that the fee would be imposed. And, of course, if you regularly give your landlord rubber checks, don't be surprised if you receive a tenancy termination notice or, at least, a demand that you pay the rent by money order or another cash equivalent.

Like late charges, bounced check charges must be reasonable. Some states regulate the amount landlords can charge; in the absence of such regulation, your landlord should charge no more than the amount the bank charges for a returned check, probably $25 to $30 per returned item, plus a few dollars for her trouble.

If your check has bounced, you might get a little breathing room if your landlord follows a policy of letting the bank present the check again to your bank. But don't count on it—experienced landlords instruct their banks to return bad checks after the first rejection, so they can confront the tenant and demand that the check be made good immediately.

Laws in some states allow landlords to charge interest on a bounced check, whether or not your lease or rental agreement says anything about late check charges. For example, California landlords may charge 10% per year interest on a bounced check—so, for example, on a $1,000 rent check that isn't made good for a month, the landlord can demand an additional $8.34. (Cal. Civ. Code § 3289(b).) Your state's consumer protection office should be able to tell you whether your state has a similar law. For a list of state consumer protection agencies, go to www.usa.gov/state-consumer.

Negotiating Partial or Delayed Rent Payments

Even a model tenant can suffer a temporary financial setback that makes it impossible to pay the rent on time or in full. If this happens to you, don't immediately assume that you will be evicted or even subjected to a late charge. A landlord who considers you a good tenant won't want to lose you, since it's often difficult and expensive to find and move in good tenants. This means you can probably get the landlord to accept a portion of the rent now—maybe even a small portion—and the rest later. Here are five sensible approaches to take:

1. **Give your landlord written notice (as much as possible) that you will not be able to pay on time.** By taking this responsible and courteous step, you seize the psychological high road. And even more important, you raise the issue *before* your landlord, faced with a bounced check or an empty rent envelope, has a chance to work up a righteous head of steam. This early warning approach could backfire—with your landlord simply giving you a legal demand to pay the rent or move out. But you don't have much to lose, because most landlords who receive no rent or your rubber check will promptly do exactly the same thing.

2. **Explain your difficulties and emphasize that they are only temporary.** If your landlord is a fairly decent sort and likely to empathize with your predicament, it's best to share at least some of the reasons behind your request. Emphasize your good, long-term relationship and—if you can—that your predicament will be short-lived and not likely to recur. The point, of course, is to put a human face on your situation. It's up to you to decide where your desire for privacy ends and your need to defer your rent begins.

3. **Offer to pay at least some of the rent on time.** Even if you have to borrow money, try to pay at least a portion of the rent on time. By putting even a small amount of money where your mouth is, you offer tangible evidence of your intention to

Sample Letter Asking Landlord to Accept Late Rent

123 Shady Lane
Madison, Wisconsin 00000

(608) 555-1234

January 25, 20xx

Mr. Max Mason
100 North Main Street
Madison, Wisconsin 00000

Dear Mr. Mason,

As you know, I have been your tenant at 123 Shady Lane for the past ten months, and I have always met the terms and conditions of my lease. Not only have I paid my rent fully and on time, but I have treated your property with care and respect. I enjoy living at Shady Lane and hope to stay here.

The reason for this letter is to ask you whether I may pay part of next month's rent, due on February 1st, late. I would like to pay half the rent on the 1st, and the balance on the 15th. Unfortunately and with practically no notice, I have been laid off from my job as a computer programmer as a result of downsizing at ABC Software. This layoff happened just after I had spent most of my savings on computer equipment I need for the freelance programming work I do on the side. I have been diligently looking for a new job and already have three interviews scheduled next week. I have also applied for unemployment benefits, and I expect to start receiving checks in a few weeks. After February, I should have no problem paying the rent on time.

I would greatly appreciate it if you could accommodate my request. And since my finances are already stretched, I would also appreciate it if you would waive the late fee. I will be happy to sign an agreement laying out these terms.

Please call me (555-1234) so we can discuss this further. If I don't hear from you within a few days, I'll phone you at your office. Thank you very much for your consideration.

Yours truly,

Tom Tenant

Tom Tenant

follow through with the rest of your obligation. Your landlord knows that a tenant who has paid a portion of the rent is less likely to skip out than one who has had a totally free ride.

4. **Give your landlord written assurance of your plan to pay.** Most landlords, even the most accommodating, will want a written agreement of your promise to pay the full rent by a certain date, such as the 15th of the month. Your landlord will probably ask for a date that is tied to a verifiable outside event, such as your payday or after your taxes are due. And a written agreement will protect you if, despite an oral agreement, your landlord suddenly decides to evict you for nonpayment of rent. (If, however, you've already received an overdue rent notice and make a partial rent payment, your landlord may still give you a termination notice for the balance.) A sample letter asking the landlord to accept late rent is shown above. If the landlord agrees to your request to pay rent late, you should follow up with a written note confirming your exact agreement. Send your letter "return receipt requested," so that you can prove, if need be, that the landlord received it. In some situations, the landlord may want to draw up a more formal document.

5. **Keep your promise.** If you run into further difficulties and need to ask for an additional small extension, be sure that you have at least paid an additional portion of the overdue amount first. Obviously, your ability to renegotiate is limited by the landlord's favorable opinion of you and his desire to keep you as a tenant, both of which will probably decline the more your payments are delayed.

Rent Increases

Rent increases are an inevitable part of any tenant's life. But landlords cannot raise the rent at whim. The timing of a rent increase, and the way your landlord communicates it, are governed by statute in most states.

When Your Landlord Can Raise the Rent

Except in cities with rent control, your landlord's legal right to raise the rent depends primarily on whether you have a lease or a month-to-month rental agreement.

Leases

Your landlord can't raise the rent until the end of the lease period, unless the lease itself provides for an increase or you agree. When the lease expires, the landlord can present you with a new lease that has a higher rent or other changed terms.

Rental Agreements

If you rent under a month-to-month rental agreement, the landlord can raise the rent by giving you proper written notice, which is 30 days in most states. (If you pay rent every 15 days, you may only be entitled to 15 days' notice.) In a few states, however, landlords must provide 45 or 60 days' notice to raise the rent for a month-to-month tenancy. (See "State Rules on Notice Required to Change or Terminate a Month-to-Month Tenancy" in Appendix A.)

Improper Notice

There are two ways in which landlords typically violate their notice obligations. Either they don't give enough notice before the increase is set to take effect, or they fail to provide written notice at all. Your response should depend on which error is involved.

The notice period is too short. If your landlord writes you on June 20 that your rent, due on July 1, has gone up, you haven't been given enough notice. You absolutely do not have to pay the increased rent on July 1, but, of course, you must still make your existing rent payment. However, if your landlord has complied with other notice requirements (discussed below), you *will* be expected to pay the extra rent as of 30 days from the date you got the notice. In other words, your landlord's notice is effective as soon as the legal notice period has elapsed. This might mean you have to pay the next month's rent at the old rate; but, at some point during that month (when the notice period expires), you'll need to pay a prorated share of the rent at the new rate.

> **EXAMPLE:** Simon, a month-to-month tenant, paid his rent for the coming month on the first of the month. State law requires 30 days' notice before a rent increase can take effect. Simon's landlord gave him written notice of an increase on the 20th of June. On July 1, Simon paid full rent at the old rate. On July 20, Simon owed his landlord an additional sum: the rent per day at the new rate minus the rent per day at the old rate, times 11. On August 1, he paid the full increased rent.

The notice is oral or not properly delivered. State laws all require rent increase notices to be delivered to a tenant in writing; in some states, certified mail is required. Oral notices are ineffective and, unless you specifically agree to the rent increase, you are not obligated to pay any more money. But if you ignore a polite oral notice from a landlord you know well, be prepared for an angry confrontation followed by a speedily drafted written notice and a chill in your long-term relationship.

If you receive an oral notice and don't consider it worthwhile, in the long run, to fight your landlord on this issue, be sure to put details on the rent increase (and any other changes in your rental agreement) in writing. One way to do this is to ask the landlord to prepare a new rental agreement. (Chapter 15 shows how.) Another approach is to write a letter to the landlord confirming the new terms. Ask the landlord to sign and date it and return it to you. (Letters of understanding are explained in Chapter 2.) This will protect you against any misunderstanding as to the amount of the increase. The sample letter below shows you how to lock in an oral rent raise. You would be wise to send it return receipt requested, and to keep the receipt in a safe place with your other rental papers.

RENT CONTROL
Local rent control laws also affect rent increase notices. If you live in an area covered by rent control and get a rent increase notice, be sure the notice (as well as the amount of the increase) complies with the laws of your city. Check your ordinance or contact the rent board.

Sample Letter Formalizing a Rent Increase

789 Walnut Street
Concord, CA 00000
(510) 555-4567

June 1, 20xx

Mr. Mike Moskowitz
788 Walnut Street
Pleasanton, CA 00000

Dear Mr. Moskowitz,

In a conversation today you informed me that my rent, currently $850 per month, will go up $50, to $900, as of the first of July. Please sign and date this letter confirming this understanding and return it to me at the above address.

Yours truly,

William Ames

William Ames

_____   _____
s/Mike Moskowitz   Date

How High Can the Rent Go?

In areas without rent control, there is no limit on the amount your landlord can increase the rent (except in Connecticut, where tenants can challenge increases they feel are excessive). The only exception to this rule is if a rent increase is discriminatory or is in retaliation for a tenant's exercising a legal right.

Recognizing that most tenants want to know when and by how much the rent is likely to rise, some savvy landlords announce their rent increase policy in advance. For example, your landlord may say the rent will go up every January, based on a formula tied to the Consumer Price Index. Can

you rely on this and successfully resist any other type of rent increase? It depends. If the policy is part of your written lease or rental agreement, the landlord is bound by it. But if it is an oral policy, or one that is part of another tenant's rental agreement but not yours, you'll have a very hard time convincing a judge to hold the landlord to it. If your landlord's policy is not in your lease or rental agreement, ask him to amend the lease or rental agreement to include it. (See Chapter 15 for advice on how to amend these documents.)

 CAUTION
Rent increases often trigger security deposit increases. Many states limit the amount a landlord can charge for a security deposit. Typically, deposits are capped as a multiple of the monthly rent—for example, the maximum deposit may be twice the monthly rent. But this means that if the rent has gone up legally, the security deposit may also be legally increased. For example, if the deposit is twice the monthly rent, and your $1,000 rent has gone up $100, the deposit limit rises from $2,000 to $2,200. See Chapter 4 for more on security deposit increases.

Rent Increases as Retaliation or Discrimination

No landlord may raise the rent in a discriminatory manner—for example, only for members of a certain race or religion or for families with children. (Discrimination is explained in detail in Chapter 5.) And in most states your landlord can't use a rent increase (or evict you or decrease services, either) in retaliation against you for exercising a legal right—for example, in response to your legitimate complaint to a public agency about defective conditions or your decision to withhold rent because the landlord won't fix the broken water pipes in your rental unit. (Chapters 8 and 17 discuss your rights to demand fit and habitable housing, free from the threat of eviction.)

How will you know whether a rent increase is in response to your exercise of a legal right? In some states, if you get a rent increase soon—typically, within three to six months—after you've complained about defective conditions, the landlord is presumed to have been acting in retaliation. (See "State Laws Prohibiting Landlord Retaliation" in Appendix A.) If you refuse to pay the increase and the landlord sues to evict you for nonpayment of rent, you should survive the eviction. Landlords in these states must prove to the judge that retaliation was not, in fact, the motive behind the increase. But if the increase follows a general policy that your landlord has announced before your use of a legal remedy, and if the landlord has applied the increase to all tenants, it will be hard to show that your recent exercise of a legal right such as rent withholding had anything to do with it.

For example, many landlords raise rent once a year in an amount that more or less reflects the increase in the Consumer Price Index. Other landlords use a more complicated formula that takes into account other rents in the area, as well as factors such as increased costs of maintenance or rehabilitation. They make sure to inform their tenants about the rent increase in advance and apply the increase uniformly to all their tenants. This kind of consistent approach usually protects the landlord against any claim of a retaliatory rent increase by a tenant who has coincidentally made a legitimate complaint about the condition of the premises or withheld rent.

If you think a rent hike is motivated by your assertion of a legal right, you can refuse to pay the increase; and if the landlord tries to evict you for nonpayment of rent, you can assert in court that the increase was done to retaliate against you. But before you do, ask yourself the following questions:

1. **Does state law presume landlord retaliation in some circumstances?** In some states, if rent is increased within a certain time following a tenant's legitimate complaint to a public agency, use of a remedy such as rent withholding, or exercise of a legal right such as organizing a tenants' group, the law presumes that the landlord acted improperly. This brand of antiretaliation statute gives you an important tactical advantage in the courtroom: It is up to the landlord to convince the judge that the increase was not based on retaliation. If the landlord can't convince the judge, you should win without even opening your mouth.

2. **How soon after your action did the rent increase come?** Obviously, the shorter the interval between your exercise of a legal right and the date of the increase, the more suspicious it becomes.

3. **How large was the increase?** Judges are more likely to view a large rent increase (rather than a small one) as the landlord's way to punish or drive away a troublesome tenant.

4. **Does the rent increase affect you alone, or does it apply to many others?** Your chances of proving a retaliatory motive will be greatly increased if you can show that you alone, or you and other activist tenants, but not tenants in similar units, received a rent increase.

5. **Is your landlord known for repeatedly and seriously trampling on tenants' rights?** Your landlord's reputation is certainly a relevant factor if you contemplate challenging a rent increase. You can learn whether the landlord is a frequent visitor to landlord-tenant or small claims court by asking the local tenants' organization or even your fellow tenants. Technically, you aren't supposed to argue in court that the landlord's past illegal rent raises prove guilt now, too; most judges will try to confine you to the facts of your case alone. But it's fairly easy to make sure the judge knows your landlord is a scofflaw—share your information succinctly and quickly, then listen politely while the judge gives you a little lecture on the rules of evidence.

RENT CONTROL

Check past rent control records. If you are protected by rent control, your landlord's reputation before the rent control board is just as important as his track record in court. To find out whether your landlord has been repeatedly challenged before the board, check with the local tenants' union.

6. **How disruptive or expensive, from the landlord's point of view, was your exercise of a legal right?** It's easier to win these cases where you can convince a judge that the landlord has a strong motive to get even. Did you cause the landlord considerable time, expense, aggravation, or embarrassment? For example, if you complained to the local health department that your housing is uninhabitable because the roof leaked, and the department ordered your landlord to put on a new roof, that's an expensive job that your landlord might resent highly. This anger could well, you'll claim, prompt a retaliatory rent hike. Similarly, a charge of discrimination (which the landlord might even ultimately defeat) could easily generate strong feelings of bitterness. On the other hand, your isolated request for a necessary and inexpensive repair is far less likely in the eyes of a judge to engender serious landlord revenge. Of course, this theory is based on the assumption that retaliation is always linked to important matters—and we know that some landlords are inclined toward pettiness.

EXAMPLE: Ira rents a two-bedroom unit in a large apartment complex. Within the past year, he has asked his landlord for new carpets and drapes, which were grudgingly provided; and he has organized the rest of the tenants so that they can collectively press for improvements in the property. Ira received a steep rent hike, which he refused to pay. When the landlord tried to evict him for nonpayment of the increased portion, Ira argued that the raise was in retaliation for his requests and political activities. Noting that none of the other two-bedroom tenants received similar hikes, the judge ruled in Ira's favor.

Talking the Landlord Out of a Rent Increase

Legally, there is nothing you can do about a legal rent hike that doesn't violate a rent control ordinance and is not discriminatory or retaliatory. The landlord can charge as much as the market will bear. (Connecticut tenants have some recourse, however, as noted above.) But practically, you can appeal to your landlord—to his business sense and to his heart. The first approach is built upon the *landlord's* reputation as a fair and human businessperson; the second approach emphasizes *your* good qualities as an attractive tenant. For the best results, use both.

No increase is good business. Landlording is a business, entered into to make money, but smart landlords realize that high rents are not the only route to high profits. Solvent, long-term tenants are the best tenants because they are low maintenance—they don't have to be evicted, sued, coddled, cleaned up after, scolded for breaking the rules, or interviewed and investigated as part of the time- and money-consuming new-tenant application process. If you are a good, long-term tenant and you can convince your landlord that the rent hike will make you move, your landlord might think twice, or at least moderate the increase. (On the other hand, if you have been less than straight in your dealings with the landlord, don't expect any accommodations.)

Obviously, your leverage with the landlord will increase if you can show that many other stable, long-term tenants are also upset and considering moving. If the rent hike affects others in your building, work together to present your collective plea. (See Chapter 19 for suggestions on working with other tenants.) Remember, even in a tight rental market, lots of long-term tenants are hard to find.

The increase is morally unfair. If you think your landlord will respond to an appeal based on kindness and fairness, give it a try. Design your appeal on the assumption that the landlord is a decent person who wants to be a fair and honest landlord (hopefully, this won't be too much of a stretch). Let the landlord know you're sure that only some unusual circumstance would have led to the request for such an increase. Ideally, after reading your letter your landlord will be convinced that insisting on a big rent increase would be an uncharacteristic, somewhat embarrassing thing to do.

Sample Letter in Response to a Rent Increase

787, 788, & 789 Cherry Street
St. Louis, MO 00000
(314) 555-4567

June 15, 20xx

Mr. Joe Jacks, Owner
790 Cherry Street
St. Louis, MO 00000

Dear Mr. Jacks,

We were dismayed to receive your notice of an intended rent increase of $100 per month. While we realize that you are within your legal rights to raise the rent, we would like to ask you to reconsider this decision.

As you know, the three families who have signed this letter have been your tenants and neighbors in your fourplex for the last four, five, and seven years. None of us have ever been late with the rent; we all have always responded promptly to your requests to inspect and repair various aspects of the building, and have never intentionally damaged your property. During the time that we have lived here, no one has protested the two rent increases (the last being nine months ago). We have been careful to promptly notify you of any problems, and have not insisted on unnecessary, cosmetic improvements.

Having lived in many rentals over the years, we have appreciated your prompt attention to all the large and small details involved in running your business, and we have especially appreciated your kindness and understanding when things went a little bit awry. (Remember when Jimmy Spenser's basketball went through the front window?) The increased rent, however, will make it extremely difficult for us to continue living here.

We hope that you will take a few moments to consider our request that the increase be rescinded or, at the least, lessened significantly. We have enjoyed living here and hope to continue doing so.

Yours truly,

Alex Corinthos
Benny Spenser
Cathy Webber

Above is a sample letter in response to a rent increase. Obviously, your letter will have to be closely tailored to your own situation. Note how the writers have documented the various ways in which they have been model tenants (the appeal to the landlord's business motives), and have acknowledged how decent the landlord has been in the past (the appeal to the heart). In addition, they have told the landlord, who lives in the same building, that there is a very real chance of losing quiet neighbors. Are these tenants more valuable than an extra $300 a month? Hopefully, yes.

Security Deposits

Dollar Limits on Deposits..78

How Landlords May Increase Deposits 80

Last Month's Rent 80

    Applying Last Month's Rent to Damage or Cleaning..80

    If Your Rent Goes Up 81

Nonrefundable Deposits and Fees..81

Interest on Deposits and Separate Accounts 82

    Separate Accounts 82

    Interest..82

How the Deposit May Be Used 83

If Your Landlord Sells the Property..83

Almost all landlords require their tenants to pay a deposit before moving in, typically at the time they sign a lease or rental agreement. This payment, usually called a "security deposit" or "last month's rent," can amount to several hundreds, or even thousands, of dollars. Landlords charge security deposits to assure that you'll pay rent when due and keep the rental unit in good condition. If you damage the property or leave early owing rent, your landlord can use your deposit to cover what you owe.

Security deposits constitute a big investment on your part, and they are a major source of friction between landlords and tenants. Fortunately, most states impose fairly strict rules on how landlords can collect and use deposits and how they must return them when the tenant moves out. Many states even require landlords to put deposits in a separate account and pay interest on them. Landlords who violate security deposit laws are often subject to substantial financial penalties.

RELATED TOPIC
Also covered in this book:

- Credit-check fees, holding deposits, and other fees landlords may charge: Chapter 1.
- Lease and rental agreement provisions on security deposits: Chapter 2.
- State rules on how and when deposits must be returned, and deductions allowed for cleaning, damage, and unpaid rent: Chapter 16.
- How to handle legal disputes involving deposits when you move out: Chapter 16.

Dollar Limits on Deposits

Many states limit the amount a landlord can collect as a deposit to an amount equal to one or two months of rent. (Sometimes larger deposits are allowed for furnished rentals.) In some states, the rent a landlord collects in advance for the last month is not considered part of the security deposit limit, while in others it is. (Later in this chapter we cover last month's rent.)

Rent that a landlord collects in advance for the first month is never considered part of the security deposit limit. However, a landlord who demanded several months' rent in advance would almost always run afoul of state security deposit limits. Advance rent, beyond paying for the first month of your tenancy, is considered part of the deposit in most states. In highly competitive rental areas such as New York City, tenants applying for desirable rental units occasionally offer to prepay several months' rent in order to convince landlords to choose them over other applicants. But is a landlord who collects this money (clearly in excess of the state's security deposit limit) in violation of the law? Probably not, as long as it's the tenant's idea and the landlord has not made the extra rent payment a condition of getting the unit. In short, a tenant who wants to waive this protection of the state's deposit limit may; but the landlord cannot do it unilaterally.

The deposit limit in your state may depend on factors such as:

- your age (senior citizens may have a lower deposit ceiling)
- whether the rental unit is furnished
- whether you have a month-to-month rental agreement or a long-term lease
- whether you have a pet or waterbed, and
- the number of rental properties the landlord owns (smaller landlords may be exempt from security deposit limits).

For details, see "State Security Deposit Rules" in Appendix A.

EXAMPLE: Jane, Reuben, and Sandy, who live in different states, each pay $900 rent per month for an unfurnished apartment. The maximum security deposit they may pay ranges from $900 to $2,700:

- Reuben (Hawaii) pays $900 (one month's rent)
- Jane (California) pays $1,800 (two months' rent)
- Sandy (Nevada) pays $2,700 (three months' rent).

TIP

Don't pay an excessive deposit. If your landlord is requesting a deposit that exceeds your state's limit, show him a copy of your state's security deposit statute and ask him to lower the deposit. If your landlord refuses, contact your city or district attorney's office, tenants' rights group, or state consumer protection agency for advice.

If you have a hard time coming up with the deposit, see if the landlord will reduce the deposit or allow you to pay it in installments. Here are a few tips for approaching your landlord. Obviously, these strategies are more likely to work if you have a good credit history and references and live in an area with lots of rentals. And don't ask for a lower deposit or an installment plan until you definitely have the place. A prospective landlord may be put off if you ask for special favors such as a lower deposit right off the bat. Wait until the landlord has offered you the rental unit before you start asking for special considerations.

- **Ask to pay in installments.** Offer to pay half the deposit up front with the rest on an affordable installment plan. Some landlords will say yes only if you can come up with the whole deposit in 30 to 60 days, but others will let you increase the amount a little each month until it's paid off in six months or more.

- **Suggest a cosigner.** A landlord may be reassured if a financially responsible friend or relative agrees to pay the deposit if you can't. (Chapter 2 discusses cosigners.)

- **Offer to buy renters' insurance.** A landlord who's worried about damage may be willing to reduce the deposit if you provide this extra measure of protection to cover any damage done to the rental property. (Chapter 2 explains renters' insurance.)

- **Offer to pay slightly more rent (assuming there are no rent control limits).** Some landlords may agree to a substantially lower deposit in exchange for a higher rent.

EXAMPLE: You offer to pay $25 more per month for rent in exchange for the landlord cutting the security deposit from $1,000 to $500. True, unlike the security deposit, the extra rent is not refundable. But if it allows you to rent a place you otherwise wouldn't qualify for, paying the extra money over time may be worth it. (However, if the landlord is worried about unpaid rent and intentional damage, he won't be mollified by your purchase of renters' insurance, since your policy won't cover you in these situations.)

CAUTION

Your landlord's security deposit policy cannot discriminate illegally. A landlord who charges some tenants the maximum deposit, and others less, should have a good explanation. This means if your landlord is charging the tenant next door a lower deposit because she's purchased renters' insurance, you should be in good legal shape to ask for the same deal. If the landlord refuses, without good reason, to give you an equivalent deal, you may have a discrimination claim in the offing. See Chapter 5 for information on illegal discrimination.

Where to Get More Information on Security Deposits

For more information about security deposit rules in your state, get a current copy of your state's security deposit law (statute). Start by referring to "State Security Deposit Rules" in Appendix A. This table highlights key rules, such as the deposit limit, deadline for landlord to return the deposit, and exemptions to state security deposit laws. Then read the statute at a public library, at a law library, or online. (See Chapter 20 for information on using the law library and accessing state statutes online.)

In addition, be sure to check local ordinances. Cities (particularly those with rent control) may add their own rules on security deposits, such as a limit on the amount landlords can charge or a requirement that landlords pay interest on deposits.

How Landlords May Increase Deposits

Tenants often ask whether it's legal for a landlord to raise their security deposit after they move in. The answer is that it depends on the situation.

Leases. If you have a fixed-term lease, your landlord may not raise the security deposit during the term of your lease, unless the lease allows it (most don't). Security deposits may be increased, however, when the lease is renewed or becomes a month-to-month tenancy (subject, of course, to any limitations imposed by state law).

Written rental agreements. If you have a month-to-month tenancy, a security deposit can be increased just the same way the rent can be, typically by giving you a written notice 30 days in advance of the change (see Chapter 3). Of course, the deposit can't exceed the maximum amount allowed by your state's security deposit law. (See above.)

> **EXAMPLE:** Jules rents an apartment for $750 a month in a state that limits security deposits to one month's rent. If his landlord raises the rent to $1,000, the maximum deposit his landlord may collect goes up to $1,000. But the deposit doesn't go up automatically. To raise the deposit amount, his landlord must give Jules the required 30 days' notice.

RENT CONTROL
Local rent control ordinances typically limit deposits as well as rents. (See Chapter 3 for more on rent control.)

Last Month's Rent

A landlord may want you to pay a sum of money called "last month's rent" before you move in, as a form of insurance against your leaving early and owing rent. Problems can arise when:

- the landlord tries to use last month's rent to cover repairs or cleaning, or
- the rent has gone up during the tenancy— and the landlord wants you to top off the last month's rent.

We'll look at these situations below.

Applying Last Month's Rent to Damage or Cleaning

If you have paid your landlord a sum labeled last month's rent and your tenancy is ending (voluntarily or involuntarily), chances are that you will not write a rent check for your last month. After all, you've already paid for that last month, right? Surprisingly, many tenants do pay for the last month anyway, often forgetting that they have prepaid. What happens to that last month's rent?

Ideally, you'll leave the place clean and in good repair, enabling the landlord to refund the entire last month's rent and all or most of your security deposit. But if you leave the place a mess, most states allow your landlord to treat "last month's rent" as part of the security deposit and use all or part of it for cleaning or to repair or replace damaged items.

> **EXAMPLE:** Katie's landlord required a security deposit of one month's rent, plus last month's rent. Her state law allowed a landlord to use all advance deposits to cover a tenant's unpaid rent or damage, regardless of what the landlord called the deposit. When Katie moved out, she didn't owe any back rent, but she left her apartment a shambles. The landlord was entitled to use the entire deposit, including that labeled "last month's rent," to cover the damage.

A few states, such as Massachusetts, restrict the use of money labeled as "last month's rent" to its stated purpose: the rent for the last month of your occupancy. In these states, if your landlord uses any of last month's rent to repair the cabinet you broke, he's violating the law.

EXAMPLE: Mike's landlord collected a security deposit of one month's rent, plus last month's rent. Mike's state required that landlords use money collected for the last month as last month's rent only, not for cleaning or repairs. When Mike moved out, he didn't owe any rent but he, too, left his apartment a mess. Mike's landlord had to refund his last month's rent and, when the remaining security deposit proved too little to cover the damage Mike had caused, the landlord had to sue Mike in small claims court for the excess.

Last month's rent restrictions are often developed in court cases, not statutes. For this reason, we can't give you a neat list of states that restrict your landlord's use of your last month's rent. If you want to find out how courts in your state have ruled on the use of last month's rent, see our advice on doing legal research in Chapter 20.

Your landlord may want to use money labeled last month's rent before the end of your tenancy. As explained below, the landlord may use your security deposit during your tenancy to pay for repairs that your actions have necessitated. If he also holds last month's rent, in most states he can use that during your tenancy, too, if your security deposit is insufficient.

If Your Rent Goes Up

If you've paid the last month's rent in advance, and the rent at the end of your tenancy is the same as when you began, you're paid up. However, if the rent has increased, but you have not been asked to top off the last month's rent held by the landlord, questions arise. Do you owe the landlord for the difference? If so, can he take money from your security deposit to make it up?

Unfortunately, there are no clear answers. But because landlords in every state are allowed to ask you to top off the last month's rent at the time they increase the rent, judges would probably

allow them to go after it at the end of the tenancy, too. Whether they get the difference from your security deposit or sue you in small claims court is somewhat academic.

EXAMPLE: When Rose moved in, the rent was $800 a month, and she paid this much in advance as last month's rent, plus an additional $800 security deposit. Over the years the landlord, Artie, has raised the rent to $1,000. Rose does not pay any rent during the last month of her tenancy, figuring that the $800 she paid up front will cover it. Artie, however, thinks that Rose should pay the $200 difference. Artie and Rose may end up in small claims court fighting over who owes what. They could have avoided the problem by discussing the issue of last month's rent when Rose's tenancy began.

To avoid these disputes, we suggest that you get issues involving last month's rent straight with your landlord at the outset.

Nonrefundable Deposits and Fees

A few states specifically prohibit landlords from charging any fee or deposit that is not refundable. Some states specifically allow landlords to collect a fee that is not refundable—such as for pets or cleaning. (See "State Security Deposit Rules," in Appendix A.) A few of these states require terms to be spelled out in the lease or rental agreement, but most don't, so find out your landlord's policy when you move in. A further complication is that non-refundable fees are sometimes called "deposits"—a contradiction in terms.

If your landlord is charging a nonrefundable fee or deposit, make sure it is legal. This is not always easy, because most state security deposit statutes are silent on the subject of nonrefundable fees. Contact your city or district attorney's office, state or local consumer protection agency, or tenants' rights organization for advice.

CAUTION
In states with deposit limits, creative land-lords have come up with ways to evade the law. At the beginning of the tenancy, they collect the maximum deposit and also impose nonrefundable fees for processing the tenancy (called "tenant initiation expense fees" or "introductory fees"). Tenants have challenged these as a ruse to avoid the strictures of the deposit law. At least one state (California) has allowed them, saying that there is nothing illegal in charging up-front fees that are not intended to cover damage or unpaid rent. (*Kaus v. Trinity Management Services, Inc.*, 23 Cal.4th 116 (2000).)

Interest on Deposits and Separate Accounts

Unfair as it may seem, less than half of the states require landlords to pay interest on deposits or put the money in a separate bank account. In other words, your landlord can simply put your deposit in a personal bank account and use it, as long as the money is available when you move out. A number of years ago, when deposits were small, this may not have been such a big deal. But now, when deposits are often $1,000 or more, it's extremely unfair.

Separate Accounts

Several states require landlords to put security deposits in a separate account, sometimes called a "trust" account, rather than mixing the funds with their personal or business accounts.

Some states require landlords to give tenants information on the location of this separate trust account at the start of the tenancy, usually as part of the lease or rental agreement. The idea is that by isolating these funds from the landlord's other accounts and telling the tenant where they are kept, the deposit can be easily traced, and it will become immediately evident if the money is improperly used—for example, spent by the landlord for personal purposes, or grabbed by an overeager creditor. Landlords are not usually required to set up separate accounts for every tenant, although they should maintain careful records of each tenant's contribution.

Interest

Ideally, your landlord should put your deposit into some kind of interest-bearing account and pay you the interest when you move out, After all, it's your money, not the landlord's.

Unfortunately, only a third of the states require landlords to pay interest on security deposits.

Of course, excellent landlords are willing to pay interest on your deposit as an honest business practice, even if there is no law requiring it. If your landlord doesn't volunteer to do this, there's no harm in asking.

Even among the states that require interest, there are many variations. A few states, such as Illinois, don't require small landlords (less than 25 rental units) to pay interest on deposits. Others, such as Iowa, allow the landlord to keep the interest earned during the first five years of your tenancy.

State laws typically establish detailed requirements, including:

- **The interest rate to be paid.** Usually, it's a little lower than the bank actually pays because the landlord is allowed to keep a small portion for administrative expenses.
- **When interest payments must be made.** The most common laws require payments to be made annually and/or when you leave.
- **Notification.** Landlords must tell tenants where and how the security deposit is being held and the rate of interest. This should go in the lease or rental agreement.

Chicago, Los Angeles, and several other cities (typically those with rent control) require landlords to pay or credit tenants with interest on security deposits even if the state law does not impose this duty. A few cities require that the funds be kept in separate interest-bearing accounts.

How the Deposit May Be Used

By law, your landlord must refund your deposit fairly promptly after you move out, unless there is a valid reason not to return part or all of it. Most states give landlords a set amount of time (usually from 14 to 30 days) to either return your entire deposit or provide an itemized written statement of deductions and refund the rest, if there's anything left.

Although state laws vary, your landlord can almost always withhold all or part of the deposit to pay for:

- unpaid rent
- repairing damage to the premises (except for "ordinary wear and tear") that you or a guest caused
- cleaning necessary to restore the rental unit to its level of cleanliness at the beginning of the tenancy (taking into consideration ordinary wear and tear), and
- replacing rental unit property you've taken.

TIP

Read your lease or rental agreement to be sure deposit refund procedures are spelled out. To protect yourself and avoid the all-too-common misunderstandings with your landlord, make sure your lease or rental agreement is clear on the use of security deposits and both you and your landlord's obligations. If it's not, follow our advice in "Avoiding Fights Over Deposits," in Chapter 16, and write a letter of understanding to your landlord.

Landlords don't necessarily need to wait until you move out to tap into your security deposit. Your landlord may use some of your security deposit during your tenancy—for example, because you broke something and didn't fix it or pay for it. In this case, the landlord will probably require you to replenish the security deposit.

EXAMPLE: Millie pays her landlord Maury a $1,000 security deposit when she moves in. Six months later, Millie goes on vacation, leaving the water running. By the time Maury is notified, the overflow has damaged the paint on the ceiling below. Maury repaints the ceiling at a cost of $250, taking the money out of Millie's security deposit. Maury is entitled to ask Millie to replace that money so that her deposit remains $1,000.

RELATED TOPIC

Chapter 16 provides details on rules landlords must follow when returning deposits. It covers what kinds of deductions landlords can legally make, and how to resolve disputes, including how to sue your landlord in small claims court.

If Your Landlord Sells the Property

In most states, the law requires a landlord who sells rental property to do one of two things: return the deposit to the tenant or transfer it to the new owner.

It's been known to happen, however, that a landlord does neither and simply walks off with the money. The tenant may not even be notified that the building has been sold until after the fact. Fortunately, the new owner—even one who never gets the deposit money—cannot require the tenant to replace any security deposit kept by the old landlord. And even better, in most states, whoever happens to be the landlord at the time a tenancy ends is legally responsible for complying with state laws requiring return of security deposits.

If Your Landlord Goes Bankrupt

If your landlord files for bankruptcy, your security deposit is beyond the reach of creditors. That's because, technically speaking, it's not your landlord's money—it's yours, which must be returned to you, unless you fail to pay the rent or damage the property. Chapter 15 explains what happens to your lease or rental agreement if the landlord goes bankrupt.

Discrimination

Kinds of Discrimination Prohibited by Federal Laws 87

    Race or Religion.. 88

    National Origin... 89

    Familial Status or Age 90

    Disability 93

    Sex and Sexual Harassment.. 97

Kinds of Discrimination Prohibited by State and Local Law 97

    Marital Status... 98

    Sexual Orientation and Gender Identity 98

    Source of Income 99

How to Fight Back.. 99

    Picking the Strategy That Suits Your Goals... 99

    Special Issues in Sexual Harassment Cases 100

    Negotiating With the Landlord... 101

    How Strong Is Your Case?... 102

    Complaining to a Fair Housing Agency 103

    Filing a Lawsuit in Federal or State Court 104

Not so long ago, a landlord could refuse to rent to you, or could evict you, for almost any reason—because of your skin color or religion, or because you had children or were elderly or disabled. Some landlords even discriminated against single women, believing that they would be incapable of paying the rent or would have too many overnight guests.

Recognizing that all Americans who could afford to pay the rent should have the right to live where they chose, Congress and state legislatures passed laws prohibiting housing discrimination. Most notable of these are the federal Fair Housing Act of 1968 and the federal Fair Housing Amendments Act of 1988, which outlaw discrimination based on race or color, national origin, religion, sex, familial status, or disability. (Throughout this chapter, we refer to this federal legislation as the federal Fair Housing Acts or the federal Acts.) In addition, many states and cities have laws making it illegal to discriminate based on additional factors, such as marital status or sexual orientation. Today, it is safe to say that unless a landlord has a legitimate business reason to reject a prospective tenant (for example, a poor credit history, terrible references from previous landlords, or an application from a more solvent candidate), the landlord risks a potentially costly legal challenge.

Because antidiscrimination laws are widely known, it is unusual to encounter a landlord who blatantly discriminates—for example, by stating a preference for all-white tenants or those without children. But it is still far too common to encounter more subtle—yet equally illegal—discrimination. For example, some landlords use overly restrictive occupancy standards to hide discrimination against families with children, or design advertisements that send powerful messages that applicants of a certain race are preferred. Or they may simply come up with superficially plausible—but nevertheless bogus—reasons not to rent to people of a certain race or religion.

In most situations with tenants, landlords have the upper hand. When it comes to discrimination, however, the balance of power shifts to the tenant.

Because of strong antidiscrimination laws, a determined tenant or applicant for rental housing who has been wronged can often tie a landlord in legal knots. As discussed below, tenants may complain to the U.S. Department of Housing and Urban Development (HUD), the federal agency that enforces the Fair Housing Acts, or to a state or local fair housing agency. Tenants may also file a lawsuit in federal or state court.

One of the reasons tenants have more clout in the housing discrimination area is that you don't always need to show that the landlord or manager intended to discriminate. As long as the landlord's conduct has a discriminatory effect or impact on members of a legally protected group (such as African Americans), you may successfully win a discrimination case. And knowing that outrageous cases may result in large jury verdicts, insurance companies are often quick to offer settlements outside of court.

If you think that you have been a victim of housing discrimination and you want to do something about it, you face an important choice. You can take your story to the federal or state agency in charge of enforcing the federal and state laws, and hope that an agency investigator will pursue your case (you usually won't need your own lawyer). Or, you can talk to an attorney about suing in state or federal court. Successful tenants may win an order (or leverage a settlement from the landlord's insurance company) forcing the landlord to rent to them or cease the discriminatory practice. You may also get a monetary award for your actual losses (having to rent another unit at a higher price, for example) or compensation for the humiliation you have endured.

 RELATED TOPIC
Also covered in this book:
- Legitimate reasons landlords may use to turn down prospective tenants: Chapter 1.
- Discriminatory rent increases: Chapter 3.
- Discriminatory evictions: Chapter 18.

Kinds of Discrimination Prohibited by Federal Laws

Federal, state, and local laws all forbid various kinds of discrimination against tenants. The most common kinds of discrimination—race or disability, for example—are prohibited by federal law, which must be followed by landlords in every state. (The key federal laws are the Fair Housing Acts, 42 U.S.C. §§ 3601–3619, 3631.)

Most state laws also make these forms of discrimination illegal, although some are not as inclusive as the federal laws. On the other hand, some states go even further; for example, some outlaw housing discrimination based on sexual orientation, something that is not addressed by federal law.

If you think you have been illegally discriminated against, it becomes important to know which law covers your situation, for two main reasons. First, if federal law has been violated, you can complain to a federal agency or sue in federal court; if only state law covers your situation, you are limited to state agencies and courts. If your situation is addressed by both federal and state law, you have a choice between going to a federal agency or court or a state agency or court. Second, federal law (and many state laws) doesn't apply to every rental. As discussed below, some properties are exempt. Even if your situation is covered by both laws, you'll need to know whether an exemption would force you to use one law or the other.

Since federal law governs everyone, we'll start with it. The federal Acts prohibit discrimination on the following grounds (called "protected categories"):

- race or color
- religion
- national origin
- familial status or age—includes families with children under the age of 18 *and* pregnant women and elderly persons
- disability or handicap, and
- sex, including sexual harassment.

The federal Acts apply to all aspects of the landlord-tenant relationship. A landlord may not:

- advertise or make any statement that indicates a limitation or preference based on race, religion, or any other protected category (advertising a building as a "quiet environment for mature adults" may be considered illegal familial status discrimination)
- falsely deny that a rental unit is available
- set more restrictive standards for selecting tenants
- refuse to rent to members of certain groups
- before or during the tenancy, set different terms, conditions, or privileges for rental of a dwelling unit, such as requiring larger deposits of some tenants, or adopting an inconsistent policy of responding to late rent payments
- during the tenancy, providing different housing services or facilities, such as making a community center or other common area available only to selected tenants, or
- terminate a tenancy for a discriminatory reason.

Unfortunately, not every rental is covered by the federal Acts. The following types of property are exempt:

- owner-occupied buildings with four or fewer rental units
- single-family housing rented without the use of discriminatory advertising or without a real estate broker, as long as the owner doesn't own more than three such houses at any one time
- certain types of housing operated by religious organizations and private clubs that limit occupancy to their own members, and
- with respect to age discrimination only, housing reserved exclusively for senior citizens. There are two kinds of senior citizen housing exempted: communities where every tenant is 62 years of age or older, or communities with individual units that have at least one person 55 years of age or older. To qualify as "55 and older housing," at least 80% of the occupied units in the housing facility must be occupied by at least one person 55 years or older.

TIP

State and local laws may offer additional antidiscrimination protections. If the property you rent is exempt under federal law, similar state or local anti–housing-discrimination laws may nevertheless protect you. For example, owner-occupied buildings with four or fewer rental units are exempt under federal law but not under California law.

More Information From HUD and State Agencies

For more information about the Fair Housing Act, and technical assistance on accessibility requirements, contact one of HUD's many local offices. You'll find a list of state and local offices on the HUD website at www. hud.gov. Check the tab "State Info" and then click "Get Rental Help" for your state. You can also call the agency's Housing Discrimination Hotline at 800-669-9777 (or 800-927-9275 TTY).

Your state consumer protection agency can provide more general information and referrals to state law. Many also publish free brochures on landlord-tenant law. For a list of state consumer protection agencies, go to www.usa.gov/directory/state-consumer.

Race or Religion

Discrimination based on race or religion isn't always as obvious as you might think. Especially when a person's beliefs are out of the mainstream or unpopular with other groups, it might even seem reasonable not to rent to that person. For example, a Jewish landlord might be offended by someone's anti-Semitic convictions, but nevertheless could not legally refuse to rent to that person for that reason.

EXAMPLE: Several tenants in Creekside Apartments reserved the common room for a meeting. Creekside management learned that the tenants were members of a white supremacist religion that believes in the inferiority of all nonwhites and non-Christians. Creekside management was appalled at the thought of these ideas being discussed on its premises, and denied the group the use of the common room. The tenants who were members of this group filed a discrimination complaint with HUD on the basis of freedom of religion. HUD supported the religious group and forced Creekside to make the common room available.

Unintended discriminatory messages are just as illegal as overt ones. For example, an apartment ad that says "safe Christian community" or "Sunday quiet times enforced" violates federal law, since applicants might reasonably conclude that Christians are preferred as tenants. Landlords may not legally send these subtle messages to tenants after they have moved in, either. For example, tenant rules, signs, newsletters, and other communication cannot legally convey any attempt to benefit, support, or discriminate against a racial or religious group. The following examples are based on actual fair housing complaints of illegal discrimination:

- Management extends the use of the common room to tenants for "birthday parties, anniversaries, and Christmas and Easter parties." Non-Christian tenants could understandably feel excluded.
- In an effort to accommodate Spanish-speaking tenants, management translates the move-in letter and house rules into Spanish. Regarding the use of alcohol in the common areas, the Spanish version—but not the English one —begins, "Unlike Mexico, where drinking is practiced in public places, alcoholic beverages may not be consumed in common areas ...." To many people, this phrase implies an ethnic generalization.
- The metropolitan area where you live contains large numbers of both Spanish-speaking and Cantonese-speaking people. Several apartment

complexes advertise in Spanish only and offer nothing but Spanish-language leases. As an Asian-American who speaks Cantonese (or an Anglo who speaks only English), you naturally conclude that these complexes welcome Hispanics but not you. It is always legal to advertise in English only.

National Origin

Discrimination based on national origin is illegal, whether it's practiced deliberately or unintentionally. For example, a landlord who required all residents to be U.S. citizens, or who advertised "Special discounts for members of the Irish-American Club," would likely face a charge of discrimination based on national origin.

Even if your landlord is motivated by what seems like a valid business concern, but rejects tenants in a way that singles out people of a particular nationality, it's still illegal. For example, people in the U.S. without permission can be picked up and held in custody pending deportation at any time. If that were to happen, these tenants might stop paying rent. Does this mean that landlords are entitled to ask every "foreign looking" applicant (but not others) for immigration papers or proof of citizenship? The answer is no, and the reason, of course, is because of the impact this practice is almost sure to have on applicants who look the same but are citizens or in the United States legally. If you're one of them, you're likely to reach the conclusion that you are not welcome because management assumes that everyone like you is living in the United States illegally. A fair housing agency or court would surely agree that this sort of selective "let me see your papers" policy is illegal discrimination.

On the other hand, a landlord who requires *all* prospective tenants to supply satisfactory proof of identity and eligibility to work is on solid ground. Why? Because every applicant, and not just members of one group, is subjected to an inquiry that is reasonably related to the landlord's right to choose tenants who are likely to pay rent over the tenancy term.

TIP

For information on how your landlord may legally verify your citizenship or immigration status, contact the U.S. Citizenship and Immigration Services or USCIS, a bureau of the U.S. Department of Homeland Security, at 800-375-5283, or check their website at www.uscis.gov.

Discrimination on the Basis of Immigration Status

In all areas but New York City, it has always been theoretically okay for landlords to question applicants' immigration status as long as landlords questioned every applicant. After the events of 9/11, however, landlords became more aggressive in questioning immigration status, and many tenants reacted by challenging whether even the "question one, question all" approach is legal. California landlords, however, cannot inquire as to applicants' or tenants' immigration status.

HUD clarified the issue, at least with respect to federal law, by pointing out that because illegal immigrants are not a protected class, discrimination (refusing to rent) based solely on a person's immigration status is not illegal. But, landlords could be guilty of national origin discrimination if they demanded proof of legal entry of only certain ethnic applicants. (Search "Rights and Responsibilities of Landlords and Residents in Preventing Housing Discrimination Based on Race, Religion, or National Origin in the Wake of the Events of September 11, 2001," at www.hud.gov.)

Cities in several states have passed ordinances that attempt to make it illegal for landlords to rent to people who are not legally in the United States. These ordinances direct landlords or city officials to examine applicants' immigration or citizenship papers, and fine landlords who are found to have rented to someone not legally in this country. To date, every such ordinance has been successfully withdrawn or challenged, and legal scholars uniformly doubt that these ill-conceived laws will ever withstand Constitutional scrutiny. To find out whether your city has such a law, contact your state's branch of the American Civil Liberties Union, or ACLU (the ACLU has been involved in challenging these ordinances). Go to www.aclu.org and choose "Find your local ACLU affiliate."

Familial Status or Age

A landlord may not legally turn away or evict families because they have children or because an applicant or tenant is pregnant. In addition, a landlord cannot exclude families by unreasonably limiting the maximum number of people permitted to occupy a rental unit, thereby indirectly preventing families with children from occupying smaller units. Finally, a landlord may not make tenancy decisions based on an applicant's age.

Discrimination Against Families

Discrimination based on family make-up can take unexpected forms. Even well-intentioned landlord motives will not justify a policy or rule that discriminates against families with children or younger people. Consider these examples:

- You and your 15-year-old daughter have applied to rent an apartment in an area of town that has experienced several muggings and rapes. Afraid that your daughter, when she returns from school alone each day, will be an easy mark, the manager refuses to accept your application.
- You, your spouse, and your teenage son and daughter have applied for a two-bedroom apartment. The occupancy policy is two-per-bedroom, but the landlord decides that it is inappropriate for children of different sexes to share a room.

The ban against familial status discrimination protects adults without children and singles, too. A landlord may not establish policies that adversely affect childless tenants. This means it is illegal to rent *only* to families, or even to segregate (or restrict) some tenants to certain floors or parts of a building. For example, a policy that requires tenants with children to rent ground floor units indirectly funnels childless tenants to the upper stories. A childless tenant who wanted a ground floor unit would have a valid claim of familial discrimination. Similarly, hosting "families only" social events in the common area excludes childless renters, who could raise a claim of discrimination.

Occupancy Limits: How Many People Can Live in the Rental Unit?

Landlords may try to avoid renting to families with children by setting occupancy policies that appear neutral but have the effect of discriminating. For example, a policy of no more than two people for a two-bedroom apartment would exclude a family with one or two children or a single parent with three children. To counter this subtle discrimination, the government has come up with rules that limit landlords' occupancy policies.

Illegal discrimination against families also occurs when an occupancy policy differentiates between adults and children. For example, consider the results of a landlord's policy allowing only one person per bedroom, with a couple counting as one person. Under this criterion, the landlord would rent a two-bedroom unit to a husband and wife and their one child, but would not rent the same unit to a mother with two children. The mother and her two children would have a valid discrimination claim.

Familial status discrimination also appears when a landlord applies an occupancy policy in an inconsistent manner. If in practice your landlord distinguishes between adults and children, you may be able to challenge those actions as a hidden form of familial discrimination, even if the landlord is following what he believes is a sensible and nondiscriminatory policy.

> **EXAMPLE:** Jackson owned and managed two identical one-bedroom units, one of which he rented out to three flight attendants who were rarely there at the same time. When the other unit became vacant, Jackson advertised it as a one-bedroom, two-person apartment. Harry and Sue Jones and their teenage daughter were turned away because they exceeded Jackson's occupancy limit of two people. The Jones family learned that the companion unit was rented to three people, and decided to file a complaint with HUD, whose investigator helped negotiate a settlement. Jackson saw that

he was legally in the wrong. He agreed to rent to the Jones family and to compensate them for the humiliation they had suffered as a result of being refused.

How do you know what is a reasonable occupancy limit? State and local health and safety codes typically limit the number of tenants allowed, based on the size of the unit and the number of bedrooms and bathrooms.

But the law also addresses the other end of the how-many-occupants issue, by setting policies that require a landlord to rent to *at least* a certain number of tenants per unit. The Department of Housing and Urban Development issues the federal guidelines, thus going a long way toward preventing discrimination against families with children. HUD generally considers a limit of two persons per bedroom a reasonable occupancy standard. Because the number of bedrooms is not the only factor—the size of the bedrooms, age of the children, and configuration of the rental unit are also considered—the federal test has become known as the "two per bedroom plus" standard.

States and localities can set their own occupancy standards, and many have. And this is where things get tricky: Ordinarily, when the federal government legislates on a particular subject, states and localities are free to pass laws on the subject too, as long as they're equally (or more) protective of the targeted group (in this case, tenants). But the federal government's guidance (a mere memo to regional HUD directors) emphatically stated that Congress didn't intend to develop "a national occupancy code." ("Fair Housing Enforcement—Occupancy Standards Notice of Statement of Policy," Code of Federal Regulations (C.F.R.) Vol. 63, No. 243, Dec. 18, 1998.) The memo practically invited states and localities to set their own occupancy standards, and didn't make it clear whether those standards had to be at least as generous (to tenants) as the federal guidance. As a result, some states developed occupancy standards that were less generous than the federal guidance,

while others, such as California, developed standards that were more generous.

If you are renting in a state that has its own occupancy standards (and your city may have its own, too), you'll want to check to see what they are. Landlords are on shaky ground if they follow any standard other than the most generous. To learn about state or local occupancy standards, check with your state's consumer protection agency. You'll find a state-by-state list at www.usa.gov/directory/state-consumer. A landlord may, however, set an occupancy standard that is lower than the applicable federal, state or local figure if legitimate business reasons will justify it. This is hard to do—while the inability of the infrastructure to support more tenants (perhaps the septic system or plumbing has a limited capacity) may validate a lower occupancy policy, a landlord's desire to ensure a quiet, uncrowded environment for upscale older tenants will not. If your landlord's occupancy policy limits the number of tenants for any reason other than health, safety, and legitimate business needs, it may be illegal discrimination against families.

CAUTION

Exceeding the maximum allowable number of tenants is not always a bargain. Some tenants are delighted to find a landlord who will allow them to live with more than the maximum number of residents allowable under the local health and safety laws. Your rent share will be lower and, in tight rental markets, it may mean the difference between living in a good area and a really bad one, or not even having a home at all. But unless you are desperate, beware! The fact that a landlord is willing to live outside the law tells you a lot about how seriously he takes other legal responsibilities (like repairs and maintenance). And by agreeing to live in an overcrowded rental, you hamper your ability to assert your rights—you will naturally hesitate to do anything (like complain to a housing authority about substandard conditions or utilize a repair and deduct remedy) that will bring the illegal rental to the attention of courts or building inspectors.

Age Discrimination

The federal Fair Housing Acts do not expressly ban discrimination based on age. Nevertheless, it is definitely forbidden under the broader concept of prohibiting discrimination on the basis of familial status.

A landlord cannot refuse to rent to an older person or impose special terms and conditions on the tenancy unless these same standards are applied to everyone else. If you have excellent references and credit history, a landlord has no legal basis for refusing you, even if you are 85 and rely to some degree on the regular assistance of a nearby adult child or friend. (Of course, the landlord could legally give the rental to someone else with equal or better references or financial stability.) However, if your current landlord reveals that you suffer from advanced senility to the point that you often wander into the wrong apartment, frequently forget to pay the rent, or are unable to undertake basic housekeeping chores, the prospective landlord can refuse to rent to you based on this age-neutral evidence that you are not likely to be a stable, reliable tenant.

> **EXAMPLE:** Ethel, who is 80 years old, wants to find a smaller place closer to her daughter, Nora. She sells her home and applies for a one-bedroom apartment at Coral Shores. Ethel presents impeccable references from neighbors and employers and an outstanding credit history. Nonetheless, Lucy, the manager of Coral Shores, is fearful that Ethel, at her age, might forget to turn off the stove, fall on the front steps, or do any number of other dangerous things, and decides not to rent to her. Ethel files a fair housing complaint with HUD, which she quickly wins on the basis of Coral Shores' policy of age discrimination.

The issue of age discrimination may also arise during a well-established tenancy. Suppose you have lived alone for years and now, with advanced age, must face the question of whether you are still able to live safely by yourself. Your landlord is honestly concerned that your physical incapacity or mental inattention might result in damage to the premises and injury to you or other tenants. Can your landlord, on the basis of these fears alone, decide not to renew your lease? Absolutely not—there must be real, serious, and probably repeated violations of the criteria that apply to all tenants before nonrenewal of a lease, or eviction, would be legal.

 TIP

Elderly tenants may also qualify as disabled tenants, who are entitled to accommodation under the law. An elderly tenant who cannot meet one of the landlord's policies may be entitled to special treatment as a disabled person. (See the discussion of discrimination on the basis of disability, below.) For example, an elderly tenant who is chronically late with the rent because of sporadic disorientation might justifiably ask for a grace period, or a friendly reminder when the rent is due; a nondisabled tenant who is chronically late with the rent would not be entitled to such special treatment. And if an elderly tenant can't negotiate the stairs, the legal solution is a ramp or a move to a single-level rental, not an eviction notice.

Additional Eviction Protections for Elderly Tenants

Some states and localities, including Connecticut and New York City, protect elderly tenants in the event that their building is sold or converted to condominiums, or if the owner of their rent-controlled unit attempts to evict them in order to move in themselves (or a member of their family). For information on eviction protections for elderly tenants, check your state's fair housing agency.

The prohibition against age discrimination also applies to "emancipated" minors who have the same status as an adult and must be treated like any other adult applicant or tenant. (An emancipated minor is a 17-year-old—or possibly even a 16-year-old in some states—who is legally married, has a court order of emancipation, or is in the military.) On the other hand, a landlord can reject an under-age applicant who is not emancipated, because these minors lack the legal capacity to enter into a binding rental agreement.

Disability

Federal law prohibits discrimination against people who:

- have a physical or mental disability that substantially limits one or more major life activities—including, but not limited to, hearing, mobility, and visual impairments; chronic alcoholism (but only if it is being addressed through a recovery program); mental illness; HIV-positive status, AIDS, and AIDS-Related Complex; and mental retardation
- have a history or record of such a disability, or
- are regarded by others as though they have such a disability.

Mental or Emotional Impairments

If you had, have, or appear to have mental or emotional impairments, you must be evaluated and treated by the landlord on the basis of your financial stability and history as a tenant, not on the basis of your mental health. A landlord may reject you only if he can point to specific instances of past behavior that would make you dangerous to others (such as information from a previous landlord that you repeatedly threatened or assaulted other residents). If you cannot meet the good-tenant criteria that the landlord applies to all applicants (such as a good credit report), you may be rejected on *that* basis.

Discriminatory Questions and Actions

Landlords are not allowed to ask you whether or not you have a disability or illness, or ask to see medical records. Even if it is obvious that you are disabled—for example, you use a wheelchair or wear a hearing aid—it is nevertheless illegal to inquire how severely you are disabled. In short, your landlord's actions and questions cannot be designed to treat you differently than other tenants. The policy behind this rule is simple: No matter how well-intentioned, the landlord cannot make decisions about where and how you will live on the property that he would not make were you not disabled. For example, if there are two units for rent—one on the ground floor and one three stories up—the landlord must show both units to a wheelchair-bound applicant, however reasonable the landlord thinks it would be for the person to consider only the ground floor unit.

The Rights of Tenants With Disabilities to Live in an Accessible Place

Federal law protects disabled tenants *after* they have moved into a rental unit as well as during the application process. Landlords must:

- accommodate the needs of disabled tenants, at the landlord's own expense (42 U.S.C. § 3604(f)(3)(B)), and
- allow disabled tenants to make reasonable modifications to their living unit at their expense, if needed for the person to comfortably and safely live in the unit. (42 U.S.C. § 3604(f)(3)(A)).

Let's look briefly at each of these requirements. (You can find more information at www.hud.gov (search for "accessibility requirements").)

Accommodations

As a tenant with a disability, you may expect your landlord to reasonably adjust rules, procedures, or services in order to give you an equal opportunity to use and enjoy your dwelling unit or a common space. Accommodations can include such things as:

- parking—if the landlord provides parking in the first place, providing a close-in, spacious parking space for a tenant who uses a wheelchair
- service animals—allowing a dog or other animal that is individually trained to do work or perform tasks for the benefit of someone with a disability

- rent payment—allowing a special rent payment plan for a tenant whose finances are managed by someone else or by a government agency
- reading problems—arranging to read all communications from management to a blind tenant, and
- phobias—for example, providing a washtub and clothesline for a clinically diagnosed tenant whose anxiety about machines makes her unable to use the facility's washer and dryer.

Does your landlord's duty to accommodate tenants with disabilities mean that you can expect every rule and procedure to be changed at your request? No. Although landlords are expected to accommodate "reasonable" requests, they need not undertake changes that would seriously impair their ability to run their business. For example, if an applicant in a wheelchair prefers the third-story apartment in a walk-up building constructed in 1926 to the one on the ground floor, the landlord does not have to rip the building apart to install an elevator. HUD would consider the expense to be unreasonable.

Modifications

Fortunately, where your landlord's legal duty to reasonably accommodate the needs of tenants with disabilities ends, his obligation to allow you to modify your living space may begin. You have the right to modify your living space to the extent necessary to make the space safe and comfortable, as long as the modifications will not make the unit unacceptable to the next tenant, or you agree to undo the modification when you leave. Examples of modifications undertaken by a tenant with a disability include:

- lowering countertops for a tenant who uses a wheelchair
- installing special faucets or door handles for persons with limited hand use
- modifying kitchen appliances to accommodate a blind tenant, and
- installing a ramp to allow a tenant who uses a wheelchair to negotiate two steps up to a raised living room.

Service Animals and Comfort or Emotional Support Animals

A lot of uncertainty surrounds the public's understanding of the meaning of a "service animal" and, recently, a "comfort" or "emotional support" animal. The confusion is understandable, because different rules apply to housing and public places such as shops, restaurants, and theaters. In the housing context, a service animal is not limited to a dog, as it is in other, public contexts. This change came about in 2011, when the Department of Justice revised its regulations interpreting the Americans with Disabilities Amendments Act. A tenant with a legal disability who has a trained animal other than a dog (such as a monkey), that performs work or tasks to help that person live safely and comfortably in his or her home, may ask the landlord to accommodate the animal. But in a public place like a shop, the shopkeeper need not allow the monkey into the shop with his or her owner.

A comfort animal (one that supplies emotional support, well-being, comfort, or companionship, but does no work or tasks) is not part of the definition of a service animal when that animal is in a public place, such as a restaurant. For example, a dog whose presence calms its owner but who is not trained to do work would not qualify as a service animal and a restaurant or shop would not be expected to accommodate its presence. But for purposes of rental housing, it seems that landlords are required to accommodate the presence of such a comfort animal if they can reasonably do so.

The practical result of two sets of rules is apparent: What is the legally disabled tenant with a trained pig expected to do when he or she leaves her apartment and wants to go shopping or to a restaurant?

Keep in mind that before any of these questions can be raised, let alone answered, a tenant must be able to establish that he or she is, in fact, a person with a legal disability. No landlord need accommodate any service or comfort animal unless requested by someone who is covered by the law—that is, someone with a disability, as that term is defined by law.

These modifications must be reasonable and made with prior approval. A landlord is entitled to ask for a description of the proposed modifications, proof that they will be done in a workmanlike manner, and evidence that you are obtaining any necessary building permits. In addition, if you propose to modify the unit in a way that will require restoration when you leave (such as the repositioning of lowered kitchen counters), the landlord may require you to pay into an interest-bearing escrow account the amount estimated for the restoration. (The interest belongs to you.)

Unless the property is in Massachusetts or is federally financed, tenants pay for the modification. But if the building opened for occupancy on or after March 13, 1991, and the modification is needed because the building doesn't comply with HUD's accessibility requirements, the landlord must pay.

Verification of Disabled Status

Landlords are also entitled to ask for proof that the accommodation or modification you have requested will address your needs. For years, landlords asked for a doctor's letter. Now, according to a HUD and Department of Justice guidance memo, they must be willing to listen to less formal sources. (*Reasonable Accommodations Under the Fair Housing Act,* Joint Statement of the Department of Housing and Urban Development and the Department of Justice, May 17, 2004.) Sources of reliable information include:

- **The individual himself.** A person can prove that he has met the requirements for having a legal disability (and that a modification or accommodation addresses that disability) by giving the landlord a "credible statement." Unfortunately, the guidance does not define this term.
- **Documents.** A person who is under 65 years of age and receives Supplemental Security Income or Social Security Disability Insurance Benefits is legally disabled. Someone could establish disability by showing a landlord relevant identification cards. Likewise, license plates showing the universal accessibility logo, or a driver's license reflecting the existence of a disability, are sufficient proof.
- **Doctors or other medical professionals, peer support groups, nonmedical service agencies.** Information from these sources might come through letters, phone calls, or personal visits.

- **Reliable third parties.** This wide-open source of information could include friends, associates, and roommates.

If you choose to ask a doctor or therapist to write a letter, ask for a letter attesting that what you are asking for will meet your needs. To protect your privacy, carefully explain to the physician or other writer that he need not explain the disability; he need only certify that the changes you would like are appropriate to your situation. A sample letter, in which the physician describes the tenant's requests but not the disability, is presented below.

New Buildings and Accessibility

The Fair Housing Amendments Act (42 U.S.C. §§ 3604 (f)(3)(C) and 3604(f)(7)) imposes requirements on new buildings of four or more units that were first occupied after March 1991. All ground-floor units and every unit in an elevator building must be designed or constructed so that:

- the main building is accessible and on an accessible route
- the public and common areas are "readily accessible to and usable by" the people with disabilities, including parking areas (a good rule of thumb is to reserve 2% of the spaces)
- any stair landing shared by more than one rental unit is handicapped-accessible. (*U.S. v. Edward Rose & Sons,* 384 F.3d 258 (6th Cir. 2004).)
- entryway doorways have 36" of free space *plus* shoulder and elbow room; and interior doorways are at least 32" wide
- interior living spaces have wheelchair-accessible routes throughout, with changes in floor height of no more than ¼"
- light switches, outlets, thermostats, and other environmental controls are within the legal "reach range" (15" to 48" from the ground)
- bathroom walls are sufficiently reinforced to allow the safe installation of "grab bars," and
- kitchens and bathrooms are large enough to allow a wheelchair to maneuver within the room (40" turning radius minimum) and have sinks and appliances positioned to allow side or front use.

Sample Letter
Attesting to the Appropriateness of an Accommodation or Modification

Marcus Welby, M.D.
400 Professional Way, Suite 100
Anytown, Colorado 00000
(719) 555-9999
September 19, 20xx

Hilda Hanson, Manager
Royal Crest Apartments
Anytown, Colorado 00000

Dear Ms. Hanson:

John Anderson, who resides at Royal Crest Apartments, is a patient under my care. He has informed me that he will soon be asking you to modify certain aspects of his apartment. He will also ask you to make some accommodations regarding management policies at Royal Crest.

Modifications

1. Disconnect the electric doorbell and install a hand-knocker on the front door.
2. Allow Mr. Anderson to install curtain rods in the bedroom that will support heavy, light-blocking drapes.
3. Allow Mr. Anderson to put wall-to-wall carpet in the bedroom, which is currently bare hardwood.

Accommodations

1. Communicate any management requests in writing, left in Mr. Anderson's mailbox, rather than by phone.
2. Open the laundry room at 7 a.m., one hour earlier than the current schedule.
3. When management at Royal Crest calls a tenants' meeting to discuss and vote on issues of concern to tenants and management, allow Mr. Anderson to send a proxy who may speak and vote in his place.

In my professional opinion, these requests are necessary and appropriate to enable Mr. Anderson to live at Royal Crest in a safe and enjoyable manner.

Yours truly,

Marcus Welby, M.D.

Marcus Welby, M.D.

cc: Mr. John Anderson

Limited Protection for Alcoholics and Drug Users

Federal fair housing law extends limited protection to two carefully defined groups:

- **Recovering alcoholics.** An alcoholic who is "in recovery" may not be denied housing on the basis of his status as an alcoholic. Unfortunately, there is no clear definition of what "recovery" means, nor when it begins; but someone who actively and regularly participates in a medically based treatment or AA program probably qualifies.
- **Former drug addicts.** People who were previously addicted to illegal drugs cannot be denied housing on that basis alone. It is also illegal for a landlord to discriminate based on a conviction for illegal drug use. This protection does not extend to current addiction, nor does it protect someone who has a conviction for drug dealing or manufacture.

It is important to remember that other aspects of a recovering alcoholic's (or a former drug addict's) past might legally serve as the basis for a denial of housing. For example, if the recovering alcoholic also has bad credit, a spotty employment history, or negative references from previous landlords, a landlord may reject the applicant for these reasons just as readily as any other applicant with these flaws. What a landlord *cannot* do is reject the former addict or the recovering alcoholic on the basis of their *status* as former addicts or recovering alcoholics.

EXAMPLE: Patsy applied for an apartment one morning and spoke with Carol, the manager. Patsy said she would have to return that afternoon to complete the application form because she was due at an Alcoholics Anonymous meeting. Carol decided on the spot that she did not want Patsy for a tenant, and she told Patsy that the unit "had just been rented," which was a lie. (Patsy continued to see the newspaper ad for the unit.)

Patsy filed a complaint with HUD, alleging that she was a recovering alcoholic who had been discriminated against. Because Carol could not point to any reason for turning Patsy away other than her assumption that Patsy, as an alcoholic, would be a bad tenant, the judge awarded Patsy several thousand dollars in damages.

Sex and Sexual Harassment

You cannot be denied a place to live (or have special rules imposed on you) solely because you're female or male. Even well-intentioned policies are off-limits—for example, fearful that single women are more likely to be burglarized and assaulted than male tenants, a landlord cannot require single females to live in upper-story apartments, even if, in fact, those units are less prone to break-ins. Whether the landlord considers it good intentions or unacceptable paternalism, it's illegal.

A landlord's policy that favors one sex over another may justify a claim of discrimination by either sex. In the example above, the landlord is discriminating against female applicants who want ground-floor apartments, *and* against male applicants who want an upper-story apartment that is reserved for single women.

Sexual harassment is another form of sexual discrimination. For example, it's illegal to refuse to rent to a person who resists the landlord's sexual advances or to make life difficult for a tenant who has resisted such advances. In the rental housing context, courts have defined sexual harassment as:

- a pattern of persistent, unwanted attention of a sexual nature, including the making of sexual remarks and physical advances, or a single instance of highly egregious behavior. A manager's persistent requests for social contact, or constant remarks concerning a tenant's appearance or behavior, could constitute sexual harassment, as could a single extraordinarily offensive remark.
- a situation in which a tenant's rights are conditioned upon the acceptance of the owner's or manager's attentions. For example, a manager who refuses to fix the plumbing until the tenant agrees to a date is guilty of sexual

harassment. This type of harassment may be established on the basis of only one incident.

EXAMPLE: Oscar, the resident manager of Northside Apartments, repeatedly asked Martha, a Northside tenant, for dates. Martha always turned Oscar down and, after his fourth proposition, asked that he leave her alone. Oscar didn't back off, and began hanging around the pool whenever Martha used it, watching her intently and making suggestive remarks about her to the other tenants.

Martha stopped using the pool and filed a sexual harassment complaint with HUD, claiming that Oscar's unwanted attentions made it impossible for her to use and enjoy the pool and even to comfortably live at Northside. Oscar refused to consider a settlement when the HUD investigator spoke to him and Martha about his actions. As a result, HUD pursued the case in court, where a federal judge ordered Oscar to leave Martha alone and awarded her several thousand dollars.

Deciding how to respond to an act of sexual harassment involves considerations that go beyond the usual housing discrimination case, because sexual harassment involves proving certain facts that aren't involved in other sex discrimination lawsuits. In "How to Fight Back," below, we suggest ways to evaluate the strength of your case and include suggestions as to how best to respond to sexual harassment.

Kinds of Discrimination Prohibited by State and Local Law

Most state and local laws prohibiting housing discrimination echo federal antidiscrimination law in that they outlaw discrimination based on race or color, national origin, religion, familial status, disability, and sex. But state and local laws often go into more detail and may also forbid some kinds of discrimination—such as discrimination based on marital status—that aren't covered by federal law.

For example, in states that prohibit discrimination based on marital status, it would be illegal to refuse to rent to divorced people, something that is not covered by federal law.

Here we explain some of the common antidiscrimination laws that states and localities have adopted. For more information on state and local housing discrimination laws, contact your state fair housing agency. See "More Information From HUD and State Agencies" earlier in this chapter for contact information.

Marital Status

In most states, landlords may legally refuse to rent to you if you are an unmarried couple. About 20 states ban discrimination on the basis of marital status, and most of these extend protection to married couples only. Only a few states—Alaska, California, Massachusetts, Michigan, and New Jersey—have clearly ruled that the term "marital status" refers to *unmarried* couples. Oddly, courts in Maryland, Minnesota, New York, and Wisconsin have ruled that the term "marital status" only protects *married* people from being treated differently from single people, not vice versa.

Zoning Ordinances and Living Together

Some communities have adopted zoning ordinances that prohibit groups of unrelated people from living together (the U.S. Supreme Court has upheld these laws). Most of these ordinances are aimed at barring groups, foster families, shelters, or boarding houses. Very few prohibit two unrelated adults from living together. If you are an unmarried couple, straight or gay, find out whether the neighborhood you're interested in has been zoned only for people related by "blood, marriage, or adoption." If such an ordinance does apply, a landlord could use it to justify refusing to rent to you, though the landlord would be on shaky ground if the law exempts two adults.

Some landlords resist renting to unmarried couples on the grounds that cohabitation violates their religious beliefs. Courts in California and Massachusetts have refused to allow landlords to reject unmarried couples as tenants for this reason.

TIP

Unmarried couples may be protected by a city or county ordinance prohibiting discrimination on the basis of sexual orientation. Although usually passed to protect the housing rights of gay and lesbian tenants, most local laws forbidding discrimination based on sexual orientation also protect unmarried heterosexual couples as well. In addition, unmarried people may be able to challenge a landlord's refusal to rent to them on the basis of sex discrimination, which is covered by the federal Acts.

Arbitrary Discrimination Is Illegal in California

Federal and state laws clearly prohibit discrimination based on race, religion, sex, and so on. But what about tenant-selection criteria that don't fit into these categories? Can a landlord exclude bearded men and lawyers?

In California, at least, the answer is probably no. Courts have ruled that although California's Unruh Civil Rights Act (Cal. Civ. Code §§ 51–53, 54.1–54.8) contains only the phrases "sex, race, color, religion, ancestry, national origin, disability or medical condition, genetic information, marital status, or sexual orientation" to describe types of illegal discrimination, these categories are just examples. The courts have construed the Unruh Act to forbid discrimination on the basis of a "personal characteristic or trait"—also known as "arbitrary discrimination." Other common examples of arbitrary discrimination include obesity, occupation, or style of dress.

Sexual Orientation and Gender Identity

Housing discrimination based on sexual orientation and gender identity is prohibited in at least 18 states and the District of Columbia: California, Colorado, Connecticut, Delaware, Hawaii, Illinois, Iowa, Maine, Maryland, Massachusetts, Minnesota, New Jersey, Nevada, New Mexico, Oregon, Rhode Island, Vermont, and Washington. In addition, three states prohibit housing discrimination based on sexual orientation (but not gender identity): New Hampshire, New York, and Wisconsin. Many cities prohibit discrimination against gays and lesbians, including Atlanta, Chicago, Detroit, Miami, New York, Pittsburgh, St. Louis, and Seattle. For more information on state or local law, contact the National LGBTQ Task Force, 202-393-5177 or www. thetaskforce.org.

As of early 2012, housing programs run by HUD may not discriminate on the basis of sexual orientation, gender identity, or familial status.

Source of Income

In several states, including California, Connecticut, the District of Columbia, Maine, Massachusetts, Minnesota, New Jersey, North Dakota, Oklahoma, Oregon, Utah, Vermont, and Wisconsin, applicants who receive public assistance may not be turned away or otherwise discriminated against because of this fact. This doesn't mean, however, that being on public assistance entitles you to be considered for every rental. A landlord may refuse to rent to you if your available income (regardless of its source) falls below an established level, as long as that standard is applied to every applicant. (See "How Landlords Reject Tenants," in Chapter 1, for information on how landlords may legally use income as a selection criterion.)

How to Fight Back

If you believe that a landlord has unlawfully discriminated against you, you don't just have to take it or move on. You can try to work things out with the landlord, or you can take advantage of the powerful antidiscrimination laws discussed earlier.

Your options (discussed in detail below) include:

- trying to negotiate an acceptable settlement with the landlord, possibly with the help of a neutral mediator
- filing a complaint with a federal, state, or local government fair housing agency, or
- filing a lawsuit in federal or state court.

Any of these strategies may force the landlord to do one or more of the following:

- Rent you a particular unit.
- Pay you "actual" or "compensatory" damages. This amount covers your trouble in finding another rental, plus any additional rent you had to pay to rent elsewhere. In addition, you are entitled to money for any humiliation or emotional distress—if the landlord's conduct was truly awful, this amount can be substantial.
- Pay you punitive damages—extra money as punishment for especially outrageous, intentional discrimination. It is not uncommon for juries to make large awards—$25,000 and up—if a landlord has persistently and obnoxiously violated fair housing laws.
- Pay your attorneys' fees (if you hired an attorney to file a lawsuit).
- Pay a penalty to the federal government. The maximum penalty under the federal Fair Housing Acts is $19,787 for a first violation and $98,935 for a third violation within seven years. Many states have comparable penalties.

Picking the Strategy That Suits Your Goals

Before you can make an intelligent decision about what strategy to pursue, you need to sit down and ask yourself what you're trying to achieve.

If you simply want the offensive or unfair behavior to stop, and aren't interested in seeking compensation for humiliation, inconvenience, or added expense, you won't want to file a complaint or lawsuit right away. For example, if you're an established tenant, you may want a quick resolution of your own beef with the landlord, and be less interested in money damages. A frank discussion with the landlord, perhaps in the company of a mediator or other neutral third party, may work better than a frontal legal assault. Many a landlord will listen up quite quickly if you explain, for example, how an occupancy policy discriminates against families. With luck (and the specter of a lawsuit), the landlord may make amends. And if informal techniques don't work, you can still sue or complain to a government agency.

If, on the other hand, you see the incident as part of a bigger issue that ought to be settled for the sake of others to come, you may not want to broker your own separate peace. If you reach an informal resolution of your discrimination claim, you may be left with the disquieting thought that the same illegal behavior will simply be practiced on the next, unwitting applicant or tenant. Sexual harassment, in particular, is not likely to end as the result of one person's courageous confrontation.

Lawsuits and agency complaints, however, are adversarial and drawn-out procedures. As anyone who has been involved in a court case will tell you, it is no picnic—even if you win. If you have a strong case and can get a quick court order from a judge, your experience will be mercifully short. Or, if your facts are compelling and your lawyer good, you may be able to settle for a sizable amount of money without going to trial.

Not every case, however, proceeds so easily. If the landlord or his insurance company digs in their heels, it may take months, even years; in the meantime, the lawsuit may come to feel like an albatross around your neck. For example, you will need to be available for depositions (long, drawn-out sessions with the other side's lawyers in which you are questioned under oath) and court dates that are set without much, if any, consideration for your personal or business schedule. As the court or hearing day approaches, your stomach will be in knots and your mind consumed by the battle to come. Many litigants, including the successful ones, come out of the experience vowing never again to go near a lawyer or a courthouse if they can possibly avoid it.

Another important downside of filing a fair housing complaint or lawsuit is that it may hurt your chances of renting later. Future background checks done by prospective landlords will probably reveal the fact that you filed a discrimination complaint. In spite of the existence of some legal protections against direct landlord retaliation (see Chapter 15), the reality is that you have no idea how this information will be used. It would be an unusual landlord indeed who would consider a lawsuit against a former landlord as a mark in your favor, even if your suit was totally justified.

Before making a final decision as to which path to take, ask for the opinion of a trusted and reasonable friend. Discrimination can be a highly emotional subject, and it's always a good idea to seek the counsel of someone who is not involved.

Special Issues in Sexual Harassment Cases

Sexual harassment cases are handled the same way as are other fair housing claims. But because of their special psychological and legal aspects, these cases involve several additional considerations.

As with other kinds of housing discrimination cases, you can directly confront the harasser or seek help from HUD (or a state fair housing agency) or a lawyer. Generally, annoying but not outrageous behavior merits an informal response, but serious, unbearable harassment needs the resources of professionals and courts. Is the behavior threatening? Or does it amount to the social ineptitude of one person? It is usually helpful to share your experience with a wise friend and ask for a candid evaluation of your perceptions.

If you conclude that the landlord's or manager's behavior warrants a confrontation, demand that it stop. Do so in writing or, at least, follow up your conversation with a written demand. Surprisingly often—some experts say up to 90% of the time—this works, especially in cases where the behavior is fairly low level, such as comments about your appearance, tacky photos on the apartment manager's bulletin board, or off-color jokes. Repeat your demands if necessary.

If the offensive behavior continues in spite of your oral and written requests that it stop, you'll need to consider your next step. In general, you have three options:

Stay put and hope for the best. It's not a good idea to choose this option unless you simply cannot move or file a complaint. Many hard-core harassers escalate their behavior over time.

Break the lease and move out. The landlord has a legal responsibility to make sure you have the undisturbed, quiet enjoyment of your leased home. If a court decides that a landlord has not met this responsibility, the tenant is excused from the lease.

What this amounts to in the context of sexual harassment is that, if the landlord, manager, or employee is harassing you and interfering with your ability to enjoy your tenancy, you may be able to point to this as a justification for breaking the lease. But the harassment must be serious and persistent in order for this strategy to work, and if your landlord challenges your decision to move without giving proper notice, you must be prepared to produce convincing evidence—for example, copies of your written demands that the behavior stop and, if possible, testimony from other tenants who have experienced similar mistreatment.

File a fair housing claim or lawsuit. In general, consider this option only if you can show clearly that the advances were unwanted, rebuffed, repeated, and fairly serious; that you lost no time in confronting the harasser and, when repeated requests were unheeded, you promptly filed a complaint. Filing a sexual harassment complaint is almost sure to be a painful experience, especially if you alone have endured the mistreatment. The other side will probably base much of its defense on trying to discredit you.

To prove a claim of sexual harassment, you must usually show that the behavior was *unwanted*. This can be hard to do, since it's usually a matter of your word ("I told him to stop and he persisted") against the harasser's ("She was just playing hard to get"). To help your lawyer or HUD investigator establish your case, you should:

- **Collect evidence.** Keep any offensive cards, notices, or photographs; photograph evidence (such as off-color jokes or cartoons posted on bulletin boards) that you cannot seize.
- **Keep a detailed journal.** Keep a detailed journal of every offensive incident. Include the names of everyone involved, dates, times, and locations. If your case goes to court, the contents of your journal may be admitted to substantiate your testimony; in any event, it will be an invaluable aid to the lawyer or investigator preparing your case.
- **Talk with other tenants.** If your story is echoed by other women, it's harder for the harasser to claim that you are lying or unreasonably interpreting his ardent but innocent interest. Talk to other tenants and find out whether others are in the same boat. (Chapter 19 discusses ways for tenants to act together effectively.)
- **Talk with friends.** Promptly sharing your experience with trusted friends serves two purposes: First, it helps you sort out your emotions and relieves the burden of keeping an upsetting secret. Second, it creates potentially valuable witnesses who can testify that you were angry or upset. It will also preclude a harasser's inevitable argument that, had you been truly offended, you would have turned to a friend for solace and advice.

Negotiating With the Landlord

If the landlord's insurance company or lawyer realizes you have complained (or are about to do so) to a fair housing agency or are poised to file a lawsuit, they may offer to settle. Be wary of dealing with these professional types without the presence of a neutral third party—a mediator, for example. Chapter 19 explains the mediation process in detail, and gives you information on locating and working with a mediator.

During negotiations, you might be offered $5,000 to settle a sexual harassment or race-based discrimination claim. If you think that figure is too low, you may be tempted to go shopping for a lawyer in hopes of getting more money. Fine, but remember, once the lawyer's fee and pretrial expenses are figured in, you'll have to get quite a bit more in order to come out ahead.

EXAMPLE: Your landlord offers you $5,000 to settle your discrimination claim. Thinking that you can get more, you hire a lawyer, agreeing to an attorney's fee of one-third of your settlement or jury verdict plus court costs. Assuming costs amount to $1,500, this means you'll have to recover almost $10,000 in order to actually receive $5,000—what you were offered in the first place. If you end up getting only a couple of thousand dollars more with a lawyer than without, you'll recover less than you were originally offered.

How Strong Is Your Case?

If you've thought it through and decided you do want to file a complaint with a fair housing agency or sue the landlord, you need to evaluate the strength of your case and the chances of your success. How serious was the discrimination, and how convincing is your proof?

Severity of the Illegal Act

The more serious the harm you suffered, the more likely you are to win. For example, if you are a family of four and encounter a landlord who clearly uses occupancy standards to discriminate against families with children, an investigator at the local HUD office may be quite interested in your case. The key issue—being able to rent as a family—is extremely important. Less serious acts of discrimination might be better addressed in a meeting with the landlord.

Be realistic in your assessment of the harm. Remember, your fate will depend on how a judge, jury, or insurance adjuster reacts to the landlord's behavior. For example, when a manager screams racial epithets at minority tenants, it's a big case in anyone's book; if he puts all families with kids in the back of the building, it's less so.

Also try to determine whether the act was part of a pattern. Landlords who repeatedly discriminate against applicants and tenants are of far greater interest to enforcement agencies than those who commit an isolated wrong. Judges and juries, too, are more prone to punish inveterate bigots than first-timers.

Intentional vs. Unintentional Discrimination

Housing discrimination comes in two forms:
- intentional, such as a statement that the owner doesn't rent to African Americans, and
- unintentional, such as a policy that lets only two people occupy a two-bedroom flat. This indirectly discriminates against families, even if the landlord's genuine reason is to limit noise and congestion.

Even though the law bans both kinds of discrimination, landlords who practice intentional discrimination are, in general, far more vulnerable to a fair housing charge. Indirect discrimination cases often must be proved by argument and statistics—you must show that the landlord's behavior or policy tends to hurt a protected group more than tenants in general. Also, intentional discrimination carries with it the possibility of punitive damages, which makes the case more attractive to a private attorney and often pressures landlords into settling.

Coming Up With Proof

However right you may be, to win in an administrative hearing or in court you'll have to prove it. If you're lucky, you can use the landlord's own words—like a printed ad that asks for "mature adults only"—as proof. But it's just as likely that there will be no hard proof of discrimination, and that your case will come down to your word against the landlord's.

For example, consider the landlord who tells you during the application process, when no one else is present, that he doesn't rent to single women because he is afraid of his liability if a woman is assaulted on his property. He can be expected to deny having made that statement. In this situation, your case would be greatly strengthened if you could find other women with decent credit and employment records who had also been turned down by this landlord.

How Landlords Get Caught

Landlords who turn away prospective tenants on the basis of race, ethnic background, or other group characteristics don't come out and admit what they're doing. But especially if they own many rental units, their illegal practices often become known to private fair housing advocacy groups (sometimes known as "fair housing councils") or HUD investigators, who hear repeated complaints.

Commonly, a person who's a member of a racial minority or other protected group is told that no rentals are available, or that his income and credit history aren't good enough. If this person suspects that he isn't being told the truth, he contacts a private fair housing group or HUD. Both groups are adept at uncovering this discriminatory practice by having people called "testers" apply to the same landlord. Typically, a white tester applies for the same housing, listing credit and income information that is similar—or sometimes not even as good—as that given by the minority applicant. A landlord who offers to rent to a white tester, after having rejected the minority applicant with the same or better qualifications, is very likely to become the subject of a fair housing complaint or lawsuit.

Landlords are also sometimes caught by amateur testers. For example, if you are an African American and think that you have been treated differently only because of your race, there is nothing to stop you from asking friends who are not African American to apply for the same vacancy. Be sure that your "testers" have background and credit histories that are similar to yours. If they are offered the apartment, it's strong evidence that you were rejected because of your race.

Complaining to a Fair Housing Agency

You may file a discrimination complaint with HUD (if you believe a federal law has been violated) by phone (800-669-9777), mail, or on the HUD website (see Fair Housing/Equal Opportunity under Program Offices on www.hud.gov). You can also file a complaint with a state antidiscrimination agency (if your state's antidiscrimination law has been violated), and in some places also with a local fair housing agency. State and local fair housing agencies are listed on the HUD website at www.hud.gov (check the tab "State Info" and then click "Get Rental Help" for your state). You can also get information by calling HUD's Housing Discrimination hotline at 800-669-9777. A phone call to the state or regional federal agency should provide you with the complaint-filing procedure.

How It Works

A federal HUD complaint must be filed within one year of the alleged violation; state statutes and local ordinances may set shorter deadlines. The complaint form for HUD is short, simple, and easily completed without the help of a lawyer. (In fact, you can file the complaint online, at www.hud.gov (search for "housing discrimination complaint")). If the complaint is filed with HUD, the agency should (but doesn't always) conduct an investigation within 180 days. The response time of state housing agencies varies.

After HUD investigates (and this is true of most state agencies as well), it will decide whether to dismiss your complaint or take it further. If the agency proceeds with your complaint, they'll attempt to produce a conciliation agreement (compromise) between you and the landlord. For example, you might agree to drop your complaint in exchange for a sum of money and the landlord's written promise to rent you an apartment or, if you're a current tenant, to stop discriminatory policies.

If conciliation is unsuccessful, the fair housing agency will hold an administrative hearing, which is like a trial without a jury, to determine whether discrimination has occurred. If the administrative law judge decides there was a fair housing violation, he or she will order the landlord to pay you money damages, rent you the unit you were denied, or take other appropriate action.

State or Federal Fair Housing Agency: Which Is Better?

If the fair housing violation you've encountered involves both federal and state law, you'll have a choice as to which enforcement agency to approach. Some points to consider are:

- **Your time frame.** HUD cases are typically long, drawn-out affairs—some have dragged on for years. If you want a court order that a landlord offer you a particular rental, you probably won't get quick action from HUD, but you could receive money damages later. Some states handle their cases more quickly. Call your state's fair housing agency and ask how long it takes to resolve a typical case.

- **What you must prove.** It may be tougher to prove your case under one law than another. For example, the federal Fair Housing Acts do not require you to prove that the landlord acted intentionally, but some state laws (California's Unruh Act, for one) do. It may be wise to talk to a fair housing group or lawyer to compare the available laws.

- **What you may win.** Some state statutes put a cap on money damages, both compensatory and punitive; federal law does not. If your case is serious, you may give up a substantial amount of money by choosing a state agency.

- **Your state's reputation for protection of tenant rights.** A state fair housing agency will mirror the general attitude of the state toward tenants' rights. If you live in California, Massachusetts, or New York, for example, you can expect more protection than if you live in a hands-off state such as Alabama. If you aren't familiar with your state's approach to housing discrimination law, you'll have to do a bit of homework, such as going to the public library and asking the reference librarian to guide you to helpful articles or resources. The same questions may be asked of a librarian in your local law library. (See Chapter 20 for information on doing legal research.)

Filing a Lawsuit in Federal or State Court

If you have experienced clear and outrageous discrimination, going directly to court may be quicker and more rewarding than going to a government agency. You'll need the help of an experienced lawyer if you choose this route. With her help, you may be able to force the landlord to rent you the premises and to pay you money damages.

You may sue in federal court or state court even if you have filed a complaint with a fair housing agency (deciding whether to do both is one of the reasons you'll need to hire a good lawyer). The exceptions to this rule are if you have signed a conciliation agreement, or if a formal HUD administrative hearing has already begun. If you file in federal court, you must do so within two years of the alleged violation.

How It Works

Your attorney may decide to file papers asking the court for an expedited hearing (often within a few days), with the hope that a judge will find that the landlord's actions or policies are discriminatory and order the landlord to cease them immediately. These orders are called "temporary restraining orders" (TROs) or sometimes "preliminary injunctions." They are granted only if you convince the judge that:

- You have a good chance of winning the case (that is, the landlord really did illegally discriminate).
- You will suffer irreparable harm if immediate relief isn't granted.

In theory, the TRO remains in place until a more formal hearing is held. In practice, when discrimination is clear enough for a judge to issue a TRO, normally the parties settle out of court. A typical settlement might involve the tenant getting the rental unit plus attorney fees, plus money damages—which, depending on the severity of the discrimination, might be $2,000 to $20,000 or more.

Hiring a Lawyer

Finding a lawyer to represent you in a federal or state lawsuit of this kind may be tough. In the past, legal aid attorneys, hired by government-financed law clinics, often handled discrimination cases for people with low incomes, but federal cutbacks have greatly reduced the availability of legal aid services. As a result, you will probably need to work with a private attorney. (Chapter 20 offers tips on how to find and work with a lawyer.)

If you have a strong case, an attorney may take it "on contingency." This means you pay nothing up front but agree to give the attorney a percentage, usually 20% to 40%, of whatever you win or agree to in a settlement. But the lawyer is reimbursed for the costs of filing the lawsuit and other expenses, such as those for depositions, investigators, and expert witnesses, before the award is divided and distributed.

An attorney who is not confident your case is a winner will require an up-front retainer of at least several thousand dollars, to cover the costs of preparing the legal papers and filing the suit. When the case is over, the lawyer will return to you any amount that was not needed for costs and fees. If you have won, the whole award is divided according to your contingency fee agreement (since you've already paid for expenses). If the case settles or ends in your favor, you may also be awarded court costs, attorneys' fees, and damages, but you can't count on it.

As explained above, if you've gotten a reasonable settlement offer from a landlord, your lawyer needs to win considerably more for you in order for you to come out ahead. To ensure that a lawyer doesn't end up actually costing you money, one strategy is to insist on paying a percentage of only the portion of any award or settlement that exceeds the amount you were already offered. If the lawyer balks at this, it's probably because she believes that the case isn't worth much more than your original offer. On the other hand, a lawyer who thinks that the case is really worth a lot more (for example, $25,000 to $50,000) will be pleased to base her fee on only a percentage of any recovery over $5,000.

CAUTION

If your lease or rental agreement has an "attorneys' fees" clause, it may not apply to a discrimination lawsuit. Typically, these clauses, which require the loser to pay the winner's attorneys' fees in a lawsuit between the landlord and tenant, apply only when the lawsuit is over a lease clause. For example, if you don't pay the rent and your landlord evicts you, the clause will apply, because paying rent is part of the lease. But if your landlord's discriminatory behavior does not involve a lease term—you sue for sexual harassment, for example—the fees clause won't apply.

Who Gets Sued or Targeted in a Complaint

Landlords and their employees aren't the only targets of fair housing enforcement. Newspapers that publish discriminatory ads are also covered by the federal fair housing rules, and many have been sued or named by fair housing enforcement agencies for ads like "quiet and mature neighborhood" and "Tenant wanted: Christian handyman." Publishers are especially attractive targets, since they usually have hefty insurance policies that can pay a settlement or court judgment. Online publishers are also covered by fair housing laws, and can be sued for posting discriminatory ads.

Management companies hired by landlords to oversee their rental properties may also be sued. Frequently, it's the company's manager who commits the discriminatory act—for example, by improperly screening tenants or setting discriminatory policies. Usually the company is every bit as liable as if the owner himself had done the deed; sometimes, an administrative judge or jury decides that both owner and management company are responsible. Large management companies that handle hundreds of rentals are often more solvent (have "deeper pockets") than the small-fry landlords they represent.

Inspecting the Rental Unit and Moving In

How to Inspect the Rental Unit 108

   Filling Out a Landlord-Tenant Checklist 108

   Signing the Checklist 114

Photographing the Rental Unit 114

How to Handle Problems 114

   Serious Problems 114

   Nonessential Repairs or Improvements 115

Clarifying Important Terms of the Tenancy 115

Organizing Your Rental Records 116

Using Email or Text Messages for Notice or a Letter of Understanding 116

Legal disputes between tenants and landlords have gained a reputation for being almost as emotional as divorce court battles. One of the most common disputes doesn't even occur until your relationship with the landlord is over. Of course, we refer to the problem that occurs when your landlord keeps all or part of your security deposit, claiming you left the place filthy or damaged it—for example, stained the rug, cracked the bathroom mirror, or left behind a major cockroach problem, a grease-covered stove, or a broken garbage disposal. Not surprisingly, you probably disagree for one of several reasons:

- the problems existed when you moved in
- the property damaged was so old that it wasn't worth anything in the first place or was impossible to clean, or
- the landlord is substantially exaggerating the cost of cleaning up or fixing damage that did occur.

You consider suing your landlord in small claims court for your full deposit, but decide against it because you have no way to prove your case.

This chapter shows how you can avoid such disputes by inspecting and photographing the rental unit *before* you move in. (Chapter 16 covers the subject of moving out and getting your security deposit returned in detail.) This chapter also discusses the value of keeping organized records and why it's best to send important notices and requests to the landlord in writing (rather than relying only on email communications).

How to Inspect the Rental Unit

When you first visited your new place, you got a general impression of the rental unit's condition. To avert all sorts of future arguments with your landlord, you need to go much further. It is absolutely essential that you check the place over for damage, dirt, mildew, and obvious wear and tear before moving in—ideally, before you've signed a lease or rental agreement or paid your first month's rent and deposit.

Filling Out a Landlord-Tenant Checklist

Filling in a Landlord-Tenant Checklist, inventorying the condition of the rental property at the beginning (and end) of the tenancy, is an excellent way to protect yourself when it comes time to getting your security deposit returned. It's also the law in some states, as you'll see on "State Security Deposit Rules" and "Required Landlord Disclosures" in Appendix A.

FORM
A sample Landlord-Tenant Checklist is shown below, and the Nolo website includes a downloadable copy. See Appendix B for the link to the forms in this book.

You and your landlord or manager should fill out the checklist together. If that's impossible, complete the form on your own. It's a good idea to take along a friend as a potential witness, who could testify in court if there's a dispute over security deposit deductions when you move out.

The checklist is in two parts. The first side covers the general condition of each room; the second covers furnishings.

You will be filling out the first column—*Condition on Arrival*—before you move in. The last two columns—*Condition on Departure* and *Estimated Cost of Repair/Replacement*—are for use when you move out and ideally the two of you inspect the unit again. At that time the checklist will document any damage to the rental unit during your tenancy, which the landlord may attempt to recoup by withholding all or part of your security deposit. (Chapter 16 discusses how to complete the Landlord-Tenant Checklist when you move out.)

General Condition of Rental Unit and Premises

In the *Condition on Arrival* column, you should note both serious problems, such as a broken heater or leaking roof, and minor flaws such as stained kitchen counters. Be sure to note areas or items (especially in the kitchen or bathroom) that are dirty, including mildew, pest, or rodent problems.

Landlord-Tenant Checklist

GENERAL CONDITION OF RENTAL UNIT AND PREMISES

572 Fourth St.	Apt. 11	Washington, D.C
Street Address	Unit No.	City

	Condition on Arrival	Condition on Departure	Estimated Cost of Repair/ Replacement
Living Room			
Floors & Floor Coverings	OK		
Drapes & Window Coverings	Miniblinds discolored		
Walls & Ceilings	OK		
Light Fixtures	OK		
Windows, Screens, & Doors	Window rattles		
Front Door & Locks	OK		
Smoke Detector	OK		
Fireplace	OK		
Other	N/A		
Other			
Kitchen			
Floors & Floor Coverings	Cigarette burn hole		
Walls & Ceilings	OK		
Light Fixtures	OK		
Cabinets	OK		
Counters	Stained		
Stove/Oven	Burners filthy (grease)		
Refrigerator	OK		
Dishwasher	N/A		
Garbage Disposal	OK		
Sink & Plumbing	OK		
Smoke Detector	OK		
Other			
Other			
Dining Room			
Floors & Floor Coverings	OK		
Walls & Ceilings	Crack in ceiling		
Light Fixtures	OK		
Windows, Screens, & Doors	OK		
Smoke Detector	OK		
Other			

	Condition on Arrival		Condition on Departure		Estimated Cost of Repair/ Replacement
Bathroom(s)	Bath #1	Bath #2	Bath #1	Bath #2	
Floors & Floor Coverings	OK				
Walls & Ceilings	Wallpaper peeling				
Windows, Screens, & Doors	OK				
Light Fixtures	OK				
Bathtub/Shower	Tub chipped				
Sink & Counters	OK				
Toilet	Base of toilet very dirty				
Other					
Other					
Bedroom(s)	Bdrm #1	Bdrm #2	Bdrm #3	Bdrm #1	Bdrm #2	Bdrm #3	
Floors & Floor Coverings	OK	OK					
Windows, Screens, & Doors	OK	OK					
Walls & Ceilings	OK	OK					
Light Fixtures	Dented	OK					
Smoke Detector	OK						
Other	Water stains in closet						
Other							
Other							
Other							
Other Areas						
Heating System	OK				
Air Conditioning	OK				
Lawn/Garden	OK				
Stairs and Hallway	OK				
Patio, Terrace, Deck, etc.	N/A				
Basement	OK				
Parking Area					
Other					
Other					
Other					
Other					
Other					

☐ Tenants acknowledge that all smoke detectors and fire extinguishers were tested in their presence and found to be in working order, and that the testing procedure was explained to them. Tenants agree to promptly notify Landlord in writing should any smoke detector appear to be malfunctioning or inoperable. Tenants will not refuse Landlord access for the purpose of inspecting, maintaining, repairing, or installing legally-required smoke detectors.

FURNISHED PROPERTY

	Condition on Arrival		Condition on Departure		Estimated Cost of Repair/ Replacement
Living Room					
Coffee Table	Two scratches on top				
End Tables	OK				
Lamps	OK				
Chairs	OK				
Sofa	OK				
Other					
Other					
Kitchen					
Broiler Pan	N/A				
Ice Trays	N/A				
Other					
Other					
Dining Room					
Chairs	OK				
Stools	N/A				
Table	Leg bent slightly				
Other					
Other					
Bathroom(s)	Bath #1	Bath #2	Bath #1	Bath #2	
Mirrors	OK				
Shower Curtain	Torn				
Hamper	N/A				
Other					
Bedroom(s)	Bdrm #1	Bdrm #2	Bdrm #3	Bdrm #1	Bdrm #2	Bdrm #3	
Beds (single)	OK	N/A					
Beds (double)	N/A	OK					
Chairs	OK	OK					
Chests	N/A	OK					
Dressing Tables	OK	OK					
Lamps	OK	OK					
Mirrors	OK	OK					
Night Tables	OK	N/A					

	Condition on Arrival	Condition on Departure	Estimated Cost of Repair/ Replacement
Other			
Other			
Other Areas			
Bookcases	N/A		
Desks	N/A		
Pictures	Hallway picture frame chipped		
Other			
Other			

Use this space to provide any additional explanation:

_____

_____

_____

_____

_____

_____

_____

_____

_____

_____

_____

_____

_____

Landlord-Tenant Checklist completed on moving in on _____ May 1, 20xx _____ and approved by:

Bernard Cohen _____ and *Maria Crouse* _____
Landlord/Manager   Tenant

                                                                          Sandra Martino _____
                                                                          Tenant

                                                                          _____
                                                                          Tenant

Landlord-Tenant Checklist completed on moving out on _____ and approved by:

_____ and _____
Landlord/Manager   Tenant

                                                                          _____
                                                                          Tenant

                                                                          _____
                                                                          Tenant

Mark "OK" next to items that are in satisfactory condition—basically, clean, safe, sanitary, and in good working order.

Make a note—as specific as possible—on items that are broken, stained, worn, grime-covered, scratched, leaking, smelly, dented, chipped, or simply not in the best condition. For example, instead of writing "stove dirty," state that the burners are covered with grease. Don't simply note that the refrigerator "needs fixing" if an ice maker doesn't work. It's just as easy to write "ice maker broken, should not be used." This way, the landlord can't claim you broke the ice maker and should pay for its repair or replacement.

RESOURCE

Home inspection resources. For helpful articles, search online for "how to inspect an apartment."

Furnishings

The second part of the checklist covers furnishings, such as lamps or shower curtains. Obviously, you can simply mark "Not Applicable" or "N/A" in most of these boxes if your unit is not furnished.

If your rental property has rooms or furnishings not listed on the checklist, note them in "Other Areas" or cross out something that you don't have

---

What to Look For

Structure
- holes or cracks in floors, walls, or ceiling
- dark round spots on the ceiling or dark streaks on the walls, indicating water leaks or mold

Plumbing
- toilet takes too long to flush or leaks on the floor
- tap water is discolored
- low water pressure (scalding hot water in the shower when you flush the toilet)
- water drains slowly in sinks, tubs, and showers
- mold stains on walls, ceilings

Heating
- no heat or inadequate or dangerous heating facilities

Light and Ventilation
- poor ventilation in bathrooms (no outside window or fan)
- inadequate natural light through windows
- poor lighting in hallways, stairs, entranceways, or parking areas

Wiring and Electricity
- loose or exposed wiring
- insufficient outlets or light fixtures

Insects, Vermin, and Rodents
- rodent trails or excrement
- evidence of cockroaches in cupboards, in closets, or behind appliances
- bedbugs (under carpets, within light fixtures)

Security
- flimsy or inadequate locks on doors and windows
- windows don't open and close easily (painted or nailed shut)

Fire Safety
- smoke detectors absent or not working
- fire extinguishers absent or not working
- exits leading to street or hallway unsafe or full of litter
- combustible materials in storage rooms, garages, or basements

Trash and Garbage Receptacles
- inadequate garbage and trash storage and removal

Other Issues
Depending on where you live, you may note other problems—for example, earthquake and flooding hazards are important issues in some parts of the country.

and write in the changes. If you are renting a large house or apartment or providing many furnishings, you may want to attach a separate sheet. Just make a separate list for additional items and staple it to the checklist.

Test Smoke Detectors and Fire Extinguishers

State and local laws often require landlords to provide fire extinguishers and smoke detectors in rental units.

As part of your move-in procedures, make sure the landlord tests all smoke detectors and fire extinguishers in your presence and shows them to be in good working order. Be sure you understand how to:

- test the fire extinguisher and smoke detector
- recognize the signs of a failing detector—for example, a beeping noise, and
- replace the smoke detector battery.

Do not disable a smoke detector. Not only is it foolish—it could expose you to liability if a fire causes damage that could have been prevented had there been a working detector. Consider, for example, Texas Prop. Code Section 92.211, which will also impose a civil fine for disabling a detector even if there is no fire.

The box on the bottom of the second page of the checklist acknowledges that you tested the smoke detector and fire extinguisher in the landlord's presence and found them to be in working order.

CAUTION

Don't forget carbon monoxide detectors. Some states, such as California, require these, so be sure to check them as well as smoke detectors and fire extinguishers.

Signing the Checklist

After you and your landlord agree on all of the particulars on the rental unit, you each should sign and date every page of the checklist, including any attachments. The landlord will probably keep the original and give you a copy. If you filled out the checklist on your own, make sure the landlord reviews your comments, notes any disagreement, and returns a copy to you promptly. You should ask the landlord to make the checklist part of your lease or rental agreement, as explained in Chapter 2.

A savvy landlord will update the checklist after making repairs or replacing, adding, or removing items after you move in. You should both initial and date any changes.

Photographing the Rental Unit

Taking photos of the unit before you move in is another excellent way to avoid disputes over your responsibility for damage and dirt. In addition to the checklist, you'll be able to compare "before" and "after" pictures when you leave. This should help refresh your landlord's memory, and if you end up in small claims court fighting over the security deposit, documenting your point of view with photos or videos will be invaluable.

Whether you take a photo with your phone or use a separate camera, print out two sets of the photos as soon as possible. Give one set to your landlord. Each of you should date and sign both sets of photos. If you make a video, clearly state the time and date when the video was made and send the landlord a copy.

You should repeat this process when you leave. Chapter 16 discusses moving out.

How to Handle Problems

If you discover any problems, try to get your new landlord to fix them before you move in.

Serious Problems

The landlord must fix certain defects—such as a broken heater or leaking roof—under state and local housing codes. (Chapter 8 discusses landlords' repair and maintenance responsibilities.) A landlord who does not immediately agree to fix serious problems probably isn't taking the obligation to repair very seriously. You're probably best off refusing to rent the place and reporting the landlord to your local housing or building inspector.

If the landlord promises to make repairs or alterations after you move in, be careful. First, ask other tenants how good the landlord is at keeping promises. Second, get the promises in writing and signed, ideally as part of the lease or rental agreement (see Chapter 2). Your written agreement should specify the:

- exact repair or alteration—for example, installation of a deadbolt lock
- deadline by which repairs will be made, and
- consequence for the landlord's failure to complete repairs by the promised date—for example, a certain reduction in your rent.

Some samples are shown below.

Sample Agreements Regarding Repairs

Serious Problem:

> Landlord will clear the drains and fix the leaking toilet by February 28, the day before the Tenant's rental agreement begins. If Landlord fails to fix these plumbing problems by March 1, Tenant may withhold rent until Landlord fixes the problem.

Nonessential Repair or Improvement:

> Landlord will supply up to $250 worth of "Color Pro" paint and painting supplies. Tenant will paint the living room, hall, and two bedrooms, using off-white latex paint on the walls and ceiling and water-based enamel paint on all wood surfaces (doors and trim). Paint and supplies will be picked up by Tenant from ABC Hardware and billed to Landlord.

Nonessential Repairs or Improvements

If repairs are not essential—such as a new coat of paint or more electrical outlets in the study—try to work something out.

Many landlords are open to making reasonable improvements and alterations, especially in higher-rent areas where there are lots of places for rent and not too many people looking, or if you've impressed the landlord as a good, responsible tenant.

You might offer to pay part of the expense of nonessential repairs or improvements, such as upgrading the electrical system to accommodate your electronic equipment or fixing the backyard fence so that your dog can't get out. If you want the apartment painted, offer to do the work if the landlord buys the paint. Chapter 10 provides advice on how to convince the landlord to improve or alter the premises, and how to keep your monetary outlay to a minimum.

If the landlord seems completely unreasonable, or really put out simply by your request, beware. This doesn't sound like a good way to start the tenancy.

> **TIP**
> **If you are a disabled person seeking modification of your living space to meet your needs, your landlord will not be able to legally stand in your way.** Under the federal Fair Housing Amendments Act of 1988, you are entitled to make reasonable modifications to your rental to make it safe and enjoyable. Chapter 5 explains how to go about obtaining permission to perform necessary modifications.

Clarifying Important Terms of the Tenancy

A good lease or rental agreement should cover the basic issues of your tenancy, including rent, deposits, rent increases, and sublets. (Chapter 2 discusses leases and rental agreements.)

If your landlord does little more than sign a tersely worded lease or rental agreement and hand you a key, make sure you have all necessary information before you move in. For example, be sure you know:

- the landlord or manager's phone numbers (day and night) and emails

- how to report maintenance and repair problems
- any rules for the use of grounds, garage, and storage space
- location of garbage cans, recycling programs, and trash pickup days, and
- other issues that affect the particular rental, such as pool hours or use of a laundry room.

Organizing Your Rental Records

Establishing a simple system to record all correspondence with your landlord, such as repair requests, will provide a valuable paper trail should disputes later develop—for example, regarding your landlord's failure to make necessary repairs. Without good records, the outcome of a dispute may come down to your word against your landlord's, always a precarious situation.

To get started right, set up a file folder for the following documents:

- a copy of your rental application, references, and credit report (keeping these will also save you some work next time you move)
- your copy of the signed lease or rental agreement
- any building rules and regulations or move-in letter from the landlord
- deposit information, including the amount and (if known) the location and interest rate terms of your deposit (Chapter 4 discusses basic security deposit rules), and
- Landlord-Tenant Checklist and photos or video taken at move-in.

After you move in, add these documents to your file:

- your landlord's written requests for entry (Chapter 11 discusses tenant privacy rights)
- rent increase notices
- records of your repair requests, including how and when they were handled (Chapters 8, 9, and 10 discuss repairs, maintenance, improvements, and alterations), and
- any other correspondence with your landlord, including copies of emails.

Using Email or Text Messages for Notice or a Letter of Understanding

You and your landlord are probably a lot more likely to send each other messages by email or text rather than by post—for example, if you're trying to schedule a time for the landlord to fix your heater. But will those electronic communications serve you as well as a mailed letter, if you need evidence that the message was received at the other end?

Suppose, for example, that you want to give notice of your intention to end your month-to-month tenancy, and do so by sending an email that's 30 days in advance of your planned departure. Or, say you need to send your landlord a request for repairs (this is the first, necessary step before you can use a remedy like repair-and-deduct, if the landlord fails to take action). If you end up in a legal dispute and your landlord challenges you in court, saying that you never told him about your decision to leave or alerted him to the repair problem, you'll need confirmation that the emails or text messages were received.

> ## CAUTION
> **Read the statute (or the lease) for notice instructions!** Now and then, a statute will tell you exactly how to deliver notices and demands to the other party. As email and text communications become more and more common, lawmakers will begin to incorporate specifications for email and text communication in their laws. And lawyers will draft leases with notice clauses that take email and text into account. For now, however, you'll mostly see the generic requirement that demands and notices be delivered "in writing," which doesn't help very much.

Two laws confirm the acceptability of electronic notices: "UETA" (the Uniform Electronic Transactions Act), adopted in some form by 47 states and the District of Columbia, and "ESIGN" (Electronic Signatures in Global and National Commerce Act), a federal law. Unless some other law prohibits it, UETA and ESIGN permit the use of electronic signatures and electronic notices.

Put another way, under both of these laws, a legal notice cannot be denied admission in court simply because it is electronic (and not on paper).

Three states (Illinois, New York, and Washington) have not adopted the UETA, but have statutes pertaining to electronic transactions. Some sophisticated services such as RPost (www.rpost.com) allow you to send tamper-proof attachments and electronic signatures, and offer reasonably priced individual plans; these may be worth it to a tenant who sends critical emails to their landlord a few times per month.

 **CAUTION**
Text messages are hard to track, and evidence of receipt isn't available short of complex searches through users' accounts. Rarely would a landlord/tenant dispute support the expense of such a search. If you're worried about being able to prove the receipt of a text, you'd be best served to also print it and mail it return receipt requested … the old-fashioned way. Consider doing the same for your emails (if you don't use a service such as RPost).

Why It's Difficult to Prove That Your Landlord Received Your Email

You may think that you'll be able to produce evidence of the landlord's receipt of your emails, by using your computer's stored files or receipt requests. Think again. Here are some common myths about how to prove that email messages were delivered.

The email didn't return to you. Emails that cannot be delivered to an account often come back with an error message. If you don't receive an error message, you might feel confident that the email was delivered. But how can you prove it? The best you can do is to print the email and hope that it shows that there was no response like "Re: Undelivered email" or something similar. There's a problem with this approach, however. Because of the large volume of spam, many email servers will send undeliverable email to one big account, rather than generating individual "cannot deliver" replies. So the absence of a "cannot deliver" email may not prove that the message was delivered to your landlord. In short, archived email shows what you sent (though you can easily alter the text after you've sent it), but no legal proof that the original email was received by the other side.

Printed email. Printing your sent message provides no proof that the other side got it. Printed emails can easily be challenged for authenticity (the text can be altered after the message was sent). For this reason, it won't be admitted in court.

A delivery confirmation request. This method asks the recipient to send back a message (just a click) that he got the email. But here, too, problems abound: The recipient can simply decide not to send the message, and many large email servers (like Yahoo and Hotmail) don't support these features.

Request read receipt. This is a feature on most email systems, and it simply asks the user who receives the message to send you a receipt. Again, it's dependent on the user agreeing to send the receipt. A landlord who doesn't want to give you proof of the date of your repair request is not likely to send a receipt.

Hidden scripts. These bits of software are embedded in your email, and secretly trigger a notification when the message is read. But most current email programs will detect the presence of the script, and warn you that the message you're about to open contains possibly unsafe content. Most email users will not open those emails.

Roommates, Guests, and Airbnb

Renting a Place With Others..120

    If One Roommate Doesn't Pay Rent...121

    If One Roommate Violates the Lease or Rental Agreement...121

    Agreements—and Disagreements—Among Roommates..122

    Domestic Violence Situations...125

    If You Fear Violence...126

    When a Roommate Leaves...127

Adding a New Roommate...129

    Getting the Landlord's Approval..129

    Adding a Roommate to the Lease or Rental Agreement..130

    More Roommates, More Rent..130

    Security Deposit Increases..130

Guests...131

Tenant Rights to Use Airbnb and Similar Vacation Rental Services............................131

    Read Your Lease or Rental Agreement..131

    Work Something Out With Your Landlord..131

    Research Your Local Zoning or Land Use Laws...132

Taking In a Roomer..132

Many tenants decide to share a home rather than live alone. For some, living with roommates not only saves money but is also a social boon. Whatever the reasons you have roommates, one thing is likely: The makeup of your living group will change over time as jobs, schooling, friendships, love, and even illness or death play their part in rearranging the names on your mailbox. Unfortunately, most landlords are not as flexible as you might wish when it comes to adding new roommates or letting one out of a lease.

This chapter discusses key issues about sharing rental housing, such as:

- your legal obligations and responsibilities with respect to your roommate
- moving in a roommate and what to do if your landlord objects
- what to do if your roommate becomes nasty or won't pay the rent
- your rights to bring in paying "guests" through Airbnb and similar services, and
- whether or not you can rent space to a roomer.

 RELATED TOPIC
Also covered in this book:

- How to find a compatible roommate: Chapter 1.
- Lease or rental agreement limits on number of occupants and restrictions on overnight guests, sublets, and assignments: Chapter 2.
- Your right to sublet your apartment for a while, and what happens if your landlord objects: Chapter 15.
- Whether you can get someone else to take over the rest of your lease and, if you do, whether you are off the financial hook: Chapter 15.
- What happens if you break your lease and move out early: Chapter 15.
- Getting your security deposit back if you leave but your roommates stay: Chapter 16.

Renting a Place With Others

When two or more people all sign the same rental agreement or lease—or enter into the same oral rental agreement—they are cotenants and share the same legal rights and responsibilities. Most of the time, cotenants sign the rental document at the same time, when the tenancy begins for all of them. A person can become a cotenant later, too, by moving in when an original cotenant leaves, and either signing the existing lease or rental agreement or being accepted and treated as a full-fledged cotenant by the landlord.

With cotenants, there's a special twist. One cotenant's negative behavior—not paying the rent, for example—can affect everyone's tenancy. The sections below explain how this works.

Common Terms

Original tenant. The initial tenant (or tenants) who signed the lease or rental agreement. This is a shortcut term with no precise legal meaning.

Tenant. Someone who has signed a lease or a rental agreement, or whose residency—or rent payment—has been accepted by the landlord.

Cotenants. Two or more tenants who rent the same property under the same lease or rental agreement. Each is 100% responsible for carrying out the agreement (lawyers call this "joint and several liability"), including paying all the rent.

Roommates. Two or more people, usually unrelated, living under the same roof and sharing rent and expenses. Roommates are usually cotenants, but a roommate may be a subtenant of the original tenant. In other situations, a roommate may have the legal status of a long-term guest, with no formal legal relationship with the landlord.

Joint and several liability. This refers to the sharing of legal obligations by two or more people. When cotenants are "jointly and severally liable" for rent, it means each of them can be held responsible for paying the entire rent. You and your cotenants are jointly and severally liable for rent and other obligations—*even if your lease or rental agreement does not include this clause.* It applies to oral leases, too.

Roomer. A person who rents space in your home. If you are a tenant, the roomer is your subtenant, and you are her landlord.

If One Roommate Doesn't Pay Rent

Cotenants may decide to split the rent equally or unequally, depending on their own personal wishes. However, such agreements don't have any impact on the landlord. Each cotenant is independently liable to the landlord for all of the rent. Landlords often remind cotenants of this obligation by inserting into the lease a chunk of legalese that says that the tenants are "jointly and severally" liable for paying rent and adhering to terms of the agreement. (See "Common Terms," above.) If one tenant can't pay a share of the rent in a particular month, or simply moves out, the other tenant(s) must still pay the full rent.

> **EXAMPLE:** James and Helen sign a month-to-month rental agreement for an apartment rented by Blue Oak Properties, for $800 per month. James and Helen agree between themselves to each pay half of the rent. After three months, James moves out without notifying Helen or Blue Oak. Helen is legally obligated to pay Blue Oak all the rent until she legally ends the tenancy. (This usually requires 30 days' written notice.) If Helen can't pay the rent, Blue Oak may evict her.
>
> In the meantime, if she can prove the existence of her agreement with James, Helen could try to recover James's share of the rent by suing him in small claims court.
>
> If, instead of leaving, she gets a new roommate who pays half the rent, Helen can recover from James only the extra rent she had to pay before the new person moved in.

Landlords often insist on receiving one rent check for the entire rent—they don't want to be bothered with multiple checks from cotenants, even if each cotenant pays on time and the checks add up to the full rent. As long as you have been advised of this policy in the rental agreement or lease, it's legal for your landlord to impose it.

If One Roommate Violates the Lease or Rental Agreement

Although it is painful for an innocent tenant to hear, the landlord can, legally, hold all cotenants responsible for the negative actions of just one, and terminate everyone's tenancy with the appropriate notice. For example, two cotenants can be evicted if one of them seriously damages the property, moves in an extra roommate on the sly, keeps a dog in violation of a no-pets rule, or otherwise violates the lease or rental agreement.

> **EXAMPLE:** Dan and Mike were cotenants whose lease prohibited pets. Dan's friend Kate implored him to take Ralph, her cat, when she joined the Peace Corps. Mike didn't like the idea, but Dan won him over by promising that both he and Ralph would move if the landlord found out. To Mike's dismay, when the landlord discovered Ralph, he sent both Mike and Dan termination notices.

In practice, however, landlords sometimes ignore the legal rule that all tenants are equally liable for lease violations, and don't penalize a blameless one. If the nonoffending roommates pay the rent on time, do not damage the landlord's property, and can differentiate themselves from the bad apple in the landlord's eyes, the landlord will probably want to keep them.

If you want to remain after a cotenant gets the boot, you would do well to understand the landlord's principal concerns—to have good, stable tenants who pay the rent on time. If you can convince the landlord that throwing everyone out and starting over doesn't best serve those goals, the landlord may decide not to evict all of you. Of course, you will have to absorb the departed tenant's share of the rent for the time it takes to find an acceptable new cotenant. And, your landlord will need to approve any new cotenant. ("Adding a New Roommate," below, shows the best way to find a roommate who passes your landlord's muster.)

Unfortunately, if you can't handle the increased rent until you find a new tenant, or the landlord feels you can't be trusted to find a trustworthy one, the landlord is likely to evict all of you at the same time. It's far simpler and quicker than first evicting the troublemaker for the lease violation and then later ousting the rest of you when you fail to come up with the entire rent.

Agreements—and Disagreements— Among Roommates

Roommates make lots of informal agreements about splitting rent, occupying bedrooms, and sharing chores. Your landlord isn't bound by these agreements, and has no power to enforce them. For all sorts of reasons, roommate arrangements regularly go awry. If you have shared an apartment or house, you know about roommates who play the stereo too loud, never wash a dish, always pay their share of the rent late, have too many overnight guests, leave their gym clothes on the kitchen table, or otherwise drive you nuts. If the situation gets bad enough, you'll likely end up arguing with your roommates about who should leave.

Only Landlords Can Evict Tenants

As a general rule, you can't terminate your roommate's tenancy by filing an eviction action. (The situation is different if you rent to a subtenant; see "Taking In a Roomer," below.)

The exception involves rentals governed by the few rent control statutes, such as the one in San Francisco, that allow a landlord to designate a "master tenant"— usually a long-term tenant who was there first—to perform many of the functions of a landlord. Master tenants have the right to choose—as well as to evict— tenants. If your municipality is subject to rent control, find out whether the scheme includes a provision for a master tenant.

The more you can anticipate possible problems from the start, the better prepared you'll be to handle disputes that do arise. First, try to choose compatible housemates. (Follow our advice in Chapter 1.) Before you move in, sit down with your roommates and create your own agreement covering major issues, such as:

1. **Rent.** What is everyone's share? Who will write the rent check if the landlord requires only one check?

2. **Space.** Who will occupy which bedrooms? How will you divvy up the extra closet?

3. **Household chores.** Who's responsible for cleaning, and on what schedule?

4. **Food sharing.** Will you be sharing food, shopping, and cooking responsibilities? How will you split the costs and work?

5. **Noise.** When should stereos be turned off or down low?

6. **Overnight guests.** Is it okay for boyfriends/ girlfriends to stay over every night?

7. **Moving out.** If one of you decides to move, how much notice must be given? Must the departing tenant find an acceptable substitute?

It's best to put your understandings in writing. (See the sample roommate agreement, below.) Oral agreements are too easily forgotten or misinterpreted after the fact.

Be as specific as possible, especially on issues that are important to you. If dirty dishes in the sink drive you up the wall, write it down. If occasional guests are no problem, but you can't stand the thought of your roommate's (nonrent-paying) boyfriend hogging the bathroom every morning, make sure your agreement is clear on guests.

Most of this kind of agreement isn't legally binding—that is, a judge won't order a tenant to clean the bathroom. Judges will, however, enforce financial agreements, such as how rent is to be shared.

> **EXAMPLE:** Roommates Janet and Jacob orally agree that Jacob will get the larger bedroom and pay 60% of the rent, and Janet will pay 40%. Right after they move in, Jacob loses his job and is unable to pay his share. Janet pays the whole amount for two months, until finally she talks Jacob into moving. Six months later, after landing a good job, Jacob still hasn't paid Janet, who sues him in small claims court. Jacob admits in court that he owes Janet his share of two months' rent, but says there was never a deal to split it 60-40. The judge, faced with two

Sample Roommate Agreement

Alex Andrews, Brian Bates, and Charles Chew are cotenants at Apartment 2, 360 Capitol Avenue, Oakdale, Kentucky, under a year-long lease that expires on February 1, 20xx. They have all signed a lease with the landlord, Reuben Shaw, and have each paid $500 toward the security deposit of $1,500. Alex, Brian, and Charles all agree as follows:

1. **Rent.** The rent of $1,500 per month will be shared equally, at $500 per person. Alex will write a check for the total month's rent and take it to the manager's office on the first of each month (or the next day if the 1st falls on a holiday). Brian and Charles will pay their share to Alex on or before the due date.

2. **Bedrooms.** Alex and Brian will share the large bedroom with the adjacent deck; Charles will have the small bedroom.

3. **Food.** Each cotenant is responsible for his own food purchases.

4. **Cleaning.** Charles will clean his own room and Alex and Brian will clean theirs. The household chores for the rest of the apartment—living room, dining room, kitchen, and bathroom—will rotate, with each cotenant responsible for vacuuming, dusting, mopping, and bathroom maintenance on a weekly basis.

   Each cotenant will promptly clean up after himself in the kitchen. No one will leave dishes in the sink for more than 24 hours, and everyone will promptly clean up when asked.

5. **Utilities.** Everyone will pay an equal share of the electricity, gas, Internet, and cable bills. Alex will arrange for these services and will pay the bills. Within three days of receiving the bills, Charles and Brian will each pay Alex one-third of the total.

6. **Guests.** Because of the apartment's small size, each tenant agrees to have no more than one overnight guest at a time and to inform the others in advance, if possible. Each cotenant agrees to no more than four guests overnight in a month.

7. **Exam Periods.** During midterm and final exam periods, no cotenant will have overnight guests or parties.

8. **Violations of the Agreement.** The cotenants agree that repeated and serious violations of one or more of these understandings will be grounds for any two cotenants to ask the other to leave. If a cotenant is asked to leave, he will do so within two weeks, and will forfeit any outstanding prepaid rent.

9. **Leaving Before the Lease Ends.** If a cotenant wants to leave before the lease expires on February 1, 20xx, he will give as much notice as possible (and not less than one month) and diligently try to find a replacement tenant who is acceptable to the remaining cotenants and the landlord.

Sample Roommate Agreement (continued)

10. **Security Deposits.** The cotenant who leaves early (voluntarily or involuntarily) will get his share of the security deposit returned, minus costs of repairs, replacement, and cleaning attributable to the departing tenant, when and if an acceptable cotenant signs the lease and contributes his share to the security deposit. If an acceptable cotenant cannot be found, the departing tenant will not receive any portion of his share of the security deposit.

11. **Dispute Resolution.** If a dispute arises concerning this agreement or any aspect of the shared living situation, the cotenants will ask our town's Mediation Service for assistance before they terminate the cotenancy or initiate a lawsuit. This will involve all three tenants sitting down with a mediator in good faith to try to resolve the problems.

Alex Andrews
_____
Alex Andrews

February 1, 20xx
_____
Date

Brian Bates
_____
Brian Bates

Feb. 1, 20xx
_____
Date

Charles Chew
_____
Charles Chew

Feb. 1, 20xx
_____
Date

different stories and nothing in writing, decides to split the rental obligation 50-50.

If Janet and Jacob had shared the rental for some time and given separate rent checks to the landlord every month (Jacob paying 60% and Janet 40%), Janet would probably have been able to convince the judge of the 60-40 agreement by producing her string of canceled checks. Of course, a written and signed Roommate Agreement that reflected the 60-40 split would have won the case for Janet.

By far the greatest value of committing your understanding of cotenant rights and responsibilities to writing is that it forces you and your housemates to take your cotenancy responsibilities seriously. To underline this commitment, it's always wise to include a clause requiring cotenants to participate in mediation before one of you breaks the agreement by moving out or running off to court. Our sample roommate agreement, above, includes such a clause. Chapter 19 discusses how mediation works.

It is usually best not to involve your landlord in disputes among roommates. The reasons—both practical and legal—include the following:

- The landlord can't enforce any decisions among tenants. For example, short of continual—and, of course, illegal—monitoring of your living situation, how could a landlord make tenants share housecleaning?
- Any complaint you make about a cotenant is likely to be reciprocated, with the result that your landlord is likely to receive a negative picture of all of you. Especially if you have a month-to-month tenancy, your landlord may get tired of your constant complaining and decide to get rid of the whole bunch of you.

> **CAUTION**
> **Don't change the locks.** If a roommate dispute gets serious—especially if your cotenant hasn't paid the rent—you may be tempted to change the locks or ask the landlord to do so. Don't. A landlord cannot legally bar entry to a tenant without a court order. Similarly, if you unilaterally bar your roommate from the rental, you, too, risk legal liability if the locked-out roommate is forced to find shelter elsewhere and sues you for the cost of alternate housing. Finally, changing the locks without your landlord's permission is almost always prohibited in the lease, and gives your landlord a legal justification to evict all of you.

Domestic Violence Situations

Most states extend special protections to victims of domestic violence. (See "State Laws in Domestic Violence Situations," in Appendix A.) If you are dealing with domestic violence, take steps to protect your personal safety, and consider contacting local law enforcement or a battered women's shelter for help. Your state may have laws that will protect you from negative actions from your landlord, such as the following:

- **Antidiscrimination status and eviction protection.** Many states prohibit landlords from refusing to rent to applicants who have restraining orders, whether it's refusing to renew leases or terminating on the basis of domestic violence status alone. (Increasingly, however, states are allowing termination when the situation poses a threat to other tenants.)
- **Early termination rights.** Many states allow victims of domestic violence to terminate a lease and move without responsibility for the balance of the rent. Tenants must present evidence of domestic violence status, such as a police report (each state specifies the types of admissible evidence).
- **Confidentiality.** Some states prohibit landlords from disclosing to prospective landlords a former tenant's status as a victim of domestic violence.
- **Evicting the aggressor.** Some states allow a landlord to evict only the wrongdoer, leaving the lease intact for the victim.
- **Locks.** Most states require landlords to change the locks once an abuser has left.

In the absence of a state law giving victims of domestic violence early termination rights or other domestic violence protections, don't assume your landlord will say "No" to an early termination or other related request. First, because a blanket policy will usually affect female, not male, tenants, it can be attacked in court as indirectly discriminating on the basis of sex (several lawsuits brought in states without statutory protections have succeeded on this theory). Aside from the landlord's vulnerability to being sued, emphasize that it may be essential to your safety to allow you to quickly move. Finally, point out that the landlord's bottom line may benefit from allowing the tenancy to end immediately— what the landlord may lose in rent may pale in comparison with what its repair costs may be if the property is damaged, not to speak of the fallout from negative publicity if the situation escalates.

Although your state (and the federal law mentioned above) may give some special protections to domestic violence victims, these accommodations do not prohibit the landlord from terminating, if necessary, for nonpayment of rent. Unfortunately, all too often the abuser will leave the property but the remaining victim struggles to pay the rent. Landlords may legally terminate the tenancy of a domestic violence victim who falls behind in the rent, just as it would any tenant who hasn't paid.

If You Fear Violence

If you ever fear for your immediate physical safety (or that of one of your cotenants), or when serious law-breaking such as drug dealing is involved, call the police. Short of that, if you have a sound factual basis to believe that one of your roommates intends to harm you (he's purchased a gun or has repeatedly told others he's going to get you), communicate these fears to your landlord, who may begin proceedings to evict the aggressor. Your landlord will probably be motivated by self-interest as much as a desire to protect you. A landlord who fails to sensibly intervene where violence is clearly threatened may be successfully sued by the victim if the aggressor in fact carries through with the threat. (See a related discussion of assaults by one tenant against another tenant in Chapter 14.)

In the meantime, if you fear violence from a cotenant, consider taking the following precautions:

- **Get out of harm's way.** This may mean spending a few days with a friend or at a motel, but if you feel seriously threatened, the inconvenience and possible cost of removing yourself from danger will be well worth it. If continuing your cotenancy turns out to be impossible, taking a breather may give you a chance to plan your exit.
- **Contact the local police department, the court clerk's office, or a battered women's shelter for information on obtaining a temporary restraining order.** In most areas, it's fairly quick and easy to bring this type of problem before a judge, without needing to pay a lawyer. And if the judge decides that the situation merits it, he or she will issue an order forbidding the aggressor from coming near you. Temporary restraining orders (TROs)—and how to use them—are explained in Chapter 14.

RESOURCE
For information and referrals to local agencies, call the National Domestic Violence Hotline (www.thehotline.org) at 800-799-SAFE. This organization's website also includes links to state coalitions against domestic violence. Another useful resource is WomensLaw.org, which includes extensive information on state laws relevant to domestic violence, sexual assault, and stalking.

If you and other blameless cotenants want to stay, follow our suggestions for bringing in a substitute tenant as explained below in "Adding a New Roommate."

EXAMPLE: Andy and his roommate Bill turned out to be completely incompatible. Before long, arguments about housekeeping, regular guests, and late rent payments by Andy escalated to the point where Bill felt physically threatened.

Bill asked their landlord, Anita, to evict Andy. Andy responded by telling Anita that he had never threatened Bill, and that Bill's complaints were a clear illustration of how paranoid and hard to live with he was.

After listening to Andy's and Bill's complaints, Anita referred them to a local mediation service. Both agreed to participate. The mediator's influence worked for a while, but Andy and Bill were soon back at loud, unpleasant shouting matches. After satisfying herself that Andy really had made a series of physical threats, Anita initiated eviction proceedings against him, on the grounds that he posed a real danger to the safety of another tenant. The lawsuit made Andy even madder, and Bill sensibly moved in with his girlfriend for a week, until Andy moved out. Bill posted a "roommate wanted" notice on a bulletin board at work and eventually found Charlie, who had a solid employment and rental history. After confirming Charlie's qualifications, Anita added him to the lease in place of Andy. Although Bill ended up paying some of Andy's share of the rent, he wisely decided that his peace of mind and safety were worth more than the money, and did not sue Andy for the debt.

If your living situation has deteriorated to the point that the police have paid you a visit, or you think that they will soon, you may find yourself being asked by police whether they can come in and look around. When the police have a search or arrest warrant, you must let them in (they'll force their way in if you refuse); and they may enter without a warrant if they are in "hot pursuit" of a fleeing criminal, or need to preserve evidence of a serious crime. But if they have no warrant, and no other justification for warrantless entry, and your roommate is present and objects to a proposed search of your home or apartment, your roommate's objection should stop the entry (the cops will have to return with a warrant). If your roommate is absent, however, you have the power to consent to the search. (*Georgia v. Randolph*, 547 U.S. 103 (2006).)

When a Roommate Leaves

A cotenant who wants to leave in the middle of a tenancy is legally responsible, if the resident is a month-to-month tenant, for giving the landlord proper written notice and paying rent through the end of the notice period. If there's a lease, the tenant must either get permission from the landlord to leave early or, if this is impossible, find a new tenant (acceptable to the landlord) to take over. If a cotenant simply leaves, the fallout can be serious. Chapter 15 explains in detail the likely consequences to the departing tenant. Here we discuss the predicament of the remaining cotenants.

What to Do If You Want to Stay

The unauthorized departure of a cotenant gives the landlord the option of evicting the rest of you, even if you can pay the full rent. The landlord has this option because breaking the lease or rental agreement is a violation of a key lease term (the length of stay), for which all tenants are liable. (See "Renting a Place With Others," above.)

In practice, however, your landlord will probably let you stay if it will keep a steady stream of rent money coming in and keep the place occupied by stable, nondestructive tenants. So if you pay the rent after a cotenant has broken the lease and left, the landlord will probably not evict you and other tenants unless:

- You are a troublesome tenant, and this is a golden opportunity to be rid of you.
- Your income doesn't appear sufficient to cover the rent in the future. In this case, if you can assure the landlord that you can promptly bring in a good, law-and-lease-abiding new cotenant, you might be able to salvage your tenancy. In the meantime, you may need to ask permission to pay the rent late or in installments. Or, ask the landlord to use the departed tenant's share of the security deposit to help pay the rent until you find an acceptable replacement. See Chapter 3 for ideas on how to approach your landlord.

(!) **CAUTION**
Always get your landlord's approval before moving in a new roommate. If a cotenant takes off and leaves you facing the entire rent, you may be tempted to simply move in another roommate, bypassing the landlord's application process. Don't! Your lease or rental agreement probably prohibits unauthorized sublets. If it does, bringing in a new tenant—even a great one—without your landlord's okay violates your agreement and gives your landlord a watertight reason to evict you. Instead, keep your relationship on an honest footing and get your landlord's approval for a replacement tenant. "Adding a New Roommate," below, shows how.

How to Deal With a Departing Roommate

Remaining roommates need to cover their legal flanks with respect to the departed tenant as well as the landlord. If your housemate has left during the middle of a lease or without proper notice in a month-to-month tenancy, leaving you responsible for all the rent, your personal relations will be rocky at best. Probably the last thing you want is to have your errant roommate reappear expecting to move back in.

To avoid such surprises, try to get your former roommate to sign an agreement, making it clear that the departing tenant will do all of the following:

- Pay a stated amount of rent and utilities. If you rent under a written rental agreement, this will normally be rent and utilities for 30 days from the date the departing tenant gave written notice (or left without notice) unless a new roommate comes in earlier and covers these costs. If you rent under a lease, the amount owed will depend on when a new cotenant, acceptable to the landlord, is ready to take over. If, despite your best efforts, you cannot find an acceptable replacement, the departing tenant will be liable for the rent for the balance of the lease.

- Pay for any damage she caused to the rental unit. (See the Chapter 16 discussion of how landlords charge for damage. You can apply the same strategy.)
- Pay for rent and damage no later than a stated date.
- Move out for good and give up any claim to be a tenant.

Chapter 16 discusses what happens to the departing cotenant's security deposit.

But what if you and the departing roommate can't work things out, and the departed cotenant shows no signs of paying? If your roommate is long gone or out of state, you may want to grit your teeth, pay his share and forget it, since trying to find him, sue him, and then collect the judgment is likely to be more trouble than it's worth.

On the other hand, if your ex-roommate is still in town and has a source of income, consider taking the time to sue him in small claims court for unpaid rent, damage to the rental unit, unpaid utilities, and your costs to find a replacement cotenant, such as advertising. Then, if your ex-roommate still doesn't pay up, you can collect what you won in court from his bank account or wages. (Landlords often use these methods; see Chapter 16.)

What to Do If You Want to Move Out, Too

If your cotenant skips out, leaving you in the lurch, you may decide that it's not worth the hassle of trying to stay and rustle up another roommate.

To ease your departure and forestall the landlord from keeping your security deposit to make up for unpaid rent, or reporting you as a deadbeat to the credit bureau, follow these steps:

- If you are a month-to-month tenant, give the required amount of written notice (usually 30 days) immediately. Don't wait until you can't pay the next month's rent and receive a termination notice. (Chapter 15 shows how to give proper notice.)

- If you have a lease, let the landlord know in writing that you plan to move because you cannot afford the rent without your cotenant. Before you move, be extra accommodating when it comes to showing the unit to prospective renters. Facilitating a quick rerental is not just a courtesy to your landlord, but is to your advantage as well, since the sooner a new tenant takes over, the sooner your liability for the balance of the rent due under the lease ends. In addition, do your best to find an acceptable replacement tenant yourself. (See Chapter 15 for an explanation of the landlord's responsibility to look for a new tenant, and "Adding a New Roommate," below, for advice on finding and presenting a replacement.)

Adding a New Roommate

Suppose now that love, poverty, or the desire for some friendly conversation convinces you to add a roommate—or you just need to replace a departing one. Most landlords will insist that the new roommate become a cotenant, having the same rights and responsibilities that you do. This is normally best for you, too, but in a few situations, you may want the newcomer to be a subtenant, who rents from you and has no direct relationship with the landlord. For example, if you want to have the power to evict your new roommate, you'll need to set up a subtenancy. Either way, though, you'll need the consent of the landlord. Here, we explain how to bring the roommate in as a cotenant. "Taking In a Roomer," below, discusses how to sublet to a roomer.

Getting the Landlord's Approval

Obviously, you want to be sure that your choice of a new roommate is financially stable and compatible with you.

But even if you satisfy yourself as to your intended cotenant's stellar qualifications, it doesn't mean the landlord will take your word for it. Landlords have their own good-tenant criteria. To increase your chances of getting an official okay, consider these questions before approaching the landlord:

- **Will adding a roommate exceed the occupancy limit?** Landlords are entitled to set reasonable limits on the number of occupants per rental unit. (See Chapter 5.)
- **Will the new roommate meet your landlord's good-tenant criteria?** Many landlords subject prospective tenants to a thorough screening process, checking credit, employment, rental history, and references. Put yourself in your landlord's shoes and find out as much as you can about the person's financial status and rental history. It not only will help assure the landlord's approval, but will also protect you from getting saddled with a deadbeat roommate. Ask your prospective roommate to request a credit report on himself. (See Chapter 1.) If the credit report is good, you'll want to hand it to the landlord with your proposed new tenant's application. Since the landlord will almost surely do this as well, doing it first gives you the opportunity to develop a plausible explanation for any negative information—for example, a prior eviction or bankruptcy.

Unless you are on fairly close personal terms with your landlord, it's usually a good idea to write your landlord a note about your desire to add a roommate. This gives the landlord an unpressured opportunity to think about it. It is also your chance to sell your proposal by pointing out that your rental is big enough for another tenant and, assuming you already have someone lined up, that your new roommate will be a great tenant. A sample letter is shown below.

Sample Letter Requesting Permission to Add a Roommate

January 5, 20xx

Barrie Newsome
247 Oakleaf Road
St. Paul, Minnesota 00000

Dear Ms. Newsome,

As you know, I rent a spacious one-bedroom apartment, #3A, at 250 Main Street, St. Paul, Minnesota. I would like to add my friend Marilyn Mason to my lease, as a cotenant. Marilyn has just learned that her lease will not be renewed at the end of February because the owners of her flat, where she has lived for five years, have decided to move in themselves.

Marilyn and I have been friends for years. She works with me in the fulfillment department of Better Graphics, Ltd., and has been there for ten years. Her supervisor, Jim Barton, will be happy to answer any questions you might have, and Marilyn will be glad to provide a recent copy of her credit report. You can also contact her current and former landlords for references.

I would like to drop by the rental office this week and pick up a rental application for Marilyn.

Thank you very much for your consideration of my request.

Yours truly,

Tanya Tenant
Tanya Tenant

Adding a Roommate to the Lease or Rental Agreement

If your intended roommate passes the landlord's credit and background checks, the landlord will probably ask both of you to sign a new lease or written month-to-month agreement. From your landlord's point of view, this is far more than a formality, since it makes the new arrival a cotenant who is 100% liable to pay rent and make good on any damage. It's also desirable from your perspective, because it makes it completely clear that your new roommate shares the same legal rights and responsibilities that you do.

More Roommates, More Rent

A landlord who agrees to an additional cotenant will probably ask for a rent increase, on the theory that more residents means more wear and tear. By signing a new lease or rental agreement, you are in effect starting a new tenancy, so the landlord can increase rent immediately, rather than give you the usual 30 days' notice (for a month-to-month rental agreement) or wait until the lease ends.

Unless your rental unit is covered by rent control —or if the landlord is using a big rent increase as a not-so-subtle way to discriminate against you for an illegal reason (see Chapter 5)—your landlord can ask for as much extra money as the market will bear.

 TIP

Negotiate the rent increase. Just because your landlord asks for a big rent increase doesn't mean you have to say yes. One good approach is to counteroffer a lower amount. Let the landlord know that you may rethink adding a roommate, or even move out yourself, if you can't reach an acceptable compromise.

Security Deposit Increases

The landlord also has the legal right to change other conditions of your tenancy when you add a roommate and sign a new agreement. One change that is particularly likely is an increase in the security deposit. However, this is one area where the sky is not the limit, because many states limit the amount of security deposits. Usually the limit is a multiple of the monthly rent. (See "State Security Deposit Rules" in Appendix A.) Keep in mind that if the deposit is already at the maximum, but the landlord raises the rent for the new occupant, the maximum security deposit goes up, too.

Guests

You should always be clear with your roommates regarding how you feel about overnight guests, whether you have a written roommate agreement (as we recommend early in this chapter) or you just discuss the subject before you move in. You might not be happy about your roommate's boyfriend staying over every night and hogging up the shower in the morning; and you certainly might not want your roommate renting out your place on Airbnb during winter break (issues regarding Airbnb are discussed in the following section). Your personal preferences regarding guests aren't the only issues to consider: Your lease or rental agreement may set some restrictions, such as time limits, on guest stays (see "Guest Policies" in Chapter 2 for details).

Tenant Rights to Use Airbnb and Similar Vacation Rental Services

If you're a renter, you may be tempted to earn some extra cash by renting out your apartment on a short-term basis though websites such as Airbnb, HomeAway, or FlipKey. But the result may be the landlord filing an eviction lawsuit against you. Here are some things you should do before engaging in short-term hosting.

Read Your Lease or Rental Agreement

As discussed in Chapter 2, your lease likely prohibits sublets without your landlord's prior written consent (and may even specifically forbid your use of services such as Airbnb). If you violate a no-sublets provision, or a lease clause limiting guest stays, your landlord may terminate your rental and, if you refuse to move, evict you.

Work Something Out With Your Landlord

Most renters who do short-term hosting on sites such as Airbnb never tell their landlords about it (especially if their landlord lives out of town and rarely stops by the rental). But if the neighbors complain or the landlord otherwise discovers what you're doing, you could be in trouble. Instead of taking this chance, consider asking your landlord's permission before you list your apartment on Airbnb or another short-term hosting site. Offering to split with your landlord part of the money you earn, or pay more rent, may seal the deal.

There are other things you can do as well to make your landlord more amenable to your short-term hosting, such as:

- promise to have paying guests only on an occasional basis, rather than all the time
- carefully screen your Airbnb, HomeAway, FlipKey, and similar guests, and
- rent out only a portion of your apartment, rather than the entire unit, so you'll be present to deal with the guests (and limit problems with neighbors).

If you do get your landlord's permission to short-term host, be sure to summarize your agreement in writing.

If you don't have it already, you should also obtain renters' insurance (discussed in Chapter 2) with plenty of liability coverage. That said, having renters' insurance may not, in the end, cover you if a paying "guest" causes damage. The insurance company may claim that its coverage extends only to damage caused by you and your true guests, not damage caused by a paying occupant. And be forewarned: If you approach your insurance company proactively, asking whether they will cover you for your short-term rentals, the insurance company may respond by canceling your policy outright.

If your landlord won't agree to permit you to short-term host, don't do it. The extra money you might earn likely won't make up for getting evicted.

Research Your Local Zoning or Land Use Laws

Many cities restrict or prohibit short-term rental hosting (they may set maximum days per year for short-term rentals, require the host to be present, restrict such activities to specified neighborhoods, and so on). If short-term rentals are regulated where you live, unless you can comply with the restrictions, forget about it—even if it's okay with your landlord.

Taking In a Roomer

What if you're reluctant to completely share your home with a roommate, but want someone to share costs of your rental? The answer may be to take in a roomer as a "subtenant," making it clear that this person is not a full-fledged cotenant.

When you take in a subtenant, you're that person's landlord. We suggest that you sign a month-to-month rental agreement, specifying rent and any restrictions on the roomer's use of your home. And although your roomer doesn't sign the rental document you have with *your* landlord, he must comply with its rules as well as yours. Think of the arrangement as a set of nesting dolls: You live within your landlord's rules and regulations, and your subtenant lives within yours. So if your landlord prohibits using the pool after 10 p.m., you can't promise your roomer the joy of midnight swims.

The main advantage of making your roomer a subtenant instead of a cotenant is that it gives you the legal right to terminate the roomer's tenancy if things don't work out as planned. By contrast, you can't end the tenancy of a roommate who is a full-fledged cotenant—only the landlord can do this.

Don't get too enthusiastic about bringing someone in as a roomer without first talking with your landlord. You'll need your landlord's approval to create a subtenancy—and many landlords would rather not. Even if your landlord gives approval, you may have problems getting a roomer out. You'll probably have to follow the same procedures all landlords use to terminate a tenancy.

For more on the pros and cons of subtenancies, see the discussion of subletting in Chapter 15.

 CAUTION

The New York Roommate Law is special. Tenants in New York enjoy the benefits of its Roommate Law (N.Y. Real Prop. Law § 235(f)), which gives tenants the right to bring in specified roommates, subject only to local laws on overcrowding. For more information on New York laws, see www.tenant.net.

Major Repairs and Maintenance

Your Basic Right to Livable Premises...134

State Laws and Local Housing Codes...135

    Local Ordinances...135

    State Housing Laws...136

Court-Imposed Rules...136

Your Repair and Maintenance Responsibilities...137

Making Tenants Responsible for Repairs...137

How to Get Action From Your Landlord..138

    Put Repair Requests in Writing..138

    Deliver Your Repair Request to the Landlord..139

    Keep Notes on All Conversations and Copies of All Emails......................................140

    Put the Landlord's Promises in Writing...140

What to Do If the Landlord Won't Make Repairs..141

    Reporting Code Violations to Housing Inspectors..142

    Withholding the Rent...142

    Making Repairs and Deducting the Cost—"Repair and Deduct"..............................146

    Moving Out...148

    Suing the Landlord..150

In almost every state, you are legally entitled to rental property that meets basic structural, health, and safety standards and is in good repair. But suppose a landlord comes up short? Depending on the state, you may have the legal right to:

- withhold rent
- pay for repairs yourself and deduct the cost from the rent
- sue the landlord, or
- move out without notice.

This chapter describes your right to basic, important things, such as hot water, a floor that will not collapse under your feet, decent heat, and a roof that doesn't leak—in other words, your right to a safe and livable home. It also provides practical advice on how to get a reluctant landlord to perform needed repairs. Less important maintenance and repair issues—such as unclogging kitchen drains or mowing the front lawn—are covered in the next chapter.

 RELATED TOPIC
Also covered in this book:

- How to be sure your lease or rental agreement has clear provisions on repair and maintenance: Chapter 2.
- How to use a Landlord-Tenant Checklist to keep track of the condition of the premises before and after you move in: Chapter 6.
- Landlord's responsibility for minor repairs such as small plumbing jobs: Chapter 9.
- How to make improvements or alterations to your rental unit without violating your lease or rental agreement or donating your property to the landlord: Chapter 10.
- Landlord's liability for injuries caused by defective housing conditions: Chapter 12.
- Landlord's liability for cleaning up environmental hazards, such as asbestos and lead: Chapter 13.
- Landlord's responsibility to provide safe, reasonably crime-free rental housing: Chapter 14.

Your Basic Right to Livable Premises

Every landlord except those in Arkansas is legally required to offer livable premises when they originally rent a unit and to maintain it in that condition throughout the rental term. In legal terminology, this is given the lofty-sounding name "the implied warranty of habitability." If a landlord persists in failing to fulfill the obligation to provide habitable housing, tenants in most states may legally withhold rent or take other strong measures. (See "What to Do If the Landlord Won't Make Repairs," below.)

The vast majority of American tenants have the right to a decent place to live even if they've moved into a place that's clearly below habitability standards, or even if the lease states that the landlord doesn't have to provide a habitable unit. In a rare showing of unanimity, almost all courts have rejected these sleazy arguments of tenant "waivers" and landlord "disclaimers." Except for a handful of states in very limited circumstances (including Florida, Maine, and Texas), neither a tenant waiver (at the beginning of the tenancy or during its life) nor a disclaimer in the lease will relieve the landlord of the responsibility to provide housing that begins—and remains—fit and habitable.

The landlord's responsibility to provide habitable housing generally includes:

- keeping basic structural elements of the building, including floors, stairs, walls, and roofs, safe and intact
- maintaining all common areas, such as hallways and stairways, in a safe and clean condition
- keeping electrical, plumbing, sanitary, heating, ventilating, and air-conditioning systems and elevators operating safely
- supplying cold and hot water and heat in reasonable amounts at reasonable times
- providing trash receptacles and arranging for their removal, and
- exterminating infestations of rodents and other vermin.

In some states, the building codes alone define what it means for housing to be habitable, while in others, court decisions define the concept. And in still other states, both apply. It can be important for you to know which source (building codes, court decisions, or both) is the basis for the implied warranty of habitability in your state. The source of the warranty can define the landlord's responsibilities and determine your options for dealing with the landlord.

Are You Covered?

Every state except Arkansas has adopted the implied warranty of habitability. However, some local governments in Arkansas may have enacted housing codes that protect their urban residents in ways similar to the implied warranty. And tenants in Arkansas who do *not* have the benefit of local laws may enjoy some of the same protections against dilapidated premises under a legal doctrine called the "covenant of quiet enjoyment." This rather quaint phrase amounts to an implied promise by your landlord to safeguard your ability to use the rented premises.

Examples of landlords' violations of the covenant of quiet enjoyment include:

- tolerating a nuisance, such as piled-up garbage or a major rodent infestation
- failing to provide sufficient electrical outlets, so that tenants cannot use appliances, and
- failing to fix a leaky roof, which deprives a tenant the use of that room.

Unfortunately, the covenant of quiet enjoyment is not as legally powerful or far-reaching as the implied warranty of habitability—that is, landlords can get away with more in Arkansas. For example, unless your landlord has promised a fit dwelling, you may not be able to break the lease and move out if he doesn't make needed repairs. Hopefully, your landlord will be subject to local government ordinances that impose specific requirements that make up for your state's lackadaisical approach.

State Laws and Local Housing Codes

If your state or local government has enacted building and housing laws, your landlord must comply with them. This section explains what these laws typically require of a landlord; if yours runs afoul of them, see the discussions below, for what to do.

Local Ordinances

City or county building or housing codes regulate structural aspects of buildings and usually set specific space and occupancy standards, such as the minimum size of sleeping rooms. They also establish minimum requirements for light and ventilation, sanitation and sewage disposal, heating, water supply (such as how hot the water must be), fire protection, and wiring (such as the number of electrical outlets per room). In addition, housing codes typically make property owners responsible for keeping hallways, lobbies, elevators, and the other parts of the premises the owner controls clean, sanitary, and safe.

Exemptions for Older Buildings

When a new housing code is adopted, or an old one changed, it doesn't necessarily mean that all existing buildings are illegal because they are not "up to code." Especially when it comes to items that would involve major structural changes, lawmakers will often exempt older buildings by writing a "grandfather clause" into the code, exempting all buildings constructed before a certain date. Typically, however, a landlord who later undertakes major renovations or remodeling must comply with the new rules. If you suspect that major work is being planned or done without bringing the building up to code, contact your local housing department. If you fear landlord retaliation, do so anonymously, if possible. (Tenants' protections against retaliatory conduct are discussed in Chapter 15.)

Other new code requirements that are easy and inexpensive to make—for example, installing locks, peepholes, or smoke detectors—must be made regardless of the age of the building.

Most local housing codes also have a catch-all provision that prohibits something called "nuisances." A nuisance is something that is dangerous to human life, detrimental to health, or morally offensive and obnoxious—for example, overcrowding a room with occupants, providing insufficient ventilation or illumination, inadequate sewage or plumbing facilities, permitting illegal activities, or allowing excessive noise or commotion, making it impossible to use or enjoy one's property. Drug use and dealing on the premises is also a legal nuisance.

Your local building or housing authority, and health or fire department, may have an informational booklet that describes the exact requirements your landlord must meet. In most urban areas, these local codes are more thorough than the state's general housing law—for example, many cities require landlords to install smoke detectors and some security items, such as dead bolt locks and peepholes, in exterior doors. However, local laws usually don't explain what you can do—withhold rent, for example—if your landlord fails to comply. To find out, you'll need to consult your state's general housing law.

State Housing Laws

Legislatures in most states have enacted general laws requiring landlords to keep rental units in habitable condition. If you live in an urban area covered by a detailed building or housing code, the vaguer state regulations are likely to be of little importance to you. However, if you live in a small town or rural area not covered by a detailed building code, you'll want to refer to your state housing law. Some states have detailed laws—for example, requiring certain kinds of locks.

To find out whether your state has statutes that pertain to the maintenance of your rental, follow these steps:

- Refer to "State Landlord-Tenant Statutes" in Appendix A. You'll need to look through these statutes in a law library or online. (See Chapter 20 for a lesson on how to access your state and local statutes online, and for advice on using the law library.)
- Check out the laws that apply to you in more detail by looking in the index to your state's

statutes for subentries under "Landlord-Tenant" such as "Landlord Obligations to Maintain Premises," "Repairs," and "Duty to Maintain."
- Contact your state consumer protection agency to see if it publishes pamphlets or brochures that describe landlords' repair and maintenance responsibilities in less legalistic terms. (For a list of state consumer protection agencies, see www.usa.gov/state-consumer.)

What's "Common Law"?

This book often refers to "the common law." This term refers to the law that has been created and modified by courts over almost 1,000 years of English and U.S. history. Since it's made by judges, common law is different from statutory law, which is written by legislators and set out in code books.

In the landlord-tenant field, judges, not legislators, make a good portion of the rules. This means that researching the law often involves finding and understanding key court cases as well as statutes. (See Chapter 20 for a discussion of legal research sources.) Some legal concepts (for example, the implied warranty of habitability) are a mixture of both judge-made common law and statutory law.

Court-Imposed Rules

In many states, your right to habitable housing doesn't depend only on a state or local housing code. In these states, housing must be up to code *and* "fit for human occupation" or "fit and habitable." While a serious housing code violation will almost always qualify as a breach of the warranty of habitability, other shortfalls will constitute a violation of the warranty, too. This means that if your locality has nonexistent or poorly written housing codes, a judge could still find that your landlord breached the warranty because, in the judge's opinion, the premises are not fit for human habitation. And even if there are local housing or building codes, a court may require more of a landlord than do the codes.

In evaluating whether or not a landlord is providing habitable housing, courts may also consider the weather, the terrain, and where the rental property is located. Features or services that might be considered nonessential extras in some parts of the country are legally viewed as absolutely necessary components of habitable housing in others. For example, in climates with severe winters, storm windows may be considered basic equipment.

Finally, keep in mind that the meaning of the term "habitable housing" is not static, and court decisions are made in light of changes in living conditions and technology. For example, these days courts consider the prevalence of crime in urban areas when determining what constitutes habitable housing; and the presence of mold may make some dwellings unfit. Good locks, security personnel, exterior lighting, and secure common areas are now seen, in some cities, to be as important to tenants as are water and heat. (Chapter 14 discusses your rights to adequate security measures.)

Your Repair and Maintenance Responsibilities

You now know that you can expect your landlord to provide safe and habitable housing and adhere to basic norms of cleanliness and behavior under a variety of overlapping legal rules. But your landlord isn't the only one with legal responsibilities. State and local housing laws generally require you to:

Keep your rental unit as clean and safe as the condition of the premises permits. For example, if your kitchen has a rough, unfinished wooden floor that is hard to keep clean, you should not be expected to keep it shiny and spotless—but a tenant with a new tile floor would be expected to do a decent job. If you don't, and your landlord has to do a major clean-up when you move out, expect a hefty deduction from your security deposit.

Dispose of garbage, rubbish, and other waste in a clean and safe manner. For instance, if mice or ants invaded your kitchen because you forgot to take out the garbage before you left on a two-week vacation, you would be responsible for paying any necessary extermination costs.

Keep plumbing fixtures as clean as their condition permits. For example, bathtub caulking that has sprouted mold and mildew may render the tub unusable (or at least disgusting), but since it could have been prevented by proper cleaning, you are responsible. On the other hand, if the bathroom has no fan and the window has been painted shut, the bathroom will be hard to air out; resulting mildew might be your landlord's responsibility.

Use electrical, plumbing, sanitary, heating, ventilating, air-conditioning, and other facilities and other systems, including elevators, properly. Examples of abuse by tenants include overloading electrical outlets and flushing large objects down the toilet.

Fix things you break or damage. If you cause a serious habitability problem in your unit—for example, you carelessly break the heater—you are responsible. A landlord who finds out about the problem can insist that you pay for the repair. Legally, you can't just decide to live without heat for a while to save money. If you drag your feet, the landlord can use your security deposit to pay for it, and if that isn't enough, sue you besides. Your landlord can't, however, charge you for problems caused by normal wear and tear—for example, a carpet that has worn out from use. (Chapter 16 discusses the difference between normal wear and tear and damage.)

Making Tenants Responsible for Repairs

Your landlord may legally delegate some repair and maintenance responsibilities to you, typically in exchange for less rent. He cannot, however, force you to give up your rights to habitable housing.

Landlords rarely try to get tenants to take responsibility for major repair and maintenance duties (such as roof repairs and other structural work) in apartment rentals, since tenants do not have the time, skill, or interest to devote to extensive construction. (Taking on responsibility for minor repairs and maintenance is discussed in Chapter 9.) In addition, many states have specific rules regarding the types of repairs that can be delegated and only allow licensed contractors to do the work.

Damage Caused by Criminals

If a burglar breaks into your home, smashing the cupboards and generally making a mess, who pays? Usually, the landlord, as long as your carelessness (failing to lock a window, for example) didn't facilitate the intruder's entry. If you *were* careless, are you 100% liable for the damage? If your landlord sues you and a jury is asked to apportion the blame between you and the burglar, it's anyone's guess what figure they'll come up with.

Carelessness is not the only way you might be liable for a criminal's acts. For example, if you and your landlord agree that you will maintain the doors and windows in your single-family rental and you fail to do so, you may be held partially liable for the burglar's damage. (If you live in Louisiana, you are required by law to maintain the locks. La. Civ. Code art. 2716.) And if the criminal happens to be someone whom you have let into the building, a jury will almost surely hold you responsible if they conclude that you knew or should have known that a criminal incident was likely.

The picture is often different, however, when you rent a single-family residence. In several states, the landlord and tenant may agree in writing that the tenant will perform some of the landlord's legal duties—for example, arranging for garbage disposal, running water, hot water and heat, or other specified repairs. (In other states, agreements like this are void.) States allowing this arrangement typically require that each side completely understands their rights and responsibilities and that neither pressures the other (otherwise, a court won't enforce the agreement).

How to Get Action From Your Landlord

Knowing that you have a legal right to habitable housing and getting it are, obviously, horses of very different colors. A lot depends on the attitude of your landlord. Here are some tips to maximize your chances of getting quick results.

Put Repair Requests in Writing

By far the best approach is to put every repair and maintenance request in writing, keeping a copy for your files. You may want to call first, but be sure to follow up with a written request. (Send your letter certified, "return receipt requested," to confirm delivery.)

Written communications to your landlord are important because they:

- are far more likely to be taken seriously than face-to-face conversations or phone calls, because it's clear to the landlord you're keeping a record of your requests
- are less likely to be forgotten or misunderstood
- satisfy the legal requirement that you give your landlord a reasonable opportunity to fix a problem before you withhold rent or exercise other legal rights (see below), and
- serve as potential evidence in case you ever need to prove that the serious problems with your unit were the subject of repeated repair requests.

In Chapter 6, "Using Email or Text Messages for Notice or a Letter of Understanding" explains why it's best to send important communications, such as repair requests, by mail or delivery service, rather than email or text messages.

In your repair request, be as specific as possible regarding the problem, its effect on you, what you want done and when. For example, if the thermostat on your heater is always finicky and often doesn't function at all, explain that you have been without heat during the last two days during which the nighttime low was below freezing—don't simply say "the heater needs to be fixed." If the problem poses a health or safety threat, such as a broken front door lock or loose step, say so and ask for it to be fixed immediately. Competent landlords will respond extra quickly to genuinely dangerous, as opposed to merely inconvenient, situations. Finally, be sure to note the date of the request and how many requests, if any, have preceded this one. For more tips on writing a persuasive repair request, see Chapter 9.

Sample Request for Repair or Maintenance

TO: Kay Sera, Landlord
        Stately View Apartments

FROM: Will Tripp
        376 Seventh Avenue
        Apartment No. 45
        Brighton, New Jersey 00000

RE: Roof leak

DATE: March 10, 20xx

As I mentioned to you on the phone yesterday, on March 9, 20xx, I noticed dark stains on the ceilings of the upstairs bedroom and bath. These stains are moist and appear to be the result of the recent heavy rains. I would very much appreciate it if you would promptly look into the apparent roof leak. If the leak continues, my property may be damaged and two rooms may become unusable. Please email or call me so that I'll know when to expect you or a repairperson. You can reach me at work during the day (555-1234) or at home at night (555-4546). My email is wtrip@tripp.com.

Thank you very much for your attention to this problem. I expect to hear from you within the next few days, and expect that the situation will be corrected within a couple of weeks.

Yours truly,

Will Tripp

Will Tripp

If your landlord provides a repair request form, use it. If not, do your own. (See the sample shown above.) Always make a copy of your request and keep it in a safe place in your files.

> ⓘ **CAUTION**
>
> **In dangerous situations, you must take precautions, too.** Once you're aware of a dangerous situation, you must take reasonable steps to avoid injury. Don't continue to use the outlet when you see sparks fly from the wall; don't park in the garage at night if the lights are burned out and there is a safer alternative. If you don't take reasonable care and are injured and sue the landlord, you can expect a judge or jury to hold the landlord only partially responsible. (See Chapter 12.)

Deliver Your Repair Request to the Landlord

If your landlord has an on-site office or a resident manager, deliver your repair request personally. If you mail it, consider sending it certified (return receipt requested), or use a delivery service (such as FedEx) that will give you a receipt establishing delivery. If you email your request, ask for a call (or a return email) acknowledging receipt. Although taking steps to verify delivery will cost a little more, it has two major advantages over regular mail:

- It will get the landlord's attention and highlight the fact that you are serious about your request.
- The signed receipt is evidence that the landlord did, in fact, receive the letter. You may need this in the event that the landlord fails to make the repair and you decide to do it yourself or withhold rent. If a dispute arises as to your right to use a self-help measure, you'll be able to prove in court that you satisfied the legal requirement of notifying the landlord first.

If your first request doesn't produce results—or at least a call or note from the landlord telling you when repairs will be made—send another. Mention that this is the second (or third) time you have brought the matter to the landlord's attention. If the problem is getting worse, emphasize this fact. And, of course, be sure to keep a record of all repair requests.

Keep Notes on All Conversations and Copies of All Emails

Besides keeping a copy of every written repair request, don't neglect to keep a record of oral communications, too. If the landlord calls you in response to your repair request, make notes during the conversation or immediately afterward; write down the date and time that the conversation occurred and when you made your notes. These notes may come in handy to refresh your memory and help you reconstruct the history of your case. In most states, if a dispute ends up in court, and you are unable to remember the details of the conversation, your notes can be introduced in court to fill the gap.

You can keep track of other kinds of communications, too. For example, if your dealings with your landlord are accomplished online, simply print out each message. But keep in mind that email does not provide the type of legal proof that you'd get with a written communication sent certified mail or return receipt requested. See "Using Email or Text Messages for Notice or a Letter of Understanding" in Chapter 6 for details.

> **CAUTION**
> **Think twice before taping telephone conversations.** Many tenants are tempted to tape phone conversations with their landlords or managers, figuring that this is one sure-fire way to preserve evidence of a promise to repair. Under federal law (18 U.S.C. § 2511), some phone conversations can be taped with the consent of one party (you), but laws in many states require the consent of all parties before a conversation can be recorded. Penalties include fines and, in some instances, jail time. While it is unlikely that a one-time offender will be prosecuted, it is likely that this illegal conduct will weaken your case should you wind up in court defending your use of a tenant repair option. And it is possible that a landlord will turn around and sue *you* for your conduct.

Sample Letter of Understanding Regarding Repairs

1234 Appian Way, #3
Bloom City, Indiana 00000

September 3, 20xx

Ms. Iona Lott, Landlord
100 Civic Center Drive
Bloom City, Indiana 00000

Dear Ms. Lott,

Thank you for calling me yesterday, September 2, 20xx, regarding my request for repairs, dated August 27, 20xx. In that request, I told you that the hot water in my unit is very hot (123° F. on my thermometer), even though the temperature gauge on the water heater is turned down as far as it can go. I am concerned that my young daughter may be injured by this scalding water, and am anxious that the temperature be lowered as soon as possible.

As I understand it, you agreed to have Ralph, your handyman, come check the problem on Saturday morning, September 6, between 9 and 10 a.m. Ralph will bring along a new thermostat should he need to replace the old one.

Please let me know if your recollection of our conversation and plans differs from mine.

Yours truly,
Howard Hillman
Howard Hillman

Put the Landlord's Promises in Writing

If you and your landlord agree on a plan of action, it's especially wise to write down your understanding of this agreement. Send a copy to the landlord, inviting a reply if the landlord thinks that you have missed or misstated anything. (This is called a letter of understanding, which we explain in Chapter 2.) If the landlord doesn't write back, the law presumes that he agreed with your version of the conversation. See the sample Letter of Understanding Regarding Repairs, above.

What to Do If the Landlord Won't Make Repairs

If your persistent and businesslike requests for repairs are ignored, you can take stronger measures. Your options will probably include one or more of what we call the "big sticks" in a tenant's self-help arsenal. (See "State Laws on Rent Withholding and Repair and Deduct Remedies," in Appendix A.) These remedies include:

- calling state or local building or health inspectors
- withholding the rent (if allowed by your state law)
- repairing the problem (or having it repaired by a professional) and deducting the cost from your rent (if allowed by your state law)
- moving out, or
- paying the rent and then suing the landlord for the difference between the rent you paid and the value of the defective premises.

If the landlord hasn't fixed a serious problem that truly makes your rental unit uninhabitable—rats in the kitchen, for example—you will want to take fast action. But not every case is so clear-cut. Before you withhold rent, move out, or adopt another extreme remedy, make sure every one of these conditions is met:

- **The problem is serious, not just annoying, and imperils your health or safety.** Not every building code violation or annoying defect in your rental home (like your water heater's ability to reach only 107° F, short of the code-specified 110°) justifies use of a "big stick" against the landlord.
- **You (or a guest) did not cause the problem, either deliberately or through carelessness or neglect.** If so, you can't pursue the self-help options.
- **You told the landlord about the problem and gave him a reasonable opportunity to get it fixed, or the minimum amount of notice required by state law.** You can't use big-stick options without first notifying the landlord and giving him a chance to fix the problem. You'll need to check your state's law for the exact requirements for the specific option you are pursuing.

- **You are willing to risk termination of your tenancy by an annoyed landlord.** Exercising any of the rights discussed here will not endear you to your landlord. Many states forbid your landlord from retaliating against you by raising the rent or terminating your tenancy, but, unfortunately, some states don't. If your lease is about to run out (or you're a month-to-month tenant) and your state does not protect you from retaliatory rent increases or evictions, a complaint to health inspectors or use of a self-help big stick could end up causing you to lose your rental. (Chapter 15 discusses retaliation and gives information on state laws.)

- **You are willing to risk eviction if a judge decides that you shouldn't have used the big stick, and your credit report can bear this negative mark.** Even if you're sure that you were justified in using a big stick, a judge may decide otherwise. For example, if you withhold rent, the landlord may sue to evict you based on nonpayment of rent. In most states and in most situations, you'll have a second chance to pay the balance before being sued for eviction, but not always. (See Chapter 17.) For some tenants, additional negative marks on their credit records will cause extremely serious problems for future rentals, loans, and employment.

- **If you move out, either voluntarily or because the building is closed due to code violations you have reported, you can find a comparable or better unit.** In some states, landlords whose buildings are closed due to code violations must help their tenants with relocation expenses.

TIP
Before doing repairs yourself, withholding rent, or using another "big stick," make sure you have proof of how bad the problem was. One good approach is to take pictures of the problem; another is to have witnesses. Also consider asking an experienced and impartial contractor or repairperson to examine the situation and give you a written description of the problem and estimate for repair. Be sure the description is signed and dated.

Reporting Code Violations to Housing Inspectors

There are several ways a local building, health, or fire department inspector may discover code violations, such as hazardous electrical wiring or a leaking roof. A tenant complaint may trigger an inspection, as may a change in property ownership or financing—for example, if the owner takes out a new loan. Code violations may also be discovered through routine inspections (discussed in Chapter 11).

If You Must Move Because of Building Code Violations

If a judge decides that a building's condition substantially endangers the health and safety of its tenants, and repairs are so extensive they can't be made while tenants inhabit the building, the result may be an order to move. You usually won't have a chance to come to the court hearing to object to this dire consequence—you'll simply be told to get out, sometimes within hours.

In some states, the landlord must pay your rent in comparable temporary housing nearby. Some statutes also make the landlord cover moving expenses and utility connection charges and give you the first chance to move back in when the repairs are completed. In other states, however, you may be out of luck, which explains why tenants are often reluctant to call the inspectors.

If you're tempted to call the inspectors for major habitability problems, it might be wise to find out whether you can get relocation assistance if the building is closed. There's nothing to prevent you from calling the housing department for your city or state and simply asking, without registering a complaint. Or, you can check your state statutes (listed in "State Landlord-Tenant Statutes" in Appendix A). Look in the index to your state's codes, under "Landlord-Tenant," for subheadings such as "Relocation Assistance" or "Padlock Orders." (See Chapter 20 for general advice on using the law library.)

After discovering a code violation, the housing inspector will give the owner an order to correct the problem. Fines and penalties usually follow if the owner fails to comply within a certain amount of time (often five to 30 business days). If there's still no response, the city or county may sue the landlord. In many cities, a landlord's failure to promptly fix cited violations of local housing laws is a misdemeanor (minor crime) punishable by hefty fines or even imprisonment. In rare cases, especially if tenants' health is imperiled, local officials may even require that the building be vacated.

In many areas, reporting a landlord to a building inspector is a very big deal—an inspector who finds lots of problems can force the landlord to clear them up immediately. But there is wild variation as to the effectiveness of building inspectors. Some cities have woefully few inspectors compared to the number of tenant complaints, and courts are largely unable to follow up on the properties that are cited.

Withholding the Rent

If you conclude that your landlord has not met the responsibility of keeping your unit livable, you may be able to stop paying any rent to the landlord until the repairs are made. This is called rent withholding. Many states have established rent withholding, either by statute or by court decision. See "State Laws on Rent Withholding and Repair and Deduct Remedies" in Appendix A.

The term "withholding" is actually a bit misleading, since in some states and cities you can't simply keep the rent money until your landlord fixes the problem. Instead, you often have to deposit the withheld rent with the court or a neutral third party or escrow account set up by a local court or housing agency until the repairs are accomplished. (And even if your statute doesn't require it, it's a good idea to escrow the rent yourself, as explained below.)

Before you can properly withhold the rent, three requirements must be met:

- The lack of maintenance or repair has made your dwelling unlivable (we discuss habitability requirements above).
- The problems were not caused by you or your guest, either deliberately or through neglect.
- You told the landlord about the problem and gave him a reasonable time to fix it, or the minimum amount required by state law.

In addition, under most rent withholding laws, you cannot withhold rent if you are behind in the rent or in violation of an important lease clause. In short, you need to be squeaky clean.

The Consequences of Withholding Rent

Your landlord will not be pleased when your rent check fails to arrive. The landlord's response will typically be to terminate your tenancy for nonpayment of rent and file for eviction if you don't move voluntarily. This may seem particularly unfair if you are meeting all your state requirements for withholding rent.

If you have met the requirements explained above and have carefully followed the procedures set out in your rent withholding statute, you'll have a good defense to the landlord's eviction lawsuit. You may feel confident enough to head into court without a lawyer, or you may want to consult with an attorney first. If you have improperly used the remedy (for a minor repair, for example), you'll be evicted. Because of the possibility of this dire consequence, it's crucial to understand your rent withholding law and use it appropriately.

How to Withhold Rent

Here are the steps to follow when considering whether to withhold rent.

Step 1: Research the law.

If rent withholding is allowed in your state, the statute (law) will be listed in Appendix A. Also,

check if any local laws apply. In a few localities subject to rent control, the procedure may be part of your local ordinance. In either case, read the law to find out:

- what circumstances justify rent withholding
- whether you must give the landlord a certain amount of notice (ten to 30 days is typical) and time to fix the defect, or whether the notice and response time simply be "reasonable" under the circumstances, and
- whether you must place the unpaid rent in a separate bank account or deposit it with a court or local housing agency, and how this is done.

We explain how to find and look up your state's law in the library and online in Chapter 20.

Illegal Lease Clauses: Your Landlord Can't Limit Your Right to Withhold the Rent Under State Law

Some landlords insert clauses in their leases and rental agreements purporting to prohibit a tenant from withholding the rent, even if a property is uninhabitable. In many states, the rent withholding law itself makes this practice flatly illegal. But even where a state statute or court decision does not specifically disallow this side step, these clauses may be tossed out if a tenant nevertheless withholds rent and is served with an eviction notice for nonpayment of rent. Why? Because a judge will approve your supposed waiver of your right to withhold rent only if your "waiver" has been the subject of real negotiations between you and the landlord, and not something the landlord insisted upon unilaterally. And since most leases are preprinted forms that tenants are given in a take-it-or-leave-it situation, a judge is likely to decide that the so-called "waiver" was in fact imposed by the landlord and, consequently, invalid.

Step 2: Notify your landlord.

Give your landlord written notice of the problem and your intent to withhold rent. A sample letter is shown below. Refer to your state's law or statute that allows withholding and include a copy of it. We recommend that you include in your letter a proposal that if for any reason your landlord disagrees that repairs are needed, you quickly mediate the dispute. (Chapter 19 discusses mediation services.) Send the letter "return receipt requested."

Step 3: Collect evidence.

In case your landlord tries to evict you for nonpayment of rent, you will want to prepare your defense from day one. You'll need to prove that the problem truly is serious and that you complied with the notice requirements of the rent withholding law. Of course, you'll want to keep copies of all correspondence with the landlord, plus photographs of the problem. Be sure to consider other ways (besides your own testimony) you can convince the judge that the problem was real and serious. For example, if your heater delivers a frigid blast, you'll want an estimate from a heating repairperson that corroborates the fact that the heater doesn't work. And because evictions are usually handled in a regular trial court, which has stricter rules of evidence than small claims court, you cannot simply present a repairperson's written description of the problem. The repairperson would have to appear in court and testify about the condition of the repair job. Introducing evidence is covered in detail in "Rules of Evidence in Formal Court" in Chapter 18.

Step 4: Repeat your request for repairs.

If the landlord hasn't responded satisfactorily to your first letter, give the landlord one last deadline—say, 48 hours or whatever period you feel is reasonable under the circumstances.

Sample Letter Telling the Landlord You Intend to Withhold Rent

58 Coral Shores, #37
Sandy Bay, FL 00000
407-555-5632

August 5, 20xx

Mr. Roy Hernandez
3200 Harbor Drive
Sandy Bay, FL 00000

Dear Mr. Hernandez:

My family and I are your tenants at the above address. As you know, I called you on August 3 to report that the front porch has collapsed from dry rot at the top of the stairs, making it impossible to enter the flat except by the back door. You assured me that you would send a contractor the next day. No one came on August 4.

Under Florida Statutes Section 83.51(b), you are responsible for keeping the porch in good repair. Florida law gives tenants the right to withhold rent if you fail to do so and the condition is serious (Florida Stat. § 83.201). Tenants may begin withholding if the landlord, after receiving 20 days' notice, fails to fix the problem.

By hand-delivering this notice to you today, August 5, I am giving you the notice as required by law. If the porch is not repaired by August 25, I will withhold rent until it is.

Yours truly,

Alicia Sanchez

Alicia Sanchez

Enclosure: Florida Statutes Sections 83.51 & 83.201

Step 5: File any court papers.

Under some state laws, you must ask a local court for permission to withhold rent, providing compelling reasons why your rental is not livable, and follow specific procedures. This filing process usually isn't difficult and doesn't require the use of a lawyer. You can get the necessary information and forms from the court or housing department that is named in your rent withholding statute.

Step 6: Deposit your rent in escrow.

In some states, you may have to deposit your rent with the specified local court or housing agency or in a separate bank account. Some states do not require a separate escrow account.

Even if your statute does not require this, we recommend that you deposit the withheld rent into an escrow account held by a neutral third party. This will dispel any suggestion that you are withholding rent simply in order to avoid paying it.

If a court or housing department is not set up to handle withheld rent, try asking a mediation service if it will establish an account for this purpose. Or, if you have an attorney, ask her to deposit the withheld rent in her "trust account." You can also set up a separate bank account of your own and use it only for withheld rent. If you must pay for any of these services, you can ask the court to order the landlord to reimburse you if the landlord brings an eviction action.

What Happens to the Withheld Rent

If the rent money is being held by a court or housing authority, landlords can sometimes ask for release of some of the withheld rent to pay for repairs. While repairs are being made, you may continue to pay the entire rent to the court or housing authority, or you may be directed to pay some rent to the landlord and the balance to the court or housing authority. When the dwelling is certified as fit by the local housing authorities or the court, any money in the account is returned to the landlord, minus court costs and inspection fees.

If your withholding law does not require you to escrow the rent and a court has not been involved, you and the landlord are free to make your own arrangements as to the distribution of the money. Once your landlord has made the repairs, he will probably expect full payment of the withheld rent. If you don't pay up, you can expect your landlord to file an eviction lawsuit for nonpayment of rent.

Depending on your state's law, whether or not a court is involved, the severity of the repair problem, and your landlord's willingness to negotiate, you may seek compensation for the time you have spent living in a substandard home. You may want a retroactive reduction in rent, starting from the time that the premises became uninhabitable. (Some states will limit you to a reduction starting from the time you notified the landlord of the problem.) Reducing the rent is known in legalese as rent "abatement."

You may get a retroactive rent abatement through a court process or through negotiation with your landlord. The following section describes how a judge will determine how much the landlord should compensate you for the inconvenience of having lived in a substandard rental unit. If a court is not involved, you can use this same system in negotiating with your landlord.

Determining the Value of a Defective Rental Unit

How does a judge determine the difference between the withheld rent and what a defective, unlivable unit was really worth? There are two widely used ways:

Figuring the market value. In some states, statutes or court cases say that if the landlord leaves your unit in a defective condition, all you owe the landlord is the fair market value of the premises in that condition. For example, if an apartment with a broken heater normally rented for $1,200 per month but was worth only $600 without operable heating, the landlord would be entitled to only $600 per month from the escrowed funds. Of course, the difficulty with this approach—as with many things in law—is that it is staggeringly unrealistic. An apartment with no heat in winter has *no* market value, because no one would rent it. As you can see, how much a unit is worth in a defective condition is extremely hard to determine.

By percentage reduction. Another slightly more sensible approach is to start by asking what part of the unit is affected by the defect, and then to calculate the percentage of the rent attributable to that part. For example, if the roof leaked into the living room of your $900 per month apartment, rendering the room unusable, you could reduce the rent by the percentage of the rent attributable to the living room. If the living room were the main living space and the other rooms were too small to live in comfortably, the percentage of loss would be much greater than it would be in more spacious apartments. Obviously, this approach is far from an exact science, too.

We recommend you use both methods to calculate the unit's reduced, real value. Sometimes, the calculations will be simple—for example, using the fair market value approach, if a broken air conditioner reduces your flat to an oven, its rental value can be determined by consulting ads for non–air-conditioned flats in your area. The percentage reduction method might, in some situations, yield a lower rental value. After you've used both methods, ask the judge to adopt the lower figure and to rule that the landlord is entitled only to that amount of rent per month, times the number of months that you endured the substandard conditions. The difference between the full rent and the realistic rent should go to you.

> **EXAMPLE:** When Henry and Sue moved into their apartment, it was neat and well-maintained. Soon after, the building was sold to an out-of-state owner, who hired an off-site manager to handle repairs and maintenance. Gradually, the premises began to deteriorate. At the beginning of May, 15 months into their two-year lease, Henry and Sue could count several violations of the building code, including the landlord's failure to maintain the common areas, remove the garbage promptly, and fix a broken water heater.
>
> Henry and Sue sent numerous requests for repairs to their landlord over a two-month period, during which they gritted their teeth and put up with the situation. Finally they had enough and checked out their state's rent withholding law. They learned a tenant could pay rent into an escrow account set up by their local court. Henry and Sue went ahead and deposited their rent into this account.
>
> In response, Henry and Sue's landlord filed an eviction lawsuit. In their defense, Henry and Sue pointed to the numerous code and habitability violations. The court agreed with the couple, did not allow the eviction, and ordered the following:
>
> - During the time that they lived in these uninhabitable conditions, Henry and Sue were not required to pay full rent. Using the "market value" approach, the court decided that their defective rental was worth half its stated rent. Accordingly, since the landlord owed them a refund for portions of their rent for May and June, Henry and Sue would be paid this amount from the escrow account.
> - The balance of the rent in the account would be released to the landlord (less the costs of the escrow and the tenants' attorney fees), but only when the building inspector certified to the court that the building was up to code and fit for human habitation.
> - Henry and Sue could continue to pay 50% of the rent until needed repairs were made and certified by the building inspector.

Making Repairs and Deducting the Cost—"Repair and Deduct"

You may, depending on where you live, also be eligible to use another powerful legal remedy called "repair and deduct." Most states and some large cities allow it. (See "State Laws on Rent Withholding and Repair and Deduct Remedies" in Appendix A.) If your state doesn't allow repair and deduct, check your local housing ordinances to determine whether your city has independently adopted it. If your state or city does not have a repair and deduct statute, this procedure is not available to you.

It works like this: If you have tried and failed to get the landlord to fix a serious defect, you can hire a repairperson to fix it and subtract the cost from the following month's rent. In most states, the amount you can spend and deduct is limited to a specific figure or a percentage of the month's rent. Most states also limit the frequency with which you can use the procedure and require that you notify the landlord in writing and give him a specified or reasonable amount of time to repair the problem. Be sure to read your state statute for details on the repair and deduct option,

Reducing the Rent on Your Own

If your state doesn't have a rent withholding statute, you may be tempted to reduce the rent on your own. For example, if the water heater is broken and the landlord won't fix it despite your repeated requests, you may feel like paying a few hundred dollars less per month, figuring that your cold-water flat is only worth that much.

It's very risky to give your landlord a short rent check. You can expect a speedily delivered termination notice, followed by an eviction lawsuit, for nonpayment of rent. Your theory—that the landlord was entitled to less rent because the premises weren't livable—is not likely to be well-received in a state that hasn't taken the issue seriously enough to establish orderly procedures (rent withholding) to ensure that landlords live up to their duty to provide habitable housing. If you lose, you'll lose your rented home.

If your state does not give you the option of rent withholding, use one of the other remedies mentioned here, including repair and deduct (if available), moving out, or filing a lawsuit in small claims court asking for a retroactive rent reduction for substandard conditions.

State laws vary greatly as to the amount of rent you can withhold and the frequency you can use this remedy for repairs. For example, in Massachusetts, you can spend up to four months' rent (for health code violations certified by an inspector only).

(Mass. Gen. Laws ch. 111, § 127L.) In California, you can spend only one month's rent, and only use this option twice a year. (Cal. Civ. Code §§ 1941 to 1942.5.) And in Louisiana, there is practically no guidance at all: You are simply allowed to repair and deduct for "indispensable" repairs that are the landlord's responsibility. (La. Civ. Code art. 2694.)

Sample Letter Telling the Landlord You Intend to Repair and Deduct

8976 Maple Avenue
Carson, WA 00000
360-555-6543

January 14, 20xx

Hattie Connifer
200 Capitol Expressway, Suite 300
Carson, WA 12345

Dear Ms. Connifer:

On January 10, I called your office and spoke to you about a major problem: I have no hot water. As I explained on the phone, on the evening of January 9 the water heater for my flat sprang a leak. Luckily, I was home and was able to divert the water to the outside with a hose, turn off the intake valve, and shut off the pilot.

At the end of our conversation on January 10, you assured me that you would send a repairperson to the flat the next day, January 11. As of today, no one has showed up, and I am enduring my fourth day of no hot water.

Under Washington law, I am entitled to remedy the problem and deduct the cost from my rent if you do not attend to the problem within 24 hours (Washington Rev. Code § 59.18.100). I intend to do this if the heater is not replaced within 24 hours after you receive this letter, which I am personally delivering to your office. As required by law, I have enclosed an estimate of the replacement cost: A-1 Appliance Repair has estimated the cost of a new, comparable heater at $400.

Yours truly,

Wanda Wright

Wanda Wright

Enclosure: Estimate of A-1 Appliance Repair

These restrictions make the repair and deduct remedy a poor choice for tenants when it comes to big-ticket projects such as a major roof repair. Obviously, if you're limited to a twice-a-year expenditure of half your monthly rent, you are not going to be able to pay for a $20,000 roof retrofit. Sometimes, however, a number of tenants might pool their dollar limits to accomplish a costly repair. (Tenants working together is covered in Chapter 19.)

> **CAUTION**
>
> **Most repair and deduct statutes require you to spend only a reasonable amount of money on repairs.** In Washington, for example, you have to go with the lowest bid. If your landlord challenges the amount you spent on the repair, you'll need to be able to prove that the cost was the going rate for the job. Get bids from several reputable contractors or licensed repairpersons, and choose wisely—in most states, not necessarily the lowest bid, but the best value for a decent job.

Moving Out

If your dwelling isn't habitable and hasn't been made so despite your complaints and repair requests, you also have the right to move out—either temporarily or permanently. These drastic measures are justified only when there are truly serious problems, such as the lack of essential services, the total or partial destruction of the premises, or the presence of environmental health hazards such as lead paint dust. (Chapter 13 explains your right to move out because of environmental toxins. This section covers the other two situations that justify moving out.)

The Landlord's Failure to Keep the Unit Habitable

The 49 states and the District of Columbia that recognize your right to habitable housing allow you to move out if you don't get it. Depending on the circumstances, you may move out permanently, by terminating the lease or rental agreement, or

temporarily. This approach is borrowed directly from consumer protection laws. Just as the purchaser of a seriously defective car may sue to undo the contract or return the car for a refund, you can consider the housing contract terminated and simply return the rental unit to the landlord if the housing is unlivable.

The law, of course, has a convoluted phrase to describe this simple concept. It's called "constructive eviction," which means that the landlord, by supplying unlivable housing, has for all practical purposes "evicted" you. Once you have been constructively evicted (that is, you have a valid reason to move out), you have no further responsibility for rent.

Your state statute may have specific details, such as the type of notice you must provide before moving out because of a major repair problem. You may need to give your landlord anywhere from five to 21 days to fix it, depending on the state and, sometimes, the seriousness of your situation. Check your state law for details.

Temporary moves. In many states, if the landlord fails to provide heat or other essential services, you may procure reasonable substitute housing during the period of the landlord's noncompliance. You may recover the costs (as long as they're reasonable) of substitute housing up to an amount equal to your rent.

Permanent moves. If you move out permanently because of habitability problems, you may also be entitled to money from the landlord to compensate you for out-of-pocket losses. For example, you may be able to recover moving expenses and the cost of a hotel for a few days until you find a new place. Also, if the conditions were substandard during prior months when you did pay the full rent, you may sue to be reimbursed for the difference between the value of the defective dwelling and the rent paid. In addition, if you are unable to find comparable housing for the same rent, and end up paying more rent than you would have under the old lease, you may be able to recover the difference.

Damage to the Premises

If your home is totally damaged by natural disaster or any other reason beyond your control, it only makes sense that you have the legal right to consider the lease at an end and to move out.

Partial destruction, however, is another matter. If you must find another place to live because of damage to or significant destruction of the premises —no matter the cause—you must decide whether to terminate the lease or rental agreement or just suspend it while repairs are made. Depending on your situation, there are advantages to either course.

> ! CAUTION
> **Check your lease or rental agreement for a clause covering what happens if the premises are partially damaged or destroyed.** The landlord may have reserved for himself the choice as to whether to terminate your rental or merely suspend it. If you disagree with the landlord's call, you'll need to try some negotiation to see if you can change his mind.

Terminating the lease or rental agreement. You'll want to terminate the lease if you can find new housing of comparable quality and cost. You won't have to live with the uncertainty of when you'll move back to the original dwelling, and it will save you the time and aggravation of an extra household move. And if your new housing comes with a lease, you may *have* to terminate the old one, since a lease won't allow you to move when you want.

If you decide to terminate the original lease or rental agreement, finalize the decision in writing. Have the landlord write "Terminated" on each page of your lease or rental agreement. Both of you should sign and date each page. Your landlord should refund your security deposit according to your state's procedures. (See Chapter 16.)

Leaving temporarily without terminating the lease. If your rental is a particularly great deal, the local market is very tight, or the repairs can be accomplished within a reasonable time, you'll want to hang on to your unit. If you are protected by rent control and you have lived in your rental for a significant period of time, you'll probably be loath to move. Find a month-to-month rental while the original unit is repaired.

You and the landlord should add a page to the lease entitled "Suspension," which states that the landlord's and tenant's responsibilities have been suspended from a certain date until the day you move back in. Be sure to include the landlord's promise to notify you promptly as soon as the rental is ready. If relocation costs are being covered by the landlord, note them. Both of you should sign and date this document.

In some circumstances, and regardless of whether you decide to terminate or just suspend the original lease, you may have the legal right to financial assistance from the landlord to pay for temporary substitute housing. It depends on how your rental unit was destroyed. If a natural disaster struck, the landlord is less likely to be obligated than if your home was destroyed by fire caused by the landlord botching an electrical repair job. And if your home burns down because of your own carelessness, don't expect financial help—in fact, the landlord may be able to sue *you*.

Natural or third-party disasters. If your unit is destroyed by earthquake, tornado, flood, or arson, your duty to pay rent is at an end. State laws vary on the extent of the landlord's responsibility to aid you with relocation or temporary housing costs. If you have renters' insurance, your best bet is to file a claim for help in resettlement and coverage for your lost or destroyed possessions. (Renters' insurance is covered in Chapter 2.)

If you have a month-to-month tenancy, the landlord may be required by law to pay for your substitute housing for 30 days. If you have a lease, the landlord is probably obligated to pay for substitute housing for a longer period—often until you find a comparable replacement or, if you drag your feet, until a court thinks you should have been able to.

Destruction that is traceable to the landlord. If the landlord or his employees were even partially responsible for the damage, your legal right to assistance almost surely increases. Even if your tenancy is just month to month, the landlord is likely to be obligated by state law to pay for a reasonable period of temporary housing. If the permanent substitute housing you find is more expensive, the landlord may be obliged to pay the difference between your old rent and the new rent for one or two months. If you have a lease, the landlord's responsibility to pay the difference may extend to the end of your lease term.

If the landlord or his insurance company doesn't offer you a fair settlement, you may want to bring a lawsuit to recover the cost of temporary and substitute housing and the value of your lost possessions. Often, cases like these settle before trial, since your claims are likely to be covered by the landlord's insurance policy. (Business policies generally include coverage for the landlord's negligent acts, but they exclude coverage for natural disasters.)

Suing the Landlord

A consumer who purchases a product—be it a car, a hair dryer, or a steak dinner—is justified in expecting a minimum level of quality, and is entitled to compensation if the product is seriously flawed. The same goes for tenants. Except in Arkansas, if your rental is not habitable, you can sue the landlord— whether or not you move out. You can probably use small claims court, which allows claims of up to several thousand dollars. (For your state's ceiling, see the table in Chapter 19.) You won't need to hire a lawyer.

Suing the landlord makes sense only if you can safely continue to live in your rental. For example, if the roof leaks only into the second bedroom, and you can move the kids into the living room for a while, you might want to stay and sue in order to avoid the hassle of moving, arranging for the repair yourself (repair and deduct), or figuring out the complications of rent withholding. But you wouldn't want to stay and sue if you are without heat in the winter or in danger of electrocution every time you use the kitchen stove.

What are the pros and cons of suing your landlord instead of using repair and deduct or rent withholding? On the positive side, if you lose your lawsuit you'll have lost some time and money, but you won't be evicted, as can happen with the unsuccessful use of repair and deduct or rent withholding. But suing isn't entirely risk-free, especially if you're a month-to-month tenant or nearing the end of a lease you would like to renew. Your annoyed landlord may simply decide to terminate or not renew. Tenants who are protected by state antiretaliation laws will have some protection, but to assert your rights you'll have to bring a lawsuit, a dreary prospect. (Landlord retaliation is covered in Chapter 15.)

In your lawsuit, you ask the judge to rule that your unrepaired rental was not worth what you've paid for it. You want to be paid the difference between the monthly rent and the real value of the unit, times the number of months that you've lived with the substandard conditions. In short, you'll ask for a retroactive rent decrease. In addition, you can sue your landlord for:

- lost or damaged property—for example, furniture ruined by water leaking through the roof
- compensation for personal injuries—including pain and suffering—caused by the defect (see Chapter 12), and
- your attorneys' fees and court costs if you had to hire a lawyer to sue the landlord (Chapter 2 discusses attorneys' fees).

In some states, you may ask the court for an order directing the landlord to repair the defects, with rent reduced until they are fixed. In others, small claims courts can only order the landlord to pay you for your losses, but usually the money judgment gets the landlord's attention and he makes the repairs.

Minor Repairs and Maintenance

Minor Repairs: What Are They? 152

The Landlord's Responsibilities 152

    Building Codes 153

    Landlord-Tenant Laws 154

    Promises in the Lease or Rental Agreement 154

    Promises in Ads 154

    Promises Made Before You Rented the Unit 154

    Implied Promises 155

Tenant Responsibilities 155

Getting the Landlord to Make Minor Repairs 157

    Appealing to Your Landlord 157

    Reporting Code Violations 159

    Suing in Small Claims Court 159

Making Minor Repairs Yourself 161

    Evaluating Your Skills and Time 161

    Getting the Landlord's Permission 161

Ask a group of tenants which rental problem is most annoying, and chances are you'd hear "Repairs!" And most wouldn't be referring to major problems that make a unit unlivable. What really bugs tenants are the day-to-day but nonetheless important problems: leaky faucets, malfunctioning appliances, security devices that don't work, worn carpets, noisy heaters, hot water heaters that produce a pathetic quantity of tepid water, and dozens of other frustrating breakdowns.

Unfortunately, if your landlord refuses to attend to minor repairs, you don't have much legal clout. You can't withhold rent, move out, or use most of the other "big stick" legal weapons discussed in Chapter 8. Even so, there are several proven strategies for getting results.

 RELATED TOPIC
Also covered in this book:

- How to clarify repair and maintenance duties at the start of your tenancy: Chapter 2.
- How to use a Landlord-Tenant Checklist to note problems with the rental unit when you move in: Chapter 6.
- Dealing with serious problems that make housing uninhabitable: Chapter 8.
- Your responsibilities to keep your rental unit clean, safe, and in good condition: Chapter 8.
- Making improvements or alterations to your rental on your own: Chapter 10.
- Your landlord's liability for injuries caused by defective premises: Chapter 12.

Minor Repairs: What Are They?

If a landlord balks at making repairs, your first step is to decide whether the problem is major (affecting the habitability of your rental unit) or minor. This distinction is necessary because you have different legal options depending on your conclusion.

Minor repair and maintenance includes:

- small plumbing jobs, like replacing washers and cleaning drains
- system upkeep, like changing heating filters

- structural upkeep, like replacing excessively worn flooring
- small repair jobs like fixing broken light fixtures or replacing the grout around bathtub tile, and
- routine repairs to and maintenance of common areas, such as pools, spas, and laundry rooms.

Don't assume that inexpensive repairs are always minor repairs. Sometimes an extremely important repair costs very little. For example, if the only thing between you and a heated apartment is the replacement of a $45 furnace part, the repair is "major" because an unheated dwelling is uninhabitable, even though the repair cost is insignificant. And because this is true, if the landlord didn't replace the furnace part promptly, you would probably be entitled to withhold rent or use one of the other "big stick" strategies discussed in Chapter 8. By contrast, replacing the living room carpet, which is worn but not a hazard, will be very expensive, but will be considered a minor repair because the consequence of not replacing it is not an unfit dwelling.

Most often, minor repairs are the landlord's responsibility. But landlords are not required to keep the premises looking just like new—ordinary wear and tear does not have to be repaired during your tenancy. (When you move out, however, the cost of dealing with ordinary wear and tear will fall on the landlord and cannot come out of your security deposit. See Chapter 16.)

The Landlord's Responsibilities

Not every minor problem is, legally, your landlord's responsibility. If you or one of your guests caused it, carelessly or intentionally, you are responsible for repairing it—or, if your lease or rental agreement prohibits you from doing so, for paying the landlord to do it. Typically, landlords deduct the cost from your security deposit, as discussed in Chapter 16.

If you had nothing to do with the repair problem and it's not a cosmetic issue, chances go way up that your landlord is responsible, for one of the following reasons:

Common Misconceptions About Routine Maintenance

Many tenants (and landlords) are under the mistaken impression that every time a rental unit turns over, or a certain number of years have passed, the landlord must supply a new paint job or clean drapes and carpets or some other kind of refurbishing. Unfortunately for tenants, the law almost never mandates cosmetic changes—even badly needed ones. (Of course, if the landlord doesn't spruce up the place now and then, it may be hard to find and keep tenants. But that's a market, not a legal, issue.)

Here are some of the common misconceptions regarding rental sprucing-up:

Paint. No state's law requires landlords to repaint the interior every so often. (Very rarely, local ordinances such as those in New York City may impose minimal repainting obligations.) Unless the paint creates a habitability problem—for example, it's so thick around a window that the window can't be opened, or flaking lead-based paint poses obvious health risks—it should comply with the law. (Lead-based paint creates so many potential problems that we discuss it separately in Chapter 13.)

Drapes and Carpets. So long as drapes and carpets are not so damp or mildewy as to amount to a health hazard, and so long as carpets don't have dangerous holes that could cause someone to trip and fall, your landlord isn't legally required to replace them.

Windows. You're responsible for fixing (or paying to fix) a broken window that you or your guest intentionally or carelessly break. If a burglar, vandal, or neighborhood child breaks a window, however, the landlord is usually legally responsible for the repair. (Broken windows can sometimes be a habitability problem; see Chapter 8.)

Keys and Locks. Unfortunately, in many areas of the country, landlords are not legally required to change the locks for new tenants or even to provide serious, heavy-duty door and window locks. (The trend, however, is to require such items.) However, if you tell a landlord in writing that you are worried about renting a unit secured by locks for which previous tenants (and perhaps their friends) have keys, most landlords rekey the locks. (If the landlord knows of your concern but does not respond, and you are attacked or your place is burglarized by someone using an old key, the chances of the landlord being held liable in a lawsuit go way up. See Chapter 14.)

- A state or local building code requires that the landlord keep the damaged item (for example, a kitchen sink) in good repair.
- A state or local law specifically makes it the landlord's responsibility.
- A lease or rental agreement provision or advertisement describes or lists particular items, such as hot tubs, trash compactors, and air conditioners; by implication, this makes the landlord responsible for maintaining or repairing them.
- The landlord made explicit promises when showing you the unit—for example, regarding the security or air conditioning system.
- The landlord has obligated himself to maintain a particular feature, such as a whirlpool bathtub, because the landlord has fixed or maintained it in the past.

Each of these reasons is discussed below. If you're not sure whether a minor repair or maintenance problem is the landlord's responsibility, scan the discussion to find out.

Building Codes

States (and sometimes cities) write building codes that cover structural requirements, such as roofs, flooring, and windows, and essential services, such as hot water and heat. If your repair problem is also a violation of the building code, you may be facing a habitability problem, as discussed in Chapter 8. But building codes often cover other, less essential details as well. For example, codes may specify a minimum number of electrical outlets per room; if a broken circuit breaker means that you have fewer working outlets, the consequence is probably not an unfit dwelling, but the landlord is still legally required to fix the problem.

Landlord-Tenant Laws

Some state laws place responsibility for specific minor repairs and maintenance on the landlord. A common example is providing garbage receptacles and arranging for garbage pickup. Many states have their own special rules. In Alaska, for example, the law makes landlords responsible for maintaining vacuum cleaners, dishwashers, and other appliances supplied by them. (Alaska Stat. § 34.03.100 and following.)

In many states, renters of single-family residences may agree to take on responsibilities that would otherwise belong to the landlord, such as disposing of garbage. For details, check your state's landlord-tenant codes under "State Landlord-Tenant Statutes," which are listed in Appendix A.

Promises in the Lease or Rental Agreement

When it comes to legal responsibility for repairs, your own lease or rental agreement is often just as important (or more so) than building codes or state laws. If your written agreement describes or lists items such as drapes, washing machines, swimming pools, saunas, parking places, intercoms, or dishwashers, your landlord must provide them in decent repair. And the promise to provide them carries with it the implied promise to maintain them.

Promises in Ads

If an advertisement for your unit described or listed a feature that was included in the rent, such as cable TV service, and this significantly affected your decision to move into the particular rental unit, you have the right to hold the landlord to these promises. Even if your written rental agreement says nothing about appliances, if the landlord's ad listed a dishwasher, clothes washer and dryer, and microwave oven, you have a right to expect that all of them will be repaired by the landlord if they break through no fault of yours.

EXAMPLE: Tina sees Joel's ad for an apartment, which says "heated swimming pool." After Tina moves in, Joel stops heating the pool regularly because his utility costs have risen. Joel has violated his promise to keep the pool heated.

The promise doesn't have to be in words.

EXAMPLE: Tom's real estate agent showed him a glossy color photo of an available apartment, which featured a smiling resident using an intercom to welcome a guest. The apartment Tom rented did not have a working intercom, and he complained to the management, arguing that the advertisement implied that all units were so equipped. The landlord realized that he would have to fix the intercom.

Promises Made Before You Rented the Unit

It's a rare landlord or manager who refrains from even the slightest bit of puffing when showing a rental to a prospective tenant. You're quite likely to hear rosy plans for amenities or services that haven't yet materialized ("We plan to redo this kitchen—you'll love the snappy way that trash compactor will work!"). Whenever you hear promises like these, you would be wise to get them in writing, as part of (or attached to) your lease or rental agreement or, at the very least, in a prompt letter of understanding that cannot be repudiated later.

If this advice is coming to you now a bit late, and you don't in fact have anything in writing, don't give up hope. The oral promise is valid and enforceable—it's just a little harder to prove that it was made. If the promised trash compactor never appears, it's your word against the landlord's unless you have witnesses to the conversation. You'll be in a stronger position, proof-wise, if the promised feature is present in your unit but just doesn't work or breaks down after you move in, as explained just below.

EXAMPLE: When Joel's rental agent shows Tom around the building, she goes out of her way to show off the laundry room, saying, "Here's the laundry room—we have two machines now, but will be adding two more soon." Tom rents the apartment. Two months go by and Joel still hasn't added the new machines. Joel has violated his promise to equip the laundry room with four machines.

Implied Promises

Suppose your rental agreement doesn't mention a garbage disposal, and neither does any ad you saw before moving in. And, in fairness, you can't remember your landlord ever pointing it out when showing you the unit. But there is a garbage disposal, and it was working when you moved in. Now the garbage disposal is broken and, despite repeated requests, your landlord hasn't fixed it. Do you have a legal leg to stand on in demanding that your landlord make this minor repair? Yes. Many courts will hold a landlord legally responsible for maintaining all significant aspects of your rental unit. If you rent a unit with certain features— light fixtures that work, doors that open and close smoothly, faucets that don't leak, tile that doesn't fall off the wall—many judges reason that the landlord has made an implied contract to keep them in workable order throughout your tenancy.

The flip side of this principle is that if you pay for a hamburger, the waiter doesn't have to deliver a steak. In other words, if your rental was shabby when you moved in, and the landlord never gave you reason to believe that it would be spruced up, you have no legal right to demand improvements— unless, of course, you can show health hazards or code violations. As when you buy secondhand goods "as is" for a low price, legally you are stuck with your deal. (But "Getting the Landlord to Make Minor Repairs," below, suggests some strategies—based on subtly showing your landlord the consequences of ignoring minor repairs—that may convince a reluctant landlord to take better care of business.)

Another factor that is evidence of an implied contract is the landlord's past conduct. If your landlord has consistently fixed or maintained a particular feature of your rental, he has made an implied obligation to continue doing so.

EXAMPLE: Tina's apartment has a built-in dishwasher. When she rented the apartment, neither the lease nor the landlord said anything about the dishwasher or who was responsible for repairing it. The dishwasher has broken down a few times and whenever Tina asked Joel to fix it, he did. By doing so, Joel has established a practice that he—not the tenant—is responsible for repairing the dishwasher.

> **TIP**
> **Check your lease.** Landlords who want to avoid responsibility for appliance repairs often insert clauses in their leases or rental agreements warning that the appliances are not maintained by the landlord. (See "Typical Provisions in Leases and Rental Agreements" in Chapter 2.)

> **TIP**
> **Using the Landlord-Tenant Checklist at the start of your tenancy will give you a record of appliances and features—and their condition.** If something needs repairs, you'll be able to use the Checklist as proof of its original condition.

Tenant Responsibilities

Leases and rental agreements usually include a general statement that you are responsible for keeping your rental unit clean, safe, and in good condition, and for reimbursing your landlord for the cost of repairing damage you cause. Your lease or rental agreement will probably also say that you can't make alterations or repairs, such as painting the walls, installing bookcases, or fixing electrical problems, without your landlord's permission. (See Chapter 2.)

Landlords who are tired of maintenance and repair jobs may use the lease, rental agreement, or separate contract to give these responsibilities to a tenant. Especially if you rent a single-family home or duplex, you may be asked to agree to mow the lawn, trim the bushes, and do minor plumbing jobs and painting.

Many state laws regulate the kind of repairs and maintenance that landlords can hand off to tenants. In general, if the landlord is not required to provide an item in the first place (a sauna, for example), the lease or rental agreement can delegate to the tenant responsibility for repairing it (which would normally be the landlord's, as discussed above). Landlords cannot, however, make tenants responsible for repairing or maintaining essential features of any rental, which are required by law. (See Chapter 8.) Also, laws in some states limit duties that landlords can delegate to tenants in multiunit buildings, while allowing tenants in single-family dwellings and duplexes to assume more responsibilities.

Commonly, a landlord proposes a rent reduction in exchange for some work. Or the landlord may offer other perks (a parking space, for example), or will offer an amenity if the tenant will perform the maintenance—for example, a hot tub in exchange for your promise to clean it.

Although usually legal, these arrangements often lead to dissatisfaction—typically, the landlord feels that the tenant has neglected certain tasks, or the tenant feels that there is too much work. If the dispute boils over, the landlord tries to evict the tenant.

Here's how to protect yourself and avoid disputes:

- **Sign an employment agreement separate from your rental agreement or lease.** This is especially important if you plan to do considerable work for your landlord on a continuing basis, such as keeping hallways, elevators, or a laundry room clean or maintaining the landscaping. Tenants who are also building managers are in this position. Ask your landlord to pay you for your work, rather than give you a rent reduction. That way, if the landlord claims that the job is not done right, the worst that can happen is that you will be fired; your tenancy should not be affected. But if your maintenance duties are tied to a rent reduction and things go wrong, you and the landlord will have to amend the lease or rental agreement in order to reestablish the original rent. And if the maintenance jobs are spelled out in a lease clause, the landlord also has the option of terminating the lease, on the grounds that your poor performance constitutes a breach of the lease.

- **Clearly write out your responsibilities and the landlord's expectations.** List your tasks and the frequency with which your landlord expects them to be done. Weekly tasks might include, for example, cleaning the laundry room, sweeping and wet mopping the lobby, and mowing the grass between April 1 and November 1.

- **Make sure the agreement is fair.** Ideally, your landlord will pay you a fair hourly rate. If your only choice is a rent reduction, make sure the trade-off is equitable. If you're getting only a $50 rent reduction for work that would cost the landlord $200 if he hired a cleaning service, you're being ripped off.

- **Discuss problems with the landlord and try to work out a mutually satisfactory agreement.** If the landlord has complained about your work, maybe it's because he's underestimated what's involved in cleaning the hallways and grounds. Your landlord may be willing to pay you more for better results or shorten your list of jobs. If not, cancel the arrangement. In extreme cases, you may need to move out.

Watch Out for Illegal Retaliation

A landlord's delegation of some tasks does not relieve him of all repair and maintenance responsibilities. For example, if you and your landlord agree that you will do gardening work in exchange for a rent reduction, and he feels that you are not doing a proper job, he is not permitted to respond by shutting off your water.

⚠ **CAUTION**
Don't perform repairs involving hazardous materials. Any repair involving old paint or insulation (opening up a ceiling or wall cavity, for example) may expose you or others to dangerous levels of toxic materials. For example, sanding a surface for a seemingly innocuous paint job may actually create lead-based paint dust; the quick installation of a smoke alarm could involve disturbing an asbestos-filled ceiling. See Chapter 13 for more information on environmental hazards.

Getting the Landlord to Make Minor Repairs

By now you should have a pretty good idea as to whether or not your landlord is legally responsible for fixing the particular minor problem that is bedeviling you. Your next job is to get the landlord to do it. First, try to get the landlord to cooperate. If you can't, it may be time to take a confrontational approach.

Appealing to Your Landlord

Chances are you have already asked your landlord or manager to make repairs, only to be put off, ignored, or even told to forget it. Your next step is to write a formal demand letter—or, if you have already done it, a second one.

Before you pick up your pen or turn on your computer, take a minute to think about what words will most likely get action. Begin by remembering your landlord's overriding business concerns: to make money, avoid hassles with tenants, and stay out of legal hot water. A request that zeroes in on these issues will likely get the job done.

How to Write a Persuasive Repair Request

Whether this is your first or second formal demand letter, frame your repair request along one or more of the following lines, if possible:

- **It's a small problem now, but has the potential to be a very big deal.** A bathtub faucet that drips badly may be simply annoying now, but devastating later if the washer gives out while you're not home, flooding the tub and ruining the floor and downstairs neighbor's ceiling. When you ask that the faucet be repaired, point out the risk of letting things go.

- **There is a potential for injury.** Landlords hate to be sued. If a potential injury-causing problem is brought to their attention, it's likely that their fear of lawsuits will overcome their lethargy, and you'll finally get results. Say, for instance, you have asked your landlord to repair the electrical outlet in your kitchen so that you can use your toaster. If you've received no response, try again with a different pitch: Point out that, on occasion, you have observed sparks flying from the wall, and a short in the wiring could cause an injury or fire.

- **There is a security problem that imperils your safety.** Landlords are increasingly aware that they can also be sued for criminal assaults against tenants if the premises aren't reasonably secure. (Chapter 14 discusses this topic in detail.) If you can figure out a way to emphasize the security risks of not fixing a problem—for example, a burned-out lightbulb in the garage or a door that doesn't always latch properly— you may motivate the landlord to act promptly.

- **The problem affects other tenants.** If you can point to a disaster-waiting-to-happen that affects more than one tenant, you will greatly increase your chances of some action. For example, accumulated oil puddles in the garage threaten the safety of all tenants and guests, not just you. Faced with the possibility of a small army of potential plaintiffs, each accompanied by an eager attorney, even the most slothful landlord may spring into action. See Chapter 19 for tips on working with other tenants to accomplish common goals.

- **You're willing to try to fix it, but may make the problem worse.** Finally, you might try offering to fix the problem yourself in a way that is likely to elicit a quick "No thanks, I'll call my contractor right away!" This is a bit risky, since your bluff might be called, but even the most dense landlord will think twice when you offer to make an electrical repair with a chisel and masking tape.

See the sample letter below for more ideas on writing a persuasive repair request.

A written demand for repair or maintenance lets your landlord know that you are serious about the issue and are not content to just let it go. In addition, if your dispute ends up in small claims court, the demand letter can usually be introduced as evidence. Like this sample letter, your demand letter should:

- be neatly typed and use businesslike language
- concisely and accurately state the important facts (this is important in case your letter ends up before a judge, who will need to be made familiar with the situation)
- be polite and nonpersonal. Obviously, a personal attack on your landlord may trigger an equally emotional response. Since you are appealing to the landlord's business interests, you want to encourage her to evaluate the issue soberly, not out of anger.
- state exactly what you want—a new paint job, for example.

Special Concerns for Month-to-Month Tenants

If you have a month-to-month tenancy, your landlord can, in most states, terminate your tenancy with just 30 days' notice. That means you should think twice before trying one of the adversarial strategies discussed below—reporting your landlord for building code violations or suing in small claims court—over minor problems with your rental.

An antiretaliation law, if one is in force where you live, may protect you from a termination notice. (See "State Laws Prohibiting Landlord Retaliation" in Appendix A for details on your state rules.) But if you have to go to court to argue about it all, you may end up wishing you'd never complained about that cracked tile. Remember, you can end your tenancy with 30 days' notice, too—so if you're really unhappy with your place, maybe you should look for another.

Sample Letter Asking for Minor Repairs

90 Willow Run, Apartment 3A
Morgantown, Arizona 00000

February 28, 20xx

Mr. Lee Sloan
37 Main Street, Suite 100
Morgantown, Arizona 00000

Dear Mr. Sloan:

I would appreciate it if you could schedule an appointment with me to look at three problems in my apartment that have come up recently.

First, the kitchen sink is dripping, and it's getting worse. I'm concerned that a plate or dish towel might stop up the drain, leading to an overflow. At any rate, the water bill is yours, and I'm sure that you don't want to pay for wasted water.

I've also been having trouble opening the sliding doors on the bedroom closet. The track appears to be coming away from the wall, and the doors wobble and look like they might fall into the room when I open and close the closet.

Thanks very much for thinking about my requests. I hope to hear from you soon.

Yours truly,

Chris Jensen
Chris Jensen

 CAUTION

Think twice about using email or text messages. In Chapter 6, "Using Email or Text Messages for Notice or a Letter of Understanding" explains why it's best to send important communications, such as repair requests, by mail (certified or return receipt requested) or delivery service, rather than email or text messages.

Always keep a copy of the letter for your files, and hand-deliver the letter or send it "return-receipt requested."

Proposing Mediation

If your demand letter does not produce results, consider involving the help of a local mediation center. Most community services handle lots of landlord and tenant problems, for free or at a very low cost. If they can coax the landlord to talk with you (and they're very good at doing that), you have a decent chance of ending up with an agreement. See Chapter 19 for more information on mediation.

Reporting Code Violations

If appealing to your landlord's business sensibilities doesn't work, other strategies are available to pry minor repairs out of your landlord.

If the problem you want fixed constitutes a code violation, such as inadequate electrical outlets or low water pressure, you should find an ally in the building or housing agency in charge of enforcing the code. (Chapter 8 covers how to find and what to expect from these local agencies.) Whether you'll get any action out of the agency will depend on the seriousness of the violation, the workload of the agency, and its ability to enforce its compliance orders. Since by definition your problem is minor, don't expect lots of help if code enforcement officials are already overworked.

Suing in Small Claims Court

If you can reasonably argue that you aren't getting what you paid for, you might decide to sue in small claims court. But before you do, write a second demand letter. Like the first letter (see the sample above), your second letter should describe the problems and alert the landlord to the negative consequences (to him, not just to you) that may follow if repairs aren't made. In addition, state that you intend to sue if you don't get results. This may get the landlord's attention and save you a trip to the courthouse.

EXAMPLE: Chris Jensen wrote to her landlord on February 28, requesting repairs as shown in the sample letter above. She got no reply. Ten days later, she sent a second letter that summarized the first and concluded with this paragraph:

"If you are unable to attend to these repairs, I'll need to call in a handyman to repair the faucet and doors, and I will seek reimbursement from you in small claims court if necessary. Of course, I sincerely hope that this will not be necessary."

If the second letter doesn't produce results, it's time to head for small claims court. You won't need a lawyer; just go to the court and ask for the forms you need to sue someone. In small claims court, you can't get an order from the judge directing your landlord to paint, fix the dishwasher, or repair the intercom. You may, however, be compensated in dollars for living in a rental unit with repair problems. Here's how it works.

When you file your small claims court suit, you'll ask for an amount that reflects the difference between your rent and the value of the unit with repair problems. (To calculate this amount, use one of the methods described in "What to Do If the Landlord Won't Make Repairs" in Chapter 8.) In court, your argument will be that you are not getting the benefit of what you're paying rent for— for example, a functioning dishwasher, presentable paint, or a working air conditioner.

You're more likely to succeed with this line of argument if you have a lease rather than a month-to-month agreement. If you have a long-term lease, you can argue that you are locked into a set rent for an extended period of time and should be compensated accordingly—that is, month after month, you receive less than what you are obligated to pay for. In contrast, a month-to-month tenant has no long-standing obligation; if you don't like the fact that the shower door now won't close, you can leave after giving relatively short notice, with no legal liability for future rent. A judge is likely to point this out and to tell you that, in effect, you agreed to the increasing shabbiness every month when you failed to send in a termination notice.

> **CAUTION**
>
> **Don't stop paying rent.** Although fairness dictates that if your rental unit is full of repair problems you ought to pay less rent, it's a mistake to pay your landlord less than the full monthly rent. Rent withholding, as discussed in Chapter 8, is legally appropriate only for major repairs. If you withhold even a portion of the rent because of a minor repair problem, you risk eviction for nonpayment of rent.

Your goal in small claims court is to convince the judge that these problems really make your rental unit worth less money. Use common sense—don't go running to court for small things. A small claims court judge is not going to adjust your rent because a little grout is missing from your bathroom tile. But if your dishwasher is broken, three faucets leak noisily, and the bathroom door won't close properly, your chances of winning go way up. You'll need to show the judge that:

- there are lots of minor defects, not just an isolated one, and
- you've given the landlord plenty of time and notice to fix the problems.

Bring evidence. Winning in small claims court depends more on what you bring into court to prove your story than on what you say. Examples of key evidence include:

- copies of letters you've written asking for repairs
- your written notes on your landlord's response to your repair requests, including the number of times they were ignored or promised repairs didn't materialize
- witnesses—a family member, for example, who can describe the inoperable air conditioner
- photographs—your pictures of the cracked, flaking plaster, for example

- a copy of the local building or housing code, if the problem is covered there
- your lease or rental agreement, if it lists any of the items that need repair
- your lease or rental agreement, if it prohibits you from making repairs yourself
- a copy of the Landlord-Tenant Checklist, which you should have completed when you moved in and which is signed by you and the landlord, showing that the problem did not exist at the start of your tenancy, and
- ads, brochures, or For Rent signs describing features of your rental that are missing or malfunctioning.

For more advice on preparing for and filing a small claims court case, see Chapter 16.

EXAMPLE: Judy signed a one-year lease for a studio apartment at $750 a month. When she moved in, the place was in good shape. But six months into her tenancy, the condition of the apartment began to deteriorate. A water leak from the roof stained and buckled several areas of the hardwood floors; the kitchen cabinets, which were apparently badly made, warped and would not shut; the dishwasher became so noisy the neighbor banged on the wall when it was in use; the soap dish fell off the bathroom wall; and the white entryway rug started to fall apart. Judy asked her landlord to attend to these problems and followed up with several written demand letters. Two months after her original request, Judy wrote a final demand letter.

When the landlord still did nothing, Judy filed suit in small claims court, asking the judge to award her damages (money) representing the difference between her rent and the value of the deteriorated apartment. After considering Judy's evidence, including copies of her demand letter, photographs of the defects, and the testimony of her neighbor, the judge agreed with Judy. She figured that the deteriorated apartment would have rented for $150 less a month, and ordered the landlord to pay Judy $450 to make up for the three months she had lived with the defects. Judy's landlord was quick to make repairs after learning this expensive lesson in court.

RESOURCE

Everybody's Guide to Small Claims Court, by Cara O'Neill (Nolo), has all the details you need to file a small claims court lawsuit.

Making Minor Repairs Yourself

If you've concluded that a repair job isn't your landlord's responsibility, that means it's in your lap.

Before you head out to the hardware store, pause for a moment. You need to know, first, whether it makes sense from a practical point of view for you to do the repair or maintenance, and, second, whether it's legal.

Evaluating Your Skills and Time

Before you embark on a job, realistically assess its magnitude and your skills, tools, and time. Seemingly easy repairs often have hidden complexities. A simple job, like replacing the flexible hoses under the sink that connect the pipes to the faucet, may require special wrenches because of the cramped workspace. Do you have this equipment, or are you willing to purchase it? Time is also an issue: Are you willing to commit precious weekend or evening time to a plumbing project? Only an experienced, equipped handyperson (or one willing to consult a good do-it-yourself manual) should consider doing most home repairs.

You must also consider whether or not you are willing to take the risk of being held liable if one of your repair projects goes awry and results in property damage or, worse, someone's injury. Your landlord's insurance policy will not cover your misdeeds, and unless you have renters' insurance, you stand to lose a lot of money.

EXAMPLE: Colin decided to replace a window that was broken by his daughter's basketball. He removed the shards of glass, fitted a new pane in place and caulked the circumference. Colin mistakenly used the wrong type of caulk, and a year later it had cracked, allowing rainwater to seep onto the windowsill and down the wall. The landlord was furious when he realized that he would have to replace the sill and the drywall, simply because Colin had not done a workmanlike job. The cost of these repairs was taken out of Colin's security deposit.

Getting the Landlord's Permission

First, look at your lease or rental agreement. You may see a clause that forbids you from undertaking any "repairs, alterations, or improvements" without the landlord's consent. (Alterations and improvements are discussed in Chapter 10.) It may seem unfair, but such a clause is legal. And a "no repairs without consent" clause keeps the landlord in control of the property, while making you pay for it.

If your lease has a "no repairs" clause, you'll have to convince the landlord to give you permission. (See the sample letter below.) And even if you have such a clause, check with the landlord first, anyway. You won't need to do this if the repair or replacement is truly insignificant and nontechnical (or if it's unlikely to be noticed by the landlord), like replacing the entryway rug or installing miniblinds where old ones used to be.

But for jobs that have the potential to get complicated, expensive, or have dire consequences if things go wrong, you'll want to have the official okay before proceeding. It may prevent your landlord from legally charging you if things go awry. Of course, a potential negative outcome may be the very reason your landlord will say "No way" and call for the bonded repair person. But many landlords—if they trust you—will be happy to save themselves the time and trouble of lining up a worker, scheduling a time to be in your apartment, getting you to pay the bill, or deducting the expense from your security deposit and then getting you to bring the deposit up to its original level.

To protect yourself, put your repair proposal in writing, phrase it in a way that tells the landlord you'll proceed unless you hear to the contrary within a reasonable amount of time, and keep a copy for your records. That way, you have a record that your work was undertaken with the landlord's consent. A sample letter is shown below; notice how the tenant has communicated the problem, her experience with similar repairs, and a plan for repairing the item, all of which are designed to inspire the landlord's confidence.

Sample Letter Requesting Permission to Do a Minor Repair

890 Market Street, #3
Central City, Texas 00000
214-555-7890

January 4, 20xx

Jackson Montgomery
234 Fourth Street
Central City, Texas 00000

Dear Mr. Montgomery,

Last night, a fork accidentally fell into my garbage disposal, jamming the blades and causing the unit to stop. The disposal will have to be taken out and the blade assembly examined. The shear key, which prevents the engine from seizing, will need to be replaced.

I am familiar with the installation and maintenance of these appliances, having worked on one at my former residence. I have the tools to do the job. I'll proceed with this repair unless I hear from you to the contrary. Please leave me a note or call me before January 10 if you do not wish me to do the job. If I don't hear from you by then, I'll go ahead.

Yours truly,

Janet Green

Janet Green

Making Improvements and Alterations

Improvements That Become Part of the Property... 164

Improving Your Rental Unit Without Enriching Your Landlord...165

Cable TV Access...167

Previously Unwired Buildings..167

Exclusive Contracts With Cable Providers..168

Satellite Dishes and Other Antennas..168

Devices Covered by the FCC Rule...168

Permissible Installation of Satellite Dishes and Antennas 169

Restrictions on Installation Techniques..169

Placement and Orientation of Antennas and Reception Devices 170

Supplying a Central Antenna or Satellite Dish for All Tenants...170

How to Handle Disputes About the Use and Placement of Antennas
and Satellite Dishes 171

Your lease or rental agreement probably includes a clause prohibiting you from making any alterations or improvements to your unit without the express, written consent of the landlord. (Often, your landlord will forbid you to undertake repairs, too. This issue is discussed in Chapter 9.) Landlords use these clauses—some of which contain a long list of prohibitions—so that tenants don't change the light fixtures, knock out a wall, install a built-in dishwasher, or even pound in a nail to hang a picture unless the landlord agrees first.

But what if you make one of these alterations or improvements without getting your landlord's permission—for example, you bolt a closet storage system to the wall? In most states, unless you get the landlord's permission to remove the item, such improvements and additions become the landlord's property when you leave.

Discovering too late that you must leave behind what you thought of as a portable improvement can be a real blow. To help you avoid problems, this chapter explains:

- what types of improvements and alterations become the landlord's property
- what you can do, ahead of time, to forestall losing your property
- how to minimize your losses if your landlord insists that the improvement remain on the property, and
- special rules for cable TV access and satellite dishes.

 RELATED TOPIC
Also covered in this book:

- Typical lease and rental agreement restrictions on tenant improvements and alterations: Chapter 2.
- Disabled tenants' rights to modify their living space: Chapter 5.
- Performing minor repairs with the landlord's consent: Chapter 9.

Improvements That Become Part of the Property

Anything you attach to a building, fence, or deck, or the ground itself belongs to the landlord, absent an agreement saying it's yours. (Lawyers call such items "fixtures.") This is a basic legal principle, and it's also spelled out in most leases and rental agreements. This means when you move out, the landlord is legally entitled to refuse your offer to remove the fixture and return the premises to its original state. In addition, many leases and rental agreements make it even clearer what types of improvements belong to the landlord. A typical clause looks something like this: "Any alterations, installations, or improvements, including shelving and attached floor coverings, will become the property of the owner and will remain with and as part of the rental premises at the end of the term."

In some cases, a landlord and departing tenant can't agree on who owns a particular piece of property, and the dispute ends up in court. Judges use a variety of legal rules to determine whether an object—an appliance, flooring, shelving, or plumbing—is something that you can take with you or is a permanent fixture belonging to your landlord. Here are some of the questions judges ask:

- **Did you get the landlord's permission?** If you never asked the landlord to install a closet organizer, or you did and got no for an answer, a judge is likely to rule for your landlord—particularly if your lease or rental agreement prohibits alterations or improvements.
- **Did you make any structural changes that affect the use or appearance of the property?** If so, chances are that the item will be deemed the landlord's, because removing it will often leave an unsightly area or alter the use of part of the property. For example, if you modify the kitchen counter to accommodate a built-in dishwasher and then take the dishwasher

with you, the landlord will have to install another dishwasher of the same dimensions or rebuild the space. The law doesn't impose this extra work on landlords, nor does it force them to let you do the return-to-original work yourself.

- **Is the object firmly attached to the property?** In general, additions and improvements that are nailed, screwed, or cemented to the building are likely to be deemed "fixtures." For example, hollow-wall screws that anchor a bookcase might convert an otherwise free-standing unit belonging to the tenant to a fixture belonging to the landlord. Similarly, closet rods bolted to the wall become part of the structure and would usually be counted as fixtures. On the other hand, shelving systems that are secured by isometric pressure (spring-loaded rods that press against the ceiling and floor) involve no actual attachment to the wall and for that reason are not likely to be classified as fixtures. Even if you have a very good reason for firmly attaching your addition—bolting a bookcase to the wall for earthquake protection, for example—you may still end up having to leave it behind.

- **What did you and the landlord intend?** Courts will look at statements made by you and the landlord to determine whether there was any understanding as to your right to remove an improvement. In some circumstances, courts will even infer an agreement from your actions—for instance, if your landlord stopped by and gave permission for you to install what you've described as a portable air conditioner, or helped you lift it into place. (Your chances of convincing the judge would be greatly enhanced if you had gotten permission in writing, as explained below.) By contrast, if you remove the landlord's light fixtures and, without his knowledge, install a custom-made fixture that could not be used

in any other space, it is unlikely that you could convince a judge that you reasonably expected to take it with you at the end of your tenancy.

Improvements That Plug or Screw In

The act of plugging in an appliance doesn't make the appliance a part of the premises. The same is true for simple wiring or pipe attachments to join an appliance to an electrical or water source. For example, a refrigerator or free-standing stove remains the property of the tenant. Similarly, portable dishwashers that connect to the kitchen faucet by means of a coupling may be removed.

Improving Your Rental Unit Without Enriching Your Landlord

Your best protection against losing an item you love is not to attach it to a wall in your unit. Fortunately, hundreds of items are on the market—bookcases, lighting systems, closet organizers, and even dishwashers—that you can take with you when you leave. To get some good ideas, visit a large hardware store, a home improvement center, or a business devoted to closet organization systems.

If you are determined to attach something to the wall or floor, talk to the landlord before you get out your tools. If you can, get the landlord to agree to pay for the improvement or to let you remove it when you leave.

Decide beforehand which option you prefer. For example, since a custom-made track lighting system won't do you any good if you take it with you, find out whether the landlord will pay for it in the first place. On the other hand, if you want to take the fixture with you, impress upon the landlord your intent to carefully restore the property to its original condition. Keep in

Agreement Regarding Tenant Improvements to Rental Unit

Mark Henderson _____ ["Tenant"]

and _____ Robin Reese _____ ["Landlord"]

agree as follows:

Tenant may make the following alterations to the rental unit at: _____ 370 Alpine Way, San Jose, _____

California 00000

Install window unit air conditioner in the master bedroom. _____

_____ .

Tenant will accomplish the improvements by using the following materials and procedures:

Purchasing a Cold Spot window air conditioner unit, Model 34A, and anchoring it to the window frame

using manufacturer's enclosed brackets. _____ .

Landlord and Tenant further agree that (*check either 1 or 2*)

☑ 1. The improvement will become Landlord's property and is not to be removed by Tenant. Landlord will reimburse Tenant for (*check a or b or both*)

    ☑ a. the cost of material, and/or

    ☐ b. labor costs at a rate of $_____ per hour, after Tenant provides receipts and the Landlord determines that the work has been done in a workmanlike and acceptable manner.

    Landlord will reimburse Tenant (*check c or d*):

    ☑ c. by lump sum payment, within a reasonable time, or

    ☐ d. by reducing Tenant's rent, according to the following schedule: _____

    _____

☐ 2. The improvement will considered Tenant's personal property, and as such may be removed by Tenant at any time up to the end of the tenancy. Tenant promises to return the premises to their original condition upon removing the improvement. If Tenant fails to do this, Landlord may deduct the cost of restoring the premises to their original condition from Tenant's security deposit.

Mark Henderson _____ _May 10, 20xx_ _____
Landlord   Date

Robin Reese _____ _May 10, 20xx_ _____
Tenant   Date

mind that if your restoration attempts are less than acceptable, the landlord will be justified in deducting from your security deposit the amount of money necessary to do the job right. And if the deposit is insufficient, the landlord can sue you in small claims court for the excess.

Approach your landlord as one businessperson dealing with another. If the improvement will remain and you seek reimbursement, point out that it will make the property more attractive. It might even justify a higher rent for the next tenant and thus pay for itself over the long run. Your landlord might agree to reduce your rent a little each month or simply reimburse you all at once. (You could also mention that the IRS will end up paying for a portion of the improvement, since it will be deductible as a business cost.)

If you and the landlord reach an understanding, put it in writing. As shown in the sample agreement above, you will want to carefully describe the project and materials and state whether you are to be reimbursed or allowed to take the improvement with you.

FORM

The Nolo website includes a downloadable copy of the Agreement Regarding Tenant Improvements to Rental Unit form. See Appendix B for a link to the forms in this book.

TIP

Save all receipts for materials and labor. Whether you will be reimbursed or will take the fixture with you when you leave, it is important to keep a good record of the amount of money you spend on the project. That way, there can be no dispute as to what you're owed if you are to be reimbursed. If the landlord changes his mind and doesn't let you remove the improvement at the end of your tenancy, you'll have receipts to back up your small claims lawsuit for the value of the addition.

Cable TV Access

If you're lucky, the wonders of cable TV may already be in the rental property through coaxial cables that are strung along telephone poles or underground and into the building, with a single plug on the exterior of the structure and with branches to individual units. To sign up for service, you need only call the cable provider to activate the existing cable line to your unit. But what happens if the building does not have cable access now? And if the landlord has a contract with one provider, can you insist that he open his lines to another, competing provider?

Providing cable access is a bit more complicated than the situation you face when you ask to install a bookcase or paint a room. The federal government has something to say under the Federal Telecommunications Act of 1996 (47 U.S.C. §§ 151 and following). In this Act, Congress decreed that all Americans should have as much access as possible to information that comes through a cable or over the air on wireless transmissions. The Act makes it very difficult for state and local governments, zoning commissions, homeowners' associations, and landlords to impose restrictions that hamper a person's ability to take advantage of these new types of communications.

Previously Unwired Buildings

Fortunately, most residential rental properties are already wired for cable. In competitive urban markets especially, landlords have figured out that they'll have a hard time attracting tenants if they do not give them the option of paying for cable. However, in the event that the property does not have cable, your landlord is entitled to continue to resist modernity and say "No" to tenants who ask for access. If this is the response you get from your landlord, you may want to consider mounting a satellite dish. See "Satellite Dishes and Other Antennas," below, for rules governing these devices.

Exclusive Contracts With Cable Providers

Many multifamily buildings have been wired for cable. In competitive markets, some landlords have signed exclusive contracts with service providers, claiming that these contracts enable them to obtain better service, at better prices, and that these savings are being passed on to tenants. Some states disagreed with what they saw as an anticompetitive setup, and many passed laws forbidding exclusive contracts. On the federal level, however, the FCC gave its blessing to exclusive contracts in residential settings.

Everything changed in October 2007, when the FCC reversed its position and ruled that in every state, not only are exclusive contracts unenforceable, but exclusive clauses in existing contracts will not be enforced. The new order means that any exclusive clauses your landlord may now have in its contracts are unenforceable, and it may not enter into any new ones. The landlord does *not*, however, have to let any cable company that asks into its building, though pressure from tenants may lead the landlord to open up.

TIP
Don't confuse "forced access" with your wish to obtain alternate service. "Forced access" refers to the technology that lets consumers choose from among several ISPs when they subscribe to a cable modem-based broadband service. The argument around forced access is between cable providers and ISPs. Many states require cable companies to provide open access, but these laws typically do not mean that landlords must open their buildings to any cable provider.

Satellite Dishes and Other Antennas

Wireless communications have the potential to reach more people with less hardware than any cable system. But there is one, essential piece of equipment: a satellite dish with wires connecting it to the television set or computer.

You may be familiar with the car-sized dishes often seen in backyards or on roofs of houses—the pink flamingo of the modern age. Now, smaller and cheaper dishes, two feet or less in diameter, are available. Wires from the dishes can easily be run under a door or through an open window to a TV or computer. Tenants have attached these dishes to interior walls and also to roofs, windowsills, balconies, and railings. Landlords have reacted strongly, in particular to the outside placements, citing their unsightly looks and the potential for liability if one should fall and injure someone.

Fortunately, the Federal Communications Commission (FCC) has provided considerable guidance on residential use of satellite dishes and antennas (Over-the-Air Reception Devices Rule, 47 C.F.R. § 1.4000, further explained in the FCC's Fact Sheet, "Over-the-Air Reception Devices Rule"). Basically, the FCC prohibits landlords from imposing restrictions that unreasonably impair your ability to install, maintain, or use an antenna or dish that meets the criteria described below. Here's a brief overview of the FCC rule.

RESOURCE
Complete details on the FCC's rule on satellite dishes and antennas. See www.fcc.gov/guides/installing-consumer-owned-antennas-and-satellite-dishes, or call the FCC at 888-CALLFCC (toll free). The FCC's rule was upheld in *Building Owners and Managers Assn. v. FCC*, 254 F.3d 89 (D.C. Cir. 2001).

Devices Covered by the FCC Rule

The FCC's rule applies to video antennas, including direct-to-home satellite dishes that are less than one meter (39.37 inches) in diameter (or any size in Alaska); TV antennas; and wireless cable antennas. These pieces of equipment receive video programming signals from direct broadcast satellites, wireless cable providers, and television broadcast stations. Antennas up to 18 inches in diameter that transmit as well as receive fixed wireless telecom signals (not just video) are also included.

Exceptions: Antennas used for AM/FM radio, amateur ("ham"), and Citizen's Band ("CB") radio or Digital Audio Radio Services ("DARS") are excluded from the FCC's rule. Landlords may restrict the installation of these types of antennas in the same way that they can restrict any modification or alteration of rented space, as explained in the first sections of this chapter.

Permissible Installation of Satellite Dishes and Antennas

Tenants may place antennas or dishes only in their own, exclusive rented space, such as inside the rental unit or on a balcony, terrace, deck, or patio. The device must be wholly within the rented space (if it overhangs the balcony, the landlord may prohibit that placement). Also, landlords may prohibit you from drilling through exterior walls, even if that wall is also part of your rented space.

The FCC rule specifies that you cannot place a reception device in common areas, such as roofs, hallways, walkways, or the exterior walls of the building. Exterior windows are no different from exterior walls—for this reason, placing a dish or antenna on a window by means of a series of suction cups is impermissible under the FCC rule (obviously, such an installation is also unsafe). Tenants who rent single-family homes, however, may install devices in the home itself or on patios, yards, gardens, or other similar areas.

Restrictions on Installation Techniques

Landlords are free to set restrictions on how the devices are installed, as long as the restrictions are not unreasonably expensive or are imposed for safety reasons or to preserve historic aspects of the structure. The landlord cannot insist that his maintenance personnel (or professional installers) do the work (but the landlord may set reasonable guidelines as to how the devices should be installed, as explained below).

Expense

Landlords may not impose a flat fee or charge you additional rent if you want to erect an antenna or dish. On the other hand, the landlord may be able to insist on certain installation techniques that will add expense—as long as the cost isn't excessive and reception will not be impaired. Examples of acceptable expenses include:

- insisting that an antenna be painted green in order to blend into the landscaping, or
- requiring the use of a universal bracket which future tenants could use, saving wear and tear on the building.

 TIP

Rules for mounting satellite dishes or antennas shouldn't be more restrictive than those that apply to artwork, flags, clotheslines, or similar items. After all, attaching telecommunications items is no more intrusive or invasive than bolting a sundial to the porch, screwing a thermometer to the wall, or nailing a rain gauge to a railing. If your landlord's standards for telecommunications devices are much stricter than guidelines for other improvements or alterations, you may have a good argument that he's violating the FCC rules. See below for information on how to respond to unreasonable landlord rules.

Safety Concerns

Landlords can insist that you place and install devices in a way that will minimize the chances of accidents and will not violate safety or fire codes. In fact, the FCC directs landlords to give tenants written notice of safety restrictions, so that tenants will know in advance how to comply. For example, it's not a good idea to place a satellite dish on a fire escape, near a power plant, or near a walkway where passersby might accidentally hit their heads. Your landlord may also insist on proper installation techniques, such as those explained in the instructions that come with most devices. What if proper installation (attaching a dish to a wall) means that the landlord will have to eventually patch and paint a wall? Can the landlord use this as reason for preventing installation? No—unless there are legitimate reasons for prohibiting the installation, such as a safety concern. When you move out and remove the device, however, your landlord may charge you for the cost of repairing the attachment spot (such as replastering and repainting).

> **CAUTION**
> **A savvy landlord will require tenants who install antennas or dishes to carry renters' insurance.** If the device falls and injures someone, your policy will cover any claim.

Preserving the Building's Historical Integrity

Your landlord may argue that the historical integrity of his property will be compromised if an antenna or satellite dish is attached. This isn't an easy claim to make. A landlord can use this argument only if the property is included in (or eligible for) the National Register of Historic Places, the nation's official list of buildings, structures, objects, sites, and districts worthy of preservation for their significance in American history, architecture, archaeology, and culture. For more information on what's required to qualify for the Register and for a database of registered places, see www.nps.gov/nr.

Placement and Orientation of Antennas and Reception Devices

Tenants have the right to place an antenna where they'll receive an "acceptable quality" signal. As long as the tenant's chosen spot is within the exclusive rented space, not on an exterior wall or in a common area as discussed above, the landlord may not set rules on placement—for example, the landlord cannot require that an antenna be placed only in the rear of the rental property if this results in the tenant's receiving a "substantially degraded" signal or no signal at all.

Reception devices that need to maintain line-of-sight contact with a transmitter or view a satellite may not work if they're stuck behind a wall or below the roofline. In particular, a dish must be on a south wall, since satellites are in the southern hemisphere. Faced with a reception problem, you may want to move the device to another location or mount it on a pole, so that it clears the obstructing roof or wall. Tenants who have no other workable exclusive space may want to mount their devices on a mast, in hopes of clearing the obstacle. Depending on the situation, you may have the right to do so.

- **Single-family rentals.** Tenants may erect a mast that's 12 feet above the roofline or less without asking permission first—and the landlord must allow it if the mast is installed in a safe manner. If the mast is taller than 12 feet, the landlord may require the tenant to obtain permission before erecting it—but if the installation meets reasonable safety requirements, the landlord should allow its use.
- **Multifamily rentals.** Tenants may use a mast as long as it does not extend beyond their exclusive rented space. For example, in a two-story rental, a mast that is attached to the ground-floor patio and extends into the air space opposite your own second floor would be permissible. On the other hand, a mast attached to a top-story deck, which extends above the roofline or outward over the railing, would not be protected by the FCC's rule—a landlord could prohibit this installation because it extends beyond the tenant's exclusive rented space.

Supplying a Central Antenna or Satellite Dish for All Tenants

Faced with the prospect of many dishes and antennas adorning an otherwise clean set of balconies, some landlords have installed a central antenna or dish for use by all.

Landlords may install a central antenna and restrict the use of individual antennas by tenants only if the central device provides:

- **Equal access.** The tenant must be able to get the same programming or fixed wireless service that he could receive with his own antenna.
- **Equal quality.** The signal quality to and from the tenant's home via the antenna must be as good as or better than what the tenant could get using his own device.
- **Equal value.** The costs of using the central device must be the same as or less than the cost of installing, maintaining, and using an individual antenna.
- **Equal readiness.** Landlords can't prohibit individual devices if installation of a central antenna will unreasonably delay the tenant's ability to receive programming or fixed wireless services—for example, when the central antenna won't be available for months.

If a landlord has installed a central antenna after tenants have installed their own, the landlord may require removal of the individual antennas, as long as the central device meets the above requirements. Your landlord will have to pay you for the removal of your device and compensate you for the value of the antenna.

How to Handle Disputes About the Use and Placement of Antennas and Satellite Dishes

In spite of the FCC's attempts to clarify tenants' rights to reception and landlords' rights to control what happens on their property, there are many possibilities for disagreements. For example, what exactly is "acceptable" reception? If the landlord requires antennas to be painted, at what point is the expense considered "unreasonable?"

Ideally, your landlord will avoid disputes in the first place, by setting reasonable policies. But, if all else fails, here are some tips to help you resolve the problem with a minimum of fuss and expense.

Discussion, Mediation, and Help From the FCC

First, approach the problem the way you would any dispute—talk it out and try to reach an acceptable conclusion. Follow our advice in Chapter 16 for settling disputes on your own—for example, through negotiation or mediation. You'll find the information on the FCC website very helpful. The direct broadcast satellite company, multichannel distribution service, TV broadcast station, or fixed wireless company may also be able to suggest alternatives that are safe and acceptable to both you and your landlord.

Get the FCC Involved

If your own attempts don't resolve the problem, you can call the FCC and ask for oral guidance. You may also formally ask the FCC for a written opinion, called a Declaratory Ruling. For information on obtaining oral or written guidance from the FCC, follow the directions as shown on the FCC website at www.fcc.gov/consumers/guides/installing-consumer-owned-antennas-and-satellite-dishes. Fortunately for tenants, unless the landlord's objections concern safety or historic preservation, the landlord must allow the device to remain pending the FCC's ruling.

Go to Court

When all else fails, you can head for court. If the antenna or satellite dish hasn't been installed yet and you and the landlord are arguing about the reasonableness of the landlord's policies or your plans, you can ask a court to rule on who's right (just as you would when seeking the FCC's opinion). You'll have to go to a regular trial court for a resolution of your dispute, where you'll ask for an order called a "Declaratory Judgment." Similarly, if the antenna or dish *has* been installed and the landlord wants a judge to order it removed, the landlord will have to go to a regular trial court and ask for such an order. (Unfortunately, the simpler option of small claims court will not usually be available in these situations, because most small courts handle only disputes that can be settled or decided with money, not requests about whether it's acceptable to do (or not do) a particular task.)

Needless to say, being in regular trial court means that the case will be drawn out and expensive. You could handle it yourself, but be forewarned—you'll need to be adept at arguing about First Amendment law and Congressional intent and be willing to spend long hours in the library preparing your case. In the end, you may decide that it would have been cheaper to follow the Yankees on cable TV.

Your Right to Privacy

Entry by the Landlord..174

    Allowable Reasons..174

    Notice Requirements..177

    Clarifying Access Rules..178

    Cooperating With Requests to Enter...179

Entry by Others...179

    Health, Safety, or Building Inspections..179

    Law Enforcement...180

    Your Landlord's Right to Let Others In...180

Other Invasions of Privacy...181

    Giving Information About You to Strangers..181

    Bothering You at Work...181

    Unduly Restricting Guests...182

    Spying on You...182

    Self-Help Evictions...182

    Sexual Harassment or Assault..182

What to Do About Invasions of Privacy...182

    Step 1. Talk to the Landlord or Manager..183

    Step 2. Write a Tough Letter..183

    Step 3. Sue Your Landlord...184

    Step 4. Move Out...185

There's no place like home—unless, of course, you have a landlord who doesn't respect your right to privacy. The problem typically arises with a landlord or manager who cannot stop fussing over the property or who frequently tries to wangle an invitation into your home to look around. Even worse are landlords and managers who use a passkey to enter without notice when you're not at home and there is no emergency. The idea that a landlord might at any time violate your private space and even go through your personal belongings is, obviously, scary.

This chapter covers your basic rights to privacy and what to do about a landlord or manager who violates these rights. You can sue your landlord for entering unlawfully—but it's rarely worth the time or trouble. Unfortunately, the law won't solve all problems inherent in dealing with difficult people. In some instances, you may find that you'll either have to grin and bear the actions of an intrusive landlord or move on.

RELATED TOPIC

To avoid problems with obnoxious landlords at your next place, be sure to talk with other tenants before you move in. Chapter 1 provides advice on checking out prospective landlords. Also, see Chapter 2 for typical lease and rental provisions regarding landlord right of access.

State Laws on Landlord's Entry

About half the states have statutes specifying when and how landlords may legally enter rented property. (See "State Laws on Landlord's Access to Rental Property" in Appendix A for details.) In other states, your right to privacy is determined by your state's and the federal Constitution, as interpreted by the courts. If you want to know its precise extent, you'll have to research the law yourself or get help from a lawyer or tenants' rights group. See Chapter 20 for information on legal research.

Entry by the Landlord

When you rent residential property, the rental unit is your home and should be respected as such. Your landlord must have a good reason to enter your apartment and must meet legal notice requirements.

Allowable Reasons

Landlords always can come in when you give permission or any time there is a genuine emergency that threatens life or property, like a fire or a serious water leak. Nearly every state has, by judicial decision or statute, decided that landlords can also enter, after notifying you beforehand, to:

- make needed repairs or improvements or assess the need for them, or
- show property to prospective tenants or purchasers.

In addition, a landlord who believes you have abandoned the property—that is, skipped out without giving any notice or returning the key—may legally enter.

The following sections provide details on each of these reasons.

Entry With Your Permission

Obviously, your landlord can always enter rental property if you agree. But don't let your landlord coerce your permission. A landlord who pressures you, perhaps implying or even threatening eviction if you don't allow immediate or virtually unrestricted access, is clearly violating your privacy rights. See "What to Do About Invasions of Privacy," below, for advice on how to deal with this situation.

Emergencies

In all states, landlords can enter your rental unit without giving notice to respond to a true emergency that threatens injury or property damage. Here are some examples:

- Smoke is pouring out of your apartment window. Your landlord calls the fire department and uses a master key—or even breaks in if necessary—to try to deal with the fire.
- Your landlord sees water coming out of the bottom of your back door. It's okay to enter and find the water leak.
- You hear screams coming from the rental unit next door and call the manager. She knocks on the apartment door, but gets no answer. After calling the police, the manager uses her passkey to enter and see what's wrong.
- Your family and friends, worried that you haven't been at work or reachable by phone over the long weekend, ask your landlord to enter your apartment to make sure everything's okay. He does so and finds nothing amiss; you show up a day later, having taken a spur-of-the moment vacation.

On the other hand, a property owner's urge to repair a problem that's important but doesn't threaten life or property—say, a stopped-up drain that is not causing any damage—isn't a true emergency.

A landlord who does need to enter your apartment in an emergency should leave a note or call you explaining the circumstances and the date and time. If you don't get this kind of notification, make it clear in writing that you expect it.

 TIP
Your landlord is legally entitled to a key to your rental unit. Check your lease or rental agreement; many forbid tenants from rekeying, adding additional locks, or installing a security system without the landlord's permission. If a landlord does grant you permission to change or add locks, you may need to provide duplicate keys. If you install a security system, you may need to give your landlord the name and phone number of the alarm company or instructions on how to disarm the system in an emergency.

Repairs

Many states, either by statute or court decision, allow a landlord or repairperson to enter rental property to make necessary or agreed-upon repairs, alterations, or improvements—for example, to fix a broken oven or replace the carpet. This includes the landlord's entry to assess the need for or cost of repairs.

In these situations, the landlord generally must enter only at reasonable times and must give you at least the required amount of notice, usually 24 hours. (Notice requirements are discussed below.) However, if this is impracticable—for example, a repairperson is available on a few hours' notice—a landlord will probably be on solid ground by explaining the situation to you and giving shorter notice. Of course, if you agree to a shorter notice period, your landlord has no problem.

> **EXAMPLE:** Amy told her landlord Brett that her bathroom sink was stopped up and draining very slowly. Brett called the plumber, who said that he had several large jobs in progress, but would be able to squeeze in Amy's repair at some point within the next few days. The plumber promised to call Brett before he came over. Brett relayed this information to Amy, telling her he would give her at least four hours' notice before the plumber came.

 TIP
Avoid hassles with repair people. Here's how:
- Be sure your landlord knows and trusts the service and repair people allowed to enter your rental unit. If new service providers are used, their references should be checked, and your landlord or manager should be present at all times.
- Try to be home (or ask your landlord to be present) when repairs will be made to avoid possible loss of or damage to your belongings or the rental unit.
- Always get the repairperson's phone number in advance, so you can reschedule if need be.
- Make sure your landlord notifies you if plans change. You may be justifiably annoyed if the repairperson shows up late or not at all.

Maintenance While You're Away

Several states with privacy statutes give landlords the legal right to enter rental premises if you are away for an extended period, often defined as seven days or more. The landlord is allowed to maintain the property as necessary and to inspect for damage and needed repairs. For example, if you live in a cold-weather place such as Connecticut, your landlord may want to check the pipes in your house to make sure they haven't burst when you are away for winter vacation.

While many states do not address this issue, either by way of statute or court decision, your landlord is probably on safe legal ground to enter your rental unit during your extended absence if there is a genuine need to protect the property from damage. But your landlord should enter only if something really needs to be done—that is, something you would do if you were home as part of your obligation to keep the property clean, safe, and in good repair. (See Chapter 8 for a discussion of tenant repair and maintenance responsibilities.) For example, if you leave your windows wide open just before a driving rainstorm, your landlord would probably be justified in entering to close them.

TIP

Check if your lease or rental agreement requires you to report extended absences. It may require you to inform your landlord when you will be gone for an extended time, such as two weeks, and give the landlord the right to enter the premises during these times. For example, in Alaska, where tenants are required by law to notify their landlords if they plan to be absent more than seven days, a landlord may enter without notice if the tenant has been gone for more than seven days without notification. (Alaska Stat. §§ 34.03.140, 34.03.230(b).) In general, if you plan to be gone for an extended time, it makes good sense to inform your landlord. Your landlord may be able to do the things (like draining the pipes) that will obviate the need to enter while you're gone.

Inspections

Some conscientious landlords schedule regular safety and maintenance inspections of their rental properties once or twice a year, in an effort to find small problems before they become big ones.

If this is your landlord's practice, your lease or rental agreement probably gives your landlord the right to enter your unit—after giving reasonable notice—to make this inspection. Even if it doesn't, your state law probably allows this type of entry. All states with privacy statutes grant landlords the right to inspect rental property. (See "State Laws on Landlord's Access to Rental Property" in Appendix A.)

CAUTION

Don't put up with unnecessary, repeated inspections. No unit should need inspecting more than once or twice a year absent a very specific reason—for example, to track down the source of a water leak, or to check the point of entry of a persistent ant or rodent infestation. If your landlord asks to inspect your unit too frequently, it may constitute illegal harassment. "What to Do About Invasions of Privacy," below, shows how to deal with this situation.

Showing the Property to Prospective Tenants or Purchasers

Most states with access laws allow landlords to enter rented property to show it to prospective tenants. If your landlord doesn't plan to renew your about-to-expire lease, or you have given or received a notice terminating your month-to-month tenancy, your landlord may show prospective new tenants around during the last few weeks (or even months) of your stay.

Also, a landlord may show your rental unit—whether an apartment in a multiple-unit building, single-family house, or condominium unit—to potential buyers or mortgage companies.

Your landlord must follow the notice procedures discussed below. Typically, you are entitled to at least 24 hours' notice, and the landlord must enter at reasonable times.

It's no fun to have your last weeks or months in your current place constantly interrupted by prospective new tenants or buyers—after all, you are still paying the rent. Especially if you're not moving out voluntarily, it can seem like an intolerable intrusion to have your landlord or rental agent constantly parading people through.

For Sale or For Rent Signs

Occasionally, friction is caused by landlords who put "For Sale" or "For Rent" signs in front of an apartment building or a rented single-family house. Although your landlord may otherwise be very conscientious about respecting your privacy, putting a sign on the property is a flagrant invitation to prospective buyers or renters to disturb you.

With online multiple-listing services, many real estate offices can, and commonly do, sell rental houses and buildings without ever placing a For Sale sign on the property, except perhaps when an open house is in progress. If a real estate office puts a sign in front of your building, you should insist that it clearly state a telephone number to call and warn against disturbing you, using words like "Inquire at 555-1357— Do Not Disturb Occupant." If this doesn't do the trick, and informal conversations with the landlord do not result in removal of the sign, write a firm letter explaining why your privacy is being invaded and ask your landlord to remove the sign. If this doesn't work, remove the sign yourself and return it to the landlord. If your landlord simply replaces the sign, you may sue for invasion of privacy, just as if the landlord personally had made repeated illegal entries.

If the landlord regularly wants to show the unit to prospective tenants or buyers on short notice, you have two options:

Notify your landlord in writing to follow the law or you will sue for invasion of privacy. If you are planning to move out anyway, you might have nothing to lose by fully asserting your legal rights. But if you don't have a place lined up and are banking on a good recommendation, it just doesn't make sense to give your landlord a hard time.

Allow the unit to be shown on shorter notice in exchange for a reduction in the rent. This is a fair proposition since, after all, you are giving up some of the value of your rental home by letting lots of strangers waltz though. A smart landlord may well agree to pay a little something for your cooperation. For example, you might work out a deal with your landlord that two-hour notice is reasonable for up to three rental showings a week when you are home and three when you aren't, in exchange for having your rent reduced by a certain amount. Depending on how much you will be inconvenienced, a 10%–30% rent reduction might be reasonable.

> **CAUTION**
> **Under no circumstances should your landlord place a key-holding "lockbox" on the door.** A lockbox is a metal box that attaches to the front door. It can be opened with a key, and inside there's a key to the house. If the house is on the Multiple Listing Service, the box will likely be an electronic model, which opens when the user types in an acceptable code. Each member of the MLS has his or her own code, which means that any of these folks can gain entry into the home. Because either type of box allows users to gain entry at any time, without notice, they should not be used in an occupied rental.

Notice Requirements

Most state access laws require landlords to give you 24 hours' to two days' notice before entering your rental unit in nonemergency situations. A few states simply require landlords to provide "reasonable" notice. See "State Laws on Access to Rental Property," in Appendix A.

In many situations, you may not care a bit about getting the legally required amount of notice. You may be so delighted that your landlord is making needed repairs that you'll be standing by the door offering coffee and a piece of cake. However, sometimes a landlord's request to enter to fix or inspect something is totally unreasonable. You won't welcome a surprise knock at your door by a landlord who wants to make a nonemergency repair or inspection when you are in the middle of cooking dinner for your book group, taking a nap, or finishing your income taxes. In such a situation, you have a legal right to deny entry and ask that a later appointment be scheduled. If you do so politely and in a cooperative spirit, it shouldn't cause a problem.

Similarly, if your building is for sale and an overeager real estate salesperson shows up on your doorstep with clients in tow, or your landlord calls on 20 minutes' notice and asks to be let in to show the place to a potential tenant, you are entirely within your rights to say politely but firmly, "I'm busy right now—try again in a day or so after we've set a time convenient for all of us."

> **TIP**
>
> **Be sure your landlord knows how to reach you to give you notice of entry.** Without your cell and/or work phone number, your landlord may be unable to give you adequate notice.

What's Reasonable Notice?

If your state only requires your landlord to give you "reasonable" notice before entering your rented home, you'll naturally want to know how this translates into hours and days. Twenty-four hours is generally presumed to be reasonable notice. In some circumstances, less notice (say, ten or 15 hours) might be fine—for example, if your landlord finds out Thursday evening that an electrician is available Friday morning to put extra outlets in your apartment. Except for an emergency, less than four hours' notice is not ordinarily considered reasonable.

To find out precisely how your state's courts have interpreted the concept of reasonable notice, you'll need to look up their recent court decisions. (Chapter 20 explains how to find statutes and the cases that have dealt with them.)

> **TIP**
>
> **Disabled tenants may be entitled to special notice.** A landlord who knows of a disabled tenant's unusual needs for privacy will be expected to accommodate the tenant's needs in all but true emergencies. (Chapter 5 discusses the rights of disabled tenants.)

Must Notice Be in Writing?

Not all states require that notice be in writing. But it's a good idea to ask your landlord for written notice whenever possible, especially if the landlord has entered without permission previously. Keep copies of these written notices in your rental file, and also make a note of any oral or email requests for entry. Most important, if your landlord has entered without your permission or without giving proper notice, make a note of the time, date, and circumstances, listing the names of anyone else who witnessed or knows about the incident. This information will come in handy should you end up in a legal dispute with your landlord over this issue.

Time of Day Landlord May Enter

Most state access laws either do not specify what hours a landlord may enter your rental unit or simply allow entry at reasonable times. Weekdays between 9 a.m. and 6 p.m. would seem to be reasonable times, and perhaps Saturdays between 10 a.m. and 1 p.m. Some statutes are more specific.

Clarifying Access Rules

To make sure you and your landlord are operating on the same wavelength, be sure your lease or rental agreement includes a clause regarding landlord access to the property. If it doesn't, you may want to add a clause, or write a letter of understanding after you and the landlord have discussed the issue and come to an agreement. (Chapter 2 covers how to write a letter of understanding. Chapter 15 explains how to amend a lease or rental agreement.)

Spelling out clear guidelines is especially important if your state does not set specific rules regarding your landlord's entry. Ask your landlord to give you at least 24 hours' notice before entering your unit, except when there is a genuine emergency or you invite the landlord to enter. You might point out that this is the standard in many states. See the suggested lease clause in Chapter 2 for a good model.

Cooperating With Requests to Enter

Common sense suggests that if your landlord does not have a history of invading your privacy, you're better off accommodating requests for entry, especially if the purpose is to make repairs that will benefit you. By taking a reasonably cooperative approach, you'll go a long way toward avoiding disputes and legal problems. Here's why.

You might be evicted. In every state, your landlord has certain legal rights of access, regardless of any desire you have to be left alone. As long as your landlord complies with your state law as to reasons for entry and notice periods, your refusal to allow access can result in an eviction lawsuit.

Your tenancy might be terminated. Unless you have a long-term lease or live in a rent control city that requires the landlord to state a good reason (just cause) for eviction, you face the threat of losing your rental unit if your landlord concludes you are too difficult to deal with. Even though you may feel you are within your legal or moral rights to deny your landlord access to your rental unit, your landlord may simply give you a 30-day notice and terminate your tenancy (or decline to renew your lease) rather than put up with you.

Your landlord might be less cooperative when you want a favor. If your landlord considers your desire for absolute privacy hard to cope with, don't expect much help when you make other requests. And you may get a negative reference when you eventually move on.

Adopting a reasonable attitude to landlord requests doesn't mean you should surrender your right to privacy and let your landlord enter at all hours of the day or night. No question—you should respond quickly to a landlord (or manager) who is entering without notice or good reason and make it clear that you won't tolerate clear violations of your privacy. But don't be hard-nosed just for the principle involved.

Entry by Others

Your landlord is not the only one who may enter your rental unit. This section describes situations when other people, such as municipal inspectors, may want entry to your home.

Health, Safety, or Building Inspections

While your state may give you significant protections against entry by your landlord, the rules are different for entry by state or local health, safety, or building inspectors.

Neighbor's Complaints

If inspectors have credible reasons to suspect that your unit violates housing codes or local standards—for example, a credible source has complained about noxious smells coming from your home or about your 20 cats—they will usually knock on your door and ask permission to enter. Except in the case of genuine emergency, you have the right to say no.

Inspectors have ways to get around tenant refusals. A logical first step (maybe even before they stop by your rental unit) is to ask your landlord in advance to let them in. Since your landlord can usually enter on 24 hours' notice, this is probably the simplest approach. If inspectors can't reach your landlord or get cooperation, their next step will probably be to get a search warrant based on the information from your neighbor. The inspectors must first convince a judge that the source of their information—the neighbor—is reliable, and that there is a strong likelihood that public health or safety is at risk. Inspectors who believe that you will refuse entry often bring along police officers who, armed with a search warrant, have the right to do whatever it takes to overcome your objections.

Random Inspections

Fire, health, and other municipal inspectors sometimes randomly inspect apartment buildings even if they don't suspect noncompliance. These inspection programs have become increasingly popular, not only because they uncover substandard housing conditions, but because they are a revenue-generating scheme in some cities (landlords pay an inspection fee). These inspections may be allowed under state law or local ordinance. (Most ordinances exempt single-family homes and condominiums.) The inspectors may contact your landlord first and ask permission to enter. If the landlord says yes and gives you 24 hours' notice (or whatever your state requires), the inspection can proceed. If the landlord refuses entry, the inspector will almost surely have a judge issue a search warrant, allowing him to enter to check for fire or safety violations. Again, if there is any expectation that you may resist, a police officer will usually accompany the inspector.

An inspector who arrives when you're not home may ask the landlord to open your door on the spot, in violation of your state's privacy laws. If the inspectors come with a warrant, the landlord can probably give consent, since even you couldn't prevent entry. But if the inspector is there without a warrant, your landlord probably cannot speak for you and say "Come on in." However, the answer will depend on each state's interpretation of its laws regarding warrantless entries. Since municipal inspection programs are relatively new, few courts have decided the issue. Cautious landlords will ask an inspector without a warrant to enter after the landlord has given you the proper amount of notice under your state's law or the terms of your lease or rental agreement.

Inspection Fees

Many cities impose fees for inspections, on a per unit or building basis or a sliding scale based on the number of a landlord's holdings. Some fees are imposed only if violations are found. If your ordinance imposes fees regardless of violations, you may find the inspection cost passed on to you in the form of a rent hike. It's not illegal for your landlord to do this, and even in rent-controlled cities, the cost of an inspection might justify a rent increase. (See Chapter 3 for information on how landlords may legally increase rents.)

If your ordinance imposes a fee only when violations are found, your landlord should not pass the cost on to you if the noncompliance is not your fault. For example, if inspectors find that the landlord has failed to install state-mandated smoke alarms, the landlord should pay for the inspection; but if you have allowed garbage to pile up in violation of city health laws, you can expect the inspector's bill.

Law Enforcement

Even the police may not enter your rental unit unless they can show you or your landlord a recently issued search or arrest warrant, signed by a judge. The police do not need a search warrant, however, if they need to enter to prevent a catastrophe, such as an assault or fire, if they are in hot pursuit of a fleeing criminal, or if they need to enter to preserve evidence of a serious crime. Also, different rules may apply if law enforcement suspects terrorist activity by a tenant.

Your Landlord's Right to Let Others In

Your landlord has no right to give others permission to enter your home. (Municipal inspections and the police, however, may pose an exception.)

Occasionally a landlord or resident manager will be faced with a very convincing stranger who will tell a heart-rending story:

- "I'm Nancy's boyfriend, and I need to get my clothes out of her closet now that I'm moving to New York."

- "If I don't get my heart medicine that I left in this apartment, I'll die on the spot."
- "I'm John's father, and I just got in from the North Pole, where a polar bear ate my wallet, and I have no other place to stay."

Of course, if the landlord asks you and you authorize entry, there's no problem. But what if the landlord can't contact you at work or elsewhere to ask whether it's okay to let the desperate individual in? This is one reason why your landlord should always know how to reach you during the day.

The story the desperate person tells your landlord may be the truth, and chances are that if you could be contacted, you would say "Yes, let Uncle Harry in immediately." But the landlord can't know this, and letting anyone enter your home without your permission invades your privacy. The landlord risks being legally responsible should your property be stolen or damaged. If your landlord does let a stranger in without your permission, you can sue her for any loss you suffer as a result.

Other Invasions of Privacy

Entering your home without your knowledge or consent isn't the only way a landlord can interfere with your privacy. Here are a few other common situations, with advice on how to handle them.

Giving Information About You to Strangers

Your landlord may be asked by strangers, including creditors, banks, and prospective landlords, to provide credit or other information about you. Did you pay the rent on time? Did you maintain the rental property? Cause any problems? As with letting a stranger into your home, what your landlord says may cause you considerable anxiety.

Basically, your landlord has a legal right to give out truthful business information about you to people and businesses who ask and have a legitimate reason to know—for example, your bank when you apply for a loan or a prospective landlord who wants a reference. An extra-cautious landlord will ask for your written permission to release credit and similar information, but as long as the landlord's answer is in response to a legitimate request, a formal release is not legally required. (See the release form at the bottom of the rental application in Chapter 1.)

If a landlord gives out negative information on you, it should be absolutely factual. If your landlord spreads false stories about you—for example, says you filed for bankruptcy if this isn't true—and you suffer a loss as a result (for example, you don't get a job)—you can sue the landlord for defamation (libel or slander).

A landlord (or, more typically, an on-site manager) who makes a big effort to spread negative information (whether or not true) risks an invasion of privacy lawsuit. Examples include calling other landlords in your area to bad-mouth you, broadcasting that you haven't paid the rent, or telling others that you drink too much. This sort of gossip has no legitimate purpose and is malicious and damaging. It amounts to an invasion of privacy for which you may have a valid reason to sue.

Bothering You at Work

Your landlord should have your cell and/or your work phone number in case there's an emergency. However, situations justifying a landlord calling you at work are fairly rare. If a landlord calls you to complain about late rent payments or other problems, politely say you'll talk when you're at home. If this doesn't work, follow up with a brief note.

If the landlord persists or tries to talk to your boss or other employees about the problem ("Tell your deadbeat employee I'll evict her if she doesn't pay the rent"), your privacy is definitely being invaded. Write a letter asking the landlord to stop immediately. If the conduct continues, consider going to small claims court to sue for damages. If as a result of the landlord's conduct you lose your job or a promotion, see a lawyer. You may have the basis for a successful lawsuit.

Unduly Restricting Guests

Some landlords limit guests' visits—for example, no more than ten days in any six-month period—to avoid having a guest turn into an illegal cotenant or subtenant. (See Chapter 7 for an explanation on how a resident can gain the status of a tenant.) A few landlords, overly concerned about possible new occupants, go overboard in keeping tabs on legitimate guests who stay overnight or for a few days. Some leases, rental agreements, or rules and regulations will require you to register any overnight guest. While your landlord has a legitimate concern about persons who begin as guests becoming permanent unauthorized residents of the property, it is overkill to require you to inform your landlord of a guest whose stay is only for a day or two.

In short, while your landlord does have a right to control who lives in the rental unit, your social life is your own business. Extreme behavior in this area—whether by an owner or a management employee—can be considered an invasion of privacy for which you may sue.

Spying on You

A few landlords have attempted to interrogate visitors, knock on tenants' doors at odd hours to see who answers, or even peek through windows. Needless to say, this sort of conduct can give you cause to sue a landlord for invasion of privacy.

Self-Help Evictions

It is generally illegal for the landlord to come on the property and do such things as take off windows and doors, turn off the utilities, or change the locks. (Chapter 18 discusses illegal "self-help" evictions.)

Sexual Harassment or Assault

If your landlord or manager comes onto your property or into your home and harms you in any way, sexually harasses you (see Chapter 5), threatens you, or damages any of your property, see an attorney pronto. You should also report the matter to the police. Some local police departments have taken the excellent step of setting up special landlord-tenant units. The officers and legal experts in these units have been given special training in landlord-tenant law and are often helpful in settling disputes and setting straight a landlord who has taken illegal measures against a tenant.

RELATED TOPIC

You might have a discrimination claim. As we explain in Chapter 5, if you are single, female, disabled, or of a certain race, religion, or ethnicity and you have been harassed by the landlord, he may be violating fair housing laws.

What to Do About Invasions of Privacy

Suppose now your landlord does violate your rights of privacy—what can you do about it?

As you have undoubtedly long since figured out, it is one thing to have a right, and quite another thing to enforce it. This is especially true for tenants who do not have a long-term lease and do not live in a city where a rent control ordinance requires just cause for eviction. In these situations, if you set about aggressively demanding your rights, you may end up with a termination notice. So perhaps a softer approach is the most sensible. None of this means you shouldn't be firm and determined in asserting your rights, but rather, that being strident may be counterproductive.

Here is a step-by-step approach that usually works in dealing with a landlord who is violating your right to privacy.

Step 1. Talk to the Landlord or Manager

As a first step, voice your concerns in a friendly but firm way. If you come to an understanding, follow up with a note to confirm it. See the Sample Letter When Landlord Violates Privacy (Friendly Approach), below. As with all important communications with your landlord, send your letter by mail, rather than email, so you'll have proof should you end up defending your privacy rights in court. In Chapter 6, "Using Email or Text Messages for Notice or a Letter of Understanding" explains why it's best to send important communications by mail (certified or return receipt requested) or delivery service, rather than email.

Sample Letter When Landlord Violates Privacy (Friendly Approach)

February 5, 20xx

Joan Smith
123 Main St.
Portland, Oregon 00000

Dear Ms. Smith:

Thanks for sending your plumber over yesterday to fix my bathtub leak. I really appreciate your prompt response. As I mentioned, I would have preferred not to be home when the plumber came because I often work at home and need to be able to count on uninterrupted periods of time. As we discussed, next time you'll give me at least 24 hours' notice so I can plan accordingly.

Thanks again.

Sincerely,

Jon Klein

Jon Klein
Green Gables Apartment #4B
526 Grover Road
Portland, Oregon 00000

TIP

Landlords often don't know what their managers are doing. If your manager is invading your privacy, don't assume the landlord is at fault. Instead, it's best to assume the landlord doesn't know and won't approve when he does. So tell the landlord promptly and politely that you expect better. Follow up with a written note if the problem continues.

TIP

Work with other tenants. Chances are that if your landlord has entered your home repeatedly and without good reason or notice, other tenants in the building or complex have had the same problem. Talk to your neighbors and find out. If so, you have a golden opportunity to organize your neighbors and exert concerted pressure by using, together, the steps outlined in this section. For all the obvious reasons, your group complaints will be taken more seriously and given more attention than if you are acting alone. (See Chapter 19 for tips on how to organize fellow tenants.)

Step 2. Write a Tough Letter

If the friendly, informal approach doesn't work, or if your landlord doesn't follow the agreement that you have worked out, it's time for a stronger, more formal letter that sets forth your legal rights and explains what you'll do if they aren't respected. Use a mail or delivery service that will provide proof of delivery (you may need this should you end up in a legal dispute with your landlord). Assuming you are willing to risk alienating your landlord—perhaps because you have a lease and don't feel vulnerable or because your relationship is already bad—your letter should threaten a small claims lawsuit if the landlord's illegal conduct doesn't stop pronto. This can be an especially effective technique if a group of tenants is working together.

A sample letter (for the get-tough approach) is shown below.

Sample Letter When Landlord Violates Privacy (Get-Tough Approach)

September 19, 20xx

Jan Roper Real Estate Co.
11 Peach Street
Cleveland, Ohio 00000

Dear Mr. Roper:

Several times in the last two months your resident manager, Pete Tuttle, has entered my apartment when I was not at home and without notifying me in advance. Following the second such visit, I wrote to you on August 20, demanding that these unannounced entries stop at once.

In spite of my letter, Pete continued to enter when I was not home and without notice. One time when I was home sick from work, he simply walked in without knocking.

In no situation was any emergency involved, and there was no real purpose for these visits. These intrusions have caused me considerable anxiety and stress, to the point that my peaceful enjoyment of my tenancy has been seriously disrupted.

This letter is to formally notify you that I value my privacy highly and insist that my legal rights to that privacy, as guaranteed to me under Ohio Rev. Code Ann. §§ 5321.04 and 5321.05, be respected. Specifically, in nonemergency situations, I am entitled to 24 hours' notice of your (or your employee's) intent to enter my home, and a clearly stated purpose of the entry.

I assume this notice will be sufficient to correct this matter. If you want to talk about this, please call me at home (555-7890) at night before 10 p.m.

Yours truly,

Sally South

Sally South
789 Porter St., #3
Cleveland, Ohio 00000

TIP

Writing a demand letter like this will greatly improve your chances of winning a small claims court lawsuit, if you decide to go ahead and sue. For advice on using small claims court, see Chapter 19.

TIP

Try mediation before filing a lawsuit. It's always preferable in terms of cost, energy, and outcome. Mediation by a neutral third party is an especially good way to resolve disputes with your landlord when you want to continue living in your current rental unit. See Chapter 19 for details on finding and using a mediation service.

Step 3. Sue Your Landlord

If, despite your second letter, the invasions of your privacy continue, document them and either see a lawyer or take your landlord to small claims court.

Depending on the circumstances, you may be able to sue your landlord for:

- Trespass: entering your rental space without consent or proper authority
- Invasion of privacy: interfering with your right to be left alone
- Breach of implied covenant of quiet enjoyment: interfering with your right to undisturbed use of your home. ("Your Basic Right to Livable Premises," in Chapter 8, discusses the implied covenant of quiet enjoyment.)
- Infliction of emotional distress: a pattern of illegal acts by someone (in this case, the landlord or manager) which caused serious emotional consequences to you.

One difficulty with a lawsuit against a landlord guilty of unlawful entry is that it may be hard to prove much in the way of money damages. Most likely, a judge will figure that you have not been harmed much by the fact that your landlord walked on your rug and opened and closed your door—and you won't be awarded much money to compensate you.

However, if you can show a repeated pattern of illegal entry (and the fact that you asked the landlord to stop it), or even one clear example of outrageous conduct, you may be able to get a substantial recovery. You'll probably want an attorney for this kind of case, especially if you bring your case in a court other than small claims court.

Here are examples of two court cases based on a landlord's unlawful entry.

> **EXAMPLE:** Debra rented a townhouse from Grace. Grace approached Debra with a suggestion that they go into business together, but Debra declined. Feeling spurned, Grace demanded that Debra's cotenant leave. She called both tenants at home and at work, changed their locks, yelled obscenities, and ripped out their phone jack. Debra moved out, losing her prepaid rent and security deposit and incurring temporary housing costs. Debra sued Grace for trespass and, because the trespass was deliberate and outrageous, for emotional distress as well. The state appellate court directed the trial court, which had initially thrown the case out, to let it go to the jury. (*Johnson v. Marcel,* 465 S.E.2d 815. Va. (1996).)

> **EXAMPLE:** In New York, a landlord entered his tenant's apartment several times without permission. Although the entries did not make the premises unusable, they violated the tenant's reasonable expectation of privacy and New York's law that required the landlord to provide habitable premises. A judge ruled that the tenant was entitled to a retroactive rent abatement of 15%. (*Steltzer v. Spesaison,* 614 N.Y.S.2d 488 (1994).)

 RELATED TOPIC
Chapter 20 shows how to find and work with a lawyer. Chapter 19 discusses small claims court suits and dollar limits in each state.

Step 4. Move Out

Repeated abuses by a landlord of your right of privacy may give you a legal excuse to break a lease or end a tenancy early, without liability for further rent. If the landlord sues you for the rent after you leave, your defense can be that repeated intrusions made it impossible for you to "quietly enjoy" your rented home—a right guaranteed to every tenant. Or you can argue that the landlord's repeated entries amounted to an eviction (lawyers call it "constructive eviction"), justifying your departure.

TIP
Don't take the law into your own hands. You do not have the right to attack a landlord who invades your privacy. If you have good reason to fear that you or your property may be harmed, call the police.

Injuries on the Premises

What to Do If You're Injured..188

    Get Immediate Medical Attention 188

    Write Everything Down..189

    Preserve Evidence 189

    Contact Witnesses 189

    Evaluate Your Case..190

    Notify the Landlord and the Insurance Carrier...190

    Negotiate, Mediate, or Sue 191

Is the Landlord Liable?..191

    The Landlord Was Unreasonably Careless..191

    The Landlord Violated a Health or Safety Law 193

    The Landlord Didn't Make Certain Repairs 194

    The Landlord Didn't Keep the Premises Habitable 194

    The Landlord Acted Recklessly..195

    The Landlord Intentionally Harmed You 195

    The Law Makes the Landlord Liable 196

If You're at Fault, Too...197

    Your Own Carelessness..197

    Your Risk-Taking..197

How Much Money You're Entitled To..198

If you have been injured on your landlord's property, you may have a good legal claim against your landlord. That doesn't mean you'll have to file a lawsuit—over 90% of valid claims against landlords are settled without trial. It may well be to your advantage to negotiate with the landlord's insurance adjuster or lawyer yourself, rather than to immediately hire a lawyer, who will typically take one-third of your recovery. If the landlord or insurer proves unreasonable, you can always hire a lawyer.

This chapter explains how to evaluate whether your landlord is liable for your injury, and what to do to maximize your chances of a just settlement or lawsuit verdict.

 RELATED TOPIC
Also covered in this book:
- Landlords' repair and maintenance responsibilities: Chapters 8 and 9.
- Landlords' legal responsibility to provide premises that are safe from criminal acts: Chapter 14.
- How to recognize and deal with common environmental hazards: Chapter 13.
- How to sue for a landlord's tolerance of a legal "nuisance": Chapter 14.
- How to research your state's laws on personal injuries: Chapter 20.
- How to choose and work with a lawyer: Chapter 20.

What to Do If You're Injured

What is the best course of action to take if you're injured? If your injury is significant and costly—it has resulted in lost work, doctor's bills, and physical or emotional discomfort—and you think the landlord is at fault, you'll want to consider legal action. But don't go rushing off to the nearest personal injury lawyer just yet. Especially if your injury isn't very severe, you may be better off—at least initially—handling the claim yourself.

But if your injury is severe, see a lawyer right away. Injuries in this category include:

- a long-term or permanently disabling injury, such as the loss of a limb
- an injury that results in medical costs and lost income over $10,000, or
- heavy-duty toxic exposure, such as pesticide poisoning.

This book can't cover all the ins and outs of pursuing a personal injury claim. Here, however, is an outline of the basic steps you should follow.

 CAUTION
An injured guest may have a hard time pinning liability on your landlord. In all states, landlords are expected to take reasonable steps to avoid tenant injuries. (See "Is the Landlord Liable," below.) But in some states, landlords get by with a lower standard of care when it comes to nontenants. If you're reading this chapter on behalf of an injured guest, you'll need to know your state's approach to injuries suffered by nontenants. Chapter 20 gives tips on how to approach a legal research task in the library.

Get Immediate Medical Attention

The success of an accident claim often depends on what you do in the first hours and days after your injury. Although you may be in pain, angry, or even depressed, attention to these details immediately following the incident will pay off later.

It is essential to get prompt medical attention for your injury, even if you consider it to be of marginal help to your physical recovery. No insurance company, judge, or jury will take your word alone for the extent of your injury, pain, and suffering. It may seem obvious to you that a sprained ankle caused immobility, swelling, and pain and made you miss a week's work. Nonetheless, you'll need the confirmation of a physician, and the professional opinion that you didn't suffer a mere soft tissue bruise, when it comes to convincing a skeptical insurance adjuster or jury of your injury's impact.

Moreover, if you intend to hold the landlord financially responsible for your injuries, the law expects you to take whatever steps are possible to lessen the extent of your injuries and speed your recovery. Oddly, the reason has little to do with concern for your physical well-being; rather, the law expects you to take reasonable steps to lessen the accident's financial impact on the landlord. In short, you'll need the verification of a doctor that you were a conscientious patient who did not prolong or ignore your injuries.

> **EXAMPLE:** May-Ling, a new tenant, slipped on a puddle of oil-slicked rainwater that habitually accumulated at the base of the garage stairs. She fell and badly twisted her back. Thinking that time would heal her wounds, she did not seek medical attention, though she did stay home from work for a week.
>
> She then filed a claim with the landlord's insurance company, seeking compensation for her pain and suffering and lost wages. The insurance adjuster questioned the severity of her injury and suggested that, had she consulted a doctor, she might have recovered sooner with the aid of muscle-relaxing medication. Unable to verify the extent of her injury and having no way to effectively answer the claim that medical attention might have helped her, May-Ling settled her claim for a disappointing amount.

Write Everything Down

As soon as possible after the accident, jot down everything you can remember about how it happened. Include a complete list of everyone who was present and what they said. For example, if, after you tripped on a loose stair, the manager rushed over and blurted out, "I told Jim [the landlord] we should have replaced that last month!" be sure to write it down and note the names of anyone who heard the manager say it.

Describe the precise nature of your injuries, including pain, anxiety, and loss of sleep. Make notes of every economic loss, such as lost wages, missed classes and events, and transportation and medical costs. If you have a conversation regarding the incident with anyone (the landlord, other tenants, an insurance adjuster, or medical personnel), make a written summary of the conversation.

Preserve Evidence

Claims are often won by the production of a persuasive piece of physical evidence: the worn or broken stair that caused the fall, the unattached throw rug that slipped when stepped on, the electrical outlet faceplate that showed burn marks from a short. Remember that physical evidence that is not preserved within a short time can be lost, modified by time or weather, repaired, or destroyed. For example, the landlord, not wanting more accidents, may quickly replace a loose stair that caused you to fall, and throw the old one away.

If preservation of the evidence would involve dismantling the landlord's property, you may have to settle for the next-best alternative, photographs or videos taken with your phone. Don't wait— make your record before repairs are made. Be sure to upload your photos to a secure place in the cloud, lest they be lost if you lose your phone. And to forestall challenges to the accuracy of your pictures (or a claim they were doctored), have someone else take them and be prepared to testify in court that they are a fair and accurate depiction of the scene. If you are experiencing pain, keep what's known as a "pain diary." Every day (and more often if appropriate), jot down how you feel, what you can and cannot do, and what medication you're taking to help yourself. This log may come in handy if you are asked to document your condition.

Contact Witnesses

Having an eyewitness can be an immeasurable help. Witnesses can corroborate your version of events and may even have seen important aspects of the situation that you missed. But you must act very quickly to find and preserve the observations and memories of those who could bolster your case—people's memories fade quickly, and strangers can be very hard to track down later.

CAUTION

Don't tell witnesses not to talk to the "other side." Witnesses have no legal obligation to talk to you, although most will if they feel you have been wronged. Similarly, you have no legal right to tell them not to talk to others. Moreover, trying to do so may come back to haunt you via a suggestion that you had something to hide. If a favorable witness tells an insurance adjuster a different story, you can expose the inconsistencies later in court.

If you find people who witnessed the incident, get their names, addresses, and as much information about what they saw as possible. Talk with them about what they saw and write it up. Ask them if they would be willing to review your summary for accuracy; if so, mail them a copy and ask them to correct it, sign it, and return it to you in the stamped envelope you have provided.

TIP

Don't overlook the witness who heard or saw another witness. It can often be important to have a witness to what another witness said or did. For example, the manager who blurted out, "I told him we should have fixed that last month" will have every incentive to deny making that statement, since it pins knowledge of the defect on the property owner, his boss. If someone besides you also heard the manager say it, he'll have a tougher time disowning it.

Evaluate Your Case

Before you go making demands for money from your landlord or an insurance company, you need to know whether you have a legal leg to stand on. That's what most of the rest of this chapter explains.

Notify the Landlord and the Insurance Carrier

Write to the owner of the rental property, stating that you have been injured and need to deal with the owner's liability insurance carrier. You should have the owner's name and address on your lease or rental agreement. If you deal with a manager or management company, you should also notify them.

If a third party is involved, it won't hurt to notify them, too, if there is some basis for thinking that they may have been at least partially responsible. For example, a contractor or subcontractor may have created or contributed to the dangerous situation, or a repair person may have done a faulty job, causing your injury.

A sample letter is shown below. If your case is substantial, you can expect that the owner will contact the insurer right away. On the other hand, a landlord who suspects that the claim is phony or trivial may hold off notifying the insurance company, fearing a rate increase or policy cancellation. You cannot force the landlord to refer the case or disclose the name of the insurer; all you can do is persevere until your persistence and the threat of a lawsuit become real enough for the landlord to call in the insurance company's help.

Sample Letter to Landlord Regarding Tenant Injury

Alex Watson
37 Ninth Avenue North
South Fork, RI 00000
401-555-4567

February 28, 20xx

Fernando Diaz
3757 East Seventh Street
South Fork, RI 00000

Dear Mr. Diaz:

On February 25, 20xx, I was injured in a fall on the front steps of the duplex that I rent from you. The middle step splintered and collapsed as I walked down the stairs. Please refer this matter to the carrier of your business liability insurance and have them contact me at the above address.

Thank you for your cooperation.

Yours truly,

Alex Watson

Alex Watson

Negotiate, Mediate, or Sue

If you are successful at reaching the landlord's insurance carrier, chances are that you'll negotiate a settlement. You may choose mediation (in which a neutral third party helps both sides reach a settlement) if you feel that the insurance company is interested in settling the matter and will deal with you fairly. (If the result isn't adequate, you can always file a lawsuit.) But if the landlord stonewalls you, refusing to refer your claim to the insurance carrier or a lawyer, you may need to consider a lawsuit. Chapter 19 gives detailed information on negotiating with, mediating with, and suing your landlord if necessary. It also helps you decide whether to take your case to small claims court yourself, saving time and the expense of hiring a lawyer, or whether you are better off in a formal court with a lawyer.

TIP

Don't wait too long before filing suit. You must file your lawsuit within the time specified by your state's "statute of limitations." Most states give you one to four years after your injury. Check your state statutes for the deadline that applies to personal injury cases. Chapter 20 gives information on how to look up a statute.

RESOURCE

How to Win Your Personal Injury Claim, by Joseph Matthews (Nolo), explains personal injury cases and how to work out a fair settlement without going to court.

Everybody's Guide to Small Claims Court, by Cara O'Neill (Nolo), provides great advice on small claims courts, which, in most states, allow you to sue for amounts up to $5,000 to $10,000.

Represent Yourself in Court: How to Prepare & Try a Winning Case, by Paul Bergman and Sara Berman (Nolo), will help you prepare and present your case should you end up in court.

Is the Landlord Liable?

It isn't always easy to determine whether the landlord is legally responsible for an injury.

Basically, your landlord may be liable for your injuries if those injuries resulted from:

- the landlord's unreasonably careless conduct
- the landlord's violation of a health or safety law
- the landlord's failure to make certain repairs
- the landlord's failure to keep the premises habitable, or
- the landlord's reckless or intentional acts.

And in rare instances, the landlord may be liable because courts or the legislature in your state have decided that landlords are automatically liable for certain kinds of injuries, even though they haven't been careless.

Keep in mind that several of these legal theories may apply in your situation, and you (and your lawyer) can use all of them when pressing your claim. The more plausible reasons you can give for your landlord's liability, the better you will do when you negotiate with the landlord's insurance company.

The Landlord Was Unreasonably Careless

Most personal injury claims against landlords charge that the landlord acted negligently—that is, acted carelessly, in a way that wasn't reasonable under the circumstances—and that the injury was caused by that carelessness.

Negligence is always determined in light of the unique facts of each situation. For example, it may be reasonable to put adequate lights in a dark, remote stairwell. If your landlord doesn't, and you're hurt because you couldn't see the steps and fell, your landlord's failure to install the lights might be negligence. On the other hand, extra lights in a lobby that's already well-lit might not be a reasonable expectation.

To determine whether or not your landlord was negligent and should be held responsible for your injury, you must answer six questions. The insurance adjuster will use these same questions to evaluate your claim. If your case looks strong, you'll probably be able to wrest a good settlement offer from the company. And if the insurance company isn't forthcoming, you'll be able to head to court confidently, where a judge or jury will use the same questions when deciding your case.

Question 1: Did your landlord control the area where you were hurt or the thing that hurt you? The law will pin responsibility on your landlord only if he had the legal ability to maintain or fix the area or item that injured you. For example, the property owner normally has control over a stairway in a common area, and if its chronic disrepair causes a tenant to fall, the owner will likely be held liable. The owner also has control over the building's utility systems. If a malfunction causes injury (like boiling water in your sink because of a broken thermostat), he may likewise be held responsible. On the other hand, if you're hurt when your own bookcase falls on you, the landlord won't be held responsible, because he does not control how the bookcase is built, set up, or maintained.

Question 2: How likely was it that an accident would occur? The landlord isn't responsible if the accident wasn't foreseeable. For example, common sense would tell anyone that loose handrails or stairs are likely to lead to accidents, but it would be unusual for injuries to result from peeling wallpaper or a thumbtack that's fallen from a bulletin board. If a freak accident does happen, chances are your landlord will not be held liable.

Question 3: How difficult or expensive would it have been for the landlord to reduce the risk of injury? The chances that your landlord will be held liable are greater if a reasonably priced response could have averted the accident. In other words, could something as simple as warning signs, a bright light, or caution tape have prevented people from tripping over an unexpected step leading to the patio, or would major structural remodeling have been necessary to reduce the likelihood of injury? But if there is a great risk of very serious injury, a landlord will be expected to spend money to avert it. For example, a high-rise deck with rotten support beams must be repaired, regardless of the cost, since there is a great risk of collapse and dreadful injuries to anyone on the deck. A landlord who knew about the condition of the deck and failed to repair it would surely be held liable if an accident did occur.

Question 4: Was a serious injury likely to result from the problem? The amount of time and money your landlord is expected to spend on making his premises safe will also depend on the seriousness of the probable injury if he fails to do so. For example, if the umbrella on a poolside table wouldn't open, no one would expect it to cause serious injury. If you're sunburned at the pool as a result, it's not likely that a judge would rule that your landlord had the duty of keeping you from getting burned. But if a major injury is the likely result of a dangerous situation—the pool ladder was broken, making it likely you'd fall as you climbed out— the owner is expected to take the situation more seriously and fix it faster.

The answers to these four questions should tell you (or an insurance adjuster or judge) whether or not there was a dangerous condition on the landlord's property that the landlord had a legal duty to deal with. Lawyers call this having a "duty of due care."

If, based on these first four questions, you think the landlord had a legal duty to deal with a condition on the premises that posed a danger to you, keep going. You have two more questions to answer.

Question 5: Did your landlord fail to take reasonable steps to prevent an accident? The law won't expect your landlord to undertake Herculean measures to shield you from a condition that poses some risk. Instead, the landlord is required to take only reasonable steps. For example, if you've demonstrated that a stair was in a dangerous condition, you also need to show that the landlord's failure to fix it was unreasonable in the circumstances.

Question 6: Did your landlord's failure to take reasonable steps to keep you safe cause your injury? This last question establishes the crucial link between the landlord's negligence and your injury. Not every dangerous situation results in an accident. You'll have to prove that your injury was the result of the landlord's carelessness, and not some other reason. Sometimes this is self-evident: One minute you're fine, and the next minute you've slipped on a freshly waxed floor and have a broken arm. But it's not always so simple. For example, in the case of the loose stair, the landlord might be able to show that the tenant barely lost his balance because of the loose stair and that he had really injured his ankle during a touch football game he'd just played.

Examples of Injuries From Landlord Negligence

Here are some examples of injuries for which tenants have recovered money damages due to the landlord's negligence:

- Tenant falls down a staircase due to a defective handrail.
- Tenant trips over a hole in the carpet on a common stairway not properly maintained by the landlord.
- Tenant injured and property damaged by fire resulting from an obviously defective heater or wiring.
- Tenant gets sick from pesticide sprayed in common areas and on exterior walls without advance notice.
- Tenant's child is scalded by water from a water heater with a broken thermostat.
- Tenant slips and falls on a puddle of oil-slicked rainwater in the garage.
- Tenant's guest injured when she slips on ultraslick floor wax applied by the landlord's cleaning service.
- Tenant receives electrical burns when attempting to insert the stove's damaged plug into the wall outlet.
- Tenant slips and falls on wet grass cuttings left on a common walkway.

The Landlord Violated a Health or Safety Law

Many state and local governments have enacted health and safety laws requiring smoke detectors, sprinklers, inside-release security bars on windows, childproof fences around swimming pools, and so on. To put real teeth behind these important laws, legislators (and sometimes the courts) have decided

that if a landlord doesn't take reasonable steps to comply with certain health or safety statutes, he will be legally considered negligent. And if that negligence results in an injury, the landlord is liable for it. You don't need to prove that an accident was forseeable or likely to be serious; nor do you have to show that complying with the law would have been relatively inexpensive. The legal term for this rule is "negligence per se."

> **EXAMPLE:** A local housing code specifies that all kitchens must have grounded power plugs. There are no grounded plugs in your kitchen. As a result, you're injured when using an appliance in an otherwise safe manner. In many states, the law would presume negligence on the part of your landlord. If you can show that the ungrounded plug caused your injury, the landlord will be held liable.

Bear in mind that landlords are only expected to take reasonable steps to comply with safety and health laws that fall within the negligence per se realm. For example, most states require landlords to supply smoke detectors. If your landlord has supplied one, but you have disabled it, your landlord won't be held responsible if you are hurt by a fire that could have been stopped had you left the detector alone.

The landlord's violation of a health or safety law may also indirectly cause an injury. For example, if the landlord lets the furnace deteriorate in violation of local law, and you are injured trying to repair it, the landlord will probably be liable unless your repair efforts are extremely careless themselves.

> **EXAMPLE:** The state housing code requires landlords to provide hot water. In the middle of the winter, your hot water heater has been broken for a week, despite your repeated complaints to the landlord. Finally, to give your sick child a hot bath, you carry pots of steaming water from the stove to the bathtub. Doing this, you spill the hot water and burn yourself seriously.

You sue the landlord for failure to provide hot water as required by state law. If the case goes to court, it will be up to the jury to decide whether the landlord's failure to provide hot water caused your injury. Many juries would think that your response to the lack of hot water was a forseeable one and, knowing this, your landlord's insurance company would probably be willing to offer a fair settlement.

The Landlord Didn't Make Certain Repairs

For perfectly sensible reasons, many landlords do not want tenants to undertake even relatively simple tasks like painting, plastering, or unclogging a drain. Your lease or rental agreement may prohibit you from making any repairs or alterations without the owner's consent, or limit what you can do. (Chapter 10 discusses this.)

But in exchange for a landlord's reserving the right to make all these repairs, the law imposes a responsibility. If, after being told about a problem, the landlord doesn't maintain or repair something you aren't allowed to touch, and you are injured as a result, the landlord is probably liable. The legal reason is that the landlord breached the contract (the lease) by not making the repairs. (The landlord may be negligent as well; remember, there is nothing to stop you from presenting multiple reasons why the landlord should be held liable.)

EXAMPLE: The Rules and Regulations attached to Lori's lease state that management will in-spect and clean the fan above her stove every six months. Jake, an affable but somewhat scat-terbrained graduate student in charge of mainte-nance at the apartment complex, was supposed to do the fan checks. But deep into his studies and social life, Jake scheduled no inspections and, ten months later, Lori was injured when the accumulated grease in the fan filter caught fire.

Lori sued the landlord, alleging that his failure to live up to his contractual promise to clean the fan was the cause of her injuries. The jury agreed and awarded her a large sum.

Some other common examples might include:

- **Environmental hazards.** If your lease forbids repainting without the landlord's consent, the landlord is obligated to maintain the painted surfaces. If an old layer of lead paint begins to crack, deteriorate, and enter the air, the landlord will be liable for the health problems that follow. (Chapter 13 covers environmental health hazards such as lead-based paint.)
- **Security breaches.** Landlords typically forbid tenants from installing locks of their own. That means your landlord may be liable if his failure to provide secure locks contributes to a crime. (See Chapter 14.)

The Landlord Didn't Keep the Premises Habitable

One of a landlord's basic responsibilities is to keep the rental property in a "habitable" condition.

Failure to maintain a habitable dwelling may make the landlord liable for injuries caused by the substandard conditions. For example, a tenant who is bitten by a rat in a vermin-infested building may argue that the owner's failure to maintain a rat-free building constituted a breach of duty to keep the place habitable, which in turn led to the injury. You must show that the landlord knew of the defect and had a reasonable amount of time to fix it.

This theory applies only when the defect is so serious that the rental unit is unfit for human habitation. For example, a large, jagged broken picture window would probably make the premises unfit for habitation in North Dakota in winter, but a torn screen door in Southern California obviously would not. The North Dakota tenant who cut herself trying to cover the window with cardboard might sue under negligence and a violation of the implied warranty of habitability, while the California tenant would be limited to a theory of negligence.

EXAMPLE: Jose notified his landlord about the mice that he had seen several times in his kitchen. Despite Jose's repeated complaints, the landlord did nothing to eliminate the problem.

When Jose reached into his cupboard for a box of cereal, he was bitten by a mouse. Jose sued his landlord for the medical treatment he required, including extremely painful rabies shots. He alleged that the landlord's failure to eradicate the rodent problem constituted a breach of the implied warranty of habitability, and that this breach was responsible for his injury. The jury agreed and gave Jose a large monetary award.

The injury sustained by Jose in the example above could also justify a claim that the injury resulted from the landlord's negligence. And, if Jose's landlord had failed to take reasonable steps to comply with a state or local statute concerning rodent control, the landlord might automatically be considered negligent. Finally, the owner may also be liable if the lease forbade Jose from making repairs, such as repairing improper sewage connections or changing the way garbage was stored. As you can see, sometimes there are several legal theories that will fit the facts and support your claim for damages.

The Landlord Acted Recklessly

In the legal sense of the word, "recklessness" usually means extreme carelessness regarding an obvious defect or problem. A landlord who is aware of a long-existing and obviously dangerous defect but neglects to correct it may be guilty of recklessness, not just ordinary carelessness.

If your landlord or an employee acted recklessly, your monetary recovery could be significant. This is because a jury has the power to award not only actual damages (which include medical bills, loss of earnings, and pain and suffering) but also extra, "punitive" damages. (See "How Much Money You're Entitled To," below.) Punitive damages are almost never given in simple negligence cases, but are appropriate to punish recklessness and to send a sobering message to others who might behave similarly. But don't count your millions before you have them: In any situation the line between ordinary negligence and recklessness is wherever the unpredictable American jury thinks it should be. The size of the punitive award is likewise up to the jury, and can often be reduced later by a judge or appellate court.

The very unpredictability of punitive damage awards, however, can be to your advantage when negotiating with the landlord. The landlord may settle your claim rather than risk letting an indignant jury award you punitive damages.

EXAMPLE: The handrail along the stairs to the first floor of the apartment house Jack owned had been hanging loose for several months. Jack attempted to fix it two or three times by taping the supports to the wall. The tape did no good, however, and the railing was literally flapping in the breeze. One dark night when Hilda, one of Jack's tenants, reached for the railing, the entire thing came off in her hand, causing her to fall and break her hip.

Hilda sued Jack for her injuries. In her lawsuit, she pointed to the ridiculously ineffective measures that Jack had taken to deal with an obviously dangerous situation, and charged that he had acted with reckless disregard for the safety of his tenants. (Hilda also argued that Jack was negligent because of his unreasonable behavior and because he had violated a local ordinance regarding maintenance of handrails.) The jury agreed with Hilda and awarded her punitive damages.

The Landlord Intentionally Harmed You

Intentional injuries are rare but, unfortunately, they occur more often than you might guess. For example, if a landlord or manager struck and injured you during an argument, obviously that would be an intentional act for which the landlord would be liable.

Less obvious, but no less serious, are emotional or psychological injuries which can, in extreme circumstances, also be inflicted intentionally. Intentional infliction of emotional distress often arises in these situations:

- **Sexual harassment.** Repeated, disturbing attentions of a sexual nature that the harasser refuses to stop, which leave the victim fearful, humiliated, and upset, can form the basis for a claim of intentional harm. (See Chapter 5 for a detailed discussion of possible responses.)

    EXAMPLE: Rita's landlord Brad took advantage of every opportunity to make suggestive comments about her looks and social life. When she asked him to stop, he replied that he was "just looking out for her," and he stepped up his unwanted attentions. Rita finally had enough, broke the lease and moved out. When Brad sued her for unpaid rent, she turned around and sued him for the emotional distress caused by his harassment. To his surprise, Brad was slapped with a multithousand dollar judgment, including punitive damages.

- **Assault.** Threatening or menacing someone without actually touching them is an assault, which can be enormously frightening and lead to psychological damage.
- **Repeated invasions of privacy.** Deliberately invading a tenant's privacy—by unauthorized entries, for example—may cause extreme worry and distress. (Chapter 11 covers tenants' privacy rights.)

The Law Makes the Landlord Liable

In a few rare circumstances, a landlord may be responsible for a tenant's injury even though the landlord did his best to create and maintain a safe environment. In other words, even if the landlord did his best to provide a safe premises—the landlord was not negligent—he's responsible. This legal principle is called "strict liability," or liability without fault. It's a very similar concept to "no fault" auto insurance—you collect without having to prove that the accident was the other person's fault.

In most states, strict liability is imposed by courts or lawmakers only when a hidden defect poses an unusually dangerous risk of harm to a group of persons unable to detect or avoid the danger. For example, Massachusetts landlords are subject to strict liability if tenants are poisoned by lead-based paint. In New York, strict liability has been applied to injuries from radon.

Dog Bites and Other Animal Attacks

It's not uncommon for tenants (or their guests) to be injured by other tenants' dogs or other animals. In some situations, the landlord as well as the animal's owner will be legally liable for your injuries.

Dangerous domestic pets. You may be able to hold your landlord responsible for an injury caused by another tenant's dangerous domestic pet, such as a vicious dog, if you can convince a judge or jury that:

- the landlord knew (or, in the circumstances, must have known) of the animal's dangerous propensities, and
- the landlord could have prevented the injury— for example, by imposing a leash-only rule or evicting the rule-breaking pet owner.

Dangerous exotic pets. Keeping a wild animal such as a monkey or wolf as a pet is an "ultrahazardous" activity. In the eyes of the law, injured victims don't have to prove that the pet was dangerous—it's presumed dangerous, period. A landlord who knows that a wild animal is on the premises will likely be held liable along with the animal's owner if the animal injures a guest or tenant.

It's always advantageous for an injured tenant or guest to be able to sue the landlord as well as the owner, since the landlord will almost always have an insurance policy to cover the claim. If the animal owner has renters' insurance, that policy will also cover a claim. Animal owners without renters' or homeowners' insurance are not covered for the consequences of their pets' misbehavior, and your ability to collect from them will depend on whether they have enough assets to satisfy a settlement or judgment.

Louisiana is the only state that makes strict liability available for a wide range of tenant injuries, but the quirkiness of the law (you must have been injured by an "original aspect" of the structure that has succumbed to "ruin") make it little used in practice. Most injured Louisiana tenants sue their landlords for negligence.

If You're at Fault, Too

If you sue your landlord for negligence, the landlord may turn right around and accuse you of negligence, too. And if you are partially to blame for your injury, the landlord's liability for your losses will be reduced accordingly.

Your Own Carelessness

If you are also guilty of unreasonable carelessness—for example, you were drunk and, as a result, didn't (or couldn't) watch your step when you tripped on a loose tread on a poorly maintained stairway—in most states the landlord's liability will be proportionately reduced.

The legal principle is called "comparative negligence." Basically, this means that if you are partially at fault, you can collect only part of the value of your losses. For example, if a judge or jury ruled that you had suffered $10,000 in damages (such as medical costs or lost earnings) but that you were 20% at fault, you would recover only $8,000.

Comparative negligence is applied in different ways in different states. In some states, injured tenants can collect something no matter how careless they were—even if they were 99% at fault. In many others, however, you can recover only if your own carelessness was not too great. In some, for example, you'll get something only if your carelessness was less than the landlord's. If it's equal to or greater than the landlord's, you'll get nothing. In a majority of states, you can recover if your negligence was *equal to* or lower than the landlord's, so if the jury concludes that you were equally at fault, you'll collect half your damages. In a few states, the doctrine of comparative negligence doesn't exist. If you were even the least bit negligent, you can collect nothing.

It's not worth your while to learn the rule in your state—it's likely to be a fairly difficult call,

anyway, and one that lawyers argue long and hard about. Instead, understand that if you are injured and intend to file a claim or lawsuit against your landlord, you'll need to consider whether your own carelessness played a part. If it did (or if you can expect the landlord to claim that it did), check with a lawyer or do your own legal research to find out what impact, if any, your carelessness will have on your chance of success.

Injuries to Guests

Will your landlord be legally liable if a guest of yours is hurt on the rental property? In most states yes, as long as the guest was there at your invitation and was hurt while involved in an activity that the landlord could reasonably expect a guest to engage in. For example, your dinner guest who trips on a poorly maintained step while on the way to your front door could fairly look to the landlord for compensation, since using the steps is something the landlord would expect your guest to do. But suppose the laundry room is clearly posted, "For tenants' use only," and your guest is hurt there? The injured guest may not prevail.

Your Risk-Taking

Carelessness on your part is not the only way that your monetary recovery can be reduced. If you deliberately chose to act in a way that caused or worsened your injury, another doctrine may apply. Called "assumption of risk," it refers to a tenant who knows the danger of a certain action and decides to take the chance anyway.

> **EXAMPLE:** In a hurry to get to work, you take a shortcut to the garage by using a walkway that you know has uneven, broken pavement. You disregard the sign posted by your landlord: "Use Front Walkway Only." If you trip and hurt your knee, you'll have a hard time pinning blame on your landlord, because you deliberately chose a known, dangerous route to the garage.

In some states, if you are injured as a result of putting yourself in harm's way, you may not be entitled to recover anything, even if the landlord's negligence contributed to the injury. In other states, your recovery will be diminished according to the extent that you appreciated the danger involved.

How Much Money You're Entitled To

If you were injured on your landlord's property and have convinced an insurance adjuster or jury that the landlord is responsible, at least in part, you can ask for monetary compensation, called "compensatory damages." Injured tenants can recover the money they have lost (wages) and spent (doctors' bills), plus compensation for physical pain and suffering, mental anguish, and lost opportunities.

Medical care and related expenses. You can recover for doctors' and physical therapists' bills, including future care. Even if your bills were covered by your own insurance company or medical plan, you can still sue for the amounts—but expect your insurance company to come after you, via a lien claim, if you recover anything in excess of your co-payments or deductibles.

Missed work time. You can sue for lost wages and income while you were unable to work and undergoing treatment for your injuries. You can also recover for expected losses due to continuing care. The fact that you used sick or vacation pay to cover your time off from work is irrelevant. You are entitled to save this pay to use at your discretion at other times. In short, using up vacation or sick pay is considered the same as losing the pay itself.

Pain and other physical suffering. The type of injury you have suffered and its expected duration will affect the amount you can expect for pain and suffering. But insurance adjusters won't take your word for the level of discomfort you're experiencing. If you can show that your doctor has prescribed strong antipain medication, you'll have some objective corroboration of your distress. And the longer your recovery period, the greater your pain and suffering.

Permanent physical disability or disfigurement. If your injury has clear long-lasting or permanent effects—such as scars, back or joint stiffness, or a significant reduction in your mobility—the amount of your damages goes way up.

Loss of family, social, career, and educational experiences or opportunities. If you can demonstrate that the injury prevented you from advancing in your job or landing a better one, you can ask for compensation representing the lost income. Of course, it's hard to prove that missing a job interview resulted in income loss (after all, you didn't yet have the job). But the possibility that you might have moved ahead may be enough to convince the insurance company to sweeten their offer.

Injuries Without Impact: Legal Nuisances

You may be able to successfully sue and recover damages in some situations where you may not appear to be physically hurt. If the landlord maintains a legal nuisance—a serious and persistent health or safety condition that adversely affects a tenant's (or neighbor's) enjoyment of the property—a tenant can sue for damages even if no physical injury occurs. For example, a tenant who is repeatedly plagued by the stench of garbage scattered about because the landlord hasn't provided enough garbage cans for the apartment building can sue for the annoyance and inconvenience of putting up with the smell. Similarly, a tenant or neighbor—or a group of them—may sue if the landlord does nothing to evict a notorious drug-dealing tenant, whose dangerous associates genuinely frighten them. (See Chapter 14 for a discussion of legal nuisances.)

And as discussed in Chapter 5, a landlord may also be sued for the nonphysical distress caused by illegal discrimination or harassment.

Emotional damages resulting from any of the above. Emotional pain, including stress, embarrassment, depression, and strains on family relationships, can be compensated. Like pain and suffering, however, it's hard to prove. If you have consulted a therapist, physician, or counselor, their evaluations of your reported symptoms can serve as proof of your problems. Be aware, however, that when you choose to sue for mental or emotional injuries, your doctor's notes and files regarding your symptoms and treatment will usually be made available to the other side.

In some cases, injured tenants can collect more than compensatory damages. Punitive damages are awarded if a judge or jury decides that the landlord acted outrageously, either intentionally or with extreme carelessness (recklessness). Punitive damages are punishments for this conduct.

Environmental Hazards

Asbestos 203

   OSHA Regulations 203

   When the Landlord Must Test for Asbestos 204

   Protection From Asbestos 204

   Alerting and Motivating Your Landlord 205

   Moving Out If Necessary 206

Lead 208

   Federal Protections 208

   Federal Rules Covering Renovations 211

   State Laws on Lead Affecting Tenants 213

   Recognizing Lead in Your Home 213

   Dealing With Lead on Your Own 214

   Getting the Landlord to Act 215

   Moving Out If Necessary 216

Radon 217

   Finding Radon 218

   Solving Radon Problems 218

   The Landlord's Responsibility 218

   Moving Out If Necessary 219

Carbon Monoxide 219

   Sources of Carbon Monoxide 219

   Preventing Carbon Monoxide Problems 219

   Responsibility for Carbon Monoxide 221

Mold 221

   Where Mold Is Found 221

   Laws on Mold Affecting Landlords 222

   Landlord Liability for Tenant Exposure to Mold 222

   Prevention—The Best Way to Avoid Mold Problems 223

   How to Clean Up Mold 224

   Testing for Toxicity 224

   Compensation for Mold Damage 225

Bedbugs...225

What's a Bedbug—And Where Does It Come From?...225

How to Deal With an Infestation 226

Exterminations and Relocation Costs: Who Pays?..227

Ruined Belongings: Who Pays? 228

Your Right to Know About a Bedbug Problem—And What to Do If Your
      Landlord Doesn't Tell the Truth..229

Because of some relatively recent changes in the law, landlords must now do more than provide housing that meets minimum health and safety standards. They are also expected to deal with some serious environmental health hazards. Simply put, laws now require the landlord to take steps to ensure that you and your family aren't sickened by several common hazards, including lead, asbestos, and radon. Recently, the presence of mold has gotten the attention of landlords, tenants, and legislators, as have bedbugs.

This chapter explains landlords' obligations and offers some suggestions on how to spot problem areas, work with the landlord (or housing authorities), and take steps to protect yourself.

This chapter includes several sample letters to send your landlord when it comes to problems with asbestos, lead, or other environmental health hazards. As with all important communications, use a mail or delivery service that will provide proof of delivery (you may need this should you end up in a legal dispute with your landlord). In Chapter 6, "Using Email or Text Messages for Notice or a Letter of Understanding" explains why it's best to send important communications by mail (certified or return receipt requested) or delivery service, rather than email or text messages.

 RELATED TOPIC
Also covered in this book:
- Your right to safe and habitable housing: Chapters 8 and 9.
- Your legal options if you are injured by defective housing conditions: Chapter 12.

Asbestos

Exposure to asbestos has long been linked to an increased risk of cancer, particularly for workers in the asbestos manufacturing industry or in construction jobs involving the use of asbestos materials. More recently, the danger of asbestos in homes has also been recognized.

Homes built before the mid-1970s often contain asbestos insulation around heating systems, in ceilings, and in other areas. Until 1981, asbestos was also widely used in other building materials, such as vinyl flooring and tiles. Asbestos that is intact (or covered up) is generally not a problem, and the current wisdom is to leave it in place but monitor it for signs of deterioration. However, asbestos that has begun to break down and enter the air—for example, when it is disturbed during maintenance or renovation work—can become a significant health problem to people who breathe it.

OSHA Regulations

Until quite recently, landlords had no legal obligation to test for the presence of asbestos absent clear evidence that it was likely to be a health hazard.

Fortunately for tenants in every state, owners of buildings constructed before 1981 must now install warning labels, train staff, and notify people who work in areas that might contain asbestos. Unless the owner rules out the presence of asbestos by having a licensed inspector test the property, the law presumes that asbestos is present.

These requirements are imposed by the U.S. Occupational Safety and Health Administration (OSHA) to protect workers. But they are also a boon to tenants. In the process of complying with OSHA's requirements to inform and protect employees or outside contractors, your landlord learns whether or not there is asbestos on the property and (based on its type and quantity) what must be done to protect the workers. Unless the landlord never hires an employee or outside contractor or learns about asbestos on the property, these precautions also benefit tenants. And once a landlord knows about the presence of any dangerous defect on the rental property, including asbestos, the law imposes a duty to take reasonable steps to make sure that tenants aren't harmed. In short, once the asbestos genie is out of the bottle, the landlord must take reasonable steps to protect your health or face the legal consequences.

Deteriorating Asbestos: An Obvious, Dangerous Defect

Problems with asbestos often arise when neither the landlord nor the tenant realizes that the material is embedded in ceilings and floors. Sometimes, however, the situation is not so subtle. Deteriorating asbestos that is open and obvious is a dangerous defect that your landlord must address pronto. It's no different from a broken front step or an inoperable front door lock. As the owner, the landlord is responsible for fixing conditions that could cause significant injury.

OSHA regulations cover two classes of materials: those that definitely contain asbestos (such as certain kinds of flooring and ceilings) and those that the law presumes contain asbestos. The second class is extremely inclusive, describing, among other things, any surfacing material that is "sprayed, troweled on, or otherwise applied." Under this definition, virtually every dwelling built before 1980 must be suspected of containing asbestos. Asbestos or asbestos-containing materials are typically found in or on:

- sprayed-on "cottage cheese" ceilings
- acoustic tile ceilings
- vinyl flooring, and
- insulation around heating and hot water pipes.

When the Landlord Must Test for Asbestos

Your landlord is required to comply with OSHA's asbestos testing and protective rules when he undertakes a major remodeling or renovation job of a pre-1981 building, as well as when he undertakes lesser projects (such as the preparation of an asbestos-containing ceiling or wall for repainting). Even relatively noninvasive custodial work—such as stripping floor tiles containing asbestos—comes within the long reach of OSHA.

OSHA has concluded that post-1981 buildings are unlikely to contain asbestos, but if your post-1981 building *does* have asbestos (perhaps the builder or remodeler used recycled building materials), OSHA regulations cover it, too.

Protection From Asbestos

OSHA is very specific regarding the level of training, work techniques, and protective clothing for employees whose work involves disturbing asbestos. But they do not specifically address the measures that a landlord must take to protect *tenants* from exposure. However, the worker protection requirements give very useful clues as to what you can reasonably expect from your landlord in the way of tenant protections. In short, the more your landlord must do to protect workers, the more he must do to warn and protect tenants, too. If he doesn't and you are injured as a result, he risks being found liable. (See Chapter 12.)

- **Custodial work.** At the low end of the asbestos-disturbing spectrum, workers doing custodial work—for example, stripping the floor tiles in the lobby—must be trained (and supervised by a trained superior) in safe asbestos-handling techniques. Your landlord should warn all tenants that the work is planned, giving you an opportunity to avoid the area if you choose. The landlord should also make sure that tenants, their guests, and children don't come into contact with the debris. Conscientious landlords will use written notices to alert tenants, and place cones and caution tape around the area.
- **Major repairs or renovations.** If renovation or repair work is planned for a pre-1981 building, the landlord must test for asbestos and provide more protection, including air monitoring, protective clothing, and medical surveillance of workers. You are entitled to appropriate warnings, and your landlord should minimize your exposure through fastidious worksite procedures and isolation of dangerous materials.

EXAMPLE: Sally returned home to her apartment to find that workers were planning to remove the ugly, stained ceiling tile in the lobby and hallways. She learned from the contractor that the project would last four days. Sally was concerned that her young sons, returning home from school in the afternoon and curious about the renovations, would hang around the halls and lobby or at least pass through them as they went in and out to play. Either way, Sally's sons would be exposed to the airborne fibers. Sally wrote a note to the landlord, explaining her concerns.

Sally's landlord recognized the reasonableness of her fears and the potential for injury. He spoke with the contractor, one who had been specially trained in asbestos removal, and arranged for the work to be done between the hours of 8 a.m. and 3 p.m. He insisted, and the contractor readily agreed, that the old tiles be removed and any asbestos-containing material covered at the end of each work day. Finally, the landlord hired two adults to monitor foot traffic in and around the renovation site, to ensure that no one lingered near the workers or came into contact with the removed materials.

Alerting and Motivating Your Landlord

Many landlords, unfortunately, have no idea about their duty to deal with the risks posed by asbestos. If you live in an older building and suspect that there is asbestos on the premises that is not being managed properly, alert your landlord and see to it that your health is protected. Here are some strategies.

When the asbestos is obvious but intact. Asbestos that is intact—for example, asbestos insulation that is covered with foil or wrapped with tape—probably does not pose a significant health risk to you, since the fibers can't enter the air. It is important, however, that asbestos be monitored for signs of deterioration. For example, if the tape wrapping is tearing or falling away, it is no longer doing its job of containment. If you are worried about whether asbestos-containing materials in your home are dangerous, ask your landlord, in writing, to have the material inspected by a trained professional.

 CAUTION

Never disturb asbestos-containing materials. You shouldn't drill holes in walls or ceilings that contain asbestos, or sand asbestos tiles in preparation for a new coat of paint. First, you want to protect your health. Second, intentionally disturbing asbestos will almost certainly reduce, if not defeat, any legal claim you might have if your health is harmed by an asbestos-related problem. The law won't hold your landlord responsible for an injury that you deliberately courted, ignoring a risk you knew about. (See Chapter 12.)

When the asbestos is obvious and airborne. Take immediate action if asbestos in your living space has begun to break down or slough off. Asbestos that has begun to break down is extremely dangerous. If it is present in your living space in any significant amount, it makes your premises legally uninhabitable. (See Chapter 8 for your legal options, which may include withholding rent. Also, below, we discuss the option of moving out.) A sample letter from a tenant concerned about deteriorating asbestos is shown below.

Sample Letter Regarding Deteriorating Asbestos

37 Ninth Avenue North
Chicago, Illinois 00000
312-555-4567

February 28, 20xx

Margaret Mears
3757 East Seventh Street
Chicago, Illinois 00000

Dear Ms. Mears:

As you know, the ceilings in my apartment are sprayed-on acoustical plaster. I have begun to notice an excessive amount of fine, white dust in the apartment, and I believe it is the result of the breakdown of the asbestos fibers in the plaster. I am quite concerned about this, since inhaling asbestos can cause serious illness. Please contact me immediately so that you can take a look and arrange for a licensed inspector to examine the ceilings.

Yours truly,

Terry Lu

Terry Lu

TIP

Keep copies of all correspondence regarding asbestos or other environmental health hazards. If your landlord fails to take the right steps and you want to move out or seek other legal remedies, you'll need to be able to prove that you notified the landlord of the problem and waited a reasonable amount of time for a response.

When custodial or repair work is done improperly. When it comes to asbestos removal, the people who suffer most from a landlord's disregard of workplace safety are the workers themselves. But improper asbestos removal or disturbance is likely to affect you, too. Fortunately, there is something you can do about it. OSHA wants to hear about violations of workplace safety rules. You can reach OSHA by calling the phone number listed below in "Asbestos Resources." Many states have state equivalents of OSHA, and you can also call your state's consumer protection agency for information.

CAUTION

Beware of landlord retaliation. A landlord who learns about your complaint to OSHA won't be pleased. Many (but not all) states have laws that prohibit landlords from taking actions against tenants (such as rent hikes, diminution of services, or ending a tenancy) after tenants have exercised their legal rights by contacting a federal or state agency regarding a violation of law. (See "State Laws Prohibiting Landlord Retaliation" in Appendix A.) If you aren't protected by an antiretaliation statute, proceed carefully and, if possible, anonymously.

Moving Out If Necessary

Sometimes it isn't possible to shield yourself from the effects of deteriorating asbestos, or even your landlord's major repairs or renovations involving asbestos. For example, if the acoustic ceilings in your apartment are being removed, it is unlikely (even if you and your landlord are prepared to take every precaution) that you can avoid inhaling some dangerous airborne fibers. In situations like this, especially if you or your family have health problems that make you especially vulnerable to the effects of asbestos, the best alternative might be to move

out temporarily until the work is completed. (See Chapter 8 for a discussion of moving out because your rental is uninhabitable.) Since the responsibility to repair and maintain the structure is the landlord's, the cost of temporary shelter should be covered by the landlord as long as you can convincingly establish that remaining on the premises would constitute a significant health risk. See the sample letter below.

If you are able to give valid reasons why you should be temporarily absent while the asbestos removal work is done, and if you have a reasonable landlord who appreciates the potentially serious legal consequences of denying your reasonable request, chances are you'll be able to come to an agreement. (Don't ask to stay at the Ritz, however!)

But what if the landlord stubbornly refuses? Obviously, to protect your health, you'll want to move out anyway. And assuming the asbestos problems really are serious, you should stand a good chance of prevailing in a small claims court lawsuit for the cost of your temporary housing. Be sure to keep a copy of the letter you have sent (preferably by certified mail) to the landlord, a record of his refusal to pay for temporary accommodations, and all receipts for your expenses.

TIP

Come to court prepared with asbestos-related information. If you go to small claims court, be prepared to explain the serious dangers of breathing asbestos fibers to the judge and why the landlord's work was so invasive that temporarily moving out was your only sensible alternative. See "Asbestos Resources," below. Also, see Chapter 19 for a discussion of small claims lawsuits.

Instead of suing in small claims court, you may be tempted to utilize what the law calls a "repair and deduct" remedy (discussed in Chapter 8) by simply deducting the cost of replacement housing from your rent. It seems logical, but a judge might not allow it. Seizing upon this uncertainty, your landlord's response will probably be to terminate your tenancy and file for eviction for nonpayment of rent. If you lose, you will not only have to pay for the cost of the temporary housing, but face eviction from your rental as well. (In addition, you may be stuck with the landlord's attorneys' fees if there is an "attorneys' fees" clause in your lease. See Chapter 2.) Far better to file a straightforward lawsuit asking for reimbursement, where the risk is simply losing the suit, not your home.

Sample Letter Requesting Reimbursement for Temporary Housing

> 1289 Central Avenue, Apartment 8
> Toofar, TX 00000
> 713-555-7890
>
> June 13, 20xx
>
> Mr. Frank Brown, Owner
> Sunshine Properties
> 75 Main Street
> Toofar, TX 00000
>
> Dear Mr. Brown:
>
> I have just received the notice you sent to all tenants on the first floor, alerting us to the fact that you intend to tear out the heating ducts and insulation during the week of July 6. The work will involve removal of heating vents inside our apartment and removal of the asbestos insulation through the openings. You estimate that the work will take two days for each apartment.
>
> I do not think that it would be a good idea for me and my elderly mother to live in the apartment during this process. I am concerned that we will inhale airborne fibers that may cause difficulties in breathing. My mother suffers from chronic bronchitis and cannot risk exposure to anything that might worsen the condition. Dr. Jones, who treats my mother, would be happy to corroborate this fact.
>
> I think that the best solution would be for us to move out while this work is being done. The nearby Best Midwestern Motel has reasonable rates and would be convenient to our jobs and transportation. Please contact me so that we might discuss this before the renovation work begins. You can call me at home at the above number most nights and weekends.
>
> Yours truly,
>
> *Sharon Rock*
>
> Sharon Rock
>
> cc: Dr. Jones

If your landlord refuses to cover temporary housing expenses, you might also want to consider moving out permanently. This option is most appropriate when the risk is great and the length of exposure relatively long. But to justify breaking the lease (and to avoid liability for future rent), you will have to be able to show that airborne asbestos really did make the premises uninhabitable. (See Chapter 8 for a full discussion of breaking the lease due to uninhabitability.) If the landlord is ripping out whole ceilings over a month's time, this argument will be strong. However, it will not amount to much if the landlord is drilling two small holes in the ceiling to install a smoke detector.

 TIP

Check to see if your state law allows the landlord to terminate a tenancy for major renovation work if he provides relocation assistance for tenants. "State Landlord-Tenant Statutes" in Appendix A gives citations to your state's landlord-tenant codes, and "State Laws on Unconditional Quit Terminations" gives citations to laws that explain when landlords may terminate your tenancy. In one or another of those sets of laws, you may find that your state requires your landlord to pay for moving expenses if your tenancy is terminated because a major project (such as wide-scale asbestos removal) makes it impossible for you to stay on the premises.

Asbestos Resources

For further information on asbestos rules, inspections, and control, contact the nearest office of the U.S. Occupational Safety and Health Administration (OSHA) (find yours at www.osha.gov or call 800-321-OSHA). OSHA has also developed interactive computer software for property owners, called "Asbestos Advisor," designed to help identify asbestos and suggest ways to handle it. It may help you, or interested members of any tenants' association in your building, to determine whether asbestos is present and whether your landlord is managing it properly. The Asbestos Advisor is available free on OSHA's website, www.osha.gov.

For additional information on asbestos, including negative health effects, see the EPA website, at www.epa.gov/asbestos.

Lead

As we all know, exposure to lead-based paint and lead water pipes may lead to serious health problems, particularly in children. Brain damage, attention disorders, and hyperactivity have all been associated with lead poisoning. Studies show that the effects of lead poisoning are lifelong, affecting both personality and intelligence. In adults, the effects of lead poisoning can include nerve disorders, high blood pressure, reproductive disorders, and muscle and joint pain.

How Lead Poisoning Occurs

Lead-laden dust caused by the deterioration of exposed lead-based paint is the greatest source of lead poisoning. Falling on windowsills, walls, and floors, this dust makes its way into the human body when it is stirred up, becomes airborne and is inhaled, or when it is transmitted directly from hand to mouth. Exterior lead-based house paint is also a potential problem because it can slough off walls directly into the soil and be tracked into the house.

Lead dust results from renovations or remodeling—including, unfortunately, those very projects undertaken to rid premises of the lead-based paint. Lead poisoning can also occur from drinking water that contains leached-out lead from lead pipes or from deteriorating lead solder used in copper pipes.

Children between the ages of 18 months and five years are the most likely to be poisoned by lead-based paint. Their poisoning is detected when they become ill or, increasingly, in routine examinations that check for elevated blood levels of lead.

Buildings constructed before 1978 are likely to contain some source of lead: lead-based paint, lead pipes, or lead-based solder used on copper pipes. In 1978, the federal government required the reduction of lead in house paint; lead pipes are generally only found in homes built before 1930, and lead-based solder in home plumbing systems was banned in 1988. Pre-1950 housing in poor and urban neighborhoods that has been allowed to deteriorate is by far the greatest source of lead-based paint poisonings.

Discovering (or being told by the landlord) that there is lead on the premises is not necessarily the end of a healthy and safe tenancy. Below, we offer advice on how to cope with a lead problem.

Federal Protections

Unfortunately, federal law does *not* require landlords to test for lead, nor does it require them to get rid of it if they know it's present. Still, federal law aimed at reducing lead poisoning does give some important benefits to tenants. Many states give additional protections.

Disclosure

Since December 6, 1996 all property owners must inform tenants, before they sign or renew a lease or rental agreement, of any information they possess on lead paint hazard conditions on the property. They must disclose information on its presence in individual rental units, common areas and garages, tool sheds, other outbuildings, signs, fences, and play areas. If the property has been tested (testing must be done only by state-certified lead inspectors), a copy of the report, or a summary written by the inspector, must be shown to tenants.

With certain exceptions (listed below), every lease and rental agreement must include a disclosure page, even if the landlord has not tested. A copy of the federally approved disclosure form "Disclosure of Information on Lead-Based Paint and/or Lead-Based Paint Hazards" is reproduced below.

If you were a tenant in your current home on December 6, 1996 your landlord must comply with these disclosure requirements according to whether you are a tenant with a lease or are renting month to month.

- **Tenants with leases.** Your landlord need not comply until your lease is up and you renew or stay on as a month-to-month tenant.
- **Month-to-month tenants.** Your landlord should have given you a disclosure statement when

you wrote your first rent check dated after December 6, 1996 (September 6, 1996, if the landlord owns five or more units).

Lead Inspections

While inspections are not required by federal law, landlords may voluntarily arrange for an inspection in order to certify on the disclosure form that the property is lead free and exempt from federal regulations. (See list of exemptions, below.) Also, when a property owner takes out a loan or buys insurance, the bank or insurance company may require a lead inspection.

Professional lead inspectors don't always inspect every unit in large, multifamily properties. Instead, they inspect a sampling of the units and apply their conclusions to the property as a whole. Giving you the results and conclusions of a building-wide evaluation satisfies the law, even if your particular unit was not tested. If, however, your landlord has specific information regarding your unit that is inconsistent with the building-wide evaluation, he must disclose it to you.

For information on arranging a professional lead inspection or using a home testing kit, see "Recognizing Lead in Your Home," below.

Information

The landlord must give all tenants the lead hazard information booklet *Protect Your Family From Lead in Your Home,* written by the Environmental Protection Agency (EPA). If they choose, landlords may reproduce the booklet in a legal-size, 8½ x 14-inch format, and attach it to the lease. The graphics in the original pamphlet must be reproduced. State agencies may develop their own pamphlets, but they may not be used in place of the EPA version unless the EPA has approved them.

If your landlord has not given you a disclosure form or an EPA booklet, ask for them. If you get no results, notify the EPA. This will probably result in no more than a letter or call from the inspectors, since the EPA will usually not cite landlords unless

their noncompliance with the laws is willful and continuing. But a landlord who continues to ignore the law may find himself subject to the penalties described below.

Enforcement and Penalties

HUD and the EPA enforce renters' rights to know about the presence of lead-based paint by using "testers," as they do when looking for illegal discrimination (see Chapter 5). Posing as applicants, testers who get the rental will document whether landlords disclosed lead paint information when the lease or rental agreement was signed. Of course, individual complaints from tenants who have not received the required booklets can trigger an investigation, too.

Landlords who fail to distribute the required information booklet, or who do not give tenants the disclosure statement, may receive one or more of the following penalties:

- a notice of noncompliance, the mildest form of reprimand
- a civil penalty, which can include fines of up to $16,773 per violation for willful and continuing noncompliance
- an order to pay an injured tenant up to three times his actual damages, or
- a criminal fine of up many thousands of dollars per violation.

Government testers are also on the lookout for property owners who falsely claim that they have no knowledge of lead-based paint hazards on their property. Here's how it often comes up: A tenant complains to HUD if he becomes ill with lead poisoning after the landlord told him that he knew of no lead-based paint hazards on the premises. If HUD decides to investigate whether, in fact, the landlord knew about the hazard and failed to tell this tenant, their investigators get access to the landlord's records. They comb leasing, maintenance, and repair files—virtually the landlord's entire business records. If HUD finds evidence that the landlord knew (or had reason to know) of lead paint hazards, such as a contract

Disclosure of Information on Lead-Based Paint and/or Lead-Based Paint Hazards

Lead Warning Statement

Housing built before 1978 may contain lead-based paint. Lead from paint, paint chips, and dust can pose health hazards if not managed properly. Lead exposure is especially harmful to young children and pregnant women. Before renting pre-1978 housing, lessors must disclose the presence of known lead-based paint and/or lead-based paint hazards in the dwelling. Lessees must also receive a federally approved pamphlet on lead poisoning prevention.

Lessor's Disclosure

(a) Presence of lead-based paint and/or lead-based paint hazards (check (i) or (ii) below):

    (i) _____ Known lead-based paint and/or lead-based paint hazards are present in the housing (explain).

_____

_____

    (ii) _____ Lessor has no knowledge of lead-based paint and/or lead-based paint hazards in the housing.

(b) Records and reports available to the lessor (check (i) or (ii) below):

    (i) _____ Lessor has provided the lessee with all available records and reports pertaining to lead-based paint and/or lead-based paint hazards in the housing (list documents below).

_____

_____

    (ii) _____ Lessor has no reports or records pertaining to lead-based paint and/or lead-based paint hazards in the housing.

Lessee's Acknowledgment (initial)

(c) _____ Lessee has received copies of all information listed above.

(d) _____ Lessee has received the pamphlet *Protect Your Family from Lead in Your Home.*

Agent's Acknowledgment (initial)

(e) _____ Agent has informed the lessor of the lessor's obligations under 42 U.S.C. 4852d and is aware of his/her responsibility to ensure compliance.

Certification of Accuracy

The following parties have reviewed the information above and certify, to the best of their knowledge, that the information they have provided is true and accurate.

Lessor	Date	Lessor	Date
Lessee	Date	Lessee	Date
Agent	Date	Agent	Date

from a painting firm that includes costs for lead paint removal or a loan document indicating the presence of lead paint, the landlord will be hard-pressed to explain why he's checked the box on the disclosure form stating that he has no reports or records regarding the presence of lead-based paint on the property. The tenant, in turn, will have good evidence to use in court.

Rental Properties Exempt From Federal Regulations

- Housing for which a construction permit was obtained, or on which construction was started, after January 1, 1978. Older buildings that have been completely renovated since 1978 are *not* exempt, even if every painted surface was removed or replaced.
- Housing certified as lead-free by a state-accredited lead inspector. Lead-free means the absence of any lead paint, even paint that has been completely painted over and encapsulated.
- Lofts, efficiencies, studios, and other "zero-bedroom" units, including dormitory housing and rentals in sorority and fraternity houses. University-owned apartments and married student housing are not exempted.
- Short-term vacation rentals.
- A single room rented in a residential home.
- Housing designed for persons with disabilities (as explained in HUD's Fair Housing Accessibility Guidelines, 24 C.F.R., ch. I, Subchapter A, App. II), *unless* any child less than six years old resides there or is expected to reside there.
- Retirement communities (housing designed for seniors, where one or more tenant is at least 62 years old), *unless* children under the age of six are present or expected to live there.

RESOURCE

The Residential Lead-Based Paint Hazard Reduction Act was enacted in 1992 to reduce lead levels. It is commonly referred to as Title X [Ten] (42 U.S.C. § 4852d).

The Environmental Protection Agency (EPA) has written regulations that explain how landlords should implement lead hazard reduction (24 C.F.R. Part 35 and 40 C.F.R. Part 745). For more information, see "Lead Hazard Resources," below.

Federal Rules Covering Renovations

When occupied rental units or common areas in buildings constructed before 1978 are renovated, EPA regulations require that current tenants receive lead hazard information before the renovation work begins. (40 C.F.R. §§ 745.80–88.) The regulations were developed under the federal Toxic Substances Control Act (15 U.S.C. §§ 2681–2692) and became effective on June 1, 1999.

The obligation to distribute lead information rests with the "renovator." If the landlord hires an outside contractor to perform renovation work, the contractor is the renovator. But if the landlord, property manager, or superintendent or other employees perform the renovation work, the landlord is the renovator and is obliged to give you the required information.

The type of information that the renovator must give to tenants depends on where the renovation is taking place. If an occupied rental unit is being worked on, resident tenants must get a copy of the EPA pamphlet *The Lead-Safe Certified Guide to Renovate Right* (even if you already got one when you moved in). If common areas will be affected, the landlord must distribute a notice to every rental unit in the building.

What Qualifies as a Renovation?

According to EPA regulations, a "renovation" is any change to an occupied rental unit or common area of the building that disturbs painted surfaces. Here are some examples:

- removing or modifying a painted door, wall, baseboard, or ceiling
- scraping or sanding paint, or
- removing a large structure like a wall, partition, or window.

Not every renovation triggers the federal law, though. There are four big exceptions:

Emergency renovations. If a sudden or unexpected event, such as a fire or flood, requires emergency repairs to a rental unit or to the property's common areas, there's no need to distribute lead hazard information to tenants before work begins.

Minor repairs or maintenance. Minor work that affects two square feet or less of a painted surface is also exempt. Minor repairs include routine electrical and plumbing work, so long as no more than two square feet of the wall, ceiling, or other painted surface gets disturbed by the work.

Renovations in lead-free properties. If the rental unit or building in which the renovation takes place has been certified as containing no lead paint, the landlord isn't required to give out the required information.

Common area renovations in buildings with three or fewer units. Tenants in buildings with three or fewer units are not entitled to information about common area renovations.

If your landlord has repainted a rental unit in preparation for your arrival, this won't qualify as a "renovation" unless accompanied by sanding, scraping, or other surface preparation activities that may generate paint dust. Minor "spot" scraping or sanding can qualify for the "minor repairs and maintenance" exception if no more than two square feet of paint is disturbed on any surface to be painted. To learn more, go to the EPA website (www. epa.gov) and type Renovation, Repair, and Painting Program in the search box on the home page.

Receiving the EPA Pamphlet When Your Rental Is Renovated

Before starting a renovation to an occupied rental unit, the renovator must give the EPA pamphlet *The Lead-Safe Certified Guide to Renovate Right* to at least one adult occupant of the unit being occupied, preferably the tenant. This requirement applies to all rental properties, including single-family homes and duplexes, unless the property has been certified lead-free by an inspector.

The renovator (whether your landlord or an outside contractor) may mail or hand-deliver the pamphlet to you. If the renovator mails it, he or she must get a "certificate of mailing" from the post office dated at least seven days before the renovation work begins. If the renovator hand-delivers it, you'll probably be asked to sign and date a receipt acknowledging that you received the pamphlet before renovation work began in the unit. You should get the pamphlet 60 days (or less) before the work begins (delivering the pamphlet more than 60 days in advance won't satisfy the landlord's obligations under the law).

Notice of Common Area Renovation

If the building has four or more units, the renovator —be it the landlord or his contractor—must notify tenants of all "affected units" about the renovation and tell them how to obtain a free copy of the EPA pamphlet *The Lead-Safe Certified Guide to Renovate Right*. (C.F.R. § 745.84(b)(2).) In most cases, common area renovations will affect all units in the property, meaning that all tenants must be notified about the renovation. But when renovating a "limited use common area" in a large apartment building, such as the 16th floor hallway but no others, the landlord need only notify those units serviced by, or in close proximity to, the limited use common area. The EPA defines large buildings as those having 50 or more units.

To comply, the renovator must deliver a notice to every affected unit describing the nature and location of the renovation work, its location, and the dates the renovator expects to begin and finish work. If the renovator can't provide specific dates, he may use terms like "on or about," "in early June," or "in late July" to describe expected starting and ending dates for the renovation. The notices *must be delivered within 60 days before work begins.* The notices may be slipped under apartment doors or given to any adult occupant of the rental unit. Landlords may *not* mail the notices.

Penalties

Failing to give tenants the required information about renovation lead hazards can result in harsh penalties. Renovators who knowingly violate the regulations can get hit with a penalty of up to $37,500 per day for each violation. (15 U.S.C. § 2614.) Willful violations can also result in imprisonment.

State Laws on Lead Affecting Tenants

Many states have also addressed the lead issue by prohibiting the use of lead-based paint in residences and requiring the careful maintenance of existing lead paint and lead-based building materials. Some states require property owners to disclose lead hazards to prospective tenants. If your state has its own lead statute, you're entitled to its protections as well as the federal law.

If your state has its own lead hazard reduction law, you'll see that, like its federal cousin, it does not directly require the landlord to test for lead. Does this mean that the landlord need not conduct inspections? Not necessarily. In New York City, for example, landlords must perform annual visual inspections of rental units where a child under age seven resides. Landlords must inspect for "lead-based paint hazards," defined as peeling paint or deteriorated subsurfaces. New York City landlords must also visually inspect any apartments that become vacant on or after November 12, 1999 before the unit may be reoccupied. For more information on the New York City Childhood Lead Poisoning Prevention Act of 2003, commonly known as Local Law 1 (Administrative Code of City of N.Y. § 27-2012[h]), see the City's informational booklet, *What Every Tenant Should Know About LOCAL LAW 1* (type this title into your browser to access the booklet).

Recognizing Lead in Your Home

If your landlord has tested for lead and complied with federal disclosure requirements, you can skip this section. However, most landlords have not

tested for lead. (This situation will surely change as banks and insurance companies begin to require testing as a prerequisite to loans and insurance coverage.) There are several clues as to whether there is lead in or around your home, and ways that you (or, ideally, your landlord) can find out for sure.

You will need to hire a licensed lead tester to get a precise assessment of the risk of lead in your home. Unfortunately, the cost is high—a few hundred dollars at least. If you (and possibly other tenants) choose to do an assessment, you'll be in a good position to lobby the landlord to do something about containing the risk. But even if you do not get a professional's opinion, but are fairly sure that lead is present in your home, you can still act prudently on your own to reduce the risk. (Below, we explain what you can do yourself and how to get the landlord to act.)

Paint

Your first step should be to determine the age of the building. If the landlord doesn't know or won't say, go to the local building permit office and ask to see the building's construction permit. If there is no permit on file, you'll have to estimate the structure's age.

As noted above, housing that was built before January 1, 1978 is almost certain to have lead-based paint. But buildings constructed later may have it, too, since the 1978 ban did not include a recall and lead-based paint remained on the shelves.

You can do your own test for lead. Home testing kits work like this: After you swab a chemical solution over a painted surface, the swab will turn a certain color if lead is present. Kits are widely available at hardware and paint stores and are inexpensive, but unfortunately are unreliable about 30% of the time. For more reliable results, hire a professional tester who will use an X-ray gun to give an instant reading through all the layers of paint. A professional inspection will cost a few hundred dollars; if you can, share the cost with other tenants. (See "Lead Hazard Resources," below, for information on finding a HUD-approved contractor to test for lead.)

Lead Pipes

Pre-1930 construction generally used lead pipes. It's difficult to know for sure whether you have lead pipes until you examine the plumbing. When you look under the sink, you may be able to see the pipe coming out from the wall; if so, look for the tell-tale dark gray color. A plumber should be able to identify the pipes without difficulty.

Lead Solder

Lead solder was used to join sections of pipe as recently as 1988. You won't know whether it was used unless you can look at several soldered junctions; even then, you will probably need a plumber to tell you whether the solder was leaded or not.

Imported, Nonglossy Vinyl Miniblinds

Miniblinds from China, Taiwan, Indonesia, and Mexico that were manufactured before 1996, are likely to contain lead. As the surface vinyl deteriorates in the sun, lead dust enters the air. Even if your landlord knows your apartment has leaded miniblinds, he doesn't have to tell you *unless* the landlord knows that the blinds have begun to deteriorate and produce lead dust. Be smart: Ask the landlord to replace the blinds now, before a problem occurs.

Soil

For decades, American cars ran on leaded gasoline —and the effects are still with us. Exhaust from lead-burning cars contains lead, which falls to the ground where it remains, relatively inert, for years. Neighborhoods adjacent to heavily traveled roadways have significant amounts of lead in the soil; the readings drop off dramatically as the distance from the roads increases. If you live near a busy freeway or throughway, assume the worst and take care of yourself. See below for suggestions on self-help.

Dealing With Lead on Your Own

You don't need to automatically reject, or move out of, a rental that contains lead. Remember, only deteriorating lead is the culprit.

If you do discover hazardous lead, an aggressive approach is often the best idea. If you live in older housing where lead is almost surely present and deteriorating, assume a worst-case scenario and adjust your housekeeping and hygiene habits accordingly. (Ideally, you'll want the landlord to eventually take more drastic measures, such as careful repainting, as discussed below.) Here's what the experts recommend that you do:

- Vacuum thoroughly and regularly, using a "HEPA" ("high energy particle arresting") vacuum that will filter out the fine lead dust. Ask your landlord to provide one.
- Even where a unit has been repainted, the old lead paint layer will eventually be reexposed on some painted surfaces that get a lot of wear, such as door and windowsill areas. Wash them with a phosphate-based cleaner or a solution (like "Leadisolve") designed for lead pick-up.

 CAUTION

Don't disturb lead paint in buildings built before 1978. Do not sand walls, windowsills, doors, or other surfaces—it risks releasing lead into the air (possibly even from paint several layers down), creating the very hazards you are attempting to avoid. Renovations of this order should be handled by painters who have been trained and equipped to capture and remove lead dust and chips. If you intentionally disturb lead and suffer an injury, it will be difficult to place legal responsibility on your landlord.

- If your unit has lead pipes or copper pipe with lead solder, draw water out of the pipes by letting the taps run for 30 seconds before using—even if you plan to boil it for tea. Don't use hot water for cooking. Better yet, use bottled water for drinking and cooking.

- If lead is in the soil outside, provide throw rugs at each entrance or ask folks to remove their shoes before entering.
- Consider covering lead-laced soil with sod or an impermeable material.
- If your household has young children (especially those who are still crawling), use extra care to clean floors, especially around windows. Wash children's toys and hands frequently, and clean pacifiers and bottles after they fall on the floor.
- Test your children for lead poisoning. Elevated blood levels in young children can be picked up in a simple blood test. Increasingly, the test is being done as part of routine check-ups. If you live in a building that you suspect places your child at risk for lead poisoning, you need this information to protect your child. The Centers for Disease Control and Prevention recommend giving children a blood level test at age six months to one year. Do follow-up tests as needed.

CAUTION
If a child's blood lead level is very high, move promptly and see a lawyer. Evidence of lead poisoning will almost certainly entitle you to move out on the grounds of uninhabitability. (See "Moving Out If Necessary," below.) In Connecticut, a dwelling with lead is considered unfit by law. You will definitely need expert legal assistance if you sue for damages.

Getting the Landlord to Act

Getting your landlord to hire a professional to test and assess the risk of lead poisoning may be a tall order—after all, no federal or state law requires it. And it may be next to impossible to get your landlord to paint over deteriorating lead paint. But even the most penurious, callous, or short-sighted landlord may respond to an appeal to the bottom line.

Many landlords have learned (sometimes the hard way) that testing for lead and taking measures before tenants get sick is well worth the cost and time. Although landlords aren't liable for lead poisoning unless it can be shown that they knew that lead was present, these days it is increasingly difficult for landlords to plausibly argue that they were ignorant of this well-publicized issue. Lawsuits for lead poisoning can result in astronomical jury awards or settlements if the landlord is held responsible for the lifetime effects of an infant's brain damage. The cost of testing, risk assessment, and lead management pales in comparison.

If the landlord isn't aware of the potentially enormous liability for lead poisoning, suggest she read *Every Landlord's Legal Guide* (Nolo), which makes clear that tenants can bring, and win, lawsuits for lead poisoning. Many state health agencies publish their own pamphlets that also explain the risks to landowners who ignore the writing (and the paint) on the wall.

Notify the Landlord of Problems

If you discover a lead hazard on the property, tell the landlord at once, in writing. A sample letter is shown below.

Although the goal of your efforts is a safe place to live, not a successful lawsuit, don't lose sight of the fact that your landlord may avoid liability for lead injuries unless you can show that he knew (or should have known) of lead hazards and failed to take reasonable steps to reduce them. In short, if you believe there is a lead risk on your property, you want to make it impossible for the landlord to plausibly deny knowing about it. If you use a kit to test your rental unit or its water supply and find the presence of lead, send the results (certified mail) to the landlord. If your child has elevated blood levels, do the same. Keep these receipts and any other evidence of the landlord's knowledge, such as notes of a conversation in which the landlord acknowledged the presence of pre-1978, chipping paint but refused to buy a HEPA vacuum.

Sample Letter Regarding Lead Test Results

45 East Avenue North
Central City, MO 00000
816-555-7890

February 28, 20xx

Lester Levine
3757 East Seventh Street
Central City, MO 00000

Dear Mr. Levine:

We recently hired the environmental engineering firm of Checkit & Howe to test our duplex for the presence of lead-based paint. A report of their findings is enclosed. As you can see, there is indeed old, unstable lead paint on most of the windowsills and in the upstairs hall.

We are concerned about the effect that this deteriorating paint will have on the health of our children, aged three months and three years. At a minimum, we would like to discuss a safe and effective response to this problem. Please contact us as soon as possible so that we can arrange a meeting. We're home in the evenings and on weekends.

Yours truly,

Maynard G. Krebs

Zelda Krebs

Maynard G. and Zelda Krebs

Encl: Report of Checkit & Howe

Involve State, Local, or Federal Inspectors

Some states with aggressive lead-containment laws (such as Maryland, Connecticut, and California), and even some cities (such as San Francisco), have the power to inspect and order cleanups when a tenant complains to their enforcement agencies or reports a child's elevated blood level. Check whether or not your state has a lead abatement law; if so, contact the enforcing agency for help.

If your state does not have a lead hazard reduction law or effective enforcing agency, contact the EPA for advice.

Consider a Lawsuit

Some lead-management measures, such as scrupulous housekeeping, are more time-consuming than expensive. However, money enters the picture when there's so much lead dust that containment is the only reasonable response—for example, sealing lead-based paint by covering it with a durable finish. If actual removal of the painted surfaces is necessary (perhaps the underlying structure is so deteriorated that it must be replaced), considerable expense is in the offing.

Forcing the landlord to deal with lead on the property will involve asking a judge to issue an order that directs that the work be accomplished in a certain way within a certain time. Lawsuits like this cannot be filed in small claims court. These lawsuits are typically complicated affairs that require lawyers. They can be very effective when a group of tenants sue together. See Chapter 20 for suggestions on finding and working with a lawyer.

If you spend time and money dealing with lead containment—using special detergents or vacuums, devoting extra time to fastidious housekeeping, putting up with the intrusion of contractors trying to deal with the lead problem—ask your landlord to reduce the rent accordingly. (See Chapter 8 for advice on how to determine the value of a defective rental unit.) After all, these expenses are necessitated by the dilapidation of the property. If he refuses and you have a lease requiring that you live in the unit for months or years, consider going to small claims court for an order reducing your rent, and ask that you be compensated for past labor and expenses, too. See Chapter 8 and *Everybody's Guide to Small Claims Court,* by Cara O'Neill (Nolo), for help.

Moving Out If Necessary

If the risk of lead poisoning is high and cannot be controlled, the smartest move may be moving out. Here are two scenarios that usually justify a move:

The rental is permeated with lead that you cannot effectively control. If lead constitutes a serious danger to your health—perhaps deteriorating paint has caused a serious lead dust problem, or old lead pipes have contaminated the water supply—you would be justified in breaking the lease and moving out on the grounds that your unit is legally uninhabitable. (See Chapter 8 for more on this topic.) To help counter any possible lawsuit by the landlord against you for future unpaid rent, be sure that you have your evidence in hand, such as a report from an EPA inspector or a state agency in charge of enforcing your state's lead law.

Renovations will create a lead problem. If the landlord plans repairs or renovations in an effort to contain a serious lead problem, you may be wise to leave the premises. Even meticulous cleanup procedures cannot eliminate the risk of inhaling lead dust created by renovation. Some state statutes require the landlord to cover temporary housing expenses incurred during lead abatement work. Even in the absence of such a statute, however, nothing prevents you from suing in small claims court. (Above, we discuss reimbursement for housing during asbestos-removal work.)

Lead Hazard Resources

Information on the evaluation and control of lead-based paint, dust, and other hazards, disclosure forms, copies of the *Protect Your Family From Lead in Your Home* and other pamphlets, and lists of EPA-certified lead paint professionals may be obtained from the National Lead Information Center by calling 800-424-LEAD, or check the EPA website at www.epa.gov/lead. The EPA also provides pamphlets, documents, forms, and information on all lead paint hazards and federal laws and regulations on its website, www.epa.gov/lead, and useful advice on topics such as finding a contractor licensed to test for and remove lead. The EPA home page (www.epa.gov) includes a map and links to state and local websites.

State housing departments will have information on state laws and regulations. Start by calling your state consumer protection agency (find yours at www.usa.gov/state-consumer).

Radon

Radon is a naturally occurring radioactive gas that is associated with lung cancer. The U.S. Environmental Protection Agency (EPA) estimates that millions of American homes have unacceptably high levels of radon. Radon can enter and contaminate a house built on soil and rock containing uranium deposits. It can also enter through water from private wells drilled in uranium-rich soil.

Radon becomes a lethal health threat when it enters from the soil and is trapped in homes that are over-insulated or poorly ventilated. Radon is a smaller risk when it escapes from building materials that have incorporated uranium-filled rocks and soils (like certain types of composite tiles or bricks) or is released into the air from aerated household water that has passed through underground concentrations of uranium. Problems occur most frequently in areas where rocky soil is relatively rich in uranium and in climates where occupants keep their windows tightly shut to maintain heat in the winter and air conditioning in the summer. No state is immune, however—according to the EPA, high levels of radon have been detected in every state. If you smoke and your house has high radon levels, your risk of developing lung cancer is especially high.

Fortunately, there are usually simple, inexpensive ways to measure and reduce radon levels in buildings. For example, good ventilation will disperse the gas in most situations. Solutions range from the obvious (open the windows) to the somewhat complex (use fans), but none of them involves tremendous expense.

There are currently no laws that require a private landlord to try to detect or get rid of radon. The radon problem has not become the subject of national laws requiring testing or even disclosure. But if you suspect radon in your rented home, there are still things you can do.

Finding Radon

Radon is invisible and odorless. To test the air in your house, you can buy a do-it-yourself kit (make sure it says "Meets EPA Requirements") or hire a professional (get one who is certified by the EPA's Proficiency Program). Testing takes at least three days, and sometimes months. Kansas State University's National Radon Program Services (www.sosradon.org/test-kits) is a good source of discounted radon testing kits.

Testing for radon makes sense if you live in an area that is naturally rich in uranium soil and rock. (In Alaska, for instance, radon is rarely a problem.) To find out, you'll need to do a bit of sleuthing: Start with the public library or search online to find out about your local geology. City planning departments, insurance brokers (who may have experience in dealing with radon-related claims), architects (who ought to understand the local geology), environmental engineers, and neighbors may be fruitful sources.

Solving Radon Problems

If radon is present in significant amounts, it needs to be kept out or blown out of the building.

Getting it out. Once radon has entered the house, it needs to be dispelled with fans and open windows. Because of the increased costs of heating and air conditioning, and the loss of security when windows are left open, these methods should be only temporary. The only good long-term solution is keeping radon out.

Keeping it out. Sealing cracks and other openings in the foundation is a basic radon reduction technique. Another method is soil suction—sucking the radon out of the soil before it enters the foundation or basement, and venting it into the air above the roof through a pipe. Increasing the air pressure within a house can also work, because radon enters houses when the air pressure inside is less than that of the surrounding soil. Equalizing the pressure in the basement or foundation reduces this pull.

The Landlord's Responsibility

Keeping radon out of your dwelling involves major expenditures and modifications to the building's structure. Obviously, this kind of work is your landlord's responsibility.

If your landlord is unaware of the radon issue, give him a copy of the EPA booklet explaining it. (See "Radon Resources," below.) If you have grounds for concern—you notice radon detection devices in local stores, your neighborhood has several buildings that are vented for radon control, or the geology of the area suggests the presence of uranium-rich soils—suggest that your landlord hire a testing firm. As always, if a group of tenants voices their concern, the landlord is more likely to pay attention than if you act alone. Obviously, if you perform a test, send the landlord a certified letter with a copy of the report.

Keep copies of letters and reports, and write a letter of understanding to the landlord summarizing any oral discussions of the issue. (A sample letter of understanding can be found in Chapter 2.) Meticulous business practices like these impress your landlord with your seriousness and willingness to take legal action if necessary.

Radon Resources

For information on the detection and removal of radon, contact the U.S. Environmental Protection Agency Radon Hotline at 800-557-2366 or visit the EPA website (www.epa.gov/radon). The EPA site has links to state agencies that regulate radon, gives information on finding a qualified radon reduction provider, and includes a map of radon zones by state. You can also download a copy of the booklet "A Radon Guide for Tenants" and other publications, including "A Citizen's Guide to Radon."

Moving Out If Necessary

Unacceptably high levels of radon render a home unfit for habitation. If a certified tester has reached that conclusion, you have all that you need to demand that the landlord take prompt steps to remedy the problem. If the landlord fails to address it within a very short time, you can break your lease or month-to-month rental agreement and move out, citing a breach of the implied warranty of habitability (see Chapter 8). Your suspicion alone that radon is present (perhaps because your neighbor has a radon problem) will probably not protect you if the landlord sues you for unpaid rent.

It may be appropriate to move out temporarily if the landlord plans to install pumps or vents, which may take some time. See the discussion above, which suggests strategies for recouping expenses of temporary housing.

Carbon Monoxide

Carbon monoxide (CO) is a colorless, odorless, lethal gas. Unlike radon, whose deadly effects work over time, CO can build up and kill within a matter of hours. And, unlike any of the environmental hazards discussed so far, CO cannot be covered up or managed.

When CO is inhaled, it enters the bloodstream and replaces oxygen. Dizziness, nausea, confusion, and tiredness can result; high concentrations bring on unconsciousness, brain damage, and death. It is possible to be poisoned from CO while you sleep, without waking up.

Sources of Carbon Monoxide

Carbon monoxide is a byproduct of fuel combustion; electric appliances cannot produce it. Common home appliances, such as gas dryers, refrigerators, ranges, water heaters or space heaters, oil furnaces, fireplaces, charcoal grills, and wood stoves all produce CO. Automobiles and gas gardening equipment also produce CO. If appliances or fireplaces are not vented properly, CO can build up within a home and poison the occupants. In tight, "energy-efficient" apartments, indoor accumulations are especially dangerous.

TIP

If you smell gas, it's not CO. Carbon monoxide has no smell. Only a CO detector will alert you to its presence. To help identify leaking natural gas, utility companies add a smelly ingredient; when you "smell gas," you are smelling that additive. Because natural gas is so combustible, call the utility company or 911 immediately if you smell it.

Preventing Carbon Monoxide Problems

If your landlord has a regular maintenance program, it should prevent the common malfunctions that cause CO buildup. But even the most careful service program cannot rule out unexpected problems like the blocking of a chimney by a bird's nest or the sudden failure of a machine part.

Fortunately, relatively inexpensive devices, similar to smoke detectors, can monitor CO levels and sound an alarm if they get too high. If you purchase one, make sure it is UL-certified.

Avoiding Carbon Monoxide Problems

- Check chimneys and appliance vents for blockages.
- Never use portable gas grills or charcoal grills inside your home.
- Never use a gas range, clothes dryer, or oven for heating.
- If you use a nonelectric space heater, have it inspected annually. You can get recommendations from fuel suppliers.
- Never run a car engine or any gas-powered equipment in an attached garage; the fumes may seep into the house.
- Check the pilot lights of gas appliances every few months. They should show a clear blue flame; a yellow or orange flame may indicate a problem.

> ⊙ **CAUTION**
>
> **If your CO detector sounds an alarm, leave immediately and do a household head count.** Since one of the effects of CO poisoning is confusion and disorientation, get everyone out immediately—then check for signs of poisoning and call the fire department or 911.

Sample Letter Asking for CO Detector

34 Maple Avenue North, #3
Badlands, CO 00000
303-555-1234

February 14, 20xx

Cindy Cerene
1818 East Seventh Street
Badlands, CO 00000

Dear Ms. Cerene:

The kitchen in the apartment we rent from you has a gas stove and cook-top, which are about 15 years old, and there is a gas furnace in the hallway. These appliances appear to be working normally, but especially in the winter, when storm windows make the house airtight, I am concerned about the possible buildup of carbon monoxide. I would like to ask you to install a CO detector in the hallway near the bedrooms.

As you know, CO is a deadly gas that can kill within hours. We can't see it or smell it, and it could accumulate and poison us during the night. The only way to protect ourselves (besides your regular maintenance of these appliances) is with a detector. These devices are not very expensive, and can be easily installed. I would do it myself, except that our lease prevents me from undertaking alterations or improvements without your consent.

I hope that you'll give some thought to my request. Thanks very much for your consideration of this matter.

Yours truly,

Brian O'Rourke

Brian O'Rourke

Unlike smoke detectors, which are required by almost all states (or local ordinances), CO detectors are not universally required. But many states, including California, have passed laws that require builders, sellers, and landlords to install monitors, particularly in single-family homes. (For a list of states that have carbon monoxide detector laws, go to the website of the National Conference of State Legislatures (www.ncsl.org) and type "carbon monoxide detectors" into the search box on the home page. You'll get a list of state statutes—check the date for currency.)

Even if your state does not require your landlord to install a CO monitor, that doesn't mean that you cannot persuade your landlord to install one. Detectors that are connected to the interior wiring of the house and backed up with emergency batteries are best. In a letter, emphasize your concerns and the relative ease with which the landlord could put your mind at rest. A sample letter is set out above.

Responsibility for Carbon Monoxide

Most CO hazards are caused by a malfunctioning appliance or a clogged vent, flue, or chimney. It follows that the responsibility for preventing a CO buildup depends on who is responsible for the upkeep of the appliance.

Appliances. Appliances that are part of the rental, especially built-in units, are typically the responsibility of the landlord, although you are responsible for intentional or unreasonably careless damage. For example, if the pilot light on the gas stove that came with the rental is improperly calibrated and emits high amounts of CO, the landlord is responsible for fixing it. On the other hand, if you bring in a portable oil space heater that malfunctions, that is your responsibility.

Vents. Vents, chimneys, and flues are part of the structure, and their maintenance is typically handled by the landlord. In single-family houses, however, it is not unusual for landlord and tenant to agree to shift maintenance responsibility to the tenant.

If you have or suspect a CO problem that can be traced to the landlord's faulty maintenance, promptly request that the landlord fix it. If you are poisoned because your landlord failed to routinely maintain the appliances or to respond promptly to your repair request, the landlord will have a difficult time avoiding legal responsibility. (See Chapter 12.) To motivate your landlord to fix the CO-spewing gas dryer, it might be sufficient to subtly point out that failure to do so could cause a tragedy—and a lawsuit.

A sample letter bringing a CO problem to the landlord's attention is shown above. If you write such a letter, you would be smart to hand-deliver it to your landlord or manager, since the problem needs immediate attention. And in the meantime, don't use the appliance you suspect of causing the problem.

Carbon Monoxide Resources

The EPA website offers useful instructional material, including downloadable educational pamphlets, at www. epa.gov./indoor-air-quality-iaq. Local natural gas utility companies often have consumer information brochures available to their customers. You can also contact the American Gas Association for consumer pamphlets on carbon monoxide. It can be reached by calling 202-824-7000 or visiting the Association's website at www.aga.org.

Mold

Mold is the newest environmental hazard causing concern among renters. Across the country, tenants have won multimillion-dollar cases against landlords for significant health problems—such as rashes, chronic fatigue, nausea, cognitive losses, hemorrhaging, and asthma—allegedly caused by exposure to "toxic molds" in their building.

Mold is also among the most controversial of environmental hazards. There is considerable debate within the scientific and medical community about which molds, and what situations, pose serious health risks to people in their homes. Unlike lead, for example, where lead levels in blood can be accurately measured (and their effects scientifically predicted), mold is elusive. There is no debate, however, among tenants who have suffered the consequences of living amidst (and inhaling) mold spores.

Where Mold Is Found

Mold comes in various colors and shapes. The villains—with names like stachybotrys, penicillium, aspergillus, paecilomyces, and fusarium—are black, white, green, or gray. Some are powdery, others shiny. Some molds look and smell disgusting; others are barely seen—hidden between walls, under floors and ceilings, or in less accessible spots such as basements and attics.

Mold often grows on water-soaked materials, such as wall paneling, paint, fabric, ceiling tiles, newspapers, or cardboard boxes. However, all that's really needed is an organic food source, water, and time. Throw in a little warmth and the organism will grow very quickly, sometimes spreading within 24 hours.

Humidity sets up prime growing conditions for mold. Buildings in naturally humid climates of Texas, California, and the South have experienced more mold problems than residences in drier climates. But mold can grow irrespective of the natural climate, as long as moisture is present. Here's how:

- Floods, leaking pipes, windows, or roofs may introduce moisture that will lead to mold growth in any structure—in fact, these are the leading causes of mold.
- Tightly sealed buildings (common with new construction) may trap mold-producing moisture inside.

- Overcrowding, poor ventilation, numerous over-watered houseplants, and poor housekeeping may also contribute to the spread of mold.

Unsightly as it may be, most mold is not harmful to your health—for example, the mold that grows on shower tiles is not dangerous. It takes an expert to know whether a particular mold is harmful or just annoying. Your first response to discovering mold shouldn't be to demand that the landlord call in the folks with the white suits and ventilators. Most of the time, proper cleanup and maintenance will remove mold. Better yet, focus on early detection and prevention of mold, as discussed below.

Laws on Mold Affecting Landlords

Unlike other environmental hazards such as lead, landlord responsibilities regarding mold have not been clearly spelled out in building codes, ordinances, statutes, and regulations. The main reason for the lack of standards is that the problem has only recently been acknowledged. Some states have responded to mold problems in schools, but addressing residential issues has been slow to come. This is bound to change as state legislators and federal regulators begin to study mold more closely.

To do your own research on state or local ordinances covering mold, see the advice on doing legal research in Chapter 20.

Federal Law

No federal law sets permissible exposure limits or building tolerance standards for mold.

State Law

California is the first state to take steps toward establishing permissible mold standards. The "Toxic Mold Protection Act of 2001" authorizes the state's Department of Health Services (DHS) to adopt, if feasible, permissible exposure levels ("PELs") for indoor mold for sensitive populations, such as children and people with compromised immune systems or respiratory problems. If this is

not feasible, the DHS may develop guidelines for determining when the presence of mold is a health threat. In addition, the California DHS will develop identification and remediation standards, which will guide contractors, owners, and landlords in how to inspect for mold and safely remove it. California's new law also requires landlords to disclose to current and prospective tenants the presence of any known or suspected mold. (Cal. Health & Safety Code §§ 26100 and following.) (See the DHS website, given below in "Mold Resources.") Several other states have passed similar legislation, aimed specifically at the development of guidelines and regulations for mold in indoor air.

Local Law

A few cities have enacted ordinances related to mold:

- New York City's Department of Health and Mental Hygiene has developed guidelines for indoor air quality, which landlords in New York City should follow. In fact, any landlord would be wise to consult them, but you cannot force your landlord to abide by them. You can read them online at www.nyc.gov/html/doh (use the site's search function and enter the word "mold").
- San Francisco has added mold to its list of nuisances, thereby allowing tenants to sue landlords under private and public nuisance laws if they fail to clean up serious outbreaks (San Francisco Health Code § 581).

Landlord Liability for Tenant Exposure to Mold

With little law on the specific subject of mold, you'll have to rely on your landlord's general responsibility to maintain and repair rental property (the subject of Chapter 8) for guidance. The landlord's legal duty to provide and maintain habitable premises naturally extends to fixing leaking pipes, windows, and roofs—the causes of most mold. If the landlord doesn't take care of leaks and mold grows as a result, you may be able to hold the landlord responsible if you can convince a judge or jury that the mold has caused a health problem. Your position, legally, is really no different from what happens when the landlord fails to deal with any health or safety hazard on the property. For example, if the owner knows about (but fails to fix) a loose step, he'll foot the bill if someone is injured as a result of tripping on the step.

Naturally, some landlords have responded to the possibility of tenants' mold-related health claims by writing lease clauses that purport to relieve them from any liability resulting from mold growth. At least one court has refused to enforce such a clause, ruling that to do so would be against public policy. (*Cole v. Wyndchase Aspen Grove Acquisition Corp.*, 3:05-0558, 2006 U.S. Dist. LEXIS 70612 (U.S. Dist. Ct. M.D. Tenn., Nashville Div., Sept. 28, 2006).) More appellate cases from other parts of the country are sure to arise as mold litigation makes its way through the courts.

The liability picture changes when mold grows as the result of your own behavior, such as keeping the apartment tightly shut, creating high humidity, and failing to maintain necessary cleanliness. Just as you don't want the landlord to police your lifestyle, you don't want him poking his head in to examine your housekeeping habits (and in many states, privacy statutes prevent landlords from unannounced inspections, as explained in Chapter 11). When a tenant's own negligence is the sole cause of injury, the landlord is not liable.

Prevention—The Best Way to Avoid Mold Problems

A smart landlord's efforts should be directed squarely at preventing the conditions that lead to the growth of mold—and you should be the landlord's partner in this effort. This approach requires maintaining the structural integrity of the property (the roof, plumbing, and windows), which is the landlord's job. You, in turn, need to follow some practical steps and promptly report problems that need the landlord's attention.

The following steps are especially important if you live in a humid environment or have spotted mold problems in the past:

- **Check over the premises and note any mold problems; ask the landlord to fix them before you move in.** Fill out the Landlord-Tenant Checklist form in Chapter 6 and follow the advice on inspecting rental property at the start of a tenancy.
- **Understand the risks of poor housekeeping practices and recognize the factors that contribute to the growth of mold. In particular, be sure you know how to:**
  - ventilate the rental unit
  - avoid creating areas of standing water— for example, by emptying saucers under houseplants, and
  - clean vulnerable areas, such as bathrooms, with cleaning solutions that will discourage the growth of mold.

The EPA website, mentioned below, includes lots of practical tips for discouraging the appearance of mold in residential settings.

- **Immediately report specific signs of mold, or conditions that may lead to mold, such as plumbing leaks and weatherproofing problems.**
- **Ask for all repairs and maintenance needed to clean up or reduce mold—for example:**
  - Request exhaust fans in rooms with high humidity (bathrooms, kitchens, and service porches), especially if window ventilation is poor in these areas.
  - Ask for dehumidifiers in chronically damp climates.
  - Reduce the amount of window condensation by using storm windows, if they're available.

These preventive steps will do more than decrease the chances that mold will begin to grow. If you have asked for them in writing and included the underlying reason for the request, you'll have good evidence to show a judge if a landlord refuses to step forward and your possessions are damaged or you are made ill by the persistence of the problem.

EXAMPLE: The closet in Jay's bedroom begins to sprout mold along the walls and ceiling. Jay asks his landlord, Sam, to address the problem (Jay suspects that the roof is leaking). Sam refuses, and Jay begins to feel sick; his clothes and shoes are also ruined by the mold. When Jay sues Sam for the value of his ruined possessions, he shows the judge the written requests for repairs that Sam ignored. After showing the judge photos and an impressively moldy pair of shoes, Jay wins his case.

How to Clean Up Mold

Although reports of mold sightings are alarming, the fact is that most mold is relatively harmless and easily dealt with. Most of the time, a weak bleach solution (one cup of bleach per gallon of water) will remove mold from nonporous materials. You should follow these commonsense steps to clean up mold if the job is small (if a lot of work is involved or your poor housekeeping caused the problem, ask the landlord to do the work). Use gloves and avoid exposing eyes and lungs to airborne mold dust (if you disturb mold and cause it to enter the air, use masks). Allow for frequent work breaks in areas with plenty of fresh air.

- Clean or remove all infested areas, such as a bathroom or closet wall. Begin work on a small patch and watch to see if you develop adverse health reactions, such as nausea or headaches. If so, stop and contact the landlord, who will need to call in the professionals.
- Don't try removing mold from fabrics such as towels, linens, drapes, carpets, and clothing—you'll have to dispose of these infested items.
- Contain the work space by using plastic sheeting and enclosing debris in plastic bags.

For more information, check out the sites noted in "Mold Resources," below.

CAUTION

People with respiratory problems, fragile health, or compromised immune systems should not participate in cleanup activities. If you have health concerns, ask for cleanup assistance. You may want to gently remind your landlord that it's a lot cheaper than responding to a lawsuit.

Mold Resources

For information on the detection, removal, and prevention of mold, see the EPA website at www.epa.gov/mold. See their document "A Brief Guide to Mold, Moisture, and Your Home" and "Mold Remediation in Schools and Commercial Buildings Guide" (which includes multifamily properties). Publications written with the homeowner in mind are available from the California Department of Public Health at www.cdph.ca.gov (search "Mold").

Testing for Toxicity

If you discover mold on the property, should you test it to determine the nature of the mold and its harmfulness? Most of the time, no. You and the landlord are much better off directing your efforts to speedy cleanup and replacement of damaged areas. Knowing the type of mold present and whether it produces toxins will not, in most cases, affect the appropriate method of cleanup.

Properly testing for mold is also extremely costly. Unlike detecting lead paint by using a swab kit, you cannot perform a reliable mold test yourself. (Over-the-counter kits, which cost around $30, provide questionable results.) A professional's basic investigation for a single-family home can cost $3,000 or more. And to further complicate matters, there are relatively few competent professionals in this new field—unlike lead and asbestos inspectors who must meet state requirements for training and competence, there are no state or federal certification programs for mold busters.

This said, it will be necessary to call in the testers if you contemplate suing the landlord. If you're suing for significant health impairment, you'll need a lawyer. In that event, the lawyer will have the mold tested as part of the "discovery" phase of the lawsuit—that period of time when each side gets to ask for and examine the other side's facts.

Compensation for Mold Damage

If your belongings have been damaged by mold in your rented home, your recourse will depend on who is responsible for the mold (you, or the landlord?). Sometimes this is easy to know, as when the roof leaks and the resulting soggy closet has sprouted mold. But, if you are watering a large number of plants and have leaky saucers of standing water in a closed-up apartment, arguably your housekeeping habits have created the conditions ripe for mold. Alas, it's often not so clear-cut. But here, at least, are the guidelines:

- **The landlord is responsible for the conditions that lead to mold growth.** When this is the case, the landlord is legally responsible for foreseeable damages, which include ruined tenant property. A polite, written request for compensation, followed by a suit in small claims court if necessary, is your course of action. Note that the landlord's property insurance policy will not cover this situation, but the landlord's liability policy might. Whether the landlord turns the case over to his or her carrier is his decision, however.
- **The tenant is responsible for conditions that resulted in mold.** In this case, you're on your own, unless you have renters' insurance. Even with a policy, however, you may not have coverage for damage due to mold. Check your policy for its definitions of coverage and exclusions.

Bedbugs

Bedbugs are the latest scourge to plague tenants (and landlords). A single female will lay 500 eggs in her lifetime. You'll find them in sleazy digs with sloppy tenants, as well as upscale apartments with fastidious residents. They're expert hitchhikers who can catch a ride on your suitcase or clothing. No one really knows how to kill them. What are they? They're 21st century bedbugs, and if they show up at your rental property, you'll probably conclude that mold, asbestos, or even lead-based paint would be benign by comparison. If you learn nothing else from reading this section, or want to stop right here, know this: If your landlord proposes aggressive, albeit inconvenient, methods to eradicate the bugs, join in the effort.

Expert Help on Bedbugs

For detailed information on identifying and dealing with bedbugs, check out www.techletter.com, maintained by a pest management consulting firm. (Read their articles or order the comprehensive "Bedbug Handbook: The Complete Guide to Bedbugs and Their Control.") Give this information to your landlord if necessary.

What's a Bedbug—And Where Does It Come From?

Bedbugs are wingless insects that are about one-quarter inch in length, oval but flattened from top to bottom. They're nearly white (after molting) and range to tan or deep brown or burnt orange (after they've sipped some blood, a dark red mass appears within the insect's body). They seek crevices and dark cracks, commonly hiding during the day and finding their hosts at night. Bedbugs nest in mattresses, bed frames, and adjacent furniture, though they can also infest an entire room or apartment. They easily spread from apartment to apartment via cracks in the walls, heating systems, and other openings.

Relatively scarce during the latter part of the 20th century, bedbug populations have resurged recently in Europe, North America, and Australia, possibly a result of the banning of effective but toxic pesticides such as DDT. Bedbugs do not carry disease-causing germs (perhaps their one saving feature). Their bites resemble those of a flea or mosquito. Bedbugs are expert stowaways, crawling into luggage, clothing, pillows, boxes, and furniture as these items are moved from an infested home or hotel to another location. Second-hand furniture is a common source of infestation.

How to Deal With an Infestation

You'll learn that bedbugs have infested your property when you or another resident notices widespread, annoying bites that appear during the night. To minimize the outbreak and attempt to stop the spread of the pests to other rental units, take the following steps immediately. We can't emphasize this enough: Unless you and your landlord move swiftly and aggressively, identifying infested areas and treating them thoroughly, you will be doomed to a never-ending infestation.

Confirm the Infestation

First, make sure that you're in fact dealing with bedbugs and not some other pest, such as fleas. Because several kinds of insects resemble bedbugs, you'll need to capture a critter or two and study them. Go online to the sites mentioned above for more pictures of bedbugs than you ever wanted to see, and compare your samples. If it looks like a bedbug, that's good enough. Your landlord should be able to confirm it by calling a pest control outfit.

Tell the Landlord

Notify your landlord or manager immediately if you suspect a bedbug problem (even if you haven't confirmed it). You probably don't need to make a midnight phone call, but a call on the weekend is definitely in order. The following sections explain what happens when the landlord steps up and addresses the problem; below are some suggestions on what to do if the landlord will not take care of the issue.

Get Ready for an Inspection

In a multiunit building, bedbugs can travel from one unit to another, leading to the nightmare of an entirely infested building. But chances are that one unit is the original source (and it will have the highest concentrations of bedbugs). A landlord who knows what they're doing will hire a competent exterminator to measure the concentration of bugs in the complaining tenant's unit, and to also inspect and measure all adjoining units (on both sides and above and below the infested unit). You should get proper notice of the exterminator's inspection and be told what's involved (expect a competent exterminator to look closely into drawers, closets, and shelves). By "boxing" or "mapping" the source, the professional will confirm where the bedbug problem originated and learn whether and how far the problem has spread (this tells the owner whether it needs to treat adjoining units). Mapping the infestation (particularly if the exterminator does it more than once, over a period of time) may also help determine when a particular unit became infested, which the landlord may use to apportion financial responsibility for the extermination (see "Extermination and Relocation costs: Who Pays," below).

 TIP

Using an experienced exterminator is the *only* way to deal with a bedbug infestation. A can of Raid is not going to do the job.

What Kills Bedbugs?

Although bedbugs are hard to kill using today's approved materials, exterminators have three ways to go after bedbugs:

- Insecticidal dusts, such as finely ground glass or silica, will scrape off the insects' waxy exterior and dry them out.
- Contact insecticides (such as chlorfenapyr, available only to licensed pest control operators) kill the bugs when they come into contact with it.
- Insect growth regulators (IGR) interfere with the bugs' development and reproduction, and though quite effective, this takes a long time.

Pest control operators often use IGR in combination with other treatments. Most controllers will recommend multiple treatments, over a period of weeks, interspersed with near-fanatical vacuuming (to capture dead and weakened bugs). Anecdotal reports claim that even with repeated applications of pesticides, it's not possible to fully eradicate heavy infestations. Honest exterminators will not certify that a building is bedbug-free.

Declutter, Move Out, Exterminate, Vacuum—And Do It Again

Bedbugs thrive in clutter, which simply gives them more hiding places. Before you can effectively deal with the bugs, tenants in infested units must first remove clutter and neaten up (what to do with possibly-infested items is covered below). Tenants must remove all items from closets, shelves, and drawers; and wash all bedding and clothing (putting washed items in sealed plastic bags). Then, you need to move out during treatment, and return when the exterminator gives the all clear. Most of the time, you can return the same day.

Upon return, tenants must thoroughly vacuum. Experienced exterminators will recommend a second and even a third treatment, with exhaustive cleaning and clutter-removing in between. You must take these steps. If you don't and the infestation reappears and spreads, you're in for the whole process all over again.

Infested items that can't be treated must be destroyed. Do not remove infested items and simply bring them back. And use extreme care when removing infested belongings and furniture. Bag them in plastic before carting them away—otherwise, you may inadvertently distribute the bugs to the rest of the building.

Bag the Bed

Bedbugs will always be found in an infested room's bed. The only way to rid a mattress of bedbugs is to enclose it in a bag that will prevent bugs from chewing their way out (they will eventually die inside). Buy a bag guaranteed to trap bedbugs (some bags will simply deter allergens). See the articles from techletter.com, above, for more information on bed bags.

Exterminations and Relocation Costs: Who Pays?

In keeping with their obligation to provide fit and habitable housing, landlords must pay to exterminate pests that tenants have not introduced. In Florida, this duty is explicit: Since 1973, bedbugs are specified as one of the many vermin that landlords are required to get rid of, in order to maintain a fit and habitable rental. (Fla. Stat. Ann. § 83.51.) Eradicating infestations caused by the tenant, however, can rightly be put on the tenant's tab. But determining who introduced the bedbugs is often very difficult.

Bedbugs in Multifamily Buildings

In a multiunit building, if your landlord has approached a bedbug problem by "boxing" the building as explained above, it may be able to identify the most infested rental unit. But identifying the source (or most infested) unit is not the same as proving that these tenants caused the problem. For example, suppose the landlord traces the infestation to Unit 2, whose occupant moved into the building a few weeks ago. Serial mapping may show that adjoining Units 1 and 3 became infested after Unit 2 did, thereby suggesting that tenants in Units 1 and 3 were not responsible for their infestations. But the tenant in the source unit (Unit 2) may argue that the *former* occupants introduced the bedbug eggs that conveniently hatched after their departure. How will a landlord disprove this? Maybe it will discover that the new tenant came from a building that was also infested, but lacking this, the landlord will have a hard time laying responsibility on the new resident. Even if management did a thorough inspection of the unit before re-renting, there's no guarantee that it didn't miss some miniscule eggs. In short, because of the practical difficulty of identifying the tenant who introduced the bugs, the landlord will probably end up footing the bill for extermination and relocation costs.

If mapping identifies a source unit that's occupied by a long-term resident, it will be similarly difficult to develop the facts needed to prove that this tenant introduced the bugs. How will management learn about its tenants' habits, purchases, and travels, short of a full-blown lawsuit? And even if the landlord discovers, for example, that tenants bought a second-hand couch recently, how will it prove that the couch contained bedbugs? Or that bugs came home with a tenant following his recent stay in a hotel, or travel abroad? The bottom line is that landlords usually end up footing the bill for cleaning up bedbugs in multiunit buildings.

Bedbugs in Single-Family Rentals

Renters of single-family rentals may more easily be saddled with the responsibility for an infestation, simply because there won't be any other residents to look to. Especially if you are a long-term tenant, it will be difficult to avoid the conclusion that your activities resulted in the infestation. (Tenants who have just moved in might be able to argue that the former residents introduced the eggs.)

Ruined Belongings: Who Pays?

In extreme cases, bedbugs infest every nook and cranny of a rental and its contents—books, clothes, furniture, appliances. One New York landlord reported getting a phone call from his tenant who discovered bedbugs and moved out with only the clothes on his back, leaving everything—everything—behind. This tenant sued the owner for the replacement cost of his belongings, claiming that the landlord's ineffective eradication methods left him no choice. Who pays?

Should this claim get before a judge, the answer would probably depend on the judge's view of the reasonableness of the landlord's response and the tenant's reaction. The more you can show that you took immediate and effective steps to report the problem, and cooperated with every reasonable request of the landlord and the exterminator, the better you would fare.

Will Your Insurance Step Up for Bedbugs?

If you're facing a bedbug problem, you'll want to know whether your renters' insurance (or your landlord's policies) will help you with the cost of moving out and replacing any ruined belongings. Here's the scoop:

- **Expenses of moving out temporarily.** The landlord's commercial general liability policy will probably cover these expenses, which you will have to submit initially to your landlord. Your own renters' policy should also cover you.
- **Claims for lost or damaged belongings, and medical expenses.** Again, your landlord's policy should step up.

Now, suppose *you* are the source of the infestation? Your landlord may attempt to place the eradication cost on you. Here's where you'll be very glad you have renters' insurance—it should cover you, just as it would if you did any other negligent act, such as carelessly starting a fire.

Your Right to Know About a Bedbug Problem—And What to Do If Your Landlord Doesn't Tell the Truth

As the public learns about bedbugs, many applicants worry about the building's history. Knowing that full eradication is rare unless the landlord acts swiftly and thoroughly, many tenants simply won't consider renting in a property that ever had a problem, period. Knowing this, some landlords believe that disclosing a rental's bedbug past will make it unrentable, period.

State and local legislators are increasingly addressing the issue of whether landlords should be required to disclose a property's bedbug history, as well as tenant and landlord duties when an infestation appears. For a list of state laws and summaries, go to the National Conference of State Legislatures, www. ncsl.org (type "state bedbug laws" into the search box on the home page).

The majority of tenants, however, will not have the benefit of explicit disclosure laws. But that doesn't mean that you can't try to find out, and by asking, set the stage for some powerful responses on your part if the landlord is untruthful. First, if you question the landlord directly about a bedbug problem, especially if you make it clear that this issue is of critical importance to you, the landlord must answer truthfully or risk the consequences:

- **Breaking the lease.** A tenant who learns after the fact that the landlord hasn't answered truthfully will have legal grounds for breaking the lease and leaving without responsibility for future rent. Your theory is fraud, which will undo a contract and leave you free to walk away.

Electromagnetic Fields

Electromagnetic fields (EMFs) are another one of the household "environmental hazards" that concern tenants.

Power lines, electrical wiring, and appliances emit low-level electric and magnetic fields. The intensity of both fields are thousands of times lower than the natural fields generated by the electrical activity of the human heart, brain, and muscles. The farther away you are from the source of these fields, the weaker their force.

The controversy surrounding EMFs concerns whether exposure to them increases a person's chances of getting certain cancers—specifically, childhood leukemia. Although some early research raised the possibility of a link, recent scientific studies have discounted it. Interestingly, the scientific inquiry on the effects of EMFs has now shifted to the effects of cell phone reception and use. You probably have nothing to worry about regarding EMF exposure even if your rental sits under or near a set of power lines.

Since the landlord cannot insist that the power companies move their transmitters or block the emissions, the landlord is not responsible for EMFs or their effect—if any—on you. If you're worried, your only practical option is to move. If you have a month-to-month rental agreement or the lease is up, you can easily move on without legal repercussions. But what if you decide midlease that the EMFs are intolerable? Legally, you would be justified in breaking a lease or rental agreement only if the property presents a significant threat to your health or safety. (Breaking a lease when the property is unfit is explained at length in Chapter 8.) Given the professional debate regarding the danger from EMFs, it is unclear whether that a court would decide that their presence makes the property unlivable.

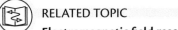 **RELATED TOPIC**
Electromagnetic field resources. The National Institute of Environmental Health Sciences has useful resources on EMFs. To find these, simply do a search on their website at www.niehs.nih.gov.

- **Increased chances of damages.** In the event that the bug problem reappears and you sue over lost or damaged possessions, costs of moving and increased rent, and the psychological consequences of having lived with the bugs, your chances of recovering will be enhanced by the owner's lack of candor. A competent lawyer will argue that its failure to disclose a potentially dangerous situation set you up for misery that could have been avoided had it been truthful.

- **Using repair and deduct or rent withholding remedies.** If your state allows you to use these remedies for serious fixes that the landlord has failed to do, you may want to consider them now (see "State Laws on Rent Withholding and Repair and Deduct Remedies" in Appendix A, and "What to Do if the Landlord Won't Make Repairs" in Chapter 8). But because an infesta-tion, particularly in a multitenant building, will be costly to address, these remedies may not practically do you much good. In a single-family rental, you may have more success.

- **Call the health inspectors.** Health inspectors are becoming increasingly aware of the seriousness of bedbug infestations. Your local department may be prepared to deal with the landlord on your behalf.

Now, suppose you don't question a landlord about a rental's bedbug history, the landlord remains silent, and a problem reappears. Will you have a strong case for breaking the lease without responsibility for future rent, or using the landlord's silence as a way to increase your chances of collecting damages? It's impossible to answer this in the abstract—like many legal questions, the answer will depend on the facts, such as how aggressively and thoroughly the owner attempted to rid the property of bugs.

Crime on the Premises

The Landlord's Basic Duty to Keep You Safe...232

    State and Local Laws...232

    The Landlord's General Responsibility 233

    The Landlord's Promises...235

Problems With Other Tenants...235

    When the Landlord Must Act...235

    What the Landlord Must Do 236

Illegal Activity on the Property and Nearby 237

    Government Lawsuits Against the Landlord...238

    Seizure of the Landlord's Property 238

    Small Claims Lawsuits Filed by Neighbors..239

Getting Results From the Landlord 240

    Evaluate the Situation 240

    Request Improvements...241

    Meet With the Landlord...243

    Get Help From the Government 243

    Withhold Rent...244

    Break the Lease...244

    Sue in Small Claims Court 245

Protecting Yourself 245

    Use Good Judgment...245

    Install Your Own Security Protections..246

    Consider Moving..246

Landlords in most states have at least some degree of legal responsibility to provide secure housing. This means they must take reasonable steps to:

- protect tenants from would-be assailants, thieves, and other criminals
- protect tenants from the criminal acts of fellow tenants
- warn tenants about dangerous situations they are aware of but cannot eliminate, and
- protect the neighborhood from their tenants' illegal and noxious activities, such as drug dealing.

If landlords don't live up to this responsibility, they may be liable for any injuries or losses that occur as a result.

This chapter explores the security measures that you can legally expect from your landlord—and how to insist on them if your landlord doesn't do enough to safeguard tenants.

 RELATED TOPIC
Also covered in this book:

- Lease and rental agreement ban on tenants' illegal activities and disturbances: Chapter 2.
- Landlords' responsibilities for repair and maintenance: Chapters 8 and 9.
- Your right to privacy: Chapter 11.
- Landlords' liability for injuries from defective housing conditions: Chapter 12.

The Landlord's Basic Duty to Keep You Safe

In every state, a landlord is expected to take reasonable precautions to protect tenants from foreseeable harm. You can't expect your landlord to build a moat around the rental property and provide round-the-clock armed security. On the other hand, your landlord can't just turn over the keys, trusting to the local constable and fate to assure your safety.

State and Local Laws

In many areas of the country, state and local building and housing codes are rich with specific rules designed to protect tenants. For example, some laws require peepholes and specific types of locks, and lighting.

Unfortunately, many state and local laws offer little specific guidance. For example, they may require "clean and safe" or "secure" housing, without defining these terms. Courts in several states have ruled that these requirements apply only to the condition of the physical structure. In other words, "safe" stairways are those that will not collapse or otherwise cause injury, not those that are well-lit, protected, and unlikely to be the site of a criminal incident.

But as the following example shows, some courts have taken a broader view of the term "safe."

EXAMPLE: The housing code in the city where Andrew owned rental property set minimum standards for apartment houses, including a requirement that all areas of rental property be kept clean and safe. The garage in Andrew's apartment building was poorly lit and accessible from the street because the automatic door worked excruciatingly slowly. The tenants met to discuss the situation and decided to send a group letter to Andrew, setting out their concerns. They had done a little legal research first, and were able to explain to Andrew that if a tenant (or guest) were hurt by an assailant who had entered through the unsecured entrance, Andrew might be liable.

Andrew showed the letter to his lawyer, who explained that the apartment building's dark and easy-to-enter parking garage violated the "clean and safe" requirement of the housing code, and that the tenants were right regarding his potential liability. Andrew fixed the door and added lights in the garage.

If your state and local laws are vague, you may want to see how local agencies or the courts have interpreted the meaning of fuzzier terms.

If your landlord does not comply with specific equipment requirements, you can complain to the agency in charge of enforcing the codes, often a local building or housing authority. (See below.)

If you are injured when a criminal takes advantage of your landlord's violation of a safety law—for example, an intruder enters your apartment building by way of a lock that's been broken for weeks—the landlord may be liable for your injuries.

TIP

To get a copy of your local housing code or ordinance, call your city manager's or mayor's office or look it up online at your local public library. In addition, you may be able to get information from a state or local housing agency or local tenants' association. To find building codes for all 50 states and major cities, check out the Building Code Reference Library at www.cmdgroup.com/building-codes.

The Landlord's General Responsibility

In addition to complying with local and state laws that require basic security measures, landlords have a general common law duty to act reasonably under the circumstances—or, expressed in legal jargon, to "act with due care." For example, common areas must be kept clean and safe, so that they do not create a risk of accidents. When it comes to security, too, courts in most states have ruled that landlords must take reasonable precautions to protect tenants from foreseeable criminal assaults and property crimes.

What precautions are reasonable depends on the situation. If you have been the victim of a crime on the premises—or are afraid you will be, sooner or later—ask yourself six questions to help you determine your landlord's responsibility:

1. Did your landlord control the area where the crime occurred?

Your landlord isn't expected to police the entire world. For example, a lobby, hallway, or other common area is an area of high landlord control. However, the landlord exerts much less control over the sidewalk outside the front door.

2. How likely is it that a crime would occur?

Landlords are duty-bound to respond to the foreseeable, not the improbable. Have there been prior criminal incidents at the particular spot you are worried about? Elsewhere in the neighborhood? A landlord who knows that an offense is likely (because of a rash of break-ins or prior crime on the property) has a heightened legal responsibility in most states to guard against future crime.

3. How difficult or expensive would it have been for the landlord to reduce the risk of crime?

If relatively cheap or simple measures could significantly lower the risk of crime, it is likely that a court would find that your landlord had a duty to undertake them, especially in an area where criminal activity is high. For instance, would reasonably inexpensive new locks and better lighting discourage thieves? However, if the only solution to the problem is costly, such as structural remodeling or hiring a full-time doorman, it is doubtful that a court would expect it of your landlord unless the danger is very great.

4. How serious an injury was likely to result from the crime?

The consequences of a criminal incident (break-in, robbery, rape, or murder) may be horrific.

If, based on these first four questions, you think the landlord had a legal duty to deal with a condition on the premises that exposed you to the risk of crime, keep going. You have two more questions to answer.

5. Did your landlord fail to take reasonable steps to prevent a crime?

As ever, "reasonableness" is evaluated within the context of each situation. The greater the danger, the more a landlord must do. Past criminal activity on the premises increases your landlord's duty to keep tenants safe. "Reasonable precautions" in a crime-free neighborhood are not the same as those called for when three apartments in the landlord's building have been burglarized within the past month.

Many courts have ruled that prior criminal activity in the neighborhood increases a landlord's duty to tenants only if the prior crimes were similar to the current one. For example, a string of car break-ins in the neighborhood will probably not obligate a landlord to provide extra security measures to prevent apartment break-ins.

> **EXAMPLE:** In New Jersey, a fight between two tenants in a downstairs apartment knocked loose their light fixture; later, another altercation between the same tenants resulted in a shotgun blast through the ceiling, injuring the upstairs tenant. The trial court found that the landlord was not negligent for failing to evict the rowdy tenants, and was not liable for the neighbor's injuries, because the second incident was not reasonably foreseeable as a result of the first. (*Williams v. Gorman*, 214 N.J. Super. 517 (1986).)

Landlords cannot eliminate all danger to tenants. In some situations, it may be enough to warn them. Just as caution tape and warning cones alert tenants to a freshly washed floor, landlords can warn tenants about possible criminal problems by using:

- newsletters that remind tenants to be on the alert and use good sense
- letters that communicate specific information, such as a physical description of an assailant who has struck nearby, and
- signs that remind tenants to use the building's safety features, such as a notice posted in the lobby asking tenants to securely lock the front door behind them.

6. Did your landlord's failure to take reasonable steps to keep you safe contribute to the crime?

You must be able to connect the landlord's failure to provide reasonable security with the criminal incident. It is often very difficult for tenants to convince a jury that the landlord's breach caused (or contributed to) the assault or burglary.

Think of it this way: If you fall because the rotten front step collapsed, you can trace the collapse directly to the landlord's failure to maintain the property. But when an intruder enters through an unsecured front door, you have another ingredient: the burglar's independent decision to commit the crime. The landlord is not responsible for the criminal's determination to break the law, and many juries simply won't place any responsibility on the landlord, even if, for example, failure to install a lock made the entry possible. To convince a jury otherwise, you must emphasize that a crime of this nature was highly foreseeable and would probably have been prevented had the landlord taken appropriate measures.

If a jury decides that the landlord didn't meet the duty to keep you safe, and that this failure facilitated the crime, it will typically split the responsibility for the crime between the landlord and the criminal. For example, jurors might decide that the landlord was 60% at fault and the criminal 40%. The landlord must compensate you accordingly. Not surprisingly, the criminal's share is usually never collected.

How Much Money You're Entitled To

To get financial compensation, you must show that you were harmed by the criminal incident. Tragically, this is often quite obvious, and the only issue that lawyers argue about is the worth, in dollars, of dreadful injuries. Compensation may also be awarded for mental anguish and continuing psychological effects of the encounter.

The Landlord's Promises

A landlord who promises specific security features —such as a doorman, security patrols, interior cameras, or an alarm system—must either provide them or be liable (at least partially) for any criminal act that they would have prevented. Remember, your lease is a contract, and if it includes a "24-hour security" promise or a commitment to have a doorman on duty at night, you have a right to expect it. Even oral descriptions of security bind the landlord if they were a factor that led you to rent the unit. You can often also rely on statements about security in advertisements.

Your landlord won't be liable for failing to provide what was promised, however, unless this failure caused or contributed to the crime. Burned-out lightbulbs in the parking lot won't mean anything if the burglar got in through an unlocked trapdoor on the roof.

EXAMPLE 1: The manager of Jeff's apartment building gave him a thorough tour of the "highly secure" building before Jeff decided to move in. Jeff was particularly impressed with the security locks on the gates of the high fences at the front and rear of the property. Confident that the interior of the property was accessible only to tenants and their guests, Jeff didn't hesitate to take his kitchen garbage to the dumpsters at the rear of the building late one evening. There he was accosted by an intruder who got in through a rear gate which had a broken lock. Jeff's landlord was held liable because he had failed to maintain the sophisticated, effective locks that had been promised.

EXAMPLE 2: The information packet given to Maria when she moved into her apartment stressed the need to keep careful track of door keys: "If you lose your keys, call the management and the lock will be changed immediately." When Maria lost her purse containing her keys, she immediately called the management company but couldn't reach them because it was after 5 p.m. and there was no after-hours emergency procedure. That evening, Maria was assaulted by someone who got into her apartment by using her lost key.

Maria sued the owner and management company on the grounds that they had completely disregarded their own standard (to change the locks promptly) and so were partially responsible (along with the criminal) for the assailant's entry. The jury agreed and awarded Maria a large sum.

Problems With Other Tenants

Sometimes danger lurks within as well as beyond the gate. And your landlord has a duty to take reasonable steps to protect you if another resident on the property (including a roommate) threatens to harm you or your property.

Your landlord should respond to a troublesome tenant in essentially the same way he would respond to a loose stair or broken front-door lock. A landlord who knows about a problem (or should know about it) is expected to take reasonable steps to prevent foreseeable harm to other tenants. If the landlord fails to do that, and you are injured or robbed by another tenant, you may sue and recover damages.

If your roommate's the problem, be sure to read the related discussion of violent roommates in Chapter 7.

When the Landlord Must Act

The landlord won't be held partially responsible for a tenant's illegal acts unless the problem tenant had done or threatened similar criminal conduct in the recent past, and the landlord knew about it. In short, you'll need to convince an insurance adjuster, judge, or jury that:

- it was reasonable to expect the landlord to know or discover the details of a tenant's past, and
- once known, the landlord could have taken steps to control or evict the troublemaker.

Unless there's a clear history of serious problems with the offending tenant, landlords usually win these cases.

EXAMPLE 1: Evelyn decided to rent an apartment to David, although she knew that he had been convicted of spousal abuse many years earlier. For two years David appeared to be a model tenant, until he hit another tenant, Chuck, in the laundry room over a disagreement as to who was next in line for the dryer. Chuck was unable to convince the jury that Evelyn should bear some responsibility for his injuries, because he could not show that the incident was foreseeable.

EXAMPLE 2: Mary rented an apartment to Carl, who appeared to be a nice young man with adequate references. Carl stated that he had no criminal convictions when he answered this standard question on the rental application. Several months later, Carl was arrested for the burglary and assault of another tenant in the building. At trial, it came out that Carl had recently been released from state prison for burglary and rape. Because Mary had no knowledge of Carl's criminal past, she was not held liable for his actions.

On the other hand, tenants sometimes win if they can show that the landlord knew about a resident's tendency toward violence and failed to take reasonable precautions to safeguard the other tenants.

EXAMPLE: Bill received several complaints from his tenants about Carol, a tenant who had pushed another resident out of the elevator, slapped a child for making too much noise, and verbally abused a tenant's guest for parking in Carol's space. Despite these warning signs, Bill didn't terminate Carol's tenancy or even speak with her about her behavior. When Carol picked a fight with a resident whom she accused of reading her newspaper and badly beat her up, Bill was held partly liable on the grounds that he knew of a potentially dangerous situation and failed to take appropriate steps to safeguard his tenants.

TIP

If you fear violence from another tenant, let your landlord know in writing. Not only does this underscore the seriousness of the situation, but it will be irrefutable proof that the landlord was on notice that problems were brewing. When more than one resident complains, the landlord will face more pressure to take action. And if there is an altercation later, the landlord cannot plausibly claim ignorance.

CAUTION

Get your facts straight before making accusations. If you believe that certain individuals are breaking the law—or just causing trouble—be certain that you have the facts straight before telling others about them. Otherwise, you might find yourself on the wrong end of a libel or slander lawsuit.

What the Landlord Must Do

A landlord who knows about the potential for danger from another tenant must do something about the problem tenant, such as warn other tenants or evict the troublemaker.

For example, suppose your neighbor bangs on the walls every time you practice the violin during the afternoon—and the pounding is getting louder. If you've tried to talk things out and been greeted with a raised fist, it's time to alert the landlord. You can reasonably expect the landlord to intervene and attempt to broker a solution—perhaps an adjustment of your practice schedule or some heavy-duty earplugs for the neighbor. If the circumstances are more threatening—for example, your neighbor brandishes a gun—your landlord might be legally expected to call the police, post a security guard, and warn other tenants pending the speedy eviction of the dangerous tenant.

To make this legal responsibility easier for landlords to meet, many states now make it relatively simple for landlords to evict troublemakers. These laws specify that harm or the threat of harm to other persons justifies a quick eviction. (See Chapter 17 for details on expedited evictions.)

Getting a Restraining Order

If you are seriously threatened by another tenant who will not leave you alone, and your landlord either won't evict the aggressor or the eviction is taking some time, consider obtaining a court restraining order.

These orders are signed by a judge after you demonstrate that you really are in danger—for example, the aggressor has made repeated verbal threats to harm you or your family. The order directs the person to stay away from you. Its principal value is that the police will react faster and more firmly than they might otherwise. To obtain a restraining order, call your local courthouse for information.

If you obtain a restraining order, make a copy and give it to your landlord and to the manager, if any. Ask him to alert other on-site personnel, such as security guards and maintenance personnel, of the existence and meaning of the order. A wise landlord will usually consider a restraining order as ample grounds for a swift termination and eviction. If the aggressor returns after he is evicted, request that the landlord order him off the property and call the police.

If you get no cooperation from your landlord and are still fearful, move. Your safety is worth far more than your right to live in a particular rental space. Your landlord may feel that you have broken the lease and may try to keep your security deposit to cover unpaid rent for the balance of the lease or rental agreement, but if you go to court to contest this, your chances of winning are good. (Chapter 16 discusses small claims suits over security deposits.) You can argue that by failing to evict the troublemaker, the landlord breached the covenant of quiet enjoyment and made your rental unfit and uninhabitable, which justified your moving out. (See Chapter 8.)

If your situation involves domestic violence, you may have specific rights (see Chapter 7, "Domestic Violence Situations," and "State Laws in Domestic Violence Situations" in Appendix A).

Intervention and eviction of the troublemaker are the usual ways that landlords meet their duty to take care that residents don't harm other residents. But the law doesn't require your landlord to have a crystal ball.

EXAMPLE: Abbot and his mother rented a duplex from Xavier, who knew that Abbot was emotionally disabled and took regular medication to control his behavior. Unknown to his mother or Xavier, Abbot began skipping his medication and eventually attacked Larry, the other tenant in the duplex, with a baseball bat. Xavier was not held liable, since it would have been illegal to refuse to rent to Abbot, a disabled person, under the Federal Fair Housing Amendments Act. Xavier did not know that Abbot had discontinued his medication, nor would it have been reasonable to expect Xavier to monitor Abbot's dosages. If Xavier had known that Abbot was off his medication, however, he would have been duty-bound to speak to Abbot and his mother and possibly warn the other resident. (Note, however, that if Abbot had a history of violent behavior toward other tenants or damaging rental property that the landlord, Xavier, was aware of when Abbot and his mother applied for the tenancy, Xavier would probably have been on solid legal ground to deny the application.)

Illegal Activity on the Property and Nearby

Illegal activities on the premises create problems for law-abiding tenants and enormous financial risks and penalties for landlords. Law-abiding tenants move out, and landlords may be hit with:

- lawsuits by tenants who are hurt or annoyed by drug dealers or other criminals
- fines by local, state, or federal authorities for tolerating a legal nuisance
- criminal charges for tolerating illegal behavior, and

- in extreme cases, loss of their rental properties when they are seized by the courts.

Nice Properties Are Not Immune

If you live in a safe neighborhood, you may think that drug crime is largely a problem in seedy neighborhoods. Think again. Illegal drug use is spread widely throughout American society—the notion that it is a ghetto phenomenon is just plain wrong. Smaller apartment complexes with some measure of security are often preferred by drug dealers over large, unprotected housing units. The reason may surprise you: A drug dealer, like a law-abiding tenant, is interested in a safe, controlled environment. But a drug dealer who's smart enough to choose a nice property isn't always smart enough not to hassle the other tenants.

Understanding your landlord's legal responsibilities and risks will help you and other tenants convince the landlord to take steps to avoid trouble before it strikes. (The balance of this chapter gives suggestions on what you can do to convince the landlord to take action against drug dealing and other activities and, at the same time, take steps to protect yourself.)

Government Lawsuits Against the Landlord

The legal meaning of "nuisance" bears only a little resemblance to its meaning in everyday life. A legal nuisance is a pervasive, continuing, and serious condition—like a pile of stinking garbage or a group of drug dealers—that threatens public health, safety, or morals. In some states, it also includes activity that is simply offensive, like excessive noise or open sexual conduct.

Every state has some type of nuisance abatement law, which allows the government, and sometimes the neighbors, to sue to stop these sorts of problems. Using public nuisance abatement laws against crime-tolerant landlords is increasingly common in large cities with pervasive drug problems. In extreme cases, where the conduct giving rise to the nuisance complaint is illegal (drug dealing or prostitution, for example), landlords themselves face civil fines or criminal punishment for tolerating the behavior.

Public nuisance laws come in two forms: civil and criminal. The table below explains the differences between the two types.

Seizure of the Landlord's Property

It's rare, but the government sometimes seizes property because of the illegal activities of one or

Civil and Criminal Nuisance Laws

	Civil Nuisance Laws	Criminal Nuisance Laws
Activities the laws target	Unhealthy, immoral, or obnoxious behavior that may be, but is not necessarily, a violation of the criminal law as well	Criminal behavior
Examples of targeted activities	Excessive noise, piles of garbage and trash, and inordinate amounts of foot or car traffic	Drug dealing, prostitution, gambling, and gang activities
Who can sue	Public agencies such as city health departments, law enforcement agencies, and, in many states, affected neighbors, who may band together and sue for large sums in small claims court (see below)	Law enforcement agencies only
Possible consequences to the landlord	A court ordering the offending tenant, and sometimes the landlord, to compensate other tenants. If a health, fire, or other enforcement agency brings the nuisance action based on many violations, it can result in a court order closing down the entire building.	Liability for money damages plus fines and imprisonment

more tenants. A successful forfeiture proceeding is absolutely devastating from the landlord's point of view. The landlord loses not only the property, but also all the rent money that the landlord received from the drug-dealing tenants.

If you're a tenant, forfeiture won't improve your lot. Few tenants want to live in government-run housing that starts off as a drug den. But a landlord who hears the word "forfeiture" will probably be highly motivated to get rid of the offending tenants.

> **EXAMPLE:** Sterling Properties hired a management firm to run several apartment buildings in a high-crime area. At one of the buildings, there were repeated drug arrests and complaints from neighbors regarding incessant comings and goings of people at all hours. The federal government initiated forfeiture proceedings. Sterling Properties argued that because it had not been informed by its management company of the situation, it had no knowledge of the illegal activities of the tenants. The court ruled that the neighborhood was a virtual "anthill" of illegality that any reasonable person would know about and that the knowledge of the management company could be imputed to the owners. The building was forfeited and became the property of the U.S. government.
>
> Other landlords in the area, shocked at this result, began meeting to work out strategies to rid their neighborhood of residents suspected of drug dealing.

Small Claims Lawsuits Filed by Neighbors

Overworked and understaffed police and health departments are often unable to make a real dent in problem-plagued neighborhoods. Determined tenants and neighbors have stepped into the breach, bringing their own lawsuits seeking the elimination of the offensive behavior. Basically, tenants and neighbors may sue a landlord for failing to take steps to clean up the property, and seek:

- monetary compensation for each of them for having put up with the situation. Each neighbor generally sues for the maximum allowed in state small claims court ($5,000 to $10,000 in most states), and the landlord often pays the maximum to *each one*. (See the discussion of small claims courts in Chapter 19.)
- an order from the judge directing the landlord to evict the troublemakers, install security, and repair the premises. Such orders are not available in all states.

Many lawsuits of this nature have been successfully filed across the nation.

Small (But Sometimes Mighty) Claims Court

The private enforcement of public nuisance laws has been creatively and successfully pursued in small claims courts in California and several other states, where groups of affected neighbors have brought multiple lawsuits targeted at drug houses. This approach makes sense whenever a landlord is confronted by a large group of tenants all suing for the small claims maximum dollar amount, thus motivating the landlord to clean up the property.

In one case in Berkeley, California, after failing to get the police and city council to close down a crack house, neighbors sought damages stemming from the noxious activities associated with a crack house. Each of the 18 plaintiffs collected the maximum amount allowed in small claims court ($3,500 at the time), avoided the expense of hiring counsel, and sent the landlord a very clear and expensive message. The problem was solved within a few weeks.

Many laws proscribing nuisances are "neighbor friendly"—that is, an offended neighbor doesn't need to have the resources of Scotland Yard to successfully use them. For example, in New York neighbors (including tenants) within 200 feet of property used as a "bawdy house" or for other illegal activity may bring a summary eviction proceeding (in a court other than small claims) against the occupants if the owner does not take steps to correct the problem after being given five days' notice. (N.Y. RPAPL § 715.) A notable aspect of the law is that the neighbors need not prove specific acts of illegality; all they need show is the ill repute of the premises or of those renting or using it.

Getting Results From the Landlord

Here are some suggestions on how to encourage your landlord to fulfill the responsibility to provide a safe place to live.

Evaluate the Situation

Before approaching your landlord with requests for improved security, collect hard evidence concerning the building's vulnerability to crime. The best way to evaluate the safety of your rented home is to conduct a security inspection of the rental property. Your goal is to answer two questions:

- If I (or a family member, roommate, or guest) were here alone at night, would I feel safe?
- If I were an assailant or a thief, how difficult would it be to get into the building or individual rental unit?

Analyze the Building

Start by circulating a letter to other residents, explaining your concerns and suggestions for improved security on the property, and solicit their comments. Call a meeting to discuss the results and plan your next moves.

You'll learn the most about your building's vulnerability if several tenants walk or drive around the rental property at different times of the day and night—you might see something at 11 p.m. that you wouldn't notice at 11 a.m. A reasonably safe and secure single-family home, duplex, or multiunit rental will have strong locks on windows and doors, good interior and exterior lighting, and other features that will hinder unwanted intrusions. To see how your rental unit, building, and grounds measure up, use the checklist of Important Security Features, below.

You may also want to get a security evaluation and advice from your renter's insurance agent.

Because insurance companies are potentially liable for large settlements or awards, they are concerned with reducing crime on rental property. So talk to your insurance company and, even more important, encourage your landlord to do the same and learn about equipment and safety systems that can prevent break-ins and assaults.

Involve Other Tenants

If you are a renter in a multiunit building, chances are that you aren't the only one concerned with safety. Working with other tenants on this issue (or others) has definite advantages:

- **Landlords respond to armies more readily than to individuals.** Once you get other tenants involved, your chances of getting the landlord to implement anticrime measures greatly increase. The consequences of rent withholding, complaints to the police, or small claims actions are much greater if done by a group than by a sole tenant. (These tactics are discussed below.)
- **Involving others reduces the chances of retaliation.** Tenants in most states are protected against landlord retaliation (such as terminations, rent hikes, and withdrawal of services) for exercising their rights to voice their opinions to the landlord, complain to enforcement agencies, and organize collectively. (See Chapter 15 for a thorough explanation of antiretaliation laws.) But if your state does not protect you against retaliation, acting as a group may make it harder for your landlord to retaliate—few landlords want instantly empty buildings or, worse, buildings full of angry residents.
- **You'll learn more about security problems.** For example, maybe the upstairs neighbor, who is home during the day, can tell you that the 24-hour security guard really lounges in the manager's office all afternoon, watching the soaps.
- **Involving others increases your safety.** Once you and your neighbors realize that you are all in the same boat, it is more likely that you will look out for each other.

See Chapter 19 for tips on working with other tenants.

Important Security Features

- Exterior lighting directed at entranceways and walkways that is activated by motion or a timer, and not dependent on the memory of managers or tenants to turn it on. The absence or failure of exterior lights is regarded by many security experts as the single most common failing that facilitates break-ins and crime.
- Good, strong interior lights in hallways, stairwells, doorways, and parking garages.
- Sturdy dead bolt door locks on individual rental units and solid window and patio door locks, as well as peepholes (with a wide-angle lens for viewing) at the front door of each unit. Lobby doors should have deadbolt locks. Solid metal window bars or grills over ground floor windows are often a good idea in higher-crime neighborhoods, but landlords may not be able to install them due to restrictions of local fire codes. All grills or bars should have a release mechanism allowing the tenant to open them from inside. Too many tenants have tragically died in fires because they could not escape an apartment with window bars or grills that had no release mechanism.
- Intercom and buzzer systems that allow you to control the opening of the front door from the safety of your apartment.
- Neat and compact landscaping that does not obscure entryways or afford easy hiding places adjacent to doorways or windows.
- In some areas, a 24-hour doorman is essential and may do more to reduce crime outside the building than anything else.
- Driveways, garages, and underground parking that are well lit and secure from unauthorized entries. Fences and automatic gates may be a virtual necessity in some areas.
- Elevators that require a passkey for entry. If this won't solve the problem, you may even want to request that the landlord install closed-circuit monitoring. Having someone watch the monitor is expensive, but it may be worth suggesting if your building has fairly high rents or is in a particularly crime-prone area.

Consider the Neighborhood

The extent of your vulnerability depends on not only the security systems in your building, but also on the surrounding neighborhood. If there has been little or no crime in your area, you have less to worry about and less legal reason to expect your landlord to equip the property with extensive security devices. On the other hand, if crime is a problem where you live, gather information on local crime from people in the neighborhood and the police department. Then, armed with what you have learned, you are in a good position to suggest ways both your landlord and other tenants can keep the rental property safe.

Request Improvements

Once you and other tenants have gathered information about your vulnerability to crime and what can be done to reduce your risk, you'll be ready to take specific steps to make your lives safer.

It's quite likely that you know more about the security needs of the rental units and building (and landlords' legal responsibilities) than the owner, especially if the owner is an absentee landlord. To improve security in your rental, you may first have to educate your landlord about:

- **Statutory security requirements.** If local or state ordinances or laws require specific security devices, such as dead bolts, peepholes, or window locks, start by asking your landlord to comply with the law. Put your request in writing. (Of course, keep copies of all correspondence.) Attach a copy of the ordinance or statute to your request. If you get no response, submit a second request. Then, if there is still no compliance, consider your options. (See "Protecting Yourself," below.)
- **Promised security measures that are missing or malfunctioning.** If the landlord has promised security beyond the basics dictated by law—such as an advertisement promising garage parking or security personnel—you have a legal

right to expect that the landlord deliver; see "The Landlord's Basic Duty to Keep You Safe," above. Send a written reminder to the landlord and attach a copy of the advertisement or lease provision that backs up your request.

• **Security required by the surroundings and circumstances.** Your own assessment of the property and the neighborhood may lead you to conclude that the landlord is shirking his duty to protect tenants. But if you do not have a clear-cut ordinance or statute to point to, you will have to do some extra work motivating the landlord. Use the information you've gathered to convince the landlord that, given the area's crime problems, more effective security measures are required—and that if security isn't improved, the landlord could be legally liable for injuries that result.

Oral requests sometimes get results, but more often they are ignored. Putting security requests in writing and having them signed by as many tenants as possible is a far better way to get results. Even the most dim-witted landlord understands that if tenants have a written record of their complaints about personal safety issues—especially when the landlord has not kept promises to provide security systems—and nothing is done, the chances of a successful lawsuit go way up.

So write a letter even if you think it's hopeless, even if your landlord is notoriously stingy or impossibly stubborn. By creating a paper trail, you have provided the landlord with a considerably increased incentive to take action. Your letter should:

• remind the landlord that he has control of the problem

• set out the foreseeable consequence (an assault) of not dealing with the property's obvious lack of security

• propose that the solution is relatively easy, and

• suggest that the consequences—a burglary or assault—are serious.

A sample letter alerting the landlord to dangerous conditions is shown below.

Sample Letter Alerting the Landlord to Dangerous Conditions

789 Westmoreland Avenue, #5
Central City, WA 00000
555-123-4567

January 3, 20xx

Mr. Wesley Smith, Landlord
123 East Street
Central City, WA 00000

Dear Mr. Smith:

As tenants of the Westmoreland Avenue building, we are concerned that there is a dangerous condition on the property that deserves your prompt attention.

As you know, the large sliding windows on the bottom floor (in the lobby) are secured by turn locks that can be easily forced open. On occasion we have seen a dowel placed in the track to prevent the windows from being opened, but lately the dowels have often been missing. Several times, the windows have even been left open all night.

We are worried that an intruder will have an easy time of getting into the building. There have been several burglaries in the neighborhood within the past two months. The situation would be greatly helped if you could send a glass repair person to replace the locks with much stronger ones. Needless to say, a burglary or assault is a worrisome prospect.

Thank you for your prompt consideration of this matter.

[signed by as many tenants as possible]
_____
_____
_____

 TIP

Contact the landlord's insurance company. If you can find out who insures the landlord (a tenant who has filed any type of previous claim may know) and the landlord persists in not taking reasonable safety precautions, send copies of all your correspondence to the company. Since it may have to pay a substantial claim or jury award if a tenant is assaulted, it has an obvious interest in getting the landlord to act, now. Pressure from the insurance company (and the worry that it may cancel the policy or increase rates) may have an immediate effect on a lazy or stubborn landlord.

Meet With the Landlord

If your written requests don't produce results, invite your landlord to meet with you (and other tenants, if possible) to discuss your concerns. You may want to involve a local mediation service, which has the advantage of giving you a skillful and neutral moderator. You'll be especially glad for the presence of the mediator if your landlord arrives with an attorney. If you or other tenants end up in court over your landlord's failure to keep the premises safe, the refusal to discuss the situation with you will hardly help the landlord's case. (Chapter 19 gives suggestions on finding and working with a mediator.)

TIP

Ask other tenants if they're willing to pay for better security. For example, you may find that fellow tenants will agree to a small rent increase in order to get a doorman, a locking garage gate, or an intercom system. A landlord may be very interested in such a proposal.

Get Help From the Government

If gentle (or even concerted) persuasion fails to get desired security improvements, call in the reinforcements. Depending on what the exact problem is and where you live, contact either building or health inspectors or local law enforcement agencies, who have the power to order the landlord to comply with the law. For example, if there is a local ordinance requiring dead bolts on all exterior doors, it probably names the agency (such as the health department or the building

inspectors) responsible for enforcing the code. Often, all you need to do is to contact that agency and begin the complaint procedure. Send copies of your complaint (signed by as many tenants as possible) to the landlord. This alone may result in the landlord taking the desired actions.

The effectiveness of turning to building or health inspectors varies hugely. In some areas, such as New York City, inspectors are so overwhelmed with complaints that they are rarely able to respond promptly. On the other hand, enforcement agencies are quite effective in many areas, and you may get a quick and satisfying response. Since they respond fastest to situations that pose serious and immediate threats to health or safety, emphasize the seriousness of the problem.

EXAMPLE: When Lucy moved into her apartment two years ago, the neighborhood was reasonably safe and untroubled. In the last two months, however, Lucy's street had become the site of rival gang activity. After two muggings nearby and a burglary next door, Lucy was worried about her safety and decided to do something about it.

Lucy looked at her city ordinances online, which included a requirement that multiunit rental property be equipped with dead bolts and locks on lower-level windows. Along with several other tenants, she also evaluated the property and concluded that the shrubbery needed trimming, the exterior lights were inadequate, and the parking garage was unsafe. They talked with the other tenants, and decided to present their concerns to the landlord as a group.

When a meeting failed to produce significant change, they contacted the building inspector, who cited the landlord for code-related violations of the dead bolt lock law. At that point, another tenant had an idea that proved to be a small stroke of genius: She complained to the fire department about the condition of the bushes, which resulted in a scheduled inspection. Even though the size of the bushes might not have resulted in a citation, notification of the inspection was enough to motivate the landlord to immediately cut them back.

Finally, realizing that the tenants were determined to make changes—and to avoid being hassled in the future—the landlord hired a regular landscaper, installed floodlights, and added a locking gate to the garage.

Withhold Rent

If your rented home becomes truly dangerous, it may be legally considered uninhabitable—which means that you might be justified in withholding rent. (Chapter 8 explains this option.)

Because this is a relatively new and fast-developing area of the law, we cannot give you a neat list of the states in which these options are available for serious security problems. We can, however, suggest some guidelines that must be met by any claim that a unit is uninhabitable because of high crime danger.

- **The problem is truly serious now, not merely annoying or a potential problem.** For example, having to walk past dope dealers on your way through the front hall is unavoidable, frightening, and loaded with potential for violence. On the other hand, unverified stories regarding prostitution in your neighborhood or even in your building are less compelling.
- **You've given the landlord notice of the problem and time to respond.** In general, as discussed in Chapter 8, you must tell the landlord about it and give him time to respond, either by fixing the problem or approaching the legal authorities (police or city attorney) who are better equipped to deal with it. For example, if drug dealers have moved in next door, you must alert the landlord and give him time to begin eviction procedures; if gangs have invaded your neighborhood, you must complain to the landlord and give the police time to act.

CAUTION

Withholding rent, even if it's totally justified, may prompt the landlord to terminate your tenancy if you're a month-to-month renter. Although many states have laws that are supposed to protect you from such retaliation, you may still have to fight it out in court if your landlord sues to evict you. (See Chapter 8.)

Break the Lease

If your rented home is legally considered uninhabitable, you might be justified in moving out, for the same reasons you may be able to withhold rent.

You may also be justified in breaking the lease and moving out if the promised security was an important factor in your decision to rent your place, and the landlord failed to follow through on that promise (see "The Landlord's Basic Duty to Keep You Safe," above). This remedy is explained in Chapter 8 in connection with repairs or maintenance that has been promised but not delivered.

EXAMPLE: Wendy, a flight attendant, rented her apartment in Safe Harbor after reading its advertisement in the local newspaper that promised "Security personnel on duty at all times." When she was shown around the property, Wendy told the manager that she often came home late at night. She was assured that there was a 24-hour guard service. However, after coming home several nights in the early morning hours and discovering that there were no security guards on duty, Wendy confronted the management and was told that financial constraints had made it necessary to cut back on the guards' hours. Wendy wrote the landlord a letter asking that the guard service be restored. When it wasn't, she promptly moved out.

Safe Harbor kept Wendy's entire security deposit (one month's rent), claiming that her departure violated the lease and that management had been unable to find a replacement tenant for four weeks. Wendy sued Safe Harbor for the return of her entire deposit, arguing that in fact it was Safe Harbor who had broken the lease by failing to provide security as promised. The judge decided that the promise of 24-hour security was an important part of Safe Harbor's obligations and that its failure to deliver constituted a breach of the lease, which excused Wendy from her obligation to stay and pay rent. And the judge ordered Safe Harbor to refund Wendy a portion of the rent she had already paid, on the grounds that she had paid for an apartment with a guard but had not received it.

You may be able to break a lease and move with little or no financial consequence. In most states, your landlord will have a duty to make reasonable efforts to rerent your unit and apply the new rent to what you owe on the balance of your lease. (This duty is discussed in detail in Chapter 15.) If the rental market is tight and your rental is reasonably attractive and competitively priced, your landlord may have little excuse for not rerenting quickly. Of course, if the dangerous conditions that prompted your early departure are noticed by prospective tenants (who reject the rental for that reason), the landlord may have a hard time rerenting. Fortunately for you, the harder it is for the landlord to rerent, the stronger your case that the rental was unacceptably unsafe, justifying your breaking the lease. In short, you win either way.

Sue in Small Claims Court

Your most effective response to inadequate security or dangerous surroundings might be aggressive action in small claims court. Interestingly, small claims court can be an appropriate tool to deal both with simple problems like the installation of a dead bolt and complex ones like ridding the building of drug-dealing tenants.

If you're lucky, the difference between a secure apartment and an unsecured one might be the simple addition of a code-mandated door or window lock, trimming some bushes, or replacing burned-out lightbulbs in the garage or hall. If your repeated requests for action have fallen on closed ears, and local inspectors can't or won't come to your aid, what should you do?

Small claims court might be the answer. Simply perform the work yourself (preferably with other tenants) and then sue the landlord for the cost. This route does, however, put you at risk, especially if your lease or rental agreement says "no improvements or alterations without the landlord's consent." Your risk of eviction for violating a lease clause will probably be less if the job you do is required by local law, such as a code-required dead bolt, rather than a modification like trimming the bushes that *you* have concluded is required for your safety. In short, if it's something clearly required of the landlord, he'll have a hard time laying blame on you for doing his job, and your lease clause violation will appear almost necessary.

Protecting Yourself

Faced with an unsafe living situation, your only option may be to pursue self-help remedies such as installing your own security protections or moving out.

Use Good Judgment

If you live in a dangerous building or high-crime neighborhood, your first thought must be to watch out for yourself. Just as defensive driving techniques may do more to keep you safe than confronting dangerous drivers or equipping your car with every imaginable safety device, you'll want to rely primarily on your own good judgment and willingness to change your habits.

If you have identified vulnerable aspects of your building or rental unit, chances are that others have, too. If you were a burglar or mugger, how would you strike? Avoid dangerous situations—for example:

- Don't use an isolated parking lot late at night.
- Consider curtailing your evening's activities. No late-night movie is worth the risk of an assault.
- Use a fan for air circulation instead of opening easily accessible windows at night.

Install Your Own Security Protections

In some situations, you may be able to take matters into your own hands, at least as regards your own rented space. Although your lease may prohibit you from making alterations or repairs without the landlord's permission (see Chapter 10), lots of effective security devices do not require permanent installation. For example, sliding windows can often be secured with removable interior blocks, and sliding doors can be tightly locked with specially designed rods. In addition, local or state law may expressly permit you to install certain devices when the landlord has failed to do so. In Texas, the tenant may install code-required locks and peepholes. (Tex. Prop. Code §§ 92.151 to 170.) (For suggestions on supplying code-required equipment and not footing the bill, see "Getting Results From the Landlord," above.)

CAUTION

Involve your landlord if you install an alarm or permanent locks. Many tenants install locks or alarms, no matter what the law or their lease says. If you live in a high-crime area, your landlord may not squawk as long as you provide keys to the locks and a way to disarm the alarm.

Remember, your landlord has the right to enter in an emergency, and you cannot make this impossible. (Chapter 11 discusses your landlord's right of entry.) We suggest that you ask your landlord before you install locks or alarms, since installation of these devices constitutes an "improvement or alteration" that your lease or rental agreement may prohibit. If you don't get the landlord's okay, the lease violation could serve as grounds to terminate your tenancy.

Consider Moving

Sad to say, often your most effective response to a dangerous rental situation is to move. Many tenants on a tight budget believe they can't afford any better alternatives. While understandable, this view is often wrong. Look around your area for places where low rents don't mean high crime. Although sometimes well-kept secrets, these neighborhoods often exist. Or consider the possibility of getting a roommate or sharing a house so you can afford to live in a better part of town.

If you have a month-to-month rental agreement, you can usually move out with 30 days' notice. Breaking a lease may be a little more difficult, unless you're moving out because your rental is uninhabitable or your landlord failed to follow through with promised security measures, as discussed above. (Chapter 15 discusses notice requirements for ending a tenancy.)

How Tenancies End or Change

Changing Terms During Your Tenancy...248

    Amending a Month-to-Month Rental Agreement..248

    Preparing a New Rental Agreement..250

How Month-to-Month Tenancies End..250

    How Landlords May End a Tenancy..250

    How You Can End a Month-to-Month Tenancy...251

How Fixed-Term Leases End...254

    What to Do Before the Lease Expires...255

    Staying On and Paying Rent Without a New Lease..255

    When a Lease Ends and Your Landlord Wants You Out...256

Retaliation and Other Illegal Tenancy Terminations...257

    Illegal Discrimination..257

    Retaliation...257

How to Stay When Your Landlord Wants You Out...258

    Promptly Ask for a Meeting...258

    Prepare Your Case in Advance...258

    Negotiate With Your Landlord..258

    Try Mediation...258

    If You're Successful, Sign a New Lease or Rental Agreement..259

Getting Out of a Lease...259

    Getting the Landlord to Cancel the Lease...260

    Terminating the Lease and Providing a New Tenant...261

    Assigning Your Lease...262

    Subletting Your Home Temporarily...263

    Breaking the Lease..267

Condominium Conversions...270

If the Landlord Sells or Goes Out of Business..271

If the Landlord Declares Bankruptcy...271

If the Rental Property Is Foreclosed..272

    Eviction Protection After a Foreclosure...272

    Paying Rent—Before or After Foreclosure...272

    Repairs and Maintenance Preforeclosure..273

ooner or later, all tenancies end. Whether you move often or tend to stay put for years, you should understand the important legal issues that arise at the end of a tenancy, including:

- the type of notice a landlord or tenant must provide to end a month-to-month tenancy
- legal restrictions on your landlord's ability to end a month-to-month tenancy, including the ban on "retaliatory evictions"
- what happens if you leave without giving required notice
- the landlord's legal options if you don't leave after receiving (or giving) a termination notice or after the lease has expired
- your options if you want to get out of a lease early or sublet your home temporarily, and
- what happens if your landlord goes out of business or declares bankruptcy.

This chapter starts with a brief discussion of a related topic—how your landlord may change your lease or rental agreement during your tenancy. For example, your landlord would be a pretty rare bird if he never increased the rent for a month-to-month tenancy. And you, too, may want to make a change—for example, by adding a roommate or bringing in a pet.

RELATED TOPIC
Also covered in this book:
- Lease and rental agreement provisions on notice required to end a tenancy: Chapter 2.
- Notice required for rent increases: Chapter 3.
- Getting your security deposit back after you leave: Chapter 16.
- When the landlord can terminate your tenancy because you violated the lease or rental agreement: Chapter 17.
- Overview of eviction lawsuits: Chapter 18.

Changing Terms During Your Tenancy

Once you sign a lease or rental agreement, it's a legal contract between you and your landlord. All changes should be in writing and signed by both of you.

SKIP AHEAD
If you have a lease, your landlord cannot unilaterally change its terms until the lease period ends. After all, the whole point of a lease is to fix the terms of the tenancy—including rent—for the length of the lease. If you have a lease, skip ahead to "How Fixed-Term Leases End."

Amending a Month-to-Month Rental Agreement

A landlord who wants to change something in a month-to-month rental agreement doesn't need your consent. Legally, your landlord need simply send you a notice of the change. The most common reason landlords amend a rental agreement is to increase the rent. Chapter 3 provides a detailed discussion of this issue.

To change a month-to-month tenancy, most states require 30 days' notice, subject to any local rent control ordinances. (See "State Rules on Notice Required to Change or Terminate a Month-to-Month Tenancy" in Appendix A for a list of each state's notice requirements.) In most states, the landlord can deliver the notice by first-class mail.

A landlord doesn't legally have to redo the entire rental agreement in order to make a change or two. It's just as legal and effective to attach a copy of the notice making the change to the rental agreement. However, many landlords will want the change to appear on the written rental agreement itself.

If the change is small and simply alters part of an existing clause—such as increasing the rent or making the rent payable every 14 days instead of every 30 days—your landlord can cross out the old language in the rental agreement, write in the new and sign in the margin next to the new words. The landlord will probably also want you to sign and date the change.

If the changes are lengthy, your landlord may either add an amendment page to the original document or prepare a new rental agreement, as discussed below. If an amendment is used, it should clearly refer to the agreement it's changing and be signed by the same people who signed the original agreement. See the sample amendment below.

Amendment ___A___ to Lease or Rental Agreement

This is an Amendment to the lease or rental agreement dated _____March 1, 20xx_____ ["the Agreement"]

between _____Olivia Matthew_____ ["Landlord"]

and _____Steve Phillips_____ ["Tenant"]

regarding property located at _____1578 Maple St., Seattle, WA_____ ["the premises"].

Landlord and Tenant agree to the following changes and/or additions to the Agreement:

1. Beginning on June 1, 20xx, Tenant shall rent a one-car garage, adjacent to the main premises, from Landlord for the sum of $75 per month.

2. Tenant may keep one German shepherd dog on the premises. The dog shall be kept in the back yard and not in the side yard. Tenant shall clean up all animal waste from the yard on a daily basis. Tenant agrees to repair any damages to the yard or premises caused by his dog, at Tenant's expense.

Olivia Matthew _____ _May 20, 20xx_ _____
Landlord/Manager   Date

Steve Phillips _____ _May 20, 20xx_ _____
Tenant   Date

_____ _____
Tenant   Date

_____ _____
Tenant   Date

FORM

The Nolo website includes a downloadable copy of the Amendment to Lease or Rental Agreement form. See Appendix B for the link to the forms in this book.

Preparing a New Rental Agreement

A landlord who is adding a new clause or making several changes to your rental agreement will probably find it easiest to substitute a whole new agreement for the old one. For example, your landlord will probably want a new agreement if you're adding or replacing a roommate or if a "no pets" clause is being added. If your landlord prepares an entire new agreement, it's best that you both write "Canceled by mutual consent, effective [*date*]" on the old one, and sign it. All tenants (and any cosigner or guarantors) should sign the new agreement. (Chapter 7 discusses having a roommate sign a new agreement.) The new agreement should take effect on the date the old one is canceled.

How Month-to-Month Tenancies End

This section discusses how you or the landlord can end a month-to-month tenancy.

RELATED TOPIC

Ending a rental agreement involuntarily. If your landlord terminates your tenancy on the grounds that you have violated a rental clause—for example, by not paying rent or by disturbing your neighbors—turn to Chapter 17.

How Landlords May End a Tenancy

It's easy for a landlord to end a month-to-month tenancy. No reasons are required in most states. (New Hampshire and New Jersey are exceptions, because landlords in these states must have a just cause or valid reason to end a tenancy.) A landlord can simply give you a written notice to move, allowing you the minimum number of days required by state law (typically 30) and specifying the date on which your tenancy will end. (See "State Rules on Notice Required to Change or Terminate a Month-to-Month Tenancy" in Appendix A.) After that date, you no longer have the legal right to occupy the premises.

RENT CONTROL

Protections of rent control. Most rent control laws do not allow a landlord to terminate a month-to-month tenancy except for just cause, or a legally recognized reason. Chapter 3 discusses rent control rules.

If you want more security, your only real alternative is to sign a fixed-term lease. But if you want to stay after getting a 30-day notice telling you to leave, either for a short time (until you find another place) or indefinitely, there is nothing to stop you from negotiating with the landlord. ("How to Stay When Your Landlord Wants You Out," below, gives some practical advice on how to approach this.)

Each state, and even some cities, has its own very detailed rules and procedures for how landlords must prepare and serve termination notices. For example, some states specify that the notice be printed in a certain size or style of typeface. If your landlord doesn't follow these procedures, the notice terminating your tenancy may be invalid. But once you point out the mistake, either informally or as a defense to an eviction lawsuit, your landlord will probably do it right the next time. If you want information on your state's exact requirements, consult your state statutes. (See "State Landlord-Tenant Statutes" in Appendix A.) Your state consumer protection agency or local tenants' rights organization may also have useful advice.

If you stay on despite receiving a properly written and served termination notice, you'll be a candidate for an eviction lawsuit.

TIP

The 30-day period may start on the day the notice is mailed, not received. Say your landlord mailed a 30-day notice on June 1, asking you to be out by July 1. If you don't get the notice until June 4, you might believe you are legally entitled to stay until July 4, even though the notice gives a July 1 termination date. Not necessarily. In some states, putting the notice in the mail is enough to start the 30-day notice period running. If you need every day possible to move out and can't arrange a compromise date with your landlord, check this point in your state's statutes. (Chapter 20 discusses how to look up a statute.)

How You Can End a Month-to-Month Tenancy

The landlord isn't the only one who can end a month-to-month tenancy easily and quickly; you can do it, too. In fact, the overwhelming number of rental relationships are ended when the tenant voluntarily decides to move on.

How and When to Give Notice

In most states, and for most rentals, you must provide the same amount of notice as (sometimes less than) a landlord—typically, 30 days.

For details on your state's rules, see "State Rules on Notice Required to Change or Terminate a Month-to-Month Tenancy" in Appendix A. You'll see that in some states, if you pay rent more frequently than once a month, you can give notice to terminate that matches your rent payment interval. For example, if you pay rent every two weeks, you need give only 14 days' notice.

TIP

If your state allows you to mail your termination notice, use certified mail, and mail it a few days early. You'll get a receipt that shows exactly when the landlord received it. Depending on the state, it may be legal to mail your 30-day notice exactly 30 days before you wish to end your tenancy, even though the landlord gets it a few days later. But in other states, a landlord is entitled to receive the notice at least 30 days before you plan to leave. If you intend to leave on July 1 and mail your notice on June 1, your landlord might not get it until June 4. If the notice period is 30 days, your tenancy won't end until July 4. Your landlord might try to withhold four days' worth of "unpaid rent" from your security deposit if you move out as planned on July 1.

To protect yourself, mail a notice in plenty of time to give the landlord 30 days' notice. To be on the safe side, don't count the last day if it falls on a Sunday or holiday. Or, if time is tight, deliver it in person, requesting a receipt.

It's not a good idea to give your notice orally. Even if you know the landlord well and feel that your word is enough, the law usually requires written notice. Use our form Tenant's Notice of Intent to Move Out. A filled-out sample is shown below.

FORM

The Nolo website includes a downloadable copy of the Tenant's Notice of Intent to Move Out form. See Appendix B for the link to the forms in this book. Copy this form, fill it out, and give it to your landlord.

In most states, you can give notice at any time. In other words, you don't have to give notice so that your tenancy will end on the last day of the month or the last day of your rental cycle. If your tenancy ends midmonth, you'll be paying rent until that date. For example, if you pay rent on the first of the month but give notice on the tenth, you will be obliged to pay for ten days' rent for the next month, even if you move out earlier. To calculate the amount, prorate the monthly rent.

The only exception to this general rule comes if your rental agreement states that notice may be given only on a certain date, typically the date the rent is due. This means that if you decide on the tenth that you need to move, you'll have to wait until the first to give notice and will be obliged to pay for the entire next month, even if you leave earlier.

You are legally free to give your landlord more notice than is required by law. But giving extra notice does not give you an initial period of time in which to change your mind. For example, if you give 45 days' notice in a state that legally requires 30, you have no legal right to change your mind during the first 15 days.

Tenant's Notice of Intent to Move Out

April 3, 20xx
_____
Date

Anne Sakamoto
_____
Landlord

888 Mill Avenue
_____
Street Address

Nashville, Tennessee 00000
_____
City and State

Dear _____ Ms. Sakamoto _____ ,
                                 Landlord

This is to notify you that the undersigned tenants, _____ Patti and Joe Ellis _____

_____ , will be moving from

_____ 999 Brook Lane, Apartment Number 11, Nashville, Tenn. _____ ,

on _____ May 3, 20xx _____ , _____ 30 days _____ from today.

This provides at least _____ 30 days' _____ written notice as required in our rental agreement.

Sincerely,

Patti Ellis
_____
Tenant

Joe Ellis
_____
Tenant

_____
Tenant

If You Change Your Mind

For all sorts of reasons, you may change your mind after giving your landlord formal notice of your intent to move. But if you can't convince the landlord to reinstate your tenancy, or the unit has already been rented again, it's too late. You'll have to move.

If you now want to stay on, promptly call the landlord, explain your change of heart, and ask for a meeting. Explain why your plans have changed—for example, you were moving because you thought you had just bought a house, but the deal collapsed in escrow. You are more likely to influence the landlord to reinstate your tenancy if you can show that you now plan to stay for an extended period of time, not just a few weeks.

If the landlord agrees to reinstate your tenancy informally—perhaps over the phone—fine, but be sure to follow up with a confirming letter. If your landlord doesn't immediately write back disagreeing with your understanding, this is probably enough to legally reinstate the old rental agreement. But, to be safe, offer to sign a new rental agreement. A sample letter to a landlord is shown below. Note how the tenant has built in a favorable outcome: The letter states that if she doesn't hear from her landlord within a reasonable time, the old rental agreement will be back in force. (Locking the landlord into your position is the essence of this kind of letter, which is explained in detail in "Oral Leases and Rental Agreements" in Chapter 2.)

If you are having trouble communicating with your landlord, see if a local mediation program can help. (See Chapter 19 for more on mediating landlord-tenant disputes.)

Paying Rent After You've Given or Received Notice

If your landlord accepts rent (excluding past-due rent) any time after your notice period has ended, it cancels the termination notice and creates a new month-to-month tenancy. This means you (or your landlord) must give another 30-day notice to start the termination process again.

Sample Letter Requesting Reinstatement of Tenancy

945 Willow Road, #8
Marysville, RI 00000

June 10, 20xx

Mr. Paul Johnston
123 Capitol Mall
Capital City, RI 00000

Dear Mr. Johnston,

On June 1, I gave you written notice of my intent to move on the first of July, in order to accept a transfer to my company's headquarters in New York.

After I gave notice, however, my job transfer was canceled, and I would like to continue living here. I hope that you have not rented my apartment already, and will cancel my 30-day notice and continue to rent to me as you have done for the past two years. My hope is to continue to live here for at least six months.

Thank you very much for considering my request. Assuming I can stay on, I would be happy to sign another rental agreement or, if you prefer, we can resume using the old agreement. If I don't hear from you within a few days, I'll assume that we'll be operating under the old rental agreement. I have enclosed a copy of my supervisor's recent memo canceling my job transfer.

Yours truly,

Sally Blum

Sally Blum

Extending Your Tenancy a Few Days

Suppose that, after giving notice, you need a little more time to move. Assuming no new tenant is set to move in right away, your landlord may be willing to let you pay prorated rent for a specified number of extra days. If so, you should sign an agreement setting out what you have agreed to.

If your landlord refuses your request to stay a few days and you simply don't move at the end of the notice period, you'll probably receive a termination notice from the landlord right away. The landlord will probably also promptly file papers to evict you or, if it's allowed in your state, go directly to court.

Leaving on Short Notice

There are times when even the most conscientious tenant may not be able to give the landlord the required amount of notice (usually 30 days). Perhaps a family medical emergency or a new job requires you to move out immediately. If you leave without giving enough notice, you lose your right to occupy the premises, but are still obligated to pay rent through the end of the required notice period. (In some states, there's an exception for victims of domestic violence, who have early termination rights. See "Renting a Place With Others" in Chapter 7 for more information.)

> **EXAMPLE:** Edna moves out after giving her landlord 15 days' written notice of her intent to move. Since Edna lives in a state that requires 30 days' notice, she owes rent for an additional 15 days. Of course, Edna's landlord may let her leave early without paying the additional rent, especially if another tenant is ready to move in very soon. But if the landlord can't rent the apartment within 15 days, he can deduct any unpaid rent from Edna's security or last month's rent deposit.

TIP
Many landlords must try to minimize their losses when tenants leave early. In many states, your landlord has a legal duty to try to limit ("mitigate," in legalese) the amount lost because you leave early. To do that, the landlord must try to rerent the property promptly. (This responsibility is discussed in detail in "Getting Out of a Lease," below.) But few courts expect a landlord to accomplish this in less than a month. So if you leave without giving enough notice, expect to pay rent for the next month.

Special Rules for Tenants Who Enter Military Service

Tenants who enter military service after signing a lease or rental agreement have a federally legislated right to get out of their rental obligations. (War and National Defense Servicemembers' Civil Relief Act, 50 App. U.S. Code Ann. §§ 501 and following.) You must mail written notice of your intent to terminate your tenancy for military reasons to the landlord or manager.

Rental agreements. Once you have mailed or delivered the notice, the tenancy will terminate 30 days after the day that rent is next due. For example, if rent is due on the first of June and you mail a notice on May 28, the tenancy will terminate on July 1. This rule takes precedence over any longer notice periods that might be specified in your rental agreement or by state law. If state law or your agreement provides for shorter notice periods, however, the shorter notice will control. Recently, many states have passed laws that offer the same or greater protections to members of the state militia or National Guard.

Leases. A tenant who enters military service after signing a lease may terminate the lease by following the procedure for rental agreements, above. For example, suppose you sign a one-year lease in April, agreeing to pay rent on the first of the month. You enlist October 10 and mail a termination notice to the landlord on October 11. In this case, your tenancy will terminate on December 1, 30 days after the first time that rent is due (November 1) following the mailing of your notice. You will have no continuing obligation for rent past December 1, even though this is several months before the lease expires.

The Act also restricts the landlord's ability to evict covered active-duty personnel and their dependents for nonpayment of rent.

How Fixed-Term Leases End

A lease lasts for a fixed term, typically one year. As a general rule, neither you nor your landlord may unilaterally end the tenancy, unless you have violated the terms of the lease or the landlord has failed to meet a responsibility, such as to provide a habitable place to live.

If you and your landlord both live up to your promises, however, the lease simply ends of its own accord at the end of the lease term. At this point, you must either:

- move
- sign a new lease (with the same or different terms), or
- stay on as a month-to-month tenant with your landlord's approval.

If you do none of these things and your landlord wants you to move on, you are considered a "holdover" tenant and will probably be evicted.

 RENT CONTROL
Your lease renewal may be protected in a rent control area. If your tenancy is covered by rent control, your landlord may be required to renew your lease unless there is a legally approved reason (just cause) not to. (See Chapter 3 for more on rent control.) Reasons such as your failure to pay rent or your landlord's desire to move in a close relative commonly justify nonrenewal. If your landlord does not renew your lease, but the reason given does not meet the city's test, you will probably become a month-to-month tenant. Your landlord will still need a good reason to get you out. Check your city's rent control ordinance carefully.

What to Do Before the Lease Expires

A lease clearly states when it will expire, and you are responsible for knowing this date. Some states or cities (especially those with rent control), however, require landlords to remind you in writing a reasonable period (often 30 days) before the lease expiration date if they want you to leave.

If you want to renew your lease or stay on as a month-to-month tenant, talk to your landlord well before your lease expires. If you have been a good tenant, your landlord will probably want you to stay, assuming you agree to any new terms such as, possibly, a rent increase. This is also the time to suggest changes you want—for example, if you want to add a roommate or bring in a pet.

If you plan to leave at the end of the lease, it's courteous to give your landlord notice of your intent. If you plan to move but need an extra few days, weeks, or even months, chances are your landlord will be accommodating, unless the unit has already been rented or advertised as available on a date earlier than when you want to leave.

Staying On and Paying Rent Without a New Lease

It's fairly common for landlords and tenants not to care, or not even to notice, that a lease has expired. The tenant keeps paying the rent, and the landlord keeps cashing the checks. Is everything just the same as it was before the lease expired? The answer depends on where you live.

Creating a month-to-month tenancy. In most states, you will have created a new, oral month-to-month tenancy on the terms that appeared in the old lease. Now your landlord can treat you as a month-to-month tenant—for example, the rent can be raised with 30 days' notice.

EXAMPLE: Shawn's lease ended on July 1, but neither he nor his landlord Helen realized that the lease was up. Shawn paid the regular month's rent on July 1. On July 20, Helen realized that the lease had expired, and decided that she wanted Shawn to stay—but at a higher rent. She decided not to offer Shawn another lease, since rents were going up in her area and she wanted to be able to raise his rent as she saw fit. She sent him a note telling him that he would have to pay $100 more on August 1.

When Shawn got Helen's note, he realized that he was no longer renting under his old lease. But he understood that, by accepting rent on July 1, Helen had created a month-to-month tenancy. This meant that Helen could not change any terms unless she gave Shawn the proper amount of notice—30 days in their state. Since Helen gave notice on July 20, Shawn's rent could not go up until August 20.

Of course, your landlord can belatedly present you with a new lease. If you decide not to sign it, you can stay on as a month-to-month tenant, under the terms of the old lease, until the landlord gives you proper written notice to move on. As discussed above, this is usually 30 days.

Automatically renewing the lease. However, in a few states the rule is quite different. If your lease expires and your landlord continues to accept rent, the two of you have created a new lease for the same length (such as one year) and terms (such as the amount of rent) as in the old lease. In other words, you have automatically renewed the lease. The effects are dramatic: You and the landlord are now legally obligated for a new lease with the same term as the old one.

To avoid inadvertently signing up for an entire new term, never pay rent past the date the lease expires without discussing it first with your landlord.

When a Lease Ends and Your Landlord Wants You Out

Once the lease expires, your landlord doesn't have to keep you on as a tenant. If you stay on after the lease ends and offer rent that your landlord *does not* accept, you're a "holdover" tenant. In some states, the landlord must still give you notice, telling you to leave within a few days; if you don't leave at the end of this period, you can be evicted. A few states allow the landlord to file for eviction immediately, as soon as the lease expires.

Unless you have a reasonably good chance of proving that your landlord's refusal to renew the lease is illegal (see "Retaliation and Other Illegal Tenancy Terminations," below), or you believe you can work out a compromise with your landlord (see "How to Stay When Your Landlord Wants You Out," below), it's probably time to pack up and move. There's no reason to head into an eviction lawsuit that's a pretty sure loser.

First, if your intent is to buy time, you'll get relatively little of it by staying on and going to court. That's because holdover eviction lawsuits where the tenant has no good defense are given speedy treatment in most states. And while the exact time will vary depending on state law and how fast the landlord jumps through required procedural hurdles, it can often be accomplished in two to three weeks. (See the overview of evictions in Chapter 18.)

Second, take a good look at your lease or rental agreement. Chances are it has an "attorney fees and costs" clause in it. (See "Typical Provisions in Leases and Rental Agreements" in Chapter 2.) This means that if you lose (or even if you capitulate on the courthouse steps before the actual hearing), you'll probably be on the hook for your landlord's attorneys' fees and costs. Those can add up to a few thousand dollars for even the most perfunctory eviction lawsuit. These costs will come out of your security deposit. If that doesn't cover them, the landlord can come after your wages or bank account.

Finally, remember that the fact that an eviction lawsuit was filed against you will show up on any credit report perused by future employers, banks, landlords, and stores where you wish to establish credit. In short, holding on to your apartment for no legally defensible reason in an effort to avoid moving for a few weeks is very rarely worth the negative consequences.

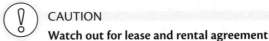 **CAUTION**

Watch out for lease and rental agreement clauses that make holdover tenants pay a higher rent. Your landlord may attempt to discourage you from staying past the end of your tenancy by making you agree, in advance, to pay as much as three times the rent if you do. Clauses like this may not be legal—they are a form of "liquidated damages" (damages that are set in advance, without regard to the actual harm suffered by the landlord), which are illegal in residential rentals in many states, including California. (However, they have been upheld in Texas.) The clause would probably not hold up in a rent control city; nor would it survive a challenge if the clause describes the rent hike as a "penalty."

Retaliation and Other Illegal Tenancy Terminations

Landlords can terminate a tenancy for a variety of reasons, such as nonpayment of rent, serious violations of the lease, and illegal activity such as drug-dealing on the rental property. And unless state or local laws require a reason, a landlord can, with proper notice, terminate a month-to-month rental agreement or decline to renew a lease without giving any reason at all. But they can't terminate a tenancy for the *wrong* reason—in retaliation against you for exercising your legal rights or in a way that discriminates illegally.

Illegal Discrimination

Just as landlords can't engage in illegal discrimination when they rent a unit and manage it during your tenancy, they can't unlawfully discriminate when it comes to terminating a month-to-month tenancy or deciding not to renew a lease—for example, by deciding not to continue to rent to persons of a certain ethnicity. Discrimination is covered in detail in Chapter 5, which also explains what you can do if you think you have been illegally discriminated against. All of the options discussed there—such as complaining to the federal Department of Housing and Urban Development and filing a lawsuit—are available to you if your lease or rental agreement is not renewed for discriminatory reasons.

Retaliation

The second major landlord "no-no" when it comes to tenancy nonrenewals is retaliation. In most states, landlords may not end a tenancy in retaliation for your legally protected activities, such as complaining to a building inspector that a rental unit is uninhabitable. If they do, and you stay on despite the landlord's wishes, you can defend yourself against a lawsuit to evict you by proving retaliation.

Prohibitions against retaliatory evictions were the natural outgrowth of tenant protection laws that began to appear in the 1970s. Lawmakers reasoned, quite rightly, that it made no sense to arm tenants with the legal right to insist on fit and habitable housing (see discussion in Chapter 8) if the landlord could simply evict a tenant who exercised this right. Only eight states—Georgia, Idaho, Indiana, Louisiana, Missouri, North Dakota, Oklahoma, and Wyoming—do not have statutes or court decisions protecting tenants against retaliation. The rest protect you if you have:

- complained to government agencies, such as housing authorities, health departments, or fire departments
- exercised your First Amendment rights to assemble and present your views collectively, as in joining or organizing a tenant union, and
- availed yourself of strategies allowed by your state's law, such as deducting money from the rent and using it to fix defects in the rental unit, or even withholding the rent entirely for an uninhabitable unit (see Chapter 8).

See "State Laws Prohibiting Landlord Retaliation" in Appendix A for the specifics of these state laws.

How do you prove your landlord is trying to retaliate against you? In the real world, landlords are rarely so foolish as to say directly, "If you complain to the housing department, I'll evict you!" Instead, they're likely to terminate a tenancy for a trumped-up reason, hoping to mask the fact that the real motive is to get rid of a tenant whom they regard as a troublemaker. Common examples of cover-ups that are really retaliations are:

- a termination that follows hard on the heels of a long-term tenant's legitimate decision to withhold the rent
- an unexplained refusal to renew a lease following a tenant's complaint to the health department, and
- sending a termination notice alleging misuse of common facilities after a tenant has used the common room to bring tenants together to fight a proposed rent increase.

Fortunately, however, many states give tenants an edge when it comes to unmasking illegal reasons to end a tenancy. In 21 states, the landlord is presumed to be retaliating against you if a tenancy is ended (or services decreased) within a certain amount of time, typically six months but sometimes 90 days or one year, following your exercise of a legal right. These rights include such things as withholding rent, complaining to a public agency about safety problems, or legitimately using any of the other remedies discussed in Chapter 8. (For a related discussion of rent hikes as retaliation, see Chapter 3.)

How to Stay When Your Landlord Wants You Out

Even if you do not have a legally valid response to your landlord's tenancy termination notice—for example, you can't convincingly claim that your landlord is retaliating for your exercise of a legal right, or you can't characterize it as an instance of illegal discrimination—all is not necessarily lost. In fact, your best chance of staying comes not from legal arguments but from honest negotiations. Not only does this strategy save the money and aggravation that you would otherwise spend defending yourself in an eviction lawsuit, but it also allows you to clear the air with your landlord. Even if your landlord has been behaving in a highly unreasonable way, it is still in your interest to try to arrive at an acceptable compromise. The following steps may help get your lease or rental agreement renewed.

Promptly Ask for a Meeting

Set up an appointment with the landlord or manager. Don't wait—the more time that passes, the less chance you have to get the landlord to come around. If possible, save the specifics of what you want to talk about until you meet face to face. It's harder to say no across a table than it is on the phone.

Prepare Your Case in Advance

If the termination or nonrenewal is apparently not based on something the landlord thinks you did wrong (these situations are covered in Chapter 17), try to figure out the reason behind the landlord's

decision before you meet. The manager (if any) or other tenants may have some insight.

Common reasons for a landlord to end a tenancy include:

- **A misunderstanding.** For example, maybe your landlord's been told—incorrectly—that you'll be moving in a couple of months, and wants to rent the unit now, when a renter is lined up.
- **A matter of personal taste.** Your landlord is annoyed with the family parties you hold around the outdoor grill every Saturday night or has been influenced by the manager, who doesn't like you, your teenage son, or any one of a dozen other things.
- **Irrational whim.** Your landlord likes to periodically rotate tenants, even stable ones, on the theory that—contrary to accepted landlord lore—regular turnover makes it easier to push through rent increases.

Negotiate With Your Landlord

When you meet with your landlord, explain why you want to stay, and be prepared with convincing arguments to counter the landlord's concerns. Chapter 19 discusses how to negotiate with your landlord.

Try Mediation

If you're unsuccessful negotiating your own case, enlist the help of a neutral third-party mediator, often available at little or no cost. Chapter 19 discusses how to find and use an outside mediator.

TIP

Look for hidden, illegal reasons behind your landlord's termination. It's just possible that, in the process of negotiation, you'll discover that the true motivation is, indeed, illegal—such as your proper exercise of a repair and deduct statute or the addition of a baby to an apartment that is roomy enough to accommodate another occupant. In that event, you may want to stay and fight, even up to and including an eviction lawsuit. Chapter 18 gives you some tips on how to defend an eviction lawsuit.

If You're Successful, Sign a New Lease or Rental Agreement

Sage negotiators never leave the table without a written version of the conclusions reached. Neither should you. Ask to sign a new lease or rental agreement or, at the very least, write a summary of your understandings, date it, and ask the landlord to sign it. If that can't be accomplished, immediately write a letter of understanding detailing the promises made by each of you, including the reinstatement of your tenancy. Letters of understanding are explained in Chapter 2.

Getting Out of a Lease

Ideally, you'll sign a lease for just the amount of time you need the rental—a year to attend school, for instance. But despite your best efforts to match your lease term with your plans, you may need to move, temporarily or permanently, before the lease is up.

If you have no intention of returning, one option is to simply move out without sweating the legalities. Leaving before a fixed-term lease expires without paying the remainder of the rent due under the lease is called breaking the lease.

Breaking the lease may not cost you much. If the landlord rerents the property quickly, all you'll be responsible for paying is the rent for the brief time the unit was vacant.

But if you want to leave early, there are better options than just moving out and hoping your landlord gets a new tenant quickly. There's a lot you can do to minimize your financial responsibility—and ensure a good reference from the landlord when you're looking for your next place to live.

This section discusses all your options:

1. **Get the landlord to cancel the lease.** By far the most painless method.

2. **Find a new tenant to sign a new lease.** A little more trouble, but usually worth it if the landlord won't just let you off the hook.

3. **Assign your lease.** Turn over your lease to someone else—not a bad choice, but it keeps you on the legal hook to some extent.

When Breaking a Lease Is Justified

There are some important exceptions to the blanket rule that a tenant who breaks a lease owes the rent for the entire lease term. You may be able to legally move out without providing the proper notice in the following situations:

- **The rental unit is unsafe or otherwise uninhabitable.** If your landlord does not provide habitable housing—for example, if the unit violates health or safety codes—a court would probably conclude that you have been "constructively evicted." That releases you from further obligations under the lease. (See Chapter 8.)

- **State or federal law allows you to leave early in the circumstances.** A few states' laws list reasons that allow a tenant to break a lease. For example, in Delaware you need only give 30 days' notice to end a long-term lease if you must move because your present employer has relocated or because of health problems (yours or a family member's). In New Jersey, a tenant who has suffered a disabling illness or accident can break a lease and leave after 40 days' notice upon presenting proper proof of disability. In many states, victims of domestic violence have early termination rights (see "Renting a Place With Others" in Chapter 7). Some states, such as Georgia, allow members of the military to break a lease because of a change in orders. In all states, tenants who enter active duty after signing a lease must be released after delivering proper notice (see "Special Rules for Tenants Who Enter Military Service," above). If you have a good reason for a sudden move, check your state's law. Check the "Changing or Breaking Your Lease" section in the tenants' area of www.nolo.com for details.

- **The rental unit is damaged or destroyed.** If your home is significantly damaged—either by natural disaster or any other reason beyond your control—you have the right to consider the lease terminated and to move out. (See Chapter 8.)

- **Your landlord harasses you or violates your privacy rights.** (See Chapter 11.)

4. **Sublet, leave temporarily, and return later.** Subletting makes sense only if you truly want go back to your rental later.

5. **Break the lease.** The landlord probably has a legal duty to try to find a new tenant, so you may not lose much by following this simple route.

Getting the Landlord to Cancel the Lease

Lots of tenants assume that their landlord will never agree to end their lease early. This is a mistake. And anyway, it can't hurt to ask. Depending on the circumstances, your landlord may actually be delighted to see you go.

Reasons why your landlord may cheerfully tear up your lease include:

- **It's a chance to raise the rent.** Especially if you are a long-term tenant and your rent is below the current going rate, your departure gives your landlord the chance to offer the unit at a higher rate.

RENT CONTROL

Most rent control cities, including those in California and Washington, DC, let landlords raise rent to the market rate when a tenant moves out. This gives landlords a huge financial incentive to get rid of old tenants. In the few rent control cities that limit rent increases even when a tenant voluntarily moves out, the landlord's profit motive to end your tenancy will be weaker. (Chapter 3 discusses rent control.)

- **The landlord will be able to make major repairs or renovations.** Laws in many states require the landlord to pay for relocation and temporary housing costs if a tenant must move because of renovations or repairs. Or the landlord might have to reduce the rent if a part of an apartment becomes unusable. (See Chapter 8.) So landlords usually put these jobs off until the unit is vacant; your departure might be just what your landlord was waiting for.

- **The landlord doesn't like you.** Here is one situation where a less-than-perfect tenant might have an edge. If, in your landlord's eyes, you are a pain in the neck (but your actions have not justified eviction), your request to leave early might be met with a sigh of relief.

- **Your landlord is a decent sort.** If you have been honest and considerate with the landlord, and you have a good reason for leaving—for example, to nurse a sick parent or find a new job after getting laid off—your landlord might be willing to extend you the favor of letting you go. In fact, your landlord may be legally required to allow you to leave early because of a job change or health problem. (See "When Breaking a Lease Is Justified," above.)

When you ask to get out of your lease, be prepared to sweeten the deal by offering to pay a little bit extra. In the world of big business, this is known as a "buyout." There's no reason why you can't do it, too. For example, if you want to leave three months early, you might offer to pay half a month's extra rent and promise to be extra accommodating when the landlord wants to show the unit to prospective tenants. A sample Buyout Agreement is shown below.

If your landlord agrees to let you out of your lease early—even if your parting is friendly—it's vital to get the agreement in writing. (See the sample Landlord-Tenant Agreement to Terminate Lease, below.) It protects you in the event that the landlord changes his mind (or sells to a new owner) and tries to hold you responsible for future rent or damages done by the next tenant.

Help With Moving Costs From Your Employer

If you need to move because of a new job or transfer, check to see if your company will cover the cost of getting out of a lease. Many will, recognizing that relocation expenses aren't limited to hiring movers and storing furniture. Especially if your transfer is involuntary or you have been aggressively courted by a new company, use your leverage as a valued employee to ask the company to buy out at least a month or two of your lease. In most areas, that should give the landlord plenty of time to find a new tenant.

Sample Buyout Agreement Between Landlord and Tenant

This Agreement is entered into on January 3, 20xx, between Colin Crest, Tenant, who leases the premises at 123 Shady Lane, Capitol City, California, and Marie Peterson, Landlord.

1. Under the attached lease, Tenant agreed to pay Landlord monthly rent of $1,200. Tenant has paid rent for the month of January, 20xx.

2. Tenant's lease expires on June 30, 20xx, but Tenant needs to break the lease and move out on January 15, 20xx.

3. Landlord agrees to release Tenant on January 15, 20xx, from any further obligation to pay rent in exchange for Tenant's promise to pay one-and-one-half month's rent ($1,800) by January 15, 20xx.

4. Tenant agrees to allow Landlord to show his apartment to prospective new tenants on two hours' notice, seven days a week. If Tenant cannot be reached after Landlord has made a good-faith effort to do so, Landlord may enter and show the apartment.

5. If Tenant does not fulfill his promises as described in paragraphs 3 and 4 above, the attached lease, entered into on January 3, 20xx, will remain in effect.

Colin Crest   _1/3/xx_
Colin Crest, Tenant   Date

Marie Peterson   _1/3/xx_
Marie Peterson, Landlord   Date

 FORM

The Nolo website includes a downloadable copy of the Landlord-Tenant Agreement to Terminate Lease form. See Appendix B for the link to the forms in this book.

Terminating the Lease and Providing a New Tenant

If your landlord is not willing to end your lease early, another approach will probably let you break your lease at little or no cost. Simply present your landlord with an acceptable substitute tenant, who will take over right away and continue the flow of rent uninterrupted. Another benefit of this strategy is that it prevents the landlord from passing along to you the costs of finding a new tenant.

To come up with an acceptable new tenant, you'll need to advertise the unit and screen applicants. Doing this is similar to finding someone to be a cotenant. (See Chapter 7.) If you find a good person whom the landlord accepts, be sure the landlord signs a termination of lease form, shown below.

In many states, your landlord is legally bound to accept a suitable tenant you propose or to try to find one without your help. (See the discussion below.) But what if your landlord simply refuses to talk to the perfectly acceptable people you find, and demands that you pay rent for the rest of the lease? You'll need to preserve the evidence that you presented one or more good, new tenants, and that the landlord unreasonably refused to consider them or unreasonably rejected them. Without good evidence, you may lose your deposit, be liable for unpaid future rent, and suffer other negative consequences of breaking a lease.

 TIP

Keep good records of suitable new tenants. This should include their employment and rental history and letters of reference. Better yet, have candidates fill out the rental application in Chapter 1 and give you a copy of their credit report. If your prospective sub's background and credit history is as good as or better than your own, the landlord is going to have a tough time explaining a rejection to a judge if the dispute ever goes to court.

Landlord-Tenant Agreement to Terminate Lease

_____Robert Chin_____ ["Landlord"]

and ____Carl Mosk_____ ["Tenant"]

agree that the lease they entered into on _____November 1, 20xx_____ , for premises at

__56 Alpine Terrace, Hamilton, Tennessee_____ ,

will terminate on ___January 5, 20xx_____ .

_Robert Chin_____   _December 28, 20xx_____
Landlord/Manager   Date

_Carl Mosk_____   _December 28, 20xx_____
Tenant   Date

Assigning Your Lease

If you intend to leave permanently, but your landlord will not cancel the lease, consider the third option: assignment. True, you may still have to hustle up a new tenant, but your landlord may be willing to go along with this arrangement, as explained below. But because you face some potential legal liability with assignments, this option is always less attractive than the previous two.

How Assignments Work

Assigning a lease means you turn over the entire rest of your lease to another person, called an "assignee." (You're the "assignor.") You move out, and the new person takes over the lease and moves in. If a dispute erupts over the lease—for example, the assignee fails to pay the rent or the landlord fails to maintain the property—the new tenant can sue or be sued by the landlord.

But making an assignment doesn't completely sever your legal relationship with the landlord. _Unless you agree otherwise, you remain responsible for the rent if the assignee fails to pay._ You are not, however, liable for damage to the premises caused

by the assignee. The bottom line: It's much better to get your lease officially terminated and have the new tenant sign a new lease. Then you're totally off the hook.

Generally, the landlord and new tenant are bound by all the terms of the lease you, the original tenant, signed. For example, a lease provision in which the landlord agreed to return the security deposit in a certain manner is still in effect, but it now benefits the new tenant. Only in very unusual situations, where a lease provision is personal, does the obligation not transfer. For example, under the law of most states, a promise by a tenant to do a landlord's housekeeping in exchange for a rent reduction would not automatically pass to an assignee.

Some landlords will agree to an assignment when they might not agree to terminate your tenancy and simply rent to a new tenant. The reason is obvious: Under an assignment, you are still legally responsible to pay the rent if the assignee doesn't. In a sense, you've become a rent guarantor. Of course, if you are moving out of state and will be beyond the power of a local court, the landlord is unlikely to be able to collect from you.

Finding an Assignee

Finding someone to take over your lease is little different from finding an acceptable new tenant. The advice in Chapter 7 will help you locate and present someone whom your landlord is likely to accept.

There is one important added consideration, however. Because you remain on the hook financially if the new tenant falls behind on the rent, you will want to be absolutely sure that the assignee is solvent and responsible. In short, you may want to be even fussier than your landlord. Once you move, you never want to hear about your old rental unit again.

If You Take Over Someone's Lease

If you move in as an assignee of an old tenant's lease, your legal position is very good. You can stay until the lease runs out and enjoy all the rights of a regular tenant—for example, you can sue your landlord for failure to fix a hole in the roof, insist on the use of a parking space as promised in the lease, or use your state's repair and deduct statute for appropriate repairs. Be aware that if you don't pay the rent, you'd still get evicted; but if it turns out that the original tenant is easier to locate or collect from, the landlord may even pursue that person, not you.

But keep in mind that if you take over a lease that has only a few more months to run, you may face a rent increase if you want to stay longer. It might be better to sign a new, year-long lease and lock in the current rent, if the landlord agrees.

How to Assign a Lease

Accomplishing an assignment isn't difficult. One simple, legal approach is to print "Assigned to John Doe" on your current lease at each place your name appears. This will usually be the first clause that identifies the "parties" of the lease and the signature line at the end of the lease. The new tenant, you, and the landlord should then sign your

names next to the words "Assigned to John Doe," each place these words are inserted on the lease.

However, there is a less messy approach. Simply present your landlord with a formal "Consent to Assignment of Lease," like the sample shown below. Using this form protects you in two important respects:

- It tells the newcomer (the assignee) that he is responsible for every term and condition of the lease.
- It gives you an opportunity to have the landlord agree that, contrary to the default rule explained above, you are off the hook even if the new tenant fails to pay the rent.

In this assignment document, the landlord specifically gives up the right to collect any further rent from you. The landlord may balk and demand that this provision be removed. But then again, lots of landlords, not that worried about this aspect of assignments (or unaware that it exists), may just go ahead and sign.

FORM
The Nolo website includes a downloadable copy of the Consent to Assignment of Lease form. See Appendix B for the link to the forms in this book.

Subletting Your Home Temporarily

If you have a fairly long lease and a particularly wonderful rental, you may want to move out for a while but then move back in. If you really want to keep your place, you can try to sublet it—that is, rent it to a short-term tenant who will leave when you wish to return.

Subletting may sound good, but think long and hard before you dive in. There are some serious drawbacks, explained below. As a general rule, sublease only if all four of these conditions are met:

- You are completely confident of the integrity, financial stability, and housekeeping habits of your intended subtenant.

Consent to Assignment of Lease

Carolyn Friedman _____ ["Landlord"] and

Joel Oliver _____ ["Tenant"]

and Sam Parker _____ ["Assignee"]

agree as follows:

1. Tenant has leased the premises at _____ 5 Fulton, Indianapolis, Indiana _____

   _____

   from Landlord.

2. The lease was signed on _____ April 1, 20xx _____ and will expire on

   _____ March 31, 20xx _____.

3. Tenant is assigning the balance of Tenant's lease to Assignee, beginning on ____ November 1, 20xx ____,

   and ending on _____ March 31, 20xx _____.

4. Tenant's financial responsibilities under the terms of the lease are not ended by virtue of this

   assignment. Specifically, Tenant understands that:

   a. If Assignee defaults and fails to pay the rent as provided in the lease, namely on ____ the first of ____

      ____ the month ____, Tenant will be obligated to do so within ____ three ____ days of being notified by

      Landlord; and

   b. If Assignee damages the property beyond normal wear and tear and fails or refuses to pay for

      repairs or replacement, Tenant will be obligated to do so.

5. As of the effective date of the assignment, Tenant permanently gives up the right to occupy the

   premises.

6. Assignee is bound by every term and condition in the lease that is the subject of this assignment.

Carolyn Friedman _____   _October 1, 20xx_ _____
Landlord/Manager   Date

Joel Oliver _____   _October 1, 20xx_ _____
Tenant   Date

Sam Parker _____   _October 1, 20xx_ _____
Assignee   Date

- Your landlord has approved the person you have presented.
- You are sure you will return.
- You really want your old rental unit back.

EXAMPLE: Denis has lived in his apartment in a university town for 20 years. His landlord, Sally, happily renews the lease every year, appreciating the fact that Denis pays the rent on time and takes good care of the property. When Denis began planning a four-month trip to Europe, he asked Sally if he could sublet to his cousin Ralph, who would be a visiting professor during that time.

Sally was hesitant, having heard from other landlords that sublets were loaded with legal problems. But Denis gave Sally a copy of Ralph's excellent résumé and explained that he just couldn't afford to leave the unit empty for four months; he might have to move out permanently if Sally didn't let Ralph take over. After checking Ralph's references and credit report, Sally agreed to the sublet. The subtenancy proceeded without a hitch and Denis returned to a well-kept home.

Downsides of Subletting

Here are some important issues to consider before you go hunting for a subtenant.

You're still on the hook, financially. If the new tenant (the subtenant) fails to pay the rent or damages the premises, you will be 100% legally responsible.

It's hard to find good subtenants. The pool of reliable short-term tenants is fairly small: visiting students or professors, people waiting for escrow to close on a home they've purchased, and so on. And it's important to find a very, very reliable subtenant; if you don't, you may end up getting sued by the landlord for losses caused by the subtenant. (See Chapter 7 for advice on choosing a replacement tenant.)

Your landlord may refuse. Most leases require the landlord's permission before you can sublet. (See Chapter 2.) But your landlord will probably prefer to end your tenancy and rent to a new tenant, let you assign the rest of your lease to a new tenant, or, if you want a roomer (discussed in Chapter 7), insist that the new occupant become a full-fledged cotenant.

	Comparing Subleases and Assignments	
	Sublease	**Assignment**
Rent	New tenant (subtenant) is liable to the original tenant, not to the landlord. Original tenant is liable to landlord.	New tenant (assignee) is liable to the landlord. Absent an agreement to the contrary, old tenant is liable if new tenant doesn't pay.
Damage to premises	Original tenant is liable for damage caused by new tenant.	Absent an agreement to the contrary, original tenant is not liable for damage caused by new tenant.
Violations of lease	Landlord can't sue new tenant for money losses caused by violating lease, because new tenant never signed lease. New tenant can't sue landlord for lease violations, either.	New tenant and landlord are bound by all terms in lease except those that were purely personal to the landlord and old tenant.
Eviction	Landlord can sue to evict new tenant for any reason old tenant could have been evicted. But to evict subtenant, landlord must also evict old tenant.	Landlord can evict new tenant for any reason old tenant could have been evicted.

The big reason is that if the subtenant screws up, the landlord may not be able to sue the subtenant directly. For example, in some states, if a subtenant ruins the premises and the security deposit doesn't cover the loss, the landlord can only sue you, the tenant, not the subtenant who caused the damage. If you are far away and suddenly decide not to return, the landlord has a big problem. Or if the subtenant's behavior is grounds for eviction—for example, the subtenant is dealing drugs on the rental property or disturbing the neighbors—the landlord may need to evict you in order to get rid of the subtenant.

From a landlord's perspective, there are other problems as well:

- If the subtenant won't move out when you return, the landlord could become embroiled in a lawsuit between you and the subtenant.
- Few landlords are willing to grant eviction powers to tenants, fearing that sooner or later the power will be abused.

The subtenant might refuse to leave when you return. This puts you in an awkward legal situation. The only way the landlord may be able to evict the subtenant is to evict you, too.

A subtenant can turn into a tenant. If you and the landlord treat a subtenant like a tenant, that subtenant can gain the legal status of the landlord's tenant. For example, a subtenant who repeatedly pays rent directly to the landlord and not to you may be able to claim the status of a tenant. And once that happens, the new tenant has all the rights and responsibilities of a cotenant, which can have important legal consequences for you. (See the Chapter 7 discussion of cotenants and the joint and several liability rule.) To avoid this, make sure that the subtenant pays *you* the rent, no matter what it says in a written subtenancy agreement. Either send it to the landlord or, better yet, deposit it in your account and write a personal check for the rent.

Housesitters as Subtenants

Many tenants use housesitters to stay in their homes when they will be gone for an extended period of time, especially if they have a dog or cat that needs care. It may surprise you to learn that unless your housesitter will be there for just a few days—a period of time that would make her a guest, per the terms of your lease or rental agreement—that housesitter is poised to become a subtenant (or an unauthorized occupant, if your landlord doesn't accept your housesitter as a subtenant). The question is, should you take the time and trouble to alert the landlord and create a sublease, as the rest of this section explains?

The answer depends entirely on your relationship with the landlord, the circumstances of the rental, and how comfortable you are with taking a chance that your tenancy will be imperiled unless you operate "by the book." Don't take a chance if you have a touchy relationship with the landlord, who is itching to find a reason to boot you, and who is likely to find out about the arrangement. Long-term tenants with rent control have a lot to lose, in particular. On the other hand, if the landlord will probably not find out, and neighboring tenants in the building have been alerted and have no issues, you may do just fine going under the radar.

If you do decide to approach the landlord, emphasize the value of having someone on-site during your absence, and assure the owner that the sitter has every intention to depart. Still, follow the suggestions in this section for choosing your sitter wisely and documenting the arrangement with a sublease, signed also by the landlord.

CAUTION
Carefully choose your dog walkers. Because these people will not be living in your home, legally speaking they are guests to whom you've given a key. Unless their presence creates a nuisance, the landlord should have no legal basis for objecting to their comings and goings. But obviously, choose the dog walker with care: Not only are you entrusting your pet, but the entire contents of your home will be at the walker's fingertips. Look for a service that is bonded, incorporated (or is an LLC), and has an established, good reputation.

Creating a Sublease

If you have decided to sublease—and have gotten your landlord's okay—you have just donned a new legal hat: You are your subtenant's landlord. As a landlord, it makes sense to take steps to protect your interests and, above all, ensure that your tenant will not do anything that will jeopardize your own tenancy.

You'll need a clear written agreement, signed by you and the subtenant, that will specify rent, duration of the tenancy, a security deposit, and so on. For example, you'll need to state whether the subtenant has a month-to-month tenancy or a lease for a certain period. One way is to simply use the same form you signed with your landlord, changing the title from "Lease" to "Sublease" and making yourself the sublessor and the other person the subtenant. Attach a copy to your original lease, the terms and conditions of which the sublessee agrees to follow as well.

Now That You're a Landlord

Once you take on a subtenant, you must meet your responsibilities as a landlord. Follow these steps to make sure you cover the basics:

- Screen and choose your subtenant carefully.
- Get a security deposit equal to the maximum allowed by law.
- Do your best to provide the subtenant a safe place to live. As you would do for your own safety, alert the property owner about any hazards and clean up any dangerous situation you've created within your rental unit.
- Use a Landlord-Tenant Checklist to note the condition of the premises when the subtenant moves in.
- Use the Landlord-Tenant Checklist again when the subtenant moves out and promptly refund the security deposit, less any legitimate deductions for unpaid rent, cleaning, or damage. If you make deductions, immediately give the subtenant a written explanation.

CAUTION

Don't discriminate illegally. As a sublessor, you must abide by fair housing laws. (See Chapter 5.) Be especially careful in your advertisements. An index card tacked to a grocery store bulletin board advertising "Room to rent, single Christian woman preferred" may be a violation of your state's law. On the other hand, if you spread word of your search by informal word-of-mouth only, you'll probably be okay.

Ending a Subtenancy

If your subtenant rents month to month and you'd like to end the arrangement, you'll need to give the amount of notice required by your state to terminate a month-to-month tenant. Typically, this is 30 days. (Appendix A lists every state's rule.) If your subtenant has a lease that you would prefer not to renew, send a reminder toward the end of the term that the end is approaching and that you do not intend to renew the lease or start a month-to-month relationship.

If the tenant doesn't leave, do not accept any more rent. You'll probably need to follow regular eviction procedures, like any other landlord.

You also may find it necessary to evict if the subtenant hasn't paid you the rent, or has broken the house rules or a lease clause. You'll probably need to follow your state's procedures for eviction "for cause." (Chapter 17 discusses termination notices for tenant wrongdoing. Read Chapter 18 for an overview of evictions.)

RENT CONTROL

Rent control may limit your options. Check your ordinance to see if it applies to subtenants. If it's unclear, ask the local rent control board or a tenants' group.

Breaking the Lease

When you sign a lease, you are legally bound to pay rent for the full lease term, whether or not you continue to occupy the dwelling. Simply moving out, even if you notify the landlord in advance, does not get you off the hook as far as paying rent is concerned.

There's good news, though: You may not have to pay much, if any, additional rent. In most states, you must pay only the amount your landlord loses because you moved out early. If the rental market is tight, the landlord will probably get a new tenant quickly, at the same rent you paid (or even more). Once there's a new rent-paying tenant, that ends your obligation to pay rent.

Your Landlord's Duty to Find a New Tenant

Most states require a landlord to take reasonable steps to keep losses to a minimum—in legalese, to "mitigate damages." (Each state's rule is listed in "Landlord's Duty to Rerent" in Appendix A.) So if you break your lease and move out without legal justification, your landlord usually can't just sit back and wait until the end of the lease, and then sue you for the total amount of lost rent. In most states, your landlord must try to rerent the property reasonably quickly and subtract the rent received from new tenants from the amount you owe. The landlord can also, however, add legitimate expenses to your bill—for example, the cost of advertising the property or using credit reporting agencies to investigate potential renters.

 TIP

Negotiate over the landlord's normal tenant-finding expenses. Why should you pay for the landlord's costs of advertising, showing the apartment, and screening applicants? After all, these are expenses that your landlord would have incurred anyway if you had stayed and left at the end of your term.

Especially if you left only a month or so early, tell the landlord that you are willing to pay lost rent, but shouldn't have to underwrite regular business expenses. If the landlord doesn't buy it and withholds a sizable portion of your security deposit for this purpose, consider suing in small claims court. Many judges will conclude that your landlord should bear at least a portion of the cost of finding a new tenant. (Chapter 16 explains the use of small claims court to dispute security deposit deductions.)

Your landlord is required to make reasonable efforts to rerent the property to a good tenant at a reasonable rent. The landlord does not need to relax standards for acceptable tenants—for example, to accept applicants with poor credit or shady rental histories. Also, the landlord is not required to rent the premises for below their fair market value or to immediately turn all her attention to renting your unit, disregarding other business.

EXAMPLE: Susan rented an apartment from Stephen in January for a term of one year, at the monthly rent of $1,000. At the end of August, Susan gave notice of her intent to move at the end of September to be closer to her invalid mother. Susan is legally liable to Stephen for $3,000—the rent for October, November, and December.

However, Stephen posts an ad, checks out prospective tenants, and rents the apartment again on October 15. The new tenant pays $500 for the last half of October and $1,000 in November and December. Stephen must subtract this $2,500 from Susan's $3,000 debt. This leaves her liable for only $500, plus Stephen's advertising costs of $20 and credit check fees of $30, for a total of $550.

If the Landlord Sues You

If you move out and break your lease, your landlord can, and probably will, charge you for the time and cost of advertising for a new tenant, particularly if the rental market is slow.

Your landlord will probably first use your security deposit to cover these amounts. (See Chapter 16.) But if your deposit does not cover what you owe, your landlord may sue you. The landlord can go to court as soon as the property is rented again. At this point, his losses—his expenses and the rent differential, if any—are known. In many states, the landlord has up to four, or even five, years to sue.

If you are sued, you will receive legal documents setting out the landlord's claim. Read them carefully, to see if the amount the landlord asks for is fair. As explained above, if you took the proper steps to protect yourself by finding an acceptable replacement tenant who was unreasonably turned down by your landlord, your landlord's suit may be bogus, and you will definitely want to defend yourself.

Chances are you'll be sued in small claims court, assuming the amount the landlord claims isn't above the court's upper limit—about $3,000 to $10,000 in most states. But if it is, and if your lease contains a clause allowing your landlord to recover attorneys' fees, he may file in regular court, where you stand to lose much more.

Termination Fees

If your lease contains a termination fee clause—a provision requiring you to pay the landlord a certain amount of money if you break the lease—the landlord may sue you for that amount. In some states, liquidated damages clauses like this in residential leases are flatly illegal. (Florida, however, specifically allows them under certain circumstances). This means that the landlord would not be able to automatically collect this amount. The court would probably, however, allow the landlord to prove his actual losses, which you'd have to pay if the landlord could convince the judge that his reasonable efforts could not produce a suitable tenant and that he spent a certain amount of money in trying to find one.

Even in some states that allow liquidated damages, the termination fee must not be excessive. If the amount you are supposed to pay greatly exceeds what the landlord actually lost—or would have lost if she had actively looked for another tenant—a court may consider it an invalid "penalty" and order you to compensate the landlord only for actual losses. But even if you ultimately don't have to pay the whole amount, you'll expend considerable time and energy fighting your landlord in court.

EXAMPLE: Cree has a year's lease at $800 per month. She moves out with six months ($4,800 of rent) left on the lease. Cree's landlord, Robin, cannot find a new tenant for six weeks, and when she finally does, the new tenant will pay only $600 per month.

Unless Cree can show Robin acted unreasonably, Cree would be liable for the $200 per month difference between what she paid and what the new tenant pays, multiplied by the number of months left in the lease at the time she moved out. Cree would also be responsible for $1,200 for the time the unit was vacant, plus Robin's costs to find a new tenant. Cree would thus owe Robin $2,400 plus advertising and applicant screening costs. If Robin sues Cree for this money and uses a lawyer, if there is an "attorneys' fees and costs" in her lease Cree will also owe Robin these costs, which can be upwards of a few thousand dollars.

If you are sued in small claims court for an amount that seems excessive, simply tell the judge your side of the case. Bring with you any witnesses and documentation that would help tell your story —for example, any evidence that the landlord did not advertise the rental unit, failed to consider prospective tenants you suggested or overpriced the unit, making it harder to find new tenants.

In some states, in order to win *you* may be required to prove that the landlord took no steps to find a new tenant. In other states, it's up to the landlord to prove that he *did* take reasonable steps. To be on the safe side, assume that the burden of proof will be on you, and be prepared to make your case in court if your landlord sits back and makes no attempts to rerent.

Chapter 16 discusses how to defend yourself in small claims court. If you are sued in regular court and want legal advice, see Chapter 20, which covers how to find and work with a lawyer.

RESOURCE

Everybody's Guide to Small Claims Court, by Cara O'Neill (Nolo), explains how to defend yourself against a landlord who sues you in small claims court.

For more information on the mechanics of a civil lawsuit and how to conduct yourself in court, see *Represent Yourself in Court: How to Prepare & Try a Winning Case,* by Paul Bergman and Sara Berman (Nolo).

Condominium Conversions

Landlords can sometimes make a lot of money by converting their rental properties into condominiums, which will often mean the end of your tenancy. Condo conversions can be especially attractive to landlords in areas with rent control, because rent control restricts the profit a landlord can make by renting, but doesn't regulate the selling price of condominiums.

Many states regulate the conversion of rental property into condominiums—that is, they limit the number of conversions and give existing tenants considerable rights, as explained below. Here are some of the basic issues that your state's condo conversion law may address:

Government approval. An owner who intends to convert rental property to condos must usually get a plan approval (often called a "subdivision map approval") from a local planning agency. If the property is subject to rent control, there are probably additional requirements.

Public input. In most situations, the public—including current tenants—can speak out at planning agency hearings regarding the proposed condominium conversion and its impact on the rental housing market. Owners are usually required to give tenants notice of the time and place of these hearings.

Tenants' right of first refusal. Most condominium conversion laws demand that the owner offer the units for sale first to the existing tenants, at prices that are the same as or lower than the intended public offering. Often, to keep tenant opposition

to a minimum, landlords voluntarily offer existing tenants a chance to buy at a significantly lower price.

Tenancy terminations. Month-to-month tenants who don't buy their units will receive a notice to move at some point during the sales process. Tenants with leases usually have a right to remain through the end of the lease. The entire condo conversion approval process typically takes many months—time enough for current leases to expire before the final okay has been given.

Renting after the conversion has been approved. If you sign a lease or rental agreement *after* the condo conversion has been approved, many states require the owner to give you plenty of clear written warnings (in large, bold-faced type) that your unit may be sold and your tenancy terminated on short notice. Knowing this, landlords who continue to rent units after they've gotten their subdivision approval usually do so on a month-to-month basis, so the short notice really won't be any different from what any month-to-month tenant would receive.

Relocation assistance and special protections. Some statutes require owners to pay current tenants a flat fee to help with relocation. Some also require owners to provide more notice or additional relocation assistance for elderly tenants or those with small children. There is nothing to stop you from bargaining with the owner for additional compensation—in exchange for your agreement to vacate earlier, for example.

What can you do if your landlord fails to comply with your state or city's conversion laws? Generally, you may be able to delay the conversion and possibly obtain money damages (if you sue your landlord), but you can rarely, if ever, stop the process.

RELATED TOPIC

Legal research on condo conversions. For advice on researching your state's statutes and court cases on condominium conversions, see the discussion of legal research in Chapter 20.

If the Landlord Sells or Goes Out of Business

What happens to your lease if your landlord goes out of the business of renting residential property before the end of the lease term? If a new owner buys the property, in most cases the new owner must honor the existing leases.

If a landlord no longer wants to be a landlord (suppose he wants to take the property out of circulation in order to fix it up for sale), you can't just be tossed out. The regular rules discussed just above apply. If you don't have a lease, the landlord can give you a 30-day notice. If you do have a lease, it must be honored. But when your lease is up, the landlord has no obligation to continue renting to you or anyone else. A landlord who really wants leaseholding tenants out early will offer to buy them out.

RENT CONTROL

Phony going-out-of-business ploys. Some landlords in rent-control situations claim to go out of business and then pop up a few months later, in order to charge a market-rate rent—which may be higher than the current, controlled rent—to a new batch of tenants. To prevent this, a rent control ordinance may require withdrawn property to remain off the market for a lengthy amount of time (penalties result if the landlord rerents too soon). It may also specify that former tenants be given the right of first refusal when the property is returned to the residential rental market.

If the Landlord Declares Bankruptcy

If your landlord files for bankruptcy, your tenancy will not automatically end. To explain what will happen, we need to give you a little background information. First, if the landlord has filed a Chapter 7 bankruptcy, his assets will be used to pay off as many debts as possible (the rest are wiped out). The bankruptcy court will appoint someone called a bankruptcy trustee to oversee the case and manage (and then sell) the landlord's property for the benefit of his creditors. If the landlord has filed a Chapter 11 bankruptcy, where the landlord comes up with a plan to pay off his debts while still running the business, the landlord stays in the picture as the trustee and is known as the "debtor in possession." (11 U.S.C. § 1101.) Both types of trustees have broad powers over the landlord's assets—and income-producing rental property is considered an asset. Your security deposit, however, is not an asset of the bankruptcy estate, because it's your money, not the landlord's. (U.S.C. § 365(h).)

Both trustees have the ability to "assume" or "reject" the landlord's leases. Very little will change for you if the trustee assumes the lease—you may even continue to pay rent to the landlord and deal with him on other matters such as repairs. If the trustee rejects the lease, you will have a choice. You can:

- treat the lease as terminated and move out, or
- stay put and retain all your rights under the lease.

As you can see, the term "rejects" is a bit misleading, since it does not mean that your tenancy will end. However, your ability to use your state-given tenant remedies, such as rent withholding and repair and deduct, will be replaced by the remedy provided by the bankruptcy code. If, for example, your landlord fails to provide heat, you'll have to apply to the bankruptcy court for an "offset" against rent—in effect, a rent abatement based on the diminished value of your rental. (11 U.S.C. § 365(h)(1)(B).)

In practical terms, your landlord's bankruptcy may not greatly affect the quality of your tenancy. In a Chapter 7 bankruptcy, the property will probably be sold eventually, in which case you'll be dealing with a new owner who will have to honor your lease (the same situation you'd face if the landlord sold the property voluntarily). In a Chapter 11 bankruptcy, if there is enough value in the property to justify its continued operation, you may notice little change. There is always the chance, however, that the trustee will decide to sell the property, in which case you will find yourself with a new owner/landlord—but again, one who will have to honor the terms of your lease.

If the Rental Property Is Foreclosed

If the landlord falls behind on mortgage payments on the rental property, the bank (or mortgage holder) can foreclose, and then sell the property to satisfy the landlord's debt out of the proceeds of the sale. At such sales, that mortgage holder usually winds up owning the property, though sometimes a third party outbids the mortgage holder and winds up with the property.

Eviction Protection After a Foreclosure

Because the federal Protecting Tenants at Foreclosure Act expired at the end of 2014, how much time a tenant has to stay in a foreclosed property now depends on state and local foreclosure laws, and whether or not the rental is in a city with "just cause" eviction protections.

State and Local Foreclosure Protections for Tenants

Many states (and some cities) give tenants protection from eviction in default and foreclosure situations. For example, some state and local laws require a foreclosing bank to give tenants notice about an impending foreclosure, require a new owner to give tenants a certain number of days' notice to vacate before starting an eviction after a foreclosure, or require a new owner to honor existing leases under specific circumstances. If you are caught in the middle between a defaulting landlord and a foreclosing bank, and you want to preserve your rental, consider consulting a local real estate or foreclosure lawyer, who should know the details of your state's laws. The website of the National Housing Law Project (nhlp.org) is also a useful resource on state and local protections for tenants in foreclosure situations.

> ### "Cash for Keys"
>
> To encourage tenants to leave quickly, banks sometimes offer tenants a cash payout in exchange for their rapid departure. Thinking that they have little choice, many tenants—even Section 8 and other protected tenants—take the deal.

Rules in Cities With Just Cause Eviction Protection

Tenants who live in cities with "just cause" eviction protection are also protected from terminations at the hands of an acquiring bank or new owner. These tenants can rely on their ordinance's list of allowable reasons for termination. Because a change of ownership, without more, does not justify a termination under the cities' lists of allowable reasons to evict, the fact that the change occurred through foreclosure will not justify a termination. However, a new owner who wants to do an "owner move-in" eviction may do so, as long as the owner complies with the ordinance's procedures.

Paying Rent—Before or After Foreclosure

The issue of who you pay rent to pending or after a foreclosure can be confusing. Here's a summary of the key issues.

Paying Rent Before the Foreclosure

Tenants who learn that their landlords are in default on the mortgage (they've fallen behind on their payments) or already in foreclosure (the lender has announced their intent to foreclose) are often confused about who is entitled to the rent money. You are likely to hear demands from many quarters—the desperate owner, a management company, or a bank. It's important to know who is—and who isn't—entitled to the rent check. First, a little background.

Lending banks (the mortgage holders) typically attach a rider, or special agreement, to the mortgage or deed of trust documents when a buyer intends to use the building as a rental. This rider, called a 1-4 Family Rider (Assignment of Rents), is used by lenders in most states for properties that have one to four rental units. Its main purpose is to give the lender the right to receive the rent when the buyer has defaulted on the mortgage.

To understand how the rider works, think like a banker for a minute. The property is generating income and the buyer is falling behind on his mortgage. In order to cut its losses as quickly and as thoroughly as possible, the lender wants to get its hands on the rent.

Foreclosures in Multifamily Properties

The 1-4 Family Rider is a standard form that's used for small properties (four or fewer rental units). Banks and buyers use a standard form because they assume that the relatively small size of the deal doesn't merit lengthy negotiations between the parties.

Larger properties almost always have the same sort of arrangement—if the owner falls behind on the mortgage payments, the lender gets the right to receive the rent. Usually, these arrangements are negotiated by the banks and the buyers' lawyers and may include unique provisions that are hammered out by the parties. But as far as the tenants are concerned, the bottom line is the same: With proper notice, you will be expected to pay the rent to the bank.

In most states, once the lender gives the owner a written notice of default, the lender has the right (except in Michigan) to receive the rent directly from the tenants. Lenders have to give written notice to the tenants, and they typically do so by letter, posted notice on the property, or in person.

Paying Rent After the Foreclosure

After the foreclosure has happened, the new owner, whether a bank or an individual who bought as an investor, can insist that the tenant comply with the lease or rental agreement that the tenant entered into with the old owner. This means that on the first rent due date after the property changes hands, you must pay the same rent to the new owner. If you don't pay, the new owner can give you a notice to pay rent or quit, and if you do neither, begin eviction proceedings.

If you receive notice that the property in which you live has been foreclosed (that is, a "trustee's sale" has been held), you should stop paying rent to the now-former owner and pay it to the new owner. If you don't know who that is, set aside your rent payment each month (to be extra careful, set up an escrow account and deposit it there), so that you can pay it to the new owner once you find out who that is. If you receive a three-day notice to pay rent or quit from the new owner, you might want to confirm with your county's Recorder's Office—usually located at the county seat—that the person or entity giving you the notice is truly the new owner.

Repairs and Maintenance Preforeclosure

Even though the bank is receiving the rent payments, all other rights and responsibilities that the owner/landlord has with respect to the tenants remain in place. Until the bank actually forecloses, the owner is still the owner. This leads to problems if you need maintenance or repairs.

Landlords are often unwilling to make repairs. Without a source of income from the rental property, most owners will be unable (or unwilling) to maintain it. For you, however, the owner's disillusionment is beside the point when it comes to safe and secure rental housing, because in every state but Arkansas, landlords must maintain fit and habitable rental housing. How does a tenant enforce this right against a demoralized (and possibly broke) owner?

The lender is not obligated to help. According to the Family Rider, the lender must apply the rent money to property management costs, including maintenance, before it applies the money to the unpaid mortgage. But the Rider explicitly does not obligate the lender to assume the maintenance duties of the owner. Unless there's a specific local or state law to the contrary, the lender's right to receive rent money doesn't turn that lender into the landlord for purposes of maintaining the property. (A few states are beginning to make banks legally responsible for maintenance. For example, in California, banks have specified maintenance duties.) If conditions seriously deteriorate to the point where the home is not fit to live in, you may find yourself stuck between an owner who has no ability to take care of business, and a lender who has no obligation to do so.

Self-help remedies are tricky. You may need to avail yourself of a tenant's "self-help" remedy, such as rent withholding and repair-and-deduct (not all states give these remedies to tenants). In many cities, housing and health departments are charged with responding to unsafe and unsanitary conditions in rental housing. They typically have powers that range from ordering the owners to take care of business (under threat of contempt of court), to taking over the property altogether and running it until they've fixed the problems (and charging the owner for the privilege).

Although these government agencies can, and should, still do their jobs, their intervention may be ineffective. The agencies will be dealing with an owner who has no resources to contribute (and who may even be impossible to locate), and a bank that has no legal duty to step up. Results will differ when the government takes over because the efficiency of local and state agencies varies tremendously.

Moving Out and Getting Your Security Deposit Back

Basic Rules for Returning Deposits 276

    Advance Notice of Deductions 276

    Deadlines 276

    Itemized Statements 277

Deductions for Cleaning and Damage 279

    Reasonable Deductions 279

    Common Disagreements 281

Deductions for Unpaid Rent 281

    Month-to-Month Tenancies 281

    Fixed-Term Leases 282

    After an Eviction 283

Avoiding Fights Over Deposits 283

    Your Cleaning Plans 284

    Cleaning Thoroughly 285

    Documenting the Condition of the Unit 285

    Arranging a Final Inspection 285

    Requesting Your Deposit in Writing 286

    Using the Deposit as Last Month's Rent 288

Security Deposits From Cotenants 290

How to Handle Deposit Disputes 291

    Call the Landlord 291

    Make a Second Written Demand 291

    Consider Compromise 292

Suing Your Landlord in Small Claims Court 293

    Preparation: The Key to Winning 294

    How to Present Your Case in Court 295

If Your Deposit Doesn't Cover What You Owe 296

Your Abandoned Property 297

    Why Did You Move Out? 297

    When You're Behind in the Rent 298

    Legal Notice Requirements 299

    What Will Happen to Your Property 299

    Landlord Liability for Damage to or Loss of Your Property 300

ights over security deposits make up a large percentage of the landlord-tenant disputes that wind up in small claims court. Many suits are brought by tenants against landlords who unfairly withheld deposit money for cleaning or refused to return the deposit at all.

Fortunately, you can take some simple steps to minimize the possibility that you'll spend hours haggling in court with your landlord. This chapter shows you how and, if you do end up in court, how to prepare a winning case. It includes advice and information on:

- when and how landlords must return deposits and what deductions are allowed under the law
- how to make sure you meet your landlord's expectations for the condition in which the unit should be left
- how to protect yourself by documenting the condition of the rental unit when you move out
- how to write demand letters for the return of your deposit
- how to negotiate with your landlord and use a mediation service, if appropriate, and
- how to sue your landlord in small claims court over your deposit.

This chapter includes several sample letters to send your landlord when it comes to problems with getting your security deposit back. As with all important communications, use a mail or delivery service that will provide proof of delivery (you may need this should you end up in court fighting about your deposit). In Chapter 6, "Using Email or Text Messages for Notice or a Letter of Understanding" explains why it's best to send important communications by mail (certified or return receipt requested) or delivery service, rather than email or text messages.

 RELATED TOPIC
Also covered in this book:
- State laws on the amount and collection of deposits and what happens to your deposit if the landlord sells the property: Chapter 4.

- How to use a Landlord-Tenant Checklist to document the condition of the rental unit when you move in: Chapter 6.
- Landlord and tenant repair and maintenance responsibilities: Chapters 8, 9, and 10.
- What happens to your deposit if the landlord files for bankruptcy or the property is foreclosed: Chapter 15.

Basic Rules for Returning Deposits

Most states hold landlords to a strict set of rules regarding security deposits. Landlords are expected to account for your money promptly or face stiff penalties. For example, in many states a landlord who deliberately violates the security deposit statute may have to return all of your deposit plus two or three times the amount wrongfully withheld, plus attorney fees and costs.

Advance Notice of Deductions

In many states, landlords must give tenants advance notice of intended deductions, which is generally done in a pre-move-out inspection (the second inspection is done when the tenant leaves). This gives tenants the opportunity to clean and perform repairs in order to avoid deductions from their deposits. But even when landlords perform these early inspections, they can still deduct at move-out for damage or uncleanliness that appeared after the first inspection, or for problems they couldn't see because of the presence of the tenant's belongings. For specifics on your state's law, see "State Security Deposit Rules" in Appendix A.

Deadlines

Depending on the state, landlords generally have between 14 and 30 days after you leave—whether voluntarily or by eviction—to return your entire deposit.

The landlord must mail the following to your last known address (or forwarding address, if known):

- your entire deposit, with interest if required (Chapter 4 lists state laws requiring interest), or
- a written, itemized statement as to how the deposit has been applied toward back rent and costs of cleaning and damage repair, together with whatever is left of the deposit, including any interest that is required. In most states, landlords send the itemization along with any deposit balance. A few states add an additional step that gives tenants time to respond to proposed deductions before they are actually made.

For specifics on your state's law, see "State Security Deposit Rules" in Appendix A.

Unfortunately, landlords in some states are not subject to any deadline or rules governing the return of deposits. If you live in one of these states, ask your landlord when you move out when you can expect to get your deposit back. A reasonable landlord should return your deposit within one month. If more than a month has passed or you suspect you may never see your deposit again, follow the steps in "How to Handle Deposit Disputes," below.

CAUTION
Make sure your landlord knows how to reach you. If you don't give your landlord a forwarding address, you may never see your deposit. In some states, a landlord is allowed to keep the deposit if you cannot be found after a reasonable effort, or after searching for a very short period, sometimes as little as 60 or 90 days. To protect yourself, send your landlord a written request for the return of your security deposit, and include your forwarding address. (A sample letter is in "Avoiding Fights Over Deposits," below.)

Itemized Statements

You are entitled to a statement that explains the purpose of each deduction and states the dollar amount withheld. Your landlord should never send a statement that simply says, "$200 deduction for cleaning and repairs." If you get this kind of vague statement, you have the legal right to ask for more details.

If cleaning and repair work have already been done, your landlord should provide details on labor and supplies, including receipts, in the final itemization. For example:

- "Carpet cleaning by ABC Carpet Cleaners, $160, required by several large grease stains and candle wax imbedded in living room rug."
- "Plaster repair, $400, of several fist-sized holes in bedroom wall."
- "$250 to replace drapes in living room, damaged by cigarette smoke and holes."

See the sample Security Deposit Itemization below.

If your landlord can't get necessary repairs made or cleaning done within the time required to return the security deposit, the statement should contain a reasonable estimate of the cost. But if you end up suing your landlord, he will need to produce receipts for the amount deducted.

If you damaged or substantially shortened the useful life of an item, it can be a little tougher to put a dollar amount on damages. In fairness, the landlord ought to take into account how old it was, how long it might have lasted otherwise, and its original cost.

EXAMPLE: Your dog ruined an eight-year-old rug that had a life expectancy of ten years. If the rug cost $1,000, your landlord would charge you $200 for the two years of life that would have remained in the rug had your dog not ruined it.

The approach illustrated in the example below amortizes the cost of the damaged item over its useful life. The tenant ends up paying for the value of the item at the time he damaged it. We think this approach is fair because it takes into account the fact that items wear out through normal use and landlords must shoulder the cost of replacing them. If you've shortened the useful life of an item, it's fitting that you should compensate the landlord for the fact that he'll have to make a capital expenditure earlier than he'd planned.

Security Deposit Itemization

Date: _November 8, 20xx_

From: _Rachel Tolan_

123 Larchmont Lane

St. Louis, Missouri

To: _Lena Coleman_

456 Penny Lane, #101

St. Louis, Missouri

Property Address: _789 Cora Court, St. Louis, Missouri_

Rental Period: _January 1, 20xx to October 31, 20xx_

1. Security Deposit Received: $ _1,000_

2. Interest on Deposit (if required by lease or law): $ _N/A_

3. Total Credit (sum of lines 1 and 2): $ _1,000_

4. Itemized Repairs and Related Losses:

   Repainting of living room walls, required

   by crayon and chalk marks

   _____ $ _260_

5. Necessary Cleaning:

   Sum paid to resident manager for 4 hours

   cleaning at $20/hour: debris-filled garage,

   dirty stove, and refrigerator $ _80_

6. Total Cleaning & Repair (sum of lines 4 and 5): $ _340_

7. Amount Owed (line 3 minus line 6):

   ☐ Total Amount Tenant Owes Landlord: $ _____

   ☑ Total Amount Landlord Owes Tenant: $ _660_

Comments: _A check for $260 is enclosed._

_____

_____

_____

_____

_____

This is not the only method that landlords use, however. Some will charge you for the item's original cost, regardless of its age; and some will charge you for the full replacement cost. Both of these methods result in the tenant essentially underwriting the landlord's cost of doing business. Look back at the Example—why should you pay your landlord $1,000 (the rug's original cost) when, in two years, the landlord would have had to spend that amount to replace an item that has lost its usefulness? Even worse, if the rug would now cost more, why should you take on the additional burden of paying the inflated cost?

Unfortunately, we aren't aware of any statutes that directly address the question of how landlords should figure the cost of an item when it's ruined by a tenant. If your landlord appears to be soaking you for the original cost or the full replacement cost, you'll want to challenge him. Below we cover disputes and going to court, and give advice on how to gather evidence to support your claim for a reasonable computation of damages to a ruined item.

Deductions for Cleaning and Damage

Legally, a landlord may charge for any cleaning or repairs necessary to restore the rental unit to its condition at the beginning of the tenancy. The landlord may not use your security deposit for the cost of remedying ordinary wear and tear.

Unfortunately, it's not always easy to decide what constitutes ordinary wear and tear, or what must be done to leave a rental unit clean. Must you leave the premises perfectly clean? "Reasonably" clean?

Reasonable Deductions

In general, landlords may charge only for cleaning and repairs that are really necessary, such as replacing stained or ripped carpets or drapes (particularly smoke-contaminated ones), fixing damaged furniture, and cleaning dirty stoves, refrigerators, and kitchen and bathroom fixtures. Your landlord may also need to take care of such things as flea infestations left behind by your dog or mildew in the bathroom caused by your failure to clean properly.

Your landlord can't set unreasonable standards for cleaning. For example, if the place was less than immaculate when you moved in, your landlord has no legal right to require a perfect cleaning job now. And no judge would uphold a requirement that you clean the floor with a toothbrush.

That said, every move-out is different in its details, and there are simply no hard and fast rules on what is wear and tear (your landlord's problem) and what is your responsibility. But here are some basic guidelines:

- You should not be charged for filth or damage that was present when you moved in.
- You should not be charged for replacing an item when a repair would be sufficient. For example, if you damaged the kitchen counter by placing a hot pan on it, you shouldn't be required to replace the entire counter if an expertly done patch will do the job. Of course, you have to evaluate the overall condition of the unit—if it is a luxury property that looks like an ad in *Architectural Digest*, don't expect your landlord to make do with a patch.
- The longer you've lived in a place, the more wear and tear can be expected on things like carpets, floors, and walls.
- You should not be charged for cleaning if you paid a nonrefundable cleaning fee. Landlords in some states are allowed to charge a cleaning fee, which is separate from the security deposit and is specifically labeled as nonrefundable. (See Chapter 4.) If you paid a cleaning fee, the landlord should not deduct anything from your security deposit for cleaning.
- You should be charged a fair price for repairs and replacements. You should not be asked to foot the bill for a high-priced handyman or unreasonably expensive replacement items. Legally, your landlord is obligated to spend only what is needed to accomplish the job in a workmanlike manner.

TIP

Check prices yourself. If you believe you are being price-gouged, it might be worth your while to get a few quotes from repair persons and compare them with the landlord's bill, or to shop around for the item that the landlord replaced. Say, for example, your landlord charges you $800 to replace a stove you damaged. First, argue that you should be liable only for the value of the stove you ruined. But as a backup, agree for the purposes of argument only that you'll pay for a replacement. If you find the same stove on sale at a nearby discount warehouse for $500 (and you can't convince the judge to adopt your first theory), you have the makings of a winning small claims case if, after learning of the discrepancy, the landlord doesn't reduce your bill by $300.

See "What Can Your Landlord Charge For?" below, for some examples of what a court will consider to be ordinary wear and tear, and what crosses the line and is commonly considered to be a condition for which you must pay for cleaning, replacement, or repair.

 RENT CONTROL

Your rent control ordinance may give a clue as to what is "normal wear and tear" and what is "damage." Most rent control ordinances allow the landlord to raise the rent for specific capital expenses. Typically, maintenance expenses spent in response to normal wear and tear are

What Can Your Landlord Charge For?	
Ordinary Wear and Tear: **Your Landlord's Responsibility**	**Damage or Excessive Filth:** **Your Responsibility**
Curtains faded by the sun	Cigarette burns in curtains or carpets
Water-stained linoleum by shower	Broken tiles in bathroom
Minor marks on or nicks in wall	Large marks on or holes in wall
Dents in the wall where a door handle bumped it	Door off its hinges
Moderate dirt or spotting on carpet	Rips in carpet or urine stains from pets
A few small tack or nail holes in wall	Lots of picture holes or gouges in walls that require patching as well as repainting
A rug worn thin by normal use	Stains in rug caused by your leaking fish tank
Worn gaskets on refrigerator doors	Broken refrigerator shelf
Faded paint on bedroom wall	Water damage on wall from hanging plants
Dark patches of ingrained soil on hardwood floors that have lost their finish and have been worn down to bare wood	Water stains on wood floors and windowsills caused by windows being left open during rainstorms
Warped cabinet doors that won't close	Sticky cabinets and interiors
Stains on old porcelain fixtures that have lost their protective coating	Grime-coated bathtub and toilet
Moderately dirty miniblinds	Missing miniblinds
Bathroom mirror beginning to "de-silver" (black spots)	Mirrors caked with lipstick and makeup
Clothes dryer that delivers cold air because the thermostat has given out	Dryer that won't turn at all because it's been overloaded
Toilet flushes inadequately because mineral deposits have clogged the jets	Toilet won't flush properly because it's stopped up with a diaper

not considered capital expenses. But if the landlord must replace an item, it may qualify as a capital expense, which justifies a rent increase. Protenant rent boards have reacted against this rent-increase justification by classifying the replacement of appliances, carpets, repainting, and so on as mere "maintenance" necessitated by normal wear and tear. Your argument: If it's maintenance to the rent board, it ought to be maintenance with respect to your security deposit, too, and your deposit shouldn't be used for it.

Common Disagreements

Common areas of disagreement between landlords and tenants concern repainting, carpets, and fixtures.

Painting

Although state and local laws (with the exception of some cities, including New York City) provide no firm guidelines as to who is responsible for repainting when a rental unit needs it, courts usually rule that if you have lived in your unit for several years, it should be done at your landlord's expense, not yours. On the other hand, if you have lived in a unit for less than a year, and the walls were freshly painted when you moved in but are now a mess, your landlord is probably entitled to charge you for all costs of cleaning the walls. If repainting badly smudged walls is cheaper and more effective than cleaning, however, the landlord can probably charge for repainting.

Rugs and Carpets

If the living room rug was already threadbare when you moved in a few months ago and looks even worse now, it's pretty obvious that your footsteps have simply contributed to the inevitable, and that this wear and tear is not your responsibility. On the other hand, a brand-new good quality rug that becomes stained and full of bare spots within months has probably been subjected to the type of abuse you will have to pay for. In between, it's anyone's guess. But, clearly, the longer you have lived in a unit, and the cheaper or older the carpet was when you moved in, the less likely you are to be held responsible for its deterioration.

Fixtures

The law considers pieces of furniture or equipment that are physically attached to the rental property, such as bolted-in bookshelves, to be your landlord's property, even if you paid for them. This means that if you leave behind a row of bookshelves, your landlord can legally remove them, subtract the cost from your security deposit *and* keep the bookshelves. (Chapter 10 discusses how to avoid disputes over fixtures when you move out.)

 TIP

Report damage immediately to your land-lord. If your landlord doesn't take action and the problem gets worse, you have a record of your attempts to nip it in the bud. You shouldn't have to pay, at move-out time, for the landlord's inaction.

Deductions for Unpaid Rent

If you move out owing rent, your landlord can deduct any unpaid rent from your security deposit, including any unpaid utility charges or other financial obliga-tions required under your lease or rental agreement. Even if your debt far exceeds the amount of the security deposit, the law still requires your landlord to itemize and notify you of how the security deposit was applied to your debt.

Chapter 15 discusses how month-to-month tenancies and fixed-term leases end, including notice requirements and what happens if you leave early or stay late.

Month-to-Month Tenancies

If you rent on a month-to-month basis, ideally you'll give the right amount of notice and pay for your last month's rent. Usually, the notice period is the same as your rental period, 30 days. Then, when you leave as planned, the only issue with respect to your security deposit is whether you've caused any damage or left the place dirty. But there are three common variations on this ideal scenario, and they all result in deductions from your security deposit for unpaid rent:

- You leave as announced, but with unpaid rent behind you.
- You leave later than planned, and haven't paid for your extra days.
- You leave as announced, but you haven't given the right amount of notice.

Let's look at each situation.

Leaving Unpaid Rent Behind

If you've been behind on the rent for months, convincing a good-hearted (or lazy) landlord to let matters slide, the landlord is entitled to deduct what you owe from the security deposit—either during the tenancy or when you leave.

Staying After Your Announced Departure Date

If you fail to leave when planned (or when requested, if the landlord has terminated the rental agreement), you obviously aren't entitled to stay on rent-free. When you eventually do leave, your landlord will figure the exact amount you owe by prorating the monthly rent for the number of days you have failed to pay.

> **EXAMPLE:** Erin gives notice on March 1 of her intent to move out. She pays her landlord Ann the rent of $600 for March. But because she can't get into her new place on time, Erin stays until April 5 without paying anything more. Ann is entitled to deduct 5/30 (one-sixth) of the total month's rent, or $100, from Erin's security deposit.

Giving Inadequate Notice

When you terminate a month-to-month tenancy, you must give your landlord the legally required amount of notice before leaving; in most states, that's 30 days. You must pay rent for that entire period. If you gave less than the legally required amount of notice and moved out, your landlord is entitled to rent money for the balance of the notice period unless the place is rerented within the 30 days. (Chapter 15 covers notice requirements for terminating a tenancy.)

> **EXAMPLE:** Tom pays his rent on the first of every month. State law requires 30 days' notice to terminate a tenancy. On June 20, Tom gives notice that he will leave on July 1. The rental market is soft and Jim, his landlord, is unable to rerent for two months. Since Tom gave only ten days' notice, Jim is entitled to deduct two-thirds of a months' rent (representing the 20 days of unpaid rent) from Tom's deposit.

Fixed-Term Leases

If you leave before a fixed-term lease expires, your landlord is entitled to the balance of the rent due under the lease. That rule is softened considerably by the fact that in most states your landlord is required to try to rerent the property, and once a new tenant starts paying rent, your obligation ends.

If you leave less than a month before your lease is scheduled to end, you can be almost positive that, if the case goes to court, a judge will conclude you owe rent for the entire lease term. It would be unreasonable to expect a landlord to immediately find a new tenant to take over the few days left of your lease. But if you leave more than 30 days before the end of a lease, your landlord's duty to look for a new tenant will be taken more seriously by the courts. (See Chapter 15 for more on your landlord's duty to try to rerent the property promptly.)

> **EXAMPLE:** On January 1, Anthony rents a house from Will for $1,200 a month and signs a one-year lease. He moves out on June 30, even though six months remain on the lease, making him responsible for a total rent of $7,200. Will rerents the property on July 10, this time for $1,250 a month (the new tenants pay $833 for the last 20 days in July), which means that he'll receive a total rent of

$7,083 through December 31. That's $117 less than the $7,200 he would have received from Anthony had he lived up to the lease, so Will may deduct $117 from Anthony's deposit. In addition, if Will spent a reasonable amount of money to find a new tenant (for newspaper ads, rental agency commissions, and credit checks), he may also deduct this sum from the deposit.

After an Eviction

If you lose an eviction lawsuit, the landlord can legally expect payment for rent until you actually leave.

EXAMPLE: When Allen fails to pay May's rent of $450, Marilyn sues to evict him. On June 10, she gets an eviction judgment from the court, ordering Allen to pay rent through that date. He doesn't actually leave until June 17. Marilyn can deduct the following items from the deposit:

- costs of necessary cleaning and repair, as allowed by state law
- the amount of the judgment (for rent through June 10), and
- rent for the week between June 10 and June 17 at $15 per day, or $105.

If the security deposit is not large enough to cover everything you owe, the landlord can collect the balance in all sorts of ways—for example, by going after your wages or bank account.

Avoiding Fights Over Deposits

Most security deposit hassles between landlords and tenants concern cleaning, not repairs or replacement costs. That's because replacement and repair costs are objective and can be verified, but cleanliness is a matter of each person's individual tastes. You need to ferret out what your landlord expects, and adopt those standards if they're reasonable—at least until you've moved out.

Letter #1:
Tenant's Cleaning Plans

1492 Fraser Avenue, #363
Chicago, Illinois, 00000

May 15, 20xx

Brett Steiner
5 Hilton Ave.
Chicago, Illinois 00000

Dear Ms. Steiner:

As you know, I gave notice on April 30, 20xx that I intended to terminate my tenancy effective May 30, 20xx.

I intend to leave the apartment clean and undamaged. Specifically, I plan to:

1. Vacuum all floors and carpets and wash kitchen and bathroom floors.
2. Wash bathroom tile and all painted surfaces.
3. Clean all bathroom and kitchen appliances with cleaning products designed for these areas; clean oven and clean refrigerator.
4. Cold-water wash the curtains in the kitchen and bathroom.
5. Wash the interior surfaces of the windows.
6. Remove all rubbish and personal items.

I believe that thoroughly accomplishing these tasks will satisfy my obligations under Illinois law to leave my rental unit clean. And since my apartment has not been damaged (beyond ordinary wear and tear), I expect a full and prompt refund of my $750 security deposit. Please let me know within five days if my cleaning plan is not acceptable to you. If I don't hear from you, I'll assume that you are in agreement with it.

Yours truly,

Stephan Pierce

Stephan Pierce

Your Cleaning Plans

Some landlords are wise enough to establish fair cleaning and damage guidelines right in the lease or rental agreement, a move-out letter, or set of building rules and regulations. But what if your lease says nothing beyond obligating you to leave the unit in "clean and acceptable condition"? If you've lived in your place long enough, you may have a good idea of your landlord's standards.

But if you have any doubt, you should seize the initiative by giving your landlord written notice of your cleaning plans—for example, washing the kitchen floor, laundering the cotton bedroom curtains, thoroughly cleaning all appliances and bathroom fixtures, and so on. Your letter should also ask your landlord to respond within a few days with any comments or disagreements with your cleaning plans. See the sample letter #1 above.

Is it really necessary to take the time and trouble to give your landlord a preview of your cleaning plans? Yes.

First, giving the landlord the chance to respond in advance to your cleaning plans puts you in the driver's seat. This type of letter of understanding legally obligates your landlord to tell you if your cleaning plans aren't sufficient. If the landlord fails to respond to your letter, you can assume that she agrees with your cleaning intentions. If, later, the landlord deducts for refinishing wooden floors when you stated that you intended to do a thorough polishing only, you have solid evidence that she is being unreasonable (assuming the floors are in decent shape).

But keep in mind that you must do a thorough job on the tasks you set yourself, and that it is always possible for you and the landlord to argue about whether you washed the floor well enough.

Telling your landlord in advance how you intend to clean might save you some trouble, too. For example, if your landlord intends to replace the bedroom drapes that you plan to dry clean, repaint the walls you intend to clean, or junk the old stove you plan to scrub, she might let you know, saving you a pile of work.

Letter #2: Tenant's Cleaning Plans

1492 Fraser Avenue, #363
Chicago, Illinois, 00000

May 15, 20xx

Brett Steiner
5 Hilton Ave.
Chicago, Illinois 00000

Dear Ms. Steiner:

As you know, on April 30, 20xx I gave notice to terminate my tenancy effective May 30, 20xx.

When I moved in on October 1, 20xx, the previous tenant had just left a day earlier. There were full garbage bags in the kitchen and entry hall; the kitchen, hallway and bathroom floors had been swept but not washed; the kitchen cabinets had peeling, sticky shelf paper; the windows had not been washed; the refrigerator still had containers of food; the oven had not been cleaned and the burners on the stove were encrusted with charred spills. After we toured the apartment and noted all of these problems on the Landlord-Tenant Checklist (copy attached), you promised to have a cleaning service come the next day.

Despite my written reminder to you the next day (copy attached), the cleaning crew never materialized. I was forced to spend six hours dealing with the mess. In case you don't remember just how bad it was, I have a set of date-stamped photos showing all the disgusting details, which I'd be happy to show you. I also have receipts for my cleaning materials.

Under state law, I am required to return the rental unit to you in substantially the same condition as I found it, minus ordinary wear and tear. I intend to live up to my legal duty. In fact, the condition of the apartment is far better than it was when I moved in. I will be here to go over the apartment with you on my last day as we arranged, and will have with me our original Checklist, my camera, and my friend Ray, who helped me clean when I moved in.

Yours truly,

Stephan Pierce

Stephan Pierce

A letter of understanding may also save you money. For example, when you suggest washing the walls with a strong cleaner, your landlord may react in horror, saying that it could strip the paint of its glossy finish. If you don't know about these risks and your cleaning makes things worse, you can be sure that your landlord will tap into your deposit.

Legally speaking, you are required only to return your rental in the same condition in which you found it, minus ordinary wear and tear. If your rental was on the grubby end of the cleanliness spectrum when you moved in, you'll hardly be in the mood to return it any cleaner. But leaving a dirty apartment, even for good reason, all but guarantees that your landlord will dip into your deposit for cleaning charges. Knowing this, you must be willing and equipped to assert your rights in a lawsuit in small claims court if you wish to get the entire deposit back. To win, you'll need to have a good deal of evidence of the rental unit's original filthy or damaged condition (such as a signed Landlord-Tenant Checklist, photos, and witnesses).

The sample letter #2 above shows you how to set up a less-than-perfect cleaning job for an apartment that was presented in less-than-perfect shape. Note how the tenant, Stephan, lets his landlord know that he has plenty of hard evidence concerning the miserable condition of the unit when he moved in.

Of course, there is the possibility that your landlord will use your letter as a point of departure, adding extra tasks from replacing degraded tile grout to painting the ceiling. If so, politely refuse, explaining that such requests are excessive.

Cleaning Thoroughly

You can't expect to get your deposit back if you've left the place a mess. So clean the place thoroughly, including all the items you promised in the letter (if any) you sent to your landlord. This doesn't normally mean you have to dry clean the drapes or wash the ceiling. A good thorough cleaning, including all appliances, fixtures, floors, and window coverings, should be adequate. Be sure to apply some extra elbow grease when cleaning the kitchen and bathrooms.

Remove all your belongings before you leave. That includes bags of garbage, clothes, food, newspapers, furniture, appliances, dishes, plants, cleaning supplies, or other items. Leaving them causes extra work for your landlord, which you'll end up paying for from your deposit. If you leave items of value behind, your landlord may, in some states, dispose of them or keep them for his benefit. Below we explain how landlords handle abandoned property.

Documenting the Condition of the Unit

In Chapter 6, we recommend that you fill out a Landlord-Tenant Checklist when you move in, documenting the condition of the rental unit. We also suggest you photograph and videotape the unit. You should do the same when you move out. Pictures will provide great visual proof of your claim if you later have to sue the landlord to get your deposit returned. (See Chapter 6 for suggestions on taking photos that you can rely on later.)

Also be sure to keep all your receipts for cleaning and repair materials, such as rental of a carpet cleaning machine or hiring a professional cleaning service, as evidence that you did clean in case you later have to sue in small claims court in order to get your deposit back.

Finally, be sure to have a friend or neighbor witness the final result. A person who helped clean often makes a very convincing witness. Make sure it's someone who will be willing to give you a signed declaration as to the condition of the unit pre- and post-cleaning; or better, someone who will testify in court on your behalf, if necessary, should you end up in court.

Arranging a Final Inspection

After you've moved your belongings out and cleaned up, and just before you return the key, ask your landlord to inspect the unit in your presence to determine whether any deductions from your security deposit are warranted.

Try to avoid having your landlord do the final inspection alone. A landlord is less likely to claim dirty or damaged conditions when a tenant is present. A few states, including Arizona and California, actually give the tenants the legal right to be present when landlords conduct the final inspection. But wherever you live, you'll want to insist on being there. Write the landlord a brief note such as the one below.

Request to Be Present at Inspection

1492 Fraser Avenue, Apt. #363
Chicago, Illinois 00000

May 24, 20xx

Brett Steiner
5 Hilton Ave.
Chicago, Illinois 00000

Dear Ms. Steiner:

As you know, on April 30, 20xx I gave notice to terminate my tenancy effective May 30, 20xx. On May 15, I wrote to you explaining my plans for cleaning the apartment. Since I didn't hear back from you, I went ahead and cleaned as planned.

I would like to arrange to meet you and conduct a final inspection of my apartment this week. Saturday morning is best for me, but I can be somewhat flexible. I have a copy of the Checklist we completed when I moved in two years ago. I'm sure that you will be pleased with the condition of the apartment.

Please call me at 123-4567 so that we can arrange for a convenient time to meet.

Yours truly,

Stephan Pierce

Stephan Pierce

When you meet to tour the apartment together, give your landlord a copy of the Landlord-Tenant Checklist you completed when you moved in and any other before-and-after proof you have that the unit is in essentially the same condition, excluding normal wear and tear. Any item that your landlord claims needs cleaning, repair, or replacement should be noted in the middle column, Condition on Departure. Where possible, also note the estimated cost of repair or replacement in the third column. An excerpt of the Checklist is shown below. See Chapter 6 for a complete Checklist.

Be ready to calmly and pleasantly assert your point of view, backed up, if possible, with photos showing the condition of the unit when you moved in. Try to work out any disagreements on the spot. If your landlord points to a damaged or dirty item that would be inexpensive to clean or replace, be willing to compromise. It is usually better to give up a few dollars than go to all the trouble of suing later. (You would sue for the portion improperly withheld.) If you come to an agreement, ask the landlord to return your security deposit before you leave.

If your landlord claims that your unit needs more cleaning or repairs, ask for a second chance to do it. By law, at least one state (Montana) requires landlords to offer tenants a second chance at cleaning (if it's done within 24 hours) before deducting cleaning charges from the security deposit.

As long as you are still technically a tenant (your 30-day notice period hasn't run out), you should have no problem. But if your time to move out is up and your landlord needs to get the apartment ready quickly for another tenant, the answer may be no, especially if repairs are required, not just cleaning.

If that happens, put your request in writing. (A sample letter is shown below.) A written request that is also turned down might serve you well if you decide later to sue over deposit money withheld for cleaning. Especially if the case is close, a judge is likely to look askance at a landlord who refused your repeated offers to do a better job.

Requesting Your Deposit in Writing

It's always a good idea to ask for the return of your deposit in a letter to your landlord. In some states, you *must* make a written "demand" for its return—if you don't, you risk losing it altogether. Even if

Request to Clean Further

75 Bolton Road
Evanston, Illinois, 00000

May 28, 20xx

Brett Steiner
5 Hilton Ave.
Chicago, Illinois 00000

Dear Ms. Steiner:

Thank you for meeting me today to go over the condition of my old apartment on Fraser Avenue (#363). My tenancy expires on May 30, although I have already moved my belongings and have moved out. I had hoped that you would approve completely of my cleaning job.

It is my understanding that you approved of the condition of the apartment except for the bathroom walls and tiles. I used a conventional household cleaner, not wanting to risk marring the surface of the tiles with anything stronger. As a result, I could not remove every bit of discoloration and mildew in the grout. You expressed disappointment at this and stated that you would have to hire a cleaning crew to do the job over, and would deduct two hours of their time (at $40 an hour) from my security deposit.

I asked you at the time, and I repeat the request now, to have the opportunity to do the work myself. I am sure that I can remove the offending stains with a stronger cleanser just as well as a cleaning company could. I know that this will mean that you will need to inspect again, but since you visit the property daily, it seems to me that this would not be an undue imposition. And because I am no longer occupying the unit, you would need to look at this one room only, since the rest of the apartment is acceptable. I can arrange to meet you at any time.

Please extend me the favor of another 10-minute inspection of the bathroom walls. Getting my entire security deposit ($750) back is very important to me, since I am facing a hefty security deposit obligation in my new duplex.

Yours truly,

Stephan Pierce

Stephan Pierce

---

your state does not require it, promptly writing to your landlord when your tenancy is up is important for several reasons:

- **Your letter gives the landlord your forwarding address.** This simple, essential information is often overlooked by tenants in a hurry to pack up and move. In some states, your landlord may keep the deposit if he can't locate you within a specified amount of time.

- **Writing a demand letter is another opportunity to build your case if you decide later to sue for the return of your security deposit.** Writing down what you think your landlord owes invites one of two responses: paying up or disputing your version. If your landlord doesn't pay and doesn't take the time or trouble to discuss the matter with you, you're in a good position to argue in court that he lost his opportunity to work things out and should now pay up.

- **Your letter makes it more likely that you'll get penalty damages if the landlord fails to follow the law.** Laws in many states penalize landlords who intentionally break security deposit laws. If you have written a clear letter that tells the landlord exactly what to do and you still don't get your deposit, the landlord certainly can't claim ignorance of the law or of your whereabouts.

If you're asking for your entire deposit back, use our form, "Demand for Return of Security Deposit" (a sample is shown below). Fill in the date and the landlord's (or manager's or management company's) address at the top. Consult your state law to calculate when, by law, your landlord should have returned the deposit. Give the landlord at least ten days before you resort to stronger measures (court).

You'll want to do your own letter, tailored to fit your circumstances, if you and the landlord have reached an understanding as to specific deductions, as illustrated in the "Demand for Partial Return of Security Deposit," below. Either send the letter certified mail (return receipt requested), or use a delivery service that will give you a receipt establishing delivery. Keep a copy of your letter and the delivery receipt—you'll need them if you end up in court.

FORM
The Nolo website includes a downloadable copy of the Demand for Return of Security Deposit form. See Appendix B for the link to the forms in this book.

If Stephan doesn't hear from Brett within a month, he'll want to send a stronger letter. An example is shown in "How to Handle Deposit Disputes," below.

Using the Deposit as Last Month's Rent

If you have not paid the rent for your last month of residence, the landlord can always apply your security deposit to this unpaid sum. It's just another way of saying that the deposit can be used to cover unpaid rent. In fact, this is exactly what you may want the landlord to do. It saves you from writing a check for the last month's rent and having to wait until after you move out to get your deposit refund.

(If your landlord collected a separate sum labeled "last month's rent," see Chapter 4.)

Demand for Partial Return of Security Deposit

75 Bolton Road

Evanston, Illinois, 00000

June 2, 20xx

Brett Steiner

5 Hilton Ave.

Chicago, Illinois 00000

Dear Ms. Steiner:

As you doubtless remember, I was your tenant in Apartment #363 at 1492 Fraser Avenue in Chicago. I paid you a deposit of $750. My tenancy ended on May 30.

Thanks for giving me the opportunity to redo the bathroom tiles and clean them to your satisfaction. We agreed yesterday that the entire apartment was clean and in good condition but for two cracked tiles on the counter. We agreed that you would deduct $75 for this damage. Since I have no unpaid rent to account for, I expect that my security deposit will be refunded in the amount of $675 to the address above.

Yours truly,

Stephan Pierce

Stephan Pierce

Landlord-Tenant Checklist

GENERAL CONDITION OF RENTAL UNIT AND PREMISES

572 Fourth St.	Apt. 11	Washington, D.C
Street Address	Unit No.	City

	Condition on Arrival	Condition on Departure	Estimated Cost of Repair/ Replacement
Living Room			
Floors & Floor Coverings	OK	OK	Ø
Drapes & Window Coverings	Miniblinds discolored	Miniblinds missing	$75
Walls & Ceilings	OK	Several holes in wall	$100
Light Fixtures	OK	OK	Ø
Windows, Screens, & Doors	Window rattles		Ø
& Locks	OK		

Demand for Return of Security Deposit

May 25, 20xx

Ms. Samuel

100 East Tenth Street

Mayflower, ME 00000

Dear _____ Ms. Samuel _____ :

On _____ April 1, 20xx _____ , we vacated the apartment at _____ 7 Bonny Court _____

and gave you our new address and phone number. As of today, we haven't received our $ 1,000 _____ security deposit, nor any accounting from you for that money. We were entitled to receive our deposit by _____ May 1, 20xx _____ . You are now _____ 25 days _____ late.

We left our apartment clean and undamaged, paid all of our rent, and gave you proper notice of our intention to move. In these circumstances, it's difficult to understand your oversight in not promptly returning our money.

Perhaps your check is in the mail. If not, please put it there promptly. Should we fail to hear from you by _____ June 5, 20xx _____ , we'll take this matter to small claims court. And please understand that if we are compelled to do this, we shall also sue you for any additional punitive damages allowed by state law.

Please mail our deposit immediately to the address below. If you have any questions, please contact us at the number below.

Very truly yours,

Michael Burns
Michael Burns

Theresa Burns
Theresa Burns

2520 Homestead Lane

Mayflower, ME 00000

555-123-4567
Home phone

555-456-7890
Work phone

If you want your landlord to apply your deposit for the last month's rent, get approval in writing. Why should your landlord object? Because the landlord can't know in advance what the property will look like when you leave. If you leave the property a mess, but the whole security deposit has gone to pay the last month's rent, there will be nothing left to use to repair or clean the property. The landlord will have to absorb the loss or sue you.

If you're a fastidious tenant who is almost sure to leave the unit in tip-top shape, your landlord may decide to take a chance that the deposit won't be needed for repairs or cleaning. Offer to let the landlord make a quick inspection first, to see that the property is clean and undamaged. Be forewarned, however, that many landlords will refuse to do a preinspection, arguing that the presence of all of your belongings will make it difficult to get an accurate picture of the condition of the entire unit.

Even if your landlord objects to your decision not to write a final rent check, the chances that you will be evicted for nonpayment of rent are slim, since you'll be out of there in a month anyway. (But don't expect a stellar recommendation from this landlord when your next one calls for a reference.)

> ⚠ **CAUTION**
>
> **If the landlord doesn't agree to your request, be sure you know your state's law before deciding not to write your last month's rent check.** In a few states, acting without your landlord's approval can be disastrous. For example, in Kansas, if you attempt to use the security deposit for the last month's rent, you lose the entire deposit and can be sued for the last month's rent besides. Minnesota and Texas also impose statutory penalties when tenants try this maneuver. Court cases in other states may reach similar conclusions. Check your state's statutes and the cases that have interpreted them before you act. (Citations to the statutes mentioned above are in "State Security Deposit Rules" in Appendix A.)

Security Deposits From Cotenants

A common dispute among roommates is what happens to the security deposit when one leaves and the others stay. If you're the one leaving, you would most certainly like your share of the deposit back when you move out. Unfortunately, you may have to wait a while.

When cotenants all sign a lease or rental agreement together, your landlord has no legal duty to return or account for any portion of the deposit until they all leave. Practically speaking, this means cotenants must work out among themselves what to do when one roommate leaves.

It's common for a new tenant to pay a departing one his share of the deposit. From the new tenant's point of view, however, this is wise only if the unit is being maintained properly, since the new tenant won't want to end up paying for damage that was caused before he moved in. If no one is replacing you, see if the other cotenants will chip in and pay you your share—but be prepared to accept less if there is damage that's attributable to you that the landlord will eventually deduct for.

Some landlords, however, will refund your share of the deposit when you leave even though it's not legally required. However, as part of doing so, the landlord will probably want to inspect the property. That's good for the new tenant, too, who gets to start with a clean slate, knowing that all damage has been noted and paid for from the former tenant's portion of the security deposit.

> **EXAMPLE:** Bill and Mark were cotenants who had each contributed $500 toward the $1,000 security deposit. Bill needed to move before the lease was up, and asked Len, their landlord, if he would accept Tom as a new cotenant. Len agreed.
>
> Bill wanted his $500 back, and although Tom was willing to contribute his share of the deposit, he did not want to end up paying for damage that had been caused before he moved in. To take care of this, Len agreed to inspect if Tom would first give him a check for $500. When he got the check, Len inspected and found $200 worth of damage. Bill disagreed, and they compromised on $150. Len deducted this amount from Bill's share of the deposit and wrote Bill a check for $350. Len left it

up to Bill and Mark to fairly apportion the responsibility for the damage.

If the landlord refuses your request to inspect and return a portion of the security deposit to the departing tenant, get together with your roommates and realistically appraise the situation. The new cotenant should be asked to pay the departing tenant a full share of the deposit if there is no damage, or a portion if there is damage attributable to the departing tenant.

How to Handle Deposit Disputes

Let's assume that several weeks have passed since you moved out and wrote to your landlord asking for your deposit to be returned. However, you haven't gotten either a check or an explanation of why the landlord is keeping your money. Or maybe you have received an itemization from the landlord—and you're convinced that the deductions are unjustified. Or maybe your landlord has violated another law, such as a requirement that you receive interest on your deposit.

Clearly, it's time to take action. Start with a simple phone call to your landlord, follow up with a letter, and, if all else fails, go to court.

Call the Landlord

Start by phoning the landlord to discuss the problem. Especially if your deposit is only a few days late, there may be a reasonable explanation for your landlord's tardiness—maybe the landlord is waiting for some repair work and doesn't yet know its exact cost. Make a note of the date and time of your phone call, and write down as many specifics of the conversation as you can remember. If you go to court, you may need to show these notes to the judge.

Make a Second Written Demand

If you didn't get a good answer and a firm promise that you'll get the deposit or itemization right away, it's time for stronger action. Write another demand letter like the one shown below. (If this if your first letter, you might want to soften the tone a bit.)

If you're tempted to skip this step because you're sure it's a waste of time, don't. Your demand letter may serve as a catalyst to get your landlord to agree to a fair settlement. Even if the landlord never reads it, setting out your case in a formal letter gives you an excellent opportunity to prepare your case for small claims court. And remember: Some state security deposit statutes require you to make a written request; and in some states, small claims court rules require you to write a demand letter before you can sue.

Your letter should lay out the reasons your landlord owes you deposit money and make it clear that if you don't get it, you plan to go to small claims court. Now, instead of being just another cranky voice on the telephone, you and your dispute assume a sobering reality to your landlord. Your landlord will realize that you won't simply go away and stop bothering him, but plan to have your day in court.

Here are some tips on writing a demand letter:

1. Concisely review the main facts. If you end up in small claims court, your letter will be read by a judge. It should explain what happened.

2. Be polite. Don't personally attack your landlord—even if you think it's deserved. The more annoying you are, the more you invite your landlord to respond similarly. Your goal is to get your landlord to make a businesslike analysis of the dispute and ask:

- What are my risks of losing?
- How much time will a defense take?
- Do I want the dispute to be decided in public?
- Even if I think the tenant is partly at fault, isn't it more cost-effective to return the deposit?

3. Ask for exactly what you want. For example, if you want your full deposit returned, ask for it.

4. Explain your legal rights. Cite state security deposit law, using the summaries in this book and the "State Security Deposit Rules" chart in Appendix A.

If your state allows extra, punitive damages when a landlord intentionally withholds a deposit, point out that you are entitled to them now. (Check your state security deposit statute for details on punitive damages.)

Second Demand for Return of Security Deposit

75 Bolton Road
Evanston, Illinois, 00000

July 15, 20xx

Brett Steiner
5 Hilton Ave.
Chicago, Illinois 00000

Dear Ms. Steiner:

As you know, until May 30, 20xx, I rented apartment #363 at 1492 Fraser Avenue in Chicago. When I moved out, the apartment was thoroughly cleaned. I recleaned the bathroom and you inspected it May 28, pronouncing the bathroom (and the rest of the unit) acceptable. Actually, I left the place in far better shape than it was when I moved in. In addition, the apartment was not damaged other than for two chipped tiles, which we agreed would cost me $75. I left owing no rent.

On June 2, 20xx, I sent you a letter asking that my deposit be refunded in the amount of $675 and gave you my new address. I called you on June 20 to remind you about returning my deposit and again gave you my new address. You assured me that you'd "Get right on it in a day or two."

As of today, I have received neither my $675 security deposit nor any accounting from you for that money. Under Illinois law (Ill. Rev. Stat. ch. 765 para. 710, 715), I was entitled to receive my deposit, including an itemization of any deductions, 30 days after my tenancy ended—that is, by June 30, 20xx. You are now over two weeks late.

If I do not receive my money by July 25, I will regard your retention of my deposit as showing bad faith and will sue you in small claims court for $1,350, which is double the amount of the deposit due as allowed under Illinois law.

Please mail my deposit immediately to the above address.

Very truly yours,

Stephan Pierce

Stephan Pierce

5. Conclude by stating you will promptly sue in small claims court if necessary. If you will be suing for extra (punitive) damages allowed under your state law, make this point, too. It will be hard for your landlord to claim blissful ignorance of the law or simple inadvertence—which might protect her from being hit by punitives—when you show the judge the letters you've written.

Keep a copy of all correspondence. You'll need them if you go to court.

Consider Compromise

If you've written your landlord a demand letter and you don't get a satisfactory response, in most states you are eligible to file suit immediately. (Some states require that you try mediation first; check your state's statute.) But before you do, try to meet the landlord halfway. You don't need to go overboard trying to reach a compromise, especially if you believe your landlord's original assessment of the cost of repairs and cleaning was grossly unfair and you believe you can prove your position in court. Just the same, it usually doesn't make sense for you to prepare a small claims case and spend time in court to argue over $50 or even $100. This is especially true because, fair or not, some judges are prone to split the difference between the landlord's and the tenant's claims.

If you and the landlord reach a compromise, it's wise to sign an agreement right away. Writing things down gives you a chance to make sure you and your landlord really agree. And if the landlord fails to honor the agreement, you can take it to small claims court. You won't have to argue over any of the underlying facts (concerning your clean or not-so-clean apartment, for example); the agreement will clearly show that the landlord promised you a certain amount of money. A sample agreement is shown below.

If you and your landlord can't arrive at a reasonable compromise, you may wish to try mediation. That's a procedure in which you meet with a neutral third person who helps you arrive at your own solution. Many cities, counties, and nonprofit organizations offer mediation services designed to help tenants and landlords. In addition, mediation may be an essential prerequisite to filing a lawsuit in small claims court. Check your state's small claims court procedures, and read the discussion on how to negotiate with landlords on various issues in Chapter 19. It also covers mediation.

Sample Agreement Regarding Return of Security Deposit

Brett Steiner, Landlord, and Stephan Pierce, Tenant, agree as follows:

1. Tenant's tenancy at 1492 Fraser Avenue, Apartment #363, Chicago, terminated on May 30, 20xx. Landlord holds a $750 security deposit.

2. Tenant left owing no unpaid rent. Landlord and Tenant have agreed that Tenant had caused $75 worth of damage to the bathroom counter tiles.

3. Tenant requested the return of $675 but has not yet received any of it.

4. Landlord will deduct an additional $25 from the deposit for recleaning of the bathroom tiles and will return $650 to Tenant by mailing a check no later than three days after the date of this Agreement.

5. In exchange for receiving the $650 as required by this Agreement, Tenant will not sue Landlord for failing to return the deposit within the time required by state law.

6. This Agreement is a final and complete resolution of the dispute over use and retention of Tenant's security deposit.

Brett Steiner	*8/20/xx*
Brett Steiner, Landlord	Date
Stephan Pierce	*8/20/xx*
Stephan Pierce, Tenant	Date

Suing Your Landlord in Small Claims Court

If the formal demand doesn't work and there is no reasonable prospect of compromise, consider suing your landlord in small claims court. It's inexpensive, usually $10 to $50, to file a case. You don't need a lawyer, and disputes typically go before a judge (there are no juries) within 30 to 60 days. The trial itself, which consists of both sides explaining what happened from their point of view and presenting any evidence or witnesses, seldom takes more than 15 or 20 minutes. The judge either announces a decision right there in the courtroom or mails it out within a few days.

By Any Other Name

We use the term small claims court here, but the exact name depends upon the state. These courts are called "Justice of the Peace," "Conciliation," "District," "Justice," "City," or "County" in different places.

You can sue your landlord for your security deposit and for interest if it's required in your state or city. In many states, you can also sue for extra punitive damages if the landlord intentionally failed to return your deposit on time. (See "Basic Rules for Returning Deposits," above.) Whether the landlord's conduct was bad enough to entitle you to punitive damages is up to the judge, but it never hurts to ask. In practice, your chances of collecting significant punitive damages will be good only if the landlord has delayed a considerable time and has no plausible explanation for his tardiness. As a general rule, you have to request damages when you file your suit. If you win, the judge will add court costs, such as filing fees, later.

The maximum amount for which you can sue in small claims court varies among the states, but in most states it's about $5,000 to $10,000. (Appendix A lists each state's limit.)

TIP

Don't wait to file your case. Each state limits the time within which lawsuits can be filed. In a dispute over a written rental agreement or lease, you probably have up to four or five years to sue. Just the same, it's foolish to wait very long, since the memories of witnesses fade (or the witnesses themselves may be impossible to find), and your landlord may even go out of business. Also, judges are not very sympathetic to old disputes.

RESOURCE

The Small Claims Court & Lawsuits section of www.nolo.com includes useful articles on each state's small claims court rules, as well as general articles, such as how to prepare evidence for a small claims suit. Also, *Everybody's Guide to Small Claims Court*, by Cara O'Neill (Nolo), explains small claims court strategy and procedure, including how and where to serve court papers, how to collect your money, and details on appeals.

Preparation: The Key to Winning

Winning your small claims court case can be easy or difficult, depending on the facts of the situation and how much homework you do before appearing in court.

First, get a copy of your state's security deposit law and any local ordinances that apply. Read these thoroughly before you go to court. You can get copies from the library or online. (See Chapter 20 for advice on legal research.)

Second, gather tangible evidence. If you simply testify that your apartment was clean and in good shape, and your landlord says just the opposite, the judge is stuck making a decision that is little more than a guess. Most judges will split the difference. If your landlord comes to court with a witness who reads off a long list of damaged and dirty conditions he claims you left behind, you may even lose.

To win, you must have enough evidence to convince the judge you are right. Ideally, preparation should start when you move into the rental unit and make a record of its condition. When you moved

out, you should have made another similar written record and taken photos. (See above.)

But even if you weren't so thorough, there are still good ways to convince the judge that you left the place in good shape. Here are kinds of evidence you can take to court:

- A clear statement of how much money your landlord owes you, the interest (if any) owed, penalties you seek, and expenses such as cleaning supplies.
- A copy of your signed lease or rental agreement and any written guidelines your landlord provided on cleaning, damage repair, and security deposits.
- Photos or a video of the premises before you moved in, which show how dirty or damaged the place was.
- Photos or a video after you left, which show no additional mess or damage.
- One, or preferably two, witnesses who were familiar with the property, saw it just after you left and will testify that the place was clean or that certain items were not damaged.
- If it's difficult for a witness to come to court, a signed letter or a statement (declaration) signed "under penalty of perjury" can be used in most states. Make sure the statement includes the date of the event, exactly what the witness saw, any credentials that make the person qualified to testify on the subject, and any other facts that bear on the dispute.
- Details on the amount of time you spent cleaning the unit.
- Copies of receipts for cleaning supplies you used in the final cleanup or for professional cleaning (such as carpets and drapes) or repair.
- A copy of the Landlord-Tenant Checklist that you filled out with the landlord when you moved in and when you moved out, signed by both you and your landlord. This is particularly important if the landlord admitted, on the Checklist, to damaged or dirty conditions when you moved in.

- Copies of all correspondence: a letter outlining your cleaning plans (if any), the demand letters, and written notes of your conversations about the deposit.
- If the landlord is overcharging for cleaning or repairs, a written estimate from another cleaning or repair service showing it would have done the job for less. For example, if your landlord claims to have paid $400 for cleaning, you could submit a statement from ABC cleaning that they charge $30 per hour and can clean a one-bedroom apartment in six hours, for a total bill of $180.
- If the landlord is charging you for a ruined item's full replacement cost or original cost, an estimate of the item's age, its expected useful lifetime, and its original cost. Amortize the cost over the item's life, and agree to pay the remaining value only. Check with appliance stores or do some research online to get original cost figures for rugs or appliances and their expected (or proven) lifetime. This process is a bit inexact but worth it if you're being hit with a hefty replacement bill for something that was on its last legs already.
- If you dispute your landlord's claim that you broke or damaged an item such as an appliance, the opinion of a repair person or other expert as to why the appliance failed.

If you take the trouble to understand your state's law and to gather good evidence, you should have no trouble convincing a judge to rule in your favor.

EXAMPLE: Shawna's landlord claims that Shawna is responsible for the broken refrigerator ice maker, claiming that she must have caused the problem by blocking the air circulation when she stuffed too much food in the freezer. Shawna, who rarely has more than a half-gallon of ice cream in her freezer, is not about to stand by and give up the $400 the landlord claims it will cost to fix the ice maker, which she is convinced was on its last legs when she moved in.

To fight back, Shawna talks to a local refrigerator repair person. He scoffs at the idea that the problem could be caused by overfilling the freezer and tells Shawna that this particular model is notorious for ice maker failures. Shawna asks him to write a letter to the court saying this, and then follows up by looking in *Consumer Reports* magazine, which lists this brand of ice maker as a problem. Shawna brings the letter and article to court, shows them to the judge, testifies that she never misused the freezer, and wins the case.

How to Present Your Case in Court

Small claims courts are informal places, intended to be used by regular folks presenting their own cases. If you do not have any experience with a court, consider watching a few cases a day or two before your case. You will see that it is a very simple procedure. Many small claims courts also provide helpful pamphlets, videos, and even computer tutorials on how small claims courts work. A few offer free legal adviser programs to help you prepare your case properly.

A few days before your case will be heard, practice your presentation in front of a tough-minded friend acting as the judge. Present your case from start to finish, introducing any witnesses and explaining evidence. Chances are that your presentation will be awkward, and you may even forget key points. Fine, keep practicing until you can make your presentation in an efficient and convincing way. Keep in mind that the judge will give you only a few minutes to make your case. Stick to the important facts.

On the day your case is to be heard, get to the court a little early and check for your courtroom (in some places referred to as a "department"). Tell the clerk or bailiff that you are present, and sit down and wait until your case is called. When your turn comes, stand at the large table at the front of the room to speak. Remember, judges hear many cases every day and will not be particularly excited by yours. If you are long-winded, your judge may stop listening and start thinking about lunch.

Start your presentation with the problem; for example, "Brett Steiner hasn't returned my security deposit to me, and it's been almost two months since I moved out of her apartment at 1492 Fraser Avenue. State law says she is supposed to return it within 30 days." Then present the directly relevant facts that explain why you should win; for example, "The apartment was clean, my rent was paid in full, and we had agreed that my deposit of $750 would be returned but for $75 in damage costs." Again, be brief and to the point; don't ramble. You may show pictures and documents to the judge. When you are done with your oral presentation, tell the judge you have witnesses who want to testify.

The landlord, of course, will also have a chance to speak. In most states, the landlord has the responsibility of proving that he's entitled to keep all or part of a deposit. If the landlord exaggerates the extent of any damage or dirt, stay cool. You should get another chance to speak—and your evidence should back up your version. If you don't have a lot of tangible evidence or witnesses, simply state the facts as you see them. For example, you might say, "Your Honor, when I moved in three years ago, the walls had not been freshly painted. And since the previous tenant lived in the unit for two years, I'm pretty sure it's been at least five years since the unit was painted. The fact that they need freshening up now is due to ordinary wear and tear, and it should be the landlord's responsibility."

If Your Landlord Doesn't Show Up

In the unlikely event your landlord doesn't show up, you'll probably win. In most states, the judge will ask you to briefly state the basic facts of your case and to provide some evidence, such as a set of photos showing the condition of the rental unit when you moved in and out. The judge may also check to see that your landlord was properly served with the court papers and may ask you a question or two to make sure there is no obvious flaw in your case. Of course, you'll still have to collect the judgment, and the landlord may appeal in some cases.

TIP

When to see a lawyer. Although generally it's not cost-effective to hire a lawyer when you head to small claims court, there is one possible exception to this rule. If your lease or rental agreement requires you to pay the landlord's attorneys' fees if the landlord wins a lawsuit, then in most states, you, too, are entitled to attorney fees if you win a lawsuit. In short, if there's a fair sum of money involved and you're confident of winning, you might look for a lawyer experienced in representing tenants to handle the matter for you if your state allows lawyers to appear in small claims court. (If it doesn't, the lawyer can at least advise you, and you should be able to collect for that, too.) Be sure you thoroughly discuss fee arrangements ahead of time. (See Chapter 20 for advice on finding and working with an attorney.)

If Your Deposit Doesn't Cover What You Owe

Tenants aren't the only ones who can use small claims court. If the security deposit doesn't cover what you owe for back rent, cleaning, or repairs, your landlord may file a small claims suit against you.

If you are sued, you should show up in court even if you think the landlord is in the right or you know you can't pay what you owe. Even if your landlord has a good case, it gives you a chance to present any facts that might reduce the amount of the judgment a little. Also, in some states, you can ask the judge to allow you to make payments in installments.

If you don't show up, the landlord will probably win by default and can collect the judgment by garnishing your wages or going after other assets, like a bank account. The judgment can be collected against you for many years and will be a negative mark on your credit file.

If you have good evidence of a valid defense, you definitely want to argue your side of things. For example, if you feel that the landlord charged too much for the cleaning job, get estimates from at least two reputable cleaning firms as to how much they would have charged. Calmly and clearly present your side of the dispute. If you have no proof about the dispute itself, you'll need to demonstrate that the landlord's case is flawed in some procedural respect—for example, the landlord failed to send an itemized list of proposed deductions, as required by your state's law.

Your Abandoned Property

If you've handled your move-out in a way that maximizes your chances of getting your security deposit back—cleaning thoroughly and doing a final walk-through with the landlord—it's unlikely that you'll be leaving anything behind, least of all items of value. Even the most organized tenant, however, can inadvertently miss something—for example, you might neglect a closet or forget the storage area in the garage; or walk out thinking that your partner had picked up everything ("What? I thought *you* had the laptop!"). And, let's face it—when the U-Haul is packed and the engine is running, the temptation to leave a bag full of junk for the landlord to deal with may be just too great to resist. Far too often, however, you realize later that the bag contained something you really wanted to keep.

Tenants who leave involuntarily face a higher risk of leaving something behind. If your tenancy is terminated on short notice and you decide to leave rather than fight, you may not have the time to double-check for missed belongings. Tenants who have lost an eviction lawsuit and wait until the sheriff or constable arrives to take their belongings off the property for them face the greatest danger of not being able to account for all of their possessions when the dust settles.

Regardless of the reason why your things are still on the landlord's property, you'll want to know how, if at all, you can get them back. First, understand that if the items are obvious trash, the landlord can dispose of them immediately. This means that if a reasonable person would conclude that an item had no value, the landlord is on solid ground when he tosses it—even if, to you, it has enormous sentimental value or is even a valuable

antique or collectible. Landlords aren't expected to be sensitive to your sentiments, nor need they be professional appraisers.

But for things that are clearly of some value—such as a bicycle, a stereo, clothes, or furniture—it's another story. In some states, landlords face serious liability for disposing of your personal property (other than obvious trash) unless they follow specific state rules. Typically, the more valuable the property left behind by a tenant, the more formalities the landlord must comply with when disposing of it. Not surprisingly, states that heavily regulate other aspects of landlords' dealings with tenants also impose complicated requirements on how they must handle abandoned property. States with fewer laws governing the landlord-tenant relationship tend to pay scant attention to this subject.

This section provides an overview of how to go about reclaiming your abandoned property. Because state laws vary so much, we cannot give you detailed state-by-state information on what to do and expect from your landlord. For this reason, it is critical that you read your own state statute for details on issues such as how your landlord must notify you and how much time you'll have before the landlord may dispose of or sell your things. In addition, you would be wise to check with your local tenants' association or state consumer protection agency to make sure that the process set out in your statute is all you need to know. In some states, courts have modified the procedures in the statutes, often imposing additional requirements—and unfortunately, legislatures don't always revisit their statutes to bring them into line with court-ordered changes. The "State Laws on Handling Abandoned Property" chart in Appendix A gives you citations to your state's statutes and includes some case citations.

Why Did You Move Out?

In many states, the landlord's options when dealing with your property will differ depending on the circumstances of your departure. To understand the issue, let's look at the reasons tenants leave. Here are typical scenarios:

- You decide to move at the end of a lease or after giving a termination notice. In this situation, many states give the landlord maximum flexibility to dispose of leftover belongings.
- You decide to move after receiving a termination notice (even one for cause, such as nonpayment of rent). Many states give the landlord maximum flexibility to dispose of leftover belongings in this situation.
- You are physically evicted along with your personal belongings, which may be dumped on the street or sidewalk by the sheriff. Some states require landlords to take more pains with the property of a tenant who has been evicted—though some require less efforts.
- You simply move out without notice. In a few states, property belonging to tenants who move out unexpectedly must be treated differently from property that's left after a clearly deliberate move.

When you read your state's law, be on the lookout for different rules based on the reason for your departure.

Planned Moves

If you have left voluntarily, in most states the landlord will have considerable latitude when it comes to dealing with abandoned property. The reasoning here is that tenants who decide upon and plan their own departure—even the ones who leave after receiving a three-day notice—have time to pack or dispose of their belongings themselves. Tenants who fail to take care of business are in no position to demand that the landlord handle their property with kid gloves—and many state laws don't require that landlords do so.

Evicted Tenants

Law enforcement officials who physically evict tenants will also remove property from the rental unit. In these situations, tenants arguably have less opportunity to arrange for proper packing, storing, or moving than they would if they were moving voluntarily (even though most states give tenants a few days' warning of the sheriff's impending visit). For this reason, landlords in some states must make more of an effort to preserve the property, locate the tenant, and wait before selling or disposing of items left behind. Typically, law enforcement officials are permitted to place the tenant's possessions on the sidewalk or street; then the landlord may be required to step in and store the possessions.

Paradoxically, some states take the opposite approach, reasoning that a tenant who has lost an eviction lawsuit isn't entitled to special treatment when it comes to reclaiming items left in the rental unit.

Unannounced Departures

Odd as it seems, it's not unusual for tenants to simply disappear with no notice, leaving considerable belongings behind. Sometimes, the tenant is behind on the rent and figures that abandoning his possessions will be cheaper, in the long run, than paying the rent. Here again, your state may impose special procedures that may require the landlord to store the property for a significant time or make extra efforts to locate the tenant.

Although landlords chafe at the notion that they must take special care of the belongings of someone who has left without notice, there is a very good reason behind the rule. It protects tenants who have *not* abandoned the tenancy or their possessions, but have gone on an extended trip or vacation and simply didn't tell the landlord. By making the landlord take special pains to determine that the tenant is gone for good, it's likely that the landlord will learn that you plan to return. In the meantime, your goods will be safe.

When You're Behind in the Rent

If you have moved voluntarily, been evicted, or simply disappeared but also owe back rent or money for damages, you might expect that your landlord would take or sell whatever property of value that's left behind. As tempting as this course appears, it's a risky one in many states—even if the landlord has a court judgment for money damages.

Distress and Distraint

A few states still have statutes on the books that provide for "distress" or "distraint." These were medieval procedures that allowed a landlord who was owed money, after or even during the tenancy, to simply grab his tenant's possessions. In the words of one judge, it "allowed a man to be his own avenger." In America, the practice of requiring security deposits was developed in states that did not allow a landlord to use distress and distraint.

This crude, quick, and drastic remedy was the ultimate in self-help. It won't surprise you to learn that in states that still have laws providing for distress or distraint, courts have stepped in and ruled them unconstitutional, or have added so many safeguards (notice, a hearing, and so on) that the original process is unrecognizable. If you encounter a distress or distraint statute when reading your state's laws, don't assume that your landlord will swoop in and grab your stuff. Chances are your state's courts have imposed so many restrictions that the process is too complicated to be worth it.

Some states do allow the landlord to keep or sell abandoned property if the tenant owes money, even if there is no court judgment directing the tenant to pay. In legal parlance, the landlord has an "automatic lien" on your belongings. This differs from the normal lien process, which involves formally recording the creditor's claim (the landlord's lien) against the tenant's property, then "getting in line" in case others have filed ahead of the landlord.

If your state statute gives your landlord a lien on a tenant's property, you may not see it again, although some statutes require the landlord to publicize their intent to keep an item before it definitively becomes theirs. Many states that give landlords an automatic lien will exempt certain

items, such as season-appropriate clothing, blankets, tools, and things needed for a minor child's education, from the landlord's grasp. If the landlord takes an item on which you still owe money (furniture purchased with an installment plan, for example), he may end up in a fight with the merchant, but that spat doesn't concern (or benefit) you.

Legal Notice Requirements

Many states require landlords to provide tenants written notice that they are holding abandoned property. A few states even provide a form, which you'll see printed right in the statute. Typically, the notice must give the tenant a set amount of time to reclaim the property, after which the landlord can take specific steps. Some state rules require specific information in the notice, such as:

- **A detailed description of the property left behind.** This inventory of the abandoned property should be specific but need not involve snooping. Landlords shouldn't open locked trunks or suitcases; photographs or videotapes are often used.
- **The estimated value of the abandoned property.** This is basically the landlord's estimate of what he could get for it at a well-attended flea market or garage sale.
- **Where the property may be claimed.** Many states sensibly require landlords to provide the address of the rental premises or an outside storage place.
- **The deadline for the tenant to reclaim property, such as seven or ten days.** This is usually set by state law.
- **What will happen if property is not reclaimed.** This also may be set by state law.

What Will Happen to Your Property

Getting property back begins with some very commonsense steps: Contact the landlord and give a definite day and time when you'll be back to pick it up. If the landlord has stored it, you will have to pay a reasonable fee. If you've received a notice from the landlord that the property is being held, follow the instructions on the notice for reclaiming your goods.

In some states, landlords are pretty much free to do what they want if the tenant does not respond within the specified amount of time, such as 30 days—that is, they may throw the property out, sell it, or donate it to a nonprofit organization that operates second-hand stores. In some states, as explained above, landlords can use the property to satisfy unpaid rent or damages, or may even be allowed to keep it when there's no debt. Other states require them to give the property to the state. Depending on how thoroughly your state has legislated in this area, there may be rules on the following issues:

- **Procedures based on the value of the property.** Several states allow landlords to keep or dispose of property only if the expense of storing or selling it exceeds a specified figure (such as a few hundred dollars) or the property's value.
- **Sale of abandoned property.** Some states require landlords to inventory, store, and sell tenants' property. A few require landlords to sell the property at a public sale (supervised by a licensed and bonded public auctioneer), after first publishing a notice in the newspaper.
- **Proceeds of sale of property.** States that require landlords to store and sell the property on behalf of the tenant also allow them to use any money they make from the sale to cover the costs of advertising and holding the sale and storing the property. For example, you may be charged for the prorated daily rental value for keeping the property on the landlord's premises or any out-of-pocket costs the landlord incurs for renting storage space (including moving the property to the storage space). As explained

above, some states allow landlords to use the proceeds to pay for any money owed by the tenant—for example, for unpaid rent or damage to the premises. In many states, the excess proceeds of selling the tenant's property belongs to the tenant, or the landlord may be required to pay the balance to a government agency, such as the State Treasurer.

Landlord Liability for Damage to or Loss of Your Property

Although there are lots of states with laws governing how landlords should handle abandoned property, there is no guarantee that your landlord will comply. There's always the possibility that the landlord will dispose of it, keep it, sell it, or return it damaged. Your options depend on how extensively your state has protected you in this situation (you must read and understand your state's law). In general, here's what you can expect.

Property Returned But Damaged

A landlord will not generally be held liable for damage to property unless this occurs through his or her negligent care of your property. Whether the landlord has been negligent will depend on the circumstances. For example, storing your laptop outside, exposed to the sun and weather, would be considered negligent by most judges. Placing your photo albums in a garage where they were gnawed on by mice might not be.

If you decide to seek legal redress for damage to your property, begin by writing a letter explaining the problem and the amount you want. If this produces no results, write another letter and mention that you'll sue if the matter isn't resolved. Then, sue if necessary. Unless the amount exceeds your state's small claims limit, you'll want to use that in court. Follow the advice in Chapter 19 for presenting a case in small claims court.

Property the Landlord Has Kept or Sold

As explained above, some states allow landlords to sell or keep property to satisfy outstanding tenant debts for damage or back rent. After checking your state's law and rechecking your own records, you may conclude that the landlord had no basis to keep or sell the property. If so, follow the advice just above by writing a letter and suing if necessary. Your legal theory will be that the landlord has "converted" the property to his own use, without your permission.

When the Landlord Hasn't Followed the Rules Exactly

After checking your state's law, you may discover that the landlord followed the procedure, but not exactly—and now you don't have your goods. For example, the landlord may have given you notice and time to respond, but the time to collect may have been shorter than provided by the statute. You may feel that, had you been given the proper amount of time to get your things, you would have done so. But now they're gone. What to do? Unfortunately, you won't necessarily have a rock-solid case against the landlord for the value of your belongings. State statutes vary tremendously in how they'll punish landlords who haven't followed the rules. Keep in mind that many judges simply won't penalize a landlord who attempted to comply with the law—especially in view of your carelessness in leaving the items behind.

Termination Notices Based on Nonpayment of Rent and Other Illegal Acts

Termination Notices.. 304

    Required Grace Periods 305

    Paying Rent After You Get a Termination Notice.. 305

Other Violations of the Lease or Rental Agreement.. 306

Violations of Your Legal Responsibilities as a Tenant 307

Illegal Activity on the Premises... 308

Negotiating With the Landlord 308

    When You're at Fault.. 309

    When You've Done Nothing Wrong.. 309

Getting Help From a Mediator 310

Refusing to Move Out 310

    When You're in the Right 310

    When the Landlord Is Retaliating.. 312

    Buying Time (at a Price).. 312

Cutting Your Losses and Moving... 312

I f a tenant screws up in any of a hundred possible ways—by paying the rent late, keeping a dog in violation of a no-pets clause in the lease, throwing loud parties that disturb neighbors—the landlord can terminate the tenancy. Termination is the first step toward an eventual eviction. The landlord sends you a notice announcing that your tenancy is over and that if you don't leave, he'll go to court and sue for eviction. Or the notice may give you a few days to clean up your act (pay the rent, find a new home for the dog). If you leave (or reform) as directed, no one goes to court.

Eviction itself—that is, physically throwing you and your possessions out of the property—generally can't be done until the landlord has gone to court and proved that you've done something wrong that justifies eviction. And even if the landlord wins the eviction lawsuit, he can't just move you and your things out onto the sidewalk. In most states, he has to hire the sheriff or marshal to perform that unpleasant task.

This chapter explains when and how a landlord can terminate your tenancy. It also explains some strategies you may want to consider if you are the unhappy recipient of a landlord's pink slip.

 RELATED TOPIC

Also covered in this book:

- Terminations when you haven't done anything wrong: Chapter 15.
- Overview of the eviction process, including illegal "self-help" evictions: Chapter 18.
- State laws that require your landlord to give you proper notice before beginning an eviction: Appendix A.

Termination Notices

In most states, landlords must follow specific rules and procedures to end a tenancy. Before filing an eviction lawsuit (sometimes called an unlawful detainer, or UD lawsuit), the landlord must give you a properly written notice describing a valid reason why the landlord wants you to leave.

An eviction lawsuit may be thrown out if the termination notice is not written and delivered correctly. Most states require termination notices to be written and delivered ("served") according to very picky rules that dictate the information contained and dates mentioned. Some states even specify the type size of the notice and method of delivery. Check your state's statutes to determine whether the notice you received complies with the law. If it does not, you may be able to defeat the landlord's eviction lawsuit on this basis. But a determined landlord will be simply delayed, not deterred. If you prove that the landlord's notice was faulty, you'll probably receive a correct one very soon after.

If a landlord wants you to leave because of some wrongdoing on your part, you'll receive one of three different types of termination notices. Although terminology varies somewhat from state to state, the substance of the three types of notices is remarkably the same.

- **Pay Rent or Quit** notices are used when the tenant has not paid the rent. You are given a few days (three to five in most states) to pay or move out ("quit"). If you don't, the landlord can file for eviction. But not every state requires a landlord to give you this chance to pay the rent; in a few states, if you fail to pay rent on time, the landlord can simply demand that you leave (see "Unconditional Quit," below).
- **Cure or Quit** notices are typically given after a violation of a term or condition of the lease or rental agreement, such as a no-pets clause or the promise to refrain from making excessive noise. Typically, you are given a set amount of time in which to correct, or "cure," the violation; if you fail to do so, you must move in order to avoid an eviction lawsuit.
- **Unconditional Quit** notices are the harshest of all. They order you to vacate the premises with no chance to pay the rent or correct your violation of the lease or rental agreement. In

most states, unconditional quit notices are allowed only when the tenant has repeatedly:

- violated a lease or rental agreement clause
- been late with the rent
- seriously damaged the premises, or
- engaged in illegal activity.

Many states have all three types of notices on the books. But Unconditional Quit notices are the only notice statutes in Louisiana and Texas. Of course, Louisiana and Texas landlords may voluntarily give you a chance to pay the rent or correct your behavior, but no state law requires them to do it.

The tables in Appendix A ("State Laws on Termination for Nonpayment of Rent," "State Laws on Termination for Violation of Lease," and "State Laws on Unconditional Quit Terminations") give the details and citations to your state's statutes.

The number one reason for getting kicked out of a rental is—surprise!—not paying the rent on time. If you are late with the rent, landlords in most states can immediately send you a termination notice.

Fortunately, in most states the termination notice must give you a few days—usually three to five—in which to pay up. The exact number of days varies from state to state. (For details, see "State Laws on Termination for Nonpayment of Rent" in Appendix A.)

EXAMPLE: Willy's $1,200 rent was due on the first of the month. When he had not paid by the third, his landlord sent him a five-day Pay or Quit notice. Willy understood that he had to pay his rent by the end of the eighth day of the month in order to avoid being sued for eviction. On the seventh, Willy paid the entire rent of $1,200, avoiding a lawsuit that would have surely led to his eviction.

Unfortunately, if your state does not require the landlord to give you a few days to scrape the rent together, your landlord may immediately terminate your tenancy for not paying the rent. Usually, you have a few days before the landlord can file for eviction. Of course, even in the harshest states, some landlords will allow you to stay on if you pay

reasonably quickly and convincingly argue that you'll pay your rent on time in the future.

Required Grace Periods

A handful of states do not let the landlord send a termination notice (either a Pay or Quit notice or an Unconditional Quit notice) until the rent is a certain number of days late. In these states, tenants enjoy a statutory "grace period." (Details are in "State Laws on Termination for Nonpayment of Rent" in Appendix A.) If you live in one of these states, haven't paid the rent, and receive a Pay or Quit notice, you have a pretty good cushion before your landlord can file for eviction: the grace period plus the time specified in the Pay or Quit notice.

EXAMPLE: Lara, a Maine tenant, couldn't pay her rent on time. State law required the landlord to wait until the rent was seven days late before he could send a termination notice. He did so on the eighth, giving Lara notice that she must pay or move within seven days. In all, Lara had 14 days in which to pay the rent before her landlord could file for eviction.

TIP
Late rent fees are unaffected by Pay or Quit time periods or statutory grace periods. If you are subject to late rent fees, they'll kick in as soon as your lease or rental agreement (or in some states, state law) says they can. The number of days specified in your Pay or Quit notice will not affect them, nor will a legally required grace period. (Chapter 3 discusses late fees.)

Paying Rent After You Get a Termination Notice

If you are late with the rent and get a termination notice—whether or not it gives you a few days to pay the rent—call the landlord immediately and try to work something out. "Negotiating With the

Landlord," below, offers some pointers on dealing with the landlord. Here are the legal rules.

Paying the Whole Rent

If the landlord has sent you a termination notice but then accepts rent for the entire rental term, you are entitled to stay for that period. In most states, it's as if you paid on time in the first place.

> **EXAMPLE:** Zoe's rent was due on the first of the month. She didn't pay on time, and her landlord sent her a three-day Pay or Quit notice. Zoe borrowed money from her parents and paid on the third day, saving her tenancy and avoiding an eviction lawsuit.

In some states, however, your late payment may come back to haunt you if you are late again, as explained below.

If You're Chronically Late

In several states, landlords don't have to give you a second chance to pay the rent if you are habitually late. Typically, they are legally required to give you a chance to pay and stay only once or twice within a certain period.

Some states insist that the landlord must have given you a written Pay or Quit notice for the first late payment, so that there is proof that you were late. Other statutes allow the Unconditional Quit notice merely for "repeated lateness." In that case, the landlord need not have given you a notice to pay or quit for the first tardiness.

 CAUTION

Don't wear your landlord's patience thin. Even if your landlord accepts late rent without giving you a Pay or Quit notice ("writing you up," landlords call it), don't count on endless forbearance. Remember, unless you have a lease, in most states the landlord can terminate your tenancy with a 30-day notice. Even if you live in a rent control area that requires landlords to have good reason to evict you, repeatedly paying late is ample legal reason to evict. ("Negotiating With the Landlord," below, explains how to protect yourself when negotiating late rent payments.)

If you receive a Pay or Quit notice, don't assume that you have to pack up and move immediately. "Negotiating With the Landlord," below, explores your options.

Making a Partial Rent Payment

Some tenants believe that having the landlord accept a partial payment of overdue rent after receiving a Pay or Quit (or Unconditional Quit) notice means that the landlord can't go ahead with an eviction. Sorry, but the most that you've bought is a little time. If the landlord accepts an amount of rent that covers only part of what you owe (for past months or even just the current month), that will, in most states, cancel the effect of the notice. But your landlord can pocket your offering with one hand and simultaneously serve you with a new notice with the other, demanding that you pay the new balance or leave.

> **EXAMPLE:** Danny's rent of $950 was due on the first of the month. Danny didn't pay January's rent and didn't have enough for February, either. On February 2, his landlord sent him a three-day notice to pay $1,900 or leave. Danny paid $950 on February 3 and thought that he'd saved his tenancy. He was amazed when, later that day, his landlord handed him a new three-day notice to pay $950 or leave. The landlord filed for eviction on February 7 when Danny failed to pay.

Other Violations of the Lease or Rental Agreement

In addition to nonpayment of rent, landlords may terminate a tenancy if you violate other terms of the lease or rental agreement. Common examples are:

- keeping a pet in violation of a no-pets rule
- bringing in an unauthorized tenant
- subleasing or assigning without the landlord's permission, and
- repeatedly violating "house rules" that are part of the lease or rental agreement, such as

using common areas improperly, making too much noise, having unruly guests, or abusing recreation facilities.

"Waste" and "Nuisance"

If you receive a termination notice based on your behavior, you may encounter two archaic legal terms that need a bit of explaining:

Waste. A tenant who either intentionally or through extreme carelessness damages the landlord's property is said to have committed waste. Waste does not include normal wear and tear or accidents that are the result of simple carelessness. For example, a carpet that needs to be replaced because your fish tank inexplicably sprung a leak would probably not constitute waste; but if you turn the dining room into a motorcycle repair shop, ruining the carpet in the process, you can expect a termination notice based on waste.

Nuisance. Public nuisances are activities that result in a substantial danger to the health or safety of occupants or neighbors, such as drug dealing. Private nuisances are activities, not necessarily illegal, that seriously limit the neighbors' ability to use and enjoy their homes, such as playing music so loudly that no one can sleep or using the backyard for midnight volleyball tournaments every Friday and Saturday night. Many state statutes allow a landlord to terminate a tenancy based on either form of nuisance. (Chapter 14 explains how to use public nuisance laws to pressure a landlord to evict troublemaking tenants.)

The laws in most states insist that the landlord give you an opportunity to correct, or "cure," the violation before the tenancy can end. You'll get a "Cure or Quit" notice, giving you about five to 30 days to mend your ways. However, there are two important "but ifs" that can limit your chances to clean up your act and avoid the premature end of your tenancy:

Repeated violations. If you have violated the same lease clause two or more times within a certain period of time, you'll probably lose the right to a second chance. The landlord may give you an Unconditional Quit notice instead.

The violation cannot be corrected. Some lease violations cannot be corrected because the effect of the violation is permanent. For instance, suppose your lease contains the common prohibition against making alterations or improvements without the landlord's consent. Without asking, you remove and discard the living room wallpaper, which you think is surpassingly ugly but your landlord considers a national treasure. He can hardly demand that you cease violating the lease clause, because it is simply too late to save the wallpaper. If a lease violation cannot be cured, the landlord may serve you with an Unconditional Quit notice.

If you get a notice telling you to cease a curable violation of your lease or rental agreement, your response will depend on the legitimacy of the landlord's claim. See "Negotiating With the Landlord," below, for suggestions.

Violations of Your Legal Responsibilities as a Tenant

Virtually every state allows landlords to terminate a tenancy if a tenant has violated basic responsibilities imposed by law. These include the duty to maintain at least minimally acceptable housekeeping standards and to refrain from highly disruptive activities. For example, a tenant who commits any of the following acts is a likely candidate for a termination notice:

- grossly deficient housekeeping practices that cause an unhealthy situation, such as allowing garbage to pile up
- seriously misusing appliances, like damaging the oven while attempting to clean it with steel wool
- repeatedly interfering with other tenants' ability to peacefully enjoy their homes, such as hosting late parties, playing incessant loud music, or running a noisy small business (repairing cars in the driveway of a rental duplex, for example)
- substantially damaging the property—for instance, knocking holes in the walls or doors, and

- allowing or participating in illegal activities on or near the premises, such as drug dealing or gambling.

Many careful landlords incorporate these obligations into their leases or rental agreements. But even if they are not mentioned in these documents, you are still legally bound to observe them.

If you or your guests substantially damage the premises, expect an Unconditional Quit notice. The law does not require landlords to give tenants accused of serious misbehavior a second chance. You'll probably get only five to ten days to move out. The details are in "State Laws on Unconditional Quit Terminations" in Appendix A.

Illegal Activity on the Premises

In recent years, many states have responded aggressively to widespread drug dealing in residential neighborhoods by making it easier for landlords to evict based on these activities. Indeed, in some states a landlord must evict known drug dealers or users or risk having authorities close down or even confiscate the entire property. (This process, known as "forfeiture," is explained in Chapter 14). To say the least, the threat of losing their rental property has motivated many landlords to quickly evict tenants they suspect are engaging in illegal acts.

The landlord usually doesn't have to wait until the tenant is convicted of a crime or even arrested. In some states, landlords may evict as long as they have a "reasonable suspicion" that illegal activity is afoot and the tenant or the tenant's guests are involved. By contrast, in others an eviction for illegal drug activity may not begin unless there's been a criminal conviction for criminal acts on the rented premises.

Evictions based on criminal activity are often called "expedited evictions" because courts push them through and send law enforcement out to finish the job quicker than for a normal eviction. Expedited evictions are preceded by an Unconditional Quit notice that tells the tenant to move out (and do it quickly). If the tenant stays, the landlord can go to court and file for eviction. The court hearing on the eviction is typically held within a few days, and, if the landlord wins, the tenant is given little time to move. Details are set out in "State Laws on Unconditional Quit Terminations" in Appendix A.

Negotiating With the Landlord

If you receive a termination notice, you may experience at least a momentary surge of panic, despair, or anger. Do you have to move immediately, or can you buy some time? What if you think the landlord is wildly exaggerating the problem? What will happen if you don't move out when you're supposed to?

Your best response to a termination notice will depend on whether and how long you would like to stay and whether you have a good defense to the landlord's justification for giving you the termination notice. You'll also want to consider the big picture: the time and trouble it will take you to fight an eviction, and the possible effect a lawsuit may have on your credit rating and chances for future rentals, even if you win.

If you don't want to move, negotiation should be your first response—regardless of the merits of your defense. For example, if there is some validity behind your landlord's termination notice—if you are, in fact, late with the rent, or your last two parties truly were a bit raucous—your best bet is to meet with your landlord and agree on making some changes in the future. Don't be shy about negotiating. After all, from your landlord's point of view, striking a deal can make far more sense than going to court to evict you. Remember, lawsuits are time-consuming, expensive, and filled with technicalities; they are certainly a lot less attractive, businesswise, than negotiating a firm settlement that the landlord believes you will abide by.

It goes without saying that a landlord who perceives you as an inveterate troublemaker is unlikely to want to bargain. And, of course, some landlords are so unapproachable or irrational that meeting on a one-to-one basis is sure to be fruitless. If so, you'll have to consider one of the options covered in the two sections below.

Suggestions on how to negotiate with the land-lord are also covered in Chapter 15. All of the considerations explained there also apply in the situations discussed in this chapter. But there are additional strategies to consider.

When You're at Fault

If the landlord has a valid reason for terminating your tenancy, you'll find that negotiation is most likely to work under two conditions:

- you have generally been a stable, law-abiding tenant, and
- the alleged violation is relatively minor and can be completely remedied.

For example, if you've kept your son's dog for a couple of weeks in violation of the no-pets rule, and the animal has not caused substantial damage or annoyance, your landlord might give you a few extra days (beyond the time specified in the Cure or Quit notice) to find a home for the pooch. Similarly, if the landlord is mad because you've had an overnight guest a few too many times in violation of the lease clause, offer proof of your changed ways, in that your pal has:

- moved on (show him your friend's new lease)
- agreed not to stay over on a regular basis in the future, or
- wants to become a tenant (your roommate) for a reasonable increase in your rent.

If you're late with the rent, an offer to pay part now and the rest on your next payday might mollify the landlord. (It's even better to tell the landlord if you anticipate a payment problem and set up a partial payment agreement in advance; see Chapter 3.) Other strategies include offering to make payments in person for the next three months or, if checks have been bouncing, paying with a money order rather than a check. To ensure that there will be a sure source of rent money, offer to add a parent or friend as a cosigner on the lease or rental agreement.

As you negotiate, keep these points in mind:

- Emphasize your track record as a desirable tenant.
- Explain that the problem can be easily resolved, will leave no lasting ill effects, and won't happen again.
- If possible, offer to compensate the landlord in place of moving out—for example, if the landlord is furious at your "remodeling" work in the kitchen, which he believes was done badly, offer to pay for further work that will remedy the situation.
- As subtly as possible, point out to the landlord that compromising with you is far less expensive and time-consuming than going to court to evict you.
- Remember that it may be to your advantage, too, to live with a less-than-perfect solution rather than take the time to respond to—and possibly lose—an eviction lawsuit.

TIP
If the manager is unreasonable, try to meet and deal with the owner.

When You've Done Nothing Wrong

If a termination notice accuses you of something you did not do—or, at least, did not intend to do—you're in a difficult position. True, if the case goes to court, the landlord will have the job of proving your misdeeds. But short of that, during informal negotiations you must convince the landlord that you're not guilty. And, of course, it's never easy—and sometimes impossible—to get some people to contemplate the possibility that they have exaggerated the situation or are just plain mistaken. Here are some approaches that may be useful in your situation:

- **The landlord has made a mistake.** The landlord thinks you were the one responsible for the mess left in the common room, or were the host of the destructive wild party. Unlike TV lawyers, you may not be able to produce the culprit, but you may be able to bring evidence

—for example, statements from neighbors—that will establish your blamelessness. Here you need not only evidence, but a good deal of tact. Don't rub your landlord's face in his error. Not only may this poison your future relations, it's also likely to cause him to terminate your month-to-month tenancy or refuse to renew your lease when it runs out.

- **You made a good-faith error.** You violated a lease or rental agreement term, but really didn't intend to do so. For example, perhaps you made the common mistake of assuming that all tenants enjoy a legal grace period when it comes to paying rent late before a termination notice can be sent. Arriving with your entire month's rent and honestly explaining your confusion to the landlord may get results.

Getting Help From a Mediator

In many areas, community mediation programs—or sometimes even mediation programs limited to landlord-tenant disputes—are available to help feuding landlords and tenants. They can be a huge help when direct negotiation with your landlord fails or your landlord refuses to negotiate. To find out if such a program exists, call your city government (manager or mayor), county offices, or court clerk.

Even if you are sure your landlord is an unmovable rock, mediation is worth a try. One big advantage to this approach is that you don't have to call a person whom you are mad at (and who may even refuse to talk to you). Instead, case workers at the mediation program will contact the landlord for you and set up the session. At the mediation session, a skilled person—the mediator—will attempt to help you both craft an acceptable compromise. Remarkably, most mediation programs report a better-than-50% success rate working with people who believed no compromise was possible. Chapter 19 gives details on using mediation to resolve landlord-tenant disputes.

Refusing to Move Out

When the deadline in your termination notice passes, you will not be automatically evicted. In almost every state, the landlord must file and win an eviction lawsuit before the sheriff or marshal can physically evict you. It follows that if you and the landlord haven't arrived at a solution, you face two choices:

- abide by the demands of the termination notice, or
- force the landlord to start eviction proceedings.

Refusing to obey a termination notice makes sense in three situations: when the landlord's reasons for terminating your tenancy are wrong, when they are illegal, or (possibly) if you need to buy time to find another place.

Depending on the state, your case will be heard in a formal trial court, a small claims court, or an informal landlord-tenant court. If you're headed for formal court, you may want to hire a lawyer. Chapter 18 gives an overview of eviction lawsuits.

When You're in the Right

The most obvious reason to ignore a termination notice and fight an eviction lawsuit is if you're right and you're prepared to take the time and the risk of going to court to prove it. For example, suppose, despite your repeated requests over a reasonable period of time, your landlord failed to replace your broken heater, with the result that you eventually called a heater service and had it fixed yourself. After deducting the cost of the repair from the next month's rent, you received a Pay or Quit notice. If you carefully read Chapter 8 and followed your state's law allowing you to make the repair, and have documented your communications with the landlord, you will probably be in no mood to move or even compromise.

As any lawyer or citizen who has been through a lawsuit will tell you, however, being in the right is no guarantee that you will prevail in court. You must have the law and the facts on your side—and sometimes a fair amount of luck besides.

If you're headed for court, no matter what the reason, check these points:

Did the landlord comply with the notice requirements to end your tenancy? Carefully read your state's entries on the three tables in Appendix A ("State Laws on Termination for Nonpayment of Rent," "State Laws on Termination for Violation of Lease," and "State Laws on Unconditional Quit Terminations") and compare them with the notice that you have received. Here are some common landlord mistakes you'll want to check for:

- Did the landlord give you the correct notice? For example, if you received an Unconditional Quit notice when you were entitled to a Cure or Quit notice, this is a serious error. Failure to use the right notice is probably the most common landlord mistake, and often results in a judge refusing to grant an eviction. A landlord can start over with the proper notice.

- Did the landlord deliver the notice to you in the way required by your state law? For example, did the person who served the notice attempt to do so personally?

- Did the termination notice contain the legally required wording? For example, many states require the landlord to explain, in plain English, exactly what you've done (or not done) that justifies the notice. In these states, a notice is legally insufficient if it simply says that you have five days to cease violation of the lease or leave. The landlord must explain, for example, that you owe a specified amount of rent, or that the lease violation consists of your repeated use of the pool at night, which is prohibited in your lease.

- Did a lawyer who regularly collects rent debts send your notice? Under the Federal Debt Collection Practices Act ("FDCPA"), written pay or quit demands signed by attorneys who regularly collect rent debts violate federal law unless they afford you 30 days' notice (rather than the minimum required under state law) (FDCPA, 15 U.S. Code Ann. §§ 1692 et seq.; *Romea v. Heiberger & Associates*, 988 F.Supp 712 (S.D. N.Y. 1997) aff'd 163 F.3d 111 (2d Cir. 1998)). If you received a rent demand notice from a lawyer that gives you less than 30 days to pay the rent or move out, you may be able to seek damages against the lawyer under the FDCPA. A notice issued by a lawyer that provides less than 30 days' notice is nevertheless valid. If you do not pay the rent demanded or move out within the time provided, the landlord may still commence an eviction proceeding against you based on the rent demand.

> **TIP**
> **Consider doing some legal research.** You may want to go to your local law library or online to read the termination notice laws and the cases that have interpreted them before concluding whether the notice was properly chosen, drafted, and given. See Chapter 20 for advice.

- **Do you have documentary evidence?** Obviously, it's helpful in court to back up your claims with as much hard-copy evidence as possible. For example, if the basis of the termination is that you have violated a rental rule (by using the pool at midnight), yet no rule prohibiting night swimming appears in the lease or house rules, be sure that you have a copy of the lease and rules.

- **Do you have visual evidence?** The chances for winning will increase if you can give a judge or jury a real picture of the situation. If you withheld rent because of a leaking roof, take a picture of the sodden wall and your bucket of water.

- **Do you have live testimony?** A neutral witness who supports your side of the story is invaluable. For instance, if you withheld rent because the landlord refused to repair your stove, ask a repair person to examine the stove, and call him to testify as to its condition. Or, if the landlord claims that you've made excessive noise, ask a neighbor to testify that, in fact, there was really no problem.

When the Landlord Is Retaliating

In most states, landlords are not allowed to terminate your tenancy as punishment for exercising a legal right, such as complaining to a health inspector, organizing a tenants' group, or properly withholding rent or using repair and deduct. (Landlord retaliation is discussed in detail in Chapter 15.) But suppose you have spoken to a housing inspector but you are *also* late with the rent—will it do you any good to prove that the landlord's real motive is retaliation? Or, put another way, does your conduct have to be "squeaky clean" in order to get a judge to stop an eviction lawsuit based on your landlord's retaliatory conduct?

It stands to reason that you'll always be in a better position if you can present yourself as a completely blameless tenant. But even if you are less than perfect, all may not be lost. Some states address this issue in their written law; others leave it to the courts to decide. If you plan to mount a retaliatory eviction defense but you know that there is a skeleton or two hiding in your closet, be sure to read your state's retaliation statutes and look for court decisions interpreting them. (Chapter 20 gives advice on how to do basic legal research.)

Buying Time (at a Price)

If you do not have a good legal reason for ignoring a termination notice, you may still choose to force the landlord to proceed to an eviction lawsuit if you have no place to move. The process (other than expedited evictions) normally takes from two to six weeks, time which you may need in order to find another rental or finish a job or school year. And depending on the law and practice in your state, you may be able to obtain additional delays for hardship circumstances (see Chapter 18).

Understand that buying time often comes at a price: When an eviction lawsuit is filed against you, that fact will inevitably become part of your credit record, which can be consulted by future employers, landlords, banks, and stores. This negative mark will appear even if you voluntarily move (and the case is dismissed) before the landlord gets a court order that allows him to evict you. And if your lease or rental agreement allows your landlord to recover for attorneys' fees, you'll be charged for these, too. Courts in some states can order you to pay these fees even in the absence of such a clause, if the judge decides that your conduct has been extreme and outrageous. These fees can total $500 to $1,000 or even more. (Chapter 2 explains attorneys' fees.)

Cutting Your Losses and Moving

Even if you believe you are in the legal right, finding another place to live may be your best option after getting a termination notice. There are many times in life when it is not worth your time and money to fight. Consider moving to a more congenial situation if:

- You can find comparable or better housing without major inconvenience.
- The landlord has always been difficult to deal with and you can expect future hassles.
- You cannot afford the time off from work, school, or your personal life to get involved in a lawsuit, nor can you afford to hire a lawyer.
- You are not absolutely sure you will win and your lease or rental agreement contains an attorneys' "fees and costs" clause, meaning that if you lose you'll pay the landlord's costs as well as your own.

- Your credit record is shaky, you are in the process of trying to clean it up, and you are absolutely determined not to damage it further.

Moving in response to a termination notice, or even an eviction, does not mean that you forfeit your security deposit. Of course, if you have failed to pay the rent or have damaged the rental unit beyond normal wear and tear, the landlord can subtract what you owe from the deposit. (Chapter 16 discusses basic rules on returning security deposits.)

What about any future rent you owe under a lease the landlord terminates early? Chances are that even if the landlord has a good reason to end your lease early, a court will not hold you liable for rent for any period after you leave. However, this may not always be true if your conduct has been highly outrageous or illegal (dealing drugs from your bedroom, for example). In this situation, a judge might charge you for future rent and subtract it from your deposit for an additional period, to give the landlord a reasonable chance to rerent the unit.

Evictions

When to Fight—And When to Move 316

Illegal "Self-Help" Evictions 316

How Eviction Lawsuits Work 317

    What Court Hears Evictions? 317

    First Steps: The Complaint and Summons 318

    Knocking the Lawsuit Out of Court Before Trial 319

    Your Answer to the Complaint 319

    Pretrial Discovery 320

    The Trial 321

    The Judgment 321

    If You Lose: Stopping or Postponing an Eviction 321

    Eviction 323

Stopping Eviction by Filing for Bankruptcy 323

This chapter is for those readers who, despite the fact their landlord has told them to move on, have decided to stay put. If you count yourself as one of this intrepid group, read this chapter to get an idea of what you'll face if the landlord goes ahead and files a lawsuit to evict you.

We can't tell you exactly how to fight back—laws vary too much from state to state, and every situation is unique. But we can give you a good overview of the eviction procedure that follows a termination notice (see Chapter 17) and tell you what your landlord can—and cannot—do under the law. To win an eviction lawsuit, you'll need to hire a lawyer or learn the particulars of your state's laws on your own. (Chapter 20 tells you how to get started by looking up your state's eviction statutes.)

> **TIP**
>
> **Consider hiring a lawyer if your lease or rental agreement has an attorneys' fees clause.** If you will be entitled to attorneys' fees if you win, and you are confident that you have a strong case, you may want to hire an attorney. Some lawyers even take eviction defense cases on a contingency—that is, you owe nothing if you lose, and they collect their fees from the landlord if you win. (Chapter 20 discusses contingency fees.)

> **RESOURCE**
>
> **Find your state's eviction rules and procedures.** California tenants should consult *California Tenants' Rights*, by Janet Portman and J. Scott Weaver (Nolo); this book contains eviction defense information and tear-out court forms. Tenants in other states should check the Tenants section of www.nolo.com for useful state-specific articles such as on tenant defenses to evictions.

When to Fight—And When to Move

Unless you have the law and provable facts on your side, fighting a termination notice is usually short-sighted. If you lose an eviction lawsuit, you may end up hundreds (even thousands) of dollars in debt and face a negative credit rating.

So when does it make sense to fight an eviction? Here is a bare-bones list of the main legal reasons (grounds) on which to contest an eviction:

- Your landlord gave you the wrong notice—for example, an unconditional notice to quit when you were entitled, under state law, to a "Pay or Quit" notice. (Fighting an eviction on this ground only buys you a bit of time.) See Chapter 17.
- Your landlord canceled the termination notice—for example, your landlord accepted rent after giving you a Pay or Quit notice—but filed for eviction anyway. See Chapter 17.
- You got a Pay or Quit notice and you offered rent within the specified time, but the landlord wouldn't accept it. See Chapter 17.
- The premises are legally uninhabitable, which excuses you from paying rent. See Chapter 8.
- You didn't pay all the rent because you properly used a repair and deduct procedure or rent withholding. See Chapter 8.
- An agreement with your landlord justified your paying less rent—for example, because you had taken on responsibility for maintenance. See Chapter 9.
- You're being evicted because you've exercised a legal right, such as complaining to a housing inspector about your unit. See Chapter 15.
- Your landlord has an illegal discriminatory motive for eviction—for example, your race, sex, age, family status, or disability. See Chapter 5.

Illegal "Self-Help" Evictions

In years past, there was nothing to stop a landlord from changing the locks, removing the front door, cutting off the utilities, or even moving the furniture onto the street if the tenant failed to pay rent, violated a lease clause, or damaged the property. Fortunately, today practically every state has forbidden these "self-help" evictions. Instead, landlords must get a court order directing you to leave and, if you don't, authorizing a local sheriff or marshal to physically remove you.

Many states that have outlawed self-help evictions have put some teeth behind the ban. If you have been locked out, frozen out by having the heat cut off, or denied electricity or water by the landlord, you can sue not only for your actual money losses (such as the need for temporary housing, the value of food that spoiled when the refrigerator stopped running, or the cost of an electric heater when the gas was shut off), but also for penalties as well. In some states, you can collect and still remain in the premises; in others, you are entitled to monetary compensation only. (See the chart "Consequences of Self-Help Evictions," in Appendix A.)

If you decide to sue your landlord for an illegal eviction, research your state's statutes and consider consulting an experienced tenants' lawyer. (See Chapter 20 for advice on legal research and using an attorney as a coach.)

TIP

Watch out for the landlord who removes your property under the guise of handling "abandoned" property. A few states allow the landlord to freely dispose of a tenant's property when the tenant has permanently moved out. So when a landlord has locked up, taken, or moved a tenant's property, it's not surprising to hear the landlord claim that the tenant had abandoned the property—even when it's not clear. If a tenant who in fact didn't intend to abandon sues over the property, the landlord must prove by clear and decisive evidence that the tenant intended to leave permanently and turn the place (and its contents) over to the landlord. "Your Abandoned Property" in Chapter 16 explains how landlords handle abandoned property.

How Eviction Lawsuits Work

Here's a guide to the basic elements of an eviction lawsuit.

CAUTION

"Expedited evictions" are fast and do not follow the typical path. If you are being evicted for serious illegal activity, such as drug dealing or use, you may be subject to a speedy eviction procedure that will give you little, if any, time to prepare a defense. In Arizona, for example, a landlord who suspects you of engaging in serious illegal activity on the premises can immediately terminate a tenancy and get a court date within three days. (Ariz. Rev. Stat. §§ 33-1368 and 1377.)

What Court Hears Evictions?

Your landlord will file an eviction lawsuit in a formal trial court (called "municipal," "county," or "justice"), or in small claims court. Some states give landlords the choice; others confine eviction lawsuits to one or the other. If your landlord has a choice, the decision of which court to use will depend on:

- **Amount of unpaid rent.** If the landlord is also suing for unpaid rent which is higher than the small claims court's jurisdictional amount, the landlord must use a higher court. (States' small claims court jurisdictional limits are listed in Chapter 19.)
- **Attorneys' fees clause.** If your lease or rental agreement contains an attorneys' fees clause and your landlord has a strong case against you, she's likely to hire an attorney and go to formal court, figuring that the fee will come from your pocket when she wins. On the other hand, if she realizes that you have little or no funds, she'll understand that her chances of collection are dim and may choose small claims instead. Big landlords (who usually include attorneys' fees clauses in their rental contracts) are especially likely to choose the formal court, regardless of the strength of their case, since they do not have the time to go to court themselves.

A few states have separate "landlord-tenant" courts in larger cities, similar to a small claims court, specifically set up to handle evictions.

There are important differences between regular trial courts and small claims (or landlord-tenant) court:

- In small claims court, the regular rules of evidence are greatly relaxed, and you can show or tell the court your side of the story without adhering to the "foundation" requirements that apply in higher courts. ("Laying a foundation" is explained in "Rules of Evidence in Formal Court," below.)

- In regular court, you and the landlord may engage in a pretrial process called "discovery," in which you ask each other about the evidence that supports your positions. Discovery includes depositions (where witnesses are questioned under oath) and interrogatories (discussed in "Pretrial Discovery," below). This process is normally available in formal court, but not in small claims or landlord-tenant courts.

- In regular court, you and the landlord may each attempt to wash the case out of court quickly by filing pretrial requests to the court to dismiss or limit the case (discussed below). In small claims and landlord-tenant court, the idea is to decide the entire case after one efficient court hearing, and these motions are not used.

RESOURCE

Everybody's Guide to Small Claims Court, by Cara O'Neill (Nolo), describes the workings of your state's small claims court in detail.

Represent Yourself in Court: How to Prepare & Try a Winning Case, by Paul Bergman and Sara Berman (Nolo), explains how to present evidence and arguments in formal court.

First Steps: The Complaint and Summons

An eviction lawsuit begins when the landlord files a legal document called a "Complaint" or similar term. The Complaint, which is usually loaded with legal jargon, lists the facts that the landlord thinks justify your eviction. It also asks the court to order you to leave and to pay back rent, damages directly caused by your unlawfully remaining on the property, court costs, and sometimes attorneys' fees.

Normally, your landlord cannot sue you for anything but back rent and damages. Because an eviction procedure is so quick, most states do not allow a landlord to add other legal beefs to an eviction Complaint. For example, if your landlord claims that you have damaged the sofa and your security deposit won't cover the cost of replacement, he must sue you in small claims court in a separate lawsuit. Similarly, if you would like to bring up an unrelated bit of landlord misbehavior, such as your landlord's repeated violations of your privacy, you will have to do so in a separate legal action.

When the landlord files a Complaint, the clerk will assign a date on which the case will be heard by the court. That date is entered on the Summons, a piece of paper that says that you've been sued and must answer the landlord's charges and appear in court within a specified number of days or lose the lawsuit. The landlord must then give you the Complaint and the Summons, which officially inform you of your right to appear before a judge. In legal jargon, this is called "service of process."

State laws are quite detailed as to the proper way to give you, or "serve," court papers. Typically, the preferred method is "personal" service, which means that a law enforcement officer or professional process server personally hands you the papers. (Don't think that you can slam the door in his face and avoid service—when the process server leaves them on the doorstep, you're served.) In some states, any adult not involved in the lawsuit can serve papers.

If, despite repeated attempts, the process server cannot locate you, most states allow something called "substituted service." This means the process server leaves a copy of the papers with a competent adult at your home, or mails the papers first-class and also leaves a copy in a place where you'll likely see it, such as posted on your front door.

Failure to properly serve the tenant is one of the most common errors landlords make. For example, the landlord may serve the papers himself, violating the typical rule that does not permit parties to a lawsuit to serve papers. Or, the landlord may not make enough attempts at personal service before resorting to substituted service. The most common violation of the service rules is that the process server simply lies about having personally contacted you. This happens especially in rough areas of town, where process servers are afraid to go.

If your landlord did not follow state statutes correctly, you can usually ask the judge to dismiss the lawsuit before trial. However, in some states the fact that you did, in fact, receive the papers will defeat your claim. And even if you win, your landlord may be prepared with a new Summons, which will be handed to you right in court.

> **CAUTION**
> **Don't ignore a Summons.** If you have already ignored a notice telling you to move out, you may be tempted to also ignore a Summons and Complaint, too, figuring that you'll move out just before the case goes to court or the sheriff arrives to escort you out. This is usually a mistake. Far better to immediately call the landlord and negotiate a move-out date. If you owe back rent and attorneys' fees and costs which amount to more than the security deposit, maybe the landlord will agree not to sue you for the excess in exchange for your speedy departure. But don't expect more than a few days at this point.
>
> If you don't respond to the Summons and Complaint, the landlord will automatically win the eviction lawsuit. The court will grant what's called a "default judgment" against you, ordering you to pay unpaid rent and, if your lease or rental agreement has an attorneys' fees and costs clause, those expenses as well. The default will show up, to your obvious disadvantage, on future credit reports.

Knocking the Lawsuit Out of Court Before Trial

Failure to properly serve you isn't the only procedural objection you can raise to the landlord's lawsuit. Other landlord mistakes may also justify dismissal of the case before trial. To get the case dismissed, you may need to file brief documents called a "motion to dismiss" the landlord's case, or to "strike" (eliminate) a key part of it. In California, you use a response called a "demurrer." You must also serve a copy of your motion on the landlord, in the manner required by law in your state. Here are the main grounds for these challenges.

The landlord used the wrong notice. In many states, a landlord must give you a certain amount of time—often three to five days—to pay the rent or cure the lease violation before filing an eviction lawsuit. (See Chapter 17.) However, very serious misbehavior (such as damage to the property), illegal activities, or repeated late rent or lease violations may allow the landlord to serve you with an Unconditional Quit notice, which gives you no second chance to cure the problem. If you are being evicted for behavior that triggers a Pay or Quit or Cure or Quit notice, but the landlord gave you an Unconditional Quit notice instead, you can challenge it in court. If you win, the landlord will be told to start over and use the right termination notice. So you'll buy yourself some time, but you'll still have to argue the merits of the case later.

The landlord filed the lawsuit too soon. If you've been given a termination notice that does give you time to pay or cure, the landlord cannot file for eviction until that time has run out. For example, if you have five days to pay the rent or move and you don't pay, the lawsuit cannot be filed until the sixth day.

Your Answer to the Complaint

The next step in a typical eviction lawsuit involves your response to the landlord's claims that something you've done (or not done) justifies your eviction. At this point, you've gone beyond the technicalities of the way your landlord filed the lawsuit, and are meeting the reasons for the eviction head-on.

You must file a document called an Answer on or before the date printed on the Summons. Fortunately, your answer need not take the shape of a lengthy legal brief. In some states, you can even use a preprinted Answer form prepared by the court that allows you to simply check an appropriate box, depending on what you intend to argue. And even in states that still follow the old-fashioned approach of requiring documents typed up on numbered legal paper, law libraries contain form books which you can use to copy out the required language. (Lawyers use them, too.)

In general, your Answer may contain two kinds of responses:

- **Denials.** You may dispute that what the landlord says is true. For example, if you paid your rent to the manager but the landlord claims it was never received, you will simply deny that the rent is unpaid. Or, if the landlord is evicting you because you have a dog but the animal actually belongs to the tenants in the next unit, you'll also simply check the "denials" box. Or, if there is no form, you would type something like this: "Defendant denies the allegations in Paragraph X of Plaintiff's Complaint." (The landlord is the plaintiff in the lawsuit; you're the defendant.)

- **Affirmative Defenses.** The Answer is also the place to state what the law calls "affirmative defenses"—good legal reasons that excuse what would otherwise be grounds for eviction. For example, if you're being evicted for not paying the rent, you could explain that you used some of the rent money to pay for repairing a serious problem your landlord had ignored, as is allowed under your state's law. Some preprinted Answer forms actually list the common defenses, which we set out for you at the beginning of this chapter. Normally, you'll need to provide a one-paragraph statement of the facts that justify your use of the affirmative defense you have selected.

EXAMPLE: Wilson, an African American man, was sure that his termination and eviction were racially motivated. On the Answer form, he checked "Discrimination" and, below, simply wrote "Plaintiff served me with a 30-day notice because he doesn't want Black people living in his building."

Not every state, however, gives you the convenience of a list of preprinted affirmative defenses. But don't worry: You won't have to write your Answer entirely from scratch. You can find a fill-in-the-blanks form at your local law library and online at the court's website. Form books are designed to cover every typical situation, so you're sure to find a "canned" form that will fit your situation. When you sign your Answer, be sure to note under your typed name that you are appearing "Pro per" or "Pro se," which means that you are representing yourself and have not hired a lawyer. A sample is shown below.

Pretrial Discovery

You or the landlord may wish to find out more about each other's case before you go to trial. Called "discovery," this process is not available in small claims court. It can involve:

- depositions, in which witnesses, experts, or parties to the lawsuit are questioned under oath and a transcript of the session is prepared

- requests for documents, such as the landlord's repair request form or a landlord's letter to all tenants

- sets of preprinted questions, called "interrogatories," that cover information normally involved in a landlord-tenant dispute. For example, the landlord might be asked to "State the names and addresses of all owners of record of the property."

- specific statements of fact that the other side is asked, under oath, to admit or deny (called "requests for admissions"), such as a statement "Landlord does not maintain an on-site office at [your apartment complex]."

Information gathered during discovery can be used at trial.

Answer Raising Affirmative Defense

First Affirmative Defense

1. Defendant admits that she did not pay the amount of rent due as stated in the Complaint. She argues, however, that the entire rent was not due because she was legally entitled to pay less than the stated rent because of her valid use of the repair and deduct statute of the state of California, Civil Code Section 1942.

2. Plaintiff is required by law to provide hot water of at least 110 degrees Fahrenheit, as specified by California Civil Code Section 1941.1. However, the water temperature in defendant's apartment did not rise above 50 degrees as of January 4, 20xx.

3. Plaintiff had actual knowledge of the inability of defendant's water heater to deliver legally sufficient hot water, since defendant wrote him two letters (dated January 5 and 10, 20xx), asking that the situation be corrected, but he failed to do so.

4. The defective condition was not caused by any willful or negligent act of the defendant or any person acting under her authority.

5. As a direct and proximate result of plaintiff's failure to correct the violation of law within a reasonable time, defendant hired a plumber on January 25, 20xx, to inspect and repair the water heater. The heater was fixed by installing a new valve, at a reasonable cost of $125.

6. Defendant deducted $125 from her rent check on February 1, 20xx.

7. Defendant has not used this state's repair and deduct statute more than the number of times allowed by law, nor is the amount deducted more than one month's rent.

THEREFORE, DEFENDANT ASKS THAT:

1. Plaintiff take nothing by his action;
2. Costs of this action be awarded to defendant; and
3. Defendant be awarded such further relief as the Court considers proper.

February 9, 20xx   _Sally Strong_
Date   Sally Strong, in Pro Per

The Trial

The way your trial will look and sound will depend primarily on whether it's in a formal court or a small claims or landlord-tenant court. In formal court, you'll have to abide by your state's rules of evidence. But in an informal court, you may be able to introduce letters and secondhand testimony ("I heard her say that …"). Also, you can introduce evidence without elaborate "foundations." (See "Rules of Evidence in Formal Court," below.) See Chapter 19 for an explanation of the kinds of evidence you'll need to win.

The Judgment

If you win, the landlord cannot evict you, and you'll likely get a judgment for your court costs and fees. You may also be awarded money damages if the landlord acted illegally, as in the case of discrimination. If the landlord wins, you must move out. The landlord may also be awarded unpaid rent, damages, court costs, and attorneys' fees.

If you win by asserting a habitability defense, the court may hold onto your case even after the trial is over. That's because the court doesn't want to simply return you to an unfit dwelling. In some states, a judge may order the landlord to make repairs while the rent is paid into a court account; when an inspector certifies that the dwelling is habitable, the judge will release the funds.

If You Lose: Stopping or Postponing an Eviction

If you lose the eviction lawsuit, you can expect your landlord to move quickly to physically remove you from the property. In rare instances, you may be able to get the trial judge to stop the eviction, but only if you can convince the court of two things:

- Eviction would cause a severe hardship for you or your family. For example, you may be able to persuade the judge that alternate housing is unavailable and your job will be in jeopardy if you are forced to move.

Rules of Evidence in Formal Court

Depending on the state, evictions are heard in a formal trial court, small claims court, or an informal landlord-tenant court. In small claims court, you can present any evidence you want to the judge. But if you are in a formal court, the judge will not examine documentary evidence until you have established that it is likely to be trustworthy. Presenting the legal background of evidence is called "laying a foundation." Here are a few hints on how to prepare evidence for formal court:

- **Photographs.** If your landlord's termination notice is based on your knocking a hole in the kitchen wall, you'll want to show the judge a photograph of the place where, in fact, there is a mere scuff mark. But before the picture can be admitted into evidence, someone will have to testify that the picture is a fair and accurate depiction of the way the wall looked. It's best to ask a neutral witness to come to your apartment, look at the wall, and come to court prepared to testify that, yes, the photo is an accurate portrayal. Your witness need not take the photo.

- **Letters.** You may have received a termination notice because your landlord thinks that you improperly used the repair and deduct remedy by failing to notify him of the problem in the first place. In court, this means you'll need to introduce into evidence your copy of the letter you sent your landlord requesting repairs as proof that you complied with this requirement. To do this, you can simply testify that the letter is a true copy, that the signature is your own, and that you mailed or handed it to your landlord.

- **Petitions.** Perhaps your defense to your termination and eviction is that the landlord is retaliating against you because you circulated a petition asking for cleaner common areas or because you protested a rent increase. To introduce the petition, you can testify that you circulated it or, even better, have someone who signed it testify that it is genuine.

- **Government documents.** If you've withheld rent because of what you claim are uninhabitable conditions (an inoperable toilet, for example), your landlord may attempt to evict you for nonpayment of rent. If you made a complaint to a local health department and they issued a report critical of your landlord, you'll want to have the report considered by the court (admitted into evidence). You'll have to have the inspector testify that he wrote the report as part of his normal duties when investigating possible health violations. To get him to court, you'll need to use an order, called a "subpoena," that you can serve on the inspector.

- You are willing and able to pay any back rent owed (and the landlord's costs to bring the lawsuit) and future rent, as well.

It's very unusual for a judge to stop an eviction, for the simple reason that if your sympathetic predicament (and sufficient monetary reserves) weren't persuasive enough to win the case for you in the first place, it's unlikely that these arguments can prevail after the trial.

It may, however, be more realistic to ask for a postponement of the eviction. Typically, evictions are postponed in three situations:

- **Pending your appeal.** If you file an appeal, you may ask the trial judge to postpone ("stay") the eviction until the appellate court decides the case. If you've been evicted in small claims court, in a few states you may enjoy an automatic postponement during the appeal. Of course, this is one reason why smart landlords never use small claims court in these states.

- **Until your circumstances improve.** You may be able to persuade a judge to give you a little more time to find a new home.

- **Until the weather improves.** Contrary to popular belief, judges in many cold-climate states are not required to postpone an eviction on frigid days. But there's nothing to stop you from asking the judge, anyway. In the District of Columbia, however, a landlord may not evict on a day when the National Weather Service predicts at 8 a.m. that the temperature at the National Airport will fall below freezing within the next 24 hours. (D.C. Code § 45-2551(k).)

To convince a judge to order your eviction postponed, you'll need to show that it would pose an extreme hardship to you or your family, and that your continued presence will not harm the landlord. This will at least involve proving that you are capable of continuing to pay the rent.

Eviction

In most states, a landlord cannot move your belongings out on the street, even after winning an eviction lawsuit. (See "Illegal 'Self-Help' Evictions," above.) Typically, the landlord must give the judgment to a local law enforcement officer, along with a fee that you've been charged as part of the landlord's costs. The sheriff or constable gives you a notice telling you that he'll be back, sometimes within just a few days, to physically remove you if you aren't gone. At this point, it's time to move. No one, even the most outrageously wronged tenant, wants the experience of being tossed out.

Stopping Eviction by Filing for Bankruptcy

Tenants with significant financial burdens may decide to declare bankruptcy. There are several kinds of bankruptcy; the most common are "Chapter 7," in which most debts are wiped out after as many creditors as possible have been paid; or "Chapter 13," in which qualifying debts get wiped out after paying into a court-approved plan for three to five years.

If you have filed for either Chapter 7 or Chapter 13 bankruptcy and are behind in the rent, or become unable to pay the rent, or if you violate another term of your tenancy (such as having a dog in spite of a no-pets clause), the landlord cannot deliver a termination notice or proceed with an eviction. This prohibition is known as the "automatic stay," and it means that the landlord must go to the federal bankruptcy court and ask the judge to "lift," or

remove the stay. (U.S.C. § 365(e).) In most cases, the judge will lift the stay within a matter of days and the landlord can proceed with the termination and eviction. (The landlord won't have to go to court if the tenant is using illegal drugs or endangering the property, as explained below in "Bankrupt Tenants, Drugs, and Damage.")

What Happens to Your Lease

Filing for a Chapter 7 bankruptcy affects your tenancy even if you are not behind in the rent or otherwise in violation of your lease. After you file, the Chapter 7 "bankruptcy trustee" (a person appointed by the bankruptcy court to oversee the case) must decide whether to assume your lease or rental agreement (take it over) or reject it.

A trustee who assumes your residential contract will step into your shoes. The trustee gets no more than what you contracted for and must pay whatever you owe, including the monthly payment and any past due amount. Doing so can be expensive, so it will happen only if you pay below-market rent, and when subletting your place (assigning your agreement to someone else) will net your creditors a profit. If you're paying the current market rate, or your contract forbids subletting, there won't be any profit to be made and the trustee will let you keep the lease.

It works a bit differently in a Chapter 13 bankruptcy. As long as you're current on your payments, you won't have to worry about losing your residential rental, because the Chapter 13 trustee doesn't sell or liquidate your property.

However, if you're behind in the rent, you must pay unpaid rent regardless of the chapter that you file. (11 U.S.C. §§ 365(b)(1)(A), (B), & (C).)

The automatic stay does not apply, however if the landlord completed the eviction proceeding and got a judgment for possession before the tenant filed for bankruptcy. Under the Bankruptcy Abuse Prevention and Consumer Protection Act of 2005, landlords can proceed with the eviction without having to go to court and ask for the stay to be lifted.

In very narrow circumstances, and only for evictions based on rent nonpayment, a tenant can stop the eviction even if the landlord got a judgment before the tenant filed for bankruptcy. A tenant has only 30 days after filing for bankruptcy to try this. Here are the specifics:

- You must go to court and file a paper certifying that state law allows you to avoid eviction by paying the unpaid rent, even after the landlord has won a judgment for possession. Very few states extend this option to tenants. The certification must be served on the landlord.

- You must deposit with the clerk of the bankruptcy court any rent that would be due 30 days from the date the petition was filed and,

- You must certify to the bankruptcy court (and serve the landlord with this certification) that you have paid the back rent.

At any point during these 30 days, the landlord can file an objection to the tenant's certification. The judge will schedule a hearing in the bankruptcy court within ten days. If the landlord convinces the judge that the tenant's certifications are not true, the court will lift the stay and the landlord can proceed to recover possession of the property.

Bankrupt Tenants, Drugs, and Damage

Landlords may need to evict a tenant who is using illegal drugs, even off-site, or endangering the property. If the tenant files for bankruptcy before the landlord wins a judgment for possession, the landlord will be able to proceed with the eviction without asking the bankruptcy judge to lift the stay. In the unlikely event that you find yourself at the other end of such a proceeding, here is how it will go down, which depends on the timing:

- **When the landlord has begun an eviction case but doesn't have a judgment.** The landlord will file a certification, or sworn statement, that he has begun an unlawful detainer case based on the tenant's endangerment of the property or use of illegal drugs (or such use by the tenant's guests).

- **When the landlord hasn't yet filed an eviction lawsuit.** The landlord will file a certification, or sworn statement, that the activity described above has happened within the past 30 days.

In either situation, the landlord will then file the certification with the bankruptcy court and serve the tenant as he would serve any legal notice.

If the tenant does not file an objection within 15 days of being served, the landlord can proceed with the eviction without asking the court for relief from the stay.

Now, suppose the tenant objects? You must file with the court, and serve on the landlord, a certification challenging the truth of the landlord's certification. The bankruptcy court will hold a hearing within ten days, at which you must convince the court that the situation the landlord describes did not exist or has been remedied. If the court rules for the landlord, he may proceed with the eviction without asking that the stay be lifted; but if the tenant wins, the landlord may not proceed.

Resolving Problems Without a Lawyer

How to Negotiate a Settlement 326

Using a Mediator 327

    How to Find a Mediation Group 328

    How Mediation Works 328

Suing in Small Claims Court 328

    Learning the Rules 329

    How Much Can You Sue For? 329

Tenants Working Together 329

    What Tenants' Groups Can Do 330

    Getting Tenants Together 330

    How to Structure Your Group 331

    Petitioning the Landlord and Taking Action 331

    Meet With the Landlord 333

Legal disputes between tenants and landlords come in all shapes and sizes. Here are some of the more common ones:

- **Rent.** You disagree about the validity, timing, or method of a rent increase.

- **Habitability.** You've complained several times about the leaky roof that has made the living room unusable. After getting no response from your landlord, you don't pay the next month's rent. Your landlord is threatening eviction.

- **Privacy.** You don't want the landlord to show your apartment to prospective new tenants on very short notice and at inconvenient times. Your landlord thinks you're being unreasonable.

- **Security deposits.** At the end of your tenancy, you claim that you left the rental unit reasonably clean and undamaged. The landlord says it didn't pass the white glove test.

- **Lease or rental agreement violation.** Your landlord complains that you are violating your lease by having noisy parties and frequent overnight guests. You feel your private life is your business, and that your landlord is mostly mad that you have more fun than she does.

How you handle problems with your landlord can have a profound effect on your ability to enjoy your rental home. In some cases, such as when a landlord persistently refuses to attend to major repairs, enters unannounced, and generally makes your life miserable on a number of fronts, your best bet may be simply to end the tenancy and move to a more congenial place. Or, if you are the victim of serious discrimination or other illegal acts, your best bet might be to go straight to a lawyer.

Often, however, you can take steps that will improve matters—or at least resolve the dispute in your favor. But rarely should lawyers, lawsuits, and all their attendant expenses and tensions be your first approach. Instead, try:

- negotiation
- mediation, or
- small claims court.

In many cases, you will be dealing with your landlord either alone or with your roommates. But if other tenants will share your concerns, you'll find it effective to approach your landlord as a group. We show you how later in this chapter.

How to Negotiate a Settlement

No matter how serious the problem, you're almost always better off trying to resolve disputes directly with your landlord. This is especially true if your concerns don't warrant the use of a heavy-duty legal strategy in the first place. So put aside the possibility of suing—except possibly in small claims court (see below)—and instead direct your efforts toward negotiating a settlement.

You'll be most successful if you focus on what exactly you want the landlord to do, rather than fighting for the principle involved. Berating your landlord for insensitivity or ignorance may give you a sense of righteous vindication, but not necessarily better results.

Here are some helpful pointers for negotiating with landlords:

- **Set up an appointment to discuss the problem.** Try to arrange sufficient time, without distractions such as children, so you can both express your concerns and work out an agreement.

- **Solicit the landlord's point of view.** Once the landlord starts talking, listen closely and don't interrupt, even if some points are not true or some opinions are inflammatory.

- **State that you understand and respect the landlord's key points.** Even if you strongly disagree with your landlord's position, it's often a good idea to accurately restate his concerns. This should discourage him from endlessly repeating the same point.

- **Avoid personal attacks.** Even if true, suggesting that your landlord is a slumlord or is profiteering at the expense of tenants will only raise the level of hostility and make settlement more difficult. Equally important, it's usually best to stay calm and not to react impulsively or emotionally to your landlord's misstatements.

- **Be courteous, not weak.** If the law is on your side or you have the firm backing of most other tenants, let the landlord know that you're coming from a position of strength. Make it clear that you prefer negotiating an agreement but that, if necessary, you have the resources and evidence to fight and win.

- **Emphasize problem solving.** Try to structure the negotiation as a mutual attempt to solve a problem. For instance, if you're complaining about a landlord's policy of entering tenants' apartments to make unannounced repairs, seek solutions that recognize the interests of both parties—for example, an understanding that repairs are necessary and even desirable but most can be prearranged.

- **Put yourself in the landlord's shoes.** How would you want to work with unhappy tenants if roles were reversed? Your answer may be something like, "I'd want to feel that I've won." As it turns out, this is a great insight—the best settlements are often those in which both sides feel they've won, or at least not given up anything fundamental.

- **If you reach an understanding with your landlord, promptly write it down and sign it.** You should volunteer to prepare the first draft. If you agree to pay the landlord some money as part of the settlement, make it clear that the payment fully satisfies the landlord's claim: "Tenant's $200 payment of August 1, 20xx, fully satisfies any claim Landlord has against Tenant regarding damaged patio furniture."

RESOURCE

Getting to Yes: Negotiating Agreement Without Giving In, by Roger Fisher, William Ury, and Bruce Patton (Penguin Books). This classic book offers a strategy for coming to mutually acceptable agreements in all kinds of situations, including landlord-tenant disputes.

Using a Mediator

If you're unsuccessful negotiating a settlement with your landlord, or relations are so strained that no meeting seems possible, you may be ready to give up on the idea of negotiation. This would be a mistake. Instead, your best approach is often to enlist the help of a neutral third-party mediator. Even if your landlord won't speak to you, a skilled and experienced mediator may get him to the table.

Many people confuse mediation with arbitration, which is seldom, if ever, used in residential landlord-tenant disputes. While both are nonjudicial ways to resolve disputes, there's a huge difference: Arbitration, like lawsuits, results in a binding decision. Mediators, by contrast, have no power to impose a decision. Their job is simply to help the parties work out a mutually acceptable solution to their dispute. Put another way, if you and your landlord don't agree on a solution, there is no solution.

Mediation can make especially good sense if:

- your landlord doesn't realize what a poor job the resident manager or management company has been doing, and you want the opportunity to bring this up

- you are dealing with a good or at least halfway decent landlord, and you think there's hope for resolution, or

- you think the landlord is savvy enough to want to avoid a protracted court battle.

TIP

Mediation can also help resolve roommate disputes. If you and your roommate disagree about noise, overnight guests, or some other issue, consider trying mediation.

Does mediation really work? Surprisingly, yes. One big reason is the cooperative spirit that emerges. By agreeing to mediate a dispute in the first place, you and the landlord implicitly agree to solve your own problems. Also, the fact that no judge or arbitrator has the power to impose what may be an unacceptable solution reduces fear and defensiveness on both sides. This, in turn, often means both landlord and tenant take less extreme—and more conciliatory—positions.

Sometimes mediation is not the best approach. For example, if your landlord has discriminated against you based on your race, sex, or some other illegal reason, you should probably file a fair housing complaint or a lawsuit, as explained in Chapter 5.

How to Find a Mediation Group

Many cities offer free or low-cost community mediation programs that handle landlord-tenant disputes. For information, call your mayor's or city manager's office and ask for the staff member who handles landlord-tenant mediation matters or housing disputes. That person should refer you to the public office or community group that attempts to informally—and at little or no cost—resolve landlord-tenant disputes before they reach the court stage. You can also get referrals for fee-based mediation services from the American Arbitration Association (visit their website at www.adr.org) or a neighborhood dispute resolution center.

> **TIP**
>
> **If there's a charge for the mediation service, offer to split it with your landlord.** That way, you'll both feel equally vested in the outcome.

How Mediation Works

Mediation in landlord-tenant disputes is fairly informal. More likely than not, the mediator will have you and your landlord sit down together. Each side is usually asked to discuss all issues they consider important—even emotional ones. This process of airing the entire dispute often cools people off considerably and can lay the foundation for a fairly quick compromise.

If the dispute is not resolved easily, the mediator may suggest ways to resolve the problem, or may even keep everyone talking long enough to realize that the real problem goes deeper than the one being mediated. Typically this is helped along through a caucus process, where each side is asked to occupy a separate room, with the mediator shuttling back and forth with offers and counteroffers. When settlement appears near, everyone gets back together, and the mediator helps guide the parties to an agreement everyone approves.

For example, assume you and you landlord are mediating because you have threatened to withhold rent due to a serious defect in the premises, such as a broken heater. In a court hearing, this issue would be the only one considered. In contrast, the mediator may use the looser mediation process to discover that a major part of your grievance is that the manager has been slow to make all types of repairs, and the heat problem is simply the final straw.

You're not the only one who will have a chance to discuss other issues. You may discover that your landlord is angry at you for letting your kids run wild and ruin the garden, or is sick and tired of getting calls from the police responding to noise complaints filed by your neighbors. Once all of this is on the table, a compromise solution may fall easily into place: You may agree to provide better supervision of your kids and cut out overly loud parties in exchange for the manager getting the heat fixed and doing other repairs quickly.

And to keep future conflicts from developing, both sides might agree to meet monthly so that misunderstandings can be resolved before they grow into major battles.

Suing in Small Claims Court

If your attempts at settling a dispute with your landlord fail, you may end up in a lawsuit. Fortunately, there are many situations when you can competently and efficiently represent yourself in court. This is almost always true when your case is worth less than a few thousand dollars and you choose to use small claims court.

You can use small claims court for many legal problems:

- to force a landlord to perform needed major repairs (see Chapter 8)
- to pressure a landlord to do minor repairs (see Chapter 9)
- to deal with a landlord who repeatedly and seriously intrudes upon your privacy (see Chapter 11)
- to win a money judgment against a landlord who has failed to get rid of drug-dealing tenants (see Chapter 14), or
- to get your security deposit back (see Chapter 16).

Most people who go to small claims court handle their own cases. In fact, in some states, lawyers aren't allowed to represent clients in small claims court. (Some states allow attorneys in certain situations, such as with permission of the court or only when both sides have counsel.) In any event, representing yourself is almost always the best choice—after all, the main reason to use the small claims court is because the size of the case doesn't justify the cost of hiring a lawyer.

Learning the Rules

Small claims court procedures are relatively simple and easy to master. Basically, you pay a small fee, file your lawsuit with the court clerk, see to it that the papers are served on your landlord (this can often be done by mail), show up on the appointed day, tell the judge your story, and present any witnesses and other evidence.

Evidence that backs up your story is usually the key to winning in small claims court. For example, if you are suing your landlord to get your security deposit returned, all you need to win is a photograph of a clean and undamaged apartment and the convincing testimony of someone who helped you clean up. (Chapter 16 explains how to gather and present evidence in small claims court disputes about security deposits.)

Court rules that cover such things as where you file your lawsuit, how legal papers must be delivered to your opponent ("service of process"), and how promptly you must sue are usually available from the small claims clerk. In addition, clerks in small claims court are expected to explain procedures to you. In some states, they may even help you fill out the necessary forms, which are quite simple anyhow. If necessary, be persistent. If you ask enough questions, you'll get the answers you need to handle your own case comfortably. Also, in some states such as California, you can consult a free small claims court adviser.

How Much Can You Sue For?

Exactly how much can you sue for in small claims court? The maximum varies from state to state. In most, it is $5,000 to $10,000. (See "State Small Claims Court Limits" in Appendix A, or ask your court clerk for the most current limit.)

Don't assume that your case can't be brought in small claims court if it's slightly over the limit. Rather than hiring a lawyer or trying to go it alone in formal court, your most cost-effective option may be to sue for the small claims maximum and forget the rest.

RESOURCE

Everybody's Guide to Small Claims Court, by Cara O'Neill (Nolo), provides detailed advice on bringing or defending a small claims court case, preparing evidence and witnesses for court, and collecting your money judgment when you win. Especially if you have never been to small claims court, you'll want to closely study the material on how to present your testimony and witnesses in court. *Everybody's Guide to Small Claims Court* will also be useful in defending yourself against a landlord who sues you in small claims court—for example, claiming that you owe money for damage to the premises.

Tenants Working Together

When it comes to tenants confronting a recalcitrant landlord, one strategy is potentially more productive than all others: Working together with other tenants. A landlord who has the resources and determination to outwait, outspend, or outmaneuver one tenant will often be much more willing to compromise when a number of tenants all threaten to act together. For example, you and other tenants could file a complaint with a government agency, sue, threaten a rent strike, or move out.

Keep in mind, however, that a group of tenants will be effective only if they speak with a clear, consistent voice. For a variety of reasons, it can be hard or even impossible to form a tenants' group—for example, if tenant turnover is high or many tenants fear or dislike one another. But even if it's only a handful of tenants, you may find that there's power in numbers.

What Tenants' Groups Can Do

A tenant organization can be an informal group that comes together on one major issue, such as getting the landlord to make repairs or fighting a rent increase. Or a group can be more formally organized with regular meetings and address a wide variety of issues, such as getting the landlord to stop arbitrary mistreatment of tenants or making the building safer.

The tenant organization may use negotiation or mediation to convince the landlord to work more cooperatively with tenants. If push comes to shove, however, the tenants' group may even sue the landlord in small claims court. Faced with a multitenant lawsuit, many landlords suddenly become more willing to sign a formal agreement giving the tenants all or some of what they request. A cohesive tenant organization should be able to convince the landlord to deal with it on a continuing basis.

Tenants' organizations can also help work out problems among tenants. As any tenant in a multiunit building knows, a neighbor with a loud stereo (or child, dog, or spouse) can cause more day-to-day misery than the most obnoxious landlord. To deal with ongoing problems, an effective tenants' group can set up a voluntary mediation procedure to help members settle problems before they fester. And when it comes to drugs, prostitution, and gang activity, a tenants' organization can be very effective in pressuring the landlord to evict the troublemaker.

CAUTION

Beware of retaliation against tenant groups. Laws in most states protect tenants from landlord retaliation when the tenant exercises a legal right such as withholding rent when conditions justify it. Unfortunately, some states don't extend this legal protection to activist tenants, which means that a hostile landlord may try to get rid of those who organize or participate in tenant groups. Of course, the stronger and more unified the group, the harder this will be to do. See "State Laws Prohibiting Landlord Retaliation" in Appendix A and the discussion of retaliation in Chapter 15. Proceed at your own risk if tenants' organizing activities are not protected by your state's antiretaliation laws.

Getting Tenants Together

Two or three concerned tenants can start an effective tenants' group. Start by holding a meeting so people can get to know each other and speak about problems they have had with the building or the landlord.

You'll need a small group to get things started. If there are members of different races or ethnic groups on the property, get someone from each group to participate in your core organizing group. If you live in a large apartment complex or more than one building is involved, make sure you have the active involvement of someone from each building.

To get other tenants interested, identify one or more problems most tenants face. A big rent increase, fear of crime, safety of children, and parking problems are common. Focus on problems that should concern most tenants, not just your personal beef with your landlord.

Set a convenient meeting time and place to discuss these issues, and contact tenants individually to ask them to come. If you and the other organizers can afford the time, do this in person, door-to-door. Post or distribute notices only as a last resort or as a supplement to personal contact. Don't be too confrontational. You don't want to present yourselves to moderate tenants as a bunch of hotheads, and, of course, you don't want to alienate the landlord, whom you hope to persuade to work with your group.

The first meeting should begin informally. People should be given a chance to get to know each other and see that they really do have common problems that can be tackled by a group.

Try to anticipate and deal with tenants' fears about participating in the group. Some people may worry about being evicted if they ask for better treatment, while others may be concerned that the tenants' group is controlled by unreasonable or self-centered people. Even if not expressed, these fears are likely to be present. If they are not brought into the light and dealt with, they may cause tenants to drop out later, when the action starts.

At the close of your first meeting, assuming you have clearly identified one or more key problems that badly need to be addressed, you'll want to assign a little legal homework. For example, if your landlord has refused to repair the front door lock, someone needs to see if state or local laws require specified security equipment. Fortunately, the research you need to do shouldn't be difficult. If this book doesn't answer your questions, Chapter 20 goes into considerable detail about how you can learn more.

TIP

Bring a copy of laws that back up your position. Wavering tenants are often convinced to support a tenants' group when they see that the law is on their side. If you have a copy of your state's antiretaliation statute or repair and deduct statute, for example, it will reassure other tenants.

How to Structure Your Group

At some point, your group will need to decide how to structure itself. Do you want a formal organization, with officers, committees, chairpersons, and regular meetings? Or are you content with a looser, as-needed organization that requires less work and commitment? If you are lucky enough to have a relatively small, committed group of long-term tenants, you may be able to create a cohesive, structured organization. But in most places, the tenant population is ever-changing, and tenants are not particularly connected to each other. Most tenant organizations look less like a labor union and more like a group of neighbors responding to a particular problem.

TIP

Contact groups that are concerned with tenants' rights. Many communities, especially those with rent control, have active tenant associations that can furnish technical and legal advice as well as publicity and moral support. Examples of tenants' rights groups in California include the San Francisco Tenants Union (www.sftu.org) and Tenants Together (www.tenantstogether.org); a useful online resource for tenants in New York is www.tenant.net. To find local tenant advocacy groups, check out the Tenant Rights section of the U.S. Department of Housing and Urban Development (HUD) website (www.hud.gov). HUD provides a wide variety of local resources, including links to tenant unions and legal aid organizations for each state; even if you don't qualify for legal aid services, you will find useful information on tenant rights on many legal aid websites. Also, be sure to see the links to tenant rights' guides by state in the Tenants section of Nolo.com.

RENT CONTROL

If you live in a city covered by rent control, be sure to study the ordinance and its regulations. You may be able to bring your group's grievance before the rent board, and you may be required to do so before going to court.

Petitioning the Landlord and Taking Action

Especially if you face a serious problem, your group's second meeting should be devoted to developing a strategy to deal with the landlord. First, report on what you've found out about the legal options available to you. For example, if you all are fed up with the building's lack of hot water and have determined that its temperature often falls below the minimum mandated by your state's building codes, you will probably have learned that it's legal to withhold rent until the situation is corrected. (See Chapter 8.) But you should have

Petition to the Landlord

Harbor View Apartments
3700 Marina Way
Shady Bay, OR 00000

September 1, 20xx

PETITION TO RENEE ECKER, LANDLORD

We are all tenants at Harbor View Apartments. We direct your attention to the following problems, and ask that prompt action be taken to correct them.

1. **Closed laundry facility.** Because advertisements for Harbor View state that there are two on-site laundry facilities, and the apartment tour includes a visit to one of the two laundry rooms, we are entitled to the use of both rooms. Since June 15, 20xx, the laundry room in the West building has been closed, forcing all tenants to use the one remaining room. There are not enough washing machines in that room to reasonably accommodate the needs of the tenants.

2. **Inadequate security.** We request that the security of Harbor View be improved. At present, there are no deadbolt locks on residents' doors, no peepholes in front doors, and no lighting (other than a softly lit decorative sign) in the front of the building. This situation is intolerable given the fact that there have recently been three burglaries at a neighboring apartment building, Sea Breeze. In addition, Officer Friday, who covers this beat on a regular basis, has informed us that there has been an increase in the number of robberies, car thefts, and incidents of vandalism in this neighborhood.

   We ask that you immediately install deadbolt locks, peepholes, and better lighting. We also ask that you consult a security specialist to develop an overall plan for improved building security.

3. **Dirty common areas.** We request that the cleanliness and maintenance of our building be improved. As the landlord, you have the responsibility under state law to keep these common areas neat and clean by maintaining them on a regular basis. The lobby, hallways, and stairways are not being cleaned on a regular basis. Specifically, the lobby has large dustballs, piles of discarded junk mail, and unwashed windows. The stairways and halls are not regularly swept and washed, and the exterior breezeways have not been thoroughly cleaned since last spring.

We would like to meet with you to discuss these issues. Please contact Andy Ableson, in Apartment 3C, within the next five days to arrange for a mutually convenient time and place. A weekday evening in the Clubhouse common room might work best. We look forward to talking with you and working out a solution to these concerns.

Signed,

[Signed by as many tenants as possible]

also learned that you cannot legally do this until you have notified the landlord in writing and given her a reasonable amount of time in which to attend to the problem. (This is a good idea, regardless of whether it's legally required or not.)

Draw up a list of your complaints and concerns, present them to the landlord, and ask for a meeting. Your letter or petition should:

- be worded politely but firmly
- clearly set out your requests, and
- ask for a response within a specific time (such as seven days).

Unless the situation is extremely serious (for example, drug dealers are shooting at each other in the parking lot, or the building's sewage systems are backing up daily), your first letter should not threaten specific repercussions if the landlord is not coopera-tive. Better to have your letter carry the clear implica-tion that your group takes its requests seriously and that it will act in some as-yet-unspecified way if a favorable response is not forthcoming. To reinforce this point, it is usually best if all the tenants in the group sign the petition. See the sample Petition to the Landlord, above.

Meet With the Landlord

Follow our suggestions for negotiating, above. But be careful not to overwhelm the landlord with sheer numbers. Consider nominating one or two people to speak on behalf of the group.

If that doesn't work, follow through with media-tion and then, as a final resort, sue in small claims court or take other appropriate court action.

Lawyers and Legal Research

How a Lawyer Can Help You 336

Finding a Good Lawyer 336

    Compile a List of Prospects 337

    Shop Around 338

Fee Arrangements With Lawyers 339

    Lawyers' Billing Practices..339

    Saving on Legal Fees 339

Resolving Problems With Your Lawyer...340

Doing Your Own Legal Research 341

    Statutes and Ordinances..341

    State Statutes 342

    Court Decisions..343

Throughout this book, we point out instances when an attorney's advice or services may be useful—usually, disputes that involve lots of money or are very complicated. For example, if you become involved in a lawsuit over housing discrimination, withhold rent because your rental unit is uninhabitable, or claim that your landlord's wrongful acts resulted in your being seriously injured, you'll likely benefit from a lawyer's help. This chapter explains how to work with a lawyer efficiently, to get the most for your money.

But, if you attempt to buy much legal information at the rates lawyers charge—$150 to $250 an hour—you'll quickly go broke. Fortunately, you don't need a lawyer to acquire a good working knowledge of the basic legal principles that apply to problems with landlords. You've probably learned a lot already by reading this book. When more questions come up, turn to this chapter for advice on how to research the law for yourself.

How a Lawyer Can Help You

Here are some important ways lawyers can help tenants:

Make a quick phone call or write a letter to the landlord. For example, say your landlord persists in entering your apartment to perform nonemergency repairs upon 20-minutes' notice and ignores your complaints about these intrusions. In this case, a letter from your lawyer explaining your state's interpretation of "reasonable notice" requirements should do the trick, especially if it outlines repercussions of your landlord's continued violation of the law.

Help you with research. A lawyer can point you to the statutes, regulations, and possibly court cases that apply in a given situation, if you can't find them yourself.

Help with a complicated case. If you're being sued for eviction, a lawyer can help prepare your defense. Or, you may want a lawyer to confirm that you have a good claim, especially in cases involving significant amounts of money.

Handle big lawsuits for a contingency fee. If you have a legal problem that may involve a big recovery, such as a personal injury lawsuit or discrimination charge, the lawyer may be willing to accept a contingency fee, which means the lawyer gets paid only if you win.

Represent you in disputes over terms of your lease or rental agreement. If the lease or agreement has an "attorneys' fees" clause and your position appears to be a solid winner, the landlord will end up paying for the lawyer if you win. Obviously, this provision makes your case more attractive to a lawyer.

Review a long-term lease before you sign it. Most people don't need to involve a lawyer when they sign a lease. But if you plan to lease a place for several years, and especially if you're adding custom provisions such as an option to purchase, the advice of a knowledgeable lawyer will probably be worth the expense.

Finding a Good Lawyer

Most lawyers in general practice have limited experience in landlord-tenant legal issues. (In fact, by now you may know more than many of them.) So if you just pick a name out of the telephone book or you find online, or go with the attorney who prepared your will, you're unlikely to get someone who's qualified to deal with your problem. And the lawyers who are thoroughly familiar with landlord-tenant law often represent property owners; they may be unwilling to take a tenant's case—or charge so much that you can't afford them anyway.

But the good news is that in every metropolitan area there are competent tenants' lawyers who charge fairly for their services. Not only do these attorneys already know the law (you don't pay while they look it up), they understand how the landlord-tenant business works and can often suggest effective strategies that general practitioners don't even know about.

RESOURCE

Looking for a lawyer? Asking for a referral from someone you trust can be a good way to find legal help. Someone looking to hire a lawyer, even if only for consultation, can also try these excellent and free resources:

Nolo's Lawyer Directory. Nolo has an easy-to-use online directory of lawyers, organized by location and area of expertise. You can find the directory and its comprehensive profiles at www.nolo.com/lawyers.

Lawyers.com. At Lawyers.com you'll find a user-friendly search tool that allows you to tailor results by area of law and geography. You can also search for attorneys by name. Attorney profiles prominently display contact information, list topics of expertise, and show ratings—by both clients and other legal professionals.

Martindale.com. Martindale.com allows you to search not only by practice area and location, but also by criteria, such as by law school. Whether you look for lawyers by name or expertise, you'll find listings with detailed background information, peer and client ratings, and even profile visibility.

Keep in mind that these online resources are simply modern versions of the Yellow Pages: The listed lawyers have paid to have their names show up on the relevant pages.

Compile a List of Prospects

The best way to find a suitable attorney is through one or more of these sources:

A trustworthy person or organization with experience in the landlord-tenant field. A local tenants' organization is often a good place to get a referral.

Organizations that focus on a particular area of the law, or special interest groups. Fair housing groups can give referrals for discrimination cases. Women's organizations, such as the National Women's Law Center (www.nwlc.org), may recommend attorneys who handle sexual harassment cases; groups representing the rights of disabled people, such as the Disability Rights Education and Defense Fund (DREDF), may recommend attorneys who specialize in disability rights litigation (see www.dredf.org).

An experienced local lawyer. Ask for a referral to someone who regularly represents tenants. For example, if you or a friend has been pleased with the services of a local family law practitioner, chances are that this attorney will steer you to an equally good tenants' lawyer.

Local legal aid (legal services) office. Legal aid usually has lawyers experienced in representing tenants. If you have a limited income, you may be eligible for their services. Even if you are not eligible, ask for a reference—the legal aid office may know local lawyers who are experienced, honest, and skillful.

RENT CONTROL

Where there's rent control, there are lawyers. Because many rent control ordinances are complicated or poorly written, attorneys are almost always on the scene. Ask the rent control board, or visit a meeting or hearing and see who shows up on behalf of the tenants.

Attorneys who write articles about landlord-tenant law in trade magazines and newspapers. Even if these lawyers live in other parts of the country, it can make sense to track them down. Experts in this increasingly complex field share information at national conferences or online, and may be able to provide top-notch referrals in your area.

Your state's continuing legal education program—usually run by a bar association, a law school, or both. These programs offer seminars and publications for attorneys and can often identify lawyers with expertise in landlord-tenant law.

TIP

Don't forget your renters' insurance. If you followed our advice in Chapter 2 and purchased renters' insurance, you have bought legal representation if you are sued by your landlord, a guest, or other tenant for specified acts. (Your policy does not entitle you to a lawyer in an eviction or if you are the one who intends to file a lawsuit.) Contact your insurance company immediately if you are served with legal papers (usually called a Complaint and Summons).

Help From Nonlawyers

In large metropolitan areas, look to tenants' organizations and legal typing services (often called independent paralegals) for help if you're sued for eviction. Some tenants' groups provide free one-on-one eviction defense help, and others offer classes or seminars on particular issues, such as eviction defense or rent withholding.

Legal typing services, on the other hand, are private businesses that help consumers do their own legal paperwork, for fees that are usually much lower than lawyers. They normally specialize in typing your eviction papers (such as your Answer to the landlord's Complaint) so they'll be accepted by the court, arranging for filing, and then serving court papers on the landlord. Typically, they charge by the page or by the document.

Typing services can't give legal advice about your specific case and can't represent you in court at the eviction trial. You must decide what steps to take in your case and provide the information to complete the needed forms.

To find a nonlawyer typing service, search online or in your phone book for "Eviction Services" or "Paralegals" in your area. Ask how many years they have been in business, and also ask for and check references.

Shop Around

After several reliable organizations or individuals give you the names of prospective lawyers, your job has just begun. First, take a look at your list of names. If several people recommend the same attorney, start with that one.

The best way to evaluate a prospective lawyer is to arrange a brief meeting to evaluate your case. If your case has the potential for a significant monetary award (as do discrimination or personal injury cases), many lawyers will be glad to speak to you for a half hour or so at no charge, or at a reduced rate.

When you meet, briefly explain your legal problem and how much work you plan to do yourself. Try to get a feeling for the lawyer's experience and accessibility.

Does the lawyer frankly answer your questions about fees, experience in landlord-tenant matters, and your specific legal issue? Stay away from lawyers who make you feel uncomfortable asking questions. And be sure you understand how the lawyer charges for services. (We discuss various fee arrangements below.)

Will the lawyer provide the kind of legal help you want? If you plan to be actively involved in dealing with your legal problem, look for a lawyer who doesn't resent your participation. If it will make the lawyer uncomfortable, you have the wrong lawyer.

Does the lawyer clearly lay out all your options? A good lawyer should almost always discuss the possibility of trying to resolve your dispute through negotiation or mediation instead of immediately going to court.

Will the lawyer be accessible? This is a huge issue —probably the most common complaint against lawyers is that they don't return phone calls or faxes and are not available to their clients in times of need. If every time you have a question there's a delay of several days before you can talk to your lawyer, you'll lose precious time, not to mention sleep. So be sure to discuss with any lawyer how fast you can expect to have phone calls returned and how you can contact the lawyer in an emergency.

Is the lawyer experienced in your particular legal problem? If your property is in a rent-controlled city, be sure the lawyer knows its particular rent control laws and practices.

Does the lawyer represent landlords, too? Chances are that a lawyer who represents both landlords and tenants has the knowledge to do a good job for you. On the other hand, you'll want to steer clear of lawyers who represent landlords almost exclusively, since their sympathies and world view are likely to be different from yours.

TIP
Talk with other tenant clients. It's a good idea to ask for references from some of the lawyer's other tenant clients, particularly those with similar legal problems. Find out how satisfied other tenants were with the lawyer's work.

Fee Arrangements With Lawyers

How you pay your lawyer depends on the type of legal service you need and the amount of legal work involved. Once you choose a lawyer, ask for a written fee agreement explaining how fees and costs will be billed and paid. In some states, a written agreement is required by law; even if it isn't, it's always a good idea. Be sure to include an overall cap on what you can be billed absent your specific agreement.

If your case involves a significant amount of attorney time, and your lawyer will be delegating some of the work to a less experienced associate, paralegal, or secretary, the delegated work should be billed at a lower hourly rate. Be sure this information is recorded in your written fee agreement.

Lawyers' Billing Practices

There are four basic ways that lawyers charge for their services.

Hourly fees. In most parts of the United States, you can get competent representation for $125 to $300 an hour. Most lawyers bill in ten- or 15-minute increments. If you're doing much of the legal legwork yourself, and just want specific questions answered, you'll probably be billed this way. Comparison shopping among lawyers can help you avoid overpaying, but only if you are comparing lawyers with similar expertise. A highly experienced tenants' attorney may be cheaper in the long run than a general practitioner, even at a higher hourly rate. The fact that the tenants' attorney is further along the learning curve means it should take less time to come up with good answers and advice.

Flat fees. Sometimes a lawyer will quote you a flat fee for a specific job—for example, to defend you in an eviction lawsuit. In a flat fee agreement, you pay the same amount regardless of how much time the lawyer spends on the particular job. If a lawyer is highly recommended by others as trustworthy and the flat fee is moderate, this can be a great arrangement for you.

Contingency fees. This is a percentage—commonly, one-third—of the amount the lawyer obtains for you in a negotiated settlement or through a trial. If the lawyer recovers nothing for you, you pay only for the costs of filing suit and other expenses (for example, expert fees and depositions). Contingency fees are common in personal injury and discrimination cases, but relatively unusual for eviction defense. (For more details on contingency fees, see Chapter 5.)

The landlord pays. If your lease or written rental agreement has a two-way ("loser pays") attorneys' fees provision (discussed in Chapter 2), you are entitled to recover your attorneys' fees if you win a lawsuit that concerns the meaning or implementation of that agreement. The clause does not cover fees if the dispute arose independently of the lease or rental contract, such as a discrimination claim, personal injury lawsuit, or sexual harassment case. If you have a strong case that's backed up with a loser-pays clause, many lawyers will take your case for little or nothing, in the expectation that they will get paid by the losing landlord.

Saving on Legal Fees

Here are some key ways to hold down the cost of legal services:

Do your own research. Read any consumer-oriented legal materials in your state or city, such as informational booklets prepared by your state's attorney general's office or consumer protection agency. The HUD website (www.hud.gov) includes many useful links for each state. Search "[name of your state] tenant rights" to get started. Also, see the suggestions in "Doing Your Own Legal Research," below, as to how you can easily find relevant statutes, ordinances, and court decisions that affect your problem.

Be organized. Especially when you are paying by the hour, it's important to gather important documents, write a short chronology of events, and concisely explain a problem to your lawyer. Since papers can get lost in a lawyer's office, keep a copy of everything that's important, such as your lease or rental agreement, move-in letter from your landlord, correspondence with the landlord, repair requests, and other records.

Be prepared before you meet your lawyer. Whenever possible, put your questions in writing and email, mail, fax, or deliver them to your lawyer before all meetings or phone conversations. That way your lawyer can be prepared to answer your questions and won't have to schedule another conference or phone conversation. Early preparation also helps focus the meeting so there is less chance of digressing (at your expense) into unrelated topics.

How Legal Costs Can Mount Up

In addition to the fees they charge for their time, lawyers bill for a variety of items as well—and if you're not wary, these costs can add up quickly. Costs can include charges for:

- photocopying
- faxes
- overnight mail
- messenger service
- expert witness fees
- court filing fees
- long distance phone calls
- process servers
- work by investigators
- work by legal assistants or paralegals
- deposition transcripts
- online legal research, and
- travel.

Many lawyers absorb the cost of photocopying, faxes, local phone calls, and the like as normal office overhead—part of the cost of doing business—but that's not always the case. So in working out the fee arrangements, ask for a list of costs you'll be expected to pay. If a lawyer seems intent on nickel-and-diming you to death, look elsewhere. For example, if you learn the law office charges $3 or more for each page it faxes, red flags should go up. On the other hand, it is reasonable for a lawyer to pass along expenses like court costs, process server fees, and work by investigators.

Carefully review lawyer bills. Like everyone else, lawyers make mistakes. For example, a ".1" of an hour (six minutes) may be transposed into a "1." (one hour) when the data are entered into the billing system. That's $200 instead of $20 if your lawyer charges $200 per hour. Don't hesitate to politely question your bill. You have the right to a clear explanation of costs.

Resolving Problems With Your Lawyer

If you see a problem emerging with your lawyer, don't just sit back and fume; call or write your lawyer. Whatever it is that rankles—a shockingly high bill or a missed deadline—have an honest discussion about your feelings.

Your Rights as a Client

As a client, you have the right to expect the following:

- courteous treatment by your lawyer and staff members
- an itemized statement of services rendered and a full advance explanation of billing practices
- charges for agreed-upon fees and no more
- prompt responses to phone calls, emails, and letters
- confidential legal conferences, free from unwarranted interruptions
- up-to-date information on the status of your case
- diligent and competent legal representation, and
- clear answers to all questions.

If you can't frankly discuss these sometimes sensitive matters with your lawyer, fire that lawyer and hire another one. If you don't, you'll surely waste money on unnecessary legal fees and risk having matters turn out badly.

If you decide to change lawyers, be sure to fire your old lawyer before you hire a new one. If you don't, you could find yourself being billed by two lawyers at the same time. Also, be sure to get all important legal documents back from the first lawyer. Tell your new lawyer what your old one has done to date and pass on the file.

Here are some tips on resolving specific problems:

- If you have a dispute over fees, the local bar association may be able to mediate it for you, although the extent to which they are willing to go after one of their own varies greatly.

- If a lawyer has violated legal ethics—for example, had a conflict of interest, overbilled you, or didn't represent you zealously—the state agency that licenses lawyers may discipline or even disbar the lawyer. Although lawyer oversight groups are typically biased in favor of the legal profession, they will often take action if your lawyer has done something seriously wrong.

- Where a major mistake has been made—for example, a lawyer missed the deadline for filing your papers in response to an eviction lawsuit—you can sue for malpractice. Many lawyers carry malpractice insurance, and your dispute may be settled out of court.

Doing Your Own Legal Research

Using this book is a good way to educate yourself about the laws that affect your rights as a tenant. But given the fact that the laws and court decisions of 50 states, plus the ordinances of many thousands of municipalities, are involved, no one book can do the whole job. If you face a serious problem with your landlord, sooner or later you'll probably need more information. For example, if you were assaulted in the hall of your apartment building, you'll almost surely want to look up your state court decisions involving similar incidents.

Lawyers aren't the only source for legal help. There's a lot you can do on your own. You can get the text of key federal and state statutes (except Louisiana) free on many states' websites. Rules put out by federal and state regulatory agencies are often available, too, and the Internet's legal resources grow every day.

If you don't have access to the Internet, law libraries are full of valuable information, such as state statutes that regulate the landlord-tenant relationship. Your first step is to find a law library that's open to the public. You may find such a library in your county courthouse or at your state capitol. Publicly funded law schools generally permit the public to use their libraries, and some private law schools grant access to their libraries—sometimes for a modest fee.

Don't overlook the reference department of the public library if you're in a large city. Many large public libraries have a fairly decent legal research collection. Also, ask about using the law library in your own lawyer's office. Some lawyers, on request, will share their books with their clients.

 RESOURCE

Recommended reading on legal research. We don't have space here to show you how to do your own legal research in anything approaching a comprehensive fashion. To get started, go to Nolo's website at www. nolo.com/legal-research. Here you'll find articles on legal research, advice on finding local ordinances and court cases, and more. To go further, we recommend *Legal Research: How to Find & Understand the Law*, by Stephen Elias and the Editors of Nolo (Nolo). This nontechnical book gives easy-to-use, step-by-step instructions on how find legal information.

Statutes and Ordinances

Every tenant and every landlord is governed by a mix of state, local, and federal law, with state law almost always being the most important. In some areas, such as discrimination, federal, state, and local laws overlap. When this happens, the laws that give tenants the most protection usually prevail.

If you're starting out to find the answer to a legal question, it's usually best to start by looking for a state, federal, or local law that covers your issue.

State Statutes

State law regulates, among other things, rent rules, deposits, your right to privacy, housing standards, maintenance responsibilities, and eviction procedures. Your state consumer protection agency or attorney general may provide helpful publications or phone advice summarizing and explaining these laws. (Find yours at www.usa.gov/state-consumer.)

If you need more information, begin with the legal references (citations) to your state's key landlord-tenant laws contained in this book. Armed with the citation, go online to your state's official website (www.[state abbreviation].gov). Every state has posted its statutes online, although each has presented them in a unique way, so we can't give you precise directions for locating a law in your state. But in general, you'll find links to state legislation or state laws, and once in that section of the site, you should be able to plug in your citation and get to the law you want to read.

The website maintained by the Cornell Legal Information Institute (www.law.cornell.edu) also provides access to federal and state statutes, cases, and informative articles.

If you want to find out how courts have interpreted the law you're dealing with, you'll need to go to a physical law library and read the law in an "annotated code" collection (annotated code sets aren't available for free online). These are books that include not only the statutes, but cases that have involved them. You may find similar cases to yours, which could be very helpful. Annotated codes have comprehensive indexes by topic, and are kept up to date with paperback supplements ("pocket parts") stuck inside the back cover of each volume.

CAUTION
Never rely on old law. Many laws change every year. Make sure you are up to date by referring to the insert you'll almost always find inside the back cover of code books. (If there isn't an insert, it's because the hardbound book was published that year and is completely current.)

These pocket parts, which are organized by code number, should contain all law changes through the end of your state's last legislative session.

Local Ordinances

Local ordinances, such as rent control rules, noise regulations, health and safety standards, requirements for interest on tenants' security deposits, and antidiscrimination rules will also affect your tenancy. Many municipalities have local ordinances online—just search for the name of a particular city. Sometimes this presence is nothing more than a not-so-slick public relations page, but sometimes it includes a large body of information, including local ordinances available for searching and downloading.

Be sure to check out State and Local Government on the Net (www.statelocalgov.net), and www.municode.com, good sources for finding local governments online.

Finally, your local public library or office of the city attorney, mayor, or city manager can provide information on local ordinances that affect tenants. If you rent in a city with rent control, be sure to get a copy of the ordinance, as well as all rules issued by the rent board covering rent increases and hearings.

Federal Statutes and Regulations

Congress has enacted laws, and federal agencies such as the U.S. Department of Housing and Urban Development (HUD) have adopted regulations, that cover important aspects of landlord-tenant law. Examples include antidiscrimination laws, wage and hour rules that affect the employment of tenant-managers, and statutes requiring the disclosure of environmental health hazards.

Federal laws affecting tenants are contained in a multivolume series of books called the U.S. Code. It consists of 50 separate numbered titles. Each title covers a specific subject matter. For example, the federal Fair Housing Acts are contained in title 42 and begin with Section 3601.

Federal regulations which explain the law in detail are usually published in the Code of Federal

Regulations (C.F.R.), organized by subject into 50 separate titles. For example, regulations issued by the Environmental Protection Agency interpreting the federal lead paint legislation ("Title Ten") can be found in Title 24, Part 35, and Title 40, Part 745.

To access the U.S. Code online, see the "Federal Law Resources" on Nolo's website (in the Legal Research section), or see the Cornell Legal Information Institute at www.law.cornell.edu. Finally, check www.usa.gov, the official website for U.S. government information.

Court Decisions

Sometimes the answer to a legal question cannot be found in a statute. This happens when:

- court cases and opinions have greatly expanded or explained the statute, taking it beyond its obvious or literal meaning, or
- the law that applies to your question has been made by judges, not legislators.

Court Decisions That Explain Statutes

Statutes and ordinances rarely explain themselves. For example, a state law may guarantee you the right to housing that is weatherproofed, but that statute alone may not tell you whether that means your landlord must provide storm windows. However, other tenants may have asked the same question and ended up in court. If a judge interpreted the statute and wrote an opinion on the matter, that written opinion, once published, will become the law as much as the statute itself. If a higher court (an appellate court) has also examined the question, then its opinion becomes the law statewide.

To find out if there are written court decisions that interpret a particular statute or ordinance, a good place to start is an annotated code (discussed above). If a case that seems to answer your question or relate to your problem is listed in the code, your first step is to find and read it.

Next, if you find a court decision that's useful to your case, make sure the decision is still good law—

that a more recent opinion from a higher court has not reached a different conclusion. To do this, use a set of books known as *Shepard's*. Explaining how to do this takes more space than is available here, but a friendly law librarian can guide you. *Legal Research: How to Find & Understand the Law*, by Stephen Elias and the Editors of Nolo (Nolo), has a good, easy-to-follow explanation of how to use the *Shepard's* system to expand and update your research.

Court Decisions That Make Law

Some laws that govern your rights will not have a starting point in a statute or ordinance. These laws, which are entirely court-made, are known as common law. An example of common law in many states is the landlord's responsibility to provide tenants with habitable housing, discussed in Chapter 8.

Researching common law is more difficult than researching statutory law, because you do not have the launching pad of a statute or ordinance. But with a little perseverance, you can find your way to the court cases that have developed and explained the legal concept you wish to understand. It's rather challenging to find cases about a topic online when you don't have a statute as a starting point. For example, if you're interested in a landlord's liability for burglary committed after the landlord installed a faulty lock, you may not have a statute to begin with. If you're online, try using a search engine to see if you get results that include cases (or reports of cases). This is an area where you'll be hampered if you are relying solely on free online resources.

At the physical law library, you will have access to materials that will help you get to the relevant cases. A good beginning is to ask the librarian for any lawyer's practice guides in the field of landlord-tenant law (these are not available for free online). These outlines of the law, which are written to provide basic information to lawyers, are usually up to date. Because lawyers' practice guides are so popular, they are usually kept behind the reference counter and cannot be taken out of the library.

How to Read a Case Citation

If you find a citation to a case that looks important, you may want to read the opinion. You'll need the title of the case and its citation, which is like an address for the set of books, volume, and page where the case can be found. Ask the law librarian for help.

Although it may look about as decipherable as hieroglyphics, once understood, a case citation gives lots of useful information in a small space. It tells you the names of the people or companies involved, the volume of the reporter (series of books) in which the case is published, the page number on which it begins, and the year in which the case was decided.

EXAMPLE: *Smith v. Jones Int'l,* 123 N.Y.S.2d 456 (1994). Smith and Jones are the names of the parties having the legal dispute. The case is reported in volume 123 of the New York Supplement, Second Series, beginning on page 456; the court issued the decision in 1994.

	Common Abbreviations in Case Citations	
Abbreviation	**Title**	**Courts Covered**
A. and A.2d	Atlantic Reporter (first and second series)	Connecticut, Delaware, the District of Columbia, Maine, Maryland, New Hampshire, New Jersey, Pennsylvania, Rhode Island, and Vermont
N.E. and N.E.2d	Northeastern Reporter (first and second series)	Illinois, Indiana, Massachusetts, New York (except for appellate court decisions), and Ohio
N.Y.S.	New York Supplement (first and second series)	New York appellate court
N.W. and N.W.2d	Northwestern Reporter (first and second series)	Iowa, Michigan, Minnesota, Nebraska, North Dakota, South Dakota, and Wisconsin
P. and P.2d	Pacific Reporter (first and second series)	Alaska, Arizona, California (except for appellate court decisions), Colorado, Hawaii, Idaho, Kansas, Montana, Nevada, New Mexico, Oklahoma, Oregon, Utah, Washington, and Wyoming
Cal. Rptr.	California Reporter (first and second series)	California appellate court
S.E. and S.E.2d	Southeastern Reporter (first and second series)	Georgia, North Carolina, South Carolina, Virginia, and West Virginia
So. and So.2d	Southern Reporter (first and second series)	Alabama, Florida, Louisiana, and Mississippi
S.W. and S.W.2d	Southwestern Reporter (first and second series)	Arkansas, Kentucky, Missouri, Tennessee, and Texas
U.S.	United States Reports	U.S. Supreme Court
S.Ct.	Supreme Court Reporter	U.S. Supreme Court
F.2d or F.3d	Federal Reporter (second or third series)	Federal court other than the U.S. Supreme Court
F. Supp.	Federal Supplement	Federal court other than the U.S. Supreme Court

Most states publish their own official state reports. All published state court decisions are also included in seven regional reporters. There are also special reports for U.S. Supreme Court and other federal court decisions. (See "Common Abbreviations in Case Citations," above.)

Law Review Articles

Law schools and other state and local bar associations publish periodicals that may contain timely articles on legal issues that affect tenants. But academic journals rarely contain useful, practical information. Local bar association journals and other publications aimed at practicing lawyers are likely to be much more helpful.

Computerized Research Services: Helpful but Costly

Two companies, West Publishing and Lexis, offer full-scale legal research services that make it relatively easy to search a huge database of statutes, court decisions, regulations, and legal articles. The cost is very high.

If you are not connected with a large law office or law school, you will likely find it difficult to get access to either Westlaw or Lexis for free. A small but growing number of law libraries or public libraries, however, offer these services.

Keep in mind that it takes time and training to learn how to navigate these legal research systems efficiently. However, if you are already savvy on how to use computerized information retrieval services, you may want to give it a try.

State Landlord-Tenant Law Charts

State Landlord-Tenant Statutes...348

State Rent Rules...349

State Rules on Notice Required to Change or Terminate a
    Month-to-Month Tenancy 351

State Security Deposit Rules...354

Required Landlord Disclosures 364

State Laws in Domestic Violence Situations...378

State Laws on Rent Withholding and Repair and Deduct Remedies............................383

State Laws on Landlord's Access to Rental Property...385

State Laws on Handling Abandoned Property...387

State Laws Prohibiting Landlord Retaliation...388

State Laws on Termination for Nonpayment of Rent 390

State Laws on Termination for Violation of Lease 393

State Laws on Unconditional Quit Terminations...395

State Small Claims Court Limits...402

Landlord's Duty to Rerent..408

Consequences of Self-Help Evictions..410

How to Use the State Landlord-Tenant Law Charts

The State Landlord-Tenant Law Charts are comprehensive, 50-state charts that give you two kinds of information:

- citations for key statutes and cases, which you can use if you want to read the law yourself or look for more information (see the legal research discussion in Chapter 20), and
- the state rules themselves, such as notice periods and deposit limits—in other words, what the statutes and cases say.

When you're looking for information for your state, simply find your state along the left-hand list on the chart, and read to the right—you'll see the statute or case, and the rule.

State Landlord-Tenant Statutes

Here are some of the key statutes pertaining to landlord-tenant law in each state. In some states, important legal principles are contained in court opinions, not codes or statutes. Court-made law and rent stabilization—rent control—laws and regulations are not reflected in this chart.

Alabama	Ala. Code §§ 35-9-1 to 35-9-100; 35-9A-101 to 35-9A-603	**Mississippi**	Miss. Code Ann. §§ 89-7-1 to 89-8-29
Alaska	Alaska Stat. §§ 34.03.010 to 34.03.380	**Missouri**	Mo. Rev. Stat. §§ 441.005 to 441.880; §§ 535.010 to 535.300
Arizona	Ariz. Rev. Stat. Ann. §§ 12-1171 to 12-1183; 33-1301 to 33-1381; 33-301 to 33-381	**Montana**	Mont. Code Ann. §§ 70-24-101 to 70-27-117
		Nebraska	Neb. Rev. Stat. §§ 76-1401 to 76-1449
Arkansas	Ark. Code Ann. §§ 18-16-101 to 18-16-306; 18-16-501 to 18-16-509; 18-17-101 to 18-17-913	**Nevada**	Nev. Rev. Stat. Ann. §§ 118A.010 to 118A.530; 40.215 to 40.425
California	Cal. Civ. Code §§ 1925 to 1954.05; 1954.50 to 1954.605; 1961 to 1995.340	**New Hampshire**	N.H. Rev. Stat. Ann. §§ 540:1 to 540:29; 540-A:1 to 540-A:8; 540-B:1 to 540-B:10
Colorado	Colo. Rev. Stat. §§ 38-12-101 to 38-12-104; 38-12-301 to 38-12-302 38-12-401 to 38-12-402; 38-12-501 to 38-12-511; 38-12-701; 13-40-101 to 13-40-123	**New Jersey**	N.J. Stat. Ann. §§ 46:8-1 to 46:8-50; 2A:42-1 to 42-96
		New Mexico	N.M. Stat. Ann. §§ 47-8-1 to 47-8-51
Connecticut	Conn. Gen. Stat. Ann. §§ 47a-1 to 47a-74	**New York**	N.Y. Real Prop. Law §§ 220 to 238; Real Prop. Acts §§ 701 to 853; Mult. Dwell. Law (all); Mult. Res. Law (all); Gen. Oblig. Law §§ 7-101 to 7-109
Delaware	Del. Code Ann. tit. 25, §§ 5101 to 5907		
Dist. of Columbia	D.C. Code Ann. §§ 42-3201 to 42-3610; D.C. Mun. Regs., tit. 14, §§ 300 to 311	**North Carolina**	N.C. Gen. Stat. §§ 42-1 to 42-14.2; 42-25.6 to 42-76
Florida	Fla. Stat. Ann. §§ 83.40 to 83.683	**North Dakota**	N.D. Cent. Code §§ 47-16-01 to 47-16-41
Georgia	Ga. Code Ann. §§ 44-7-1 to 44-7-81	**Ohio**	Ohio Rev. Code Ann. §§ 5321.01 to 5321.19
Hawaii	Haw. Rev. Stat. §§ 521-1 to 521-82	**Oklahoma**	Okla. Stat. Ann. tit. 41, §§ 101 to 136
Idaho	Idaho Code §§ 6-301 to 6-324; §§ 55-208 to 55-308	**Oregon**	Or. Rev. Stat. §§ 90.100 to 91.225
Illinois	735 Ill. Comp. Stat. §§ 5/9-201 to 321; 765 Ill. Comp. Stat. §§ 705/0.01 to 742/30; 765 Ill. Comp. Stat. §§ 750/1 to 750/35	**Pennsylvania**	68 Pa. Cons. Stat. Ann. §§ 250.101 to 399.18
		Rhode Island	R.I. Gen. Laws §§ 34-18-1 to 34-18-57
Indiana	Ind. Code Ann. §§ 32-31-1-1 to 32-31-9-15; 36-1-24.2-1 to 36-1-24.2-4	**South Carolina**	S.C. Code Ann. §§ 27-40-10 to 27-40-940
Iowa	Iowa Code Ann. §§ 562A.1 to 562A.37	**South Dakota**	S.D. Codified Laws Ann. §§ 43-32-1 to 43-32-32
Kansas	Kan. Stat. Ann. §§ 58-2501 to 58-2573	**Tennessee**	Tenn. Code Ann. §§ 66-28-101 to 66-28-521
Kentucky	Ky. Rev. Stat. Ann. §§ 383.010 to 383.715	**Texas**	Tex. Prop. Code Ann. §§ 91.001 to 92.355
Louisiana	La. Rev. Stat. Ann. §§ 9:3251 to 9:3261; La. Civ. Code Ann. art. 2668 to 2729	**Utah**	Utah Code Ann. §§ 57-17-1 to 57-17-5, 57-22-1 to 57-22-7
		Vermont	Vt. Stat. Ann. tit. 9, §§ 4451 to 4469a
Maine	Me. Rev. Stat. Ann. tit. 14, §§ 6000 to 6046	**Virginia**	Va. Code Ann. §§ 55-217 to 55-248.40
Maryland	Md. Code Ann. [Real Prop.] §§ 8-101 to 8-604	**Washington**	Wash. Rev. Code Ann. §§ 59.04.010 to 59.18.912
Massachusetts	Mass. Gen. Laws Ann. ch. 186, §§ 1A to 29; ch. 186a, §§ 1 to 6	**West Virginia**	W.Va. Code §§ 37-6-1 to 37-6A-6
Michigan	Mich. Comp. Laws §§ 554.131 to 554.201; 554.601 to 554.641	**Wisconsin**	Wis. Stat. Ann. §§ 704.01 to 704.95; Wis. Admin. Code ATCP §§ 134.01 to 134.10
Minnesota	Minn. Stat. Ann. §§ 504B.001 to 504B.471	**Wyoming**	Wyo. Stat. §§ 1-21-1201 to 1-21-1211; 34-2-128 to 34-2-129

State Rent Rules

Here are citations for statutes that set out rent rules in each state. When a state has no statute, the space is left blank. See the "Notice Required to Change or Terminate a Month-to-Month Tenancy" chart in this appendix for citations to raising rent.

State	When Rent Is Due	Grace Period	Where Rent Is Due	Late Fees
Alabama	Ala. Code § 35-9A-161 (c)		Ala. Code § 35-9A-161 (c)	
Alaska	Alaska Stat. § 34.03.020(c)		Alaska Stat. § 34.03.020(c)	
Arizona	Ariz. Rev. Stat. Ann. §§ 33-1314(C), 33-1368(B)		Ariz. Rev. Stat. Ann. § 33-1314(C)	Ariz. Rev. Stat. Ann. § 33-1368(B) [1]
Arkansas	Ark. Code Ann. § 18-17-401	Ark. Code Ann. §§ 18-17-701, 18-17-901	Ark. Code Ann. § 18-17-401	
California	Cal. Civ. Code § 1947		Cal. Civ. Code § 1962	*Orozco v. Casimiro*, 121 Cal. App.4th Supp. 7 (2004) [2]
Colorado				
Connecticut	Conn. Gen. Stat. Ann. § 47a-3a	Conn. Gen. Stat. Ann. § 47a-15a	Conn. Gen. Stat. Ann. § 47a-3a	Conn. Gen. Stat. Ann. §§ 47a-4(a)(8), 47a-15a [3]
Delaware	Del. Code Ann. tit. 25, § 5501(b)		Del. Code Ann. title 25, § 5501(b)	Del. Code Ann. tit. 25, § 5501(d) [4]
D.C.		D.C. Code Ann. § 42-3505.31		D.C. Code Ann. § 42-3505.31 [5]
Florida	Fla. Stat. Ann. § 83.46(1)			
Georgia				
Hawaii	Haw. Rev. Stat. § 521-21(b)		Haw. Rev. Stat. § 521-21(b)	Late charge cannot exceed 8% of the amount of rent due.
Idaho				
Illinois	735 Ill. Comp. Stat. Ann. § 5/9-218		735 Ill. Comp. Stat. Ann. § 5/9-218	
Indiana	*Watson v. Penn*, 108 Ind. 21 (1886), 8 N.E. 636 (1886)			
Iowa	Iowa Code Ann. § 562A.9(3)		Iowa Code Ann. § 562A.9(3)	Iowa Code Ann. § 562A.9 [6]
Kansas	Kan. Stat. Ann. § 58-2545(c)		Kan. Stat. Ann. § 58-2545(c)	
Kentucky	Ky. Rev. Stat. Ann. § 383.565(2)		Ky. Rev. Stat. Ann. § 383.565(2)	
Louisiana	La. Civ. Code Ann. art. 2703		La. Civ. Code Ann. art. 2703	
Maine		Me. Rev. Stat. Ann. tit. 14, § 6028		Me. Rev. Stat. Ann. tit. 14, § 6028 [7]
Maryland				Md. Code Ann. [Real Prop.] § 8-208(d)(3) [8]
Massachusetts		Mass. Gen. Laws Ann. ch. 186, § 15B(1)(c); ch. 239, § 8A		Mass. Gen. Laws Ann. ch. 186, § 15B(1)(c) [9]
Michigan	*Hilsendegen v. Scheich*, 21 N.W.2d 894 (1885)			

[1] Late fees must be set forth in a written rental agreement and be reasonable. (Arizona)

[2] Late fees will be enforced only if specified language is included in a written lease or rental agreement. (California)

[3] Landlords may not charge a late fee until 9 days after rent is due. (Connecticut)

[4] To charge a late fee, landlord must maintain an office in the county where the rental unit is located at which tenants can pay rent. If a landlord doesn't have a local office for this purpose, tenant has 3 extra days (beyond the due date) to pay rent before the landlord can charge a late fee. Late fee cannot exceed 5% of rent and cannot be imposed until the rent is more than 5 days late. (Delaware)

[5] Fee policy must be stated in the lease, and cannot exceed 5% of rent due, nor be imposed until rent is five days late (or later, if lease so provides). Landlord cannot evict for failure to pay late fee (may deduct unpaid fees from security deposit at end of tenancy). (D.C.)

[6] When rent is $700 per month or less, late fees cannot exceed $12 per day, or a total amount of $60 per month; when rent is more than $700 per month, fees cannot exceed $20 per day or a total amount of $100 per month. (Iowa)

[7] Late fees cannot exceed 4% of the amount due for 30 days. Landlord must notify tenants, in writing, of any late fee at the start of the tenancy, and cannot impose it until rent is 15 days late. (Maine)

[8] Late fees cannot exceed 5% of the rent due. (Maryland)

[9] Late fees, including interest on late rent, may not be imposed until the rent is 30 days late. (Massachusetts)

State Rent Rules (continued)

State	When Rent Is Due	Grace Period	Where Rent Is Due	Late Fees
Minnesota				Minn. Stat. Ann. § 504B.177 [10]
Mississippi				
Missouri	Mo. Rev. Stat. § 535.060			
Montana	Mont. Code Ann. § 70-24-201(2)(c)		Mont. Code Ann. § 70-24-201(2)(b)	
Nebraska	Neb. Rev. Stat. § 76-1414(3)		Neb. Rev. Stat. § 76-1414(3)	
Nevada	Nev. Rev. Stat. Ann. § 118A.210		Nev. Rev. Stat. Ann. § 118A	Nev. Rev. Stat. Ann. § 118A.200(3)(g), (210/5)(c) [11]
New Hampshire				
New Jersey		N.J. Stat. Ann. § 2A:42-6.1	N.J. Stat. Ann. § 2A:42-6.1	N.J. Stat. Ann. § 2A:42-6.1 [12]
New Mexico	N.M. Stat. Ann. § 47-8-15(B)		N.M. Stat. Ann. § 47-8-15(B)	N.M. Stat. Ann. § 47-8-15(D) [13]
New York				
North Carolina		N.C. Gen Stat. § 42-46		N.C. Gen. Stat. § 42-46 [14]
North Dakota	N.D. Cent. Code § 47-16-20			
Ohio				
Oklahoma	Okla. Stat. Ann. tit. 41, § 109	Okla. Stat. Ann. tit. 41, § 132(B)	Okla. Stat. Ann. tit. 41, § 109	*Sun Ridge Investors, Ltd. v. Parker*, 956 P.2d 876 (1998) [15]
Oregon	Or. Rev. Stat. § 90.220	Or. Rev. Stat. § 90.260	Or. Rev. Stat. § 90.220	Or. Rev. Stat. § 90.260 [16]
Pennsylvania				
Rhode Island	R.I. Gen. Laws § 34-18-15(c)	R.I. Gen. Laws § 34-18-35	R.I. Gen. Laws § 34-18-15(c)	
South Carolina	S.C. Code Ann. § 27-40-310(c)		S.C. Code Ann. § 27-40-310(c)	
South Dakota	S.D. Codified Laws Ann. § 43-32-12			
Tennessee	Tenn. Code Ann. § 66-28-201(c)	Tenn. Code Ann. § 66-28-201(d)	Tenn. Code Ann. § 66-28-201(c)	Tenn. Code Ann. § 66-28-201(d) [17]
Texas		Tex. Prop. Code Ann. § 92.019 [18]		
Utah				
Vermont	Vt. Stat. Ann. tit. 9, § 4455			
Virginia	Va. Code Ann. § 55-248.7(C)		Va. Code Ann. § 55-248.7(C)	
Washington				
West Virginia				
Wisconsin				
Wyoming				

[10] Late fee policy must be agreed to in writing, and may not exceed 8% of the overdue rent payment. The "due date" for late fee purposes does not include a date earlier than the usual rent due date, by which date a tenant earns a discount. (Minnesota)

[11] A court will presume that there is no late fee provision unless it is included in a written rental agreement, but the landlord can offer evidence to overcome that presumption. (Nevada)

[12] Landlord must wait 5 days before charging a late fee, but only when the premises are rented or leased by senior citizens receiving Social Security Old Age Pensions, Railroad Retirement Pensions, or other governmental pensions in lieu of Social Security Old Age Pensions; or when rented by recipients of Social Security Disability Benefits, Supplemental Security Income, or benefits under Work First New Jersey. (New Jersey)

[13] Late fee policy must be in the lease or rental agreement and may not exceed 10% of the rent specified per rental period. Landlord must notify the tenant of the landlord's intent to impose the charge no later than the last day of the next rental period immediately following the period in which the default occurred. (New Mexico)

[14] Late fee when rent is due monthly cannot be higher than $15 or 5% of the rental payment, whichever is greater (when rent is due weekly, may not be higher than $4.00 or 5% of the rent, whichever is greater); and may not be imposed until the rent is 5 days late. A late fee may be imposed only one time for each late rental payment. A late fee for a specific late rental payment may not be deducted from a subsequent rental payment so as to cause the subsequent rental payment to be in default. (North Carolina)

[15] Preset late fees are invalid. (Oklahoma)

[16] Landlord must wait 4 days after the rent due date before imposing a late fee, and must disclose the late fee policy in the rental agreement. A flat fee must be "reasonable." A daily late fee may not be more than 6% of a reasonable flat fee, and cannot add up to more than 5% of the monthly rent. (Oregon)

[17] Landlord can't charge a late fee until the rent is 5 days late (the day rent is due is counted as the first day). If day five is a Sunday or legal holiday, landlord cannot impose a fee if the rent is paid on the next business day. Fee can't exceed 10% of the amount past due. (Tennessee)

[18] Late fee provision must be included in a written lease and cannot be imposed until the rent remains unpaid one full day after the date it is due. The fee is valid only if it is a reasonable estimate of uncertain damages to the landlord that are incapable of precise calculation. Landlord may charge an initial fee and a daily fee for each day the rent is late. (Texas)

State Rules on Notice Required to Change or Terminate a Month-to-Month Tenancy

Except where noted, the amount of notice a landlord must give to increase rent or change another term of the rental agreement in a month-to-month tenancy is the same as that required to end a month-to-month tenancy. Be sure to check state and local rent control laws, which may have different notice requirements.

State	Tenant	Landlord	Statute	Comments
Alabama	30 days	30 days	Ala. Code § 35-9A-441	No state statute on the amount of notice required to change rent or other terms
Alaska	30 days	30 days	Alaska Stat. § 34.03.290(b)	
Arizona	30 days	30 days	Ariz. Rev. Stat. Ann. § 33-1375	
Arkansas	30 days	30 days	Ark. Code Ann. § 18-17-704	No state statute on the amount of notice required to change rent or other terms
California	30 days	30 or 60 days	Cal. Civ. Code § 1946; Cal. Civ. Code § 827a	30 days to change rental terms, but if landlord is raising the rent, tenant gets 60 days' notice if the sum of this and all prior rent increases during the previous 12 months is more than 10% of the lowest rent charged during that time. 60 days to terminate (landlord), 30 days (tenant).
Colorado	21 days	21 days	Colo. Rev. Stat. § 13-40-107	
Connecticut		3 days	Conn. Gen. Stat. Ann. § 47a-23	Landlord must provide 3 days' notice to terminate tenancy. Landlord is not required to give a particular amount of notice of a proposed rent increase unless prior notice was previously agreed upon.
Delaware	60 days	60 days	Del. Code Ann. tit. 25, §§ 5106, 5107	After receiving notice of landlord's proposed change of terms, tenant has 15 days to terminate tenancy. Otherwise, changes will take effect as announced.
District of Columbia	30 days	30 days	D.C. Code Ann. § 42-3202	No state statute on the amount of notice required to change rent or other terms
Florida	15 days	15 days	Fla. Stat. Ann. § 83.57	No state statute on the amount of notice required to change rent or other terms
Georgia	30 days	60 days	Ga. Code Ann. §§ 44-7-6, 44-7-7	No state statute on the amount of notice required to change rent or other terms
Hawaii	28 days	45 days	Haw. Rev. Stat. §§ 521-71, 521-21(d)	
Idaho	One month	One month	Idaho Code §§ 55-208, 55-307	Landlords must provide 15 days' notice to increase rent or change tenancy.
Illinois	30 days	30 days	735 Ill. Comp. Stat. § 5/9-207	
Indiana	One month	One month	Ind. Code Ann. §§ 32-31-1-1, 32-31-5-4	Unless agreement states otherwise, landlord must give 30 days' written notice to modify written rental agreement.
Iowa	30 days	30 days	Iowa Code Ann. §§ 562A.34, 562A.13(5)	To end or change a month-to-month agreement, landlord must give written notice at least 30 days before the next time rent is due (not including any grace period).
Kansas	30 days	30 days	Kan. Stat. Ann. § 58-2570	No state statute on the amount of notice required to change rent or other terms
Kentucky	30 days	30 days	Ky. Rev. Stat. Ann. § 383.695	

State Rules on Notice Required to Change or Terminate a Month-to-Month Tenancy (continued)

State	Tenant	Landlord	Statute	Comments
Louisiana	10 days	10 days	La. Civ. Code Art. 2728	No state statute on the amount of notice required to change rent or other terms
Maine	30 days	30 days	Me. Rev. Stat. Ann. tit. 14 §§ 6002, 6015	Landlord must provide 45 days' notice to increase rent.
Maryland	One month	One month	Md. Code Ann. [Real Prop.] § 8-402(b)(3), (b)(4)	Two months' notice required in Montgomery County (single-family rentals excepted) and Baltimore City.
Massachusetts	See comments	See comments	Mass. Gen. Laws Ann. ch. 186, § 12	Interval between days of payment or 30 days, whichever is longer.
Michigan	One month	One month	Mich. Comp. Laws § 554.134	
Minnesota	See comments	See comments	Minn. Stat. Ann. § 504B.135	For terminations, interval between time rent is due or three months, whichever is less; no state statute on the amount of notice required to change rent or other terms
Mississippi	30 days	30 days	Miss. Code Ann. § 89-8-19	No state statute on the amount of notice required to change rent or other terms
Missouri	One month	One month	Mo. Rev. Stat. § 441.060	No state statute on the amount of notice required to change rent or other terms
Montana	30 days	30 days	Mont. Code Ann. §§ 70-24-441, 70-26-109	Landlord may change terms of tenancy with 15 days' notice.
Nebraska	30 days	30 days	Neb. Rev. Stat. § 76-1437	No state statute on the amount of notice required to change rent or other terms
Nevada	30 days	30 days	Nev. Rev. Stat. Ann. §§ 40.251, 118A.300	Landlords must provide 45 days' notice to increase rent. Tenants 60 years old or older, or physically or mentally disabled, may request an additional 30 days' possession, but only if they have complied with basic tenant obligations as set forth in Nev. Rev. Stat. Chapter 118A (termination notices must include this information).
New Hampshire	30 days	30 days	N.H. Rev. Stat. Ann. §§ 540:2, 540:3	Landlord may terminate only for just cause.
New Jersey	One month	One month	N.J. Stat. Ann. §§ 2A:18-56, 2A:18-61.1	Landlord may terminate only for just cause.
New Mexico	30 days	30 days	N.M. Stat. Ann. §§ 47-8-37, 47-8-15(F)	Landlord must deliver rent increase notice at least 30 days before rent due date.
New York	One month	One month	N.Y. Real Prop. Law § 232-b	No state statute on the amount of notice required to change rent or other terms
North Carolina	7 days	7 days	N.C. Gen. Stat. § 42-14	No state statute on the amount of notice required to change rent or other terms
North Dakota	30 days	30 days	N.D. Cent. Code §§ 47-16-15, 47-16-07	Tenant may terminate with 25 days' notice if landlord has changed the terms of the lease.
Ohio	30 days	30 days	Ohio Rev. Code Ann. § 5321.17	No state statute on the amount of notice required to change rent or other terms
Oklahoma	30 days	30 days	Okla. Stat. Ann. tit. 41, § 111	No state statute on the amount of notice required to change rent or other terms

State Rules on Notice Required to Change or Terminate a Month-to-Month Tenancy (continued)

State	Tenant	Landlord	Statute	Comments
Oregon	30 days or 72 hours (lack of bedroom exit only)	Landlord may not increase the rent during the first year, and must give 90 days' notice for any rent increases thereafter.	Or. Rev. Stat. §§ 91.070, 90.427, 90.460	To terminate, 30 days for occupancies of one year or less; 60 days for occupancies of more than one year (but only 30 days if the property is sold and other conditions are met). Tenant may terminate on 72 hours' notice if landlord's failure to provide proper bedroom emergency exit, properly noticed, has not been corrected. Temporary occupants are not entitled to notice. (Or. Rev. Stat. § 90.275.)
Pennsylvania			No statute	
Rhode Island	30 days	30 days	R.I. Gen. Laws §§ 34-18-16.1, 34-18-37	Landlord must provide 30 days' notice to increase rent.
South Carolina	30 days	30 days	S.C. Code Ann. § 27-40-770	No state statute on the amount of notice required to change rent or other terms
South Dakota	One month	One month	S.D. Codified Laws Ann. §§ 43-32-13, 43-8-8	If tenant (or spouse or minor child) is in the active duty in the military, landlord must give two months' notice, in the absence of tenant misconduct, sale of the property, or passing of the property into the landlord's estate.
Tennessee	30 days	30 days	Tenn. Code Ann. § 66-28-512	No state statute on the amount of notice required to change rent or other terms
Texas	One month	One month	Tex. Prop. Code Ann. § 91.001	Landlord and tenant may agree in writing to different notice periods, or none at all. No state statute on the amount of notice required to change rent or other terms
Utah		15 days	Utah Code Ann. § 78B-6-802	No state statute on the amount of notice required to change rent or other terms
Vermont	One rental period, unless written lease says otherwise	30 days	Vt. Code Ann. tit. 9, §§ 4467, 4456(d)	If there is no written rental agreement, for tenants who have continuously resided in the unit for two years or less, 60 days' notice to terminate; for those who have resided longer than two years, 90 days. If there is a written rental agreement, for tenants who have lived continuously in the unit for two years or less, 30 days; for those who have lived there longer than two years, 60 days.
Virginia	30 days	30 days	Va. Code Ann. §§ 55-248.37, 55-248.7, 55-225.32	Rental agreement may provide for a different notice period. No state statute on the amount of notice required to change rent or other terms, but landlord must abide by notice provisions in the rental agreement, if any.
Washington	20 days	20 days	Wash. Rev. Code Ann. §§ 59.18.200, 59.18.140	Landlord must give 30 days' notice to change rent or other lease terms.
West Virginia	One month	One month	W.Va. Code § 37-6-5	No state statute on the amount of notice required to change rent or other terms
Wisconsin	28 days	28 days	Wis. Stat. Ann. § 704.19	No state statute on the amount of notice required to change rent or other terms
Wyoming			No statute	

State Security Deposit Rules

Here are the statutes and rules that govern a landlord's collection and retention of security deposits. Many states require landlords to disclose, at or near the time they collect the deposit, information about how deposits may be used, as noted in the Disclosure or Requirement section. Required disclosures of other issues, such as a property's history of flooding, are in the chart, "Required Landlord Disclosures."

Alabama

Ala. Code § 35-9A-201

Exemption: Security deposit rules do not apply to a resident purchaser under a contract of sale (but do apply to a resident who has an option to buy), nor to the continuation of occupancy by the seller or a member of the seller's family for a period of not more than 36 months after the sale of a dwelling unit or the property of which it is a part.

Limit: One month's rent, except for pet deposits, deposits to cover undoing tenant's alterations, deposits to cover tenant activities that pose increased liability risks.

Deadline for Landlord to Itemize and Return Deposit: 60 days after termination of tenancy and delivery of possession.

Alaska

Alaska Stat. § 34.03.070

Limit: Two months' rent, unless rent exceeds $2,000 per month. Landlord may ask for an additional month's rent as deposit for a pet that is not a service animal, but may use it only to remedy pet damage.

Disclosure or Requirement: Orally or in writing, landlord must disclose the conditions under which landlord may withhold all or part of the deposit.

Separate Account: Required.

Advance notice of deduction: Not required.

Deadline for Landlord to Itemize and Return Deposit: 14 days if the tenant gives proper notice to terminate tenancy; 30 days if the tenant does not give proper notice or if landlord has deducted amounts needed to remedy damage caused by tenant's failure to maintain the property (Alaska Stat. § 34.03.120).

Arizona

Ariz. Rev. Stat. Ann. § 33-1321

Exemption: Excludes, among others, occupancy under a contract of sale of a dwelling unit or the property of which it is a part, if the occupant is the purchaser or a person who succeeds to his interest; occupancy by an employee of a landlord as a manager or custodian whose right to occupancy is conditional upon employment in and about the premises.

Limit: One and one-half months' rent.

Disclosure or Requirement: If landlord collects a nonrefundable fee, its purpose must be stated in writing. All fees not designated as nonrefundable are refundable.

Advance notice of deduction: Not required.

Deadline for Landlord to Itemize and Return Deposit: 14 days; tenant has the right to be present at final inspection.

Arkansas

Ark. Code Ann. §§ 18-16-303 to 18-16-305

Exemption: Excludes, among others, occupancy under a contract of sale of a dwelling unit or the property of which it is a part, if the occupant is the purchaser or a person who succeeds to his or her interest; occupancy by an employee of a landlord whose right to occupancy is conditional upon employment in and about the premises; and landlord who owns five or fewer rental units, unless these units are managed by a third party for a fee.

Limit: Two months' rent.

Advance notice of deduction: Not required.

Deadline for Landlord to Itemize and Return Deposit: 60 days.

California

Cal. Civ. Code §§ 1950.5, 1940.5(g)

Limit: Two months' rent (unfurnished); 3 months' rent (furnished). Add extra one-half month's rent for waterbed.

Advance notice of deduction: Required.

Deadline for Landlord to Itemize and Return Deposit: 21 days.

Colorado

Colo. Rev. Stat. §§ 38-12-102 to 38-12-104

Limit: No statutory limit.

Advance notice of deduction: Not required.

Deadline for Landlord to Itemize and Return Deposit: One month, unless lease agreement specifies longer period of time (which may be no more than 60 days); 72 hours (not

State Security Deposit Rules (continued)

counting weekends or holidays) if a hazardous condition involving gas equipment requires tenant to vacate.

Connecticut

Conn. Gen. Stat. Ann. § 47a-21

Exemption: Excludes, among others, occupancy under a contract of sale of a dwelling unit or the property of which the unit is a part, if the occupant is the purchaser or a person who succeeds to his interest; and occupancy by a personal care assistant or other person who is employed by a person with a disability to assist and support such disabled person with daily living activities or housekeeping chores and is provided dwelling space in the personal residence of such disabled person as a benefit or condition of employment.

Limit: Two months' rent (tenant under 62 years of age); one month's rent (tenant 62 years of age or older). Tenants who paid a deposit in excess of one month's rent, who then turn 62 years old, are entitled, upon request, to a refund of the amount that exceeds one month's rent.

Separate Account: Required.

Interest Payment: Interest payments must be made annually (or credited toward rent, at the landlord's option) and no later than 30 days after termination of tenancy. The interest rate must be equal to the average rate paid on savings deposits by insured commercial banks, rounded to the nearest 0.1%, as published by the Federal Reserve Board Bulletin.

Advance notice of deduction: Not required.

Deadline for Landlord to Itemize and Return Deposit: 30 days, or within 15 days of receiving tenant's forwarding address, whichever is later.

Delaware

Del. Code Ann. tit. 25, §§ 5514, 5311

Limit: One month's rent on leases for one year or more. For month to month tenancies, no limit for the first year, but after that, the limit is one month's rent (at the expiration of one year, landlord must give tenant a credit for any deposit held by the landlord that is in excess of one month's rent). No limit for furnished units. Tenant may offer to supply a surety bond in lieu of or in conjunction with a deposit, which landlord may elect to receive.

Separate Account: Required. Orally or in writing, the landlord must disclose to the tenant the location of the security deposit account.

Advance notice of deduction: Not required.

Deadline for Landlord to Itemize and Return Deposit: 20 days.

District of Columbia

D.C. Code Ann § 42-3502.17; D.C. Mun. Regs. tit. 14, §§ 308 to 310

Exemption: Tenants in rent-stabilized units as of July 17, 1985 cannot be asked to pay a deposit.

Limit: One month's rent.

Disclosure or Requirement: In the lease, rental agreement, or receipt, landlord must state the terms and conditions under which the security deposit was collected (to secure tenant's obligations under the lease or rental agreement).

Separate Account: Required.

Interest Payment: Interest payments at the prevailing statement savings rate must be made at termination of tenancy.

Advance notice of deduction: Not required.

Deadline for Landlord to Itemize and Return Deposit: 45 days.

Florida

Fla. Stat. Ann. §§ 83.49, 83.43 (12)

Exemption: Occupancy under a contract of sale of a dwelling unit or the property of which it is a part in which the buyer has paid at least 12 months' rent or in which the buyer has paid at least 1 month's rent and a deposit of at least 5 percent of the purchase price of the property; cooperative properties, condominiums, and transient residencies.

Limit: No statutory limit.

Disclosure or Requirement: Within 30 days of receiving the security deposit, the landlord must disclose in writing whether it will be held in an interest- or non-interest-bearing account; the name of the account depository; and the rate and time of interest payments. Landlord who collects a deposit must include in the lease the disclosure statement contained in Florida Statutes § 83.49.

Separate Account: Landlord may post a security bond securing all tenants' deposits instead.

State Security Deposit Rules (continued)

Interest Payment: Interest payments, if any (account need not be interest-bearing) must be made annually and at termination of tenancy. However, no interest is due a tenant who wrongfully terminates the tenancy before the end of the rental term.

Advance notice of deduction: Required.

Deadline for Landlord to Itemize and Return Deposit: 15 to 60 days depending on whether tenant disputes deductions.

Georgia

Ga. Code Ann. §§ 44-7-30 to 44-7-37

Exemption: Landlord who owns ten or fewer rental units, unless these units are managed by an outside party, need not supply written list of preexisting damage, nor place deposit in an escrow account. Rules for returning the deposit still apply.

Limit: No statutory limit.

Disclosure or Requirement: Landlord must give tenant a written list of preexisting damage to the rental before collecting a security deposit.

Separate Account: Required. Landlord must place the deposit in an escrow account in a state or federally regulated depository, and must inform the tenant of the location of this account. Landlord may post a security bond securing all tenants' deposits instead.

Advance notice of deduction: Required.

Deadline for Landlord to Itemize and Return Deposit: One month.

Hawaii

Haw. Rev. Stat. § 521-44

Limit: One month's rent. Landlord may require an additional one month's rent as security deposit for tenants who keep a pet.

Advance notice of deduction: Not required.

Deadline for Landlord to Itemize and Return Deposit: 14 days.

Idaho

Idaho Code § 6-321

Limit: No statutory limit.

Advance notice of deduction: Not required.

Deadline for Landlord to Itemize and Return Deposit: 21 days, or up to 30 days if landlord and tenant agree.

Illinois

765 Ill. Comp. Stat. 710/1; 715/1 to 715/3

Limit: No statutory limit.

Disclosure or Requirement: If a lease specifies the cost for repair, cleaning, or replacement of any part of the leased premises; or the cleaning or repair of any component of the building or common area that will not be replaced, the landlord may withhold the dollar amount specified in the lease. Landlord's itemized statement must reference the specified dollar amount(s) and include a copy of the lease clause.

Interest Payment: Landlords who rent 25 or more units in either a single building or a complex located on contiguous properties must pay interest on deposits held for more than six months. The interest rate is the rate paid for minimum deposit savings accounts by the largest commercial bank in the state, as of December 31 of the calendar year immediately preceding the start of the tenancy.

Advance notice of deduction: Not required.

Deadline for Landlord to Itemize and Return Deposit: For properties with 5 or more units, 30 to 45 days, depending on whether tenant disputes deductions or if statement and receipts are furnished.

Indiana

Ind. Code Ann. §§ 32-31-3-9 to 32-31-3-19

Exemption: Does not apply to, among others, occupancy under a contract of sale of a rental unit or the property of which the rental unit is a part if the occupant is the purchaser or a person who succeeds to the purchaser's interest; and occupancy by an employee of a landlord whose right to occupancy is conditional upon employment in or about the premises. Does apply to leases signed after July 1, 2008, that contain an option to purchase.

Limit: No statutory limit.

Advance notice of deduction: Not required.

Deadline for Landlord to Itemize and Return Deposit: 45 days.

State Security Deposit Rules (continued)

Iowa

Iowa Code Ann. § 562A.12

Limit: Two months' rent.

Separate Account: Required.

Interest Payment: Interest payment, if any (account need not be interest-bearing) must be made at termination of tenancy. Interest earned during first five years of tenancy belongs to landlord.

Advance notice of deduction: Not required.

Deadline for Landlord to Itemize and Return Deposit: 30 days.

Kansas

Kan. Stat. Ann. §§ 58-2550, 58-2548

Exemption: Excludes, among others, occupancy under a contract of sale of a dwelling unit or the property of which it is a part, if the occupant is the purchaser or a person who succeeds to the purchaser's interest; and occupancy by an employee of a landlord whose right to occupancy is conditional upon employment in and about the premises.

Limit: One month's rent (unfurnished); one and one-half months' rent (furnished); for pets, add extra one-half month's rent.

Advance notice of deduction: Not required.

Deadline for Landlord to Itemize and Return Deposit: 30 days.

Kentucky

Ky. Rev. Stat. Ann. § 383.580

Limit: No statutory limit.

Disclosure or Requirement: Orally or in writing, landlord must disclose where the security deposit is being held and the account number.

Separate Account: Required.

Advance notice of deduction: Required.

Deadline for Landlord to Itemize and Return Deposit: 30 to 60 days depending on whether tenant disputes deductions.

Louisiana

La. Rev. Stat. Ann. § 9:3251

Limit: No statutory limit.

Advance notice of deduction: Not required.

Deadline for Landlord to Itemize and Return Deposit: One month.

Maine

Me. Rev. Stat. Ann. tit. 14, §§ 6031 to 6038

Exemption: Entire security deposit law does not apply to rental unit that is part of structure with five or fewer units, one of which is occupied by landlord.

Limit: Two months' rent.

Disclosure or Requirement: Upon request by the tenant, landlord must disclose orally or in writing the account number and the name of the institution where the security deposit is being held.

Separate Account: Required.

Advance notice of deduction: Not required.

Deadline for Landlord to Itemize and Return Deposit: 30 days (if written rental agreement) or 21 days (if tenancy at will).

Maryland

Md. Code Ann. [Real Prop.] § 8-203, § 8-203.1, § 8-208

Limit: Two months' rent.

Disclosure or Requirement: Landlord must provide a receipt that describes tenant's rights to move-in and move-out inspections (and to be present at each), and right to receive itemization of deposit deductions and balance, if any; and penalties for landlord's failure to comply. Landlord must include this information in the lease.

Separate Account: Required. Landlord may hold all tenants' deposits in secured certificates of deposit, or in securities issued by the federal government or the State of Maryland.

Interest Payment: For security deposits of $50 or more, when landlord has held the deposit for at least six months: Within 45 days of termination of tenancy, interest must be paid at the daily U.S. Treasury yield curve rate for 1 year, as of the first business day of each year, or 1.5% a year, whichever is greater, less any damages rightfully withheld. Interest accrues monthly but is not compounded, and no interest is due for any period less than one month. (See the Department of Housing and Community Development website for a calculator.) Deposit must be held in a Maryland banking institution.

Advance notice of deduction: Required.

State Security Deposit Rules (continued)

Deadline for Landlord to Itemize and Return Deposit: 45 days.

Massachusetts

Mass. Gen. Laws Ann. ch. 186, § 15B

Limit: One month's rent.

Disclosure or Requirement: At the time of receiving a security deposit, landlord must furnish a receipt indicating the amount of the deposit; the name of the person receiving it, and, if received by a property manager, the name of the lessor for whom the security deposit is received; the date on which it is received; and a description of the premises leased or rented. The receipt must be signed by the person receiving the security deposit.

Separate Account: Required. Within 30 days of receiving security deposit, landlord must disclose the name and location of the bank in which the security deposit has been deposited, and the amount and account number of the deposit.

Interest Payment: Landlord must pay tenant 5% interest per year or the amount received from the bank (which must be in Massachusetts) that holds the deposit. Interest should be paid yearly, and within 30 days of termination date. Interest will not accrue for the last month for which rent was paid in advance.

Advance notice of deduction: Not required.

Deadline for Landlord to Itemize and Return Deposit: 30 days.

Michigan

Mich. Comp. Laws §§ 554.602 to 554.616

Limit: One and one-half months' rent.

Disclosure or Requirement: Within 14 days of tenant's taking possession of the rental, landlord must furnish in writing the landlord's name and address for receipt of communications, the name and address of the financial institution or surety where the deposit will be held, and the tenant's obligation to provide in writing a forwarding mailing address to the landlord within 4 days after termination of occupancy. The notice shall include the following statement in 12-point boldface type that is at least 4 points larger than the body of the notice or lease agreement: "You must notify your landlord in writing within 4 days after you move of a forwarding address

where you can be reached and where you will receive mail; otherwise your landlord shall be relieved of sending you an itemized list of damages and the penalties adherent to that failure."

Separate Account: Required. Landlord must place deposits in a regulated financial institution, and may use the deposits as long as the landlord deposits with the secretary of state a cash or surety bond.

Advance notice of deduction: Required. Not a typical advance notice provision: Tenants must dispute the landlord's stated deductions within 7 days of receiving the itemized list and balance, if any, or give up any right to dispute them.

Deadline for Landlord to Itemize and Return Deposit: 30 days.

Minnesota

Minn. Stat. Ann. §§ 504B.175, 504B.178, 504B.195

Limit: No statutory limit. If landlord collects a "prelease deposit" and subsequently rents to tenant, landlord must apply the prelease deposit to the security deposit.

Disclosure or Requirement: Before collecting rent or a security deposit, landlord must provide a copy of all outstanding inspection orders for which a citation has been issued, pertaining to a rental unit or common area, specifying code violations that threaten the health or safety of the tenant, and all outstanding condemnation orders and declarations that the premises are unfit for human habitation. Citations for violations that do not involve threats to tenant health or safety must be summarized and posted in an obvious place. With some exceptions, landlord who has received notice of a contract for deed cancellation or notice of a mortgage foreclosure sale must so disclose before entering a lease, accepting rent, or accepting a security deposit; and must furnish the date on which the contract cancellation period or the mortgagor's redemption period ends.

Interest Payment: Landlord must pay 1% simple, noncompounded interest per year. (Deposits collected before 8/1/03 earn interest at 3%, up to 8/1/03, then begin earning at 1%.) Any interest amount less than $1 is excluded.

Advance notice of deduction: Not required.

Deadline for Landlord to Itemize and Return Deposit: Three weeks after tenant leaves and landlord receives

State Security Deposit Rules (continued)

forwarding address; five days if tenant must leave due to building condemnation.

Mississippi

Miss. Code Ann. § 89-8-21

Limit: No statutory limit.

Advance notice of deduction: Not required.

Deadline for Landlord to Itemize and Return Deposit: 45 days.

Missouri

Mo. Ann. Stat. § 535.300

Limit: Two months' rent.

Advance notice of deduction: Not required.

Deadline for Landlord to Itemize and Return Deposit: 30 days.

Montana

Mont. Code Ann. §§ 70-25-101 to 70-25-206

Limit: No statutory limit.

Advance notice of deduction: Required. Tenant is entitled to advance notice of cleaning charges, but only if such cleaning is required as a result of tenant's negligence and is not part of the landlord's cyclical cleaning program.

Deadline for Landlord to Itemize and Return Deposit: 30 days; 10 days if no deductions.

Nebraska

Neb. Rev. Stat. § 76-1416

Limit: One month's rent (no pets); one and one-quarter months' rent (pets).

Advance notice of deduction: Not required.

Deadline for Landlord to Itemize and Return Deposit: 14 days.

Nevada

Nev. Rev. Stat. Ann. §§ 118A.240 to 118A.250

Limit: Three months' rent; if both landlord and tenant agree, tenant may use a surety bond for all or part of the deposit.

Disclosure or Requirement: Lease or rental agreement must explain the conditions under which the landlord will refund the deposit.

Advance notice of deduction: Not required.

Deadline for Landlord to Itemize and Return Deposit: 30 days.

New Hampshire

N.H. Rev. Stat. Ann. §§ 540-A:5 to 540-A:8; 540-B:10

Exemption: Entire security deposit law does not apply to landlord who leases a single-family residence and owns no other rental property, or landlord who leases rental units in an owner-occupied building of five units or fewer (exemption does not apply to any individual unit in owner-occupied building that is occupied by a person 60 years of age or older).

Limit: One month's rent or $100, whichever is greater; when landlord and tenant share facilities, no statutory limit.

Disclosure or Requirement: Unless tenant has paid the deposit by personal or bank check, or by a check issued by a government agency, landlord must provide a receipt stating the amount of the deposit and the institution where it will be held. Regardless of whether a receipt is required, landlord must inform tenant that if tenant finds any conditions in the rental in need of repair, tenant may note them on the receipt or other written instrument, and return either within five days.

Separate Account: Required. Upon request, landlord must disclose the account number, the amount on deposit, and the interest rate. Landlord may post a bond covering all deposits instead of putting deposits in a separate account.

Interest Payment: Landlord who holds a security deposit for a year or longer must pay interest at a rate equal to the rate paid on regular savings accounts in the New Hampshire bank, savings & loan, or credit union where it's deposited. If a landlord mingles security deposits in a single account, the landlord must pay the actual interest earned proportionately to each tenant. A tenant may request the interest accrued every three years, 30 days before that year's tenancy expires. The landlord must comply with the request within 15 days of the expiration of that year's tenancy.

Advance notice of deduction: Not required.

Deadline for Landlord to Itemize and Return Deposit: 30 days; for shared facilities, if the deposit is more than 30 days' rent, landlord must provide written agreement acknowledging receipt and specifying when deposit will be returned—if no written agreement, 20 days after tenant vacates.

State Security Deposit Rules (continued)

New Jersey

N.J. Stat. Ann. §§ 46:8-19, 44:8-21.1, 44:8-21.2, 44:8-26

Exemption: Security deposit law does not apply to owner-occupied buildings with three or fewer units unless tenant gives 30 days' written notice to the landlord of the tenant's wish to invoke the law.

Limit: One and one-half months' rent. Any additional security deposit, collected annually, may be no greater than 10% of the current security deposit.

Separate Account: Required. Within 30 days of receiving the deposit and every time the landlord pays the tenant interest, landlord must disclose the name and address of the banking organization where the deposit is being held, the type of account, current rate of interest, and the amount of the deposit.

Interest Payment: Landlord with 10 or more units must invest deposits as specified by statute or place deposit in an insured money market fund account, or in another account that pays quarterly interest at a rate comparable to the money market fund. Landlords with fewer than 10 units may place deposit in an interest-bearing account in any New Jersey financial institution insured by the FDIC. All landlords may pay tenants interest earned on account annually or credit toward payment of rent due.

Advance notice of deduction: Not required.

Deadline for Landlord to Itemize and Return Deposit: 30 days; five days in case of fire, flood, condemnation, or evacuation.

New Mexico

N.M. Stat. Ann. § 47-8-18

Limit: One month's rent (for rental agreement of less than one year); no limit for leases of one year or more.

Interest Payment: Landlord who collects a deposit larger than than one month's rent on a year's lease must pay interest, on an annual basis, equal to the passbook interest.

Advance notice of deduction: Not required.

Deadline for Landlord to Itemize and Return Deposit: 30 days.

New York

N.Y. Gen. Oblig. Law §§ 7-103 to 7-108

Limit: No statutory limit for nonregulated units.

Disclosure or Requirement: If deposit is placed in a bank, landlord must disclose the name and address of the banking organization where the deposit is being held, and the amount of such deposit.

Separate Account: Statute requires that deposits not be co-mingled with landlord's personal assets, but does not explicitly require placement in a banking institution (however, deposits collected in buildings of six or more units must be placed in New York bank accounts).

Interest Payment: Landlord who rents out nonregulated units in buildings with five or fewer units need not pay interest. Interest must be paid at the "prevailing rate" on deposits received from tenants who rent units in buildings containing six or more units. The landlord in every rental situation may retain an administrative fee of 1% per year on the sum deposited. Interest can be subtracted from the rent, paid at the end of the year, or paid at the end of the tenancy according to the tenant's choice.

Advance notice of deduction: Not required.

Deadline for Landlord to Itemize and Return Deposit: A "reasonable time."

North Carolina

N.C. Gen. Stat. §§ 42-50 to 42-56

Exemption: Not applicable to single rooms rented on a weekly, monthly, or annual basis.

Limit: One and one-half months' rent for month-to-month rental agreements; two months' rent if term is longer than two months; may add an additional "reasonable" nonrefundable pet deposit.

Disclosure or Requirement: Within 30 days of the beginning of the lease term, landlord must disclose the name and address of the banking institution where the deposit is located.

Separate Account: Required. The landlord may, at his option, furnish a bond from an insurance company licensed to do business in the state.

Advance notice of deduction: Not required.

Deadline for Landlord to Itemize and Return Deposit: 30 days; if landlord's claim against the deposit cannot be finalized within that time, landlord may send an interim accounting and a final accounting within 60 days of the tenancy's termination.

State Security Deposit Rules (continued)

North Dakota

N.D. Cent. Code § 47-16-07.1

Limit: One month's rent. If tenant has a pet that is not a service or companion animal that tenant keeps as a reasonable accommodation under fair housing laws, an additional pet deposit of up to $2,500 or two months' rent, whichever is greater. To encourage renting to persons with felony convictions, landlords may charge up to two months' rent as security.

Separate Account: Required.

Interest Payment: Landlord must pay interest if the period of occupancy is at least nine months. Money must be held in a federally insured interest-bearing savings or checking account for benefit of the tenant. Interest must be paid upon termination of the lease.

Advance notice of deduction: Not required.

Deadline for Landlord to Itemize and Return Deposit: 30 days.

Ohio

Ohio Rev. Code Ann. § 5321.16

Limit: No statutory limit.

Interest Payment: Any deposit in excess of $50 or one month's rent, whichever is greater, must bear interest on the excess at the rate of 5% per annum if the tenant stays for six months or more. Interest must be paid annually and upon termination of tenancy.

Advance notice of deduction: Not required.

Deadline for Landlord to Itemize and Return Deposit: 30 days.

Oklahoma

Okla. Stat. Ann. tit. 41, § 115

Limit: No statutory limit.

Separate Account: Required.

Advance notice of deduction: Not required.

Deadline for Landlord to Itemize and Return Deposit: 45 days.

Oregon

Or. Rev. Stat. § 90.300

Limit: No statutory limit. Landlord may not impose or increase deposit within first year unless parties agree to modify the rental agreement to allow for a pet or other

cause, and the imposition or increase relates to that modification.

Advance notice of deduction: Not required.

Deadline for Landlord to Itemize and Return Deposit: 31 days.

Pennsylvania

68 Pa. Cons. Stat. Ann. §§ 250.511a to 250.512

Limit: Two months' rent for first year of renting; one month's rent during second and subsequent years of renting.

Disclosure or Requirement: For deposits over $100, landlord must deposit them in a federally or state-regulated institution, and give tenant the name and address of the banking institution and the amount of the deposit.

Separate Account: Required. Instead of placing deposits in a separate account, landlord may purchase a bond issued by a bonding company authorized to do business in the state.

Interest Payment: Tenant who occupies rental unit for two or more years is entitled to interest beginning with the 25th month of occupancy. Landlord must pay tenant interest (minus 1% fee) at the end of the third and subsequent years of the tenancy.

Advance notice of deduction: Not required.

Deadline for Landlord to Itemize and Return Deposit: 30 days.

Rhode Island

R.I. Gen. Laws § 34-18-19

Limit: One month's rent.

Advance notice of deduction: Not required.

Deadline for Landlord to Itemize and Return Deposit: 20 days.

South Carolina

S.C. Code Ann. § 27-40-410

Limit: No statutory limit.

Advance notice of deduction: Not required.

Deadline for Landlord to Itemize and Return Deposit: 30 days.

South Dakota

S.D. Codified Laws Ann. § 43-32-6.1, § 43-32-24

State Security Deposit Rules (continued)

Limit: One month's rent (higher deposit may be charged if special conditions pose a danger to maintenance of the premises).

Advance notice of deduction: Not required.

Deadline for Landlord to Itemize and Return Deposit: Two weeks and must supply reasons if withholding any portion; 45 days for a written, itemized accounting, if tenant requests it.

Tennessee

Tenn. Code Ann. § 66-28-301

Limit: No statutory limit.

Exemption: Does not apply in counties having a population of less than 75,000, according to the 2010 federal census or any subsequent federal census.

Separate Account: Required. Orally or in writing, landlord must disclose the location of the separate account (but not the account number) used by landlord for the deposit.

Advance notice of deduction: Required.

Texas

Tex. Prop. Code Ann. §§ 92.101 to 92.109

Limit: No statutory limit.

Advance notice of deduction: Not required.

Deadline for Landlord to Itemize and Return Deposit: 30 days. Landlord need not refund deposit if lease requires tenant to give written notice of tenant's intention to surrender the premises.

Utah

Utah Code Ann. §§ 57-17-1 to 57-17-5

Limit: No statutory limit.

Disclosure or Requirement: For written leases or rental agreements only, if part of the deposit is nonrefundable, landlord must disclose this feature.

Advance notice of deduction: Not required.

Deadline for Landlord to Itemize and Return Deposit: 30 days.

Vermont

Vt. Stat. Ann. tit. 9, § 4461

Limit: No statutory limit.

Advance notice of deduction: Not required.

Deadline for Landlord to Itemize and Return Deposit: 14 days; 60 days if the rental is seasonal and not intended as the tenant's primary residence.

Virginia

Va. Code Ann. § 55-248.15:1

Exemption: Single-family residences are exempt where the owner(s) are natural persons or their estates who own in their own name no more than two single-family residences subject to a rental agreement. Exemption applies to the entire Virginia Residential Landlord and Tenant Act.

Limit: Two months' rent.

Advance notice of deduction: Not required.

Deadline for Landlord to Itemize and Return Deposit: 45 days. Lease can provide for expedited processing and specify an administrative fee for such processing, which will apply only if tenant requests it with a separate written document. Landlord must give tenant written notice of tenant's right to be present at a final inspection.

Washington

Wash. Rev. Code Ann. §§ 59.18.260 to 59.18.285

Exemption: Security deposit rules do not apply to a lease of a single-family dwelling for a year or more, or to any lease of a single-family dwelling containing a bona fide option to purchase by the tenant, provided that an attorney for the tenant has approved on the face of the agreement any lease so exempted. Rules also do not apply to occupancy by an employee of a landlord whose right to occupy is conditioned upon employment in or about the premises; or the lease of single-family rental in connection with a lease of land to be used primarily for agricultural purposes; or rental agreements for seasonal agricultural employees.

Limit: No statutory limit.

Disclosure or Requirement: In the lease, landlord must disclose the circumstances under which all or part of the deposit may be withheld, and must provide a receipt with the name and location of the banking institution where the deposit is being held. No deposit may be collected unless the rental agreement is in writing and a written checklist or statement specifically describing the condition and cleanliness of or existing damages to the premises and furnishings is provided to the tenant at the start of the tenancy.

State Security Deposit Rules (continued)

Separate Account: Not required.

Advance notice of deduction: Not required.

Deadline for Landlord to Itemize and Return Deposit: 21 days.

West Virginia

W.Va. Code § 37-6A-1 et seq.

Deadline for Landlord to Itemize and Return Deposit: 60 days from the date the tenancy has terminated, or within 45 days of the occupancy of a subsequent tenant, whichever is shorter. If the damage exceeds the amount of the security deposit and the landlord has to hire a contractor to fix it, the notice period is extended 15 days.

Wisconsin

Wis. Admin. Code ATCP 134.04, 134.06; Wis. Stat. § 704.28

Exemption: Security deposit rules do not apply to a dwelling unit occupied, under a contract of sale, by the purchaser of the dwelling unit or the purchaser's successor in interest; or to a dwelling unit that the landlord provides free to any person, or that the landlord provides as consideration to a person whom the landlord currently employs to operate or maintain the premises.

Limit: No statutory limit.

Disclosure or Requirement: Before accepting the deposit, landlord must inform tenant of tenant's inspection rights, disclose all habitability defects, and show tenant any outstanding building and housing code violations, inform tenant of the means by which shared utilities will be billed, and inform tenant if utilities are not paid for by landlord.

Advance notice of deduction: Not required.

Deadline for Landlord to Itemize and Return Deposit: 21 days.

Wyoming

Wyo. Stat. §§ 1-21-1207, 1-21-1208

Limit: No statutory limit.

Disclosure or Requirement: Lease or rental agreement must state whether any portion of a deposit is non-refundable, and landlord must give tenant written notice of this fact when collecting the deposit.

Advance notice of deduction: Not required.

Deadline for Landlord to Itemize and Return Deposit: 30 days, when applying it to unpaid rent (or within 15 days of receiving tenant's forwarding address, whichever is later); additional 30 days allowed for deductions due to damage.

Required Landlord Disclosures

Many states require landlords to inform tenants of important state laws or individual landlord policies, either in the lease or rental agreement or in another writing. Common disclosures include a landlord's imposition of nonrefundable fees (where permitted), tenants' rights to move-in checklists, and the identity of the landlord or landlord's agent or manager. Disclosures concerning the security deposit are in the chart, "State Security Deposit Rules."

Alabama

Owner or agent identity: Landlord must disclose to the tenant in writing at or before the commencement of the tenancy the name and address of the person authorized to manage the premises, and an owner of the premises or a person authorized to act for and on behalf of the owner for the purpose of service of process and for the purpose of receiving notices and demands. (Exception: does not apply to resident purchaser under a contract of sale (but does apply to a resident who has an option to buy), nor to the continuation of occupancy by the seller or a member of the seller's family for a period of not more than 36 months after the sale of a dwelling unit or the property of which it is a part.) (Ala. Code § 35-9A-202)

Alaska

Owner or agent identity: Landlord must disclose to the tenant in writing at or before the commencement of the tenancy the name and address of the person authorized to manage the premises, and an owner of the premises or a person authorized to act for and on behalf of the owner for the purpose of service of process and for the purpose of receiving notices and demands. (Alaska Stat. § 34.03.080)

Extended absence: The rental agreement must require that the tenant notify the landlord of an anticipated extended absence from the premises in excess of seven days; however, the notice may be given as soon as reasonably possible after the tenant knows the absence will exceed seven days. (Alaska Stat. § 34.03.150)

Arizona

Nonrefundable fees permitted? Yes. The purpose of all nonrefundable fees or deposits must be stated in writing. Any fee or deposit not designated as nonrefundable is refundable. (Ariz. Rev. Stat. § 33-1321)

Move-in checklist required? Yes. Tenants also have the right to be present at a move-out inspection. (Ariz. Rev. Stat. § 33-1321)

Separate utility charges: If landlord charges separately for gas, water, wastewater, solid waste removal, or electricity by installing a submetering system, landlord may recover the charges imposed on the landlord by the utility provider, plus an administrative fee for the landlord for actual administrative costs only, and must disclose separate billing and fee in the rental agreement. If landlord uses a ratio utility billing system, the rental agreement must contain a specific description of the ratio utility billing method used to allocate utility costs. (Ariz. Rev. Stat. § 33-1314.01)

Owner or agent identity: Landlord must disclose to the tenant in writing at or before the commencement of the tenancy the name and address of the person authorized to manage the premises, and an owner of the premises or a person authorized to act for and on behalf of the owner for the purpose of service of process and for the purpose of receiving notices and demands. (Ariz. Rev. Stat. § 33-1322)

Business tax pass-through: If the landlord pays a local tax based on rent and that tax increases, landlord may pass through the increase by increasing the rent upon 30 days' notice (but not before the new tax is effective), but only if the landlord's right to adjust the rent is disclosed in the rental agreement. (Ariz. Rev. Stat. § 33-1314)

Availability of Landlord and Tenant Act: Landlord must inform tenant in writing that the residential Landlord and Tenant Act is available on the Arizona department of housing's website. (Ariz. Rev. Stat. § 33-1322)

Bedbug information: Landlords must provide existing and new tenants with educational materials on bedbugs, including information and physical descriptions, prevention and control measures, behavioral attraction risk factors, information from federal, state, and local centers for disease control and prevention, health or housing agencies, nonprofit housing organizations, or information developed by the landlord. (Ariz. Rev. Stat. § 33-1319)

Arkansas

No disclosure statutes.

Required Landlord Disclosures (continued)

California

Nonrefundable fees permitted? No. (Cal. Civ. Code § 1950.5(m))

Move-in checklist required? No

Must fee policy be stated in the rental agreement? N/A

Registered sexual offender database: Landlords must include the following language in their rental agreements: "Notice: Pursuant to Section 290.46 of the Penal Code, information about specified registered sex offenders is made available to the public via an Internet Web site maintained by the Department of Justice at www.meganslaw.ca.gov. Depending on an offender's criminal history, this information will include either the address at which the offender resides or the community of residence and ZIP Code in which he or she resides." (Cal. Civ. Code § 2079.10a)

Tenant paying for others' utilities: Prior to signing a rental agreement, landlord must disclose whether gas or electric service to tenant's unit also serves other areas, and must disclose the manner by which costs will be fairly allocated. (Cal. Civ. Code § 1940.9)

Ordnance locations: Prior to signing a lease, landlord must disclose known locations of former federal or state ordnance in the neighborhood (within one mile of rental). (Cal. Civ. Code § 1940.7)

Toxic mold: Prior to signing a rental agreement, landlord must provide written disclosure when landlord knows, or has reason to know, that mold exceeds permissible exposure limits or poses a health threat. Landlords must distribute a consumer handbook, developed by the State Department of Health Services, describing the potential health risks from mold. (Cal. Health & Safety Code §§ 26147, 26148)

Pest control service: When the rental agreement is signed, landlord must provide tenant with any pest control company disclosure landlord has received, which describes the pest to be controlled, pesticides used and their active ingredients, a warning that pesticides are toxic, and the frequency of treatment under any contract for periodic service. (Cal. Civ. Code § 1940.8, Cal. Bus. & Prof. Code § 8538)

Intention to demolish rental unit: Landlords or their agents who have applied for a permit to demolish a rental unit must give written notice of this fact to prospective tenants, before accepting any deposits or screening fees. (Cal. Civ. Code § 1940.6)

No-smoking policy: For leases and rental agreements signed after January 1, 2012: If the landlord prohibits or limits the smoking of tobacco products on the rental property, the lease or rental agreement must include a clause describing the areas where smoking is limited or prohibited (does not apply if the tenant has previously occupied the dwelling unit). For leases and rental agreements signed before January 1, 2012: A newly adopted policy limiting or prohibiting smoking is a change in the terms of the tenancy (will not apply to lease-holding tenants until they renew their leases; tenants renting month-to-month must be given 30 days' written notice). Does not preempt any local ordinances prohibiting smoking in effect on January 1, 2012. (Cal. Civ. Code § 1947.5)

Notice of default: Lessors of single-family homes and multifamily properties of four units or less, who have received a notice of default for the rental property that has not been rescinded, must disclose this fact to potential renters before they sign a lease. The notice must be in English or in Spanish, Chinese, Tagalog, Vietnamese, or Korean (if the lease was negotiated in one of these languages), and must follow the language specified in Cal. Civ. Code § 2924.85(d).

Flooding: In leases or rental agreements signed after July 1, 2018, landlord must disclose, in at least eight-point type, that the property is in a special flood hazard area of an area of potential flooding if the landlord has actual knowledge of this fact. Actual knowledge includes receipt from a public agency so identifying the property; the fact that the owner carries flood insurance; or that the property is in an area in which the owner's mortgage holder requires the owner to carry flood insurance. Disclosure must advise tenant that additional information can be had at the Office of Emergency Services' website, and must include the web address for the MYHazards tool maintained by the Office. Disclosure must advise tenant that owner's insurance will not cover loss to tenant's property, and must recommend that tenant consider purchasing renters' insurance that will cover loss due to fire, flood, or other risk of loss. Disclosure must

Required Landlord Disclosures (continued)

note that the owner is not required to provide additional information. (Cal. Govt. Code § 8589.45)

Colorado

No disclosure statutes.

Connecticut

Miscellaneous disclosures:

Common interest community: When rental is in a common interest community, landlord must give tenant written notice before signing a lease. (Conn. Gen. Stat. Ann. § 47a-3e)

Owner or agent identity: Before the beginning of the tenancy, landlord must disclose the name and address of the person authorized to manage the premises and the person who is authorized to receive all notices, demands, and service of process. (Conn. Gen. Stat. Ann. § 47a-6)

Summary of Landlord-Tenant Code: A summary of the code, as prepared by the Consumer Protection Unit of the Attorney General's office, must be given to tenants at the beginning of the rental term. Failure to do so enables the tenant to plead ignorance of the law as a defense.

Delaware

Nonrefundable fees permitted? No, except for an optional service fee for actual services rendered, such as a pool fee or tennis court fee. Tenant may elect, subject to the landlord's acceptance, to purchase an optional surety bond instead of or in combination with a security deposit. (*Stoltz Management Co. v. Phillip*, 593 A.2d 583 (1990); Del. Code Ann. tit. 25, § 5311)

Owner or agent identity: On each written rental agreement, the landlord must prominently disclose the names and usual business addresses of all persons who are owners of the rental unit or the property of which the rental unit is a part, or the names and business addresses of their appointed resident agents. (25 Del. Code Ann. § 5105)

Summary of Landlord-Tenant Law: A summary of the Landlord-Tenant Code, as prepared by the Consumer Protection Unit of the Attorney General's Office or its successor agency, must be given to the new tenant at the beginning of the rental term. If the landlord fails to provide the summary, the tenant may plead ignorance of the law as a defense. (25 Del. Code Ann. § 5118)

District of Columbia

Rental regulations: At the start of every new tenancy, landlord must give tenant a copy of the District of Columbia Municipal Regulations, CDCR Title 14, Housing, Chapter 3, Landlord and Tenant; and a copy of Title 14, Housing, Chapter 1, § 101 (Civil Enforcement Policy) and Chapter 1, § 106 (Notification of Tenants Concerning Violations).

Florida

Nonrefundable fees permitted? Yes, allowed by custom, although there is no statute.

Owner or agent identity: The landlord, or a person authorized to enter into a rental agreement on the landlord's behalf, must disclose in writing to the tenant, at or before the commencement of the tenancy, the name and address of the landlord or a person authorized to receive notices and demands on the landlord's behalf. (Fla. Stat. Ann. § 83.50)

Radon: In all leases, landlord must include this warning: "RADON GAS: Radon is a naturally occurring radioactive gas that, when it has accumulated in a building in sufficient quantities, may present health risks to persons who are exposed to it over time. Levels of radon that exceed federal and state guidelines have been found in buildings in Florida. Additional information regarding radon and radon testing may be obtained from your county health department." (Fla. Stat. Ann. § 404.056)

Georgia

Nonrefundable fees permitted? Yes, nonrefundable fees, such as pet fees, are allowed by custom, although there is no statute.

Move-in checklist required? Landlord cannot collect a security deposit until he has given tenant a list of preexisting damage, but this isn't an interactive checklist. (Ga. Code Ann. § 44-7-33)

Flooding: Before signing a lease, if the living space or attachments have been damaged by flooding three or more times within the past five years, landlord must so disclose in writing. (Ga. Code Ann. § 44-7-20)

Owner or agent identity: When or before a tenancy begins, landlord must disclose in writing the names and addresses of the owner of record or a person authorized to act for the owner for purposes of service of process

Required Landlord Disclosures (continued)

and receiving and receipting demands and notices; and the person authorized to manage the premises. If such information changes during the tenancy, landlord must advise tenant within 30 days in writing or by posting a notice in a conspicuous place. (Ga. Code Ann. § 44-7-3)

Former residents, crimes: If asked by a prospective tenant, landlord must answer truthfully when questioned about whether the rental was the site of a homicide or other felony, or a suicide or a death by accidental or natural causes; or whether it was occupied by a person who was infected with a virus or any other disease that has been determined by medical evidence as being highly unlikely to be transmitted through the occupancy of a dwelling place presently or previously occupied by such an infected person. (Ga. Code Ann. § 44-1-16)

Hawaii

Nonrefundable fees permitted? No.

Other fees: The landlord may not require or receive from or on behalf of a tenant at the beginning of a rental agreement any money other than the money for the first month's rent and a security deposit as provided in this section. (Haw. Rev. Stat. § 521-43)

Owner or agent identity: Landlord must disclose name of owner or agent; if owner lives in another state or on another island, landlord must disclose name of agent on the island. (Haw. Rev. Stat. § 521-43)

Move-in checklist required? Yes. (Haw. Rev. Stat. § 541-42)

Tax excise number: Landlord must furnish its tax excise number so that tenant can file for a low-income tax credit. (Haw. Rev. Stat. § 521-43)

Idaho

No disclosure statutes.

Illinois

Utilities: Where tenant pays a portion of a master metered utility, landlord must give tenant a copy in writing either as part of the lease or another written agreement of the formula used by the landlord for allocating the public utility payments among the tenants. (765 Ill. Comp. Stat. § 740/5)

Rent concessions: Any rent concessions must be described in the lease, in letters not less than one-half inch in height consisting of the words "Concession Granted," including a memorandum on the margin or across the face of the lease stating the amount or extent and nature of each such concession. Failure to comply is a misdemeanor. (765 Ill. Comp. Stat. §§ 730/0 to 730/6.)

Radon: Landlords are not required to test for radon, but if the landlord tests and learns that a radon hazard is present in the dwelling unit, landlord must disclose this information to current and prospective tenants. If a tenant notifies a landlord that a radon test indicates the existence of a radon hazard in the rental unit, landlord must disclose that risk to any prospective tenant of that unit, unless a subsequent test by the landlord shows that a radon hazard does not exist. Requirements do not apply if the dwelling unit is on the third or higher story above ground level, or when the landlord has undertaken mitigation work and a subsequent test shows that a radon hazard does not exist. (420 Ill. Comp. Stat. §§ 46/15, 46/25)

Indiana

Owner or agent identity: Landlord's agent must disclose in writing the name and address of a person living in Indiana who is authorized to manage the property and to act as the owner's agent. (Ind. Code Ann. § 32-31-3-18)

Iowa

Owner or agent identity: Landlord must disclose to the tenant in writing at or before the commencement of the tenancy the name and address of the person authorized to manage the premises, and an owner of the premises or a person authorized to act for and on behalf of the owner for the purpose of service of process and for the purpose of receiving notices and demands. (Iowa Code § 562A.13)

Utilities: For shared utilities, landlord must fully explain utility rates, charges, and services to the prospective tenant before the rental agreement is signed. (Iowa Code § 562A.13)

Contamination: The landlord or a person authorized to enter into a rental agreement on behalf of the landlord must disclose to each tenant, in writing before the commencement of the tenancy, whether the property is listed in the comprehensive environmental response compensation and liability information system maintained by the federal Environmental Protection Agency. (Iowa Code § 562A.13)

Required Landlord Disclosures (continued)

Kansas

Move-in checklist required? Yes. Within 5 days of move-in, landlord and tenant must jointly inventory the rental. (Kan. Stat. Ann. § 58-2548)

Owner or agent identity: Landlord must disclose to the tenant in writing at or before the commencement of the tenancy the name and address of the person authorized to manage the premises, and an owner of the premises or a person authorized to act for and on behalf of the owner for the purpose of service of process and for the purpose of receiving notices and demands. (Kan. Stat. Ann. § 58-2551)

Kentucky

Move-in checklist required? Yes. Landlord and tenant must complete a checklist before landlord can collect a security deposit. (Ky. Rev. Stat. Ann. § 383.580)

Owner or agent identity: Landlord must disclose to the tenant in writing at or before the commencement of the tenancy the name and address of the person authorized to manage the premises, and an owner of the premises or a person authorized to act for and on behalf of the owner for the purpose of service of process and for the purpose of receiving notices and demands. (Ky. Rev. Stat. Ann. § 383.585)

Louisiana

Foreclosure: Before entering into a lease or rental agreement, landlord must disclose to potential tenants their right to receive notification of any future foreclosure action. If the premises are currently subject to a foreclosure action, landlord must also disclose this in writing. (La. Stat. Ann. § 9:3260.1)

Maine

Utilities: No landlord may lease or offer to lease a dwelling unit in a multiunit residential building where the expense of furnishing electricity to the common areas or other area not within the unit is the sole responsibility of the tenant in that unit, unless both parties to the lease have agreed in writing that the tenant will pay for such costs in return for a stated reduction in rent or other specified fair consideration that approximates the actual cost of electricity to the common areas. (14 Me. Rev. Stat. Ann. § 6024)

Energy efficiency: Landlord must provide to potential tenants who will pay for energy costs (or upon request from others) a residential energy efficiency disclosure statement in accordance with Title 35-A, section 10006, subsection 1 that includes, but is not limited to, information about the energy efficiency of the property. Before a tenant enters into a contract or pays a deposit to rent or lease a property, the landlord must provide the statement to the tenant, obtain the tenant's signature on the statement, and sign the statement. The landlord must retain the signed statement for at least 3 years. Alternatively, the landlord may include in the application for the residential property the name of each supplier of energy that previously supplied the unit, if known, and the following statement: "You have the right to obtain a 12-month history of energy consumption and the cost of that consumption from the energy supplier." (14 Me. Rev. Stat. Ann. § 6030-C)

Radon: By 2012 and every ten years thereafter, landlord must test for radon and disclose to prospective and existing tenants the date and results of the test and the risks of radon, using a disclosure form prepared by the Department of Health and Human Services (tenant must sign acknowledgment of receipt). (14 Me. Rev. Stat. Ann. § 6030-D)

Bedbugs: Before renting a dwelling unit, landlord must disclose to a prospective tenant if an adjacent unit or units are currently infested with or are being treated for bedbugs. Upon request from a tenant or prospective tenant, landlord must disclose the last date that the dwelling unit the landlord seeks to rent or an adjacent unit or units were inspected for a bedbug infestation and found to be free of a bedbug infestation. (Me. Rev. Stat. Ann. § 6021-A)

Smoking policy: Landlord must give tenant written disclosure stating whether smoking is prohibited on the premises, allowed on the entire premises, or allowed in limited areas of the premises. If the landlord allows smoking in limited areas on the premises, the notice must identify the areas on the premises where smoking is allowed. Disclosure must be in the lease or separate written notice, landlord must disclose before tenant signs a lease or pays a deposit, and must obtain a written acknowledgment of notification from the tenant. (14 Me. Rev. Stat. Ann. § 6030-E)

Required Landlord Disclosures (continued)

Maryland

Move-in checklist required? Yes. Before collecting a deposit, landlord must supply a receipt with details on move-in and move-out inspections, and the receipt must be part of the lease. (Md. Code Ann. [Real Prop.] § 8-203.1)

Habitation: A lease must include a statement that the premises will be made available in a condition permitting habitation, with reasonable safety, if that is the agreement, or if that is not the agreement, a statement of the agreement concerning the condition of the premises; and the landlord's and the tenant's specific obligations as to heat, gas, electricity, water, and repair of the premises. (Md. Code Ann. [Real Prop.] § 8-208)

Owner or agent identity: The landlord must include in a lease or post the name and address of the landlord; or the person, if any, authorized to accept notice or service of process on behalf of the landlord. (Md. Code Ann. [Real Prop.] § 8-210)

Massachusetts

Move-in checklist required? Yes, if landlord collects a security deposit. (186 Mass. Gen. Laws § 15B(2)(c))

Insurance: Upon tenant's request and w/in 15 days, landlord must furnish the name of the company insuring the property against loss or damage by fire and the amount of insurance provided by each such company and the name of any person who would receive payment for a loss covered by such insurance. (Mass. Gen. Laws Ann. 186 § 21)

Tax Escalation: If real estate taxes increase, landlord may pass on a proportionate share of the increase to the tenant only if the lease discloses that in the event of an increase, the tenant will be required to pay only the proportion of the increase as the tenant's leased unit bears to the property being taxed (that proportion must be disclosed in the lease). In addition, the lease must state that if the landlord receives a tax abatement, landlord will refund a proportionate share of the abatement, minus reasonable attorneys' fees. (186 Mass. Gen. Laws § 15C)

Utilities: Landlord may not charge for water unless the lease specifies the charge and the details of the water sub-metering and billing arrangement. (186 Mass. Gen. Laws § 22(f))

Michigan

Move-in checklist required? Yes. However, the requirement does not need to be stated in the lease. (Mich. Comp. Laws § 554.608)

May landlord charge nonrefundable fees? Yes. (*Stutelberg v. Practical Management Co.*, 245 N.W.2d 737 (1976))

Owner or agent identity: A rental agreement must include the name and address at which notice can be given to the landlord. (Mich. Comp. Laws § 554.634)

Truth in Renting Act: A rental agreement must also state in a prominent place in type not smaller than the size of 12-point type, or in legible print with letters not smaller than 1/8 inch, a notice in substantially the following form: "NOTICE: Michigan law establishes rights and obligations for parties to rental agreements. This agreement is required to comply with the Truth in Renting Act. If you have a question about the interpretation or legality of a provision of this agreement, you may want to seek assistance from a lawyer or other qualified person." (Mich. Comp. Laws § 554.634)

Rights of domestic violence victims: A rental agreement or lease may contain a provision stating, "A tenant who has a reasonable apprehension of present danger to him or her or his or her child from domestic violence, sexual assault, or stalking may have special statutory rights to seek a release of rental obligation under MCL 554.601b." If the rental agreement or lease does not contain such a provision, the landlord must post an identical written notice visible to a reasonable person in the landlord's property management office, or deliver written notice to the tenant when the lease or rental agreement is signed. (Mich. Comp. Laws § 554.601b)

Minnesota

Owner or agent identity: Landlord must disclose to the tenant in writing at or before the commencement of the tenancy the name and address of the person authorized to manage the premises, and an owner of the premises or a person authorized to act for and on behalf of the owner for the purpose of service of process and for the purpose of receiving notices and demands. (Minn. Stat. Ann. § 504B.181)

Required Landlord Disclosures (continued)

Outstanding inspection orders, condemnation orders, or declarations that the property is unfit: The landlord must disclose the existence of any such orders or declarations before the tenant signs a lease or pays a security deposit. (Minn. Stat. Ann. § 504B.195)

Buildings in financial distress: Once a landlord has received notice of a deed cancellation or notice of foreclosure, landlord may not enter into a periodic tenancy where the tenancy term is more than two months, or a lease where the lease extends beyond the redemption period (other restrictions may apply). (Minn. Stat. Ann. § 504B.151)

Landlord and tenant mutual promises: This mutual promise must appear in every lease or rental agreement: "Landlord and tenant promise that neither will unlawfully allow within the premises, common areas, or curtilage of the premises (property boundaries): controlled substances, prostitution or prostitution-related activity; stolen property or property obtained by robbery; or an act of domestic violence, as defined by MN Statute Section 504B.206 (1)(e), against a tenant, licensee, or any authorized occupant. They further promise that the aforementioned areas will not be used by themselves or anyone acting under their control to manufacture, sell, give away, barter, deliver, exchange, distribute, purchase, or possess a controlled substance in violation of any criminal provision of chapter 152."

Mississippi

No disclosure statutes.

Missouri

Meth Labs: Landlord who knows that the premises were used to produce methamphetamine must disclose this fact to prospective tenants, irrespective of whether the people involved in the production were convicted for such production. (Mo. Rev. Stat. § 441.236)

Owner or Agent Identity: Landlord must disclose to the tenant in writing at or before the commencement of the tenancy the name and address of the person authorized to manage the premises, and an owner of the premises or a person authorized to act for and on behalf of the owner for the purpose of service of process and for the purpose of receiving notices and demands. (Mo. Rev. Stat. § 535.185)

Montana

Nonrefundable fees permitted? No. A fee or charge for cleaning and damages, no matter how designated, is presumed to be a security deposit. (Not a clear statement that such a fee isn't nonrefundable, but by implication it must be.) (Mont. Code Ann. § 70-25-101(4))

Move-in checklists required? Yes, checklists are required when landlords collect a security deposit. (Mont. Code Ann. § 70-25-206)

Owner or agent identity: A landlord or a person authorized to enter into a rental agreement on his behalf must disclose to the tenant in writing at or before the commencement of the tenancy the name and address of the person authorized to manage the premises; and the owner of the premises or a person authorized to act for the owner for the purpose of service of process and receiving notices and demands. (Mont. Code Ann. § 70-24-301)

Nebraska

Owner or agent identity: The landlord or any person authorized to enter into a rental agreement on his or her behalf shall disclose to the tenant in writing at or before the commencement of the tenancy the name and address of the person authorized to manage the premises; and an owner of the premises or a person authorized to act for and on behalf of the owner for the purpose of service of process receiving notices and demands. (Neb. Rev. Stat. § 76-1417)

Nevada

Nonrefundable fees permitted? Yes. Lease must explain fees that are required and the purposes for which they are required. (Nev. Rev. Stat. Ann. § 118A.200)

Move-in checklist required? Yes. Lease must include tenants' rights to a checklist and a signed record of the inventory and condition of the premises under the exclusive custody and control of the tenant. (Nev. Rev. Stat. Ann. § 118A.200)

Nuisance and flying the flag: Lease must include a summary of the provisions of NRS 202.470 (penalties for permitting or maintaining a nuisance); information regarding the procedure a tenant may use to report to the appropriate authorities a nuisance, a violation of a building, safety, or health code or regulation; and

Required Landlord Disclosures (continued)

information regarding the right of the tenant to engage in the display of the flag of the United States, as set forth in NRS 118A.325. (Nev. Rev. Stat. Ann. § 118A.200)

Foreclosure proceedings: Landlord must disclose to any prospective tenant, in writing, whether the premises to be rented is the subject of a foreclosure proceeding (disclosure need not be in the lease). (Nev. Rev. Stat. Ann. § 118A.275)

Lease Signed By an Agent of the Landlord Who Does Not Hold a Property Management Permit: In single-family rentals only, unless the lease is signed by an authorized agent of the landlord who holds a current property management permit, the top of the first page of the lease must state, in font that is at least twice the size of any other size in the agreement, that the tenant might not have valid occupancy unless the lease is notarized or signed by an authorized agent of the owner who holds a management permit. The notice must give the current address and phone number of the landlord. In addition, it must state that even if the foregoing has not been provided, the agreement is enforceable against the landlord. (Nev. Rev. Stat. Ann. § 118A.200)

New Hampshire

Move-in checklist required? Yes. Landlord must inform tenant that if tenant finds any conditions in the rental in need of repair, tenant may note them on the security deposit receipt or other writing (not a true checklist). (N.H. Rev. Stat. Ann. § 540-A:6)

New Jersey

Flood zone: Prior to move-in, landlord must inform tenant if rental is in a flood zone or area (does not apply to properties containing two or fewer dwelling units, or to owner-occupied properties of three or fewer units). (N.J. Stat. Ann. § 46:8-50)

Truth in Renting Act: Except in buildings of 2 or fewer units, and owner-occupied premises of 3 or fewer units, landlord must distribute to new tenants at or prior to move-in the Department of Community Affairs' statement of legal rights and responsibilities of tenants and landlords of rental dwelling units (Spanish also). (N.J.S.A. §§ 46:8-44, 46:8-45, 46:8-46)

Child Protection Windowguards: Landlords of multi-family properties must include information in the lease about tenants' rights to request windowguards. The

Legislature's Model Lease and Notice clause reads as follows: "The owner (landlord) is required by law to provide, install and maintain window guards in the apartment if a child or children 10 years of age or younger is, or will be, living in the apartment or is, or will be, regularly present there for a substantial period of time if the tenant gives the owner (landlord) a written request that the window guards be installed. The owner (landlord) is also required, upon the written request of the tenant, to provide, install and maintain window guards in the hallways to which persons in the tenant's unit have access without having to go out of the building. If the building is a condominium, cooperative or mutual housing building, the owner (landlord) of the apartment is responsible for installing and maintaining window guards in the apartment and the association is responsible for installing and maintaining window guards in hallway windows. Window guards are only required to be provided in first floor windows where the window sill is more than six feet above grade or there are other hazardous conditions that make installation of window guards necessary to protect the safety of children." The notice must be conspicuous and in boldface type. (N.J. Admin. Code § 5:10-27.1)

New Mexico

Owner or agent identity: Landlord must disclose to the tenant in writing at or before the commencement of the tenancy the name and address of the person authorized to manage the premises, and an owner of the premises or a person authorized to act for and on behalf of the owner for the purpose of service of process and for the purpose of receiving notices and demands. (N.M. Stat. Ann. § 47-8-19)

New York

Air Contamination: Landlord who receives a government report showing that the air in the building has, or may have, concentrations of volatile organic compounds (VOCs) that exceed government guidelines must give written notice to prospective tenants and current tenants. The notice must appear in at least 12-point type bold face type on the first page of the lease or rental agreement. It must read as follows: "NOTIFICATION OF TEST RESULTS The property has been tested for contamination of indoor air: test results and additional information are available upon request." (N.Y. ECL § 27-2405).

Required Landlord Disclosures (continued)

North Carolina

Going to court fees: Yes, Landlord may collect only one of the following, when specific conditions are met: Complaint filing fee, court appearance fee, and second trial fee. Failure to pay the fees cannot support a termination notice. (N.C. Gen. Stat. § 42-46)

North Dakota

Move-in checklist required? Yes. Landlord must give tenant a statement describing the condition of the premises when tenant signs the rental agreement. Both parties must sign the statement. (N.D. Cent. Code § 47-16-07.2)

Ohio

Owner or agent identity: Every written rental agreement must contain the name and address of the owner and the name and address of the owner's agent, if any. If the owner or the owner's agent is a corporation, partnership, limited partnership, association, trust, or other entity, the address must be the principal place of business in the county in which the residential property is situated. If there is no place of business in such county, then its principal place of business in this state must be disclosed, including the name of the person in charge thereof. (Ohio Rev. Code Ann. § 5321.18)

Oklahoma

Flooding: If the premises to be rented has been flooded within the past five (5) years and such fact is known to the landlord, the landlord shall include such information prominently and in writing as part of any written rental agreements. (41 Okla. Stat. Ann. § 113a)

Owner information: As a part of any rental agreement the lessor shall prominently and in writing identify what person at what address is entitled to accept service or notice under this act. Landlord must disclose to the tenant in writing at or before the commencement of the tenancy the name and address of the person authorized to manage the premises, and an owner of the premises or a person authorized to act for and on behalf of the owner for the purpose of service of process and receiving notices and demands. (41 Okla. Stat. Ann § 116)

Oregon

Nonrefundable fees permitted? No. (Or. Rev. Stat. § 90.302)

Other fees? Landlords' written rules may not provide for tenant fees, except for specified events as they arise, including a late rent payment; tenant's late payment of a utility or service charge; a dishonored check, pursuant to Or. Rev. Stat. § 30.701(5); failure to clean up pet waste in areas other than tenant's unit; failure to clean up garbage and rubbish (outside tenant's dwelling unit); failure to clean pet waste of a service or companion animal from areas other than the dwelling unit; parking violations and improper use of vehicles within the premises; smoking in a designated nonsmoking area; keeping an unauthorized pet capable of inflicting damage on persons or property; and tampering or disabling a smoke detector.)

Owner or agent identity: Landlord must disclose to the tenant in writing at or before the commencement of the tenancy the name and address of the person authorized to manage the premises, and an owner of the premises or a person authorized to act for and on behalf of the owner for the purpose of service of process and for the purpose of receiving notices and demands. (Or. Rev. Stat. § 90.305)

Legal proceedings: If at the time of the execution of a rental agreement for a dwelling unit in premises containing no more than four dwelling units the premises are subject to any of the following circumstances, the landlord must disclose that circumstance to the tenant in writing before the execution of the rental agreement:

a. Any outstanding notice of default under a trust deed, mortgage, or contract of sale, or notice of trustee's sale under a trust deed;

b. Any pending suit to foreclose a mortgage, trust deed, or vendor's lien under a contract of sale;

c. Any pending declaration of forfeiture or suit for specific performance of a contract of sale; or

d. Any pending proceeding to foreclose a tax lien.

(Or. Rev. Stat. § 90.310)

Utilities: The landlord must disclose to the tenant in writing at or before the commencement of the tenancy any utility or service that the tenant pays directly to a utility or service provider that directly benefits the landlord or other tenants. A tenant's payment for a given utility or service benefits the landlord or other tenants if the utility or service is delivered to any area other than the tenant's dwelling unit.

Required Landlord Disclosures (continued)

A landlord may require a tenant to pay to the landlord a utility or service charge that has been billed by a utility or service provider to the landlord for utility or service provided directly to the tenant's dwelling unit or to a common area available to the tenant as part of the tenancy. A utility or service charge that shall be assessed to a tenant for a common area must be described in the written rental agreement separately and distinctly from such a charge for the tenant's dwelling unit. Unless the method of allocating the charges to the tenant is described in the tenant's written rental agreement, the tenant may require that the landlord give the tenant a copy of the provider's bill as a condition of paying the charges. (Or. Rev. Stat. § 90.315)

Recycling: In a city or the county within the urban growth boundary of a city that has implemented multifamily recycling service, a landlord who has five or more residential dwelling units on a single premises must notify new tenants at the time of entering into a rental agreement of the opportunity to recycle. (Or. Rev. Stat. § 90.318)

Smoking policy: Landlord must disclose the smoking policy for the premises, by stating whether smoking is prohibited on the premises, allowed on the entire premises, or allowed in limited areas. If landlord allows smoking in limited areas, the disclosure must identify those areas. (Or. Rev. Stat. § 90.220)

Carbon monoxide alarm instructions: If rental contains a CO source (a heater, fireplace, appliance, or cooking source that uses coal, kerosene, petroleum products, wood, or other fuels that emit carbon monoxide as a by-product of combustion; or an attached garage with an opening that communicates directly with a living space), landlord must install one or more CO monitors and give tenant written instructions for testing the alarm(s), before tenant takes possession. (Or. Rev. Stat. § 90.316, 90.317)

Flood zone: If a dwelling unit is located in a 100-year flood plain, the landlord must provide notice in the dwelling unit rental agreement that the dwelling unit is located within the flood plain. If a landlord fails to provide a notice as required under this section, and the tenant of the dwelling unit suffers an uninsured loss due to flooding, the tenant may recover from the landlord the lesser of the actual damages for the uninsured loss or two months' rent. (Or. Rev. Stat. § 90.228)

Renters' insurance: Landlord may require tenants to maintain liability insurance (certain low-income and subsidized tenancies excepted), but only if the landlord obtains and maintains comparable liability insurance and provides documentation to any tenant who requests the documentation, orally or in writing. The landlord may provide documentation to a tenant in person, by mail, or by posting in a common area or office. The documentation may consist of a current certificate of coverage. Any landlord who requires tenants to obtain renters' insurance must disclose the requirement and amount in writing prior to entering into a new tenancy, and may require the tenant to provide documentation before the tenancy begins. (Or. Rev. Stat. § 90.367)

Homeowner Assessments: If landlord wants to pass on homeowners' association assessments that are imposed on anyone moving into or out of the unit, the written rental agreement must include this requirement. Landlord must give tenants a copy of each assessment before charging the tenant. (Or. Rev. Stat. § 90.302)

Pennsylvania

No disclosure statutes.

Rhode Island

Owner disclosure: Landlord must disclose to the tenant in writing at or before the commencement of the tenancy the name and address of the person authorized to manage the premises, and an owner of the premises or a person authorized to act for and on behalf of the owner for the purpose of service of process and for the purpose of receiving notices and demands. (R.I. Gen. Laws § 34-18-20)

Code violations: Before entering into any residential rental agreement, landlord must inform a prospective tenant of any outstanding minimum housing code violations that exist on the building that is the subject of the rental agreement. (R.I. Gen. Laws § 34-18-22.1)

Notice of Foreclosure: A landlord who becomes delinquent on a mortgage securing real estate upon which the rental is located for a period of 120 days must notify the tenant that the property may be subject to foreclosure; and until the foreclosure occurs, the tenant must continue to pay rent to the landlord as provided under the rental agreement. (R.I. Gen. Laws § 34-18-20)

Required Landlord Disclosures (continued)

South Carolina

Owner or agent identity: Landlord must disclose to the tenant in writing at or before the commencement of the tenancy the name and address of the person authorized to manage the premises, and an owner of the premises or a person authorized to act for and on behalf of the owner for the purpose of service of process and for the purpose of receiving notices and demands. (S.C. Code Ann. § 27-40-420)

Unequal security deposits: If landlord rents five or more adjoining units on the premises, and imposes different standards for calculating deposits required of tenants, landlord must, before a tenancy begins, post in a conspicuous place a statement explaining the standards by which the various deposits are calculated (or, landlord may give the tenant the written statement). (S.C. Code Ann. § 27-40-410)

South Dakota

Meth labs: Landlord who has actual knowledge of the existence of any prior manufacturing of methamphetamines on the premises must disclose that information to any lessee or any person who may become a lessee. If the residential premises consists of two or more housing units, the disclosure requirements apply only to the unit where there is knowledge of the existence of any prior manufacturing of methamphetamines. (S.D. Codified Laws Ann. § 43-32-30)

Tennessee

Owner or agent identity: The landlord or any person authorized to enter into a rental agreement on the landlord's behalf must disclose to the tenant in writing at or before the commencement of the tenancy the name and address of the agent authorized to manage the premises, and an owner of the premises or a person or agent authorized to act for and on behalf of the owner for the acceptance of service of process and for receipt of notices and demands. (Tenn. Code Ann. § 66-28-302)

Showing rental to prospective tenants: Landlord may enter to show the premises to prospective renters during the final 30 days of a tenancy (with 24 hours' notice), but only if this right of access is set forth in the rental agreement or lease. (Tenn. Code Ann. § 66-28-403)

Texas

Nonrefundable fees permitted? Yes. (*Holmes v. Canlen Management Corp.*, 542 S.W.2d 199 (1976))

Owner or agent identity: In the lease, other writing, or posted on the property, landlord must disclose the name and address of the property's owner and, if an entity located off-site from the dwelling is primarily responsible for managing the dwelling, the name and street address of the management company. (Tex. Prop. Code Ann. § 92.201)

Security device requests: If landlord wants tenant requests concerning security devices to be in writing, this requirement must be in the lease in boldface type or underlined. (Tex. Prop. Code Ann. § 92.159)

Return of security deposit: A requirement that a tenant give advance notice of moving out as a condition for refunding the security deposit is effective only if the requirement is in the lease, underlined or printed in conspicuous bold print. (Tex. Prop. Code Ann. § 92.103)

Domestic violence victims' rights: Victims of sexual abuse or assault on the premises may break a lease, after complying with specified procedures, without responsibility for future rent. Tenants will be responsible for any unpaid back rent, but only if the lease includes the following statement, or one substantially like it: "Tenants may have special statutory rights to terminate the lease early in certain situations involving family violence or a military deployment or transfer." (Tex. Prop. Code Ann. § 92.016)

Tenant's rights when landlord fails to repair: A lease must contain language in underlined or bold print that informs the tenant of the remedies available when the landlord fails to repair a problem that materially affects the physical health or safety of an ordinary tenant. These rights include the right to repair and deduct; terminate the lease; and obtain a judicial order that the landlord make the repair, reduce the rent, pay the tenant damages (including a civil penalty), and pay the tenant's court and attorneys' fees. (Tex. Prop. Code Ann. § 92.056)

Landlord's towing or parking rules and policies: For tenants in multiunit properties, if the landlord has vehicle towing or parking rules or policies that apply to the tenant, the landlord must give the tenant a copy of the rules or policies before the lease agreement is signed.

Required Landlord Disclosures (continued)

The copy must be signed by the tenant, included in the lease or rental agreement, or be made an attachment to either. If included, the clause must be titled " Parking" or "Parking Rules" and be capitalized, underlined, or printed in bold print.) (Tex. Prop. Code Ann. § 92.0131.)

Electric service interruption: Landlord who submeters electric service, or who allocates master metered electricity according to a prorated system, may interrupt tenant's electricity service if tenant fails to pay the bill, but only after specific notice and according to a complex procedure. Exceptions for ill tenants and during extreme weather. (Tex. Prop. Code Ann. § 92.008(h))

Utah

Nonrefundable fees permitted? Yes. By custom, if there is a written agreement and if any part of the deposit is nonrefundable, it must be so stated in writing to the renter at the time the deposit is taken.

Move-in checklists required? Yes. Landlords must give prospective renters a written inventory of the condition of the residential rental unit, excluding ordinary wear and tear; give the renter a form to document the condition of the residential rental and allow the resident a reasonable time after the renter's occupancy of the unit to complete and return the form; or provide the prospective renter an opportunity to conduct a walk-through inspection of the rental. (Utah Code. Ann. § 57-22-4)

Applicant Disclosures: Before accepting an application or collecting an application fee, landlord must disclose whether the rental unit is expected to be available, and the criteria landlord will use in evaluating potential renter's application. Failure to comply will not invalidate the lease or provide tenant with a legal cause of action. (Utah Code Ann. § 57-22-4)

Vermont

No disclosure statutes.

Virginia

Move-in checklist required? Yes. Within 5 days of move-in, landlord or tenant or both together must prepare a written report detailing the condition of the premises. Landlord must disclose within this report the known presence of mold. (Va. Code Ann. § 55-248.11:1)

Owner or agent identity: Landlord must disclose to the tenant in writing at or before the commencement of the tenancy the name and address of the person authorized to manage the premises, and an owner of the premises or a person authorized to act for and on behalf of the owner for the purpose of service of process and for the purpose of receiving notices and demands. (Va. Code Ann. § 55-248.12)

Military zone: The landlord of property in any locality in which a military air installation is located, or any person authorized to enter into a rental agreement on his behalf, must provide to a prospective tenant a written disclosure that the property is located in a noise zone or accident potential zone, or both, as designated by the locality on its official zoning map. (Va. Code Ann. § 55-248.12:1)

Mold: Move-in inspection report must include whether there is any visible evidence of mold (deemed correct unless tenant objects within five days); if evidence is present, tenant may terminate or not move in. If tenant stays, landlord must remediate the mold condition within five business days, reinspect, and issue a new report indicating that there is no evidence of mold. (Va. Code Ann. § 55-248.11:2) If evidence of mold appears during the tenancy, landlord must promptly remediate, reinspect, and make available to the tenant copies of any available written information on how to get rid of mold. (Va. Code Ann. § 55-248.16)

Ratio utility billing: Landlord who uses a ratio utility billing service, who intends to collect monthly billing and other administrative and late fees, must disclose these fees in a written rental agreement. (Va. Code Ann. § 55-226.2)

Condominium plans: If an application for registration as a condominium or cooperative has been filed with the Real Estate Board, or if there is within six months an existing plan for tenant displacement resulting from demolition or substantial rehabilitation of the property, or conversion of the rental property to office, hotel, or motel use or planned unit development, the landlord or any person authorized to enter into a rental agreement on his behalf must disclose that information in writing to any prospective tenant. (Va. Code Ann. § 55-248.12(C).)

Defective drywall: Landlords who know of the presence of unrepaired defective drywall in the rental must disclose this before the tenant signs a lease or rental agreement. (Va. Code Ann. § 55-248.12:2.)

Required Landlord Disclosures (continued)

Washington

Move-in checklists required? Yes. Checklists are required when landlords collect a security deposit. If landlord fails to provide checklist, landlord is liable to the tenant for the amount of the deposit. (Wash. Rev. Code Ann. § 59.18.260)

Nonrefundable fees permitted? Yes. If landlord collects a nonrefundable fee, the rental document must clearly specify that it is nonrefundable. (Wash. Rev. Code Ann. § 59.18.285)

Fire protection: At the time the lease is signed, landlord must provide fire protection and safety information, including whether the building has a smoking policy, an emergency notification plan, or an evacuation plan. (Wash. Rev. Code Ann. § 59.18.060)

Owner or agent identity: In the rental document or posted conspicuously on the premises, landlord must designate to the tenant the name and address of the person who is the landlord by a statement on the rental agreement or by a notice conspicuously posted on the premises. If the person designated does not reside in Washington, landlord must also designate a person who resides in the county to act as an agent for the purposes of service of notices and process. (Wash. Rev. Code Ann. § 59.18.060)

Mold: At the time the lease is signed, landlord must provide tenant with information provided or approved by the department of health about the health hazards associated with exposure to indoor mold. (Wash. Rev. Code Ann. § 59.18.060)

Screening criteria: Before obtaining any information about an applicant, landlord must provide (in writing or by posting) the type of information to be accessed, criteria to be used to evaluate the application, and (for consumer reports) the name and address of the consumer reporting agency to be used, including the applicant's rights to obtain a free copy of the report and dispute its accuracy. Landlord must advise tenants whether landlord will accept a comprehensive reusable tenant screening report done by a consumer reporting agency (in which case the landlord may not charge the tenant a fee for a screening report). If landlord maintains a website that advertises residential rentals, the home page must include this information. (Wash. Rev. Code Ann. § 59.18.257)

Tenant screening fee: Landlords who do their own screening may charge a fee for time and costs to obtain background information, but only if they provide the information explained in "Screening Criteria," above. (Wash. Rev. Code Ann. § 59.18.257.)

West Virginia

Nonrefundable fees permitted? Yes. Nonrefundable fee must be expressly agreed to in writing. (W.Va. Code § 37-6A-1(14))

Wisconsin

Move-in checklist required? Yes. Tenant has a right to inspect the rental and give landlord a list of defects, and to receive a list of damages charged to the prior tenant. Tenant has 7 days after start of the tenancy to return the list to the landlord. (Wis. Admin. Code § 134.06; Wis. Stat. Ann. § 704.08)

Owner or agent identity: Landlord must disclose to the tenant in writing, at or before the time a rental agreement is signed, the name and address of: the person or persons authorized to collect or receive rent and manage and maintain the premises, and who can readily be contacted by the tenant; and the owner of the premises or other person authorized to accept service of legal process and other notices and demands on behalf of the owner. The address must be an address within the state at which service of process can be made in person. (Wis. Admin. Code § 134.04)

Nonstandard rental provisions: If landlord wants to enter premises for reasons not specified by law, landlord must disclose the provision in a separate written document entitled "NONSTANDARD RENTAL PROVISIONS" before the rental agreement is signed. (Wis. Admin. Code § 134.09)

Uncorrected code violations: Before signing a rental contract or accepting a security deposit, the landlord must disclose to the tenant any uncorrected code violation of which the landlord is actually aware, which affects the dwelling unit or a common area and poses a significant threat to the tenant's health or safety. "Disclosure" consists of showing prospective tenants the portion of the building affected, as well as the notices themselves. (Wis. Stat. §§ 134.04, 704.07(2)(bm))

Required Landlord Disclosures (continued)

Habitability deficiencies: Landlord must disclose serious problems that affect the rental unit's habitability. (Wis. Admin. Code § 134.04)

Utility charges: If charges for water, heat, or electricity are not included in the rent, the landlord must disclose this fact to the tenant before entering into a rental agreement or accepting any earnest money or security deposit from the prospective tenant. If individual dwelling units and common areas are not separately metered, and if the charges are not included in the rent, the landlord must disclose the basis on which charges for utility services will be allocated among individual dwelling units. (Wis. Admin. Code § 134.04)

Disposing of abandoned property: If landlord intends to immediately dispose of any tenant property left behind after move-out, landlord must notify tenant at the time lease is signed. (But landlord must hold prescription medications and medical equipment for seven days, and must give notice before disposing of vehicles or manufactured homes to owner and any known secured party.) (Wis. Stat. § 704.05(5))

Wyoming

Nonrefundable fees permitted? Yes. If any portion of the deposit is not refundable, rental agreement must include this information and tenant must be told before paying a deposit. (Wyo. Stat. § 1-21-1207)

State Laws in Domestic Violence Situations

Many states extend special protections, such as early termination rights, to victims of domestic violence. Here is a summary of state laws. For more information, check with local law enforcement or a battered women's shelter.

Alabama

No statute

Alaska

Alaska Stat. § 29.35.125(a)

Miscellaneous provisions: A city may impose a fee on the owner of residential property if the police go to the property an excessive number of times during a calendar year when called for assistance or to handle a complaint, an emergency, or a potential emergency. This fee may not be imposed for responses to calls that involve potential child neglect, domestic violence, or stalking.

Arizona

Ariz. Rev. Stat. §§ 33-1315, 33-1318, 33-1414

- Lease cannot include a waiver of some or all DV rights
- Landlord entitled to proof of DV status
- Early termination right for DV victim
- Lease cannot prohibit calling the police in a DV situation or otherwise penalize DV victim
- DV victim has the right to have the locks changed
- Penalty for falsely reporting domestic violence (including obtaining early termination)
- Perpetrator of DV liable to landlord for resulting damages

Arkansas

Ark. Code Ann. § 18-16-112

- Landlord entitled to proof of DV status
- Landlord cannot refuse to rent to victim of DV
- Landlord cannot terminate a victim of DV
- Lease cannot prohibit calling the police in a DV situation or otherwise penalize DV victim
- DV victim has the right to have the locks changed
- Perpetrator of DV liable to landlord for resulting damages
- Landlord or court may bifurcate the lease

California

Cal. Civ. Code §§ 1941.5, 1941.6, 1946.7; Cal. Code Civ. Proc. §§ 1161, 1161.3

- Landlord entitled to proof of DV status
- Landlord cannot refuse to rent to victim of DV
- Landlord cannot terminate a victim of DV
- Early termination right for DV victim
- DV is an affirmative defense to an eviction lawsuit
- DV victim has the right to have the locks changed
- Landlord or court may bifurcate the lease
- Landlord has limited right to evict the DV victim

Miscellaneous provisions: Protection against termination has been expanded to include elder or dependent adults.

Colorado

Colo. Rev. Stat. §§ 13-40-104(4), 13-40-107.5(5), 38-12-401, 38-12-402, 38-12-503

- Lease cannot include a waiver of some or all DV rights
- Landlord entitled to proof of DV status
- Landlord cannot terminate a victim of DV
- Early termination right for DV victim
- Lease cannot prohibit calling the police in a DV situation or otherwise penalize DV victim

Miscellaneous provisions: Legal protections extend to victims of unlawful sexual behavior and stalking, as well as domestic violence. Landlords may not disclose that tenants were victims of such acts, except with permission or as required by law. Landlord may not disclose such facts to tenant's new address if tenant terminates as permitted by law.

Connecticut

Conn. Gen. Stat. Ann. § 47a-11e

- Landlord entitled to proof of DV status
- Early termination right for DV victim

Delaware

Del. Code Ann. tit. 25, §§ 5141(7), 5314(b), 5316

- Landlord entitled to proof of DV status
- Landlord cannot terminate a victim of DV
- Early termination right for DV victim

State Laws in Domestic Violence Situations (continued)

District of Columbia

D.C. Code Ann. §§ 2-1402.21, 42-3505.07, 42-3505.08

- Lease cannot include a waiver of some or all DV rights
- Landlord entitled to proof of DV status
- Landlord cannot refuse to rent to victim of DV
- Early termination right for DV victim
- DV is an affirmative defense to an eviction lawsuit
- Lease cannot prohibit calling the police in a DV situation or otherwise penalize DV victim
- DV victim has the right to have the locks changed
- Landlord or court may bifurcate the lease

Miscellaneous provisions: Landlord must make reasonable accommodation in restoring or improving security and safety measures that are beyond the landlord's duty of ordinary care and diligence, when such accommodation is necessary to ensure the tenant's security and safety (tenant may be billed for the cost).

Florida

No statute

Georgia

No statute

Hawaii

Haw. Rev. Stat. §§ 521-80 to 521-82

- Landlord entitled to proof of DV status
- Early termination right for DV victim
- DV victim has the right to have the locks changed
- Penalty for falsely reporting domestic violence (including obtaining early termination)
- Landlord or court may bifurcate the lease

Miscellaneous provisions: Landlord may not disclose information gathered with respect to tenant's exercise of rights under these laws, unless the tenant consents in writing, the information is required or relevant in a lawsuit, or the disclosure is required by law.

Idaho

No statute

Illinois

735 Ill. Comp. Stat. 5/9-106.2; 765 Ill. Comp. Stat. 750/1 through 750/35

- Landlord entitled to proof of DV status
- Early termination right for DV victim

- DV is an affirmative defense to an eviction lawsuit
- DV victim has the right to have the locks changed
- Landlord or court may bifurcate the lease

Miscellaneous provisions: Landlord may not disclose to others that a tenant has exercised a right under the law; violations expose landlord to damages that result, or $2,000.

Indiana

Ind. Code Ann. §§ 32-31-9-1 through 32-31-9-15

- Landlord entitled to proof of DV status
- Landlord cannot refuse to rent to victim of DV
- Landlord cannot terminate a victim of DV
- Early termination right for DV victim
- Lease cannot prohibit calling the police in a DV situation or otherwise penalize DV victim
- DV victim has the right to have the locks changed

Iowa

Iowa Code §§ 562A.27A, 562A.27B, 562B.25A(3)

- Lease cannot include a waiver of some or all DV rights
- Landlord entitled to proof of DV status
- Landlord cannot terminate a victim of DV
- Lease cannot prohibit calling the police in a DV situation or otherwise penalize DV victim
- Landlord has limited right to evict the DV victim

Miscellaneous provisions: Landlord can recover from the tenant the cost to repair damage caused by emergency responders called by tenant. Cities cannot impose penalties against residents or landlords, including fines, permit or license revocations, and evictions, when they had a reasonable belief that emergency assistance was necessary, and it was in fact needed.

Kansas

No statute

Kentucky

Ky. Rev. Stat. §§ 383.300, 383.302

- Lease cannot include a waiver of some or all DV rights
- Landlord entitled to proof of DV status
- Landlord cannot refuse to rent to victim of DV
- Landlord cannot terminate a victim of DV
- Early termination right for DV victim
- DV is an affirmative defense to an eviction lawsuit
- DV victim has the right to have the locks changed

State Laws in Domestic Violence Situations (continued)

- Perpetrator of DV liable to landlord for resulting damages
- Landlord or court may bifurcate the lease

Louisiana

La. Rev. Stat. Ann. § 9:3261.1

- Lease cannot include a waiver of some or all DV rights
- Landlord entitled to proof of DV status
- Landlord cannot refuse to rent to victim of DV
- Landlord cannot terminate a victim of DV
- Early termination right for DV victim
- Lease cannot prohibit calling the police in a DV situation or otherwise penalize DV victim

Miscellaneous provisions: Statute applies only to multi-family housing of six or more units; does not apply if building has ten or fewer units and one is occupied by the owner.

Maine

Me. Rev. Stat. Ann. tit. 14, §§ 6000, 6001, 6002, 6025

- Landlord entitled to proof of DV status
- Landlord cannot terminate a victim of DV
- Early termination right for DV victim
- DV victim has the right to have the locks changed
- Perpetrator of DV liable to landlord for resulting damages
- Landlord or court may bifurcate the lease

Miscellaneous provisions: Landlord may terminate and/or bifurcate the lease with 7 days' notice when a tenant perpetrates domestic violence, sexual assault, or stalking (against another tenant, a tenant's guest, or the landlord or landlord's employee or agent), and the victim is also a tenant.

Maryland

Md. Real Prop. Law §§ 8-5A-01 through 8-5A-06

- Landlord entitled to proof of DV status
- Early termination right for DV victim

Massachusetts

186 Mass Gen. Laws §§ 24, 25, 26, and 28

- Lease cannot include a waiver of some or all DV rights
- Landlord entitled to proof of DV status
- Landlord cannot refuse to rent to victim of DV
- Early termination right for DV victim

- DV victim has the right to have the locks changed

Michigan

Mich. Comp. Laws § 554.601b

- Landlord entitled to proof of DV status
- Early termination right for DV victim
- Landlord or court may bifurcate the lease

Minnesota

Minn. Stat. Ann. §§ 504B.205, 206

- Lease cannot include a waiver of some or all DV rights
- Landlord entitled to proof of DV status
- Landlord cannot terminate a victim of DV
- Early termination right for DV victim
- DV is an affirmative defense to an eviction lawsuit
- Lease cannot prohibit calling the police in a DV situation or otherwise penalize DV victim

Miscellaneous provisions: Landlord must keep information about the domestic violence confidential. In a multitenant situation, termination by one tenant terminates the lease of all, though other tenants may reapply to enter into a new lease. All security deposit is forfeited.

Mississippi

No statute

Missouri

No statute

Montana

No statute

Nebraska

No statute

Nevada

Nev. Rev. Stat. Ann. §§ 118A.345, 118A.347, 118A.510

- Lease cannot include a waiver of some or all DV rights
- Landlord entitled to proof of DV status
- Landlord cannot terminate a victim of DV
- Early termination right for DV victim
- DV victim has the right to have the locks changed
- Perpetrator of DV liable to landlord for resulting damages

Miscellaneous provisions: Protections extend to victims of harassment, sexual assault, and stalking, as well as domestic

State Laws in Domestic Violence Situations (continued)

violence. Landlord may not disclose the fact of a tenant's early termination to a prospective landlord; nor may a prospective landlord require an applicant to disclose any prior early terminations. Antiretaliation protection extended to tenants who are domestic violence victims or who have terminated a rental agreement pursuant to law.

New Hampshire

N.H. Rev. Stat. Ann. § 540:2.VII

- Landlord entitled to proof of DV status
- Landlord cannot terminate a victim of DV
- DV victim has the right to have the locks changed
- Landlord or court may bifurcate the lease

New Jersey

N.J. Stat. Ann. §§ 46:8-9.5 through 46:8-9.12

- Lease cannot include a waiver of some or all DV rights
- Landlord entitled to proof of DV status
- Early termination right for DV victim

New Mexico

N.M. Stat. Ann. § 47-8-33(J)

- DV is an affirmative defense to an eviction lawsuit
- Landlord or court may bifurcate the lease

New York

N.Y. Real Prop. Law §§ 227-c(2) and 227–d; N.Y. Real Prop. Acts. Law § 744; N.Y. Crim. Proc. Law § 530.13(1); N.Y. Dom. Rel. Law § 240(3)

- Landlord cannot refuse to rent to victim of DV
- Landlord cannot terminate a victim of DV. Early termination right for DV victim
- Penalty for falsely reporting domestic violence (including obtaining early termination)
- Landlord or court may bifurcate the lease

Miscellaneous provisions: Anti-discrimination protection and eviction protection do not apply to owner-occupied buildings with two or fewer units.

North Carolina

N.C. Gen. Stat. §§ 42-40, 42-42.2, 42-42.3, 42-45.1

- Landlord entitled to proof of DV status
- Landlord cannot refuse to rent to victim of DV
- Early termination right for DV victim
- DV victim has the right to have the locks changed

North Dakota

N.D. Cent. Code § 47-16-17.1

- Landlord entitled to proof of DV status
- Landlord cannot refuse to rent to victim of DV
- Landlord cannot terminate a victim of DV
- Early termination right for DV victim

Miscellaneous provisions: Landlord may not disclose information provided by a tenant that documents domestic violence. Landlords who violate the provisions providing early termination are subject to damages including actual damages, $1,000, reasonable attorneys' fees, costs, and disbursements.

Ohio

No statute

Oklahoma

No statute

Oregon

Or. Rev. Stat. §§ 90.449, 90.453, 90.456, 90.459

- Landlord entitled to proof of DV status
- Landlord cannot refuse to rent to victim of DV
- Landlord cannot terminate a victim of DV
- Early termination right for DV victim
- Lease cannot prohibit calling the police in a DV situation or otherwise penalize DV victim
- DV victim has the right to have the locks changed
- Landlord or court may bifurcate the lease
- Landlord has limited right to evict the DV victim

Pennsylvania

No statute

Rhode Island

R.I. Gen. Laws §§ 34-37-1 through 34-37-4

- Landlord cannot refuse to rent to victim of DV
- Landlord cannot terminate a victim of DV
- Landlord or court may bifurcate the lease

South Carolina

No statute

South Dakota

No statute

State Laws in Domestic Violence Situations (continued)

Tennessee

Tenn. Code Ann. §§ 66-7-109(e), 66-28-517(g)

- Landlord entitled to proof of DV status
- Landlord cannot terminate a victim of DV
- Landlord or court may bifurcate the lease
- Landlord has limited right to evict the DV victim

Miscellaneous provisions: The rights granted under this law do not apply when the perpetrator is a child or dependent of any tenant. Landlord may evict a victim who allows an ousted perpetrator to return to the premises.

Texas

Tex. Prop. Code Ann. §§ 92.015, 92.016, 92.0161

- Lease cannot include a waiver of some or all DV rights
- Landlord entitled to proof of DV status
- Early termination right for DV victim
- Lease cannot prohibit calling the police in a DV situation or otherwise penalize DV victim

Miscellaneous provisions: Tenant who exercises termination rights will be released from any delinquent rent unless the lease includes a clause that specifically describes tenants' rights in domestic violence situations. Landlord may not prohibit or limit a tenant's right to call police or other emergency assistance, based on the tenant's reasonable belief that such help is necessary.

Utah

Utah Code Ann. § 57-22-5.1

- Landlord entitled to proof of DV status
- Early termination right for DV victim
- Lease cannot prohibit calling the police in a DV situation or otherwise penalize DV victim
- DV victim has the right to have the locks changed

Vermont

15 Vt. Stat. Ann. § 1103(c)(2)(B)

- Landlord or court may bifurcate the lease

Virginia

Va. Code Ann. §§ 55-225.5, 55-225.16, 55-248.18:1, 55-248.21:2, 55-248.31(D)

- Landlord entitled to proof of DV status
- Landlord cannot terminate a victim of DV
- Early termination right for DV victim
- DV victim has the right to have the locks changed
- Landlord or court may bifurcate the lease

Miscellaneous provisions: Right to change locks extends to "authorized occupants" (someone entitled to occupy a dwelling unit with the consent of the landlord, but who has not signed the rental agreement and does not have the financial obligations as a tenant under the rental agreement). Tenant/victim's right to continued possession when perpetrator is ousted does not apply if perpetrator returns to the premises and tenant fails to notify landlord.

Washington

Wash. Rev. Code Ann. §§ 59.18.570, 59.18.575, 59.18.580, 59.18.585, 59.18.352, 59.18.130(8)(b)(ii)

- Landlord cannot terminate a victim of DV
- Early termination right for DV victim
- DV is an affirmative defense to an eviction lawsuit

West Virginia

No statute

Wisconsin

Wis. Stat. Ann. § 106.50(5m)(d)

- Landlord cannot refuse to rent to victim of DV
- Landlord cannot terminate a victim of DV
- DV is an affirmative defense to an eviction lawsuit
- Landlord has limited right to evict the DV victim

Wyoming

Wyo. Stat. §§ 1-21-1301 to 1-21-1304

- Lease cannot include a waiver of some or all DV rights
- Landlord entitled to proof of DV status
- Landlord cannot terminate a victim of DV
- Early termination right for DV victim
- Landlord has limited right to evict the DV victim

State Laws on Rent Withholding and Repair and Deduct Remedies

State	Statute or case on rent withholding	Statute or case on repair and deduct
Alabama	Ala. Code § 35-9A-405	No statute
Alaska	Alaska Stat. §§ 34.03.190, 34.03.100(b)	Alaska Stat. §§ 34.03.180, 34.03.100(b)
Arizona	Ariz. Rev. Stat. Ann. § 33-1365	Ariz. Rev. Stat. Ann. §§ 33-1363 to -1364
Arkansas	No statute	No statute
California	*Green v. Superior Court*, 10 Cal.3d 616 (1974)	Cal. Civ. Code § 1942
Colorado	Colo. Rev. Stat. § 38-12-507	No statute
Connecticut	Conn. Gen. Stat. Ann. §§ 47a-14a to -14h	Conn. Gen. Stat. Ann. § 47a-13
Delaware	Del. Code Ann. tit. 25, § 5308(b)(3)	Del. Code Ann. tit. 25, §§ 5307, 5308
District of Columbia	*Javins v. First Nat'l Realty Corp.*, 428 F.2d 1071 (D.C. Cir. 1970)	No statute
Florida	Fla. Stat. Ann. § 83.60	Fla. Stat. Ann. § 83.60
Georgia	No statute	Not addressed by statute, but Georgia courts recognize a tenant's right to this remedy. See Georgia Landlord Tenant Handbook, 2012, Georgia Department of Community Affairs (http://www.dca.state.ga.us/ housing/housingdevelopment/programs/downloads/ Georgia_Landlord_Tenant_Handbook.pdf) and see *Abrams v. Joel*, 108 Ga. App. 662, 134 S.E.2d 480 (1963)
Hawaii	Haw. Rev. Stat. § 521-78	Haw. Rev. Stat. § 521-64
Idaho	No statute	No statute
Illinois	765 Ill. Comp. Stat. §§ 735/2, 735/2.2 (applies only when a court has appointed a receiver to collect rents, following landlord's failure to pay for utilities)	765 Ill. Comp. Stat. § 742/5
Indiana	No statute	No statute
Iowa	Iowa Code Ann. § 562A.24	Iowa Code Ann. § 562A.23
Kansas	Kan. Stat. Ann. § 58-2561	No statute
Kentucky	Ky. Rev. Stat. Ann. § 383.645	Ky. Rev. Stat. Ann. §§ 383.635, 383.640
Louisiana	No statute	La. Civ. Code Ann. art. 2694
Maine	Me. Rev. Stat. Ann. tit. 14, § 6021	Me. Rev. Stat. Ann. tit. 14, § 6026
Maryland	Md. Code Ann. [Real Prop.] §§ 8-211, 8-211.1	No statute
Massachusetts	Mass. Gen. Laws Ann. ch. 239, § 8A	Mass. Gen. Laws Ann. ch. 111, § 127L
Michigan	Mich. Comp. Laws § 125.530	*Rome v. Walker*, 198 N.W.2d 850 (1972); Mich. Comp. Laws § 554.139
Minnesota	Minn. Stat. Ann. §§ 504B.215(3)(d), 504B.385	Minn. Stat. Ann. § 504B.425

State Laws on Rent Withholding and Repair and Deduct Remedies (continued)

State	Statute or case on rent withholding	Statute or case on repair and deduct
Mississippi	No statute	Miss. Code Ann. § 89-8-15
Missouri	Mo. Ann. Stat. §§ 441.570, 441.580	Mo. Ann. Stat. § 441.234
Montana	Mont. Code Ann. § 70-24-421	Mont. Code Ann. §§ 70-24-406 to -408
Nebraska	Neb. Rev. Stat. § 76-1428	Neb. Rev. Stat. § 76-1427
Nevada	Nev. Rev. Stat. Ann. § 118A.490	Nev. Rev. Stat. Ann. §§ 118A.360, 118A.380
New Hampshire	N.H. Rev. Stat. Ann. § 540:13-d	No statute
New Jersey	*Berzito v. Gambino*, 63 N.J. 460 (1973)	*Marini v. Ireland*, 265 A.2d 526 (1970)
New Mexico	N.M. Stat. Ann. § 47-8-27.2	No statute
New York	N.Y. Real Prop. Law § 235-b, *Semans Family Ltd. Partnership v. Kennedy*, 675 N.Y.S.2d 489 (N.Y. City Civ. Ct.,1998)	For emergency repairs (such as broken door lock) only: N.Y. Real Prop. Law § 235-b; *Jangla Realty Co. v. Gravagna*, 447 N.Y.S. 2d 338 (Civ. Ct., Queens County, 1981)
North Carolina	No statute	No statute
North Dakota	No statute	N.D. Cent. Code §§ 47-16-13, 47-16-13.1
Ohio	Ohio Rev. Code Ann. § 5321.07 (does not apply to student tenants; or when landlord owns three or fewer rental units, as long as landlord has given written notice to tenant)	No statute
Oklahoma	Okla. Stat. Ann. tit. 41, § 121	Okla. Stat. Ann. tit. 41, § 121
Oregon	Or. Rev. Stat. § 90.365	Or. Rev. Stat. § 90.365
Pennsylvania	68 Pa. Cons. Stat. Ann. § 250.206; 35 Pa. Cons. Stat. Ann. § 1700-1	*Pugh v. Holmes*, 405 A.2d 897 (1979)
Rhode Island	R.I. Gen. Laws § 34-18-32	R.I. Gen. Laws §§ 34-18-30 to -31
South Carolina	S.C. Code Ann. § 27-40-640	S.C. Code Ann. § 27-40-630
South Dakota	S.D. Codified Laws Ann. § 43-32-9	S.D. Codified Laws Ann. § 43-32-9
Tennessee	Tenn. Code Ann. § 68-111-104	Tenn. Code Ann. § 66-28-502
Texas	No statute	Tex. Prop. Code Ann. §§ 92.056, 92.0561
Utah	No statute	Utah Code Ann. § 57-22-6
Vermont	Vt. Stat. Ann. tit. 9, § 4458	Vt. Stat. Ann. tit. 9, § 4459
Virginia	Va. Code Ann. §§ 54-248.25, 54-248.25.1, 54-248-27	No statute
Washington	Wash. Rev. Code Ann. §§ 59.18.110, 59.18.115	Wash. Rev. Code Ann. §§ 59.18.100, 59.18.110
West Virginia	No statute	No statute
Wisconsin	Wis. Stat. Ann. § 704.07(4)	No statute
Wyoming	Wyo. Stat. § 1-21-1206	No statute

State Laws on Landlord's Access to Rental Property

This is a synopsis of state laws that specify circumstances when a landlord may enter rental premises and the amount of notice required for such entry.

State	State Law Citation	Amount of Notice Required in Nonemergency Situations	Reasons Landlord May Enter				
			To Deal With an Emergency	To Inspect the Premises	To Make Repairs, Alterations, or Improvements	To Show Property to Prospective Tenants or Purchasers	During Tenant's Extended Absence
Alabama	Ala. Code §§ 35-9A-303, 35-9A-423	Two days	✓	✓	✓	✓	✓
Alaska	Alaska Stat. §§ 34.03.140, 34.03.230	24 hours	✓	✓	✓	✓	✓
Arizona	Ariz. Rev. Stat. Ann. § 33-1343	Two days (written or oral notice); notice period does not apply, and tenant's consent is assumed, if entry is pursuant to tenant's request for maintenance as prescribed in Ariz. Rev. Stat. § 33-1341, paragraph 8	✓	✓	✓	✓	
Arkansas	Ark. Code Ann. § 18-17-602	No notice specified		✓	✓	✓	
California	Cal. Civ. Code § 1954	24 hours (48 hours for initial move-out inspection)	✓	✓	✓	✓	
Colorado	No statute						
Connecticut	Conn. Gen. Stat. Ann. §§ 47a-16 to 47a-16a	Reasonable notice	✓	✓	✓	✓	
Delaware	Del. Code Ann. tit. 25, §§ 5509, 5510	Two days	✓	✓	✓	✓	
D.C.	D.C. Code Ann. § 42-3505.51	48 hours	✓	✓	✓	✓	✓
Florida	Fla. Stat. Ann. § 83.53	12 hours	✓	✓	✓	✓	✓
Georgia	No statute						
Hawaii	Haw. Rev. Stat. §§ 521-53, 521-70(b)	Two days	✓	✓	✓	✓	✓
Idaho	No statute						
Illinois	No statute						
Indiana	Ind. Code Ann. § 32-31-5-6	Reasonable notice	✓	✓	✓	✓	
Iowa	Iowa Code Ann. §§ 562A.19, 562A.28, 562A.29	24 hours	✓	✓	✓	✓	✓
Kansas	Kan. Stat. Ann. §§ 58-2557, 58-2565	Reasonable notice	✓	✓	✓	✓	✓
Kentucky	Ky. Rev. Stat. Ann. §§ 383.615, 383.670	Two days	✓	✓	✓	✓	✓
Louisiana	La. Civ. Code art. 2693	No notice specified			✓		
Maine	Me. Rev. Stat. Ann. tit. 14, § 6025	24 hours	✓	✓	✓	✓	
Maryland	No statute						
Massachusetts	Mass. Gen. Laws Ann. ch. 186, § 15B(1)(a)	No notice specified	✓	✓	✓	✓	
Michigan	No statute						
Minnesota	Minn. Stat. Ann. § 504B.211	Reasonable notice	✓	✓	✓	✓	
Mississippi	No statute						
Missouri	No statute						

State Laws on Landlord's Access to Rental Property (continued)

State	State Law Citation	Amount of Notice Required in Nonemergency Situations	Reasons Landlord May Enter				
			To Deal With an Emergency	To Inspect the Premises	To Make Repairs, Alterations, or Improvements	To Show Property to Prospective Tenants or Purchasers	During Tenant's Extended Absence
Montana	Mont. Code Ann. §§ 70-24-312, 70-24-426	24 hours	✓	✓	✓	✓	✓
Nebraska	Neb. Rev. Stat. §§ 76-1423, 76-1432	One day	✓	✓	✓	✓	✓
Nevada	Nev. Rev. Stat. Ann. § 118A.330	24 hours	✓	✓	✓	✓	
New Hampshire	N.H. Rev. Stat. Ann. § 540-A:3	Notice that is adequate under the circumstances	✓	✓	✓	✓	
New Jersey	N.J.A.C. 5:10-5.1	One day, by custom; in buildings with three or more units, one day (by regulation)	✓	✓	✓	✓	
New Mexico	N.M. Stat. Ann. §§ 47-8-24, 47-8-34	24 hours	✓	✓	✓	✓	✓
New York	No statute						
North Carolina	No statute						
North Dakota	N.D. Cent. Code § 47-16-07.3	Reasonable notice	✓	✓	✓	✓	
Ohio	Ohio Rev. Code Ann. §§ 5321.04(A)(8), 5321.05(B)	24 hours	✓	✓	✓	✓	
Oklahoma	Okla. Stat. Ann. tit. 41, § 128	One day	✓	✓	✓	✓	
Oregon	Or. Rev. Stat. §§ 90.322, 90.410	24 hours	✓	✓	✓	✓	✓
Pennsylvania	No statute						
Rhode Island	R.I. Gen. Laws § 34-18-26	Two days	✓	✓	✓	✓	✓
South Carolina	S.C. Code Ann. §§ 27-40-530, 27-40-730	24 hours	✓	✓	✓	✓	✓
South Dakota	No statute						
Tennessee	Tenn. Code Ann. §§ 66-28-403, 66-28-507	24 hours (applies only within the final 30 days of the rental agreement term, when landlord intends to show the premises to prospective renters and this right of access is set forth in the rental agreement)	✓	✓	✓	✓	✓
Texas	No statute						
Utah	Utah Code Ann. §§ 57-22-4, 57-22-5(2)(c)	24 hours, unless rental agreement specifies otherwise	✓		✓		
Vermont	Vt. Stat. Ann. tit. 9, § 4460	48 hours	✓	✓	✓	✓	
Virginia	Va. Code Ann. §§ 55-248.18, 55-248.33	For routine maintenance only: 24 hours, but no notice needed if entry follows tenant's request for maintenance.	✓	✓	✓	✓	✓
Washington	Wash. Rev. Code Ann. § 59.18.150	Two days; one day to show property to actual or prospective tenants or buyers	✓	✓	✓	✓	
West Virginia	No statute						
Wisconsin	Wis. Stat. Ann. § 704.05(2)	Advance notice	✓	✓	✓	✓	
Wyoming	No statute						

State Laws on Handling Abandoned Property

Most states regulate the way landlords must handle property left behind by departed tenants. Many set notice requirements as to how landlords must contact tenants regarding abandoned property. States may also regulate how landlords must store abandoned property and dispose of it if the tenant doesn't claim his or her belongings. For details, check your state statute, listed in this chart. Keep in mind that court cases not mentioned here may further describe proper procedures in your state.

State	Statute	State	Statute
Alabama	Ala. Code 1975 § 35-9A-423	Missouri	Mo. Rev. Stat. § 441.065
Alaska	Alaska Stat. § 34.03.260	Montana	Mont. Code Ann. § 70-24-430
Arizona	Ariz. Rev. Stat. Ann. § 33-1370	Nebraska	Neb. Rev. Stat. §§ 69-2303 to 69-2314
Arkansas	Ark. Code Ann. § 18-16-108	Nevada	Nev. Rev. Stat. Ann. §§ 118A.450, 118A.460
California	Cal. Civ. Code §§ 1965, 1980 to 1991	New Hampshire	N.H. Rev. Stat. Ann. § 540-A:3(VII)
Colorado	Colo. Rev. Stat. §§ 38-20-116, 13-40-122	New Jersey	N.J. Stat. Ann. §§ 2A:18-72 to 2A:18-84
Connecticut	Conn. Gen. Stat. Ann. §§ 47a-11b, 47a-42	New Mexico	N.M. Stat. Ann. § 47-8-34.1
Delaware	Del. Code Ann. tit. 25, §§ 5507, 5715	New York	No statute
D.C.	No statute	North Carolina	N.C. Gen. Stat. §§ 42-25.9, 42-36.2
Florida	Fla. Stat. Ann. §§ 715.104 to 715.111	North Dakota	N.D. Cent. Code § 47-16-30.1
Georgia	Ga. Code Ann. § 44-7-55	Ohio	*Ringler v. Sias*, 428 N.E.2d 869 (Ohio Ct. App. 1980)
Hawaii	Haw. Rev. Stat. § 521-56	Oklahoma	Okla. Stat. Ann. tit. 41, § 130
Idaho	Idaho Code § 6-311C	Oregon	Ore. Rev. Stat. §§ 90.425, 105.165
Illinois	735 Ill. Comp. Stat. § 5/9-318	Pennsylvania	68 P.S. § 250.505a
Indiana	Ind. Code. Ann. §§ 32-31-4-1 to 32-31-4-5, 32-31-5-5	Rhode Island	R.I. Gen. Laws § 34-18-50
		South Carolina	S.C. Code Ann. §§ 27-40-710(D), 27-40-730
Iowa	*Khan v. Heritage Prop. Mgmt.*, 584 N.W.2d 725, 730 (Iowa Ct. App. 1998)	South Dakota	S.D. Codified Laws Ann. §§ 43-32-25, 43-32-26
Kansas	Kan. Stat. Ann. § 58-2565	Tennessee	Tenn. Code Ann. § 66-28-405
Kentucky	No statute	Texas	Tex. Prop. Code § 92.014
Louisiana	La. Civ. Code § 2707, La. Civ. Proc. § 4705	Utah	Utah Code Ann. § 78B-6-816
Maine	Me. Rev. Stat. Ann. tit. 14, §§ 6005, 6013	Vermont	Vt. Stat. Ann. tit. 9, § 4462; Vt. Stat. Ann. tit. 12, § 4854a
Maryland	Md. Code, Real Property, § 8-208	Virginia	Va. Code Ann. §§ 55-225.40 to 55-225.42; 55-248.38:1 to 55-248.38:2
Massachusetts	M.G.L.A. 239 § 4	Washington	Wash. Rev. Code Ann. § 59.18.310
Michigan	No statute	West Virginia	W.Va. Code §§ 37-6-6, 55-3A-3
Minnesota	Minn. Stat. Ann. § 504B.271	Wisconsin	Wis. Stat. Ann. § 704.05(5)
Mississippi	Miss. Code Ann. §§ 89-7-31, 89-7-35, 89-8-13	Wyoming	Wyo. Stat. § 1-21-1210

State Laws Prohibiting Landlord Retaliation

State	Statute	Tenant's Complaint to Landlord or Government Agency	Tenant's Involvement in Tenants' Organization	Tenant's Exercise of Legal Right	Retaliation Is Presumed If Negative Reaction by Landlord Within Specified Time of Tenant's Act
Alabama	Ala. Code § 35-9A-501	✓	✓		
Alaska	Alaska Stat. § 34.03.310	✓	✓	✓	
Arizona	Ariz. Rev. Stat. Ann. § 33-1381	✓	✓		6 months
Arkansas [1]	Ark. Code Ann. § 20-27-608	✓			
California [2]	Cal. Civ. Code § 1942.5	✓	✓	✓	180 days
Colorado [3]	Colo. Rev. Stat. § 38-12-509	✓			
Connecticut	Conn. Gen. Stat. §§ 47a-20, 47a-33	✓	✓	✓	6 months
Delaware	Del. Code Ann. tit. 25, § 5516 ·	✓	✓	✓	90 days
D.C.	D.C. Code § 42-3505.02	✓	✓	✓	6 months
Florida [4]	Fla. Stat. Ann. § 83.64	✓	✓	✓	
Georgia	No statute				
Hawaii	Haw. Rev. Stat. § 521-74	✓		✓	
Idaho	No statute				
Illinois	765 Ill. Comp. Stat. § 720/1	✓			
Indiana	No statute				
Iowa	Iowa Code Ann. § 562A.36	✓	✓		1 year
Kansas	Kan. Stat. Ann. § 58-2572	✓	✓		
Kentucky	Ky. Rev. Stat. Ann. § 383.705	✓	✓		1 year
Louisiana	No statute				
Maine [5]	4 Me. Rev. Stat. Ann. tit. 14, §§ 6001(3)(4), 6021-A	✓	✓	✓	6 months
Maryland	Md. Code Ann. [Real Prop.] § 8-208.1	✓	✓	✓	
Massachusetts [2]	Mass. Ann. Laws ch. 239, § 2A; ch. 186, § 18	✓	✓	✓	6 months
Michigan	Mich. Comp. Laws § 600.5720	✓	✓		90 days
Minnesota	Minn. Stat. Ann. §§ 504B.285, 504B.441	✓		✓	90 days
Mississippi	Miss. Code Ann. § 89-8-17			✓	
Missouri	No statute				

[1] Only prohibits retaliation by landlord who has received notice of lead hazards. (Arkansas)

[2] Applies when a retaliatory eviction follows a court case or administrative hearing concerning the tenant's underlying complaint, membership in a tenant organization, or exercise of a legal right. In this situation, a tenant may claim the benefit of the antiretaliation presumption only if the eviction falls within six months of the final determination of the court case or administrative hearing. (California and Massachusetts) Landlord cannot terminate based on tenants' (or their associates') immigration or citizenship status. (California)

[3] Tenant is protected against retaliation only for complaints of violations of the warranty of habitability. Tenant must prove actual violation in order to prevail. Any termination, rent increase, or service decrease that follows a complaint is presumed to be not retaliatory (timing alone of such actions will not make them retaliatory.) (Colorado)

[4] Statute lists retaliatory acts as illustrative, not exhaustive, and includes retaliation after the tenant has paid rent to a condominium, cooperative, or homeowners' association after demand from the association in order to pay the landlord's obligation to the association; and when the tenant has exercised his or her rights under state, local, or federal fair housing laws. (Florida)

[5] Allows tenant to raise his complaint to a fair housing agency as an affirmative defense to an eviction; retaliation presumed if tenant is served with an eviction notice within 6 months of tenant's exercise of rights regarding bedbug infestations (does not apply to eviction for nonpayment or for causing substantial damage). (Maine)

State Laws Prohibiting Landlord Retaliation (continued)

State	Statute	Tenant's Complaint to Landlord or Government Agency	Tenant's Involvement in Tenants' Organization	Tenant's Exercise of Legal Right	Retaliation Is Presumed If Negative Reaction by Landlord Within Specified Time of Tenant's Act
Montana	Mont. Code Ann. § 70-24-431	✓	✓		6 months
Nebraska	Neb. Rev. Stat. § 76-1439	✓	✓		
Nevada [6]	Nev. Rev. Stat. Ann. § 118A.510	✓	✓	✓	
New Hampshire	N.H. Rev. Stat. Ann. §§ 540:13-a, 540:13-b	✓	✓	✓	6 months
New Jersey [7]	N.J. Stat. Ann. §§ 2A:42-10.10, 2A: 42-10.12	✓	✓	✓	
New Mexico	N.M. Stat. Ann. § 47-8-39	✓	✓	✓	6 months
New York	N.Y. Real Prop. Law § 223-b	✓	✓	✓	6 months
North Carolina	N.C. Gen. Stat. § 42-37.1	✓	✓	✓	12 months
North Dakota	No statute				
Ohio	Ohio Rev. Code Ann. § 5321.02	✓	✓		
Oklahoma	No statute				
Oregon	Or. Rev. Stat. § 90.385	✓	✓		
Pennsylvania	68 Pa. Cons. Stat. Ann. §§ 250.205, 399.11		✓	✓	6 months (for exercise of legal rights connected with utility service)
Rhode Island	R.I. Gen. Laws Ann. §§ 34-20-10, 34-20-11	✓		✓	
South Carolina	S.C. Code Ann. § 27-40-910	✓			
South Dakota	S.D. Code Laws Ann. §§ 43-32-27, 43-32-28	✓	✓		180 days
Tennessee	Tenn. Code Ann. §§ 66-28-514, 68-111-105	✓		✓	
Texas	Tex. Prop. Code § 92.331	✓	✓	✓	6 months
Utah	*Building Monitoring Sys. v. Paxton*, 905 P.2d 1215 (Utah 1995)	✓			
Vermont [8]	Vt. Stat. Ann. tit. 9, § 4465	✓	✓	✓	90 days
Virginia	Va. Code Ann. §§ 55-225.18, 55-248.39	✓	✓	✓	
Washington	Wash. Rev. Code §§ 59.18.240, 59.18.250	✓		✓	90 days
West Virginia	*Imperial Colliery Co. v. Fout*, 373 S.E.2d 489 (1988)	✓		✓	
Wisconsin	Wis. Stat. § 704.45	✓		✓	
Wyoming	No statute				

[6] Statute protects tenants or tenants' guests who reasonably request emergency assistance. Local government cannot deem the request itself to be a "nuisance." Landlord may, however, take appropriate adverse actions based on information supplied by emergency responders, as can local governments with regard to declaring a nuisance. (Nevada)

[7] If a tenant fails to request a renewal of a lease or tenancy within 90 days of the tenancy's expiration (or by the renewal date specified in the lease if longer than 90 days), a landlord may terminate or not renew without a presumption of retaliation. (New Jersey)

[8] Retaliation presumed only when landlord terminates for reasons other than rent nonpayment, after tenant has filed complaint with a governmental entity alleging noncompliance with health or safety regulations. (Vermont)

State Laws on Termination for Nonpayment of Rent

If the tenant is late with the rent, in most states the landlord cannot immediately file for eviction. Instead, the landlord must give the tenant written notice that the tenant has a specified number of days in which to pay up or move. If the tenant does neither, the landlord can file for eviction. In some states, the landlord must wait a few days after the rent is due before giving the tenant the notice; other states allow the landlord to file for eviction immediately. The following rules may be tempered in domestic violence situations, depending on state law (see "State Laws in Domestic Violence Situations" in this appendix).

State	Statute	Time Tenant Has to Pay Rent or Move Before Landlord Can File for Eviction	Legal Late Period: How Long Landlord Must Wait Before Giving Notice to Pay or Quit
Alabama	Ala. Code § 35-9A-421	7 days	
Alaska	Alaska Stat. §§ 09.45.090, 34.03.220	7 days	
Arizona	Ariz. Rev. Stat. § 33-1368	5 days	
Arkansas [1]	Ark. Stat. §§ 18-17-701, 18-16-101	5 days	
California	Cal. Civ. Proc. Code § 1161(2)	3 days	
Colorado	Colo. Rev. Stat. § 13-40-104(1)(d)	3 days	
Connecticut	Conn. Gen. Stat. §§ 47a-23, 47a-15a	9 days	Unconditional Quit notice cannot be delivered until the rent is 9 days late.
Delaware	Del. Code Ann. tit. 25, §§ 5501(d), 5502	5 days	If rental agreement provides for a late charge, but landlord does not maintain an office in the county in which the rental unit is located, due date for the rent is extended 3 days; thereafter, landlord can serve a 5-day notice.
District of Columbia	D.C. Code § 42-3505.01	30 days (nonpayment of a late fee cannot be the basis of an eviction)	
Florida	Fla. Stat. Ann. § 83.56(3)	3 days	
Georgia	Ga. Code Ann. §§ 44-7-50, 44-7-52	Landlord can demand the rent as soon as it is due and, if not paid, can file for eviction. Tenant then has 7 days to pay to avoid eviction.	
Hawaii	Haw. Rev. Stat. § 521-68	5 days	
Idaho	Idaho Code § 6-303(2)	3 days	
Illinois	735 Ill. Comp. Stat. § 5/9-209	5 days	
Indiana	Ind. Code Ann. § 32-31-1-6	10 days	
Iowa	Iowa Code § 562A.27(2)	3 days	
Kansas	Kan. Rev. Stat. §§ 58-2507, 58-2508, 58-2564(b)	10 days (tenancies over 3 months) 3 days (tenancies less than 3 months)	
Kentucky	Ky. Rev. Stat. Ann. § 383.660(2)	7 days	
Louisiana	La. Civ. Proc. art. 4701	Landlord can terminate with an Unconditional Quit notice.	
Maine	Me. Rev. Stat. tit. 14, § 6002	7 days	Notice cannot be delivered until the rent is 7 days late, and must tell tenant that tenant can contest the termination in court (failure to so advise prohibits entry of a default judgment).

[1] Willful failure to move within ten days is a misdemeanor that subjects the tenant to a misdemeanor (fine only).

State Laws on Termination for Nonpayment of Rent (continued)

State	Statute	Time Tenant Has to Pay Rent or Move Before Landlord Can File for Eviction	Legal Late Period: How Long Landlord Must Wait Before Giving Notice to Pay or Quit
Maryland	Md. Code Ann. [Real Prop.] § 8-401	Can file immediately; must give 5 days' notice to appear in court; if tenant doesn't pay and landlord wins, tenant has 4 days to vacate. If tenant pays all back rent and court costs before end if trial, tenant can stay.	
Massachusetts[2]	Mass. Ann. Laws ch. 186, §§ 11 to 12	Tenants with rental agreements or leases, in accordance with agreement, or if not addressed in the agreement, 14 days' notice (but tenant can avoid by paying rent and costs before answer); holdover tenants: landlord can file for eviction immediately.	
Michigan	Mich. Comp. Laws § 554.134(2)	Landlord may terminate immediately with 7-day notice	
Minnesota	Minn. Stat. Ann. §§ 504B.135, 504B.291	14 days' notice required if tenancy at will (no lease); 30 days' or more notice for a lease with a term of more than 20 years	
Mississippi	Miss. Code Ann. §§ 89-7-27, 89-7-45	3 days. Tenant may stay if rent and costs are paid prior to removal.	
Missouri	Mo. Rev. Stat. § 535.010	Landlord can terminate with an Unconditional Quit notice.	
Montana	Mont. Code Ann. § 70-24-422(2)	3 days	
Nebraska	Neb. Rev. Stat. § 76-1431(2)	3 days	
Nevada	Nev. Rev. Stat. Ann. § 40.251	5 days	
New Hampshire	N.H. Rev. Stat. Ann. §§ 540:2, 540:3, 540:9	7 days. Tenant also owes $15 in liquidated damages, but use of this remedy is limited to three times within twelve months.	
New Jersey	N.J. Stat. Ann. §§ 2A:18-53, 2A:18-61.1, 2A:18-61.2, 2A:42-9	30 days. Landlord must accept rent and costs any time up to the day of trial.	
New Mexico	N.M. Stat. Ann. § 47-8-33(D)	3 days	
New York State	N.Y. Real Prop. Acts Law § 711(2)	3 days	
North Carolina	N.C. Gen. Stat. § 42-3	10 days	
North Dakota	N.D. Cent. Code 47-32-01	Landlord can file for eviction when rent is 3 days overdue and can terminate with an Unconditional Quit notice.	
Ohio	Ohio Rev. Code Ann. § 1923.02(A)(9)	Landlord can terminate with an Unconditional Quit notice.	
Oklahoma	Okla. Stat. Ann. tit. 41, § 131	5 days	
Oregon[3]	Or. Rev. Stat. § 90.394(2)(a)	72 hours (3 days)	Notice cannot be delivered until the rent is 8 days late.
	Or. Rev. Stat. § 90.394(2)(b)	144 hours (6 days)	Notice cannot be delivered until the rent is 5 days late.
Pennsylvania	68 Pa. Cons. Stat. Ann. § 250.501(b)	10 days	

[2] For tenants at will who have not received notices in the preceding 12 months, 10 days to pay, 4 more to quit (unless notice is insufficient, then 14 days to pay). (Massachusetts)

[3] Landlord has a choice: Serve pay or quit notice after rent is 8 days late (tenant has 72 hours to pay or quit), or serve the notice earlier, after rent is overdue 5 days (tenant has longer, 144 hours, to pay or quit). (Oregon)

State Laws on Termination for Nonpayment of Rent (continued)

State	Statute	Time Tenant Has to Pay Rent or Move Before Landlord Can File for Eviction	Legal Late Period: How Long Landlord Must Wait Before Giving Notice to Pay or Quit
Rhode Island	R.I. Gen. Laws § 34-18-35	5 days. Tenant can stay if rent paid back prior to commencement of suit. If tenant has not received a Pay or Quit notice for nonpayment of rent within past 6 months, tenant can stay if rent and costs paid back prior to eviction hearing.	15 days.
South Carolina	S.C. Code Ann. § 27-40-710(B), § 27-37-10(B)	5 days. If there is a written lease or rental agreement that specifies in bold, conspicuous type that landlord may file for eviction as soon as tenant is 5 days late (or if there is a month-to-month tenancy following such an agreement), landlord may do so without further notice to tenant. If there is no such written agreement, landlord must give tenant 5 days' written notice before filing for eviction.	
South Dakota	S.D. Codified Laws Ann. §§ 21-16-1(4), 21-16-2	3 days, and landlord can terminate with an Unconditional Quit notice.	
Tennessee	Tenn. Code Ann. § 66-28-505	14 days to pay; additional 16 days to vacate.	
Texas	Tex. Prop. Code Ann. § 24.005	3 days' notice to move (lease may specify a shorter or longer time).	
Utah	Utah Code Ann. § 78B-6-802	3 days	
Vermont	Vt. Stat. Ann. tit. 9, § 4467(a)	14 days	
Virginia[4]	Va. Code Ann. §§ 55-225, 55-225.38(C), 55-243, 55-248.31	5 days. Tenant who pays rent, costs, interest, and reasonable attorneys' fees can stay, but may invoke this right only once in any 12-month period.	If tenant does not pay and does not move within the time alotted, for each day that the tenant remains, tenant will owe rent of up to 150% of the per diem of the monthly rent, but only if the rental agreement includes a clause specifying this result.
Washington	Wash. Rev. Code Ann. § 59.12.030(3)	3 days	
West Virginia	W.Va. Code § 55-3A-1	Landlord can file for eviction immediately, no notice required, no opportunity to cure.	
Wisconsin	Wis. Stat. Ann. § 704.17	Month-to-month tenants: 5 days; landlord can use an Unconditional Quit notice with 14 days' notice. Tenants with a lease less than one year, and year-to-year tenants: 5 days (cannot use Unconditional Quit notice). Tenants with a lease longer than one year: 30 days (cannot use Unconditional Quit notice).	
Wyoming	Wyo. Stat. §§ 1-21-1002 to 1-21-1003	Landlord can file for eviction when rent is 3 days or more late and tenant has been given at least 3 days' notice. Landlord can also terminate with an Unconditional Quit notice.	

4 If tenant does not pay and does not move within the time allotted, for each day that the tenant remains, tenant will owe rent of up 150% of the per diem of the monthly rent, but only if the rental agreement includes a clause specifying this result.

State Laws on Termination for Violation of Lease

Many states give the tenant a specified amount of time to cure or cease the lease or rental agreement violation or move before the landlord can file for eviction. In some states, if the tenant has not ceased or cured the violation at the end of that period, the tenant gets additional time to move before the landlord can file; in others, the tenant must move as soon as the cure period expires. And some states allow the landlord to terminate with an Unconditional Quit notice, without giving the tenant a chance to cure or cease the violation. The following rules may be tempered in domestic violence situations, depending on state law (see "State Laws in Domestic Violence Situations" in this appendix).

State	Statute	Time Tenant Has to Cure the Violation or Move Before Landlord Can File for Eviction
Alabama	Ala. Code § 35-9A-421	14 calendar days
Alaska	Alaska Stat. §§ 09.45.090, 34.03.220	10 days for violators of agreement materially affecting health and safety; 3 days to cure for failing to pay utility bills, resulting in shut-off, additional 2 to vacate.
Arizona	Ariz. Rev. Stat. § 33-1368	5 days for violations materially affecting health and safety; 10 days for other violations of the lease terms.
Arkansas	Ark. Stat. §§ 18-17-701, 18-17-702	Tenant has 14 days to cure a remediable violation. If violation materially affects tenant's health and safety, tenant must remedy as promptly as conditions require in case of emergency (or within 14 days after written notice by the landlord if it is not an emergency); failure entitles landlord to terminate the tenancy.
California	Cal. Civ. Proc. Code § 1161(3)	3 days
Colorado	Colo. Rev. Stat. § 13-40-104(1)(d.5),(e)	3 days (no cure for certain substantial violations).
Connecticut	Conn. Gen. Stat. Ann. § 47a-15	15 days; no right to cure for nonpayment of rent or serious nuisance.
Delaware	Del. Code Ann. tit. 25, § 5513(a)	7 days
District of Columbia	D.C. Code § 42-3505.01	30 days
Florida	Fla. Stat. Ann. § 83.56(2)	7 days (no cure for certain substantial violations).
Georgia	No statute	Landlord can terminate with an Unconditional Quit notice.
Hawaii	Haw. Rev. Stat. §§ 521-72, 666-3	10 days notice to cure: if it has not ceased, must wait another 20 to file for eviction; 24 hours to cease a nuisance: if it has not ceased in 24 hours, 5 days to cure before filing for eviction.
Idaho	Idaho Code § 6-303	3 days
Illinois	735 Ill. Comp. Stat. 5/9-210	10 days
Indiana	No statute	Landlord can terminate with an Unconditional Quit notice.
Iowa	Iowa Code § 562A.27(1)	7 days
Kansas	Kan. Stat. Ann. § 58-2564(a)	14 days to cure and an additional 16 to vacate.
Kentucky	Ky. Rev. Stat. Ann. § 383.660(1)	15 days
Louisiana	La. Civ. Proc. art. 4701	5 days
Maine	Me. Rev. Stat. Ann. tit. 14 § 6002	7 days
Maryland	Md. Real Prop. Code Ann. § 8-402.1	30 days unless breach poses clear and imminent danger, then 14 days (no cure).
Massachusetts	No statute	Landlord can terminate with an Unconditional Quit notice.
Michigan	Mich. Comp. Laws § 600.5714	For causing serious, continuous health hazards or damage to the premises: 7 days after receiving notice to restore or repair or quit (domestic violence victims excepted).

State Laws on Termination for Violation of Lease (continued)

State	Statute	Time Tenant Has to Cure the Violation or Move Before Landlord Can File for Eviction
Minnesota	Minn. Stat. Ann. § 504B.285 (Subd.4)	Landlord can immediately file for eviction.
Mississippi	Miss. Code Ann. § 89-8-13	30 days
Missouri	No statute	Landlord can terminate with an Unconditional Quit notice.
Montana	Mont. Code Ann. § 70-24-422	14 days; 3 days if unauthorized pet or person on premises.
Nebraska	Neb. Rev. Stat. § 76-1431	14 days to cure, 16 additional days to vacate.
Nevada	Nev. Rev. Stat. Ann. § 40.2516	5 days to cure
New Hampshire	N.H. Rev. Stat. Ann. § 540:3	30 days
New Jersey	N.J. Stat. Ann. §§ 2A:18-53(c), 2A:18-61.1(e)(1)	3 days; lease must specify which violations will result in eviction. (Some courts have ruled that the tenant be given an opportunity to cure the violation or condition any time up to the entry of judgment in favor of the landlord.)
New Mexico	N.M. Stat. Ann. § 47-8-33(A)	7 days
New York	N.Y. Real Prop. Acts Law §§ 711, 753(4)[NYC]	Regulated units: 10 days or as set by applicable rent regulation. Nonregulated units: No statute. Lease sets applicable cure and/or termination notice periods.
North Carolina	No statute	Landlord can terminate with an Unconditional Quit notice if lease specifies termination for violation.
North Dakota	No statute	
Ohio	Ohio Revised Code §§ 1923.02(A)(9) and 1923.04	3 days
Oklahoma	Okla. Stat. Ann. tit. 41, § 132(A), (B)	10 days to cure, additional 5 days to vacate.
Oregon	Or. Rev. Stat. §§ 90.392, 90.405	14 days to cure, additional 16 days to vacate; 10 days to remove an illegal pet.
Pennsylvania	No statute	Landlord can terminate with an Unconditional Quit notice.
Rhode Island	R.I. Gen. Laws § 34-18-36	20 days for material noncompliance.
South Carolina	S.C. Code Ann. § 27-40-710(A)	14 days
South Dakota	S.D. Codified Laws Ann. §§ 21-16-1(7), 21-16-2	Landlord must give tenant 3 days' notice to quit (no opportunity to cure) before filing for eviction, in specified situations. Other situations require no notice.
Tennessee	Tenn. Code Ann. § 66-28-505(d)	14 days
Texas	Tex. Prop. Code § 24.005	3 days
Utah	Utah Code Ann. § 78B-6-802	3 days
Vermont	Vt. Stat. Ann. tit.9 § 4467(b)(1)	30 days
Virginia	Va. Code. Ann. § 55-248.31	21 days to cure, additional 9 to quit. If tenant does not cure and does not move within the time allotted, for each day that the tenant remains, tenant will owe rent of up 150% of the per diem of the monthly rent, but only if the rental agreement includes a clause specifying this result.
Washington	Wash. Rev. Code Ann. § 59.12.030(4)	10 days
West Virginia	W.Va. Code § 55-3A-1	Landlord can immediately file for eviction; no notice is required.
Wisconsin	Wis. Stat. Ann. § 704.17	5 days, no opportunity to cure for public housing tenants who have committed drug-related violations.
Wyoming	Wyo. Stat. §§1-21-1002, 1-21-1003	3 days

State Laws on Unconditional Quit Terminations

The following rules may be tempered in domestic violence situations, depending on state law (see "State Laws in Domestic Violence Situations" in this appendix).

State	Statute	Time to Move Out Before Landlord Can File For Eviction	When Unconditional Quit Notice Can Be Used
Alabama	Ala. Code § 35-9A-421	7 days	Intentional misrepresentation of a material fact in a rental application or rental agreement, possession or use of illegal drugs in the rental or common areas, discharge of a firearm (some exceptions), criminal assault of a tenant or guest on the premises (some exceptions).
Alaska	Alaska Stat. § 34.03.220(a)(1)	24 hours	Tenant or guest intentionally causing more than $400 of damage to landlord's property or same violation of lease within 6 months
	§ 9.45.090(a)(2)(G)	24 hours to 5 days	Tenant or guest intentionally causing more than $400 of damage to landlord's property and specified illegal activity on the premises, including allowing prostitution
	§ 34.03.220(e)	3 days	Failure to pay utility bills twice within six months
	§ 34.03.300(a)	10 days	Refusal to allow the landlord to enter
Arizona	Ariz. Rev. Stat. Ann. § 33-1368	10 days	Material misrepresentation of criminal record, current criminal activity, or prior eviction record
		Immediately	Discharging a weapon, homicide, prostitution, criminal street gang activity, use or sale of illegal drugs, assaults, acts constituting a nuisance or breach of the rental agreement that threaten harm to others
Arkansas	Ark. Stat. Ann. §§ 81-17-701, 18-16-101	5 days	Noncompliance by the tenant with the rental agreement when the violation is not remediable; using (or allowing another person to use) the premises in a way constituting a common nuisance, or permitting/conducting specified criminal offenses; rent unpaid within five days of rent due date. If rent is unpaid within ten days of due date, tenant may be charged with a misdemeanor (fine only).
California	Cal. Civ. Proc. Code § 1161(4)	3 days	Assigning or subletting without permission, committing waste or a nuisance, illegal activity on the premises
Colorado	Colo. Rev. Stat. § 13-40-104(1)(e.5)	3 days	Any repeated violation of a lease clause
Connecticut	Conn. Gen. Stat. Ann. §§ 47a-23, 47a-15, 47a-15a	3 days	Nonpayment of rent, serious nuisance, violation of the rental agreement, same violation within 6 months relating to health and safety or materially affecting physical premises, rental agreement has terminated (by lapse of time, stipulation, violation of lease, nonpayment of rent after grace period, serious nuisance, occupancy by someone who never had the right to occupy), when summary eviction is justified (refusal to a fair and equitable increase, intent of the landlord to use as a principal residence, removal of the unit from the housing market), domestic or farm worker who does not vacate upon cessation of employment and tenancy
	Conn. Gen. Stat. Ann. § 47a-31	Immediately	Conviction for prostitution or gambling

State Laws on Unconditional Quit Terminations (continued)

State	Statute	Time to Move Out Before Landlord Can File For Eviction	When Unconditional Quit Notice Can Be Used
Delaware	Del. Code Ann. tit. 25, §§ 5513, 5514	7 days	Violation of a lease provision that also constitutes violation of municipal, county, or state code or statute, or same violation of a material lease provision repeated within 12 months
		Immediately	Violation of law or breach of the rental agreement that causes or threatens to cause irreparable harm to the landlord's property or to other tenants
District of Columbia	D.C. Code § 42-3505.01(c)	30 days	Court determination that an illegal act was performed within the rental unit
Florida	Fla. Stat. Ann. § 83.56(2)(a)	7 days	Intentional destruction of the rental property or other tenants' property or unreasonable disturbances; for destruction, damage, or misuse of the landlord's or other tenants' property by intentional act or a subsequent or continued unreasonable disturbance (after written warning within previous 12 months); a subsequent or continuing noncompliance within 12 months of a written warning by the landlord of a similar violation
Georgia	Ga. Code Ann. §§ 44-7-50, 44-7-52	Immediately	Nonpayment of rent more than once within 12 months, holding over
Hawaii	Haw. Rev. Stat. §§ 521-70(c), 521-69, 666-3	Immediately	Causing or threatening to cause irremediable damage to any person or property
		5 days	Second failure to abate a nuisance within 24 hours of receiving notice
Idaho	Idaho Code § 6-303	Immediately	Using, delivering, or producing a controlled substance on the property at any time during the lease term
		3 days	Assigning or subletting without the consent of the landlord or causing serious damage to the property
Illinois	735 Ill. Comp. Stat. § 5/9-210	10 days	Failure to abide by any term of the lease
	740 Ill. Comp. Stat. § 40/11	5 days	Unlawful use or sale of any controlled substance
Indiana	Ind. Code Ann. § 32-31-1-8	Immediately	Tenants with lease: holding over. Tenants without lease: committing waste
Iowa	Iowa Code Ann. § 562A.27	7 days	Repeating same violation of lease within 6 months that affects health and safety
	Iowa Code Ann. § 562A.27A	3 days	Creating a clear and present danger to the health or safety of the landlord, tenants, or neighbors within 1,000 feet of the property boundaries
Kansas	Kan. Stat. Ann. § 58-2564(a)	30 days	Second similar material violation of the lease after first violation was corrected
Kentucky	Ky. Rev. Stat. Ann. § 383.660(1)	14 days	Repeating the same material violation of the lease within 6 months of being given a first cure or quit notice
Louisiana	La. Civ. Code art. 2686, La. Code Civ. Proc. art. 4701	5 days	Failure to pay rent, using dwelling for purpose other than the intended purpose (lease may specify shorter or longer notice, or eliminate requirement of notice), or upon termination of the lease for any reason

State Laws on Unconditional Quit Terminations (continued)

State	Statute	Time to Move Out Before Landlord Can File For Eviction	When Unconditional Quit Notice Can Be Used
Maine	Me. Rev. Stat. Ann. tit. 14, § 6002	7 days	Tenants at will: Violations of law relating to the tenancy, substantial and unrepaired damage to the premises; causing, permitting, or maintaining a nuisance; causing the dwelling to be unfit for human habitation; tenant is a perpetrator of domestic violence, sexual assault, or stalking and the victim is also a tenant
Maryland	Md. Code Ann. [Real Prop.] § 8-402.1(a)	14 days	Breaching lease by behaving in a manner that presents a clear and imminent danger to the tenant himself, other tenants, guests, the landlord, or the landlord's property, lease provides for termination for violation of lease clause, and landlord has given 14 days' notice
	Md. Code Ann. [Real Prop.] § 8-401(e)(1)	30 days	Any lease violation if the lease states that tenancy can terminate for violation of the lease; and, when tenant is late with the rent three times within the past 12 months, but landlord must have won an eviction lawsuit for each prior nonpayment of rent episode (tenants may reinstate their tenancy by paying rent and court costs after the landlord has won an eviction lawsuit, but before physical eviction)
Massachusetts	Mass. Ann. Laws ch. 186, § 12	14 days	Tenant at will receiving second notice to pay rent or quit within 12 months
Michigan	Mich. Comp. Laws § 600.5714(d) and (e)	7 days	Failure to pay rent, causing or threatening physical injury to an individual (landlord must have filed a police report)
	Mich. Comp. Laws § 554.134	24 hours	Manufacture, dealing, or possession of illegal drugs on leased premises (landlord must first file a police report)
Minnesota	Minn. Stat. Ann. § 504B.135	14 days	Tenant at will who fails to pay rent when due
Mississippi	Miss. Code Ann. § 89-8-13	14 days	Repeating the same act, which constituted a lease violation and for which notice was given, within 6 months
		30 days	Nonremediable violation of lease or obligations imposed by statute
Missouri	Mo. Ann. Stat. §§ 441.020, 441.030, 441.040	10 days	Using the premises for gambling, prostitution, or possession, sale, or distribution of controlled substances; assigning or subletting without consent; seriously damaging the premises or violating the lease
Montana	Mont. Code Ann. § 70-24-422(1)(e)	5 days	Repeating the same act—that constituted a lease violation and for which notice was given—within 6 months
	Mont. Code Ann. § 70-24-422	3 days	Unauthorized pet or person living on premises; destroying or removing any part of the premises; creating a reasonable potential that the premises may be damaged or destroyed, or that neighboring tenants may be injured, due to tenant's drug, or gang-related, or other illegal activity
		14 days	Any other noncompliance with rental agreement that can't be remedied or repaired
Nebraska	Neb. Rev. Stat. § 76-1431(1)	14 days	Repeating the same act, that constituted a lease violation and for which notice was given, within 6 months
	Neb. Rev. Stat. § 76-1431(4)	5 days	When tenant or guest engages in violent criminal activity or sells a controlled substance on the premises, or acts in a way that threatens the health or safety of other tenants, landlord, landlord's employees or agents (does not apply if tenant has sought a protective order or alerted the police)

State Laws on Unconditional Quit Terminations (continued)

State	Statute	Time to Move Out Before Landlord Can File For Eviction	When Unconditional Quit Notice Can Be Used
Nevada	Nev. Rev. Stat. Ann. § 40.2514	3 days	Assigning or subletting in violation of the lease; substantial damage to the property; conducting an unlawful business; permitting or creating a nuisance; causing injury and damage to other tenants or occupants of the property or adjacent buildings or structures; unlawful possession for sale, manufacture, or distribution of illegal drugs
	§ 40.2516	Immediately	Violation of lease term that can't be cured
New Hampshire	N.H. Rev. Stat. Ann. § 540:1-a		Different rules apply depending on whether the property is "restricted" (most residential property) or "nonrestricted" (single-family houses, if the owner of such a house does not own more than 3 single-family houses at any one time; rental units in an owner-occupied building containing a total of 4 dwelling units or fewer; and single-family houses acquired by banks or other mortgagees through foreclosure).
	§ 540:2, 540:3	7 days	Restricted property: Neglect or refusal to pay rent due and in arrears, upon demand; substantial damage to the premises; failure to comply with a material term of the lease; behavior of the tenant or members of his family that adversely affects the health or safety of the other tenants or the landlord or his representatives; failure of the tenant to accept suitable temporary relocation required by lead-based paint hazard abatement; other good cause. Nonrestricted: Neglect or refusal to pay rent due and in arrears, upon demand; substantial damage to the premises; behavior of the tenant or members of his family that adversely affects the health or safety of the other tenants or the landlord or his representatives; failure of the tenant to accept suitable temporary relocation required by lead-based paint hazard abatement; failure to prepare unit for insect (including bedbug) remediation
		30 days	Nonrestricted only: For any legal reason other than those specified just above (for which 7 days' notice is required)
New Jersey	N.J. Stat. Ann. §§ 2A:18-53(c), 2A:18-61.2(a), 2A:19-61.1	3 days	Disorderly conduct; willful or grossly negligent destruction of landlord's property; assaults upon or threats against the landlord; termination of tenant's employment as a building manager, janitor, or other employee of the landlord; conviction for use, possession, or manufacture of an illegal drug either on the property or adjacent to it within the last two years, unless the tenant has entered a rehabilitation program (includes harboring anyone so convicted); conviction or civil liability for assault or terroristic threats against the landlord, landlord's family, or landlord's employee within the last two years (includes harboring); liability in a civil action for theft from landlord, landlord's family, landlord's employee, or another tenant; committing or harboring human trafficking
	N.J. Stat. Ann. §§ 2A:18-61.2(b), 2A:18-61.1	One month	Habitual failure to pay rent after written notice; continued violations, despite repeated warnings, of the landlord's reasonable rules and regulations; at the termination of a lease, refusal to accept reasonable changes of substance in the terms and conditions of the lease, including specifically any change in the term thereof

State Laws on Unconditional Quit Terminations (continued)

State	Statute	Time to Move Out Before Landlord Can File For Eviction	When Unconditional Quit Notice Can Be Used
New Mexico	N.M. Stat. Ann. § 47-8-33(I)	3 days	Substantial violation of the lease
	N.M. Stat. Ann. § 47-8-33(B) & (C)	7 days	Repeated violation of a term of the rental agreement within 6 months
New York	N.Y. Real Prop. Law § 232-a	30 days	In New York City, holdover of month-to-month tenancy
North Carolina	N.C. Gen. Stat. § 42-26(a)	Immediately	Violation of a lease term that specifies that eviction will result from noncompliance or holdover of tenancy
North Dakota	N.D. Cent. Code § 47-32-02	3 days	Holding over after the lease has expired; holding over after a sale or any judicial process ending the tenancy; violating a material term of the lease; using the property in a manner contrary to the agreement of the parties, using the property in a manner that unreasonably disturbs other tenants' peaceful enjoyment
	N.D. Cent. Code § 47-16-07.6	Not specified	Making a false claim of a legal disability, in an attempt to obtain an accommodation (waiver of landlord's no pets rule); or knowingly providing fraudulent documentation in connection with such a claim. Each violation is an infraction and entitles the landlord to evict and demand a damage fee of up to $1,000.
Ohio	Ohio Rev. Code Ann. §§ 1923.02 to 1923.04, 5321.17	3 days	Nonpayment of rent; violation of a written lease or rental agreement; when the landlord has "reasonable cause to believe" that the tenant has used, sold, or manufactured an illegal drug on the premises (conviction or arrest not required)
Oklahoma	Okla. Stat. Ann. tit. 41, § 132	Immediately	Criminal or drug-related activity or repeated violation of the lease
Oregon	Or. Rev. Stat. §§ 90.396, 90.403	24 hours	Violence or threats of violence by tenant or a guest; intentionally causing substantial property damage; giving false information on an application within the past year regarding a criminal conviction (landlord must terminate within 30 days of discovering the falsity); committing any act "outrageous in the extreme" (see statute); intentionally or recklessly injuring someone (or placing them in fear of imminent danger) because of the tenant's perception of the person's race, color, religion, national origin, or sexual orientation; second failure to remove a pet that has caused substantial damage
Pennsylvania	68 Pa. Cons. Stat. Ann., § 250.501(b) and (d)	10 days	Nonpayment of rent
		15 days (lease 1 year or less or lease of unspecified time)	Violations of the terms of the lease
		30 days (lease more than 1 year)	Violations of the terms of the lease
	68 Pa. Cons. Stat. Ann., § 250.505-A	10 days (any tenancy)	First conviction for illegal sale, manufacture, or distribution of an illegal drug; repeated use of an illegal drug; seizure by law enforcement of an illegal drug within the leased premises

State Laws on Unconditional Quit Terminations (continued)

State	Statute	Time to Move Out Before Landlord Can File For Eviction	When Unconditional Quit Notice Can Be Used
Rhode Island	R.I. Gen. Laws § 34-18-36(e)	20 days	Repeating an act which violates the lease or rental agreement or affects health or safety twice within 6 months (notice must have been given for the first violation)
	R.I. Gen. Laws §§ 34-18-24, 34-18-36(f)	Immediately	Any tenant who possesses, uses, or sells illegal drugs or who commits or attempts to commit any crime of violence on the premises or in any public space adjacent. "Seasonal tenant" whose lease runs from May 1 to October 15 or from September 1 to June 1 of the next year, with no right of extension or renewal, who has been charged with violating a local occupancy ordinance, making excessive noise, or disturbing the peace
South Carolina	S.C. Code Ann. § 27-40-710	Immediately	Nonpayment of rent after receiving one notification during the tenancy or allowing illegal activities on the property
South Dakota	S.D. Cod. Laws §§ 21-16-1, 21-16-2	3 days	Nonpayment of rent, substantial damage to the property, or holdover
Tennessee	Tenn. Code Ann. § 66-28-505(a)	7 days (applies only in counties having a population of more than seventy-five thousand (75,000), according to the 2010 federal census or any subsequent federal census)	Repeating an act that violates the lease or rental agreement or affects health or safety twice within 6 months (notice must have been given for the first violation)
	Tenn. Code Ann. § 66-7-109	3 days (applies only in counties of less than 75,000 residents, according to the 2010 federal census or any subsequent federal census; residential tenants in a housing authority; and tenants who are not mentally or physically disabled)	Committing a violent act; engaging in drug-related criminal activity; or behaving in a manner that constitutes or threatens to be a real and present danger to the health, safety, or welfare of the life or property of other tenants, the landlord, the landlord's representatives, or other persons on the premises. (If the underlying act of violence was also domestic abuse, as defined, only the perpetrator may be evicted.)
Texas	Tex. Prop. Code § 24.005	3 days (lease may specify a shorter or longer time)	Nonpayment of rent or holdover
Utah	Utah Code Ann. § 78B-6-802	3 days	Holdover, assigning or subletting without permission, substantial damage to the property, carrying on an unlawful business on the premises, maintaining a nuisance, committing a criminal act on the premises
Vermont	Vt. Stat. Ann. tit. 9, § 4467	30 days	Three notices for nonpayment or late rent within a 12-month period or any violation of the lease or landlord-tenant law

State Laws on Unconditional Quit Terminations (continued)

State	Statute	Time to Move Out Before Landlord Can File For Eviction	When Unconditional Quit Notice Can Be Used
Virginia	Va. Stat. Ann. § 55-248.31	30 days	Repeated violation of lease (after earlier violation was cured or nonremediable lease violation materially affecting health and safety). If tenant does not move within the time allotted, for each day that the tenant remains, tenant will owe rent of up 150% of the per diem of the monthly rent, but only if the rental agreement includes a clause specifying this result.
	Va. Stat. Ann. § 55-248.32	Immediately	A breach of the lease or rental agreement that is willful or a criminal act, is not remediable, and is a threat to the health or safety of others. If tenant does not move within the time allotted, for each day that the tenant remains, tenant will owe rent of up 150% of the per diem of the monthly rent, but only if the rental agreement includes a clause specifying this result.
Washington	Wash. Rev. Code Ann. § 59.12.030	3 days	Holdover, serious damage to the property, carrying on an unlawful business, maintaining a nuisance, or gang-related activity
West Virginia	W.Va. Code § 55-3A-1	Immediately	Failure to pay rent, violation of any lease provision, or damage to the property
Wisconsin	Wis. Stat. Ann. § 704.17	14 days (month-to-month tenants)	Failure to pay rent, violation of the rental agreement, or substantial damage to the property
		14 days (tenants with a lease of less than one year, or year-to-year tenants)	Failing to pay the rent on time, causing substantial property damage, or violating any lease provision more than once within one year (must have received proper notice for the first violation)
		5 days (all tenants)	Causing a nuisance on the property (landlord must have written notice from a law enforcement agency regarding the nuisance)
Wyoming	Wyo. Stat. §§ 1-21-1002, 1003	3 days	Nonpayment of rent, holdover, damage to premises, interference with another's enjoyment, denying access to landlord, or violating duties defined by statute (such as maintaining unit, complying with lease, disposing of garbage, etc.)

State Small Claims Court Limits

State	Statutes	Dollar limit	Evictions	Court Website
Alabama	Ala. Code §§ 6-3-2; 6-3-7; 12-12-31; 12-12-70; 12-12-71	$6,000	No.	www.alabamalegalhelp.org (click "Consumer Issues/ Small Claims Actions")
Alaska	Alaska Stat. §§ 22.15.040; 22.15.050	$10,000	No. (See www.courts. alaska.gov/webdocs/ forms/sc-100.pdf)	www.courts.alaska.gov/ forms/#sc (see "Small Claims" heading)
Arizona [1]	Ariz. Rev. Stat. Ann. §§ 22-501 to 22-524	$3,500	No. (www.mohave courts.com/Justice/ JCSS_SmallClaims.html)	www.azcourts.gov/self servicecenter/Self-Service- Forms#SmallClaims
Arkansas	Ark. Const. amend. 80, § 7	$5,000	No.	https://courts.arkansas. gov/sites/default/files/tree/ small_claims_info_0.pdf www.arlegalservices.org/ smallclaimspacket
California	Cal. Civ. Proc. Code §§ 116.110 to 116.950	$10,00 for individuals, except that a plaintiff may not file a claim over $2,500 more than twice a year. Limit for local public entity or for businesses is $5,000. $6,500 is the limit in suits by an individual against a guarantor that charges for its guarantor or surety services.	No.	www.courtinfo.ca.gov/ selfhelp/smallclaims www.dca.ca.gov/ publications/small_claims/ index.shtml
Colorado	Colo. Rev. Stat. §§ 13-6-401 to 13-6-417	$7,500	No.	www.courts.state.co.us/ userfiles/file/Self_Help/ smallclaimshandbook%20 finaltocourt%204-11.pdf www.courts.state.co.us/ Forms/SubCategory. cfm?Category=Small
Connecticut	Conn. Gen. Stat. Ann. §§ 47a-34 to 47a-42; 51-15; 51-345; 52-259	$5,000 (except in landlord- tenant security deposit claims)	No.	www.jud.state.ct.us/faq/ smallclaims.html
Delaware	Del. Code Ann. tit. 10, §§ 9301 to 9640	$15,000	Yes.	http://courts.delaware.gov/ JPCourt https://courts.delaware. gov/help/proceedings/ jp_startcivil.aspx
District of Columbia	D.C. Code Ann. §§ 11-1301 to 11-1323; 16-3901 to 16- 3910; 17-301 to 17-307	$10,000	No.	www.dccourts.gov/services/ civil-matters/requesting- 10k-or-less www.dccourts.gov/ sites/default/files/Small ClaimsHandbook.pdf

[1] Justice Courts, similar to small claims court but with more procedures, have a limit of $10,000. Rules can be found at Ariz. Rev. Stat. Ann. §§ 22-201 to 22-284. (Arizona)

State Small Claims Court Limits (continued)

State	Statutes	Dollar limit	Evictions	Court Website
Florida		$5,000	Yes.	www.flcourts.org/resources-and-services/family-courts/family-law-self-help-information/small-claims.stml www.flcourts.org/gen_public/family/self_help/smallclaims.shtml
Georgia	Ga. Code Ann. §§ 15-10-1; 15-10-2; 15-10-40 to 15-10-54; 15-10-80; 15-10-87	$15,000 (no limit in eviction cases)	Yes.	http://consumer.georgia.gov/consumer-topics/magistrate-court
Hawaii [2]	Haw. Rev. Stat. §§ 604-5; 633-27 to 633-36.	$5,000; no limit in landlord-tenant residential security deposit cases. For return of leased or rented personal property, the property must not be worth more than $5,000.	No.	www.courts.state.hi.us/self-help/small_claims/small_claims
Idaho	Idaho Code §§ 1-2301 to 1-2315	$5,000	No.	www.courtselfhelp.idaho.gov/small-claims
Illinois [3]	735 Ill. Comp. Stat. §§ 5/2-101 to 5/2-208; 705 Ill. Comp. Stat. § 205/11	$10,000	Yes.	www.ag.state.il.us/consumers/smlclaims.html
Indiana	Ind. Code Ann. §§ 33-28-3-2 to 33-28-3-10 (circuit court); 33-29-2-1 to 33-29-2-10 (superior court); 33-34-3-1 to 33-34-3-15 (Marion County Small Claims Court)	$6,000 ($8,000 in Marion County)	Yes, if total rent due does not exceed $6,000 ($8,000 in Marion County).	www.in.gov/judiciary/ 2710.htm
Iowa	Iowa Code §§ 631.1 to 631.17	$5,000	Yes.	www.iowacourts.gov/Court_Rules__Forms/Small_Claims_Forms
Kansas	Kan. Stat. Ann. §§ 61-2701 to 61-2714	$4,000	No.	www.kscourts.org/rules-procedures-forms/small-claims-information
Kentucky [4]	Ky. Rev. Stat. Ann. §§ 24A.200 to 24A.360	$2,500	Yes.	http://courts.ky.gov/courts/jefferson/small claims/Pages/default.aspx http://courts.ky.gov/resources/publications resources/Publications/P6SmallClaims Handbookweb.pdf

[2] Professional moneylenders and collection agents cannot sue in small claims court. (Hawaii)

[3] An alternative procedure exists for claims of $1,500 or less in Cook County's Pro Se Court. Plaintiffs represent themselves, and lawyers are allowed for defendants. See www.cookcountyclerkofcourt.org/includes/pages/community_resources/pro_se_faqs.asp. (Illinois)

[4] Professional moneylenders and collection agents cannot sue in small claims court. (Kentucky)

State Small Claims Court Limits (continued)				
State	Statutes	Dollar limit	Evictions	Court Website
Louisiana	La. Rev. Stat. Ann. §§ 13:5200 to 13:5211 (city court); La. Code Civ. Proc., Art. 4831, 4832, 4845, 4901 to 4925, and Art. 42 (justice of the peace court)	$5,000 (city court); $5,000 (justice of the peace, but no limit in eviction cases)	Available in Justice of the Peace courts only.	www.lsba.org/Public/CourtStructure.aspx http://brgov.com/dept/citycourt/civilfaqs.htm (Baton Rouge)
Maine	Me. Rev. Stat. Ann. tit. 14, §§ 7481 to 7487	$6,000	No.	www.courts.state.me.us/maine_courts/small_claims/index.shtml
Maryland	Md. Code Ann. [Cts. & Jud. Proc.] §§ 4-405; 6-403	$5,000	Yes, as long as the rent claimed does not exceed $5,000.	www.courts.state.md.us/legalhelp/smallclaims.html
Massachusetts [5]	Mass. Gen. Laws ch. 218, §§ 21 to 25; ch. 223, § 6; ch. 93A, § 9 (consumer complaints)	$7,000; no limit for property damage caused by motor vehicle	No.	www.mass.gov/ago/consumer-resources/consumer-assistance/small-claims-court.html
Michigan	Mich. Comp. Laws §§ 600.8401 to 600.8427	$6,000	No.	http://courts.mi.gov/administration/scao/forms/pages/small-claims.aspx https://michiganlegalhelp.org/self-help-tools/money-and-debt/i-have-small-claims-case
Minnesota [6]	Minn. Stat. Ann. §§ 491A.01 to 491A.03	$15,000 ($4,000 for claims involving consumer credit transactions)	No.	www.mncourts.gov/Help-Topics/Conciliation-Court.aspx
Mississippi	Miss. Code Ann. §§ 9-11-9 to 9-11-33; 11-9-101 to 11-9-147; 11-25-1; 11-51-85	$3,500	Yes.	http://courts.ms.gov/trialcourts/justicecourt/justicecourt.html
Missouri	Mo. Rev. Stat. §§ 482.300 to 482.365	$5,000	No.	www.courts.mo.gov/page.jsp?id=704 www.mobar.org/uploadedFiles/Home/Publications/Legal_Resources/Brochures_and_Booklets/small%20claims.pdf
Montana	Mont. Code Ann. §§ 25-2-118; 3-12-101 to 3-12-107 (district court); 25-33-101 to 25-33-306 (appeals); 25-35-501 to 25-35-807; 3-10-1001 to 3-10-1004 (justice court)	$7,000	No.	https://dojmt.gov/consumer/guide-to-small-claims-court
Nebraska	Neb. Rev. Stat. §§ 25-505.1; 25-2801 to 25-2807	$3,600 from July 1, 2015, through June 30, 2020 (adjusted every five years based on the Consumer Price Index)	No.	https://supremecourt.nebraska.gov/self-help/small-claims

[5] Consumer complaint small claims: (1) plaintiff must make written demand for relief at least 30 days before filing suit; (2) attorneys' fees available; (3) triple damages available. (Massachusetts)

[6] Educational institution may bring actions to recover student loans, if loans were originally awarded in the county in which it has administrative offices, even though the defendant is not county resident. (Minnesota)

State Small Claims Court Limits (continued)

State	Statutes	Dollar limit	Evictions	Court Website
Nevada	Nev. Rev. Stat. Ann. §§ 73.010 to 73.060	$10,000	No.	www.lasvegasjustice court.us/divisions/small_claims/ [Las Vegas] www.washoecounty.us/rjc/divisions/civil/small-claims-civil.php [Reno]
New Hampshire	N.H. Rev. Stat. Ann. §§ 503:1 to 503:11	$10,000	No.	www.courts.state.nh.us/district/eclaims/index.htm http://doj.nh.gov/consumer/complaints/small-claims.htm
New Jersey [7]	NJ R LAW DIV CIV PT Rule 6:1-2	$3,000 ($5,000 for claims relating to security deposits); certain landlord-tenant suits cannot be brought	No.	www.judiciary.state.nj.us/forms/10290_small_claims.pdf
New Mexico	N.M. Stat. Ann. §§ 34-8A-1 to 34-8A-10 (metropolitan court); 35-3-3, 35-3-5, 35-8-1 and 35-8-2 (magistrate court); 35-11-2, 35-13-1 to 35-13-3 (appeals)	$10,000	Yes.	https://metro.nmcourts.gov/uploads/files/Metro%20Self%20Help/Pamphlets/SH101%20-%20How%20to%20File%20a%20Lawsuit%20Rev%201-17.pdf www.nmcourts.gov/about-the-courts.aspx www2.nmcourts.gov/othercourts/magistrate_brochure.pdf
New York [8]	New York Unif. City Ct. Act §§ 1801 to 1815, 1801-A to 1814-A (commercial claims); N.Y. Unif. Dist. Ct. Act §§ 1801 to 1815, 1801-A to 1814-A (commercial claims); N.Y. Unif. Just. Ct. Act §§ 1801 to 1815; N.Y. City Civ. Ct. Act §§ 1801 to 1815; 1801-A to 1814-A (commercial claims)	$5,000 (town and village justice courts, $3,000)	No.	www.courts.state.ny.us/courthelp/smallClaims/index.shtml
North Carolina	N. C. Gen. Stat. §§ 7A-210 to 7A-232; 42-29	$10,000	Yes.	www.nccourts.org/Courts/Trial/SClaims www.legalaidnc.org/get-help/Documents/small-claims-guide/guide-to-small-claims-court.pdf

[7] The Special Civil Part, like the small claims court but with more procedures, has a limit of $15,000. See www.judiciary.state.nj.us/civil/civ-03.htm. (New Jersey)

[8] Corporations and partnerships cannot sue in small claims court, but may appear as defendants. (Does not apply to municipal and public benefit corporations and school districts.) Instead, they can bring commercial claims, which have similar rules to small claims courts but are subject to these additional restrictions: (1) Same limits and procedures as regular small claims except claim is brought by corporation, partnership, or association; (2) Business must have principal office in N.Y. state; (3) Defendant must reside, be employed, or have a business office in the county where suit is brought. (New York)

State Small Claims Court Limits (continued)

State	Statutes	Dollar limit	Evictions	Court Website
North Dakota [9]	N. D. Cent. Code §§ 27-08.1-01 to 27-08.1-08	$15,000	No.	www.ndcourts.gov/ndlshc/SmallClaims/SmallClaims.aspx
Ohio	Ohio Rev. Code Ann. §§ 1925.01 to 1925.18	$6,000	No.	www.supremecourt.ohio.gov/jcs/interpretersvcs/forms/english/5.pdf https://lasclev.org/smallclaimscourtbrochure
Oklahoma [10]	Okla. Stat. Ann. tit. 12, §§ 131 to 141; 1751 to 1773	$10,000	Yes.	www.oklahomacounty.org/158/Small-Claims www.okbar.org/public/brochures/smallclaimscourt.aspx
Oregon	Or. Rev. Stat. §§ 46.405 to 46.570; 55.011 to 55.140	$10,000	No.	www.osbar.org/public/legalinfo/1061_SmallClaims.htm
Pennsylvania [11]	42 Pa. Cons. Stat. Ann. §§ 1123; 1515	$12,000	Yes.	http://fjd.phila.gov/municipal/civil/ [Philadelphia] www.pabar.org/clips/bringingsuitBeforeDJ.pdf
Rhode Island	R.I. Gen. Laws §§ 10-16-1 to 10-16-16; 9-4-3; 9-4-4; 9-12-10 (appeals)	$2,500	No.	www.courts.ri.gov/Courts/districtcourt/Pages/Small%20Claims%20Court.aspx [currently under construction] www.ribar.com/for%20the%20public/findingandchoosingalawyer.aspx
South Carolina	S.C. Code Ann. §§ 22-3-10 to 22-3-320; 15-7-30; 18-7-10 to 18-7-30	$7,500	Yes.	www.sccourts.org/selfHelp/FAQMagistrate.pdf
South Dakota	S.D. Codified Laws Ann. §§ 15-39-45 to 15-39-78; 16-12B-6; 16-12B-12; 16-12B-16; 16-12C-8; 16-12C-13 to 16-12C-15	$12,000	No.	http://ujs.sd.gov/Small_Claims
Tennessee [12]	Tenn. Code Ann. §§ 16-15-501 to 16-15-505; 16-15-710 to 16-15-735; 16-15-901 to 16-15-905; 20-4-101; 20-4-103	$25,000. No limit in eviction suits or suits to recover personal property.	Yes.	http://tncourts.gov/programs/self-help-center http://gs4.shelbycountytn.gov/gscvinq/gscv_civildivision [Shelby]

[9] Plaintiff may not discontinue once small claims process is begun; if plaintiff seeks to discontinue, claim will be dismissed with prejudice (plaintiff cannot refile claim). (North Dakota)

[10] Collection agencies may not sue in small claims court. (Oklahoma)

[11] If claiming more than $2,000 personal injury or property damage, must submit statement of claim signed under oath (Philadelphia Municipal Court). (Pennsylvania)

[12] Tennessee has no actual small claims system, but trials in general sessions court are normally conducted with informal rules. (Tennessee)

State Small Claims Court Limits (continued)

State	Statutes	Dollar limit	Evictions	Court Website
Texas [13]	Tex. Gov't. Code Ann. § 27.060	$10,000	Separate small claims courts have been abolished as of August 2013; both small claims cases and evictions are heard in Justice Court. Evictions cases are governed by Rules 500-507 and 510 of Part V of the Rules of Civil Procedure.	www.txcourts.gov/courts/overview/about-texas-courts/trial-courts.aspx
Utah	Utah Code Ann. §§ 78A-8-101 to 78A-8-109	$11,000	No.	www.utcourts.gov/howto/smallclaims/index.asp
Vermont	Vt. Stat. Ann. tit. 12, §§ 5531 to 5541; 402	$5,000	No.	www.vermontjudiciary.org/self-help/debt-collection-small-claims
Virginia [14]	Va. Code Ann. §§ 8.01-262; 16.1-76; 16.1-77; 16.1-106; 16.1-113; 16.1-122.1 to 16.1-122.7	$5,000	No.	www.courts.state.va.us/resources/small_claims_court_procedures.pdf www.courts.state.va.us/courts/gd/home.html
Washington	Wash. Rev. Code Ann. §§ 12.36.010 to 12.40.120; 3.66.040	$5,000	No.	www.courts.wa.gov/newsinfo/resources/?fa=newsinfo_jury.scc&altMenu=smal www.atg.wa.gov/small-claims-court-0
West Virginia	W.Va. Code §§ 50-2-1 to 50-6-3; 56-1-1	$10,000	Yes.	www.courtswv.gov/lower-courts
Wisconsin	Wis. Stat. §§ 799.01 to 799.445; 421.401; 801.50; 808.03	$10,000. No limit in eviction suits.	Yes.	www.wicourts.gov/services/public/selfhelp/smallclaims.htm
Wyoming	Wyo. Stat. Ann. §§ 1-21-201 to 1-21-205; 5-9-128; 5-9-136	$6,000	No.	www.courts.state.wy.us/court_rule/rules-and-forms-governing-small-claims-cases

[13] Separate small claims courts have been abolished as of August 2013; both small claims cases and evictions are heard in Justice Court. Evictions cases are governed by Rules 500-507 and 510 of Part V of the Rules of Civil Procedure. (Texas)

[14] General district courts, similar to small claims court but with more procedures, can hear claims up to $25,000. (See Va. Code Ann. §§ 16.1-77 to 16.1-80.) (Virginia)

Landlord's Duty to Rerent

State	Legal authority	Must make reasonable efforts to rerent	Has no duty to look for or rent to a new tenant	Law is unclear or courts are divided on the issue
Alabama	Ala. Code §§ 35-9A-105, 35-9A-423	✓		
Alaska	Alaska Stat. § 34.03.230(c)	✓		
Arizona	Ariz. Rev. Stat. § 33-1370	✓		
Arkansas	*Weingarten/Arkansas, Inc. v. ABC Interstate Theatres, Inc.*, 811 S.W.2d 295 (Ark. 1991)		✓	
California	Cal. Civ. Code § 1951.2	✓		
Colorado	*Schneiker v. Gordon*, 732 P.2d 603 (Colo. 1987)	✓ [1]		
Connecticut	Conn. Gen. Stat. Ann. § 47a-11a	✓		
Delaware	25 Del. Code Ann. § 5507(d)(2)	✓		
District of Columbia	*Int'l Comm'n on English Liturgy v. Schwartz*, 573 A.2d 1303 (D.C. 1990)		✓ [2]	
Florida	Fla. Stat. Ann. § 83.595		✓ [3]	
Georgia	*Peterson v. Midas Realty Corp.*, 287 S.E.2d 61 (Ga. Ct. App. 1981)		✓	
Hawaii	Haw. Rev. Stat. § 521-70 (d)	✓		
Idaho	*Consol. Ag v. Rangen, Inc.*, 128 Idaho 228 (Idaho 1996)	✓		
Illinois	735 Ill. Comp. Stat. § 5/9-213.1	✓		
Indiana	*Nylen v. Park Doral Apartments*, 535 N.E.2d 178 (Ind. Ct. App. 1989)	✓		
Iowa	Iowa Code § 562A.29 (3)	✓		
Kansas	Kan. Stat. Ann. § 58-2565(c)	✓		
Kentucky	Ky. Rev. Stat. Ann. § 383.670	✓		
Louisiana	La. Civ. Code § 2002, *Gray v. Kanavel*, 508 So.2d 970 (La. Ct. App. 1987)	✓ [4]		✓
Maine	14 Me. Rev. Stat. Ann. § 6010-A	✓		
Maryland	Md. Code Ann., [Real Prop.] § 8-207			✓
Massachusetts	*Edmands v. Rust & Richardson Drug Co.*, 191 Mass. 123, 128 (1906) and assorted other cases Booklet from MA.gov says LL has a duty to mitigate: www.mass.gov/ocabr/docs/landlordrights.pdf. Ditto from MassLegal Help: www.mass.gov/ocabr/docs/landlordrights.pdf. But the Supreme Court has not yet ruled definitively.	✓	✓	
Michigan	*Fox v. Roethlisberger*, 85 N.W.2d 73 (Mich. 1957)	✓		
Minnesota	*Control Data Corp. v. Metro Office Parks Co.*, 296 Minn. 302 (Minn. 1973)		✓	

[1] Case law is not dispositive, but state practice seems to require mitigation. See ColoradoLegalServices.org ("Breaking a Lease—What You Need to Know").

[2] Despite this legal authority, DC attorneys report that judges take failure to mitigate into consideration when ascertaining the landlord's damages. (District of Columbia)

[3] Landlord has the option of rerenting, standing by and doing nothing (tenant remains liable for rent as it comes due), or invoking its right to a liquidated damages, or early termination, provision. Latter remedy is available only if the lease includes a liquidated damages addendum, or addition, that provides for no more than two months' damages and requires tenant to give no more than 60 days' notice. Liquidated damages provision must substantially include specified language in Fl. Stat. Ann. § 83.595. (Florida)

[4] Court decisions are uniform although more recent decisions appear to require mitigation. (Louisiana)

Landlord's Duty to Rerent (continued)

State	Legal authority	Must make reasonable efforts to rerent	Has no duty to look for or rent to a new tenant	Law is unclear or courts are divided on the issue
Mississippi	*Alsup v. Banks*, 9 So. 895 (Miss. 1891)		✓ [5]	
Missouri	*Rhoden Inv. Co. v. Sears, Roebuck & Co.*, 499 S.W.2d 375 (Mo. 1973), Mo. Rev. Stat. § 535.300	✓ [6]		
Montana	Mont. Code Ann. § 70-24-426	✓		
Nebraska	Neb. Rev. Stat. § 76-1432	✓		
Nevada	Nev. Rev. Stat. Ann. § 118.175	✓		
New Hampshire	*Wen v. Arlen's, Inc.*, 103 A.2d 86 (N.H. 1954), *Modular Mfg., Inc. v. Dernham Co.*, 65 B.R. 856 (Bankr. D. N.H. 1986)			✓
New Jersey	*Sommer v. Kridel*, 378 A.2d 767 (N.J. 1977)	✓		
New Mexico	N.M. Stat. Ann. § 47-8-6	✓		
New York	*Rios v. Carrillo*, 53 AD3d 111, 115 (2nd Dept., 2008); *Gordon v. Raymond Eshaghoff*, 60 AD3d 807, 2009 WL 711546 (2nd Dept., decided March 17, 2009) and *Smith v. James*, 22 Misc. 3d 128 (A) (Supreme Court, Appellate Term, 9th & 10th Dist., 2009)		✓	
North Carolina	*Isbey v. Crews*, 284 S.E.2d 534 (N.C. Ct. App. 1981)	✓		
North Dakota	N.D. Cent. Code § 47-16-13.5	✓		
Ohio	*Stern v. Taft*, 361 N.E.2d 279 (Ct. App. 1976)	✓ [7]		
Oklahoma	41 Okla. Stat. Ann. § 129	✓		
Oregon	Or. Rev. Stat. § 90.410	✓		
Pennsylvania	*Stonehedge Square Ltd. P'ship v. Movie Merchs.*, 715 A.2d 1082 (Pa. 1998)		✓	
Rhode Island	R.I. Gen. Laws § 34-18-40	✓		
South Carolina	S.C. Code Ann. § 27-40-730 (c)	✓		
South Dakota	No cases or statutes in South Dakota discuss this issue.			✓
Tennessee	Tenn. Code Ann. § 66-28-507 (c)	✓ [8]		
Texas	Tex. Prop. Code Ann. § 91.006	✓		
Utah	Utah Code Ann. § 78B-6-816, *Reid v. Mutual of Omaha Ins. Co.*, 776 P.2d 896 (Utah 1989)	✓		
Vermont	9 Vt. Stat. Ann. § 4462		✓	
Virginia	Va. Code Ann. §§ 55-248.33, 55-248.35	✓		
Washington	Wash. Rev. Code Ann. § 59.18.310	✓ [9]		
West Virginia	W.Va. Code § 37-6-7, *Teller v. McCoy*, 253 S.E.2d 114 (W.Va. 1978)	✓		
Wisconsin	Wis. Stat. Ann. § 704.29	✓		
Wyoming	*Goodwin v. Upper Crust, Inc.*, 624 P.2d 1192 (1981)	✓		

[5] Many Miss. attorneys believe this old case is not sound authority, and that a trial judge would find a duty to mitigate in spite of it. (Mississippi)

[6] Landlord must mitigate only if intending to use tenant's security deposit to cover future unpaid rent. (Missouri)

[7] Duty to mitigate applies in absence of any clause that purports to relieve the landlord of this duty (courts must enforce this clause). (Ohio)

[8] Applies only to counties having a population of more than 75,000, according to the 2010 federal census or any subsequent federal census. (See Tenn. Code Ann. § 66-28-102). (Tennessee)

[9] Detailed procedures must be followed when premises are vacant due to tenant's death. (See Wash. Rev. Code Ann. § 59.18.595.) (Washington)

Consequences of Self-Help Evictions

State	Amount Tenant Can Sue For	Statute Provides for Tenant's Court Costs & Attorneys' Fees	Statute Gives Tenant the Right to Stay	Statute or Legal Authority
Alabama	Self-help evictions are not allowed, but no specific penalties are provided (judge decides on consequences).	N/A	N/A	Ala. Code § 35-9A-427
Alaska	One and one-half times the actual damages. If tenant elects to terminate the lease, landlord must return entire security deposit.	No	Yes	Alaska Stat. § 34.03.210
Arizona	Two months' rent or twice the actual damages, whichever is greater. If tenant elects to terminate the lease, landlord must return entire security deposit.	No	Yes	Ariz. Rev. Stat. § 33-1367
Arkansas	Self-help evictions are not allowed, but it's up to the court to determine damages.	N/A	N/A	*Gorman v. Ratliff*, 712 S.W. 2d 888 (1986)
California	Actual damages plus $100 per day of violation ($250 minimum). Tenant may ask for an injunction prohibiting any further violation during the court action.	Yes	Yes	Cal. Civ. Code § 789.3
Colorado	Tenant may sue for any damages.	N/A	N/A	Colo. Rev. Stat. § 38-12-510
Connecticut	Double actual damages. Landlord may also be prosecuted for a misdemeanor.	Yes	Yes	Conn. Gen. Stat. Ann. §§ 47a-43, 47a-46, 53a-214
Delaware	Triple damages or three times per diem rent for time excluded, whichever is greater. Tenant may recover court costs, but not attorneys' fees.	Yes	Yes	Del. Code Ann. tit. 25, § 5313
District of Columbia	Actual and punitive damages.	No	No	*Mendes v. Johnson*, 389 A.2d 781 (D.C. 1978)
Florida	Actual damages or three months' rent, whichever is greater.	Yes	No	Fla. Stat. Ann. § 83.67
Georgia	Landlord may not resort to self-help evictions. Damages are determined by the court.	N/A	N/A	*Forrest v. Peacock*, 363 S.E. 2d 581 (1987), reversed on other grounds, 368 S.E.2d 519 (1988)
Hawaii	Two months' rent or free occupancy for two months (tenant must have been excluded "overnight"). Court may order landlord to stop illegal conduct.	Yes	Yes	Haw. Rev. Stat. § 521-63(c)
Idaho				
Illinois				
Indiana	Statute doesn't specify damages.	N/A	N/A	Ind. Code Ann. § 32-31-5-6
Iowa	Actual damages, plus punitive damages up to twice the monthly rent and attorneys' fees. If tenant elects to terminate the lease, landlord must return entire security deposit.	Yes	Yes	Iowa Code § 562A.26
Kansas	Actual damages or one and one-half months' rent, whichever is greater.	No	Yes	Kan. Stat. Ann. § 58-2563

Consequences of Self-Help Evictions (continued)

State	Amount Tenant Can Sue For	Statute Provides for Tenant's Court Costs & Attorneys' Fees	Statute Gives Tenant the Right to Stay	Statute or Legal Authority
Kentucky	Three months' rent.	Yes	Yes	Ky. Rev. Stat. Ann. § 383.655
Louisiana	Landlord may not resort to self-help evictions. Damages are determined by the court.	N/A	N/A	*Weber v. McMillan*, 285 So.2d 349 (1973)
Maine	Actual damages or $250, whichever is greater. The court may award costs and fees to landlord if it finds that the tenant brought a frivolous court lawsuit or one intended to harass.	Yes	No	Me. Rev. Stat. Ann. tit. 14, § 6014
Maryland	Landlord may not resort to self-help evictions. Damages are determined by the court.	N/A	N/A	*In re Promower, Inc., v. Scuderi, et al.*, 56 B.R. 619 (U.S. Bankruptcy Court, D. Maryland, 1986)
Massachusetts	Three months' rent or three times the actual damages.	Yes	Yes	Mass. Gen. Laws ch. 186, § 15F
Michigan	Up to three times actual damages or $200, whichever is greater.	No	Yes	Mich. Comp. Laws § 600.2918
Minnesota	Statute doesn't specify damages.	Yes	Yes	Minn. Stat. § 504B.375
Mississippi				
Missouri	Landlord may not resort to self-help evictions. Damages are determined by the court.	N/A	N/A	*Steinke v. Leight*, 235 S.W.2d 115 (1950), Mo. Stat. Ann § 441.233
Montana	Three months' rent or three times the actual damages, whichever is greater.	Yes	Yes	Mont. Code Ann. § 70-24-411
Nebraska	Up to three months' rent.	Yes	Yes	Neb. Rev. Stat. § 76-1430
Nevada	Up to $2,500 or actual damages, whichever is greater, or both. If tenant elects to terminate rental agreement or lease, landlord must return entire security deposit and any prepaid rent.	No	Yes	Nev. Rev. Stat. Ann. § 118A.390
New Hampshire	Actual damages or $1,000, whichever is greater; if court finds that landlord knowingly or willingly broke the law, two to three times this amount. Each day that a violation continues is a separate violation. Court may order a tenant who brings a frivolous suit or one intended to harass to pay landlord's costs and fees.	Yes	Yes	N.H. Rev. Stat. Ann. §§ 540-A:3, 540-A:4, 358-A:10
New Jersey	Self-help in prohibited, and landlord who engages in self-help is a "disorderly person," a criminal offense that subjects the landlord to up to six months in jail.	N/A	N/A	N.J. Stat. Ann. §§ 2A:39-1, 2C:43-8
New Mexico	A prorated share of the rent for each day of violation, actual damages, and civil penalty of twice the monthly rent.	Yes	Yes	N.M. Stat. Ann. § 47-8-36
New York	Three times the actual damages.	No	No	N.Y. Real Prop. Acts Law § 853

		Statute Provides for Tenant's Court Costs & Attorneys' Fees	Statute Gives Tenant the Right to Stay	
Consequences of Self-Help Evictions (continued)				
State	Amount Tenant Can Sue For			Statute or Legal Authority
North Carolina	Actual damages.	No	Yes	N.C. Gen. Stat. § 42-25.9
North Dakota	Triple damages.	No	No	N.D. Cent. Code § 32-03-29
Ohio	Actual damages.	Yes	No	Ohio Rev. Code Ann. § 5321.15
Oklahoma	Twice the average monthly rental or twice the actual damages, whichever is greater.	No	Yes	Okla. Stat. tit. 41, § 123
Oregon	Two months' rent or twice the actual damages, whichever is greater.	No	Yes	Or. Rev. Stat. § 90.375
Pennsylvania	Self-help evictions are not allowed, but no specific penalties are provided (it's up to the court to determine damages).	N/A	N/A	*Wofford v. Vavreck*, 22 Pa. D. & C.3d 444 (1981); *Kuriger v. Cramer*, 498 A.2d 1331 (1985)
Rhode Island	Three months' rent or three times the actual damages, whichever is greater.	Yes	Yes	R.I. Gen. Laws § 34-18-34
South Carolina	Three months' rent or twice the actual damages, whichever is greater.	Yes	Yes	S.C. Code Ann. § 27-40-660
South Dakota	Two months' rent. If tenant elects to terminate the lease, landlord must return entire security deposit.	No	Yes	S.D. Codified Laws Ann. § 43-32-6
Tennessee	Actual and punitive damages. If tenant elects to terminate the lease, landlord must return entire security deposit.	Yes	Yes	Tenn. Code Ann. § 66-28-504
Texas	A civil penalty of one month's rent plus $1,000, actual damages, court costs, and reasonable attorney's fees.	Yes	Yes	Tex. Prop. Code §§ 92.008, 92.009, 92.0081,
Utah	Self-help evictions are not allowed, but no specific penalties are provided.	No	No	Utah Code Ann. § 78B-6-814
Vermont	Unspecified damages. Court may award costs and fees to landlord if the court finds that the tenant brought a frivolous lawsuit or one intended to harass.	Yes	Yes	Vt. Stat. Ann. tit. 9, §§ 4463, 4464
Virginia	Actual damages.	Yes	Yes	Va. Code Ann. §§ 55-248.26, 55-225.2
Washington	Actual damages. For utility shut-offs only, actual damages and up to $100 per day of no service. Court may award costs and fees to the prevailing party.	Yes	Yes	Wash. Rev. Code Ann. § 59.18.300
West Virginia				
Wisconsin	Self-help evictions are prohibited. The court will determine damages.	N/A	N/A	Wis. Adm. Code ATCP § 134.09(7)
Wyoming				

How to Use the Downloadable Forms on the Nolo Website

Editing RTFs 414

List of Forms Available on the Nolo Website 414

This book comes with downloadable files that you can access online at:

www.nolo.com/back-of-book/EVTEN.html

To use the files, your computer must have specific software programs installed. The files are all RTFs. You can open, edit, print, and save these form files with most word processing programs such as Microsoft *Word*, Windows *WordPad*, and recent versions of *WordPerfect*.

Editing RTFs

Here are some general instructions about editing RTF forms in your word processing program. Refer to the form instructions in this book for help about what should go in each blank.

- **Underlines.** Underlines indicate where to enter information. After filling in the needed text, delete the underline. In most word processing programs you can do this by highlighting the underlined portion and typing CTRL-U.
- **Bracketed and italicized text.** Bracketed and italicized text indicates instructions. Be sure to remove all instructional text before you finalize your document.
- **Optional text.** Optional text gives you the choice to include or exclude text. Delete any optional text you don't want to use. Renumber numbered items, if necessary.
- **Alternative text.** Alternative text gives you the choice between two or more text options. Delete those options you don't want to use. Renumber numbered items, if necessary.
- **Signature lines.** Signature lines should appear on a page with at least some text from the document itself.

Every word processing program uses different commands to open, format, save, and print documents, so refer to your software's help documents for help using your program. Nolo cannot provide technical support for questions about how to use your computer or your software.

CAUTION

In accordance with U.S. copyright laws, the forms provided by this book are for your personal use only.

List of Forms Available on the Nolo Website

The following forms are available as RTF files at:

www.nolo.com/back-of-book/EVTEN.html

Form Title	File Name
Rental Priorities Worksheet	Priorities.rtf
Rental Application	Application.rtf
Consent to Background and Reference Check	CheckConsent.rtf
Receipt and Holding Deposit Agreement	Receipt.rtf
Landlord-Tenant Checklist	Checklist.rtf
Agreement Regarding Tenant Improvements to Rental Unit	Alteration.rtf
Amendment to Lease or Rental Agreement	Amendment.rtf
Tenant's Notice of Intent to Move Out	MoveNotice.rtf
Landlord-Tenant Agreement to Terminate Lease	Terminate.rtf
Consent to Assignment of Lease	AssignConsent.rtf
Demand for Return of Security Deposit	DepositReturn.rtf

Index

A

Abandoned property of tenant, retrieval of
  overview, 297
  damage to property, 300
  distress or distraint laws and, 299
  evicted tenants and, 297, 298–299, 317
  exceptions to state rules on, 301
  landlord fails to follow the rules, 301
  landlord keeps or sells property, 300, 301
  lawsuit against landlord for, 301–302
  liability of landlord for damage to or loss of, 300–301
  notice requirements, 299
  planned moves and, 298
  procedures to get property back, 299–300
  reason for leaving and, 297–298
  reasons property gets abandoned, 297
  sale of property, 300, 301
  state laws on, 297–298, 300–301, 387
  unannounced departures and, 298
  unpaid rent and, 298–299
Absences of tenant, extended
  abandoned belongings and, 298
  maintenance during, 175–176
  notice to landlord of, 37, 48, 176
  in written rental documents, 37, 48
Access to property by landlord
  clarifying access rules, 178–179
  cooperating with requests for, 179
  daytime phone number of tenant given to landlord, 178
  disabled tenants and notice for, 178
  emergencies and, 47–48, 174–175, 180
  and extended absences of tenant, 175–176
  for inspections, 176
  key, landlord's legal right to, 175, 246
  notice requirement, 47–48, 175, 177–179
  permission coerced by landlord, 174
  permission given by tenant, 174, 181
  and privacy, right to, 174, 182–185
  for repairs and maintenance, 47–48, 175–176
  showing the property to prospective tenants or buyers, 176–177
  state statutes listed, 385–386
  time of day landlord may enter, 178
  written notice, 178
  in written rental documents, 43, 48, 178
  See also Privacy of tenant
Access to property by others
  law enforcement, 180
  municipal inspectors, 179–180
  strangers requesting landlord for, 180–181
Accessibility accommodations and modifications, 38, 93–96
Accommodations, for disabled persons, 93–96, 178
ADA (Americans with Disabilities Act), 38, 94
Adult status, 37, 92–93
Adverse action reports, credit history and, 24, 27
Advertising
  classified, 10
  discrimination and, 87, 88–89, 105, 267
  in English, 89
  misleading statements and omissions in, 11, 16
  promises for repairs implied in, 154
  See also Craigslist
Age
  of adulthood, 37, 92–93
  condominium conversion rules protections for, 92, 270
  and deposit limits, 78
  discrimination based on, 87, 92–93
  qualifying as disability, 92
  senior citizen housing, 87
Airbnb. See Short-term paying guests
Alcoholics, discrimination and, 96–97
Alterations and improvements
  becoming part of the property, 164–165
  cable TV access, 167–168
  and evictions under rent control, 63
  and "good tenant" behavior when meeting landlord, 13
  and housing codes, 135
  negotiating for, as part of moving in, 13
  nonessential, negotiation for, 115
  plugging or screwing in appliances, 165

promised by landlord, in written rental document, 52–53

receipts for, 167

restoration of property to former condition, 165, 167

retaining ownership of, 164–167

sample Agreement Regarding Tenant Improvements to Rental Unit, 166

satellite dishes and other antennas, 7, 43, 168–172

by tenants, 43

written rental documents requiring consent for, 164, 246

See also Accessibility; Fixtures; Repairs and maintenance

Alumni associations, as source of leads on rentals, 13

Amendment of rental documents, 56, 248–250

Amenities

changes to, 49–50

in exchange for maintenance, 156

Americans with Disabilities Act (ADA), 38, 94

Android apps, 11

Animals, support/comfort/emotional support, 47, 93, 94

See also Pets

Antennas, placement of, 168–172

Antidiscrimination laws. *See* Discrimination

Apartment Owners Limited Building Policy, 45

Apartmentratings.com, 15

Appliances

and carbon monoxide, 219, 220

damage to, termination of tenancy for, 307

fixtures installed by tenant, 43

and inspection prior to move-in, 113–114

as property of tenant, 165

provision of, promises for, 154–155

repair of, responsibility for, 43, 154–155

repair or replacement of, and return of deposit, 280, 295

Arrests, in credit report, 24

Asbestos, 203–207

deterioration and disturbance of, 204, 205

moving out to avoid, 206–207

notifying the landlord, 205–206

OSHA regulations, 203–204

protection from, 204–205

resources on, 207

retaliation by landlord for reporting, 206

sample Letter Regarding Deteriorating Asbestos, 205

sample Letter Requesting Reimbursement for Temporary Housing, 207

temporary housing costs, 206–207

testing requirements, 204

Assault, as intentional injury with liability, 196

Assignment of leases

assignee rights, 263

compared to subletting, 265

ending lease early with, 262–263, 264

lease provisions and, 263

as prohibited, 41

sample Consent to Assignment of Lease, 264

successors clause, 53

termination of tenancy for, 306

vs. new lease, 263

Assumption of risk, 197–198

Attorneys. *See* Lawyers

Automatic debit, rent payment with, 66

Automatic liens, 41, 299

Automatic stay, and bankruptcy, 323, 324

B

Background checks

consent to, 17, 22, 23

of other tenants and neighbors, 15–16

rental applications and, 16–17, 100

See also Credit reports

Bankruptcy

and drug use or damage to property, 324

of landlord, and deposits, 83, 271

of landlord, and status of lease, 271–272

and leases, status of, 323

and rental applications, 24

stopping eviction by filing, 323–324

Bankruptcy Abuse Prevention and Consumer Protection Act (2005), 323–324

Bar associations, 337, 341

Bedbugs, 225–230

Bicycles, 44

Building codes. *See* Housing codes

Building inspectors

access to unit by, 179–180

complaints about security to, 243–244

habitability certified to court by, 146

random inspections by, 179–180

reporting code violations to, 141, 142

retaliation for complaints to, 257

See also Inspection of premises

Building materials, radon exposure via, 217

Burglar alarms. *See* Security

C

Cable TV access, 167–168
Carbon monoxide (CO), 219–221
Carbon monoxide (CO) detectors, 114, 219–220
  sample Letter Asking for CO Detector, 220
Carpets, 153, 280, 281
Cash, as rent payment, 67
CB radio, 169
Cell phones, and EMF exposures, 229
Character references, and sample, 23
Child care operations, 38
Children
  and condominium conversions, 270
  discrimination against, 39, 90–91
  and lead exposures, 208, 211, 213, 215
City-Data.com, 13
Classified ads, 10
Cleaning
  and bedbug eradication, 227
  deposit for, 40, 80–81, 83, 279
  housekeeping of tenant, as issue, 92, 222, 223, 225, 307
  and lead exposure, 214–215, 217
  and mold prevention, 222, 223, 224
  nonrefundable cleaning fee, 279
  plans for, sharing with landlord, 283–285
  security deposit used for, 80–81, 83, 277, 286, 287
  small claims court and evidence of, 294–295
Code of Federal Regulations (C.F.R.), 342–343
Comfort animals, 94
Committing waste, 46, 307
Common areas
  claimed abuse of, and landlord retaliation, 257
  discriminatory rules on use of, 87, 90
  lead exposure and, 211–212
  paying for utilities used in, 41
  repairs needed in, 192
  security and, 233
Common law, 136, 343
Commuting, as rental priority, 6
Comparative negligence, 197
Compensatory damages
  for discrimination, 99, 104
  for injuries on landlord's property, 198–199
Complaint, 318–319
Conciliation. *See* Small claims court
Condominium conversions
  overview, 270
  disclosures required for, 51

protection of vulnerable tenants and, 92, 270
  relocation assistance due to, 270
  rent control and, 64, 270
  termination of tenancy for, 270
Condominium rentals
  after approval of conversion, 270
  exempt from random municipal inspections, 180
  legal footing same as single-family houses, 1
  operating rules and regulations (CC&Rs), 1
  with purchase potential, 7
Consumer protection agencies
  and bounced rent check laws, 70
  and fair housing law, 88
  and housing codes, 136
  online contact information, 88
Cornell Legal Information Institute, 342
Corporate housing offices, leads on rentals from, 13
Cosigners
  for chronically late payment of rent, 309
  and credit report problems or lacks, 26, 27
  defined, 57
  for deposits, 78
  disabled applicants and, 57
  renter's insurance naming cosigner as insured, 44
  signing the document, 57
  students and, 57
Costs. *See* Fees and costs
Cotenants
  defined, 120
  and deposits, return of, 290–291
  joint and several liability of, 37, 120, 121
  subtenant becoming, 266
  See also Roommates
Courts
  decisions of, explaining or creating law (common law), 136, 343–344
  evidence, rules of, 318, 321, 322
  habitable housing requirements, 136–137
  mold litigation, 223
  rent abatement, approval of, 145–146, 150, 159–160, 185, 216, 271
  rent withholding, permission for, 144
  security litigation, 232
  small claims court compared to, 317–318
  See also Lawsuits; Small claims court
Craigslist
  checks against rent gouging with, 60
  finding a rental by advertising yourself on, 11
  finding a rental via ads on, 10

finding a roommate with, 30

scams on, 10

Credit card payment of rent, 66

Credit reports

"big stick" repair remedies and mark on, 141

bringing copy to meet landlord, 22, 26

checking prior to start of housing search, 4, 25

discrimination complaints recorded in, 100

Disposal Rule for, 24

errors in, checking for and correction of, 4, 25–26, 27

evictions recorded in, 24, 256, 312, 313

fees for credit-checks, 25

fraudulent fees for, 25

higher rent based on, 24

investigative consumer reports, 24

and moving out as response to termination notice, 312

negative-but-accurate information in, dealing with, 26

notices landlord required to give about (adverse action reports), 24, 27

of potential replacement tenants, tenant seeking, 261

rejection based on, 24, 26, 27

and rental applications, 22, 24–26

for roommates, new, 129

signing agreement for, 25

Crime and criminal behavior, 232–246

overview, 232

and civil vs. criminal nuisance laws, 238

clause in rental document forbidding, 46

in credit report, 24

eviction for (expedited), 308, 317

getting the facts before making accusations, 236

as "just cause" reason for eviction, 63

and law enforcement entering unit, 180

lawsuit for security issues and, 153, 157, 245

lawsuits for illegal activity on premises, 237–240, 245

liability for, on premises, 198, 237–240, 308

notice to landlord of potential for, 242

and rejection of application, 26–27

rental application asking about, 17

responsibility for damage caused by, 138, 153

seizure of landlord's property for, 238–239

tenant protecting self, 245–246

Criminal background checks, of other tenants and neighbors, 15–16

Cure or Quit notice, defined, 304

See also Termination of tenancy by landlord, for nonpayment of rent or violation of rental document

D

Damages

for bedbug nondisclosure, 230

for crimes, 234, 239

for discrimination, 99, 102, 104, 105

for failure to disclose lead-based paint hazards, 209

hold-over tenants clause as form of, 256

for illegal condominium conversions, 270

for injuries on landlord's property, 195–196, 198–199

for security deposit rule violation, 276

for termination notice by lawyer who regularly collects rent debts, 311

Decks, patios, and balconies, as rental priority, 7

Deposits, 78–83

alternatives to help pay, 78

bankruptcy of landlord and, 83, 271

cleaning deposits, 40, 80–81, 83, 279

and credit report issues, 26

discrimination and, 79, 87

dollar limits on, 78–79

eviction and, 313

excessive, not paying, 79

finder's fee interpreted as, 29

for furnished rentals, 78

increases in, 73, 80–81

as insurance, 40

interest on, paid to tenant, 40, 51, 64, 82

last month's rent, as separate deposit, 80–81

last month's rent, security deposit converted to, 288, 290

legal research on, 79

maximum ability to pay, 6

nonrefundable, 40–41, 46, 81–82

nonrefundable up-front fees, 82, 279

"not ready" apartment and refunding of, 48

notice to tenant of location of and amount of interest, 82

on pets, 40, 46, 78, 81

and prepayment of rent, 78

rent control and, 64

rent increases and, 73, 81

roommate additions and increases in, 130–131

and sale of property by landlord, 83

separate account for holding of, 82

service animals not requiring, 46

state law governing, 40, 46, 55, 73, 78, 80–83, 130–131, 354–363

for subletting, 267

waterbeds, 78

See also Deposits, deductions from; Deposits, return of; Holding deposits

Deposits, deductions from

for accessibility modifications, restoration of, 95

for cleaning, 80–81, 83, 277, 286, 287

for damaged property of landlord, 137, 277, 279–281

damages in lawsuit for violation of rules by landlord, 276

deadlines for return of, 276–277

deductions made during tenancy, 81, 83

and early termination rent owed, 254

for fixtures, 281

itemized statement of, 277–279

lawyer's fees taken from, 256

method of determining value of items, 279, 296

notice of deductions, 276

for painting, 281

price checking of landlord's claims, 279–281, 295, 296–297

for repairs and maintenance, 80–81, 83, 279–281, 285–286, 294–295

for rugs and carpets, 281

sample Security Deposit Itemization, 278

for unpaid rent, 81, 281–283, 288, 290

use of, allowable, 83

See also Deposits, return of

Deposits, return of, 276–301

overview, 276

address of tenant to landlord, 277, 287

calling the landlord, 291

and cleaning plans of tenant, 283–285

and cleaning, second chance at, 286, 287

compromising with landlord on, 286, 292–293

damages and penalties for failing to follow the law, 276, 287, 293

deadlines for receipt of, 276–277

disputes, how to handle, 291–296

documenting condition of the unit, 285

and inspection, final, 276, 285–286

and inspection, pre-move-out, 276

and Landlord-Tenant Checklist, 108, 285, 286, 288, 294

lawsuit against landlord for, 277, 285, 287, 293–296

mediation and, 293–294

normal wear and tear vs. damage, responsibility for, 279–280

to roommates (cotenants), 290–291

sample Agreement Regarding Return of Security Deposit, 293

sample Demand for Partial Return of Security Deposit, 288

sample Demand for Return of Security Deposit, 289

sample Letter #1: Tenant's Cleaning Plans, 283

sample Letter #2: Tenant's Cleaning Plans, 284

sample Request to be Present at Inspection, 286

sample Request to Clean Further, 287

sample Second Demand for Return of Security Deposit, 292

written demand for, second, 291–292

in written rental documents, 40–41, 83

written request for, first, 286–289

See also Deposits, deductions from

Digital Audio Radio Services (DARS), 169

Disabilities, persons with

accessibility, right to, 93–96

accommodations by landlord, 93–96, 178

ADA contact information, 38

alcoholics and drug users, 96–97

with cosigners, 57

damages for injuries resulting in, 198

definition of, 93

and discrimination, 92, 93–97

early termination rights of, 259

elderly qualifying as, 92

and home business accessibility requirements, 38

and lawyer, finding, 337

and lead regulations, housing exempted from, 211

mental or emotional impairments, 93

modifications to unit, by tenant, 43, 93, 94–95

new buildings and accessibility (post-1991), 94, 95

and notice for access to unit by landlord, 178

privacy needs, 178

questions about disability, 93

and rental priorities, 7

Sample Letter Attesting to the Appropriateness of an Accommodation or Modification, 96

verification of disabled status, 95

Disclosures by landlord

bank holding security deposits, 51

bedbugs, 229

condominium conversions, 51

criminal background of neighbors, 16

hidden defects of property, 51

of investigative consumer report request, 24
lead-based paint hazards, 51, 208–211, 212–213
lease with option to buy and, 35
legal papers, person authorized to receive, 51
mold, 222
rent control requirements, 51
state law summarizing, 364–377
utility bills not under control of tenant, 41
Discovery, 318, 320
Discrimination, 86–105
overview, 86
advertising and, 87, 88–89, 105, 267
age, 92–93
age, allowable (senior citizen housing), 87
antiterrorism laws and, 89
arbitrary (California), 98
bi-monthly rent payments and, 64–65
and children, 39
and deposit policy, 79, 87
and disability, 92, 93–97
domestic violence victims and, 125
exempt properties, 87
familial status, 90–91, 102
federal laws against, 27, 86–97, 99, 103–104
gender identity, 98–99
and income, source of, 99
indirect, defined, 102
intention and, 86, 88, 101
irrelevant questions asked by landlord, 17
and late rent policy, 87, 92
marital status, 98
mediation not appropriate for, 328
and national origin, 16, 89
online resources about, 88
personal characteristics, 98
protected categories, 87
and race, 88–89, 102, 103
and religion, 88
rent increases as, 73–75
sex (gender), 97, 126
sexual harassment, 97, 100–101
sexual orientation, 87, 98–99
state and local laws against, 86, 92, 97–99, 104
subletting and, 267
subtle techniques for, 86
and termination of tenancies, 257
uneven screening of applicants, 27
unmarried couples, 98–99

Discrimination, fighting back, 99–105
clout of tenants in, 86
complaints to a Fair Housing Agency, 100, 101, 103–104
exempt properties, 87
federal penalties, 99
future rentals affected by, 100
law covering situation, determination of, 87
lawsuits, filing, 100, 101, 104–105
lawyer for, and cost of, 101–102, 105
negotiating with the landlord, 101–102
results, potential, 99–100, 101, 104
settlement, potential, 101–102, 104
sexual harassment, 100–101
strategy, determination of, 99–100, 104
strength of case, determination of, 102–103
targets for lawsuit or complaint, 105
temporary restraining orders (TROs), 104
"testers" sent to apply with landlord, 103
Disputes with landlord
alternatives to getting a lawyer, 326
common reasons for, 326
See also Mediation; Negotiation; Small claims court
Distraint power, 41, 299
Distress power, 41, 299
District court. See Small claims court
Dog bites, 196
Dog walkers, 266
Domestic violence
antidiscrimination laws, 125
confidentiality in landlord disclosures of, 125
and early termination of tenancy, 125–126, 254, 259
evicting the aggressor, 125, 126–127
and locks, changing of, 125
police visit to house, 126, 127
resources on, 126
roommates and, 125–127
state law summarized, 378–382
temporary restraining orders and, 125, 126
and violence, threat of, 126
Drapes, 153
Drugs
former addiction to, and discriminatory refusal of applicants, 26, 96–97
and legal rejection of applicants, 26, 96
tenant dealing, from nice building, 238
tenant dealing, landlord liability for, 198, 238–240, 308

tenant using or dealing, evictions for, 308, 317, 324, 395–401

Duty of due care, 192

Duty to rerent, 245, 254, 268, 282, 408–409

E

Earthquake protection, and ownership of furnishings, 165

Electrical service
billing tenant for common-area usage, 41
outlets, legal number of, 153
repairs needed on, 153, 157, 193
tenant abuse of, 137

Electromagnetic fields (EMFs), as hazard, 229

Elevator security, 241

Email
separate account for advertising yourself on Craigslist, 11
vs. mailed communication with landlord, 116–117, 138, 139–140, 158

Emancipated minors, 37, 92–93

Emergencies
and access of landlord to unit, 47–48, 174–175, 181
and law enforcement entering unit, 180
repairs, and lead regulations, 212

EMFs (electromagnetic fields), as hazard, 229

Emotional impairments, 93

Emotional injury or suffering
invasion of privacy lawsuit against landlord for, 184
liability for, 195–196, 198–199

Emotional support animals, 94

Employer/employment. *See* Work

Entire agreement clause, 52–53

Environmental hazards, 203–230
overview, 203
bedbugs, 225–230
carbon monoxide, 219–221
electromagnetic fields (EMFs), 229
failure to repair, landlord liability for injuries caused by, 194
negligence of tenant and, 222
radon gas, 196, 217–219
strict liability for injuries caused by, 196
tenant making repairs and, 157
See also Asbestos; Lead-based paint; Mold; Personal injuries

Environmental Protection Agency (EPA)
and lead, 211, 217
and mold, 223, 224

and radon, 218

Equifax, 25

Escrow accounts
for rent payments under foreclosure, 273
for rent withholding, 142, 145
for restoration of modifications for disabled tenant, 95

Eviction lawsuits, 316–324
overview, 316
affirmative defense, 320
Answer to the Complaint, 319–320
appeals, 322
bankruptcy, effect on, 323–324
Complaint, 318–319
court choice for, 317–318
denials, 320
discovery process, 318, 320
dismissal of case before trial, 319
evidence gathering, 311–312
evidence, rules of, 318, 321, 322
fees and, 323
ignoring a Summons or Complaint, 319
the judgment, 321
lawyer or legal services for, 316, 338
loss of, and stopping or postponing an eviction, 321–323
notice of termination, checking for legality of, 311–312, 319
physical eviction by law enforcement, 298, 323
reasons to fight compared to moving out, 256, 312, 316
resources for, 316
retaliation by landlord, 312
sample Answer Raising Affirmative Defense, 320, 321
self-representation in (pro per), 320
service of process, 318–319
trial, 321
weather and, 322
witnesses, 312
See also Evictions

Evictions
and abandoned property, return of, 297, 298–299, 317
for access to unit by landlord, refusal of, 179
of all roommates for actions of one, 121
bankruptcy of tenant and, 323–324
and changes in terms of rental documents, 67–68
constructive, 148–150, 185

in credit report, 24, 256, 312, 313
for criminal activity (expedited evictions), 308, 317
and domestic violence victims, 125
elderly tenants protected from, 92
fighting. *See* Eviction lawsuits
foreclosure of property and, 272, 273
guest policies and, 39
for harm or threat of harm to other persons, 236–237
of hold-over tenants, 255
illegal self-help evictions, 182, 316–317, 410–412
"just cause" requirements, 35, 63, 272, 306
for late fees, unpaid, 69
lawsuits defending, and payment of attorney costs, 50–51
military personnel and restrictions on, 254
neighbors bringing proceeding for criminal activity, 239–240
owner move-in, 272
for "primary residence" provision, 37
rate of, checking out prospective rental for, 15
rejection based on, 26
relative move-ins, 35, 63
and rent withholding for repairs, 143, 144, 146
and rent withholding for security issues, 244
for repair "big stick" remedies, 141, 143
for security issues, 245
for short-term paying guests, 131
stated on rental application, 16
subleases and, 266, 267
and time, buying, 312
time for process to complete, 256, 312
unpaid rent following, deposit deduction for, 283
See also Eviction lawsuits; Rent control and evictions; Termination of tenancy by landlord
Evidence, rules of, 318, 321, 322
Exculpatory clauses, 46
Exotic pets, dangerous, 196
Expedited evictions, 308, 317
Experian, 25
Exterminator services, bedbugs and, 227–228

F

Fair Housing Acts (1968 and 1988), 86, 99, 342
Family
discrimination based on, 90–91, 102
eviction stopped on basis of hardship for, 321
Federal Communications Commission (FCC), 168, 171
Federal Debt Collection Practices Act (FDCPA), 311
Federal statutes and regulations, legal research and, 342–343

Federal Trade Commission (FTC), 26
Federally subsidized housing, 1, 60, 99, 272
Fees and costs
of attorney, for discrimination case, 101–102, 105
attorneys' fees paid by losing side in lawsuit, 50–51, 150, 256, 269, 296, 312, 316, 336, 339
bounced check charges, 70
for credit-checks, 25
for eviction, 323
expenses and court costs, lawyers' fees and, 105, 340
finder's fees, 10, 27, 29
of finding a new tenant, and breaking a lease, 261, 268–270
for inspections, 180
late rent fees, 40, 68–70, 305
of lead testing, 213
for mediation, 328
of mold testing, 224
for real estate broker, 12
satellite dishes and other antennas, 169, 170, 171
termination fees, 40, 269
up-front fees, nonrefundable, 82, 279
See also Deposits
Finder's fees, 10, 27, 29
Finding a rental, 4–30
advertising yourself to landlords, 11
"Apartment Wanted" signs, 10
credit report, checking on, 4
"good tenant" behavior and, 11, 13, 54
if new in town, 13
landlord and manager, checking out, 14–15
neighbors and other tenants, checking out, 15–16
online resources, 9, 10–12, 13
personal contacts and, 9
pounding the pavement, 10, 13
priorities for, 4–8, 13
property management companies, 12
real estate brokers, 12, 13
sample apartment-hunting note, 9
sample Rental Priorities Worksheet, 8
scams, avoiding, 10, 11, 25
steps to follow, 4–5
time and financial constraints as influences, 5, 9
university, alumni, and corporate housing offices, 12–13
viewing prospective rentals, 5, 13–14
waiting lists, 12
See also Craigslist; Rental applications
Fire extinguishers, 114
Fire insurance. *See* Renter's insurance

Fixtures
    defined, 164–165
    and deposit, return of, 281
    ownership of, 43, 164–167, 281, 301
    receipts for, saving, 167
    sample Agreement Regarding Tenant
      Improvements to Rental Unit, 166
FlipKey. *See* Short-term paying guests
"For sale" or "for rent" signs on property, 177
Foreclosures on rentals
    cash payouts offered for swift departure, 272
    evictions and, 272, 273
    as indication of landlord undesirability, 15
    paying the rent, before and after, 272–273
    repairs and maintenance and, 273–274
Forms
    download link, 414
    editing of, 414
    list of available at Nolo.com, 414
Fraud
    credit-check fees, 25
    finder's fees charged by landlord, 27, 29
Friends
    inspection after move-out, as witness to, 285
    inspection before move-in, as witness to, 108
    opinion of, on fighting discrimination, 100
    sharing sexual harassment experiences with, 101
Furnished rentals
    deposits for, 78
    inspection prior to move-in, 113–114
    as rental priority, 7
Furnishings
    bedbugs and, 226, 228
    renting, 7
    See also Property of tenant

G

Gambling on premises, 308
Garbage and recycling
    information about, in written rental documents, 116
    as legal responsibility of tenant, 137
    as nuisance, 198
Gender, discrimination based on (sex discrimination), 97
Gender identity, discrimination based on, 98–99
Grace period for late rent, 40, 65, 305
Guarantors. *See* Cosigners
Guests
    destruction of premises by, 83, 152, 153

injured on landlord's property, 45, 188, 193, 196, 197
    policies for, in written rental documents, 39
    roommate policy on, 123, 131
    termination of tenancy for violations of policy on, 309
    undue limitations on, as privacy invasion, 182
    See also Short-term paying guests

H

Habitable condition of premises
    complaints about, and retaliation by landlord, 73–75, 141, 322
    court-imposed rules, 136–137
    eviction defense based on, 321
    exemptions for older buildings, 135
    foreclosure of property and, 273–274
    and housing code violations, 153
    injuries caused by lack of, liability for, 194–195
    inspection before move-in, 42, 108–114
    justifying breaking of lease, 259
    and lead hazards, 215, 216–217
    local ordinances, 135–136
    and mold, 222–223
    moving out as remedy for, 148–150
    photographing the unit, 114
    and quiet enjoyment, covenant of, 135
    and radon exposure, 219
    requirements, list of, 134
    as right (implied warranty of habitability), 134–137
    sample Landlord-Tenant Checklist, 109–112
    slumlords and rent control and, 63
    state housing laws, 136
    waiver or disclaimer of right to, clause for, 42, 54–55, 134
    in written rental documents, 42, 54–55
    See also Quiet enjoyment, tenant's right to; Repairs and maintenance, remedies when landlord refuses to make
Handrail maintenance, 195
Hawaiian Humane Society, 47
Health inspectors
    access to premises, 179–180
    bedbugs and, 230
    complaint for lead exposure, 216
    intervention when property is in foreclosure, 274
    random inspections by, 179–180
    and repair-and-deduct, 147
    report of, and rent withholding, 322
    See also Inspection of premises

Health problems, and justifiable breaking of lease, 229, 259
  See also Medical care
Heat
  and carbon monoxide production, 219, 221
  habitability of unit requiring functional, 134, 145
  and housing codes, 153
  inspection by tenant prior to move-in, 114–115
  lack of, and rent abatement, 271
  repairs to, as major, 152
  and temporary housing, landlord liability for, 148
Hidden defects
  disclosure laws, 51
  strict liability for, 196–197
Historical integrity of building, and satellite dish installations, 170
Hold harmless clauses, 46
Hold-over tenants, 48, 255, 256
Holding deposits
  overview, 29–30
  be prepared to write a check, 13
  refundability of, 29
  sample Receipt and Holding Deposit Agreement, 28
Home office or business
  liability insurance for, 38
  as rental priority, 6, 7
  renter's insurance and, 44
  written leases and rental agreements and, 37–38
HomeAway. *See* Short-term paying guests
Housekeeping. *See* Cleaning
Housesitters, 266
Housing and Urban Development (HUD), U.S. Department of
  antidiscrimination rules for housing programs of, 99
  complaints for discrimination, 86, 103–104
  contact information, 103
  and immigration status, questions about, 89
  and occupancy standards, 91
  as resource, 331
  verification of disabled status, 95
Housing codes (building codes), 135–136, 153, 193, 233
  copy of, 136, 233
Housing. *See* Neighborhood; Relocation assistance; Rental units; Temporary housing, reimbursement for
Housing, subsidized, 1, 60, 99, 272
HUD. *See* Housing and Urban Development
Humane Society of the U.S., 47

I
Identity theft, and rental application disposal, 24
Illegal clauses, generally, 54–55
Immigration status, landlord questioning, 17, 88–89
Income as tenant selection criterion
  cosigners and, 57
  disabled applicants and, 57
  discrimination and, 27, 99, 103
  public assistance as source of income, 99
  rejection based on, 26
  rental application and, 17
  self-employment and, 17
  verification of, 23
Income, compensatory damages for lost, 198
Individual Taxpayer Identification Number, 17
Injuries. *See* Personal injuries
Insect growth regulators (IGR), 227
Inspection of premises
  for asbestos, 203, 205
  for bedbugs, 226, 230
  fees for, 180
  by health, safety, or building inspectors, 179–180
  for lead, 208, 209, 211, 212, 213, 216
  periodic, by landlord, 176
  prior to move-in, by tenant and landlord, 42, 108–114
  resources for, 113
  See also Building inspectors; Health inspectors; Landlord-Tenant Checklist
Insurance. *See* Liability insurance; Renters' insurance
Interest
  on account for restoration of accessibility modifications, 95
  on deposits, 40, 51, 64, 82
Internet service providers (ISPs), 168
iPhone apps, 11

J
Joint and several liability of tenants, 37, 120, 121
Justice of the Peace. *See* Small claims court

L
Landlord-Tenant Checklist
  mold problems noted on, 223
  and repairs needed later, 155
  and return of deposit, 108, 185, 286, 288, 294
  sample, 109–112, 286
  for subletting, 267

use of, during inspection prior to move-in, 108–109

what to look for, 113

and written rental documents clause for condition of unit, 42

Landlord-tenant courts, 317–318

Landlords

checking out, 14–15

contact information for, obtaining, 115

finder's fees charged by, 27, 29

"good tenant" behavior for, 11, 13, 54

identification of, in rental document, 37

and key, legal right to, 175, 246

on-site, rental priorities and, 7

references from previous, 17, 22–23, 26

reluctance to make repairs as bad sign, 114–115

visiting current rental of applicant, 23

willing to exceed occupancy limits (to break the law), 92

See also Access to property by landlord; Disclosures by landlord; Discrimination; Lawsuits; Mediation; Negotiation with the landlord; Oral agreements; Rental applications; Repairs and maintenance, remedies when landlord refuses to make; Retaliation by landlord; Termination of tenancy by landlord

Last month's rent

security deposit converted to, 288, 290

separate deposit for, 80–81

withholding rent without landlord's approval, 290

Late fees, 40, 68–70, 305

Laundry accommodations for disabled tenants, 94

Law enforcement

access to unit, 180

complaints about security to, 243–244

domestic violence and visits to house, 126, 127

physical evictions by, 298, 323

privacy violations and calls for help to, 185

Law libraries, 341, 342, 343, 345

Law review articles, 345

Lawsuits

attorney's fees and court costs paid by losing side in, 50–51, 150, 256, 269, 296, 312, 316, 336, 339

for bedbugs, 228, 230

for condominium conversions, 270

in credit report, 24

for deposit, failure to return, 277, 285, 287, 293–296

for discrimination, 100, 101, 102–103, 104–105

frivolous, 50

for lead remediation, 216, 217

lease breaking, landlord suing tenant for, 268–270

lease breaking, tenant suing landlord following, 282

mediation clause covering rental document disputes, 52

for mold exposure, 223, 224, 225

for "not ready" apartment, 48

for privacy violations by landlord, 181, 184–185

for repairs needed, 140, 150, 159–161

and satellite dishes, 171–172

for security issues, 153, 157, 245

for self-help evictions, 317

for temporary housing costs during asbestos removal, 206–207

for threat of violence, landlord ignoring, 126

See also Courts; Damages; Eviction lawsuits; Personal injuries; Small claims court

Lawyers

for discrimination cases, 101–102, 105

for eviction lawsuit, 316

finding a good lawyer, 336–338

for foreclosure of rental, 272

help from, situations needing, 336

for invasion of privacy lawsuit, 185

for lease-options, 35, 336

legal aid, 105, 337

for long-term leases, 36, 336

malpractice and, 341

Nolo.com directory of, 337

nonlawyers, help from, 338

notice of termination sent by, 311

personal injuries and need for, 188

problems with, resolving, 340–341

rent control and, 61

rights of client, 340

for small claims court, 296, 329

See also Lawyers' fees; Legal research

Lawyers' fees

billing practices, 339

contingency fee basis, 105, 336, 339

expenses and court costs, 105, 340

flat fee basis, 339

hourly fee basis, 339

lowered rate for paralegal and secretarial services, 338

mediation for disputes over, 341

paid by losing side in lawsuits, 50–51, 150, 256, 269, 296, 312, 316, 336, 339

review the bill, 340

saving on, 339–340

written agreement on, 339

Lawyers.com, 337

Lead-based paint and lead hazards

children and, 208, 211, 213, 215

complain to inspectors, 216

and delegation of repairs/maintenance to tenants, 157

disclosure form, 210

disclosures required, 51, 208–211, 212–213

exempt properties from federal laws, 211

failure to repair, liability for, 194

federal laws, 208–211, 343

health hazards of, 208

inspections for, 208, 209, 211, 212, 213, 216

lawsuit against landlord about, 216, 217

moving out if necessary, 216–217

notice required by landlord or contractor, 212

notify landlord of problem, 215–216

painting forbidden by lease, and liability for, 194

penalties for nondisclosure, 209, 213

persuading landlord to act, 215–216

places to find lead in the home, 213–214

poisoning, process of, 208

renovations and, 211–212, 216–217

resources on, 217

sample Letter Regarding Lead Test Results, 216

self-help to deal with, 214–215

state laws, 213, 216

strict liability for injuries by, 196

testing, 208, 213, 215, 216

Lead pipes, 214

Lead-Safe Certified Guide to Renovate Right, The (EPA), 211

Lead solder, 214

Lease-option-to-buy, 7, 35, 336

Leases

amendments to, 248, 249

attorney for, 36

bankruptcy of landlord and, 271–272

bankruptcy of tenant and, 323

changes to rules and regulations and, 49

compared to rental agreements, 33–35

condominium conversions and, 270

as contract, 248

conversion to month-to-month rental agreement, 34, 36, 255–256

deposit increases and, 80

deposit limits and, 78

as fixed-term, 34, 39

holding over (failing to leave), 39, 255, 256

landlord goes out of business, 271

landlord preference for, 34

lawyer for signing long-term, 36, 336

lead-paint disclosures and, 208

letter of understanding following negotiation to stay, 259

natural-disaster destruction and, 42

new, following negotiation to stay, 259

notice to change terms of, 67

with option to buy, 7, 35, 336

oral, 34, 36, 65, 120, 255

priority of having, as priority in finding a rental, 6

rent abatement requests and, 159, 216

rent control compared to, 35

rent increases built into, 34, 39

roommate departures and, 127, 129

sale of leased property, 35, 271–272

sample Amendment to Lease, 249

tenant preference for, 34–35

See also Assignment of leases; Leases, expiration of; Leases, tenant breaking; Leases, tenant options for ending early; Subletting; Termination of tenancy by landlord, for nonpayment of rent or violation of rental document; Written leases and rental agreements, provisions of

Leases, expiration of

overview, 34, 254–256

and access of landlord to show the unit, 176–177

conversion to month-to-month tenancy, 34, 36, 255–256

discrimination and refusal to renew, 257

fighting, vs. moving on, 256

hold-over tenants, 48, 255, 256

notice required from landlord, 255

notify landlord of your intent, 255

renewal denied, and age discrimination, 92

renewal of, automatic, 256

renewal of, landlord refuses, 256, 257

renewal of, under rent control, 63, 255

retaliation and refusal to renew, 257

staying on, and paying rent without a new lease, 255–256

staying on, negotiation after landlord terminates, 258–259

Leases, tenant breaking

overview, 267–268

asbestos exposures and, 207

bedbug infestation history and, 229

cost of finding a new tenant, 261, 268–270

defined as term, 259

domestic violence and early termination rights, 125–126, 259

and duty of landlord to rerent, 245, 254, 261, 268, 282, 408–409

and EMF exposure, 229

and facilitation of quick rerental, 129

financial obligations resulting from, 35

financial penalties for (termination fee, liquidated damages), 40, 269

and invasions of privacy by landlord, 185

justified legal reasons for, 259

lawsuit against landlord by tenant, 282

lawsuit against tenant by landlord, 268–270

military service and early termination rights, 34, 254, 259

moving out as remedy for repairs unmade, 148

and quiet enjoyment, violation of, 135, 237

roommate leaving, 127, 129

for security issues, 244–245, 246

for sexual harassment, 101, 196

for threat of violence from another tenant, 237

unpaid rent, deposit deductions for, 268, 282–283

See also Leases, tenant options for ending early

Leases, tenant options for ending early
overview, 259–260

assignment of lease, 262–263, 264

buyout of lease, 260, 261

cancellation of lease by landlord, 260–261, 262

employer bearing costs of, 260

providing a new tenant, 261, 269

sample Buyout Agreement Between Landlord and Tenant, 261

sample Consent to Assignment of Lease, 264

sample Landlord-Tenant Agreement to Terminate Lease, 262

subletting, 263, 265–267

See also Leases, tenant breaking

Legal aid, 105, 331, 337

Legal papers, person authorized to receive, 51

Legal research, 341–345
abbreviations in case citations, 344

annotated code sets, 342

case citations, 344–345

court decisions, 343–345

federal statutes and regulations, 342–343

law libraries, 341, 342, 343, 345

law review articles, 345

lawyer help with, 336

local ordinances, 342

online free, 341

online paid services, 345

overlapping laws, 341

resources for, 341

security deposit information, 79

state attorney general's offices or consumer protection agencies, 339

state statutes, 342

up-to-date laws, 342

Legal typing services, 338

Letters of understanding
email vs. postal mail or delivery service of, 116–117

for items not included in written agreement, 53

for late rent, 69–70, 71

for negotiation to stay after landlord terminates tenancy, 259

for oral lease or rental agreement, 36

for oral promises, 53

for promises by landlord upon moving in, 42, 52, 53, 154

rent increase, formalizing of, 73

rent increase, response to, 76

repairs requested, 140

return receipt requested for, 36, 71

for short-term paying guests, 131

See also Oral agreements; Written leases and rental agreements

Lexis, 345

Liability insurance
Apartment Owners Limited Building Policy, 45

for home businesses, 38

and injuries on landlord's property, 190

of landlord, as not covering rental unit, 43

and security, 242–243

See also Renter's insurance

Liability of landlord for injuries. *See* Personal injuries

Liens, automatic, 299

Liquidated damages, 40, 256

Local ordinances
condominium conversions, 270

legal research and, 342

See also Rent control; Zoning laws

Location. *See* Neighborhood

Locks and keys
changing between tenants, 153

domestic violence and change of, 125

landlord's legal right to a key, 175, 246

lock box on property for sale, 177

roommate disputes and changing of locks, 125

tenant adding locks or burglar alarm, 43, 175, 246
tenant changing, 246
tenant installing code-required, 246
tenant responsibility for maintaining, 138
type of, 241
See also Security

M

Maintenance by tenants. *See* Repairs and
 maintenance
Managers. *See* Property managers
Marijuana smoking, 49
Marital status, discrimination based on, 98
Marriage, adult legal status via, 37, 92–93
Martindale.com, 337
Mediation
 overview, 326
 arbitration distinguished from, 327
 clause for, 52
 community programs for, 310, 328
 for cotenants (roommates), 125, 327
 for deposit refunds, 292–293
 for discrimination, 101
 fee for, splitting with landlord, 328
 finding a mediator, 328
 of lawyer fees, 341
 for minor repair requests, 159
 for privacy invasions by landlord, 184
 process of, 328
 reasons for seeking, 327
 resource for, 327
 for security issues, 243
 to stay following landlord termination of tenancy,
  258
 for termination of tenancy for unpaid rent or
  violations of rental document, 310
Medical care
 for bedbugs, 228
 damages to pay for, 198
 health problems and breaking a lease, 229, 259
 for injuries on landlord's property, 188–189
 for mold toxicity, 225
Megan's Law, 16
Mental or emotional impairments, 93
Methamphetamine lab, landlord disclosure of prior, 51
Military service
 adult legal status via, 37, 92–93
 early termination rights due to, 34, 254, 259
 restrictions on eviction for nonpayment of rent, 254

Miniblinds, lead content in, 214
Minor repairs. *See* Repairs and maintenance, minor
Minors, considered as adults, 37, 92–93
Mold
 overview, 221
 clean up of, 224
 health hazards of, 221, 224
 landlord liability for, 222–223
 laws covering, 222
 lawsuit for, 223, 224, 225
 prevention of, 223–224, 225
 renters' insurance for damage from, 225
 resources about, 224
 sources of, 137, 221–222
 tenant negligence and, 222
 testing for toxicity, 224–225
Month-to-month rentals. *See* Rental agreements
 (month-to-month)
Motor vehicles
 abandoned by tenant, 301
 loans for, 24
Move-in date, as rental priority, 6
Moving out as remedy
 asbestos exposure, 206–207
 bedbug extermination, 227
 EMF exposure, 229
 invasions of privacy, 185
 lead exposure, 216–217
 radon exposure, 219
 repairs, refusal of landlord to make, 148–150
 security issues, 237, 244–245, 246
 termination notice received, 312–313
 threat of harm from another tenant, 237
 uninhabitable condition of unit, 148
Multiunit buildings
 bedbugs and, 226–228, 230
 and cable TV access, 168
 foreclosure and, 273
 involving other tenants in security issues, 240, 243
 lawsuits and, multitenant, 330
 lead inspections in, 209
 and limits on responsibilities of tenants in, 156
 owner-occupied, 62, 87
 and rules governing tenancy, 49
 and satellite dish installations, 170–171
 security issues and, 240, 243
 See also Neighbors within building; Tenants'
  groups, formation of

N

National Housing Law Project, 272
National origin, discrimination based on, 17, 89
National Register of Historic Places, 170
Natural disasters
destruction caused by, 42, 149
earthquake-proofing and fixture ownership, 165
renter's insurance coverage for, 45
Natural gas leaks, 219
Needs. *See* Rental priorities
Negligence
comparative, 197
of landlord, illegal clauses regarding, 55
and liability for injuries on landlord's property, 191–193, 194–195
negligence per se, 193
of tenant, and renter's insurance, 44, 45
Negotiation with the landlord
action-oriented vs. principle-oriented, 326
for breaking a lease, costs associated with, 268
on deposits, 79
for discrimination, 101–102
for discrimination, conciliation with fair housing agency, 103
late rent and late fees, 69, 70–71
for pets, allowing, 47
pointers for success in, 326–327
sample Letter Asking Landlord to Accept Late Rent, 71
for short-term paying guests, 131
to stay in unit, following termination of tenancy by landlord, 258–259
for termination of tenancy for nonpayment of rent or other violations, 308–310
and types of lease clauses, 54–55
when to negotiate, 53–54, 79
written agreement resulting from, 56, 327
See also Mediation; Small claims court
Neighborhood
exploring, as part of viewing rental, 14
as factor in security, 241, 246
as rental priority, 6
Neighbors
asking about the landlord and building, 14–15
complaints to housing code enforcement, 179–180
disgruntled, and guest policies, 39
lawsuits by, for criminal activity on premises, 239–240, 243

and short-term unapproved guests, 39, 131
See also Neighbors within building
Neighbors within building
checking out, 15–16
and housesitters, alerting to, 266
as rental priority, 7
and screening by landlord, 17
turnover of, 15
See also Tenants' groups, formation of
New York Roommate Law, 132
Newspapers
classified ads, 10
and discrimination cases, 105
Noise
checking on, at viewing of unit, 14–15
as rental priority, 7
written rental documents and, 46–47
See also Quiet enjoyment, tenant's right to
Nolo.com Lawyer Directory, 337
Nonsmoking/smoke-free rentals, 49
Normal wear and tear. *See* Ordinary wear and tear
Notice
email vs. postal mail for, 116–117
of termination, sent by lawyer who collects rent debts, 311
See also Notice by landlords; Notice by tenant
Notice by landlords
for abandoned property, 299
for access to unit, 47–48, 175, 177–179
to change terms of rental documents, 33, 67, 248
complaint and repair procedures, 41
of condominium conversion, 270
and credit reports, 24, 27
of deductions from deposit, 276
deposit location and rate of interest, 82
effective date of, 250–251
of eviction, checking for legality of, 311–312, 316
for expiration of lease, 256
for foreclosure-based termination of tenancy, 272
for lead hazards during renovations, 212
to raise rent, 33, 36, 64, 71–73
rent control requirements, 64
to terminate rental agreement, 250–251
Notice by tenant
asbestos threat, 205–206
bedbugs, 226
dangerous conditions (threat of crime), 244
effective date of, 251
email vs. postal mail to deliver, 116–117

extended absences, 37, 48, 176
fear of violence from another tenant, 236
of late rent, 70
oral rental agreements, changes to, 36, 251
privacy invasions by landlord, 177
of rent withholding, 143
of repair and deduct, 147, 322
repair requests, 141
and roommate departures, 127, 128
to terminate rental agreement, 251–252, 282
text message delivery of, 116, 117
See also Letters of understanding
Nuisance
civil vs. criminal nuisance laws, 238
damages awarded for, 198
defined, 135–136, 238, 307
and "just cause" evictions, 63

O

Occupancy limits
landlord willing to exceed the maximum, 92
legal vs. illegal limits, 38–39, 90–91
New York Roommate Law and, 132
priorities for finding a rental and, 6
and rejection of application, 27
roommates and, 129, 132
1-4 Family Rider (Assignment of Rents), 273, 274
Online publishers, discrimination and, 105
Online resources
and ads, misleading statements in, 11
Americans with Disabilities Act (ADA), 38
asbestos information, 207
bedbug laws, 229
bedbugs, 225
carbon monoxide, 221
classified ads, 10
computerized research services, 345
consumer protection agencies, state, 70, 88
credit report, annual free copy of, 25
credit report errors, 25
discrimination complaints, 103
discrimination information, 88
electromagnetic fields (EMFs), 229
email verification of receipt, 117
fair housing agencies, state, 103
fair housing agency, federal (HUD), 103
finding a rental, 9, 10–12, 13
foreclosure of rental, 272
forms, download link, 414

forms for leases and rental agreements, 35
forms, list of available on Nolo.com, 414
Google searches on landlord or manager, 15
housing codes, copy of, 233
HUD website, 339
illegal immigrants unable to rent, ordinances, 89
immigration status, legal verification of, 89
lawyer directories, 337
lead hazards and regulation, 212, 217
local ordinances, 342
mediators, 328
mold, 224
national apartment listings, 10–11
occupancy standards, 91
OSHA, 207
pet-friendly rentals, 12
pet résumés, 22
radon information, 218
renter's insurance, 44
reviews of rental properties and managers, 15
roommates, finding, 30
satellite dishes and antennas, 168, 170
sex offender databases (Megan's Law), 16
sexual orientation discrimination, 99
social media, finding a rental with, 9
state and local governments, finding online, 343
state laws under consideration, 229
state statutes, 342
tenants' associations and groups, 331
updates for book, 2
U.S. Code, 343
See also Craigslist
Oral agreements
for access to rental unit by landlord, 178
cotenants and, 120
FCC advice for satellite dishes and antennas, 171
joint and several liability and, 120
for late rent, 71
leases, 34, 36, 65, 120, 255
letters of understanding as locking in, 36, 53, 73
as notice of rent increase, 72, 73
and personal checks accepted for rent payment, 668
for reinstatement of tenancy, 253
and rent payment period, 36
rental agreements, 34, 36, 120
for repairs and maintenance, 140, 218
and returned check fees, 70
as roommate agreements, 122, 125
for security issues, 235, 242

for upper rent threshold, 73

See also Letters of understanding

Ordinary wear and tear

and deposit, return of, 277, 279–280, 313

guest policy and, 39

as landlord's responsibility, 296, 307

not required to be repaired during tenancy, 152

rent control ordinance and definition of, 280–281

and roommate policy, 130

vs. damage, 83, 137, 280–281

vs. waste, 307

See also Landlord-Tenant Checklist

Original tenant, defined, 120

OSHA (Occupational Safety and Health Administration), 207

and asbestos, 203–204, 206

P

Pain and suffering, damages for, 198

Paint and painting

asbestos exposure and preparation for, 204, 205

and cleaning plans shared with landlord, 284

as cosmetic issue (no landlord duty to repaint), 153

as habitability issue, 153, 217–218

handling painted surfaces with lead, 214

home testing for lead content, 213–214

need for, and return of deposit, 281, 296

repainting, responsibility for expense of, 280, 281, 296

sample Agreement Regarding Repairs, 115

See also Lead-based paint and lead hazards

Paralegals, independent, 338

Parking, 7, 93

Pay or Quit notice. *See* Pay Rent or Quit notice

Pay Rent or Quit notice

chronically late payers and, 306

chronically late rent and, 306

defined, 304

foreclosure of rental property and, 273

grace periods and, 305

partial rent payment following, 306

signed by lawyers who regularly collect rent debts, 311

as "writing you up," 306

See also Eviction lawsuits; Termination of tenancy by landlord

Personal checks

bounced check charges, 70

as rent payment, 66–67, 68, 70

Personal injuries, 188–199

overview, 188

assault, 196

assumption of risk and, 197

comparative negligence, 197

dog bites and other animal attacks, 196

emotional or psychological, 195–196, 198–199

evaluation of your case, 191–197

evidence, preserving, 189

examples of injuries from landlord negligence, 193

fault of tenant and, 197–198, 223

guests, injured, 188, 193, 196, 197

habitability of premises as cause of, 194–195

health or safety law violations causing, 193–194

intentional harm by landlord, 195–196

lawsuit against landlord for, 150, 188

liability of landlord, 191–197

liability without fault (strict liability) of landlord, 196–197

mediation and, 191

medical attention, immediate, 188–189

monetary compensation (damages), 195–196, 198–199

multiple reasons why landlord liable for, 191, 194, 195

negligence (carelessness) of landlord causing, 191–193, 194–195

negligence per se, 193

negotiation and, 191

notify landlord and insurance carrier, 190

nuisances, legal (no physical injury), 198

privacy, repeated invasions of, 196

recklessness of landlord causing, 195, 199

repairs not made, as cause of, 194

resources for, 191

sample Letter to Landlord Regarding Tenant Injury, 190

severe, *see* lawyer right away for, 188

sexual harassment, 196

statute of limitations on filing lawsuits, 191

third parties involved in, 190

witnesses, contacting, 189–190

write everything down, 189

See also Environmental hazards

Petitions

retaliation by landlord for, 322

sample Petition to the Landlord, 332

tenants' group developing, 330–333

Pets
   accommodation of housing and, 94
   dangerous and dangerous exotic, 196
   deposit for, 40, 47, 78, 81
   dog and other animal bites, 196
   dog walkers, 266
   housesitters, 266
   humane society programs to increase acceptance
      of, 47
   jointly and severally liable tenants and, 37
   landlord approval/meeting of, 22
   negotiating with landlord to allow, 47
   online resources for rentals allowing, 12
   references and résumés for, 22
   as rental priority, 6
   resources for rentals allowing, 10
   service/comfort/emotional support animals, 47, 93, 94
   termination of tenancy for, 306
   in written rental documents, 47
Photographing rental unit, 114, 285, 286, 294
   eviction defense and, 322
Plumbing
   checking on, at viewing of unit, 14
   fixtures, tenant care of, 137
   lead pipes, 214
   lead solder, 214
   and mold risk, 137, 222, 223
Police. *See* Law enforcement
Preliminary injunctions, 104
"Primary residence" requirement, 37
Priorities. *See* Rental priorities
Privacy of tenant, 174–185
   overview, 174
   actions to take about invasions of, 182–185
   and daytime phone number for tenant, 178
   guests unduly restricted, 182
   information about you given to strangers, 181
   lawsuit for violations of, 181, 184–185
   mediation with landlord, 184
   moving out as remedy for violations of, 185, 259
   police, calling for help for violations of, 185
   rent abatement for invasion of, 185
   repeated invasions of, as intentional injury with
      liability, 196
   sample Letter When Landlord Violates Privacy
      (Friendly Approach), 183
   sample Letter When Landlord Violates Privacy
      (Get-Tough Approach), 184
   self-help evictions as illegal, 182
   sexual harassment or assault, 182
   spying by landlord, 182
   talking with the landlord, 183
   at work, landlord contact at, 181
   write a tough letter, 183–184
   See also Access to property by landlord; Access to
      property by others
Property managers and property management
   companies
   discrimination lawsuits targeting, 105
   finder's fees charged by, 27
   finding, 12
   Google searches on, 15
   and injuries on landlord's property, 190
   on-site, rental priorities and, 7
   online reviews of, 15
Property of landlord, damage to
   by criminals, 138, 153
   deposit refunds, and normal wear and tear vs.,
      279–280
   eviction for, and bankruptcy of tenant, 324
   by guests, 83, 152, 153
   renters' insurance covering, 225
   responsibility of tenant for, 137, 307–308
   termination of tenancy for, 307–308
   in written rental documents, 46–47
   See also Deposits, deductions from
Property of tenant
   bedbugs and, 227, 228
   landlord taking (distress and distraint), 41, 299
   removal of, and return of deposit, 285
   suing landlord for damage to, 150
   See also Abandoned property of tenant, retrieval of
Protect your Family From Lead in Your Home (EPA),
   209
Protecting Tenants at Foreclosure Act (expired 2014),
   272
Public assistance recipients
   discrimination against, 99
   rent due date for, 65
   subsidized housing, 1, 60, 99, 272
Public libraries, legal research in, 341, 345
Public transit, as rental priority, 6
Punitive damages
   for discrimination, 99, 102, 104
   for injuries on landlord's property, 195–196, 199
   for security deposit, landlord failing to return, 276,
      287, 293
Purchase potential (lease-option), 7, 35

Q

Quiet, as rental priority, 7
Quiet enjoyment, tenant's right to
  defined, 47
  and habitability of premises, 135
  nuisance of tenant preventing others,' 307
  and privacy invasions by landlord, 184, 185
  and sexual harassment by landlord or agents, 101
  and threat of violence by another tenant, 237
  whether in written rental document or not, 47

R

Race, discrimination based on, 88–89, 102, 103
Radio antennas, 169
Radon gas, 196, 217–219
Real estate brokers/agents, 12, 13, 60, 177, 178
Recordkeeping by tenant, 116, 139–140
Recycling pickup, 116
References
  alerting to expect a call, 23
  character, 23
  credit report issues and need for, 26
  employer, 17, 23
  landlord (previous), 17, 22–23, 26
  for pets, 22
  sample Character Reference, 23
  written, bringing to rental viewing, 22
  written, obtaining prior to application, 23
Rejection of applicants, 24, 26–27, 96
Religion, discrimination and, 88
Religious organizations, exempt from fair housing laws, 87
Relocation assistance for condominium conversions, 270
Rent, 60–76
  ability to pay, and primary residence condition, 37
  accommodations for disabled tenants, 92, 94
  bimonthly payments, 64–65, 72, 248
  changes to where and how rent is due, 67–68
  due date, 40, 64–65
  due date falls on weekend or holiday, 65
  due date for oral leases, 65
  early payment discounts, 69
  fairness of, 60–61
  higher rent charged, based on credit history, 24, 27
  higher rent offered in exchange for lower deposit, 79
  how payment made (form of payment), 66–68
  low, 61
  maximum ability to pay, 6

  maximum percentage of income, recommended, 6
  partial, payment of, 70–71, 306, 309
  prepayment of several month's worth, 78
  reduction in, for shorter notice to show unit, 177
  reduction of (abatement) for defective rental unit, 145–146, 150, 159–160, 216, 271
  reduction of, for doing repairs and maintenance, 156
  roommates and. *See* Under Roommates
  state statutes list, 349–350
  on time, as most important thing, 60
  where to be paid, 40, 66
  withholding, for security issues, 244
  withholding, when landlord refuses to make repairs, 141, 142–146, 147, 230, 257–258, 322, 331, 333
  in written rental documents, 40
  See also Last month's rent; Rent control; Rent increases; Rent, late; Rent, unpaid
Rent control
  overview, 61–62
  compared to lease, 35
  condominium conversions and, 64, 270
  cost increases to landlord and, 62
  and deposits, interest on, 64
  disclosures required by, 51
  exemptions, 62
  finder's fees and, 29
  hold-over tenant rent increase clause and, 256
  housesitters as subtenants and, 266
  late rent, eviction for, 306
  and lawyer, finding, 337
  lease expirations/renewals and, 63, 255
  leases and rental agreements under, 36
  legal research and, 342
  liability insurance bought by landlord and, 45
  limits on rent, 62–63
  master tenant and, 122
  "normal wear and tear" vs. "damage" and, 280–281
  notice requirements, special, 64
  properties subject to, 62
  property withdrawn from rental market and, 271
  relative move-ins, 35, 63, 92
  rent control board, 61, 62
  rent increases and, 39, 62–63, 73, 130, 260
  rent increases, retaliatory, 74
  rent withholding for repairs and, 143
  resources about, 61
  slumlords under, 63
  state law restricting, 61

states and cities with, 61
subletting and, 266, 267
tenants' groups and, 331
vacancy control statutes, 62–63
vacancy decontrol statutes, 62
See also Rent control and evictions
Rent control and evictions
elderly tenants protected from, 92
just cause for, 35, 63, 272, 306
landlord going out of business, 64
notice requirements for, 64
of roommates, master tenant and, 122
Rent increases
overview, 71
amount of, 73
of hold-over tenants, 256
improper notice for, 72–73
inspection fees as cause of, 180
lease clause allowing during term of lease, 34, 39
lease expiration and, 72
as motivation for cancellation of lease by landlord, 260
notice period too short, prorated share of increase, 72
oral notice, 72, 73
policy of landlord on, 72–73
rent control and, 39, 62–63, 64, 73, 74, 260
and rental agreement (month-to-month) notice, 72–73
as retaliation or discrimination, 73–75
for roommates, additional, 130
sample Letter Formalizing a Rent Increase, 73
sample Letter in Response to Rent Increase, 76
talking the landlord out of, 75–76
written notice required for, 33, 72
Rent, late
in credit report, 24
discrimination and, 87, 92
fees for, 40, 68–70, 305
grace periods for, 40, 65, 305
landlord impatience with, 65, 306
negotiation with landlord for, 69, 70–71
Rent, unpaid
abandoned property and, 298–299
accruing after loss in eviction lawsuit, 283
and bankruptcy by tenant, 323, 324
and buying time after termination notice, 312
deposits used to cover, 83, 281–283, 288, 290
inadequate notice by tenant creating, 282

and leases, breaking, 282–283
and retaliation as factor, 312
by roommate, 120–121
for staying on after announced departure date, 282
See also Termination of tenancy by landlord, for nonpayment of rent or violation of rental document
Rental agreements (month-to-month)
and adversarial strategies for minor repairs, caution about, 158
amendment of, 248–250
changes to, 248–250
changes to rules and regulations and, 49
compared to leases, 33–35
and condominium conversions, 270
as contract, 248
and deposit increases, 73, 80–81
and deposit limits, 78
deposit return, and unpaid rent, 281–282
landlord preference for, 33–34
lead-paint disclosures, 208–209
lease converting to, 255–256
mailing notice, 251
as month-to-month/periodic, 33–34, 39
new agreement, for changes, 250
notice, effective date of, 250–251
notice to change terms of, 33, 67, 248
notice to change terms of oral agreements, 36
notice to raise rent, 33, 36, 71–73
oral, 34, 36, 120
priority of, as priority in finding a rental, 6
sample Amendment to a Rental Agreement, 249
tenant preference for, 34
See also Leases; Rent; Rental agreements (month-to-month), termination of; Written leases and rental agreements, provisions of
Rental agreements (month-to-month), termination of
discrimination by landlord, 257
extending tenancy for a few days, 253, 282
new agreement, after negotiation to stay, 259
new agreement, after reinstatement, 253
notice by landlord, 250–251
notice by tenant, 246, 251–252, 282
prorated rent for, 251, 253
rent accepted by landlord after notice to terminate, 253
retaliation by landlord, 257
sample Letter Requesting Reinstatement of Tenancy, 253
sample Tenant's Notice of Intent to Move Out, 252

state law summarized, 351–353

subtenancies and, 132

tenant changes mind and decides to stay, 253, 258–259

tenant leaves on short notice, 254

unpaid rent deducted from deposit, 281–282

See also Termination of tenancy by landlord

Rental applications, 17–30

overview, 17

background and reference check, 16–17, 100

bringing everything required for, to rental viewing, 13, 22

competitive edge over other applicants, 22

and credit history, 22, 24–26

disposal of, identity theft concerns and, 24

identifying information requested on, 17

immigration status information requested on, 17

need for, 17

rejection by landlord, 24, 26–27, 96

sample Consent to Background and Reference Check, 17, 22, 23

sample Rental Application, 18–21

and tenant seeking replacement tenant, 261

true interest in rental and, 17

truthfulness on, 23, 27

See also Holding deposits; References

Rental priorities, 4–8, 13

sample Rental Priorities Worksheet, 8

Rental units

condition of, checking out during viewing, 13–15

condition of, Landlord-Tenant Checklist as record of, 155

creative use of space in, 14

desire to live in a particular, 10, 12

exempt from antidiscrimination laws, 87

exempt from lead regulation, 211, 212

foreclosure, determining likelihood of, 15

furnished, 7, 78, 113–114

identification of, in rental document, 37

online reviews of, 15

photographing, 114, 285, 286, 294, 322

type and style of, as rental priority, 7

utilities, 41

See also Access to property by landlord; Appliances; Condominium rentals; Environmental hazards; Fixtures; Habitable condition of premises; Landlord-Tenant Checklist; Multiunit buildings; Occupancy limits; Personal injuries; Property of landlord, damage to; Repairs and maintenance;

Sale of rental property; Security; Short–term paying guests; Short–term rentals; Single–family residences

Renters' insurance

and bedbugs, 228

choosing, 44

cost of, 45

cotenants and, 46

coverage by, 45–46

and deposit reduction, 79

dog or other animal bites covered by, 196

floater policy, 44

high deductible for, 44

landlord buying liability insurance for unit, 45

landlord's insurance not covering rental unit, 43

legal services covered under, 337

legality of landlord requirement for, 45

for mold damage, 225

and natural or third-party disasters, 149

and repairs done by tenant, 161

resources for, 44

and satellite dishes and other antennas, 170

security advice from company, 240

written rental document requiring, 43–46

Repairs and maintenance, 133–150

overview, 134

and access, landlord right to, 47–48, 175–176

and asbestos exposures, 203–207

carbon monoxide prevention via, 219

checking out need for, 14

complaints about, and retaliatory rent increases, 73–75, 141

conversations and emails, keeping notes on, 140

cosmetic, no legal requirement to make, 153

criminals causing damage, responsibility for, 138, 153

of damage done by tenant, 137, 307, 308

dangerous situations, precautions taken by tenants, 139

deposit used to pay for. *See* Deposits, deductions from

destruction of premises, and early termination rights, 259

destruction of premises by natural disasters, 42, 149

destruction of premises by third parties or landlord, 149

and evictions under rent control, 64

and "good tenant" behavior when meeting landlord, 13

hassles with workers for, avoiding, 175

"last month's rent" used to pay for, 80–81, 83

lawsuit to force landlord to make, 140, 150, 159–161

lead regulations and, 211–212, 216–217

mold prevention and, 223–224

as motivation for cancellation of lease by landlord, 260

need for, reporting to landlord immediately, 281

procedure for reporting need for, 42

promised by landlord when making agreement, 42, 52–53, 114–115, 140, 154–155

sample Agreements Regarding Repairs, 115

sample Letter of Understanding Regarding Repairs, 140

sample Request for Repair or Maintenance, 139

signed receipt for written request, 139

by tenant, and "primary residence" condition, 37

by tenant, in written rental documents, 42–43, 137–138

by tenant, legal responsibilities for, 137–138

unfinished, and "not ready" rental unit, 48

written requests for, 138–140

See also Accessibility; Alterations and improvements; Habitable condition of premises; Ordinary wear and tear; Repairs and maintenance, minor; Repairs and maintenance, remedies when landlord refuses to make; Security; Temporary housing, reimbursement for

Repairs and maintenance, minor, 152–162

overview, 152

caution on adversarial approaches to, for month-to-month tenants, 158

cosmetic, 153

defined, 152

and hazardous materials, 157

implied promises for, 155

lack of clout of tenants for, 152

Landlord-Tenant Checklist as record of original condition, 155

lawsuits in small claims court, 159–161

and lead regulations, 212

legal basis of landlord's responsibility for, 152–155

mediation for, 159

permission from landlord to make repairs, 161–162

persuading the landlord to make, 157–161

reporting code violations, 159

retaliation and, 156, 158

sample Letter Asking for Minor Repairs, 158

sample Letter Requesting Permission to Do a Minor Repair, 162

tenant making repairs, 161–162

tenant responsibilities for, 154, 155–157

withholding of rent for, caution against, 160

written agreement for tenant responsibility for, 156

written request for, 157–159

written request for, electronic vs. postal delivery of, 158

Repairs and maintenance, remedies when landlord refuses to make

bankruptcy of landlord and, 271

building closed due to code violations, 141, 142

compensation for defective unit (rent abatement), 145–146, 150, 159–160, 216, 271

conditions to meet before taking action, 141

and foreclosure of property, 273–274

injuries sustained because of, 194

lawsuit against landlord, 150

lawyer sending letter or making phone call, 336

for major problems, 141

making repairs and deducting the cost ("repair and deduct"), 146–148, 230, 257–258, 322, 383–384

move-out forced by violations of code, 141, 142

moving out, 148–150

notes on conversations and emails, keeping, 140

proof of need for repairs, 141

rent withholding, 141, 142–146, 147, 230, 257–258, 322, 331, 333, 383–384

reporting code violations to housing inspectors, 141, 142

retaliation of landlord and, 141, 150, 257–258

sample Letter Telling the Landlord You Intend to Repair and Deduct, 147

sample Letter Telling the Landlord You Intend to Withhold Rent, 144

short rent checks, caution against, 147

signed receipt for written request(s) for repairs, 139

state statutes list, 383–384

substitute housing, landlord required to pay for, 141, 142, 148, 150, 260

taping telephone conversations, caution on, 140

See also Moving out as remedy; Temporary housing, reimbursement for; Tenants' groups, formation of

Residential Lead-Based Paint Hazard Reduction Act (Title X), 211

Retaliation by landlord

overview, 257–258

for asbestos complaints, 206

difficulty of fighting, 34–35

for disputes over repairs and maintenance done by tenant, 156 lateness of rent combined with, 312

lease as protection from, 34–35

for organizing tenants into group, 257, 312, 322, 330

rent increases as, 73–75

for security concerns, 240, 244

state law summarized, 257–258, 312, 388–389

and termination of tenancies, for assertion of legal rights, 141, 150, 257–258, 312

Right of first refusal, 270, 271

Risk, assumption of, 197

Rodent control, 194

Roomer, defined, 120

See also Subtenancies

Roommates, 120–132

overview, 30, 120

adding new, 120, 128, 129–130

adding new, and rent increase, 130

adding new, and security deposit increase, 130–131

adding, permission of landlord for, 128, 129–130, 132, 306

as cotenants, 120–121

defined, 120

departing in the middle of a tenancy, 127–129

deposit increases for additional, 130–131

deposit refund to departing cotenant, 290–291

disputes among, avoiding landlord involvement in, 125

and domestic violence, 125–127

eviction of all, for violation of rental document by one, 121

eviction of, by roommate, 122, 129, 132

finding, resources for, 30

guest policy among, 123, 131

joint and several liability of, 37, 120, 121

legal status when becoming, clarity on, 30

and locks, changing, 125

as long-term guest, 120

master tenant (rent control), 122

New York Roommate Law, 132

occupancy limits and, 129, 132

police visit to house, 127

and priorities, need to establish, 5

rent increases for additional, 130

rent payment by single check required, 121

rent payment when roommate departs, 127, 128

rent unpaid by individual, 120–121

renter's insurance and, 46

as roomer (subtenant), 120, 129, 132

sample Letter Requesting Permission to Add a Roommate, 130

sample Roommate Agreement, 123–124

small claims court for unpaid responsibilities, 128

written agreement with departing roommate, 128

written agreements on important issues between, 30, 122–125

written rental agreement or lease and, 120–121, 128, 130

See also Guests; Occupancy limits; Short-term paying guests

Rooms, number of, as rental priority, 7

RPost.com, 117

RTF forms, editing, 414

Rugs and carpets, 153, 280, 281

Rules and regulations, tenant, 47, 49–50, 55, 306–307

S

Sale of rental property

in bankruptcy, 271–272

deposits and, 83

elderly tenants protected against, 92

"for sale/for rent" signs on property, 177

lease option to buy, 7, 35, 336

and leases, 35, 271–272

lock box with key inside, 177

showing unit to prospective buyers, 176–177

termination of tenancy due to, 271–272

See also Condominium conversions; Foreclosures on rentals

San Francisco Society for the Prevention of Cruelty to Animals (SPCA), 47

San Francisco Tenants Union, 331

Satellite dishes and wireless antennas, 7, 43, 168–172

Savings clause, 52

Schools, as rental priority, 6

Section 8/subsidized housing, 1, 60, 99, 272

Security

overview, 232

analyzing the building, 240

checking on, at viewing of unit, 14

and crime, damage caused by, 138, 153

and crime, landlord's liability for, 233–234

and crime, lawsuit following, 153, 157, 245

dog walkers and, 266

features important to obtain, 241

habitable housing law and, 137

as housing code requirement, 135, 136

injury due to lack of, landlord liability for, 194

landlord's responsibility to act with due care, 233–234

legal requirements for, 232–233, 241

liability insurance company of landlord and, 242–243

liability of landlord for crimes, 233–234

liability of landlord for threats from other tenants, 235–237

mediation to address problems with, 243

monetary compensation for crimes, 234

moving out as remedy, 237, 244–245, 246

neighborhood as factor in, 241, 246

persuading landlord to make improvements, 240–245

promises of security features by landlord, 235, 241–242

as rental priority, 7

restraining orders, 237

sample Letter Alerting the Landlord to Dangerous Conditions, 242

tenant protecting self, 245–246

tenant responsibility for, 138

tenants in building as threat to, 235–237

tenants paying for increased, 243

tenants working together on, 240, 243

windows, 241, 246

written request for improvements, 242

See also Crime and criminal behavior; Locks and keys

Security deposits. *See* Deposits

Self-employment, and rental applications, 17

See also Home office

Self-help evictions, illegal, 182, 316–317, 410–412

Self-help remedies. *See* Repairs and maintenance, remedies when landlord refuses to make

Senior citizens housing, 87, 211

Service animals, 47, 93, 94

Sex discrimination, 97, 126

Sex offenders, 16

Sexual assault, 182

Sexual harassment, 97, 100–101, 182, 196

lawyer for, finding, 337

Sexual orientation, discrimination based on, 87, 98–99

Short-term paying guests (Airbnb, etc.)

overview, 131

frequency of, as factor in choosing a rental, 16

landlord permission for, 131

neighbor complaints and, 39, 131

and "primary residence" requirement, 37

renters' insurance/liability coverage and, 131

roommates and, 131

for short-term interim housing, 13

written agreement with landlord for, 131

zoning laws and, 132

Short-term rentals

exempt from lead regulations, 211

as option while seeking housing, 4, 12–13

and university housing offices, 12–13

Single-family residences

and bedbugs, 228, 230

carbon monoxide monitors and, 220

condominiums treated as, 1

and delegation of repair and maintenance responsibilities to tenant, 42, 138, 154, 156, 220–221

exempt from antidiscrimination laws, 87

exempt from random municipal inspections, 180

lease-option-to-buy and, 7, 35

leases as common with, 34

mold investigation in, 224

and rent control, 62

and satellite dish installations, 169, 170

security and, 240

Slumlords, and rent control, 63

Small claims court

overview, 293–296, 328–329

clerk or advisor for help with, 329

compared to regular trial courts, 317–318

cost of filing, 293

evidence for, 294–295, 329

frequency of landlord in, 74

if person being sued doesn't show up, 296

lawyer for, 296, 329

legal problems suitable for, 328–329

limiting claim to maximum allowed in, 329

limits on claims allowed in, 293, 329, 402–407

mediation as prerequisite to, 293

names for, in various states, 293

for "not ready" apartment, 48

photography of unit prior to move-in, 114

presenting your case in, suggestions for, 295–296

resources for, 270, 329

for roommates, departing, 128

rules for, 329

self-representation in, 329

tenants' group suing in, 330

time for process of, 293

time to file, 294

witnesses in, 294, 295, 329

See also Courts; Lawsuits; Small claims court situations

Small claims court situations

abandoned property, retrieval of, 300–301

asbestos exposures, temporary housing costs, 206–207

excessive late fee, 69

fraudulent finder's fees, 29

hold-over tenants, 48

landlord suing for broken lease, 268–270

landlord suing when deposit doesn't cover what tenant owes, 296–297

lead exposure, 216, 217

neighbor groups targeting drug houses, 239–240

privacy invasions by landlord, 181, 184–185

repairs landlord refuses to make, 150, 159–161

retaliatory rent increases, 74–75

and satellite dishes, 171–172

security issues, 245

Smoke detectors, 114, 135

tenant disabling, 193

Smoking

marijuana smoke, 49

nonsmoking/smoke-free rentals, 49

and radon, 217

Social media, finding a rental with, 9

Social Security Disability Insurance Benefits (SDI), as proof of disability, 95

Social Security Number, 17

Soil, lead content of, 214

State Landlord-Tenant Law Charts

abandoned property of tenant, 387

access of landlord to property, 385–386

disclosures by landlord, 364–377

domestic violence situations, 378–382

duty of landlord to rerent, 408–409

how to use, 347

landlord-tenant statutes, 348

notice required to change or terminate a month-to-month tenancy, 351–353

rent rules, 349–350

rent withholding and repair and deduct remedies, 383–384

retaliation by landlord, 388–389

security deposit rules, 354–363

self-help evictions, consequences of, 410–412

small claims court limits, 402–407

termination for nonpayment of rent, 390–392

termination for violation of lease, 393–394

Unconditional Quit terminations, 395–401

State statutes

legal research of, 342

under consideration, resource for, 229

See also State Landlord-Tenant Law Charts

Streetadvisor.com, 13

Strict liability, 196–197

Student loans, 24

Students

with cosigners, 57

housing on campus, federal regulations and, 211

leases required in college towns, 34

Subletting

compared to assigning a lease, 265

conditions to meet, 263, 265

downsides of, 265–266

ending the arrangement, 267

housesitters and, 266

permission of landlord required, 41, 265–266, 306

and rent control, 266, 267

responsibilities of, 267

for roommates. See Subtenancies

written agreement for, 267

in written rental documents, 41

Subtenancies, month-to-month, 120, 129, 132

See also Subletting

Summons, 317–318

Supplemental Security Income (SSI), as proof of disability, 95

Swimming pool, 49

T

Telephone conversations, taping, 140

Telephone service, 7

Television, 7, 43, 167–172

Temporary housing, reimbursement for

asbestos exposures, 206–207

bedbug exterminations, 228

lead exposures, 217

major repairs, 141, 142, 207, 260

"not ready" apartments, 48

radon exposure, 219

See also Relocation assistance for condominium conversions

Temporary restraining orders (TROs)

for discrimination, 104

for domestic violence, 125, 126

for threats by another tenant, 237

Tenancy. See Deposits; Finding a rental; Leases; Moving out as remedy; Notice by landlord; Notice by tenant; Rental agreements (month-to-month); Rental units; Repairs and maintenance; Termination of tenancy by landlord; Written leases and rental agreements, provisions of

Tenants
  adults in household as signing lease or rental
    agreement, 37
  changing mind about moving in, 48
  collective action by. *See* Tenants' associations;
    Tenants' groups, formation of
  forwarding address of, for return of deposit, 277, 287
  housekeeping of, as issue, 92, 222, 223, 225, 307
  identification of, on lease or rental agreement, 37
  master (rent control), 122
  prior, failing to leave (hold-over), 48, 255, 256
  recordkeeping by, 116, 139–140
  subtenants, month-to-month, 120, 129, 132
  termination of month-to-month rentals by,
    251–252, 281–282
  See also Abandoned property of tenant; Absences of
    tenant, extended; Finding a rental; Leases, tenant
    options for ending early; Notice by tenant; Oral
    agreements; Personal injuries; Privacy of tenant;
    Property of tenant; Roommates; Tenants' rights
Tenants' associations
  finding, 331
  help from, in organizing tenants' groups, 331
  legal help from, 331, 338
  rent control information from, 61
  rent fairness information from, 60
  and researching landlord frequency in small claims
    court, 74
  as resource, 36
Tenants' groups, formation of
  overview, 329–330
  bringing tenants together, 330–331
  meeting with the landlord, 333
  petitions, development of, 331–333
  problems among tenants, solving, 330
  retaliation by landlord for, 257, 312, 322, 330
  sample Petition to the Landlord, 332
  security issues and, 240, 243
  types of problems to address with, 330
  unlawful entry by landlord and, 183
Tenants' rights
  generally, 54–55
  retaliation by landlord for assertion of, 141, 150,
    257–258, 312
  See also Habitable condition of premises; Lawsuits;
    Mediation; Negotiation with the landlord;
    Quiet enjoyment; Repairs and maintenance,
    remedies when landlord refuses to make; Tenants'
    associations; Tenants' groups, formation of

Termination of tenancy by landlord
  overview, 248
  bankruptcy of landlord and, 271–272
  common reasons for, 258
  for condominium conversions, 270
  cotenants and, 121
  discrimination and, 257, 258
  foreclosure of property and, 272–274
  improper use of repair-and-deduct remedy and,
    206–207
  for major renovations, 207
  negotiation to stay, 258–259
  property withdrawn from rental market, 271
  refusal of landlord request for access to unit and, 179
  and repair requests, right to enforce, 141
  as retaliation for asserting right to habitable
    premises, 141, 150, 257–258, 312
  sale of property and, 271–272
  written rental documents and, 52
  See also Evictions; Leases, expiration of; Rental
    agreements (month-to-month), termination
    of; Termination of tenancy by landlord, for
    nonpayment of rent or violation of rental document
Termination of tenancy by landlord, for nonpayment
  of rent or violation of rental document, 304–313
  overview, 304
  and basic tenant responsibilities imposed by law,
    307–308
  buying time, 312
  chronically late payers and, 306
  correction of violation not possible, 307
  Cure or Quit notice, 304
  fault of tenant and, 309, 312
  fighting. *See* Eviction lawsuits
  grace periods, 305, 310
  illegal activity on premises and, 307, 308, 313,
    395–401
  late rent fees and, 305
  lawyer sending notice, 311
  and leases, future rent due on, 313
  mediation and, 310
  moving out, as best option, 312–313, 316
  moving out, refusal of, 310–312
  negotiating with the landlord to avoid, 308–310
  no-fault of tenant and, 309–310
  notice, checking for legality of, 311–312, 316
  notice requirements, 304–305, 311–312
  and nuisance, as term, 307
  number of days to comply, 305, 307, 311

partial rent payments and, 306, 309

paying rent after notice received, 305–306

repeated violations of rental document, 307

retaliation of landlord and, 312

state law summarized (for nonpayment of rent), 390–392

state law summarized (for violations of lease), 393–394

state law summarized (Unconditional Quit), 395–401

for unpaid rent, 304–306, 309

for violation of terms of rental document, other, 306–307

and waste, as term, 307

whole rent payments and, 306

See also Pay Rent or Quit notice; Unconditional Quit notice

Termination of tenancy by tenant, month-to-month rentals, 251–252, 281–282

See also Leases, tenant options for ending early

Terrorism, and discrimination, 89

Testers

for discrimination, 103

for lead-based paint disclosures, 209

for mold damage, 225

Text messages, notice via, 116, 117, 158

Three-Day notice. *See* Termination of tenancy by landlord, for nonpayment of rent or violation of rental document

Title X, 211

TransUnion, 25

Trespass, invasion of privacy by landlord, 184

U

Unconditional Quit notice

chronically late payers and, 306

and correction of violation not possible, 307

and damage to premises, 308

defined, 304–305

for illegal activity on premises, 308

partial rent payment following, 306

state law summarized, 395–401

See also Evictions; Termination of tenancy by landlord

Understanding. *See* Letters of understanding

University housing, and lead regulation exemptions, 211

University housing offices, 12–13, 30

Unlawful detainer (UD) lawsuit. *See* Eviction lawsuits

Unmarried couples, discrimination and, 98–99

Unruh Civil Rights Act (California), 98

Upgrades. *See* Alterations and improvements

U.S. Code, 343–344

Utilities, 41

See also Electrical service

V

Vinyl miniblinds, and lead, 214

Violence, threat of, by another tenant, 235–237

See also Domestic violence

VRBO. *See* Short-term paying guests

W

Waste, as term, 46, 307

Water

lead content in, 214

radon gas in, 217

Waterbed deposits, 78

Weather, evictions and, 322–323

Westlaw, 345

Windows

repair responsibility for, 153

security of, 241, 246

Wireless antennas, 43

Work

commuting, 6

and injuries on landlord's property, damages for, 198

in jeopardy, as eviction defense, 321

and justifiable breaking of lease, 259, 260

landlord harassment at, 181

paying for costs of breaking lease, 260

phone number for, given to landlord, 178, 181

references from, 17, 23

Written leases and rental agreements, provisions of, 33–57

access to unit, landlord's right to, 43, 48, 178

additional provisions, 52

alterations and improvements, consent required, 164

alterations and improvements, ownership of, 164

amendment of, 56, 248–250

appliances, responsibility for repairing, 43, 154–155

applicable law, 53

assignments, 41

attorneys' fees in lawsuits, 50–51, 105, 256, 269, 312, 316, 336, 339

automatic liens (distraint or distress power), 41, 299

changes to, initialing and dating, 57

changes to, prior to signing, 56

changes to rules and regulations, 49
complaint and repair request procedures, 42
deposits and fees, 40–41
difference between leases and rental agreements, 33–35
early copy of, to check conditions of the tenancy, 5
entire agreement, 52–53
exculpatory clauses, 46
extended absences of tenant, 37, 48
forms for, 35
grace periods, 40
guaranteed legal rights and, generally, 54
guest policies, 39
habitable (livable) condition of unit, 42, 54–55
hold harmless clauses, 46
hold-over tenants clause, 256
home business restrictions, 37–38
identification of landlord and tenant(s), 37
identification of the premises, 37
illegal clauses, generally, 54–55
jointly and severally liable tenants, 37, 121
Landlord-Tenant Checklist clause, 42
late fees, 40, 68
legal papers, person authorized to receive, 51
locks and burglar alarms added by tenant, 42, 175
mediation clause, 52
mold clauses, 223
"not ready" unit, 48
nuisances by tenant, 46–47
occupants, number of, 38–39
pets, 47
possession of the premises, tenant chooses not to move in, 48
"primary residence" condition, 37
property damage by tenant, 46
quiet enjoyment by tenant, right to, 47

rent amount and due date, 40
rent increase policy, 72–73
rent withholding, clause prohibiting, 143
renters' insurance, 43–46
repair and maintenance by tenant, 42–43, 137–138
and repairs promised by landlord, 42, 52–53, 114–115, 140, 154
repairs requiring consent, 161
rules and regulations, 47, 49–50, 306–307
rules or policies not covered by law, generally, 55
signing, 56–57
sublets, 41
for subtenants, 132
successors, 53
term of the tenancy, 39
termination fees (liquidated damages), 40, 269
termination of tenancy, grounds for, 52
tersely written, 115
types of clauses, 54–55
utilities, 41
validity of each part, 52
variations within the law, generally, 54
violations of law by tenant, 46
See also Cosigners; Disclosures; Leases; Letters of understanding; Negotiation with the landlord; Oral agreements; Rental agreements

Y

Yards and gardens, as rental priority, 7
Yelp, 15

Z

Zoning laws
    and groups of unrelated people living together, 98
    and home businesses, 38
    and short-term paying guests, 132

 **NOLO** **Save 15%** *off your next order*

Register your Nolo purchase, and we'll send you a **coupon for 15% off** your next Nolo.com order!

Nolo.com/customer-support/productregistration

On Nolo.com you'll also find:

Books & Software

Nolo publishes hundreds of great books and software programs for consumers and business owners. Order a copy, or download an ebook version instantly, at Nolo.com.

Online Legal Documents

You can quickly and easily make a will or living trust, form an LLC or corporation, apply for a trademark or provisional patent, or make hundreds of other forms—online.

Free Legal Information

Thousands of articles answer common questions about everyday legal issues including wills, bankruptcy, small business formation, divorce, patents, employment, and much more.

Plain-English Legal Dictionary

Stumped by jargon? Look it up in America's most up-to-date source for definitions of legal terms, free at nolo.com.

Lawyer Directory

Nolo's consumer-friendly lawyer directory provides in-depth profiles of lawyers all over America. You'll find all the information you need to choose the right lawyer.

EVTEN9